LITERARY OPINION
IN AMERICA

VOLUME II

LITERARY OPINION
IN AMERICA

Essays Illustrating the Status, Methods,
and Problems of Criticism in the
United States in the Twentieth Century

EDITED BY
MORTON DAUWEN ZABEL

THIRD EDITION, REVISED

VOLUME II

HARPER TORCHBOOKS · THE UNIVERSITY LIBRARY

HARPER & ROW, PUBLISHERS, NEW YORK AND EVANSTON

CONTENTS

VOLUME II

PART IV. THE WRITER AND CRITIC IN AMERICA

v

PART V. MODERN CRITICISM: ITS PROBLEMS,
METHODS, AND PROSPECTS

CONTENTS

PART IV
The Writer and Critic in America

MARIANNE MOORE

Henry James as a Characteristic American

[1934]

To say that "the superlative American" and the characteristic American are not the same thing perhaps defrauds anticipation, yet one must admit that it is not in the accepted sense that Henry James was a big man and did things in a big way. But he possessed the instinct to amass and reiterate, and is the rediscerned Small Boy who had from the first seen Europe as a verification of what in its native surroundings his "supersensitive nostril" fitfully detected and liked. Often he is those elements in American life—as locality and as character—which he recurrently studied and to which he never tired of assigning a meaning.

Underlying any variant of Americanism in Henry James' work, is the doctrine, embodied as advice to Christopher Newman, "Don't try to be anyone else"; if you triumph, "let it then be all you." The native Madame de Mauves says to Euphemia, "You seem to me so all of a piece that I am afraid that if I advise you, I shall spoil you," and Hawthorne was dear to Henry James because he "proved to what a use American matter could be put by an American hand. . . . An American could be an artist, one of the finest, without 'going outside' about it . . . quite, in fact, as if Hawthorne had become one just by being American enough."

An air of rurality as of Moses Primrose at the fair struck Henry James in his compatriots, and a garment worn in his childhood revealed "that we were somehow queer." Thackeray, he says, "though he laid on my shoulder the hand of benevolence, bent on my native costume the spectacles of wonder." On his return from Europe he marveled at the hats men wore, but it is hard to be certain that the knowledge-seeking American in Europe is quite so unconsciously a bumpkin as Henry James depicts him. When Newman has said, "I began to earn my living when I was almost a baby," and Madame de Bellegarde says, "You began to earn your living in the cradle?" the retort, "Well, madam, I'm not absolutely convinced I had a cradle," savors of the connoisseur. Since, however, it is over-difficult for Henry James in portrayals of us, not to be portraying himself, there is even in the rendering of the callow

American, a sharpness and tightening of the consciousness that threaten the integrity of the immaturity.

" I am not a scoffer," the fellow-countryman says to Theobald, the American painter, and if with Henry James it were a question of being either guarded or ridiculous, he would prefer to seem ridiculous. His respectful humility toward emotion is socially brave, and in diffidence, reserve, and strong feeling, he reminds one of Whittier, another literary bachelor whom the most ardent sadist has not been able to soil. We remember his sense of responsibility for the United States during the World War and that in *Notes of a Son and Brother* he says of the Civil War, "The drama of the War . . . had become a habit for us without ceasing to be a strain. I am sure I thought more things under that head . . . than I thought in all other connections together." What is said in the same book of the death of Mary Temple, the cousin who so greatly "had a sense for verity of character and play of life in others," is an instance of reverent, and almost reverend, feeling that would defend him against the charge of lightness in anything, if ever one were inclined to make it. It is not the artist, but the responsibility for living and for family, that wonders here about death and has about "those we have seen beaten, this sense that it was not for nothing they missed the ampler experience . . . since dire as their defeat may have been, we don't see them . . . at peace with victory." Things for Henry James glow, flush, glimmer, vibrate, shine, hum, bristle, reverberate. Joy, bliss, ecstasies, intoxication, a sense of trembling in every limb, the heart-shaking first glimpse, a hanging on the prolonged silence of an editor; and as a child at Mr. Burton's small theatre in Chambers Street, his wondering not if the curtain would rise but "if one could exist till then"; the bonfires of his imagination, his pleasure in "the tender sea-green" or "rustling rose-color" of a seriously best dress, are too live to countenance his fear that he was giving us "an inch of canvas and an acre of embroidery."

Idealism which was willing to make sacrifices for its self-preservation, is always an element in the conjuring-wand of Henry James. The fear of profanation is apparent in a remark in connection with the later America, that he felt "like one who has seen a ghost in his safe old house." Of "Independence Hall . . . and its dignity not to be uttered . . . halls and spreading staircase and long-drawn upper gallery . . . one of those rare precincts of the past against which the present has kept beating in vain," he says, "nothing . . . would induce me to revisit . . . the object I so fondly evoke." He would not risk disturbing his recollection of *The Wonder-Book* and *Tanglewood Tales* by reading them over, and Dickens "always remained better than the taste of over-hauling him." The value of the thing is more than the thing. New Hampshire in September was "so delicately Arcadian, like . . . an old legend, an old love-story in fifteen volumes," and "Newport . . . the dainty isle of Aquidneck" and "its perpetually embayed promontories of mossy rock,"

had "ingenuous old-time distinction . . . too latent and too modest for notation." Exasperated by the later superficiality of New York's determination
"to blight the superstition of rest," he terms the Public Libraries "mast-heads
on which spent birds sometimes alight in the expanses of ocean" and thought
Washington Irving's Sunnyside with its "deep, long lane, winding, embanked,
over-arched, such an old-world lane as one scarce ever meets in America . . .
easy for everything but rushing about and being rushed at." The "fatal and
sacred" enjoyment of England "buried in the soil of our primary culture"
leads him to regard London as "the great distributing heart of our traditional
life"; to say of Oxford, "no other spot in Europe extorts from our barbarous
hearts so passionate an admiration"; and for the two Americans in "hedgy
Worcestershire" beneath an "English sky bursting into a storm of light or
melting into a drizzle of silver . . . nothing was wanting; the shaggy, mouse-
colored donkey, nosing the turf . . . the towering ploughman with his white
smock-frock, puckered on chest and back." "We greeted these things," says
the narrator, "as children greet the loved pictures in a story-book, lost and
mourned and found again . . . a gray, gray tower, a huge black yew, a cluster of village graves, with crooked headstones. . . . My companion was overcome. . . . How it makes a Sunday where it stands!"

Henry James' warmth is clearly of our doting native variety. "Europe had
been romantic years before, because she was different from America," he says;
"wherefore America would now be romantic because she was different from
Europe." His imagination had always included Europe; he had not been al-
ienated by travel nor changed by any "love-philtre or fear-philtre" intenser
than those he had received in New York, Newport, or our American Cambridge. "Culture, as I hold, is a matter of attitude quite as much as of opportunity," he says in Notes of a Son and Brother, and "one's supreme relation,
as one had always put it, was one's relation to one's country." In alluding to
"our barbarous hearts" he had, of course, no thought of being taken at his
word—any more than Mrs. Cleve did when abusing America, and he is de-
lineating grossness in Baron de Mauves who "seemed to regard the New
World as a colossal plaisanterie." It entertained James to describe Mrs. Gereth
as aristocratically British and clannishly dowdy when she went to Church;—
as it pleased him to recall "a contemporary cousin" who "was with her stature
and shape the finest possible person to carry clothes," and even in the disillu-
sions attendant upon return to this country, he betrays a parentally local satisfaction in the American girl's fitness of costume.

Nationally and internationally "the sensitive citizen," he felt that patriotism
was a matter of knowing a country by perceiving the clue. Our understanding
of human relations has grown—more perhaps than we realize in the last
twenty years; and when Henry James disappoints us, by retaining the North-
erner's feeling about the Confederate, we must not make him directly con-

temporary, any more than we dispute his spelling peanut with a hyphen. He had had no proximity with the South and all that the bother-taking Henry James needed for doing justice to feeling, was opportunity to feel. "Great things . . . have been done by solitary workers," he says, "but with double the pains they would have cost if they had been produced in more genial circumstances." Education for him, in a large sense, was conversation. Speaking of Cambridge, he says,

When the Norton woods, nearby, massed themselves in scarlet and orange, and when to penetrate and mount a stair and knock at a door, and enjoying response, then sink into a window-bench and inhale at once the vague golden November and the thick suggestion of the room where nascent "thought" had again and again piped or wailed, was to taste as I had never done before, the poetry of the prime initiation and of associated growth.

We observe in the memoirs treasured American types: "silent Vanderpool . . . incorruptibly and exquisitely dumb" who "looked so as if he came from 'good people' . . . the very finest flower of shyness . . . a true welter of modesty, not a grain of it anything stiffer—"; "the ardent and delicate and firm John May"—student at Harvard; and there was Robert Temple—a cousin "with a mind almost elegantly impudent . . . as if we had owed him to Thackeray"; and Mary Temple, " 'natural' to an effect of perfect felicity . . . all straightness and charming tossed head, with long light and yet almost sliding steps and a large light postponing laugh." There was "a widowed grandmother who dispensed an hospitality seemingly as joyless as it was certainly boundless" and Uncle Albert, a kinsman who was " 'Mr.' to his own wife— . . . his hair bristling up almost in short-horn fashion at the sides," with "long, slightly equine countenance, his eyebrows ever elevated as in the curiosity of alarm."

To say that a child was a student of "history and custom . . . manners and types" would be saying too much, but to say that Henry James as a child was "a-throb" with the instinct for meanings, barely suggests that formidable paraphernalia which he was even then gathering. It is in "the waste of time, of passion, of curiosity, of contact—that true initiation resides," he said later; and no scene, strange accent, no adventure—experienced or vicarious—was irrelevant. The elder Henry James alludes to "the maidenly letters" of Emerson but Emerson in New York was strange and wonderful to Henry James, the child invited "to draw near to him, off the hearth-rug." He was "an apparition sinuously and elegantly slim . . . commanding a tone alien to any we heard around about"; and the school-master Louis De Coppet, in "his French treatment of certain of our native local names, Ohio and Iowa for instance, which he rendered . . . O-ee-oh and Ee-o-wah . . . opened vistas." "There hung about the Wards, to my sense, that atmosphere of apples and nuts . . .

and jack-knives and 'squrruls,' of domestic Bible-reading and attendance at 'evening lecture,' of the fear of parental discipline and the cultivated art of dodging it, combined with great personal toughness and hardihood"; and there was "'Stiffy' Norcom . . . whom we supposed gorgeous . . . (Divided I was, I recall, between the dread and the glory of being so greeted, 'Well, Stiffy—!' as a penalty for the least attempt at personal adornment.)"

"You cannot make a man feel low," his Christopher Newman says, "unless you can make him feel base," and "a good conscience" is a pebble with which Henry James is extremely fond of arming his Davids. Longmore's "truthtelling eyes" are that in him which puzzled and tormented the Baron. "They judged him, they mocked him, they eluded him, they threatened him, they triumphed over him, they treated him as no pair of eyes had ever treated him." In every photograph of Henry James that we have, the thing that arrests one is a kind of terrible truthfulness. We feel also, in the letters and memoirs, that "almost indescribable naturalness" which seemed to him as behavior, expressive of his Albany relatives; a naturalness which disappears in the fancy writing of his imitators. If good-nature and reciprocity are American traits, Henry James was a characteristic American—too much one when he patiently suffered unsuitable persons to write to him, call on him, and give him their "work." Politeness in him was "more than a form of luxurious egotism" and is in keeping with the self-effacement of his determination to remain a devotee of devotees to George Eliot "for his own wanton joy" though unwittingly requested to "take away please, away, away!" two books he had written. Mrs. Greville had lent the books as introductory, previous to her calling with Henry James on the Leweses, but no connection had been noticed between books and visitor. The same characteristic appears in the account of his meeting with Dickens. He speaks of "the extremely handsome face . . . which met my dumb homage with a straight inscrutability. . . . It hadn't been the least important that we should have shaken hands or exchanged platitudes. . . . It was as if I had carried off my strange treasure just exactly from under the merciless military eye—placed there on guard of the secret. All of which I recount for illustration of the force of action, unless I call it passion, that may reside in a single pulse of time."

Henry James belonged to "the race which has the credit of knowing best, at home and abroad, how to make itself comfortable" but there was in him an ascetic strain which causes him to make Longmore think with disgust of the Baron's friend who "filled the air with the odor of heliotrope"; and Eugene Pickering's American friend found "something painful in the spectacle of absolute inthralment, even to an excellent cause." Freedom; yes. The confidant, in comparing himself compassionately with the Eugene of their schooldays says, "I could go out to play alone, I could button my jacket myself, and sit up till I was sleepy." Yet the I of the original had not "been exposed on breezy uplands under the she-wolf of competition" and there was not about him "the impertinent odor of trade." Some persons have grudged Henry James his freedom and have called it leisure; but as Theobald, the American painter, said of art, "If we work for ourselves, of course we must hurry. If we work for her, we must often pause." James says of *The Tragic Muse* in a letter, "I took long and patient and careful trouble which no creature will recognize"; and we may declare of him as he did of John La Farge, "one was . . . never to have seen a subtler mind or a more generously wasteful passion, in other words a sincerer one." Reverting to the past of his own life, he is over-powered by "the personal image unextinct" and says, "It presents itself, I feel, beyond reason and yet if I turn from it the ease is less."

There was in him "the rapture of observation" but more unequivocally even than that, affection for family and country. "I was to live to go back with wonder and admiration," he says, "to the quantity of secreted thought in our daily medium, the quality of intellectual passion, the force of cogitation and aspiration, as to the explanation both of a thousand surface incoherences and a thousand felt felicities." Family was the setting for his country and the town was all but synonymous with family; as would appear in what is said of "the family-party smallness of old New York, those happy limits that could make us all care . . . for the same thing at once." It "is always a matter of winter twilight, fire-light, lamplight." "We were surely all gentle and generous together, floating in such a clean light social order, sweetly proof against ennui." "The social scheme, as we knew it, was, in its careless charity, worthy of the golden age— . . . the fruits dropped right upon the board to which we flocked together, the least of us and the greatest"; "our parents . . . never caring much for things we couldn't care for and generally holding that what was good to them would be also good for their children." A father is a safe symbol of patriotism when one can remember him as "genially alert and expert"—when " 'human fellowship' " is "the expression that was perhaps oftenest on his lips and his pen." "We need never fear not to be good enough," Henry James says, "if only we were social enough . . ." and he recalls his mother as so participatingly unremote that he can say, "I think we almost contested her being separate enough to be proud of us—it was too like our being proud of ourselves." Love is the thing more written about than anything else, and in the mistaken sense of greed. Henry James seems to have been haunted by awareness that rapacity destroys what it is successful in securing. He feels a need "to see the other side as well as his own, to feel what his adversary feels"; to be an American is not for him "just to glow belligerently with one's country." Some complain of his transferred citizenship as a loss; but when we consider the trend of his fiction and his uncomplacent denouements, we have no tremor about proving him to have been an American. What we scarcely dare ask is, how many Americans are there who can be included with him in his Americanism? Family affection is the fire that burned within him and America was the hearth on which it burned. He thinks of the American as "intrinsically and actively ample, . . . reaching westward, southward, anywhere, everywhere," with a mind "incapable of the shut door in any direction."

From *The Hound and Horn*, Vol. VII (April–June, 1934), pp. 363–372. Reprinted by permission.

The Poetry of Wallace Stevens
[1937]

For some of us, Wallace Stevens[1] is America's chief conjuror—as bold a virtuoso and one with as cunning a rhetoric as we have produced. He has, naturally, in some quarters been rebuked for his skill; writers cannot excel at their work without being, like the dogs in *Coriolanus*, "as often beat for barking As therefore kept to do so." But for healthy seductiveness, like the patterned correspondences in Handel's Sonata No. 1, he has not been rivaled:

> The body dies; the body's beauty lives.
> So evenings die in their green going,
> A wave, interminably flowing.

His repercussive harmonics, set off by the small compass of the poem, "prove" mathematically to admiration, and suggest a linguist creating several languages within a single language. The plaster temporariness of subterfuge is, he says,

> Like a word in the mind that sticks at artichoke
> And remains inarticulate.

And besides the multiplying of *h*'s, a characteristically ironic use of scale should be noted, in "Bantams in Pine Woods":

> Chief Iffucan of Azcan in caftan
> Of tan with henna hackles, halt!

The playfulness, that is to say humor, of such rhymings as *egress* and *negress*, *Scaramouche* and *barouche*, is just right, and by no means a joke; one's sense of humor being a clue to the most serious part of one's nature. But best of all, the bravura. Upon the general marine volume of statement is set a parachute-spinnaker of verbiage which looms out like half a cantaloupe and gives the body of the theme the air of a fabled argosy advancing.

[1] *Harmonium*, by Wallace Stevens. New York: Alfred A. Knopf, 1931. *Ideas of Order*, by Wallace Stevens. New York: Alfred A. Knopf, 1936. *Owl's Clover*, by Wallace Stevens. Alcestis Press, 1936.

MARIANNE MOORE

A harmonist need not be proud of dominating us illusorily, by causing a
flower in bloom to appear where a moment before there was none; and not
infrequently Wallace Stevens' "noble accents and lucid, inescapable rhythms"
point to the universal parent, Shakespeare. A novice of verse, required in an
examination to attribute to author or century the line, "These choirs of wel-
come choir for me farewell," might pay Wallace Stevens a high compliment.

> Remember how the crickets came
> Out of their mother grass, like little kin,

has perfectly Shakespeare's miniature effect of innocent sadness, and the consciously pertinaciously following of a word through several lines, as where we
see the leaves

> Turning in the wind,
> Turning as the flames
> Turned in the fire,

are cousin to the pun of Elizabethan drama. We feel, in the tentatively detached method of implication, the influence of Plato; and an awareness of if
not the influence of T. S. Eliot. Better say that each has influenced the other;
with "Sunday Morning" and the Prufrock-like lines in "Le Monocle de Mon
Oncle" in mind,

> Shall I uncrumple this much crumpled thing?
> .   .   .   .
> For it has come that thus I greet the spring

and the Peter Quince-like rhythmic contour of T. S. Eliot's "La Figlia Que
Piange." As if it were Antipholus of Ephesus and Antipholus of Syracuse,
each has an almost too acute concept of "the revenge of music"; a realization
that the seducer is the seduced; and a smiling, strict, Voltaire-like, straight-
seeing, self-directed humor which triumphs in its pain. Each is engaged in a
similar though differently expressed search for that which will endure.

We are able here to see the salutary effect of insisting that a piece of writing please the writer himself before it pleases anyone else; and how a poet
may be a wall of incorruptibleness against any concessive violating of the essential aura of contributory vagueness. Such tense heights of the romantic are
intimated by mere titles, that one might hesitate to make trial of the content
lest it seem bathos, but Wallace Stevens is a delicate apothecary of savors and
precipitates, and no hauteurs are violated. His method of hints and disguises
should have Mercury as their patron divinity, for in the guise of "a dark
rabbi," an ogre, a traveler, a comedian, an old woman, he deceives us as the
god misled the aged couple in the myth.

Again, and moreover, to manner and harmonics is added a fine and exultant
grasp of beauty—a veritable refuge of "blessed mornings, meet for the eye of

the young alligator"; an equivalence for jungle beauty, arctic beauty, marine beauty, meridian, hothouse, consciously urban or unconsciously natural beauty—which might be alarming were it not for the persistent foil of dissatisfaction with matter. This frugally unified opulence, epitomized by the "green vine angering for life"—in *Owl's Clover* by the thought of plundered harassed Africa, "the Greenest Continent" where "memory moves on leopard's feet"—has been perfected stroke by stroke, since the period of "the magenta Judas tree," "the indigo glass in the grass," "oceans in obsidian," the white of "frogs," of "clays," and in "withered reeds"; until now, tropic pinks and yellows, avocado and Kuniyoshi cabouchon emerald-greens, the blent but violent excellence of ailanthus silk-moths and metallic breast-feathers—as open and unpretending as Rousseau's Snake-Charmer and Sleeping Gipsy—combine in an impression of incandescence like that of the night-blooming cereus.

Despite this awareness of the world of sense—which at some points, to a prudish asceticism approximates wickedness—one notices the frequent recurrence of the word heaven. In each clime which the author visits and under each disguise, it is the dilemma of tested hope which confronts him. In *Owl's Clover* "the search for a tranquil belief," and the protest against the actualities of experience, become a protest against the death of world hope; against the unorder and chaos of this "age of concentric mobs." Those who dare to forget that "As the man the state, not as the state the man," who divert "the dream of heaven from heaven to the future, as a god," are indeed the carnivorous owl with African greenness for its repast. The land of "ploughmen, peacocks, doves," of "Leonardo," has been "Combating bushmen for a patch of gourds, Loosing black slaves to make black infantry"; "the widow of Madrid Weeps in Segovia"; in Moscow, in all Europe, "Always everything That is is dead except what ought to be"; aeroplanes which counterfeit "the bee's drone" and have the powers of "the scorpion" are our "seraphim." Mr. Stevens' book is the sable requiem for all this. But requiem is not the word when anyone hates lust for power and ignorance of power, as the author of this book does. So long as we are ashamed of the ironic feast, and of our marble victories—horses or men—which will break unless they are first broken by us, there is hope for the world. As R. P. Blackmur has said, "the poems rise in the mind like a tide." They embody hope, that in being frustrated becomes fortitude; and they prove to us that the testament to emotion is not volubility. It is remarkable that a refusal to speak should result in such eloquence and that an implied heaven could be made so definite. Unanimity of word and rhythm has been attained, and we have the seldom exhilaration of knowing that America has in Wallace Stevens at least one artist whom professionalism will never demolish.

From *Poetry: A Magazine of Verse*, Vol. XLIX (February, 1937), pp. 268–273. Reprinted by permission.

LIONEL TRILLING

Reality in America

[1950]

IT IS possible to say of V. L. Parrington that with his *Main Currents in American Thought* he has had an influence on our conception of American culture which is not equaled by that of any other writer of the last two decades. His ideas are now the accepted ones wherever the college course in American literature is given by a teacher who conceives himself to be opposed to the genteel and the academic and in alliance with the vigorous and the actual. And whenever the liberal historian of America finds occasion to take account of the national literature, as nowadays he feels it proper to do, it is Parrington who is his standard and guide. Parrington's ideas are the more firmly established because they do not have to be imposed—the teacher or the critic who presents them is likely to find that his task is merely to make articulate for his audience what it has always believed, for Parrington formulated in a classic way the suppositions about our culture which are held by the American middle class so far as that class is at all liberal in its social thought and so far as it begins to understand that literature has anything to do with society.

Parrington was not a great mind; he was not a precise thinker or, except when measured by the low eminences that were about him, an impressive one. Separate Parrington from his informing idea of the economic and social determination of thought and what is left is a simple intelligence, notable for its generosity and enthusiasm but certainly not for its accuracy or originality. Take him even with his idea and he is, once its direction is established, rather too predictable to be continuously interesting; and, indeed, what we dignify with the name of economic and social determinism amounts in his use of it to not much more than the demonstration that most writers incline to stick to their own social class. But his best virtue was real and important—he had what we like to think of as the saving salt of the American mind, the lively sense of the practical, workaday world, of the welter of ordinary undistinguished things and people, of the tangible, quirky, unrefined elements of life. He knew what so many literary historians do not know, that emotions and ideas are the sparks that fly when the mind meets difficulties.

Yet he had after all but a limited sense of what constitutes a difficulty.

Whenever he was confronted with a work of art that was complex, personal and not literal, that was not, as it were, a public document, Parrington was at a loss. Difficulties that were complicated by personality or that were expressed in the language of successful art did not seem quite real to him and he was inclined to treat them as aberrations, which is one way of saying what everybody admits, that the weakest part of Parrington's talent was his aesthetic judgment. His admirers and disciples like to imply that his errors of aesthetic judgment arc merely lapses of taste, but this is not so. Despite such mistakes as his notorious praise of Cabell, to whom in a remarkable passage he compares Melville, Parrington's taste was by no means bad. His errors are the errors of understanding which arise from his assumptions about the nature of reality.

Parrington does not often deal with abstract philosophical ideas, but whenever he approaches a work of art we are made aware of the metaphysics on which his aesthetics is based. There exists, he believes, a thing called *reality;* it is one and immutable, it is wholly external, it is irreducible. Men's minds may waver, but reality is always reliable, always the same, always easily to be known. And the artist's relation to reality he conceives as a simple one. Reality being fixed and given, the artist has but to let it pass through him, he is the lens in the first diagram of an elementary book on optics: Fig. 1, Reality; Fig. 2, Artist; Fig. 1', Work of Art. Figs. 1 and 1' are normally in virtual correspondence with each other. Sometimes the artist spoils this ideal relation by "turning away from" reality. This results in certain fantastic works, unreal and ultimately useless. It does not occur to Parrington that there is any other relation possible between the artist and reality than this passage of reality through the transparent artist; he meets evidence of imagination and creativeness with a settled hostility the expression of which suggests that he regards them as the natural enemies of democracy.

In this view of things, reality, although it is always reliable, is always rather sober-sided, even grim. Parrington, a genial and enthusiastic man, can understand how the generosity of man's hopes and desires may leap beyond reality; he admires will in the degree that he suspects mind. To an excess of desire and energy which blinds a man to the limitations of reality he can indeed be very tender. This is one of the many meanings he gives to *romance* or *romanticism,* and in spite of himself it appeals to something in his own nature. The praise of Cabell is Parrington's response not only to Cabell's elegance—for Parrington loved elegance—but also to Cabell's insistence on the part which a beneficent self-deception may and even should play in the disappointing fact-bound life of man, particularly in the private and erotic part of his life.[1]

---

[1] See, for example, how Parrington accounts for the "idealizing mind"—Melville's—by the discrepancy between "a wife in her morning kimono" and "the Helen of his dreams." Vol. II, p. 259.

The second volume of *Main Currents* is called *The Romantic Revolution in America* and it is natural to expect that the word romantic should appear in it frequently. So it does, more frequently than one can count, and seldom with the same meaning, seldom with the sense that the word, although scandalously vague as it has been used by the literary historians, is still full of complicated but not wholly pointless ideas, that it involves many contrary but definable things; all too often Parrington uses the word romantic with the word romance close at hand, meaning *a* romance, in the sense that *Graustark* or *Treasure Island* is a romance, as though it signified chiefly a gay disregard of the limitations of everyday fact. Romance is refusing to heed the counsels of experience (p. iii); it is ebullience (p. iv); it is utopianism (p. iv); it is individualism (p. vi); it is self-deception (p. 59)—"romantic faith . . . in the beneficent processes of trade and industry" (as held, we inevitably ask, by the romantic Adam Smith?); it is the love of the picturesque (p. 49); it is the dislike of innovation (p. 50) but also the love of change (p. iv); it is the sentimental (p. 192); it is patriotism, and then it is cheap (p. 235). It may be used to denote what is not classical, but chiefly it means that which ignores reality (pp. ix, 136, 143, 147, and *passim*); it is not critical (pp. 225, 235), although in speaking of Cooper and Melville, Parrington admits that criticism can sometimes spring from romanticism.

Whenever a man with whose ideas he disagrees wins from Parrington a reluctant measure of respect, the word romantic is likely to appear. He does not admire Henry Clay, yet something in Clay is not to be despised—his romanticism, although Clay's romanticism is made equivalent with his inability to "come to grips with reality." Romanticism is thus, in most of its significations, the venial sin of *Main Currents;* like carnal passion in the *Inferno,* it evokes not blame but tender sorrow. But it can also be the great and saving virtue which Parrington recognizes. It is ascribed to the transcendental reformers he so much admires; it is said to mark two of his most cherished heroes, Jefferson and Emerson: "they were both romantics and their idealism was only a different expression of a common spirit." Parrington held, we may say, at least two different views of romanticism which suggest two different views of reality. Sometimes he speaks of reality in an honorific way, meaning the substantial stuff of life, the ineluctable facts with which the mind must cope, but sometimes he speaks of it pejoratively and means the world of established social forms; and he speaks of realism in two ways: sometimes as the power of dealing intelligently with fact, sometimes as a cold and conservative resistance to idealism.

Just as for Parrington there is a saving grace and a venial sin, there is also a deadly sin, and this is turning away from reality, not in the excess of generous feeling, but in what he believes to be a deficiency of feeling, as with Hawthorne, or out of what amounts to sinful pride, as with Henry James. He tells us that there was too much realism in Hawthorne to allow him to give his faith to the transcendental reformers: "he was too much of a realist to change fashions in creeds"; "he remained cold to the revolutionary criticism that was eager to pull down the old temples to make room for nobler." It is this cold realism, keeping Hawthorne apart from his enthusiastic contemporaries, that alienates Parrington's sympathy—"Eager souls, mystics and revolutionaries, may propose to refashion the world in accordance with their dreams; but evil remains, and so long as it lurks in the secret places of the heart, utopia is only the shadow of a dream. And so while the Concord thinkers were proclaiming man to be the indubitable child of God, Hawthorne was critically examining the question of evil as it appeared in the light of his own experience. It was the central fascinating problem of his intellectual life, and in pursuit of a solution he probed curiously into the hidden, furtive recesses of the soul." Parrington's disapproval of the enterprise is unmistakable.

Now we might wonder whether Hawthorne's questioning of the naïve and often eccentric faiths of the transcendental reformers was not, on the face of it, a public service. But Parrington implies that it contributes nothing to democracy, and even that it stands in the way of the realization of democracy. If democracy depends wholly on a fighting faith, I suppose he is right. Yet society is after all something that exists at the moment as well as in the future, and if one man wants to probe curiously into the hidden furtive recesses of the contemporary soul, a broad democracy and especially one devoted to reality should allow him to do so without despising him. If what Hawthorne did was certainly nothing to build a party on, we ought perhaps to forgive him when we remember that he was only one man and that the future of mankind did not depend upon him alone. But this very fact serves only to irritate Parrington; he is put out by Hawthorne's loneliness and believes that part of Hawthorne's insufficiency as a writer comes from his failure to get around and meet people. Hawthorne could not, he tells us, establish contact with the "Yankee reality," and was scarcely aware of the "substantial world of Puritan reality that Samuel Sewall knew."

To turn from reality might mean to turn to romance, but Parrington tells us that Hawthorne was romantic "only in a narrow and very special sense." He was not interested in the world of, as it were, practical romance, in the Salem of the clipper ships; from this he turned away to create "a romance of ethics." This is not an illuminating phrase but it is a catching one, and it might be taken to mean that Hawthorne was in the tradition of, say, Shakespeare; but we quickly learn that, no, Hawthorne had entered a barren field, for although he himself lived in the present and had all the future to mold, he preferred to find many of his subjects in the past. We learn too that his romance of ethics is not admirable because it requires the hard, fine pressing of ideas, and we are told that "a romantic uninterested in adventure and

afraid of sex is likely to become somewhat graveled for matter." In short,
Hawthorne's mind was a thin one, and Parrington puts in evidence his use of
allegory and symbol and the very severity and precision of his art to prove
that he suffered from a sadly limited intellect, for so much fancy and so much
art could scarcely be needed unless the writer were trying to exploit to the
utmost the few poor ideas that he had.

Hawthorne, then, was "forever dealing with shadows, and he knew that he
was dealing with shadows." Perhaps so, but shadows are also part of reality
and one would not want a world without shadows, it would not even be a
"real" world. But we must get beyond Parrington's metaphor. The fact is that
Hawthorne was dealing beautifully with realities, with substantial things.
The man who could raise those brilliant and serious doubts about the nature
and possibility of moral perfection, the man who could keep himself aloof
from the "Yankee reality" and who could dissent from the orthodoxies of dissent and tell us so much about the nature of moral zeal, is of course dealing
exactly with reality.

Parrington's characteristic weakness as a historian is suggested by his title,
for the culture of a nation is not truly figured in the image of the current. A
culture is not a flow, nor even a confluence; the form of its existence is struggle, or at least debate—it is nothing if not a dialectic. And in any culture
there are likely to be certain artists who contain a large part of the dialectic
within themselves, their meaning and power lying in their contradictions;
they contain within themselves, it may be said, the very essence of the culture, and the sign of this is that they do not submit to serve the ends of any
one ideological group or tendency. It is a significant circumstance of American culture, and one which is susceptible of explanation, that an unusually
large proportion of its notable writers of the nineteenth century were such
repositories of the dialectic of their times—they contained both the yes and
the no of their culture, and by that token they were prophetic of the future.
Parrington said that he had not set up shop as a literary critic; but if a literary
critic is simply a reader who has the ability to understand literature and to
convey to others what he understands, it is not exactly a matter of free choice
whether or not a cultural historian shall be a literary critic, nor is it open to
him to let his virtuous political and social opinions do duty for percipience.
To throw out Poe because he cannot be conveniently fitted into a theory of
American culture, to speak of him as a biological sport and as a mind apart
from the main current, to find his gloom to be merely personal and eccentric,
"only the atrabilious wretchedness of a dipsomaniac," as Hawthorne's was
"no more than the skeptical questioning of life by a nature that knew no fierce
storms," to judge Melville's response to American life to be less noble than
that of Bryant or of Greeley, to speak of Henry James as an escapist, as an
artist similar to Whistler, a man characteristically afraid of stress—this is not

merely to be mistaken in aesthetic judgment; rather it is to examine without attention and from the point of view of a limited and essentially arrogant conception of reality the documents which are in some respects the most suggestive testimony to what America was and is, and of course to get no answer from them.

Parrington lies twenty years behind us, and in the intervening time there has developed a body of opinion which is aware of his inadequacies and of the inadequacies of his coadjutors and disciples, who make up what might be called the literary academicism of liberalism. Yet Parrington still stands at the center of American thought about American culture because, as I say, he expresses the chronic American belief that there exists an opposition between reality and mind and that one must enlist oneself in the party of reality.

II

This belief in the incompatibility of mind and reality is exemplified by the doctrinaire indulgence which liberal intellectuals have always displayed toward Theodore Dreiser, an indulgence which becomes the worthier of remark when it is contrasted with the liberal severity toward Henry James. Dreiser and James: with that juxtaposition we are immediately at the dark and bloody crossroads where literature and politics meet. One does not go there gladly, but nowadays it is not exactly a matter of free choice whether one does or does not go. As for the particular juxtaposition itself, it is inevitable and it has at the present moment far more significance than the juxtaposition which once used to be made between James and Whitman. It is not hard to contrive factitious oppositions between James and Whitman, but the real difference between them is the difference between the moral mind, with its awareness of tragedy, irony, and multitudinous distinctions, and the transcendental mind, with its passionate sense of the oneness of multiplictiy. James and Whitman are unlike not in quality but in kind, and in their very opposition they serve to complement each other. But the difference between James and Dreiser is not of kind, for both men addressed themselves to virtually the same social and moral fact. The difference here is one of quality, and perhaps nothing is more typical of American liberalism than the way it has responded to the respective qualities of the two men.

Few critics, I suppose, no matter what their political disposition, have ever been wholly blind to James's great gifts, or even to the grandiose moral intention of these gifts. And few critics have ever been wholly blind to Dreiser's great faults. But by liberal critics James is traditionally put to the ultimate question: of what use, of what actual political use, are his gifts and their intention? Granted that James was devoted to an extraordinary moral perceptiveness, granted too that moral perceptiveness has something to do with politics and the social life, of what possible practical value in our world of im-

pending disaster can James's work be? And James's style, his characters, his
subjects, and even his own social origin and the manner of his personal life
are adduced to show that his work cannot endure the question. To James no
quarter is given by American criticism in its political and liberal aspect. But in
the same degree that liberal criticism is moved by political considerations to
treat James with severity, it treats Dreiser with the most sympathetic indulgence. Dreiser's literary faults, it gives us to understand, are essentially social
and political virtues. It was Parrington who established the formula for the
liberal criticism of Dreiser by calling him a "peasant": when Dreiser thinks
stupidly, it is because he has the slow stubbornness of a peasant; when he
writes badly, it is because he is impatient of the sterile literary gentility of the
bourgeoisie. It is as if wit, and flexibility of mind, and perception, and knowledge were to be equated with aristocracy and political reaction, while dull-
ness and stupidity must naturally suggest a virtuous democracy, as in the old
plays.

The liberal judgment of Dreiser and James goes back of politics, goes back
to the cultural assumptions that make politics. We are still haunted by a kind
of political fear of the intellect which Tocqueville observed in us more than a
century ago. American intellectuals, when they are being consciously American or political, are remarkably quick to suggest that an art which is marked
by perception and knowledge, although all very well in its way, can never get
us through gross dangers and difficulties. And their misgivings become the
more intense when intellect works in art as it ideally should, when its processes
are vivacious and interesting and brilliant. It is then that we like to confront
it with the gross dangers and difficulties and to challenge it to save us at once
from disaster. When intellect in art is awkward or dull we do not put it to the
test of ultimate or immediate practicality. No liberal critic asks the question of
Dreiser whether *his* moral preoccupations are going to be useful in confronting the disasters that threaten us. And it is a judgment on the proper nature
of mind, rather than any actual political meaning that might be drawn from
the works of the two men, which accounts for the unequal justice they have
received from the progressive critics. If it could be conclusively demonstrated
—by, say, documents in James's handwriting—that James explicitly intended
his books to be understood as pleas for co-operatives, labor unions, better hous-
ing, and more equitable taxation, the American critic in his liberal and progressive character would still be worried by James because his work shows so
many of the electric qualities of mind. And if something like the opposite
were proved of Dreiser, it would be brushed aside—as his doctrinaire anti-
Semitism has in fact been brushed aside—because his books have the awk-
wardness, the chaos, the heaviness which we associate with "reality." In the
American metaphysic, reality is always material reality, hard, resistant, un-
formed, impenetrable, and unpleasant. And that mind is alone felt to be trust-

worthy which most resembles this reality by most nearly reproducing the sensations it affords.

In *The Rise of American Civilization*, Professor Beard uses a significant phrase when, in the course of an ironic account of James's career, he implies that we have the clue to the irrelevance of that career when we know that James was "a whole generation removed from the odors of the shop." Of a piece with this, and in itself even more significant, is the comment which Granville Hicks makes in *The Great Tradition* when he deals with James's stories about artists and remarks that such artists as James portrays, so concerned for their art and their integrity in art, do not really exist: "After all, who has ever known such artists? Where are the Hugh Verekers, the Mark Ambients, the Neil Paradays, the Overts, Limberts, Dencombes, Delavoys?" This question, as Mr. Hicks admits, had occurred to James himself, but what answer had James given to it? "If the life about us for the last thirty years refused warrant for these examples," he said in the preface to volume XII of the New York Edition, "then so much the worse for that life. . . . There are decencies that in the name of the general self-respect we must take for granted, there's a rudimentary intellectual honor to which we must, in the interest of civilization, at least pretend." And to this Mr. Hicks, shocked beyond argument, makes this reply, which would be astonishing had we not heard it before: "But this is the purest romanticism, this writing about what ought to be rather than what is!"

The "odors of the shop" are real, and to those who breathe them they guarantee a sense of vitality from which James is debarred. The idea of intellectual honor is not real, and to that chimera James was devoted. He betrayed the reality of what is in the interests of what ought to be. Dare we trust him? The question, we remember, is asked by men who themselves have elaborate transactions with what ought to be. Professor Beard spoke in the name of a growing, developing, and improving America. Mr. Hicks, when he wrote *The Great Tradition*, was in general sympathy with a nominally radical movement. But James's own transaction with what ought to be is suspect because it is carried on through what I have called the electrical qualities of mind, through a complex and rapid imagination and with a kind of authoritative immediacy. Mr. Hicks knows that Dreiser is "clumsy" and "stupid" and "bewildered" and "crude in his statement of materialistic monism"; he knows that Dreiser in his personal life—which is in point because James's personal life is always supposed to be so much in point—was not quite emancipated from "his boyhood longing for crass material success," showing "again and again a desire for the ostentatious luxury of the successful business man." But Dreiser is to be accepted and forgiven because his faults are the sad, lovable, honorable faults of reality itself, or of America itself—huge, inchoate, struggling toward expression, caught between the dream of raw power and the dream of morality.

"The liability in what Santayana called the genteel tradition was due to its being the product of mind apart from experience. Dreiser gave us the stuff of our common experience, not as it was hoped to be by any idealizing theorist, but as it actually was in its crudity." The author of this statement certainly cannot be accused of any lack of feeling for mind as Henry James represents it; nor can Mr. Matthiessen be thought of as a follower of Parrington—indeed, in the preface to *American Renaissance* he has framed one of the sharpest and most cogent criticisms of Parrington's method. Yet Mr. Matthiessen, writing in the *New York Times Book Review* about Dreiser's posthumous novel, *The Bulwark,* accepts the liberal cliché which opposes crude experience to mind and establishes Dreiser's value by implying that the mind which Dreiser's crude experience is presumed to confront and refute is the mind of gentility.

This implied amalgamation of mind with gentility is the rationale of the long indulgence of Dreiser, which is extended even to the style of his prose. Everyone is aware that Dreiser's prose style is full of roughness and ungainliness, and the critics who admire Dreiser tell us it does not matter. Of course it does not matter. No reader with a right sense of style would suppose that it does matter, and he might even find it a virtue. But it has been taken for granted that the ungainliness of Dreiser's style is the only possible objection to be made to it, and that whoever finds in it any fault at all wants a prettified genteel style (and is objecting to the ungainliness of reality itself). For instance, Edwin Berry Burgum, in a leaflet on Dreiser put out by the Book Find Club, tells us that Dreiser was one of those who used—or, as Mr. Burgum says, utilized—"the diction of the Middle West, pretty much as it was spoken, rich in colloquialism and frank in the simplicity and directness of the pioneer tradition," and that this diction took the place of "the literary English, formal and bookish, of New England provincialism that was closer to the aristocratic spirit of the mother country than to the tang of everyday life in the new West." This is mere fantasy. Hawthorne, Thoreau, and Emerson were for the most part remarkably colloquial—they wrote, that is, much as they spoke; their prose was specifically American in quality, and, except for occasional lapses, quite direct and simple. It is Dreiser who lacks the sense of colloquial diction—that of the Middle West or any other. If we are to talk of bookishness, it is Dreiser who is bookish; he is precisely literary in the bad sense; he is full of flowers of rhetoric and shines with paste gems; at hundreds of points his diction is not only genteel but fancy. It is he who speaks of "a scene more distingué than this," or of a woman "artistic in form and feature," or of a man who, although "strong, reserved, aggressive, with an air of wealth and experience, was *soi-disant* and not particularly eager to stay at home." Colloquialism held no real charm for him and his natural tendency is always toward the "fine:"

Moralists come and go; religionists fulminate and declare the pronouncements of God as to this; but Aphrodite still reigns. Embowered in the festal depths of the spring, set above her altars of porphyry, chalcedony, ivory and gold, see her smile the smile that is at once the texture and essence of delight, the glory and despair of the world! Dream on, oh Buddha, asleep on your lotus leaf, of an undisturbed Nirvana! Sweat, oh Jesus, your last agonizing drops over an unregenerate world! In the forests of Pan still ring the cries of the worshippers of Aphrodite! From her altars the incense of adoration ever rises! And see, the new red grapes dripping where votive hands new-press them!

Charles Jackson, the novelist, telling us in the same leaflet that Dreiser's style does not matter, remarks on how much still comes to us when we have lost by translation the stylistic brilliance of Thomas Mann or the Russians or Balzac. He is in part right. And he is right too when he says that a certain kind of conscious, supervised artistry is not appropriate to the novel of large dimensions. Yet the fact is that the great novelists have usually written very good prose, and what comes through even a bad translation is exactly the power of mind that made the well-hung sentence of the original text. In literature style is so little the mere clothing of thought—need it be insisted on at this date?—that we may say that from the earth of the novelist's prose spring his characters, his ideas, and even his story itself.[2]

To the extent that Dreiser's style is defensible, his thought is also defensible. That is, when he thinks like a novelist, he is worth following—when by means of his rough and ungainly but no doubt cumulatively effective style he creates rough, ungainly, but effective characters and events. But when he thinks like, as we say, a philosopher, he is likely to be not only foolish but vulgar. He thinks as the modern crowd thinks when it decides to think: religion and morality are nonsense, "religionists" and moralists are fakes, tradition is a fraud, what is man but matter and impulses, mysterious "chemisms," what value has life anyway? "What, cooking, eating, coition, job holding, growing,

[2] The latest defense of Dreiser's style, that in the chapter on Dreiser in the *Literary History of the United States,* is worth noting: "Forgetful of the integrity and power of Dreiser's whole work, many critics have been distracted into a condemnation of his style. He was like Twain and Whitman, an organic artist; he wrote what he knew—what he was. His many colloquialisms were part of the coinage of his time, and his sentimental and romantic passages were written in the language of the educational system and the popular literature of his formative years. In his style, as in his material, he was a child of his time, of his class. Self-educated, a type or model of the artist of plebeian origin in America, his language, like his subject matter, is not marked by internal inconsistencies." No doubt Dreiser was an organic artist in the sense that he wrote what he knew and what he was, but so, I suppose, is every artist; the question for criticism comes down to *what* he knew and *what* he was. That he was a child of his time and class is also true, but this can be said of everyone without exception; the question for criticism is how he transcended the imposed limitations of his time and class. As for the defense made on the ground of his particular class, it can only be said that liberal thought has come to a strange pass when it assumes that a plebeian origin is accountable for a writer's faults through all his intellectual life.

aging, losing, winning, in so changeful and passing a scene as this, important? Bunk! It is some form of titillating illusion with about as much import to the superior forces that bring it all about as the functions and gyrations of a fly. No more. And maybe less." Thus Dreiser at sixty. And yet there is for him always the vulgarly saving suspicion that maybe, when all is said and done, there is Something Behind It All. It is much to the point of his intellectual vulgarity that Dreiser's anti-Semitism was not merely a social prejudice but an idea, a way of dealing with difficulties.

No one, I suppose, has ever represented Dreiser as a masterly intellect. It is even commonplace to say that his ideas are inconsistent or inadequate. But once that admission has been made, his ideas are hustled out of sight while his "reality" and great brooding pity are spoken of. (His pity is to be questioned: pity is to be judged by kind, not amount, and Dreiser's pity—*Jennie Gerhardt* provides the only exception—is either destructive of its object or it is self-pity.) Why has no liberal critic ever brought Dreiser's ideas to the bar of political practicality, asking what use is to be made of Dreiser's dim, awkward speculation, of his self-justification, of his lust for "beauty" and "sex" and "living" and "life itself," and of the showy nihilism which always seems to him so grand a gesture in the direction of profundity? We live, understandably enough, with the sense of urgency; our clock, like Baudelaire's, has had the hands removed and bears the legend, "It is later than you think." But with us it is always a little too late for mind, yet never too late for honest stupidity; always a little too late for understanding, never too late for righteous, bewildered wrath; always too late for thought, never too late for naïve moralizing. We seem to like to condemn our finest but not our worst qualities by pitting them against the exigency of time.

But sometimes time is not quite so exigent as to justify all our own exigency, and in the case of Dreiser time has allowed his deficiencies to reach their logical, and fatal, conclusion. In *The Bulwark* Dreiser's characteristic ideas come full circle, and the simple, didactic life history of Solon Barnes, a Quaker business man, affirms a simple Christian faith, and a kind of practical mysticism, and the virtues of self-abnegation and self-restraint, and the belief in and submission to the hidden purposes of higher powers, those "superior forces that bring it all about"—once, in Dreiser's opinion, so brutally indifferent, now somehow benign. This is not the first occasion on which Dreiser has shown a tenderness toward religion and a responsiveness to mysticism. *Jennie Gerhardt* and the figure of the Reverend Duncan McMillan in *An American Tragedy* are forecasts of the avowals of *The Bulwark,* and Dreiser's lively interest in power of any sort led him to take account of the power implicit in the cruder forms of mystical performance. Yet these rifts in his nearly monolithic materialism cannot quite prepare us for the blank pietism of *The Bulwark,* not after we have remembered how salient in Dreiser's work has been the long surly rage against the "religionists" and the "moralists," the men who have presumed to believe that life can be given any law at all and who have dared to suppose that will or mind or faith can shape the savage and beautiful entity that Dreiser liked to call "life itself." Now for Dreiser the law may indeed be given, and it is wholly simple—the safe conduct of the personal life requires only that we follow the Inner Light according to the regimen of the Society of Friends, or according to some other godly rule. And now the smiling Aphrodite set above her altars of porphyry, chalcedony, ivory, and gold is quite forgotten, and we are told that the sad joy of cosmic acceptance goes hand in hand with sexual abstinence.

Dreiser's mood of "acceptance" in the last years of his life is not, as a personal experience, to be submitted to the tests of intellectual validity. It consists of a sensation of cosmic understanding, of an overarching sense of unity with the world in its apparent evil as well as in its obvious good. It is no more to be quarreled with, or reasoned with, than love itself—indeed, it is a kind of love, not so much of the world as of oneself in the world. Perhaps it is either the cessation of desire or the perfect balance of desires. It is what used often to be meant by "peace," and up through the nineteenth century a good many people understood its meaning. If it was Dreiser's own emotion at the end of his life, who would not be happy that he had achieved it? I am not even sure that our civilization would not be the better for more of us knowing and desiring this emotion of grave felicity. Yet granting the personal validity of the emotion, Dreiser's exposition of it fails, and is, moreover, offensive. Mr. Matthiessen has warned us of the attack that will be made on the doctrine of *The Bulwark* by "those who believe that any renewal of Christianity marks a new 'failure of nerve.' " But Dreiser's religious avowal is not a failure of nerve—it is a failure of mind and heart. We have only to set his book beside any work in which mind and heart are made to serve religion to know this at once. Ivan Karamazov's giving back his ticket of admission to the "harmony" of the universe suggests that *The Bulwark* is not morally adequate, for we dare not, as its hero does, blandly "accept" the suffering of others; and the Book of Job tells us that it does not include enough in its exploration of the problems of evil, and is not stern enough. I have said that Dreiser's religious affirmation was offensive; the offense lies in the vulgar ease of its formulation, as well as in the comfortable untroubled way in which Dreiser moved from nihilism to pietism.[3]

[3] This ease and comfortableness seem to mark contemporary religious conversions. Religion nowadays has the appearance of what the ideal modern house has been called, "a machine for living," and seemingly one makes up one's mind to acquire and use it not with spiritual struggle but only with a growing sense of its practicability and convenience. Compare *The Seven Storey Mountain,* which Monsignor Sheen calls "a twentieth-century form of the *Confessions* of St. Augustine," with the old, the as it were original, *Confessions* of St. Augustine.

The Bulwark is the fruit of Dreiser's old age, but if we speak of it as a failure of thought and feeling, we cannot suppose that with age Dreiser weakened in mind and heart. The weakness was always there. And in a sense it is not Dreiser who failed but a whole way of dealing with ideas, a way in which we have all been in some degree involved. Our liberal, progressive culture tolerated Dreiser's vulgar materialism with its huge negation, its simple cry of "Bunk!," feeling that perhaps it was not quite intellectually adequate but certainly very *strong*, certainly very *real*. And now, almost as a natural consequence, it has been given, and is not unwilling to take, Dreiser's pietistic religion in all its inadequacy.

Dreiser, of course, was firmer than the intellectual culture that accepted him. He *meant* his ideas, at least so far as a man can mean ideas who is incapable of following them to their consequences. But we, when it came to his ideas, talked about his great brooding pity and shrugged the ideas off. We are still doing it. Robert Elias, the biographer of Dreiser, tells us that "it is part of the logic of [Dreiser's] life that he should have completed *The Bulwark* at the same time that he joined the Communists." Just what kind of logic this is we learn from Mr. Elias's further statement. "When he supported left-wing movements and finally, last year, joined the Communist Party, he did so not because he had examined the details of the party line and found them satisfactory, but because he agreed with a general program that represented a means for establishing his cherished goal of greater equality among men." Whether or not Dreiser was following the logic of his own life, he was certainly following the logic of the liberal criticism that accepted him so undiscriminatingly as one of the great, significant expressions of its spirit. This is the liberal criticism, in the direct line of Parrington, which establishes the social responsibility of the writer and then goes on to say that, apart from his duty of resembling reality as much as possible, he is not really responsible for anything, not even for his ideas. The scope of reality being what it is, ideas are held to be mere "details," and, what is more, to be details which, if attended to, have the effect of diminishing reality. But ideals are different from ideas; in the liberal criticism which descends from Parrington ideals consort happily with reality and they urge us to deal impatiently with ideas—a "cherished goal" forbids that we stop to consider how we reach it, or if we may not destroy it in trying to reach it the wrong way.

From *The Liberal Imagination*, by Lionel Trilling. The Viking Press. Copyright, 1940, 1946, by Lionel Trilling. Reprinted by permission of the author and publishers. Based in part on "Parrington, Mr. Smith, and Reality" in *The Partisan Review*, Vol. VII (January–February, 1940), pp. 24–40; and on "Dreiser and the Liberal Mind" in *The Nation*, Vol. CLXII (April 20, 1946), pp. 466–472.

YVOR WINTERS

Robert Frost: or, The Spiritual Drifter as Poet

[1948]

I

ROBERT FROST is one of the most talented poets of our time, but I believe that his work is both overestimated and misunderstood; and it seems to me of the utmost importance that we should understand him with some accuracy. If we can arrive at a reasonably sound understanding of him, we can profit by his virtues without risk of acquiring his defects; and we may incidentally arrive at a better understanding of our present culture.

A popular poet is always a spectacle of some interest, for poetry in general is not popular; and when the popular poet is also within limits a distinguished poet, the spectacle is even more curious, for commonly it is bad poetry which is popular. When we encounter such a spectacle, we may be reasonably sure of finding certain social and historical reasons for the popularity. Frost is similar in his ways and attitudes and perceptions to a very large number of the more intelligent, if not the most intelligent, of his contemporaries: to the school teachers, the English professors, the more or less literate undergraduates, the journalists, and the casual readers of every class. These people are numerous and are in a position to perpetuate their ways and attitudes; this similarity, therefore, is worth examining.

Frost has been praised as a classical poet, but he is not classical in any sense which I can understand. Like many of his contemporaries, he is an Emersonian Romantic, although with certain mutings and modifications which I shall mention presently, and he has labeled himself as such with a good deal of care. He is a poet of the minor theme, the casual approach, and the discreetly eccentric attitude. When a reader calls Frost a classical poet, he probably means that Frost strikes him as a "natural" poet, a poet who somehow resembles himself and his neighbors; but this is merely another way of saying that the reader feels a kinship to him and likes him easily. Classical literature is said to judge human experience with respect to the norm; but it does so with respect to the norm of what humanity ought to be, not with respect to the norm of what it happens to be in a particular place and time. The human average has never been admirable, and in certain cultures it has departed very

417

far from the admirable; that is why in the great classical periods of literature
we are likely to observe great works in tragedy and satire, the works of a
Racine and a Molière, of a Shakespeare and a Jonson, works which deal in
their respective ways with sharp deviations from the ideal norm; and that is
why literature which glorifies the average is sentimental rather than classical.

Frost writes of rural subjects, and the American reader of our time has an
affection for rural subjects which is partly the product of the Romantic senti-
mentalization of "nature," but which is partly also a nostalgic looking back to
the rural life which predominated in this nation a generation or two ago; the
rural life is somehow regarded as the truly American life. I have no objection
to the poet's employing rural settings; but we should remember that it is the
poet's business to evaluate human experience, and the rural setting is no
more valuable for this purpose than any other or than no particular setting,
and one could argue with some plausibility that an exclusive concentration on
it may be limiting.

Frost early began his endeavor to make his style approximate as closely as
possible the style of conversation, and this endeavor has added to his reputation: it has helped to make him seem "natural." But poetry is not conversation, and I see no reason why poetry should be called upon to imitate conversation. Conversation is the most careless and formless of human utterance;
it is spontaneous and unrevised, and its vocabulary is commonly limited.
Poetry is the most difficult form of human utterance; we revise poems carefully in order to make them more nearly perfect. The two forms of expression
are extremes, they are not close to each other. We do not praise a violinist for
playing as if he were improvising; we praise him for playing well. And when
a man plays well or writes well, his audience must have intelligence, training, and patience in order to appreciate him. We do not understand difficult
matters "naturally."

The business of the poet can be stated simply. The poet deals with human
experience in words. Words are symbols of concepts, which have acquired
connotation of feeling in addition to their denotation of concept. The poet,
then, as a result of the very nature of his medium, must make a rational
statement about an experience, and as rationality is a part of the medium,
the ultimate value of the poem will depend in a fair measure on the soundness
of the rationality: it is possible, of course, to reason badly, just as it is possible to reason well. But the poet is deliberately employing the connotative
content of language as well as the denotative: so that what he must do is make
a rational statement about an experience, at the same time employing his language in such a manner as to communicate the emotion which ought to be
communicated by that rational understanding of the particular subject. In
so far as he is able to do this, the poem will be good; in so far as the subject
itself is important, the poem will be great. That is, a poem which merely

describes a stone may be excellent but will certainly be minor; whereas a poem which deals with man's contemplation of death and eternity, or with a formative decision of some kind, may be great. It is possible, of course, that the stone may be treated in such a way that it symbolizes something greater than itself; but if this occurs, the poem is about something greater than the stone. The poet is valuable, therefore, in proportion to his ability to apprehend certain kinds of objective truth; in proportion as he is great, he will not resemble ourselves but will resemble what we ought to be. It becomes our business, then, to endeavor to resemble him, and this endeavor is not easy and for this reason few persons make it. Country conversation and colloquial charm are irrelevant to the real issue. The great poets, men like Ben Jonson, Fulke Greville, and Richard Crashaw, have few readers; though some of them, like Milton, are widely admired from a distance. But they offer us, in their best efforts, the finest understanding of human experience to which we have access; some people are able and willing to understand them; and the human intelligence, however precariously, is thus kept alive. If we set up false ideals of human nature, and our best poets judge experience in terms of them and so beguile us into doing likewise, the human intelligence is to that extent diminished.

Frost has said that Emerson is his favorite American poet, and he himself appears to be something of an Emersonian. Emerson was a Romantic pantheist: he identified God with the universe; he taught that impulse comes directly from God and should be obeyed, that through surrender to impulse we become one with God; he taught that reason is man-made and bungling and should be suppressed. In moral and aesthetic doctrine, Emerson was a relativist; his most thorough-going disciples in American literature were Walt Whitman and Hart Crane. In Frost, on the other hand, we find a disciple without Emerson's religious conviction: Frost believes in the rightness of impulse, but does not discuss the pantheistic doctrine which would give authority to impulse; as a result of his belief in impulse, he is of necessity a relativist, but his relativism, apparently since it derives from no intense religious conviction, has resulted mainly in ill-natured eccentricity and in increasing melancholy. He is an Emersonian who has become sceptical and uncertain without having reformed; and the scepticism and uncertainty do not appear to have been so much the result of thought as the result of the impact upon his sensibility of conflicting notions of his own era—they appear to be the result of his having taken the easy way and having drifted with the various currents of his time.

II

I should like first of all to describe a few poems which deal with what in the hands of a more serious writer one could describe as the theme of moral choice. These poems throw more light on Frost as a whole, perhaps, than do any others, and they may serve as an introduction to his work. I have in mind especially three poems from *Mountain Interval*: the introductory piece entitled "The Road Not Taken," the post-scriptive piece entitled "The Sound of the Trees," and the lyrical narrative called "The Hill Wife"; and one poem from *A Further Range*: the poem entitled "The Bearer of Evil Tidings." These poems all have a single theme: the whimsical, accidental, and incomprehensible nature of the formative decision; and I should like to point out that if one takes this view of the formative decision, one has cut oneself off from understanding most of human experience, for in these terms there is nothing to be understood—one can write of human experience with sentimental approval or with sentimental melancholy, but with little else.

"The Road Not Taken," for example, is the poem of a man whom one might fairly call a spiritual drifter; and a spiritual drifter is unlikely to have either the intelligence or the energy to become a major poet. Yet the poem has definite virtues, and these should not be overlooked. In the first place, spiritual drifters exist, they are real; and although their decisions may not be comprehensible, their predicament is comprehensible. The poem renders the experience of such a person, and renders the uncertain melancholy of his plight. Had Frost been a more intelligent man, he might have seen that the plight of the spiritual drifter was not inevitable, he might have judged it in the light of a more comprehensive wisdom. Had he done this, he might have written a greater poem. But his poem is good as far as it goes; the trouble is that it does not go far enough, it is incomplete, and it puts on the reader a burden of critical intelligence which ought to be borne by the poet. We are confronted with a similar critical problem when the Earl of Rochester writes remarkably beautiful poems to invite us to share in the pleasures of drunkenness. The pleasures of drunkenness are real—let no one delude himself on that score—and the Earl of Rochester is one of the most brillian masters of English verse. But if the pleasures of drunkenness are regarded in what the sentimental critics are wont to term a true perspective, they are seen to be obstacles to other experiences of far greater value, and then they take on the appearance of temptations to sin. Dante would have dealt with these pleasures truly, placing them where they belong in the hierarchy of values; Rochester was not equal to the task, but Rochester gave us a good evaluation of the experience of a man in his predicament as he himself sees it. He is like the demon defined by Aquinas: good in so far as he may be said to exist, but a demon is so far as his existence is incomplete. And like the demon he is also enticing, for he has more than usual powers of persuasion. We are protected against his incompleteness and against his enticements if we understand his limitations, and we can then profit by what he possesses; but without understanding, we may be drawn to emulate him, to form ourselves upon him—we may, in a sense, become possessed by an evil power which is great enough to control us and diminish our own being.

The comparison of Rochester to Frost is unjust in one respect, for Rochester was a consciously vicious man; whereas Robert Frost would not willingly injure anyone. Yet the comparison in other ways is just, for Frost, as I shall show, has willfully refrained from careful thinking and so is largely responsible for his own condition; and his condition is less dramatic and more easily shared by large numbers of his contemporaries than was the condition of Rochester, so that he is probably a greater menace to the general intelligence. Rochester knew himself to be a sinner, and he knew that he would be regarded as one. Frost by a process of devious evasions has convinced himself that he is a wise and virtuous man, and he is regarded as a kind of embodiment of human wisdom by hundreds of thousands of Americans from high school age to the brink of senility. He embodies a common delusion regarding human nature, and he is strongly reinforcing that delusion in the minds of his contemporaries.

"The Sound of the Trees" deals with a longing to depart which has never quite been realized. The trees

> are that which talks of going
> But never gets away.

The poem ends as follows:

> I shall make the reckless choice
> Some day when they are in voice
> And tossing so as to scare
> The white clouds over them on.
> I shall have less to say,
> But I shall be gone.

The poem has the same quality of uncertainty and incomprehension as "The Road Not Taken"; it is written with about the same degree of success, with about the same charm, and with about the same quality of vague melancholy. In considering either of these poems, especially if one compares them even to minor works by sixteenth- and seventeenth-century masters, one will observe not only the limitations of intelligence which I have mentioned, but a quality, slight though it may be, of imprecision in the rendering of the detail and of the total attitude, which is the result of the limitations. Such a poem as Robert Herrick's "Night-Piece to Julia" is as sharp as a knife in comparison. Herrick knew exactly what he was saying and exactly what it was worth. Frost, on the other hand, is mistaking whimsical impulse for moral choice, and the blunder obscures his understanding and even leaves his mood uncertain with regard to the value of the whole business. He is vaguely afraid that he may be neither wrong nor right.

"The Hill Wife" is a less happy specimen than the poems just mentioned. It deals, not with a personal experience of the author, but with a dramatic situation seen from without; and the dramatic crisis is offered as something incomprehensible. The wife leaves her husband because she is lonely on their back-country farm, but there is no clear understanding of her motive; we are told that she is disturbed when the birds leave in the fall, and frightened by a casual tramp, and that a pine near the window obsesses her thoughts. The last section, characteristically entitled "The Impulse," describes her final act as a sudden and unpremeditated one. The poem has an eerie quality, like that of dream or of neurosis, but it has little else. As a study in human relationships, it amounts to nothing, and one has only to compare it to "Eros Turannos" by Robinson to discern its triviality. "The Bearer of Evil Tidings" deals with a similarly casual and sudden decision, although it is a more interesting poem. And one might mention also the poem from *A Witness Tree* entitled "A Serious Step Lightly Taken": the serious step in question is merely the buying of a farm; but the title is characteristic, and the title implies approval and not disapproval—it implies that serious steps ought to be lightly taken. But if serious steps are to be lightly taken, then poetry, at least, is impoverished, and the poet can have very little to say. Most of the world's great poetry has had to do with serious steps seriously taken, and when the seriousness goes from life, it goes from the poetry.

III

I shall consider next some of the more clearly didactic poems, which will reinforce what I have been saying. I should perhaps mention briefly as one of these, a short lyric in *West-Running Brook,* a lyric called "Sand Dunes," of which the clearly stated theme is the Emersonian notion that man can think better if he frees himself wholly from the past. The last poem in the same volume, at least as the volume originally appeared, is called "The Bear." The poem compares the wild bear to the bear in a cage; the uncaged bear is a creature of free impulse and is compared by implication to man as he would be were he guided by impulse; and the caged bear is compared to rational man as he is. The poem is amusing on first reading, but it wears thin with time. The difficulty is this, that satirical poetry is a branch of didactic poetry, for whereas purely didactic poetry endeavors to convince directly, satirical poetry endeavors to convince indirectly by ridiculing what the poet takes to be a deviation from wisdom; and both forms depend rather obviously upon the soundness of the ideas which they expound or assume. Frost tells us in this poem that reasoning man is ridiculous because he appears to labor and to change his mind; and he implies that impulsive man would be a wiser and a nobler creature. The fact of the matter is, however, that impulsive man, if he is restrained, like Frost, by conventions and habits the nature and origins of which he does not understand, is likely to be merely confused, uncertain, and melancholy; and if he is not so restrained may degenerate to madness or to criminality. Within relatively recent years, we have had two tragic examples, in Hart Crane and in Ezra Pound, of what a man of genius can do to himself and to his work by energetically living the life of impulse. It is not foolish to change one's mind; one learns by changing one's mind. Life is a process of revision in the interests of greater understanding, and it is by means of this process that men came down from the trees and out of the caves; and although civilization is very far from what it should be, nevertheless mankind has shown a marked improvement over the past ten thousand years. This improvement is the result of the fact that man is a rational animal, as I believe that a certain Greek once remarked. The uncaged bear, or the reflective caveman, is inferior to Thomas Aquinas and to Richard Hooker, to Dante and to Ben Jonson, and to assert the contrary is merely irresponsible foolishness. Frost then is satirizing the intelligent man from the point of view of the unintelligent; and the more often one reads the poem, the more obvious this fact becomes, and the more trivial the poem appears.

Frost expounds the same ideas more directly still in his poem "To a Thinker," in *A Further Range*. The idea in this poem is the same as that in "The Bear," but is even more plainly stated; we have the commonplace Romantic distrust of reason and trust in instinct. The poem ends as follows:

> So if you find you must repent
> From side to side in argument,
> At least don't use your mind too hard,
> But trust my instinct—I'm a bard.

The poem is badly written, but one couplet is momentarily amusing:

> I own I never really warmed
> To the reformer or reformed.

Yet when we examine it more carefully, there is something almost contemptible about it. There are, of course, reformers and reformers, and many of them have been ludicrous or worse. Frost is invoking the image of the soap-box politician or the street-corner preacher in order to discredit reason. But the word *reform* can be best evaluated if one separates the syllables for a moment. To reform means to re-form. And the progress of civilization has been a process of re-forming human nature. Socrates re-formed the human mind; Jesus re-formed man's moral and religious nature; Aquinas re-formed philosophical method and content; and William the Silent re-formed the idea of the state. Frost endeavors to gain his point by sleight-of-hand; he endeavors to obscure the difference between St. Thomas Aquinas and Pussyfoot Johnson.

Even Frost, with his instinct to guide him, is not proof against wavering,

however. In the same volume with the poem just described is a poem called
"The White-Tailed Hornet," in which Frost describes the activities of a hornet
and the errors it commits under the guidance of instinct, and he reprehends
mankind for having engaged in "downward comparisons":

>   As long on earth
> As our comparisons were stoutly upward
> With gods and angels, we were men at least,
> But little lower than the gods and angels.
> But once comparisons were yielded downward,
> Once we began to see our images
> Reflected in the mud and even dust,
> 'Twas disillusion upon disillusion.
> We were lost piecemeal to the animals
> Like people thrown out to delay the wolves.

Yet we have seen Frost himself engaging in downward comparisons, and
we shall see him doing it again. This is the only poem in Frost's works which
seems to represent a conscious rejection of his usual ideas, and this poem, as I
have said, even occurs in the same volume with the poem which I quoted
previously, "To a Thinker." It is possible that Frost shares the contempt felt
by Emerson and by Whitman for consistency, or he may be so inexperienced
a thinker as to be unaware of his inconsistency; the point is of little importance,
for he nowhere else takes up this argument.

   Frost has something to say of the relationship of the individual to society.
His most extensive poem on this subject is called "Build Soil—A Political
Pastoral," and was delivered at Columbia University, May 31, 1932, before
the national party conventions of that year. It will be remembered that these
were the conventions which led to the first election of Franklin D. Roosevelt,
and that the time was one of the darkest periods in the history of the nation.
The poem is Frost's most ambitious effort to deal with his social, political, and
economic views. As to his economic views, he says that if he were dictator of
the country:

>   I'd let things take their course
> And then I'd claim the credit for the outcome.

This statement, if it means anything at all, is a statement of belief in an unrestrained laissez-faire system, of the sort that Emerson would have approved;
a belief that if things are left alone they must come right. It represents a
doctrine of political drifting which corresponds to the doctrine of personal
drifting which we have already seen; in practice, it could lead only to the withdrawal from public affairs of the citizen not concerned primarily with personal
aggrandizement, and to the surrender of the nation to the unscrupulous go-
getter, who, though he may not be a drifter, is not governed by admirable

aims. It is similarly an obscurantist doctrine: it implies that this realm of human activity, like others, cannot be dealt with rationally and is better if not understood. As to the behavior of the private citizen, Frost says:

> I bid you to a one-man revolution—
> The only revolution that is coming.
> We're too unseparate out among each other—
> With goods to sell and notions to impart . . .
> We congregate embracing from distrust
> As much as love, and too close in to strike
> And so be very striking. Steal away
> The song says. Steal away and stay away.
> Don't join too many gangs. Join few if any.
> Join the United States and join the family—
> But not much in between unless a college. . . .

The individual is thus advised against any kind of political activity in a time of national collapse. The difficulties of effective political action are obvious; the English-speaking peoples have been struggling with the problems of constitutional government for centuries. But if the reality of the difficulties results in our stealing away from them, society will be taken over, as I have said, by the efficient scoundrels who are always ready to take over when everyone else abdicates. In a dictatorship by scoundrels, the Frosts and the Thoreaus, the amateur anarchists and village eccentrics, would find life somewhat more difficult than they have found it to date. Frost objects in the last passage to the commerce of minds, and he objects to it earlier in the poem:

> Suppose someone comes near me who in rate
> Of speech and thinking is so much my better
> I am imposed on, silenced and discouraged.
> Do I submit to being supplied by him
> As the more economical producer?
> No, I unostentatiously move off
> Far enough for my thought-flow to resume.

It does not occur to Frost that he might learn from his betters and improve himself; he can see only two possibilities in his relationship with them—he can be silenced by them or he can ignore them and proceed as before. There is the implication in this passage that his personal "thought-flow" is valuable merely because it is his own, that it should remain uncontaminated. He believes that the man and the nation equally will reach their fullest development through a kind of retreat to passivity, through letting things happen as they may with a minimum of influence from without.

The same sentimental dislike for society, for community of interest, can be found in the poem called "The Egg and the Machine," a poem appended

in the *Collected Poems* to the group called *West-Running Brook*. The poem
tells of a Thoreau-like adventurer who is exasperated to encounter a railroad
running through his favorite marsh. After a locomotive passes him, he proceeds to find a nestful of turtle eggs, and Frost writes:

> If there was one egg in it there were nine,
> Torpedo-like, with shell of gritty leather
> All packed in sand to wait the trump together.
> 'You'd better not disturb me any more,'
> He told the distance, 'I am armed for war.
> The next machine that has the power to pass
> Will get this plasm in its goggle-glass.'

Here are several familiar Romantic attitudes: resentment at being unable to
achieve the absolute privacy which Frost names as a primary desideratum in
"Build Soil," the sentimental regard for the untouched wilderness (the untouched wilderness would provide absolute privacy for the unique Romantic),
and the sentimental hatred for the machine. I am willing to admit, in connection with the last matter, that machinery is sometimes far from beautiful,
both in itself and in some of its effects; but its benefits have been overwhelmingly great, and the literary farmer in Vermont could scarcely hope to subsist
either as farmer or as writer without its help, any more than he could hope
to subsist unless a good many people faced moral and political realities; and
it is curiously unjust that the locomotive, that patient and innocuous draft
horse of civilization, should be selected to symbolize the viciousness of machinery. Frost's real objection to the machine, I suspect, is its social nature;
it requires and facilitates cooperation, and Frost is unwilling to recognize its
respectability mainly for this reason.

There have been other literary works dealing with resentment at the
machine and the changes it has introduced; the resentment I believe to be
foolish, but in certain settings it may have a tragic if barbarous dignity. Bret
Harte wrote a story called "Maruja," which tells of the first railroad to proceed
through the San Antonio Ranch in what is now Los Altos, California, and
of the resentment of the old Indian overseer at this destruction of the old
order. The Indian, Pereo, whose resentment against the incoming Anglo-
Americans had developed to the point of paranoia, and who had murdered one
of the newcomers by roping him about the neck from horseback and dragging
him to death, rode out against the first locomotive, roped it, and tried to drag
it from the tracks, and was himself dragged and killed. The negro ballad of
John Henry tells of a "steel-driving man" who broke his back in the attempt
to out-hammer a steam-drill. These actions are naïve and primitive, but they
are heroic in a fashion, they at least have the seriousness of honest violence.
Frost's protagonist, however, expresses his feelings by threatening to throw

a turtle-egg into the headlight of a locomotive. The turtle-egg, of course, may be intended as something more than a simple missile: it is "plasm," raw life, and hence capable of confounding (although only symbolically) the mechanical product of human reason. The trouble is again that the symbols will not stand inspection: the locomotive cannot be equated with human reason, for it is merely something created by human reason to facilitate higher activities; there is nothing either of wisdom or of greatness in the egg of a turtle; and the locomotive and human reason about equally would be quite unperturbed by the egg of a turtle. As we pursue the symbolism, we are left where we began, with a petulant and self-righteous gesture, a feeble joke.

There is a kind of half dramatic, half didactic poem occasionally, of which I shall mention two examples: "West-Running Brook" and *A Masque of Reason.* The first of these is a brief affair in the form of a dialogue between a young husband and wife who apparently have just established themselves on a farm next to a brook which runs west instead of east; they observe a ripple in the brook, in which the water is thrown upward and apparently backward against the current. The husband, in certain lines which are the chief part of the poem, comments upon the ripple:

> Speaking of contraries, see how the brook
> In that white wave runs counter to itself.
> It is from that in water we were from
> Long, long before we were from any creature.
> Here we, in our impatience of the steps,
> Get back to the beginning of beginnings,
> The stream of everything that runs away . . .
> It has this throwing backward on itself
> So that the fall of most of it is always
> Raising a little, sending up a little.
> Our life runs down in sending up the clock.
> The brook runs down in sending up our life.
> The sun runs down in sending up the brook.
> And there is something sending up the sun.
> It is this backward motion toward the source
> Against the stream that most we see ourselves in,
> The tribute of the current to the source.
> It is from this in nature we are from.

The theology of this passage, if we may call it theology, is tenuous and incomplete; it is what a certain kind of critic would call suggestive, rather than definitive; there is, in brief, very little to it. Frost seems to have suspected this, for he did not let his meditation on the ripple stand alone on its merits; he framed it in the dialogue I have mentioned and made his young people responsible for it. Yet the people are not depicted as characters, and their remarks lead to no dramatic action; the meditation gives the momentary illusion that the characters are more important than they are; the conversational framework gives the momentary illusion that the meditation is more important than it is. Thus the structure of the poem is actually a piece of deception, and the substance of the poem is negligible.

A Masque of Reason is the same kind of poem on a larger scale. The characters are God, the Devil, Job, and Job's wife. The scene is "A fair oasis in the purest desert"; the time is the Day of Judgment. Job and his wife suddenly discover the presence of the Burning Bush. She says:

> There's a strange light on everything today.

> Job: The myrrh tree gives it. Smell the rosin burning?
> The ornaments the Greek artificers
> Made for the Emperor Alexius,
> The Star of Bethlehem, the pomegranates,
> The birds, seem all on fire with Paradise.
> And hark, the gold enameled nightingales
> Are singing. Yes, and look, the Tree is troubled.
> Someone's caught in the branches.

> Wife: So there is.
> He can't get out.

> Job: He's loose! He's out!

> Wife: It's God.
> I'd know him by Blake's picture anywhere.
> Now what's he doing?
> Job: Pitching throne, I guess.
> Here by our atoll.

> Wife: Something Byzantine.

> (*The throne's a ply-wood flat, prefabricated,*
> *That God pulls lightly upright on its hinges*
> *And stands beside, supporting it in place.*)

This brief passage gives a clue to the nature of the whole poem. Job's first speech above is a piece of remarkable rhetoric: there is nothing else in the poem to equal it. It reminds one of Yeats, especially of Yeats's brilliant but whimsical poem called "Sailing to Byzantium." From that passage onward, through the references to Blake and to the plywood throne, we have details which are offered merely for the shock of cleverness; the details are irrelevant to any theme discernible in the poem. Frost, the rustic realist of *North of Boston,* appears in his old age as a standard exemplar of irresponsible Romantic irony, of the kind of irony that has degenerated steadily from the moderately low level of Laforgue, through Pound, Eliot, Cummings, and their younger imitators. The method is employed throughout the poem.

The poem falls roughly into three parts. The first of these deals with God's first explanation to Job of the treatment Job had been accorded in life. God tells him:

> You helped me
> Establish once for all the principle
> There's no connection man can reason out
> Between his just deserts and what he gets.
> Virtue may fail and wickedness succeed. . . .
> You realize by now the part you played
> To stultify the Deuteronomist
> And change the tenor of religious thought.
> My thanks are to you for releasing me
> From moral bondage to the human race.
> The only free will there at first was man's,
> Who could do good or evil as he chose.
> I had no choice but I must follow him
> With forfeits and rewards he understood—
> Unless I liked to suffer loss of worship.
> I had to prosper good and punish evil.
> You changed all that. You set me free to reign.

So far as the ideas in this passage are concerned, the passage belongs to the fideistic tradition of New England Calvinism; the ideas can be found in more than one passage in Jonathan Edwards, as well as elsewhere. The carefully flippant tone, however, is something else; it belongs to the tradition of Romantic irony which I have already mentioned, and is used to make the ideas seem trivial. The ideas and the tone together express the Romantic ennui or disillusionment which is born of spiritual laziness, the laziness which is justified by the Romantic doctrine that one can best apprehend the truth by intuition and without labor. One can find the same ennui, expressed in various ways, in Henry Adams, in Laforgue, in Eliot, and in scores of others.

The second passage of chief importance is the one in which God revises his explanation. Job insists that God's explanation is not the true one, that God is concealing something, and God makes the following admission:

> I'm going to tell Job why I tortured him
> And trust it won't be adding to the torture.
> I was just showing off to the Devil, Job,
> As is set forth in chapters One and Two.
> (Job takes a few steps pacing.) Do you mind?
> (God eyes him anxiously.)

Job: No. No, I mustn't.
         'Twas human of You. I expected more
         Than I could understand and what I get
         Is almost less than I can understand.
         But I don't mind. Let's leave it as it stood.
         The point was it was none of my concern.
         I stick to that. But talk about confusion . . .

The general idea is the same as in the preceding passage, but the debasement
of the attitude toward the idea becomes now a matter of explicit statement as
well as of stylistic tone. There is no understanding of good and evil in themselves, of the metaphysical questions involved. Good is submission to an
anthropomorphic and undignified God and is made to seem preposterous.
Evil is made equally preposterous, and for similar reasons. The poem resembles
"The Bear," but is on a larger scale. If these concepts of good and evil were
the only concepts available, or if they were the best concepts available, then
Frost's satire would be justified. But they are not, and in reading the poem one
can only be appalled at Frost's willful ignorance, at his smug stupidity.

In spite of the close relationship between the two passages which I have
quoted, however, the poem is far from unified. These two passages are separated by various outbursts of indignation on the part of Job's wife at the way
female witches are treated, in spite of the fact that male prophets have always
been received with honor; and there are other minor excursions. The concluding pages are devoted to the appearance of the Devil, who is called up by
God, so that Job's wife may photograph the three main actors in the old drama
as a memento. This passage is in itself an excursion from the main theme, but
it is employed to permit subsidiary excursions:

God: Don't *you* twit. He's unhappy. Church neglect
        And figurative use have pretty well
        Reduced him to a shadow of himself.

Job's Wife: *That* explains why he's so diaphanous
               And easy to see through. But where's he off to?
               I thought there were to be festivities
               Of some kind. We could have charades.

God: He has his business he must be about.
        Job mentioned him and so I brought him in
        More to give his reality its due
        Than anything.

Job's Wife: He's very real to me
               And always will be. Please don't go. Stay, stay
               But to the evensong and having played
               Together we will go with you along.

> There are who won't have had enough of you
> If you go now. Look how he takes no steps!
> He isn't really going, yet he's leaving.
>
> Job: (*Who has been standing dazed with new ideas*)
> He's on that tendency that like the Gulf Stream,
> Only of sand, not water, runs through here.
> It has a rate distinctly different
> From the surrounding desert; just today
> I stumbled over it and got tripped up.
>
> Job's Wife: Oh, yes, that tendency! Oh, do come off it.
> Don't let it carry you away. I hate
> A tendency. The minute you get on one
> It seems to start right off accelerating. . . .

In this passage, the satire is aimed at the word *tendency*, but the exact meaning of the word is not clear: it may mean a trivial fashion; it may mean an intellectual movement; it may indicate that Frost is unable to distinguish between a trivial fashion and an intellectual movement, just as he is unable to differentiate among reformers. The mutilated fragment from Herrick serves no purpose, but is merely an aimless effort to be funny. The poem as a whole is at loose ends; no single part of it is intelligent or even tries to be intelligent. It is a curious performance to signalize the seventieth birthday of a poet of so great a reputation. It is matched in triviality and general ineptitude by the collection of short poems entitled *Steeple Bush* and published more recently.

The best of the didactic poems is the one called "The Lesson for Today." The poem is for the most part a suavely satirical comment upon that school of contemporary criticism which holds that the modern poet is condemned to mediocrity because of the degeneracy of the age, and to this extent the poem is one with which it is hard not to sympathize. Frost addresses his hypothetical poet of the court of Charles the Great as follows:

> I can just hear you call your Palace class:
> Come learn the Latin Eheu for alas.
> You may not want to use it and you may.
> O paladins, the lesson for today
> Is how to be unhappy yet polite.
> And at the summons Roland, Olivier,
> And every sheepish paladin and peer,
> Being already more than proved in fight,
> Sits down in school to try if he can write
> Like Horace in the true Horatian vein,
> Yet like a Christian disciplined to bend
> His mind to thinking always of the end.
> Memento mori and obey the Lord.

Art and religion love the sombre chord.
Earth's a hard place in which to save the soul,
And could it be brought under state control,
So automatically we all were saved,
Its separateness from Heaven could be waived;
It might as well at once be kingdom-come.
(Perhaps it will be next millennium.)

From this subject, however, the poem wanders into a brief discussion of
mortality in general and the poet's concern with the subject; and after that
topic the poem closes on the poet's epitaph for himself:

I hold your doctrine of Memento Mori.
And were an epitaph to be my story
I'd have a short one ready for my own.
I would have written of me on my stone:
I had a lover's quarrel with the world.

These two transitions are casual rather than structural, and the poem falls
badly apart. The last lines, moreover, are extremely bad. There is a weak sentimentality about them which one perceives easily, but the reason for which deserves mention. There are good reasons for quarreling with the world, or at
least with large segments of it; much of the world is evil, and the evil had better
be recognized and taken seriously. If the quarrel can be reduced to a lover's
quarrel, it is not serious. It is as if one said to a murderer: "After all, you are
human, and you have a perfect right to your own opinions, attitudes, and
behavior; we are all human and should respect and admire each other." The
principle back of the final line is vicious and corrupts the line. And the
intellectual vagueness which is responsible for this weak ending is responsible
likewise for the fragmentary structure of the poem and for the weakness of
the other poems which I have been considering.

Frost, as far as we have examined him, then, is a poet who holds the following views: he believes that impulse is trustworthy and reason contemptible,
that formative decisions should be made casually and passively, that the individual should retreat from cooperative action with his kind, should retreat not
to engage in intellectual activity but in order to protect himself from the contamination of outside influence, that affairs manage themselves for the best if
left alone, that ideas of good and evil need not be taken very seriously. These
views are sure to be a hindrance to self-development, and they effectually cut
Frost off from any really profound understanding of human experience,
whether political, moral, metaphysical, or religious. The result in the didactic
poems is the perversity and incoherence of thought; the result in the narrative poems is either slightness of subject or a flat and uninteresting apprehension of the subject; the result in the symbolic lyrics is a disturbing dislocation

between the descriptive surface, which is frequently lovely, and the ultimate meaning, which is usually sentimental and unacceptable. The result in nearly all the poems is a measure of carelessness in the style, sometimes small and sometimes great, but usually evident: the conversational manner will naturally suit a poet who takes all experience so casually, and it is only natural that the conversational manner should often become very conversational indeed.

It is worth while to mention one other poem in connection with Frost's retreat from the serious subject. The poem I have in mind is called "The Times Table." The poem deals with a farmer who is given to commenting on death and who is reproved by Frost: Frost remarks that such comments should not be made

> Unless our purpose is doing harm,
> And then I know of no better way
> To close a road, abandon a farm,
> Reduce the births of the human race,
> And bring back nature in people's place.

We should remember that Frost is a poet and normally speaks with full consciousness of his role as poet; it is reasonable to assume that this poem applies to the poet as well as to other persons. The poet, then, should not deal with death or with comparably disturbing topics, because these topics distress and discourage people. Yet I wish to point out that all people die, that human life is filled with tragedy, and that commonly the tragedies accumulate all but overwhelmingly toward the end. To ignore the tragic subject is to leave oneself unprepared for the tragic experience; it is likely to lead to disaster and collapse. It is the business of the poet, let me repeat, to understand his subjects, and as far as may be the most difficult and important subjects, in rational terms, and at the same time to communicate the feeling which ought to be communicated by that rational understanding. The great poet judges the tragic subject completely, that is, rationally and emotionally; the nature of the human mind is such that we can enter the poet's mind by way of his poem, if we are willing to make the effort, and share his judgment. In this way we may gain both understanding and strength, for the human mind is so made that it is capable of growth and of growth in part through its own self-directed effort. This is the virtue of poetry; in so far as it is good, and we understand both its goodness and its limitations, it enables us to achieve a more nearly perfect and comprehensive being, to reduce that margin of spiritual privation which is evil. But Frost advises us to turn away from serious topics, and for the greater part he confines himself to minor topics. The major topics impinge upon his personal experience, however, for after all they are unavoidable; but his treatment of them is usually whimsical, sentimental, and evasive; and in his later years his poetry is more and more pervaded by an obscure melancholy which he can neither control nor understand.

IV

Yet Frost has a genuine gift for writing, as I have pointed out, and this gift emerges more clearly in his later work than in his earlier, though still hesitantly and momentarily. The view of human nature which we have seen Frost to hold is one that must lead of necessity to a feeling that the individual man is small, lost, and unimportant in the midst of a vast and changing universe. This feeling is expressed in the well-known poem entitled "On Going Unnoticed." The nostalgic love for the chaotic and the dream-like, which Frost inherits from the Romantic tradition, along with an habitual but unreasoned hesitancy or fear, which is the heritage of the earlier New England, keeps Frost looking two ways, unable to move decisively in either direction. He is neither a truly vigorous Romantic, such as Hart Crane, nor a truly reactionary Classicist, such as E. A. Robinson. He cannot decide whether to go or to stay, and the result is uncertainty and increasing melancholy. One may see the same difficulty in "Tree at My Window." Frost sees his own mind as similar to the vague dream-head of the tree, the thing next most diffuse to cloud, and the feeling of the poem is one of a melancholy longing to share the dream-like experience more fully. One can trace the manner in which Frost has arrived at this state of mind, and to that extent the poem is comprehensible. The feeling appears to be rendered more or less truly; that is, it seems to be an acceptable version of the feelings of a man in this predicament. But the poet does not understand the nature or the limitations of the predicament; and to that extent the poem is incomplete and not quite sure of itself. Like "The Road Not Taken" it puts on the reader a burden of critical intelligence which ought to have been borne more fully by the poet; and if the reader is not capable of the necessary intelligence, the poem is likely to draw him into a similar state of mind.

"The Last Mowing" deals with the same subject, and even more beguilingly. It describes a meadow which is being abandoned and is about to be taken over by the wild flowers before the more massive wilderness moves in:

> The place for the moment is ours,
> For you, oh tumultuous flowers
> To go to waste and go wild in,
> All shapes and colors of flowers,
> I needn't call you by name.

The next to the last line of this poem—"All shapes and colors of flowers"—is a curious triumph of rhetoric. Shape and color are named as pure abstractions; no particular shape or color is given; and what we get is an image of the shapeless and the shadowy, of haunting confusion, of longing for something unrealizable, of the fields of asphodel. This poem in its subdued and melancholy, yet somehow violent, abandonment to chaos, is one of the most explicit statements of Frost's predicament, and one of the most moving of them. "Spring Pools," from the same volume, appears to treat the same subject, but less explicitly. In paraphrase, it is a warning to the summer woods not to drink up the pools of snow water and the flowers that grow from them—these flowery waters and these watery flowers—and organize them into something greater. It is a poem on the love for the small, the fleeting, and the elusive experience of the late Romantic; in this respect, and in respect to the extraordinary sensitivity of its execution, it reminds me strongly of a poem by Paul Verlaine: *"Le Piano que baise une main frêle."* Superficially considered, the poem by Verlaine deals with a subject which is very different and more obviously decadent; but decadence is a state of mind, not a matter of the landscape which happens to provide the symbols, and in spiritual quality the two poems are remarkably similar.

The symbolic lyrics which I have been discussing are all to be found in the volume called *West-Running Brook,* the fifth collection. There is one poem in the volume, the sonnet entitled "Acquainted with the Night," which surpasses any poem thus far mentioned and which seems to me one of the two or three best poems that Frost has written. Superficially, the poem deals with the feeling of loneliness which one has when walking late at night in a strange city; but symbolically it deals with the poet's loneliness in a strange and obscure world, and the clock which tells him that the time is neither wrong nor right is a symbol of the relativism which causes his melancholy. The understanding of his predicament appears to be greater in this poem than in most of the others; he knows, at least, that it is a predicament and realizes the state of mind to which it has brought him. In the seventh volume, *A Witness Tree,* there is an even more impressive piece entitled "The Most of It." This poem represents a momentary insight into the vast and brute indifference of nature, the nature toward which Frost has cherished so sentimental a feeling through so many poems. For a moment the poet appears to be appalled. The poem deals with a protagonist who seems to have cultivated solitude, like Frost, and who heard only the echo of his own voice in the wilderness but who longed for a personal reply from nature. The reply, when it came, was not the one he had wanted. One morning he saw a splash on the far side of the lake, and something swimming toward him, and then:

> Instead of proving human when it neared
> And some one else additional to him,
> As a great buck it powerfully appeared,
> Pushing the crumpled water up ahead,
> And landed pouring like a waterfall,

And stumbled through the rocks with horny tread,
And forced the underbrush—and that was all.

Frost's buck has much the same kind of symbolic grandeur as the apocryphal beast in "The Second Coming," by Yeats, and he has the advantage of greater reality; the style combines descriptive precision with great concentration of meaning and at the same time is wholly free from decoration, ineptitude, and other irrelevancy. The poem gives one some idea of how great a poet Frost might conceivably have been, had he been willing to use his mind instead of letting it wither. In this poem especially, and to some extent in "Acquainted with the Night," the poet confronts his condition fairly and sees it for what it is, but the insight is momentary: he neither proceeds from this point to further understanding nor even manages to retain the realization that he has achieved. Much else in *A Witness Tree* is similar to the earlier work, and the next and last two books, *A Masque of Reason* (which I have described in some detail) and *Steeple Bush*, are his feeblest and least serious efforts.

There are a few other poems in the later books, however, which are impressive, and they ought to be mentioned in justice to their author, although little would be gained from a detailed account of them. In *A Further Range* there is a moderately long lyric entitled "The Vindictives," which deals with the looting of the Inca empire by the Spaniards, and with the way in which the Incas in return sacked their own country and buried the gold.

> One Inca prince on the rack,
> And late in his last hour alive,
> Told them in what lake to dive
> To seek what they seemed so to want.
> They dived and nothing was found.
> He told them to dive till they drowned.
> The whole fierce conquering pack
> Hunted and tortured and raged.
> There were suns of story and vaunt
> They searched for into Brazil
> Their tongues hanging out unassuaged.

This is probably the only poem in Frost in which one can find anything resembling heroic action; the poem is motivated by a simple and honest hatred of brutality and injustice so obvious that they cannot be overlooked. The hatred in question, however, can be justified only by certain ideas, the ideas of Christian and classical philosophy, which, although they are a part of Frost's background and influence him to this extent, he has during all of his career neglected or explicitly maligned. The poem is a little loose in construction and is occasionally careless in style; but it has an honesty and a controlled violence which make it very impressive. In *A Witness Tree* there are several other fine but minor lyrics which stay in one's mind, especially "The Rabbit Hunter," "Never Again Would Birds' Song Be the Same," and "I Could Give All to Time." "Come In" is a memorable lyric, but perhaps it contains too much of Frost's professional and somewhat sentimental charm.

In *A Witness Tree* there is a narrative of considerable interest, "The Discovery of the Madeiras." It retells a story from Hakluyt about a pair of lovers who elope from England; the captain of their vessel, who had been a slaver, tells the man a singularly brutal story about the murder of a pair of Negroes who were lovers; the man repeats it to his lady, and she withdraws to her cabin, becomes ill, and eventually dies. In style the poem resembles "The Vindictives," but it has less force at its best and is often undistinguished. It is written in eight-syllable lines rhyming in couplets and has something of the effect of a modern and sophisticated ballad. But the best of the old border ballads differ in one important respect: they deal, commonly, with an important decision consciously made, and with the resultant action, which is frequently violent but which is also important, either for good or for evil; Frost's poem deals with the accidental impingement of a brutal fact upon a morbid sensibility and the collapse of the sensibility. Frost's poem to this extent is the product of a decadent state of mind. Frost runs up against another difficulty in this poem which he encounters in all his narratives: the virtual impossibility of writing a short and purely realistic narrative which shall attain great power. The narrative, if it is to be short, must be symbolical or allegorical, it must be packed with the power of generalization; if it is to be purely realistic, it must be developed and explored fully in its capacity as a particular history. The short story writer in prose meets the same difficulty, but the short story is a longer and freer form and so has a better chance of success; and furthermore it makes a more modest claim upon our expectations, so that we are less likely to trouble ourselves about its limits.

V

These remarks have been unfair to Frost in certain respects. I have quoted most extensively from his didactic poems, and especially from those in blank verse. Frost is at his worst in didactic writing, in spite of his fondness for it: his ideas are impossible and his style is exceptionally shoddy. Furthermore, although Frost is frequently very skillful in the handling of short rhymed forms, he is extremely inept in managing blank verse; in blank verse his theory of conversational style shows itself at its worst—the rhythms are undistinguished and are repetitious to the point of deadly monotony. But it is in these poems that Frost states his ideas most unmistakably, and it is necessary to understand the ideas to form an estimate of him at all. He is at his best, as regards style, in the short rhymed lyric, but his short lyrics are less explicit in stating their themes, and unless one comes to them with a clear concept of

Frost's principal themes one may overlook the themes or mistake them. Frost is at his best in such poems as "The Most of It" and "Acquainted with the Night," in which he seems to be more or less aware of the untenability of his own position and to face his difficulty, or as "The Vindictives," in which as the result of a fortunate accident of some kind he is able simply to ignore his usual themes and write as if he had never heard of them. The bulk of his really memorable work, however, is to be found among the symbolic lyrics, of which "The Last Mowing" and "Spring Pools" are excellent examples, lyrics in which the descriptive element is beautifully handled, in which the feeling is communicated with a sufficient degree of success to make them unforgettable but with so great a degree of imprecision as to make them curiously unsatisfactory. For the feeling does not arise merely from the contemplation of the natural objects described: if it did so, it would be too strong and too mysteriously elusive for its origins; the feeling arises mainly from the concepts of which the natural objects are the symbolic vehicles, and those concepts, as I have shown, are unacceptable, and when one tries to project them clearly into terms of human action are unimaginable. Frost's instinctualism, his nostalgia for dream and chaos, are merely the symptoms of sentimental obscurantism when, as in Frost's work, they are dealt with lightly and whimsically, but if taken seriously, as in the work of Crane and Pound, they may lead to more serious difficulties. They do not lead toward intelligence, no matter how far the individual devotee may travel in their company; they lead away from intelligence. They lead away from the true comprehension of human experience which makes for great, or even for successful, poetry. The element of the unimaginable, and hence of the imprecise, which lurks in the theme of "The Last Mowing" will make it forever, and in spite of its real and extraordinary virtues, a very imperfectly successful poem; this poem simply will not stand comparison with such pieces, for example, as "Low Barometer," by Robert Bridges, as Howard Baker's poem on Psyche, or as J. V. Cunningham's epigrams on Swift and on the calculus. "The Last Mowing" will for some years be a more popular poem than these, however, for, as I have said, Frost's confusion is similar to that of the public, and most readers of poetry still regard poetry as a vague emotional indulgence: they do not take poetry seriously and they dislike serious poetry.

Frost, then, may be described as a good poet in so far as he may be said to exist, but a dangerous influence in so far as his existence is incomplete. He is in no sense a great poet, but he is at times a distinguished and valuable poet. In order to evaluate his work and profit by it, however, we must understand him far better than he understands himself, and this fact indicates a very serious weakness in his talent. If we do not so understand him, his poetry is bound to reinforce some of the most dangerous tendencies of our time; his weakness is commonly mistaken for wisdom, his vague and sentimental feeling for profound emotion, as his reputation and the public honors accorded him plainly testify. He is the nearest thing we have to a poet laureate, a national poet; and this fact is evidence of the community of thought and feeling between Frost and a very large part of the American literary public. The principles which have saved some part of Frost's talent, the principles of Greek and Christian thought, are principles which are seldom openly defended and of which the implications and ramifications are understood by relatively few of our contemporaries, by Frost least of all; they operate upon Frost at a distance, through social inheritance, and he has done his best to adopt principles which are opposed to them. The principles which have hampered Frost's development, the principles of Emersonian and Thoreauistic Romanticism, are the principles which he has openly espoused, and they are widespread in our culture. Until we understand these last and the dangers inherent in them and so abandon them in favor of better, we are unlikely to produce many poets greater than Frost, although a few poets may have intelligence enough to work clear of such influences; and we are likely to deteriorate more or less rapidly both as individuals and as a nation.

From *The Sewanee Review*, Vol. LVI (Autumn, 1948), pp. 564–596. Reprinted by permission of the author and editor.

Robinson Jeffers
[1930]

IT IS difficult to write of Mr. Jeffers' latest book[1] without discussing his former volumes; after his first collection he deals chiefly with one theme in all of his poems; and all of his works illustrate a single problem, a spiritual malady of considerable significance. Mr. Jeffers is theologically a kind of monist; he envisages, as did Wordsworth, Nature as Deity; but his Nature is the Nature of the physics textbook and not of the rambling botanist—Mr. Jeffers seems to have taken the terminology of modern physics more literally than it is meant by its creators. Nature, or God, is thus a kind of self-sufficient mechanism, of which man is an offshoot, but from which man is cut off by his humanity (just what gave rise to this humanity, which is absolutely severed from all connection with God, is left for others to decide): there is consequently no mode of communication between the consciousness of man and the mode of existence of God; God is praised adequately only by the screaming demons that make up the atom. Man, if he accepts this dilemma as necessary, is able to choose

[1] *Dear Judas*, by Robinson Jeffers. New York: Horace Liveright, 1929.

between two modes of action: he may renounce God and rely on his humanity, or he may renounce his humanity and rely on God.

Mr. Jeffers preaches the second choice: union with God, oblivion, the complete extinction of one's humanity, is the only good he is able to discover; and
life, as such, is "incest," an insidious and destructive evil. So much, says Mr.
Jeffers by implication, for Greek and Christian ethics. Now the mysticism of,
say, San Juan de la Cruz offers at least the semblance of a spiritual, a human,
discipline as a preliminary to union with Divinity; but for Mr. Jeffers a simple and mechanical device lies always ready; namely, suicide, a device to
which he has not resorted.

In refusing to take this logical step, however, Mr. Jeffers illustrates one of
a very interesting series of romantic compromises. The romantic of the ecstatic-
pantheist type denies life, yet goes on living; nearly all romantics decry the
intellect and philosophy, yet they offer justifications (necessarily foggy and
fragmentary) of their attitude; they deride literary "technique" (the mastery
of, and development of the sensitivity to, relationships between words, so that
these relationships may extend almost illimitably the vocabulary) yet they
write (of necessity, carelessly, with small efficiency). Not all romantics are
guilty of all of these confusions, nor, doubtless, is Mr. Jeffers; but all of these
confusions are essentially romantic—they are very natural developments of
moral monism. And Mr. Jeffers, having decried human life as such, and having denied the worth of the rules of the game, endeavors to write narrative
and dramatic poems—poems, in other words, dealing with people who are
playing the game. Jesus, the hero of *Dear Judas*, speaking apparently for Mr.
Jeffers, says that the secret reason for the doctrine of forgiveness is that all
men are driven by the mechanism-God to act as they do, that they are entirely
helpless; yet he adds in the next breath that this secret must be guarded, for
if it were given out, men would run amuck, would get out of hand—*they
would begin acting differently.*

The Women at Point Sur is a perfect laboratory of Mr. Jeffers' philosophy.
Barclay, an insane divine, preaches Mr. Jeffers' religion, and his disciples,
acting upon it, become emotional mechanisms, lewd and twitching conglom-
erations of plexi, their humanity annulled. Human experience, in these circumstances, having necessarily and according to the doctrine no meaning,
there can be and is no necessary sequence of events: every act is equivalent to
every other; every act is at the peak of hysteria; most of the incidents could be
shuffled around into varying sequences without violating anything save, perhaps, Mr. Jeffers' private sense of their relative intensity. Since the poem is
his, of course, such a private sense is legitimate enough; the point is that this
is not a narrative, nor a dramatic, but a lyrical criterion. A successful lyrical
poem of one hundred and seventy-five pages is unlikely, for the essence of
lyrical expression is concentration; but it is at least theoretically possible. The

difficulty is that the lyric achieves its effect by the generalization of emotion (that is, by the separation of the emotion from the personal history that gives rise to it in actual concrete experience) and by the concentration of expression. Narrative can survive in a measure without concentration, or intensity of detail, provided the narrative logic is detailed and compelling, as in the case of Balzac, though it is only wise to add that this occurs most often in prose. Now Mr. Jeffers, as I have pointed out, has abandoned narrative logic with the theory of ethics, and he has never achieved, in addition, a close and masterly style. His writing is loose, turgid, and careless; like most anti-intellectualists, he relies on his feelings alone and has no standard of criticism for them outside of themselves. There are occasional good flashes in his poems, and to these I shall return later, but they are very few, are very limited in their range of feeling and in their subject matter, and they are very far between. Mr. Jeffers has no remaining method of sustaining his lyric, then, other than the employment of an accidental (i.e., non-narrative) chain of anecdotes (i.e., details that are lyrically impure); his philosophical doctrine and his artistic dilemma alike decree that these shall be anecdotes of hysteria. By this method Mr. Jeffers continually *lays claim* to a high pitch of emotion which has no narrative support (that is, support of the inevitable accumulation of experience), nor lyrical support (that is, support of the intense perception of pure, or transferable, emotion), which has, in short, no support at all, and which is therefore simply unmastered and self-inflicted hysteria.

Cawdor alone of Mr. Jeffers' poems contains a plot that in its rough outlines might be sound, and *Cawdor* likewise contains his best poetry; the poem as a whole, and in spite of the confused treatment of the woman, is moving, and the lines describing the seals at dawn are fine, as are the two or three last lines of the apotheosis of the eagle. Most of the preceding material in the latter passage, however, like most of the material in the sections that give Mr. Jeffers' notions of the post-mortem experience of man, are turgid, repetitious, arbitrary, and unconvincing. The plot itself is blurred for lack of stylistic finish (that is, for lack of ability on the part of the poet to see every detail of sense and movement incisively down to the last preposition, the last comma, as every detail *is* seen in Racine or Shakespeare); and it remains again a fair question whether a moral monist *can* arrive at any clear conclusions about the values of a course of action, since he denies the existence of any conceivable standard of values within the strict limits of human life as such. In *The Tower Beyond Tragedy* Mr. Jeffers takes a ready-made plot, the Clytemnestra-Orestes situation, which is particularly strong dramatically, because Orestes is forced to choose between two sins, the murder of his mother and the refusal to avenge his father. But at the very last moment, in Mr. Jeffers' version, Orestes is converted to Mr. Jeffers' religion and goes off explaining (to Electra, who has just tried to seduce him) that though men may think he is

fleeing before the furies he is really just drifting up to the mountains to medi-
tate on the stars; and the preceding action is, of course, rendered morally and
emotionally meaningless.

In the present volume, the title poem, *Dear Judas,* is a kind of dilution of
The Women at Point Sur, with Jesus as Barclay, and with a less detailed
background. Mr. Jeffers' mouthpiece and hero, Jesus, is little short of revolt-
ing as he whips reflexively from didactic passion to malice, self-justification,
and vengeance. The poem shares the structural principles, or lack of them, of
The Women at Point Sur; and it has no quotable lines, save, possibly, the last
three, which are, however, heavy with dross. "The Loving Shepherdess," the
other long poem of the present volume, deals with a girl who knows herself
doomed to die at a certain time in childbirth, and who wanders over the countryside caring for a small and diminishing flock of sheep in an anguish of devotion. The events here again are anecdotal and reversible, and the emotion
is lyrical or nothing. The theme had two possibilities: the poet could have immersed the girl in a dream of approaching death, or he could have immersed
her in the sentimental pathos of the immediate situation. There are moments
when he seems to be trying for the former effect, but his perceptions are not
fine enough and the mass of anecdotal detail is too heavy; the poem succeeds
in being no more than a very Wordsworthian embodiment of a kind of maud-
lin humanitarianism—which is a curious but not an unexpected outcome of
Mr. Jeffers' sentimental misanthropy. The heroine is turned cruelly from door
to door, and the sheep fall one by one before the reader's eyes, the doors and
the sheep constituting the bulk of the anecdotal material; till finally the girl
dies in a ditch in an impossible effort to give birth to her child.

The short poems in the book deal with themes that Mr. Jeffers has handled
better before. He has written here and there impressive lines descriptive of
the sea and its rocks, and of dying birds of prey. "Hurt Hawks II," in the
Cawdor volume, is the most perfect short poem and is quite fine; there are
excellent lines scattered through other pieces. These poems are, however, limited both in paraphrasable content and in experiential implication: they glo-
rify brute nature and annihilation and are numb to the intricacies of human
feeling; they share in the latter respect the limitations of all mystical poetry.
Mr. Jeffers' insistence on another of his favorite lyrical themes, his own aloof-
ness, is becoming, by dint of repetition, almost embarrassing; one has the constant feeling that he is trying to bully the reader into accepting him at his own
evaluation.

Self-repetition has been the inevitable effect of anti-intellectualist doctrine
on all of its supporters. If life is valued, explored, subdivided, and defined,
poetic themes are infinite in number; if life is denied, the only theme is the
rather sterile and monotonous one of the denial. Similarly, those poets who
flee from form, which is infinitely variable, since every form is a definite and

an individual thing, can achieve only the uniformity of chaos; and those individuals who endeavor to escape morality, which is personal form and controlled direction, can, in the very nature of things, achieve nothing, save the uniformity of mechanism. One might classify Mr. Jeffers as a "great failure" if one meant by the phrase that he had wasted unusual talents; but not if one meant that he had failed in a major effort, for his aims are badly thought-out and are essentially trivial.

From *Poetry: A Magazine of Verse*, Vol. XXXV (February, 1930), pp. 279–286. Reprinted by permission.

ROBERT PENN WARREN

Hemingway

[1947]

THE situations and characters of Hemingway's world are usually violent. There is the hard-drinking and sexually promiscuous world of *The Sun Also Rises;* the chaotic and brutal world of war as in *A Farewell to Arms, For Whom the Bell Tolls,* many of the inserted sketches of *In Our Time,* the play *The Fifth Column,* and some of the stories; the world of sport, as in "Fifty Grand," "My Old Man," "The Undefeàted," "The Snows of Kilimanjaro"; the world of crime as in "The Killers," "The Gambler, the Nun, and the Radio," and *To Have and Have Not.* Even when the situation of a story does not fall into one of these categories, it usually involves a desperate risk, and behind it is the shadow of ruin, physical or spiritual. As for the typical characters, they are usually tough men, experienced in the hard worlds they inhabit, and not obviously given to emotional display or sensitive shrinking, men like Rinaldi or Frederick Henry of *A Farewell to Arms,* Robert Jordan of *For Whom the Bell Tolls,* Harry Morgan of *To Have and Have Not,* the big-game hunter of "The Snows of Kilimanjaro," the old bullfighter of "The Undefeated," or the pugilist of "Fifty Grand." Or if the typical character is not of this seasoned order, he is a very young man, or boy, first entering the violent world and learning his first adjustment to it.

We have said that the shadow of ruin is behind the typical Hemingway situation. The typical character faces defeat or death. But out of defeat or death the character usually manages to salvage something. And here we discover Hemingway's special interest in such situations and such characters. His heroes are not defeated except upon their own terms. They are not squealers, welchers, compromisers, or cowards, and when they confront defeat they realize that the stance they take, the stoic endurance, the stiff upper lip mean a kind of victory. Defeated upon their own terms, some of them have even courted their defeat; and certainly they have maintained, even in the practical defeat, an ideal of themselves, some definition of how a man should behave, formulated or unformulated, by which they have lived. They represent some notion of a code, some notion of honor, which makes a man a man, and which distinguishes him from people who merely follow their random impulses and who are, by consequence, "messy."

In case after case, we can illustrate this "principle of sportsmanship," as one critic has called it, at the center of a story or novel. For instance, Brett, the heroine of *The Sun Also Rises*, gives up Romero, the young bullfighter with whom she is in love, because she knows she will ruin him, and her tight-lipped remark to Jake, the newspaper man who is the narrator of the novel, might almost serve as the motto of Hemingway's work: "You know it makes one feel rather good deciding not to be a bitch."

It is the discipline of the code which makes man human, a sense of style or good form. This applies not only in isolated, dramatic cases such as those listed above, but in a more pervasive way which can give meaning, partially at least, to the confusions of living. The discipline of the soldier, the form of the athlete, the gameness of the sportsman, the technique of an artist can give some sense of the human order, and can achieve a moral significance. And here we see how Hemingway's concern with war and sport crosses his concern with literary style. If a writer can get the kind of style at which Hemingway professed, in *Green Hills of Africa*, to aim, then "nothing else matters. It is more important than anything else he can do." It is more important because, ultimately, it is a moral achievement. And no doubt for this reason, as well as for the reason of Henry James's concern with cruxes of a moral code, he is, as he says in *Green Hills of Africa*, an admirer of the work of James, the devoted stylist.

But to return to the subject of Hemingway's world: the code and the discipline are important because they can give meaning to life which otherwise seems to have no meaning or justification. In other words, in a world without supernatural sanctions, in the God-abandoned world of modernity, man can realize an ideal meaning only in so far as he can define and maintain the code. The effort to define and maintain the code, however limited and imperfect it may be, is the characteristically human effort and provides the tragic or pitiful human story. Hemingway's attitude on this point is much like that of Robert Louis Stevenson as Stevenson states it in one of his essays, "Pulvis et Umbra":

—everywhere some virtue cherished or affected, everywhere some decency of thought or carriage, everywhere the ensign of man's ineffectual goodness . . . under every circumstance of failure, without hope, without help, without thanks, still obscurely fighting the lost fight of virtue, still clinging, in the brothel or on the scaffold, to some rag of honor, the poor jewel of their souls! They may seek to escape, and yet they cannot; it is not alone their privilege and glory, but their doom; they are condemned to some nobility. . . .

Hemingway's code is more rigorous than Stevenson's and perhaps he finds fewer devoted to it, but like Stevenson he can find his characteristic hero and characteristic story among the discards of society, and like Stevenson is aware of the touching irony of that fact. But for the moment the important thing in the parallel is that, for Stevenson, the world in which this drama of pitiful aspiration and stoic endurance is played out is, objectively considered, a violent and meaningless world—"our rotary island loaded with predatory life and more drenched with blood than ever mutinied ship . . . scuds through space." Neither Hemingway nor Stevenson invented this world. It had already appeared in literature before their time, and that is a way of saying that this cheerless vision had already begun to trouble men. It is the world we find pictured (and denied) in Tennyson's "In Memoriam"—the world in which human conduct is a product of "dying Nature's earth and lime." It is the world pictured (and not denied) in Hardy and Housman, a world which seems to be presided over by blind Doomsters (if by anybody), as Hardy put it in his poem "Hap," or made by some brute and blackguard (if by anybody), as Housman put it in his poem "The Chestnut Casts Its Flambeaux." It is the world of Zola or Dreiser or Conrad or Faulkner. It is the world of, to use Bertrand Russell's phrase, "secular hurryings through space." It is the God-abandoned world, the world of Nature-as-all. We know where the literary men got this picture. They got it from the scientists of the 19th Century. This is Hemingway's world, too, the world with nothing at center.

Over against this naturalistic view of the world, there was, of course, an argument for Divine Intelligence and a Divine purpose, an argument which based itself on the beautiful system of nature, on natural law. The closely knit order of the natural world, so the argument ran, implies a Divine Intelligence. But if one calls Hemingway's attention to the fact that the natural world is a world of order, his reply is on record in a story called "A Natural History of the Dead." There he quotes from the traveller Mungo Park, who, naked and starving in an African desert, observed a beautiful little moss-flower and meditated thus:

Can the Being who planted, watered, and brought to perfection, in this obscure part of the world, a thing which appears of so small importance, look with unconcern upon the situation and suffering of creatures formed after his own image? Surely not. Reflections like these would not allow me to despair: I started up and, disregarding both hunger and fatigue, travelled forward, assured that relief was at hand; and I was not disappointed.

And Hemingway continues:

With a disposition to wonder and adore in like manner, as Bishop Stanley says [the author of A Familiar History of Birds], can any branch of Natural History be studied without increasing that faith, love and hope which we also, every one of us, need in our journey through the wilderness of life? Let us therefore see what inspiration we may derive from the dead.

Then Hemingway presents the picture of a modern battlefield, where the bloated and decaying bodies give a perfect example of the natural order of chemistry—but scarcely an argument for faith, hope, and love. That picture is his answer to the argument that the order of nature implies meaning in the world.

In one of the stories, "A Clean, Well-Lighted Place," we find the best description of this world which underlies Hemingway's world of violent action. Early in the story we see an old man sitting late in a Spanish café. Two waiters are speaking of him.

"Last week he tried to commit suicide," one waiter said.

"Why?"

"He was in despair."

"What about?"

"Nothing."

"How do you know it was nothing?"

"He has plenty of money."

The despair beyond plenty of money—or beyond all the other gifts of the world: its nature becomes a little clearer at the end of the story when the older of the two waiters is left alone, reluctant too to leave the clean, well-lighted place.

Turning off the electric light he continued the conversation with himself. It is the light of course but it is necessary that the place be clean and pleasant. You do not want music. Certainly you do not want music. Nor can you stand before a bar with dignity although that is all that is provided for these hours. What did he fear? It was not fear or dread. It was a nothing that he knew too well. It was all a nothing and a man was nothing too. It was only that and light was all it needed and a certain cleanness and order. Some lived in it and never felt it but he knew it all was nada y pues nada y nada y pues nada.[1] Our nada who art in nada, nada be thy name thy kingdom nada thy will be nada in nada as it is in nada. Give us this nada our daily nada and nada us our nada as we nada our nadas and nada us not into nada but deliver us from nada; pues nada. Hail nothing full of nothing, nothing is with thee. He smiled and stood before a bar with a shining steam pressure coffee machine.

"What's yours?" asked the barman.

"Nada."

At the end the old waiter is ready to go home:

Now, without thinking further, he would go home to his room. He would lie in bed and finally, with daylight, he would go to sleep. After all, he said to himself, it's probably only insomnia. Many must have it.

And the sleepless man—the man obsessed by death, by the meaningless of the world, by nothingness, by nada—is one of the recurring symbols in the

[1] nada y pues nada, etc.: nothing and after that nothing, etc.

works of Hemingway. In this phase Hemingway is a religious writer. The despair beyond plenty of money, the despair which makes a sleeplessness beyond insomnia, is the despair felt by a man who hungers for the certainties and meaningfulness of a religious faith but who cannot find in his world a ground for that faith.

Another recurring symbol, we have said, is the violent man. But the sleepless man and the violent man are not contradictory but complementary symbols. They represent phases of the same question, the same hungering for meaning in the world. The sleepless man is the man brooding upon nada, upon chaos, upon Nature-as-all. (For Nature-as-all equals moral chaos; even its bulls and lions and kudu are not admired by Hemingway as creatures of conscious self-discipline; their courage is meaningful only in so far as it symbolizes human courage.) The violent man is the man taking an action appropriate to the realization of the fact of nada. He is, in other words, engaged in the effort to discover human values in a naturalistic world.

Before we proceed with this line of discussion, it might be asked, "Why does Hemingway feel that the quest necessarily involves violence?" Now, at one level, the answer to this question would involve the whole matter of the bias toward violence in modern literature. But let us take it in its more immediate reference. The typical Hemingway hero is the man aware, or in the process of becoming aware, of nada. Death is the great nada. Therefore whatever solution the hero gets must, to be good, stick even against the fact of death. It has to be good in the bullring or on the battle field and not merely in the study or lecture room. In fact, Hemingway is anti-intellectual, and has a great contempt for any type of solution arrived at without the testings of immediate experience. One of his more uningratiating passages—again from "A Natural History of the Dead"—makes the point amply clear:

The only natural death I've ever seen, outside of the loss of blood, which isn't bad, was death from Spanish influenza. In this you drown in mucus, choking, and how you know the patient's dead is: at the end he turns to be a little child again, though with his manly force, and fills the sheets as full as any diaper with one vast, final yellow cataract that flows and dribbles on after he is gone. So now I want to see the death of any self-styled Humanist because a persevering traveller like Mungo Park or me lives on and maybe yet will see the actual death of members of this literary sect and watch the noble exits they make. In my musings as a naturalist it has occurred to me that while decorum is an excellent thing, some must be indecorous if the race is to be carried on since the position described for procreation is indecorous, highly indecorous, and it occurred to me that perhaps that is what these people are, or were: the children of decorous cohabitation. But regardless of how they started I hope to see the finish of a few, and speculate how worms will try that long preserved sterility; with their quaint pamphlets gone to bust and into foot-notes all their lust.

So aside from the question of a dramatic sense which would favor violence, and aside from the mere matter of personal temperament (for Hemingway describes himself on more than one occasion as obsessed by death), the presentation of violence is appropriate in his work because death is the great nada. In taking violent risks man confronts in dramatic terms the issue of nada which is implicit in all of Hemingway's world.

But to return to our general line of discussion. There are two aspects to this violence which is involved in the quest of the Hemingway hero, two aspects which seem to represent an ambivalent attitude toward nature.

First, there is the conscious sinking into nature, shall we call it. On this line of reasoning we would find something like this: if there is at center only nada, then the only sure compensation in life, the only reality, is gratification of appetite, the relish of sensation. Continually in the stories and novels one finds such sentences as this from *Green Hills of Africa*: ". . . drinking this, the first one of the day, the finest one there is, and looking at the thick bush we passed in the dark, feeling the cool wind of the night and smelling the good smell of Africa, I was altogether happy." What is constantly interesting in such sentences is the fact that happiness, a notion which we traditionally connect with a complicated state of being, with notions of virtue, of achievement, etc., is here equated with a set of merely agreeable sensations. The careful relish of sensation—that is what counts, always.

This intense awareness of the world of the senses is, of course, one of the things which made the early work of Hemingway seem, upon its first impact, so fresh and pure. Physical nature is nowhere rendered with greater vividness than in his work, and probably his only competitors in this department of literature are William Faulkner, among the modern, and Henry David Thoreau, among the older American writers. The meadows, forests, lakes, and trout streams of America, and the arid, sculpturesque mountains of Spain, appear with astonishing immediacy, an immediacy not dependent upon descriptive flourishes. But not only the appearance of landscape is important; a great deal of the freshness comes from the discrimination of sensation, the coldness of water in the "squlchy" shoes after wading, the tangy smell of dry sage brush, the "cleanly" smell of grease and oil on a field piece. Hemingway's appreciation and rendering of the aesthetic quality of the physical world is important, but a peculiar poignancy is implicit in the rendering of those qualities; the beauty of the physical world is a background for the human predicament, and the very relishing of the beauty is merely a kind of desperate and momentary compensation possible in the midst of the predicament.

This careful relishing of the world of the senses comes to a climax in drinking and sex. Drink is the "giant-killer," the weapon against man's thought of nada. And so is sex, for that matter, though when sexual attraction achieves the status of love, the process is one which attempts to achieve a meaning rather than to forget meaninglessness in the world. In terms of drinking and sex, the typical Hemingway hero is a man of monel-metal stomach and Homeric prowess in the arts of love. And the typical situation is love, with some drinking, against the background of nada—of civilization gone to pot, or war, or death—as we get it in all of the novels in one form or another, and in many of the stories.

It is important to remember, however, that the sinking into nature, even at the level of drinking and mere sexuality, is a self-conscious act. It is not the random gratification of appetite. We see this quite clearly in *The Sun Also Rises* in the contrast between Cohn, who is merely a random dabbler in the world of sensation, who is merely trying to amuse himself, and the initiates like Jake and Brett, who are aware of the nada at the center of things and whose dissipations, therefore, have a philosophical significance. The initiate in Hemingway's world raises the gratification of appetite to the level of a cult and a discipline.

The cult of sensation, as we have already indicated, passes over very readily into the cult of true love, for the typical love story is presented primarily in terms of the cult of sensation. (*A Farewell to Arms,* as we shall see when we come to a detailed study of that novel, is closely concerned with that transition.) Even in the cult of true love it is the moment which counts, and the individual. There is never any past or future to the love stories and the lovers are always isolated, not moving in an ordinary human society within its framework of obligations. The notion of the cult—a secret cult composed of those who have been initiated into the secret of nada—is constantly played up. In *A Farewell to Arms,* for instance, Catherine and Frederick are, quite consciously, two against the world, a world which is, literally as well as figuratively, an alien world. The peculiar relationship between Frederick and the priest takes on a new significance if viewed in terms of the secret cult. We shall come to this topic later, but for the moment we can say that the priest is a priest of Divine Love, the subject about which he and Frederick converse in the hospital, and that Frederick himself is a kind of priest, one of the initiate in the end, of the cult of profane love. This same pattern of two against the world, with an understanding confidante or interpreter, reappears in *For Whom the Bell Tolls*—with Pilar, the gipsy woman who understands "love," substituting for the priest of *A Farewell to Arms.*

The initiates of the cult of love are those who are aware of nada, but their effort, as members of the cult, is to find a meaning to put in place of the nada. That is, there is an attempt to make the relationship of love take on a religious significance in so far as it can give meaning to life. This general topic is not new with the work of Hemingway. It is one of the literary themes of the 19th Century—and has, as a matter of fact, a much longer history than that. But we find it fully stated in the last century in many instances. To take one, there is "Dover Beach" by Matthew Arnold. In a world from which religious faith has been removed the lovers can only turn to each other to find significance in life:

> Ah, love, let us be true
> To one another! for the world, which seems
> To lie before us like a land of dreams,
> So various, so beautiful, so new,
> Hath really neither joy, nor love, nor light,
> Nor certitude, nor peace, nor help for pain;
> And we are here as on a darkling plain
> Swept with confused alarms of struggle and flight,
> Where ignorant armies clash by night.

If the cult of love arises from and states itself in the language of the cult of sensation, it is an extension of the sinking-into-nature aspect of the typical Hemingway violence; but in so far as it involves a discipline and a search for a "faith," it leads us to the second aspect of the typical violence.

The violence, although in its first aspect it represents a sinking into nature, at the same time, in its second aspect, represents a conquest of nature, and of nada in man. It represents such a conquest, not because of the fact of violence, but because the violence appears in terms of discipline, a style, and a code. It is, as we have already seen, in terms of a self-imposed discipline that the heroes make one gallant, though limited, effort to redeem the incoherence of the world: they attempt to impose some form upon the disorder of their lives, the technique of the bullfighter or sportsman, the discipline of the soldier, the fidelity of the lover, or even the code of the gangster, which, though brutal and apparently dehumanizing, has its own ethic.

The discipline, the form, is never quite capable of subduing the world, but fidelity to it is part of the gallantry of defeat. By fidelity to it the hero manages to keep one small place "clean" and "well-lighted," and manages to retain, or achieve for one last moment, his dignity. As the old Spanish waiter muses, there should be a "clean, well-lighted place" where one could keep one's dignity at the late hour.

We have said earlier that the typical Hemingway character is tough and, apparently, insensitive. But only apparently, for the fidelity to a code, to the discipline, may be the index to a sensitivity which allows the characters to see, at moments, their true plight. At times, and usually at times of stress, it is the tough man in the Hemingway world, the disciplined man, who is actually aware of pathos or tragedy. The individual toughness (which may be taken to be the private discipline demanded by the world) may find itself in conflict with the natural human reaction; but the Hemingway hero, though he may be aware of the claims of the natural reaction, the spontaneous human emotion, cannot surrender to it because he knows that the only way to hold

on to the definition of himself, to "honor" or "dignity," is to maintain the discipline, the code. For example, when pity appears in the Hemingway world—
as in "The Pursuit Race"—it does not appear in its maximum but in its minimum manifestation.

What this means in terms of style and method is the use of understatement.
This understatement, stemming from the contrast between the sensitivity and
the superimposed discipline, is a constant aspect of the work, an aspect which
was caught in a cartoon in the *New Yorker*. The cartoon showed a brawny,
muscle-knotted forearm and a hairy hand which clutched a rose. It was entitled "The Soul of Ernest Hemingway." Just as there is a margin of victory
in the defeat of the Hemingway characters, so there is a little margin of sensitivity in their brutal and apparently insensitive world. Hence we have the
ironical circumstance—a central circumstance in creating the pervasive irony
of Hemingway's work—that the revelation of the values characteristic of his
work arises from the most unpromising people and the most unpromising situations—the little streak of poetry or pathos in "The Pursuit Race," "The
Killers,". "My Old Man," "A Clean, Well-Lighted Place," or "The Undefeated." We have a perfect example of it in the last named story. After the
defeat of the old bullfighter, who is lying wounded on an operating table,
Zurito, the picador, is about to cut off his pigtail, the mark of his profession.
But when the wounded man starts up, despite his pain, and says, "You
couldn't do a thing like that," Zurito says, "I was joking." Zurito becomes
aware that, after all, the old bullfighter is, in a way, undefeated, and deserves
to die with his coleta on.

This locating of the poetic, the pathetic, or the tragic in the unpromising
person or situation is not unique with Hemingway. It is something with which
we are acquainted in a great deal of our literature since the Romantic Movement. The sensibility is played down, and an anti-romantic surface sheathes
the work; the point is in the contrast. The impulse which led Hemingway to
the simple character is akin to that which drew Wordsworth to the same
choice. Wordsworth felt that his unsophisticated peasants were more honest
in their responses than the cultivated man, and were therefore more poetic.
Instead of Wordsworth's peasant we have in Hemingway's work the bullfighter, the soldier, the revolutionist, the sportsman, and the gangster; instead
of Wordsworth's children we have the young men like Nick, the person just
on the verge of being initiated into the world. There are, of course, differences between the approach of Wordsworth and that of Hemingway, but
there is little difference on the point of marginal sensibility. In one sense, both
are anti-intellectual, and in such poems as "Resolution and Independence" or
"Michael" one finds even closer ties.

I have just indicated a similarity between Wordsworth and Hemingway on
the grounds of a romantic anti-intellectualism. But with Hemingway it is far

more profound and radical than with Wordsworth. All we have to do to see the difference is to put Wordsworth's Preface to the *Lyrical Ballads* over against any number of passages from Hemingway. The intellectualism of the 18th Century had merely put a veil of stereotyped language over all the world and a veil of snobbism over a large area of human experience. That is Wordsworth's indictment. But Hemingway's indictment of the intellectualism of the past is that it wound up in the mire and blood of 1914 to 1918; that it was a pack of lies leading to death. We can put over against the Preface of Wordsworth, a passage from *A Farewell to Arms:*

I was always embarrassed by the words sacred, glorious, and sacrifice and the expression in vain. We had heard them, sometimes standing in the rain almost out of earshot, so that only the shouted words came through, and had read them, on proclamations that were slapped up by billposters over other proclamations, now for a long time, and I had seen nothing sacred, and the things that were glorious had no glory and the sacrifices were like the stockyards at Chicago if nothing was done with the meat except to bury it. There were many words that you could not stand to hear and finally only the names of places had dignity. . . . Abstract words such as glory, honor, courage, or hallow were obscene beside the concrete names of villages, the numbers of roads, the names of rivers, the numbers of regiments and the dates.

I do not mean to say that the general revolution in style, and the revolt against the particular intellectualism of the 19th Century was a result of the World War, 1914–18. As a matter of fact, that revolt was going on long before the war, but for Hemingway, and for many others, the war gave the situation a peculiar depth and urgency.

Perhaps we might scale the matter thus: Wordsworth was a revolutionist— he truly had a new view of the world—but his revolutionary view left great tracts of the world untouched; the Church of England, for instance. Arnold and Tennyson, a generation or so later, though not revolutionists themselves, are much more profoundly stirred by the revolutionary situation than ever Wordsworth was; that is, the area of the world involved in the debate was for them greater. Institutions are called into question in a more fundamental way. But they managed to hang on to their English God and their English institutions. With Hardy, the area of disturbance has grown greater, and what can be salvaged is much less. He, like the earlier Victorians, had a strong sense of community to sustain him in the face of the universe which was for him, as not finally for Arnold and Tennyson, unfriendly, or at least neutral and Godless. But his community underlay institutions, a human communion which as a matter of fact was constantly being violated by institutions; and this violation is, in fact, a constant source of subject matter and a constant spring of irony. Nevertheless Hardy could refer to himself as a meliorist.

But with Hemingway, though there is a secret community, it has greatly shrunk, and its definition has become much more specialized. Its members are those who know the code. They recognize each other, they know the password and the secret grip, but they are few in number, and each is set off against the world like a wounded lion ringed round by waiting hyenas. (*Green Hills of Africa* gives us the hyena symbol—the animal whose death is comic because it is all hideously "appetite"; wounded, it eats its own intestines.) Furthermore, this secret community is not constructive; Hemingway is no meliorist. In fact, there are hints that somewhere in the back of his mind, and in behind his work, there is a kind of Spenglerian view of history: our civilization is running down. We get this most explicitly in *Green Hills of Africa*:

A continent ages quickly once we come. The natives live in harmony with it. But the foreigner destroys, cuts down the trees, drains the water, so that the water supply is altered and in a short time the soil, once the sod is turned under, is cropped out and, next, it starts to blow away as it has blown away in every old country and as I had seen it start to blow in Canada. The earth gets tired of being exploited. A country wears out quickly unless man puts back in it all his residue and that of all his beasts. When he quits using beasts and uses machines, the earth defeats him quickly. The machine can't reproduce, nor does it fertilize the soil, and it eats what he cannot raise. A country was made to be as we found it. We are the intruders and after we are dead we may have ruined it but it will still be there and we don't know what the next changes are. I suppose they all end up like Mongolia.

I would come back to Africa but not to make a living from it. . . . But I would come back to where it pleased me to live; to really live. Not just let my life pass. Our people went to America because that was the place for them to go then. It had been a good country and we had made a bloody mess of it and I would go, now, somewhere else as we had always had the right to go somewhere else and as we had always gone. You could always come back. Let the others come to America who did not know that they had come too late. Our people had seen it at its best and fought for it when it was well worth fighting for. Now I would go somewhere else.

This is the most explicit statement, but the view is implicit in case after case. The general human community, the general human project, has gone to pot. There is only the little secret community of, paradoxically enough, individualists who have resigned from the general community, and who are strong enough to live without any illusions, lies, and big words of the herd. At least, this is the case up to the novel *To Have and Have Not*. In that novel and in *For Whom the Bell Tolls* Hemingway attempts to return, as it were, his individualistic hero to society, to give him a common stake with the fate of other men.

But to come back to the matter of Wordsworth and Hemingway. What in Wordsworth is merely simple or innocent is in Hemingway violent: the gangster or bullfighter replaces the leech-gatherer or the child. Hemingway's world

is a more disordered world, and the sensibility of his characters is more ironically in contrast with their world. The most immediate consideration here is
the playing down of the sensibility as such, the sheathing of it in the code of
toughness. Gertrude Stein's tribute is here relevant: "Hemingway is the shy-
est and proudest and sweetest-smelling story-teller of my reading." But this
shyness manifests itself in the irony. In this, of course, Hemingway's irony
corresponds to the Byronic irony. But the relation to Byron is even more fundamental. The pity is only valid when it is wrung from the man who has been
seasoned by experience. Therefore a premium is placed on the fact of violent
experience. The "dumb ox" character, commented on by Wyndham Lewis,
represents the Wordsworthian peasant; the character with the code of the
tough guy, the initiate, the man cultivating honor, gallantry, and recklessness,
represents the Byronic aristocrat.

The failures of Hemingway, like his successes, are also rooted in this situation. The successes occur in those instances where Hemingway accepts the
essential limitations of his premises, that is, when there is an equilibrium between the dramatization and the characteristic Hemingway "point," when the
system of ironies and understatements is coherent. On the other hand, the
failures occur when we feel that Hemingway has not respected the limitations
of his premises; that is, when the dramatization seems to be "rigged" and the
violence, therefore, merely theatrical. The characteristic irony, or understatement, in such cases, seems to be too self-conscious. For example, let us glance
at Hemingway's most spectacular failure, *To Have and Have Not*. The
point of the novel is based on the contrast between the smuggler and the rich
owners of the yachts along the quay. But the irony is essentially an irony
without center or reference. It is superficial, for, as a critic in the *Partisan
Review* indicated, the only difference between the smuggler and the rich is
that the rich were successful in their buccaneering. The revelation which
comes to the smuggler dying in his launch—"a man alone ain't got no . . .
chance"—is a meaningless revelation, for it has no reference to the actual
dramatization. It is, finally, a failure in intellectual analysis of the situation.
In the same way, the much advertised "The Snows of Kilimanjaro" is a
failure.

Much has been said to the effect that *To Have and Have Not* and *For
Whom the Bell Tolls* represent a basic change of point of view, an enlarge-
ment of what I have called the secret community. Now no doubt that is the
intention behind both books, but the temper of both books is the old temper,
the cast of characters is the old cast, and the assumptions lying far below the
explicit intention are the old assumptions.

The monotony and self-imitation into which Hemingway's work sometimes
falls is again an effect of a failure in dramatization. Hemingway, apparently,
can dramatize his "point" in only one basic situation and with only one set of

characters. As we have seen, he has only two key characters, with certain variations from them in terms of contrast or counterpoint. His best women characters, by the way, are those which most nearly approximate the men; that is, they embody the masculine virtues and point of view characteristic of Hemingway's work.

But the monotony is not merely a monotony deriving from the characters as types; it derives, rather from the limitations of the author's sensibility, which can find interest only in one issue. A more flexible sensibility, one capable of making nicer discriminations, might discover great variety in such key characters and situations. But Hemingway's successes are due, in part at least, to the close coordination which he sometimes achieves between the character and situation on the one hand, and the sensibility as it reflects itself in the style, on the other hand.

The style characteristically is simple, even to the point of monotony. The characteristic sentence is simple, or compound; and if compound, there is no implied subtlety in the coordination of the clauses. The paragraph structure is, characteristically, based on simple sequence. There is an obvious relation between this style and the characters and situations with which the author is concerned—a question of dramatic decorum. (There are, on the other hand, examples, especially in the novels, of other more fluent, lyrical effects, but even here this fluency is founded on the conjunction *and*; it is a rhythmical and not a logical fluency. And the lyrical quality is simply a manifestation of that marginal sensibility, as can be demonstrated by an analysis of the occasions on which it appears.) But there is a more fundamental aspect of the question, an aspect which involves not the sensibility of the characters but the sensibility of the author. The short simple rhythms, the succession of coordinate clauses, the general lack of subordination——all suggest a dislocated and ununified world. The figures which live in this world live a sort of hand-to-mouth existence perceptually, and conceptually, they hardly live at all.

II

A Farewell to Arms is a love story. It is a compelling story at the merely personal level, but is much more compelling and significant when we see the figures of the lovers silhouetted against the flame-streaked blackness of war, of a collapsing world, of nada. For there is a story behind the love story. That story is the quest for meaning and certitude in a world which seems to offer nothing of the sort. It is, in a sense, a religious book; if it does not offer a religious solution it is nevertheless conditioned by the religious problem.

The very first scene of the book, though seemingly casual, is important if we are to understand the deeper motivations of the story. It is the scene at the officers' mess where the captain baits the priest. "Priest every night five against one," the captain explains to Frederick. But Frederick, we see in this and later scenes, takes no part in the baiting. There is a bond between him and the priest, a bond which they both recognize. This becomes clear when, after the officers have advised Frederick where he should go on his leave to find the best girls, the priest turns to him and says that he would like for him to go to Abruzzi, his own province:

"There is good hunting. You would like the people and though it is cold it is clear and dry. You could stay with my family. My father is a famous hunter."
"Come on," said the captain. "We go whorehouse before it shuts."
"Goodnight," I said to the priest.
"Goodnight," he said.

In the preliminary contrast between the officers, who invite the hero to go to the brothels, and the priest, who invites him to go to the cold, clear, dry country, we have in its simplest form the issue of the novel.

Frederick does go with the officers that night, and on his leave he does go to the cities, "to the smoke of cafes and nights when the room whirled and you needed to look at the wall to make it stop, nights in bed, drunk, when you knew that that was all there was, and the strange excitement of waking and not knowing who it was with you, and the world all unreal in the dark and so exciting that you must resume again unknowing and not caring in the night, sure that this was all and all and all and not caring." Frederick at the opening of the novel lives in the world of random and meaningless appetite, knowing that it is all and all and all, or thinking that he knows that. But behind that there is a dissatisfaction and disgust. Upon his return from his leave, sitting in the officers' mess, he tries to tell the priest how he is sorry that he had not gone to the clear, cold, dry country—the priest's home, which takes on the shadowy symbolic significance of another kind of life, another view of the world. The priest had always known that other country.

He had always known what I did not know and what, when I learned it, I was always able to forget. But I did not know that then, although I learned it later.

What Frederick learns later is the story behind the love story of the book.

But this theme is not merely stated at the opening of the novel and then absorbed into the action. It appears later, at crucial points, to define the line of meaning in the action. When, for example, Frederick is wounded, the priest visits him in the hospital. Their conversation makes even plainer the religious background of the novel. The priest has said that he would like to go back after the war to the Abruzzi. He continues:

"It does not matter. But there in my country it is understood that a man may love God. It is not a dirty joke."
"I understand."
He looked at me and smiled.

"You understand but you do not love God."

"No."

"You do not love him at all?" he asked.

"I am afraid of him in the night sometimes."

"You should love Him."

"I don't love much."

"Yes," he said. "You do. What you tell me about in the nights. That is not love. That is only passion and lust. When you love you wish to do things for. You wish to sacrifice for. You wish to serve."

"I don't love."

"You will. I know you will. Then you will be happy."

We have here two items of importance. First, there is the definition of Frederick as the sleepless man, the man haunted by nada. Second, at this stage in the novel, the end of Book I, the true meaning of the love story with Catherine has not yet been defined. It is still at the level of appetite. The priest's role is to indicate the next stage of the story, the discovery of the true nature of love, the "wish to do things for." And he accomplishes this by indicating a parallel between secular love and Divine love, a parallel which implies Frederick's quest for meaning and certitude. And to emphasize further this idea, Frederick, after the priest leaves, muses on the high, clean country of the Abruzzi, the priest's home which has already been endowed with the symbolic significance of the religious view of the world.

In the middle of Book II (Chapter xviii), in which the love story begins to take on the significance which the priest had predicted, the point is indicated by a bit of dialogue between the lovers.

"Couldn't we be married privately some way? Then if anything happened to me or if you had a child."

"There's no way to be married except by church or state. We are married privately. You see, darling, it would mean everything to me if I had any religion. But I haven't any religion."

"You gave me the Saint Anthony."

"That was for luck. Some one gave it to me."

"Then nothing worries you?"

"Only being sent away from you. You're my religion. You're all I've got."

Again, toward the end of Book IV (Chapter xxxv), just before Frederick and Catherine make their escape into Switzerland, Frederick is talking with a friend, the old Count Greffi, who has just said that he thought H. G. Wells's novel *Mr. Britling Sees It Through* a very good study of the English middle-class soul. But Frederick twists the word *soul* into another meaning.

"I don't know about the soul."

"Poor boy. We none of us know about the soul. Are you Croyant?"

"At night."

Later in the same conversation the Count returns to the topic:

"And if you ever become devout pray for me if I am dead. I am asking several of my friends to do that. I had expected to become devout myself but it has not come."
I thought he smiled sadly but I could not tell. He was so old and his face was very wrinkled, so that a smile used so many lines that all graduations were lost.
"I might become very devout," I said. "Anyway, I will pray for you."
"I had always expected to become devout. All my family died very devout. But somehow it does not come."
"It's too early."
"Maybe it is too late. Perhaps I have outlived my religious feeling."
"My own comes only at night."
"Then too you are in love. Do not forget that is a religious feeling."

So here, again, we find Frederick defined as the sleepless man, and the relation established between secular love and Divine love.

In the end, with the death of Catherine, Frederick discovers that the attempt to find a substitute for universal meaning in the limited meaning of the personal relationship is doomed to failure. It is doomed because it is liable to all the accidents of a world in which human beings are like the ants running back and forth on a log burning in a campfire and in which death is, as Catherine says immediately before her own death, "just a dirty trick." But this is not to deny the value of the effort, or to deny the value of the discipline, the code, the stoic endurance, the things which make it true—or half true—that "nothing ever happens to the brave."

This question of the characteristic discipline takes us back to the beginning of the book, and to the context from which Frederick's effort arises. We have already mentioned the contrast between the officers of the mess and the priest. It is a contrast based on the man who is aware of the issue of meaning in life and those who are unaware of it, who give themselves over to the mere flow of accident, the contrast between the disciplined and the undisciplined. But the contrast is not merely between the priest and the officers. Frederick's friend, the surgeon Rinaldi, is another who is on the same "side" of the contrast as the priest. He may go to the brothel with his brother officers, he may even bait the priest a little, but his personal relationship with Frederick indicates his affiliations; he is one of the initiate. Furthermore, he has the discipline of his profession, and as we have seen, in the Hemingway world, the discipline which seems to be merely technical, the style of the artist or the form of the athlete or bullfighter, may be an index to a moral value. "Already," he says, "I am only happy when I am working." (Already because the seeking of pleasure in sensation is inadequate for Rinaldi.) This point appears more sharply in the remarks about the doctor who first attends to Frederick's wounded leg. He is incompetent and does not wish to take the responsibility for a decision.

Before he came back three doctors came into the room. I have noticed that doctors who fail in the practice of medicine have a tendency to seek one another's company and aid in consultation. A doctor who cannot take out your appendix properly will recommend to you a doctor who will be unable to remove your tonsils with success. These were three such doctors.

In contrast with them there is Dr. Valentini, who is competent, who is willing to take responsibility, and who, as a kind of mark of his role, speaks the same lingo, with the same bantering, ironical tone, as Rinaldi—the tone which is the mark of the initiate.

So we have the world of the novel divided into two groups, the initiate and the uninitiate, the aware and the unaware, the disciplined and the undisciplined. In the first group are Frederick, Catherine, Rinaldi, Valentini, Count Greffi, the old man who cut the paper silhouettes "for pleasure," and Passini, Manera, and the other ambulance men in Frederick's command. In the second group are the officers of the mess, the incompetent doctors, the "legitimate hero" Ettore, and the "patriots"—all the people who do not know what is really at stake, who are decided by the big words, who do not have the discipline. They are the messy people, the people who surrender to the flow and illusion of things. It is this second group who provide the context of the novel, and more especially the context from which Frederick moves toward his final complete awareness.

The final awareness means, as we have said, that the individual is thrown back upon his private discipline and his private capacity to endure. The hero cuts himself off from the herd, the confused world, which symbolically appears as the routed army at Caporetto. And, as Malcolm Cowley has pointed out, the plunge into the flooded Tagliamento, when Frederick escapes from the battle police, has the significance of a rite. By this "baptism" Frederick is reborn into another world; he comes out into the world of the man alone, no longer supported by and involved in society.

Anger was washed away in the river along with my obligation. Although that ceased when the carabiniere put his hands on my collar. I would like to have had the uniform off although I did not care much about the outward forms. I had taken off the stars, but that was for convenience. It was no point of honor. I was not against them. I was through. I wished them all the luck. There were the good ones, and the brave ones, and the calm ones and the sensible ones, and they deserved it. But it was not my show any more and I wished this bloody train would get to Mestre and I would eat and stop thinking.

So Frederick, by a decision, does what the boy Nick, in *In Our Time,* does as the result of the accident of a wound. He makes a "separate peace." And from the waters of the flooded Tagliamento arises the Hemingway hero in his purest form, with human history and obligation washed away, ready to enact the last phase of his appropriate drama, and learn from his inevitable defeat the lesson of lonely fortitude.

III

This is not the time to attempt to give a final evaluation of Hemingway's work as a whole or even of this particular novel—if there is ever a time for a "final" evaluation. But we may touch on some of the objections which have been brought against his work.

First, there is the objection that his work is immoral or dirty or disgusting. This objection appeared in various quarters against *A Farewell to Arms* at the time of its first publication. For instance, Robert Herrick, himself a respected novelist, wrote that if suppression were to be justified at all it would be justified in this case. He said that the book had no significance, was merely a "lustful indulgence," and smelled of the "boudoir," and summarized his view by calling it "garbage." That objection has for the most part died out, but its echoes can still be occasionally heard, and now and then, at rare intervals, some bigot or highminded but uninstructed moralist will object to the inclusion of *A Farewell to Arms* in a college course.

The answer to such an objection is fundamentally an answer to the charge that the book has no meaning. The answerer must seek to establish the fact that the book does deal seriously with a moral and philosophical issue, which, for better or worse, does exist in the modern world in substantially the terms presented by Hemingway. This means that the book, even if it does not end with a solution which is generally acceptable, still embodies a moral effort and is another document of the human will to achieve ideal values. As for the bad effect it may have on some readers, the best answer is perhaps to be found in a quotation from Thomas Hardy, who is now sanctified but whose most famous novels, *Tess of the D'Urbervilles* and *Jude the Obscure,* once suffered the attacks of the dogmatic moralists, and one of whose books was burned by a bishop:

Of the effects of such sincere presentation on weak minds, when the courses of the characters are not exemplary and the rewards and punishments ill adjusted to deserts, it is not our duty to consider too closely. A novel which does mortal injury to a dozen imbeciles, and has bracing results upon intellects of normal vigor, can justify its existence; and probably a novel was never written by the purest-minded author for which there could not be found some moral invalid or other whom it was capable of harming.

Second, there is the objection that Hemingway's work, especially of the period before *To Have and Have Not,* has no social relevance, that it is off the main stream of modern life, and that it has no concern with the economic structure of society. Critics who hold this general view regard Hemingway, like Joseph Conrad and perhaps like Henry James, as an exotic. There are several possible lines of retort to this objection. One line is well stated in the following passage if we substitute the name of Hemingway for Conrad:

> Thus it is no reproach to Conrad that he does not concern himself at all with the economic and social background underlying human relationships in modern civilization, for he never sets out to study those relationships. The Marxists cannot accuse him of cowardice or falsification, because in this case the charge is not relevant [though it might be relevant to *To Have and Have Not* or to *For Whom the Bell Tolls*]. That, from the point of view of the man with a theory, there are accidents in history, no one can deny. And if a writer chooses to discuss those accidents rather than the events which follow the main stream of historical causation, the economic or other determinist can only shrug his shoulder and maintain that these events are less instructive to the students than are the major events which he chooses to study; but he cannot accuse the writer of falsehood or distortion.[2]

That much is granted by one of the ablest critics of the group who would find Hemingway an exotic. But a second line of retort would fix on the word *instructive* in the foregoing passage, and would ask what kind of instruction, if any, is to be expected of fiction, as fiction. Is the kind of instruction expected of fiction in direct competition, at the same level, with the kind of instruction offered in Political Science I or Economics II? If that is the case, then out with Shakespeare and Keats and in with Upton Sinclair.

Perhaps *instruction* is not a relevant word, after all, for this case. This is a very thorny and debatable question, but it can be ventured that what good fiction gives us is the stimulation of a powerful image of human nature trying to fulfill itself and not instruction in an abstract sense. The economic and the political man are important aspects of human nature and may well constitute part of the materials of fiction. But the economic or political man is not the complete man and other concerns may still be important enough to engage worthily the attention of a writer—such concerns as love, death, courage, the point of honor, and the moral scruple. A man does not only have to live with other men in terms of economic and political arrangements; he has to live with them in terms of moral arrangements, and he has to live with himself, he has to define himself. It can truly be said that these concerns are all inter-related in fact, but it might be dangerously dogmatic to insist that a writer should not bring one aspect into sharp, dramatic focus.

And it might be dangerously dogmatic to insist that Hemingway's ideas are not relevant to modern life. The mere fact that they exist and have stirred a great many people is a testimony to their relevance. Or to introduce a variation on that theme, it might be dogmatic to object to his work on the ground that he has few basic ideas. The history of literature seems to show that good artists may have very few *basic* ideas. They may have many ideas, but the ideas

[2] David Daiches: *Fiction in the Modern World.*

do not lead a life of democratic give-and-take, of genial camaraderie. No, there are usually one or two basic, obsessive ones. Like the religious reformer Savonarola, the artist may say: "Le mie cose erano poche e grandi"—my ideas were few and grand. And the ideas of the artist are grand because they are intensely felt, intensely realized—not because, by objective standards, by public, statistical standards, "important." No, that kind of public, statistical importance may be a *condition* of their being grand but is not of the special essence of their grandeur. (Perhaps not even the condition—perhaps the grandeur inheres in the fact that the artistic work shows us a parable of meaning—how idea is felt and how passion becomes idea through order.)

An artist may need few *basic* ideas, but in assessing his work we must introduce another criterion in addition to that of intensity. We must introduce the criterion of area. In other words, his basic ideas do not operate in splendid isolation; to a greater or lesser degree, they operate in terms of their conquest of other ideas. Or again differently, the focus is a focus of experience, and the area of experience involved gives us another criterion of condition, the criterion of area. Perhaps an example would be helpful here. We have said that Hemingway is concerned with the scruple of honor, that this is a basic idea in his work. But we find that he applies this idea to a relatively small area of experience. In fact, we never see a story in which the issue involves the problem of definition of the scruple, or we never see a story in which honor calls for a slow, grinding, day-to-day conquest of nagging difficulties. In other words, the idea is submitted to the test of a relatively small area of experience, to experience of a hand-picked sort, and to characters of a limited range.

But within that range, within the area in which he finds the congenial material and in which competing ideas do not intrude themselves too strongly, Hemingway's expressive capacity is very powerful and the degree of intensity is very great. He is concerned not to report variety of human nature or human situation, or to analyze the forces operating in society, but to communicate a certain feeling about, a certain attitude toward, a special issue. That is, he is essentially a lyric rather than a dramatic writer, and for the lyric writer virtue depends upon the intensity with which the personal vision is rendered rather than upon the creation of a variety of characters whose visions are in conflict among themselves. And though Hemingway has not furnished—and never intended to furnish—document and diagnosis of our age, he has given us one of its most compelling symbols.

Used as "Introduction" to *A Farewell to Arms* by Ernest Hemingway. Copyright, 1949, by Charles Scribner's Sons. Reprinted by permission of the author and publisher. First published in *The Kenyon Review,* Vol. IX (Winter, 1947), pp. 1–28.

William Faulkner
[1946]

Malcolm Cowley's editing of *The Portable Faulkner*[1] is remarkable on two counts. First, the selection from Faulkner's work is made not merely to give a cross section or a group of good examples but to demonstrate one of the principles of integration in the work. Second, the introductory essay is one of the few things ever written on Faulkner which is not hagridden by prejudice or preconception and which really sheds some light on the subject.

The selections here are made to describe the place, Yoknapatawpha County, Mississippi, which is, as Cowley puts it, "Faulkner's mythical kingdom," and to give the history of that kingdom. The place is the locale of most of Faulkner's work. Its 2400 square miles lie between the hills of north Mississippi and the rich, black bottom lands. It has a population of 15,611 persons, composing a society with characters as different as the Bundrens, the Snopeses, Ike McCaslin, Percy Grimm, Temple Drake, the Compsons, Christmas, Dilsey, and the tall convict of *The Wild Palms*. No land in all fiction lives more vividly in its physical presence than this mythical county—the "pine-winey" afternoons, the nights with "a thin sickle of moon like the heel print of a boot in wet sand," the tremendous reach of the big river in flood, "yellow and sleepy in the afternoon," and the "little piddling creeks, that run backward one day and forward the next and come busting down on a man full of dead mules and hen houses," the ruined plantation which was Popeye's hangout, the swamps and fields and hot, dusty roads of the Frenchman's Bend section, and the remnants of the great original forests, "green with gloom" in summer, "if anything actually dimmer than they had been in November's gray dissolution, where even at noon the sun fell only in windless dappling upon the earth which never completely dried."

And no land in all fiction is more painstakingly analyzed from the sociological standpoint. The descendants of the old families, the descendants of bushwhackers and carpetbaggers, the swamp rats, the Negro cooks and farm hands, bootleggers and gangsters, peddlers, college boys, tenant farmers, country store-keepers, county-seat lawyers are all here. The marks of class, occupation, and history are fully rendered and we know completely their speech, dress, food, houses, manners, and attitudes. Nature and sociology, geography and human geography, are scrupulously though effortlessly presented in Faulkner's work, and their significance for his work is very great; but the significance is of a conditioning order. They are, as it were, aspects

[1] *The Portable Faulkner,* edited by Malcolm Cowley. New York: Viking Press.

of man's "doom"—a word of which Faulkner is very fond—but his manhood in the face of that doom is what is important.

Cowley's selections are made to give the description of the mythical kingdom, but more important, they are made to give its history. Most critics, even those who have most naïvely or deliberately misread the meaning of the fact, have been aware that the sense of the past is crucial in Faulkner's work. Cowley has here set up selections running in date of action from 1820 to 1940. The first, "A Justice," is a story about Ikkemotubbe, the nephew of a Chickasaw chief who went to New Orleans, where he received the name of *du Homme*, which became Doom; who came back to the tribe to poison his way to the Man-ship; and who, in the end (in Faulkner's "history" though not in "A Justice" itself), swaps a mile square of "virgin north Mississippi dirt" for a racing mare owned by Jason Lycurgus Compson, the founder of the Compson family in Mississippi. The last selection, "Delta Autumn," shows us Isaac McCaslin, the man who brings the best of the old order, philosopher, aristocrat, woodsman, into the modern world and who gives the silver-mounted horn which General Compson had left him to a mulatto woman for her bastard son by a relative of McCaslin's. In between "A Justice" and "Delta Autumn" fall such pieces as the magnificent "Red Leaves," the profoundly symbolic story called "The Bear," the Civil War and Reconstruction stories, "Rain" (from *The Unvanquished*) and "Wash," "Old Man" (the story of the tall convict from *The Wild Palms*), and the often anthologized "That Evening Sun" and "A Rose for Emily," and the brilliant episode of "Percy Grimm" (from *Light in August*). There are other pieces included, but these are the best, and the best for showing the high points in the history of Yoknapatawpha County.

Cowley's introduction undertakes to define the significance of place and history in Faulkner's work, that "labor of imagination that has not been equaled in our time." That labor is, as he points out, a double labor: "first, to invent a Mississippi county that was like a mythical kingdom, but was complete and living in all its details; second, to make his story of Yoknapatawpha County stand as a parable or legend of all the Deep South." The legend—called a legend "because it is obviously no more intended as a historical account of the country south of the Ohio than *The Scarlet Letter* was intended as a history of Massachusetts"—is, as Cowley defines it, this:

The South was settled by Sartorises (aristocrats) and Sutpens (nameless, ambitious men) who, seizing the land from the Indians, were determined to found an enduring and stable order. But despite their strength and integrity their project was, to use Faulkner's word, "accursed" by slavery, which, with the Civil War as instrument, frustrated their design. Their attempt to rebuild according to the old plan and old values was defeated by a combination of forces—the carpetbaggers and Snopeses ("a new exploiting class descended from the landless whites"). Most of the descendants of the old order are in various ways incompetent: They are prevented by their code from competing with the codeless Snopeses, they cling to the letter and forget the spirit of their tradition, they lose contact with the realities of the present and escape into a dream world of alcohol or rhetoric or gentility or madness, they fall in love with defeat or death, they lose nerve and become cowards, or they, like the last Jason in *The Sound and the Fury,* adopt Snopesism and became worse than any Snopes. Figures like Popeye (eyes like "rubber knobs," a creature having "that vicious depthless quality of stamped tin," the man "who made money and had nothing he could do with it, spend it for, since he knew that alcohol would kill him like poison, who had no friends and had never known a woman") are in their dehumanized quality symbols of modernism, for the society of finance capitalism. The violence of some of Faulkner's work is, according to Cowley, "an example of the Freudian method turned backward, being full of sexual nightmares that are in reality social symbols. It is somehow connected in the author's mind with what he regards as the rape and corruption of the South."

This is, in brief, Cowley's interpretation of the legend, and it provides an excellent way into Faulkner; it exactly serves the purpose which an introduction should serve. The interpretation is indebted, no doubt, to that of George Marion O'Donnell (the first and still an indispensable study of Faulkner's theme), but it modifies O'Donnell's tendency to read Faulkner with an allegorical rigidity and with a kind of doctrinal single-mindedness.

It is possible that the present view, however, should be somewhat modified, at least in emphasis. Although no writer is more deeply committed to a locality than Faulkner, the emphasis on the Southern elements may blind us to other elements, or at least other applications, of deep significance. And this is especially true in so far as the work is interpreted merely as Southern apologetics or, as it is by Maxwell Geismar, as the "extreme hallucinations" of a "cultural psychosis."

It is important, I think, that Faulkner's work be regarded not in terms of the South against the North, but in terms of issues which are common to our modern world. The legend is not merely a legend of the South, but is also a legend of our general plight and problem. The modern world is in moral confusion. It does suffer from a lack of discipline, of sanctions, of community of values, of a sense of a mission. It is a world in which self-interest, workableness, success, provide the standards. It is a world which is the victim of abstraction and of mechanism, or at least, at moments, feels itself to be. It can look back nostalgically upon the old world of traditional values and feel loss and perhaps despair—upon the world in which, as one of Faulkner's characters puts it, men "had the gift of living once or dying once instead of being diffused and scattered creatures drawn blindly from a grab bag and assembled"

—a world in which men were, "integer for integer," more simple and complete.

If it be objected that Faulkner's view is unrealistic, that had the old order satisfied human needs it would have survived, and that it is sentimental to hold that it was killed from the outside, the answer is clear in the work: the old order did not satisfy human needs—the Southern old order or any other —for it, not being founded on justice, was "accursed" and held the seeds of its own ruin in itself. But even in terms of the curse the old order, as opposed to the new order (in so far as the new is to be equated with Snopesism), allowed the traditional man to define himself as human by setting up codes, concepts of virtue, obligations, and by accepting the risks of his humanity. Within the traditional order was a notion of truth, even if man in the flow of things did not succeed in realizing that truth. Take, for instance, the passage from "The Bear":

"All right," he said. "Listen," and read again, but only one stanza this time and closed the book and laid it on the table. "She cannot fade, though thou has not thy bliss," McCaslin said: "Forever wilt thou love, she be fair."
"He's talking about a girl," he said.
"He had to talk about something," McCaslin said. Then he said, "He was talking about truth. Truth is one. It doesn't change. It covers all things which touch the heart—honor and pride and pity and justice and courage and love. Do you see now?"

The human effort is what is important, the capacity to make the effort to rise above the mechanical process of life, the pride to endure, for in endurance there is a kind of self-conquest.

When it is said, as it is often said, that Faulkner's work is "backward-looking," the answer is that the constant ethical center is to be found in the glorification of the human effort and of human endurance, which are not in time, even though in modernity they seem to persist most surely among the despised and rejected. It is true that Faulkner's work contains a savage attack on modernity, but it is to be remembered that Elizabethan tragedy, for instance, contained just such an attack on its own special "modernity." (Ambition is the most constant tragic crime, and ambition is the attitude special to an opening society; all villains are rationalists and appeal to "nature" beyond traditional morality for justification, and rationalism is, in the sense implied here, the attitude special to the rise of a secular and scientific order before a new morality can be formulated.)

It is not ultimately important whether the traditional order (Southern or other) as depicted by Faulkner fits exactly the picture which critical historical method provides. Let it be granted, for the sake of discussion, that Faulkner does oversimplify the matter. What is ultimately important, both ethically and artistically, is the symbolic function of that order in relation to the world which is set in opposition to it. The opposition between the old order and the new does not, however, exhaust the picture. What of the order to come? "We will have to wait," old Ike McCaslin says to the mulatto girl who is in love with a white man. A curse may work itself out in time; and in such glimpses, which occur now and then, we get the notion of a grudging meliorism, a practical supplement to the idealism, like Ike McCaslin's, which finds compensation in the human effort and the contemplation of "truth."

The discussion, even at a larger scope and with more satisfactory analysis, of the central theme of Faulkner would not exhaust the interest of his work. In fact, the discussion of this question always runs the risk of making his work appear too schematic, too dry and too complacent when in actual fact it is full of rich detail, of shadings and complexities of attitude, of ironies and ambivalences. Cowley's introduction cautions the reader on this point and suggests various fruitful topics for investigation and thought. But I shall make bold—and in the general barrenness of criticism on Faulkner it does not require excessive boldness—to list and comment on certain topics which seem to me to demand further critical study.

Nature. The vividness of the natural background is one of the impressive features of Faulkner's work. It is accurately observed, but observation only provides the stuff from which the characteristic effects are gained. It is the atmosphere which counts, the poetry, the infusion of feeling, the symbolic weight. Nature provides a backdrop—of lyric beauty (the meadow in the cow episode of *The Hamlet*), of homely charm (the trial scene of the "Spotted Horses" story from the same book), of sinister, brooding force (the river in "Old Man" from *The Wild Palms*), of massive dignity (the forest in "The Bear")—for the human action and passion. The indestructible beauty is there: "God created man," Ike McCaslin says in "Delta Autumn," "and He created the world for him to live in and I reckon He created the kind of world He would have wanted to live in if He had been a man."

Ideally, if man were like God, as Ike McCaslin puts it, man's attitude toward nature would be one of pure contemplation, pure participation in its great forms and appearances; the appropriate attitude is love, for with Ike McCaslin the moment of love is equated with godhood. But since man "wasn't quite God himself," since he lives in the world of flesh, he must be a hunter, user, and violator. To return to McCaslin: God "puts them both here: man and the game he would follow and kill, foreknowing it. I believe He said, 'So be it.' I reckon He even foreknew the end. But He said 'I will give him his chance. I will give him warning and foreknowledge too, along with the desire to follow and the power to slay. The woods and the fields he ravages and the game he devastates will be the consequence and signature of his crime and guilt, and his punishment.'"

There is, then, a contamination implicit in the human condition—a kind of Original Sin, as it were—but it is possible, even in the contaminating act, the violation, for man to achieve some measure of redemption, a redemption through love. For instance, in "The Bear," the great legendary beast which is pursued for years to the death is also an object of love and veneration, and the symbol of virtue, and the deer hunt of "Delta Autumn" is for Ike McCaslin a ritual of renewal. Those who have learned the right relationship to nature—"the pride and humility" which young Ike McCaslin learns from the half-Negro, half-Indian Sam Fathers—are set over against those who have not. In "The Bear," General Compson speaks up to Cass McCaslin to defend the wish of the boy Ike McCaslin to stay an extra week in the woods: "You got one foot straddled into a farm and the other foot straddled into a bank; you ain't even got a good hand-hold where this boy was already an old man long before you damned Sartorises and Edmondses invented farms and banks to keep yourselves from having to find out what this boy was born knowing and fearing too maybe, but without being afraid, that could go ten miles on a compass because he wanted to look at a bear none of us had ever got near enough to put a bullet in and looked at the bear and came the ten miles back on the compass in the dark; maybe by God that's the why and the wherefore of farms and banks."

Those who have the wrong attitude toward nature are the pure exploiters, the apostles of abstractionism, the truly evil men. For instance, the very opening of *Sanctuary* presents a distinction on this ground between Benbow and Popeye. While the threat of Popeye keeps Benbow crouching by the spring, he hears a Carolina wren sing, and even under these circumstances tries to recall the local name for it. And he says to Popeye: "And of course you don't know the name of it. I don't suppose you'd know a bird at all, without it was singing in a cage in a hotel lounge or cost four dollars on a plate." Popeye, as we may remember, spits in the spring (he hates nature and must foul it), is afraid to go through the woods ("Through all them trees?" he demands when Benbow points out the short cut), and when an owl whisks past them in the twilight, claws at Benbow's coat with almost hysterical fear ("It's just an owl," Benbow says. "It's nothing but an owl.").

The pure exploiters, though they may gain ownership and use of a thing, never really have it; like Popeye, they are impotent. For instance, Flem Snopes, the central character and villain of *The Hamlet*, who brings the exploiter's mentality to Frenchman's Bend, finally marries Eula Varner, a kind of fertility goddess or earth goddess; but his ownership is meaningless, for she always refers to him as "that man" (she does not even have a name for him), and he has only got her after she has given herself willingly to one of the bold, hot-blooded boys of the neighborhood. In fact, nature can't, in one sense, be "owned." Ike McCaslin, in "The Bear," says of the land which has come down to him: "It was never Father's and Uncle Buddy's to bequeath me to repudiate, because it was never Grandfather's to bequeath them to bequeath me to repudiate, because it was never old Ikkemotubbe's to sell to Grandfather for bequeathment and repudiation. Because it was never Ikkemotubbe's father's father's to bequeath Ikkemotubbe to sell to Grandfather or any man because on the instant when Ikkemotubbe discovered, realized, that he could sell it for money, on that instant it ceased ever to have been his forever, father to father, to father, and the man who bought it bought nothing."

The right attitude toward nature is, as a matter of fact, associated with the right attitude toward man, and the mere lust for power over nature is associated with the lust for power over other men, for God gave the earth to man, we read in "The Bear," not "to hold for himself and his descendants inviolable title forever, generation after generation, to the oblongs and squares of the earth, but to hold the earth mutual and intact in the communal anonymity of brotherhood, and all the fee He asked was pity and humility and sufferance and endurance and the sweat of his face for bread." It is the failure of this pity which curses the earth (the land in Faulkner's particular country is "accursed" by chattel slavery, but slavery is simply one of the possible forms of the failure). But the rape of nature and the crime against man are always avenged. The rape of nature, the mere exploitation of it without love, is always avenged because the attitude which commits that crime also commits the crime against men which in turn exacts vengeance, so that man finally punishes himself. It is only by this line of reasoning that one can, I think, read the last page of "Delta Autumn":

This land which man has deswamped and denuded and deriverd in two generations so that white men can own plantations and commute every night to Memphis and black men own plantations and ride in Jim Crow cars to Chicago to live in millionaires' mansions on Lake Shore Drive; where white men rent farms and live like niggers and niggers crop on shares and live like animals; where cotton is planted and grows man-tall in the very cracks of the sidewalks, and usury and mortgage and bankruptcy and measureless wealth, Chinese and African and Aryan and Jew, all breed and spawn together until no man has time to say which one is which nor cares. . . . No wonder the ruined woods I used to know don't cry for retribution! he thought: The people who have destroyed it will accomplish its revenge.

The attitude toward nature in Faulkner's work, however, does not involve a sinking into nature. In Faulkner's mythology man has "suzerainty over the earth," he is not of the earth, and it is the human virtues which count —"pity and humility and sufferance and endurance." If we take even the extreme case of the idiot Snopes and his fixation on the cow in The Hamlet (a scene whose function in the total order of the book is to show that even the idiot pervert is superior to Flem), a scene which shows the human being as close as possible to the "natural" level, we find that the scene is the most lyrical in Faulkner's work: even the idiot is human and not animal, for only human desires, not animal, clothe themselves in poetry. I think that George Marion O'Donnell is right in pointing to the humanism-naturalism opposition in Faulkner's work, and over and over again we find that the point of some novel or story has to do with the human effort to find or create values in the mechanical round of experience—"not just to eat and evacuate and sleep warm," as Charlotte Rittenmeyer says in *The Wild Palms*, "So we can get up and eat and evacuate in order to sleep warm again," or not just to raise cotton to buy niggers to raise cotton to buy niggers, as it is put in another place. Even when a character seems to be caught in the iron ring of some compulsion, of some mechanical process (the hunted Negro of "Red Leaves," the tall convict of *The Wild Palms*, Christmas of *Light in August*), the effort may be discernible. And in Quentin's attempt, in *The Sound and the Fury*, to persuade his sister Caddy, who is pregnant by one of the boys of Jefferson, to confess that she has committed incest with him, we find among other things the idea that "the horror" and "the clean flame" would be preferable to the meaninglessness of the "loud world."

Humor. One of the most important remarks in Cowley's introduction is that concerning humor. There is, especially in the later books, "a sort of homely and sober-sided frontier humor that is seldom achieved in contemporary writing." Cowley continues: "In a curious way, Faulkner combines two of the principal traditions in American letters: the tradition of psychological horror, often close to symbolism, that begins with Charles Brockden Brown, our first professional novelist, and extends through Poe, Melville, Henry James (in his later stories), Stephen Crane and Hemingway; and the other tradition of frontier humor and realism, beginning with Augustus Longstreet's *Georgia Scenes* and having Mark Twain as its best example." The observation is an acute one, for the distortions of humor and the distortions of horror in Faulkner's work are closely akin and frequently, in a given instance, can scarcely be disentangled.

It is true that the most important strain of humor in Faulkner's work is derived from the tradition of frontier humor (though it is probable that he got it from the porches of country stores and the courthouse yards of county-seat towns and not from any book), and it is true that the most spectacular displays of Faulkner's humor are of this order—for example, the "Spotted Horses" episode from *The Hamlet* or the story "Was." But there are other strains which might be distinguished and investigated. For example, there is a kind of Dickensian humor; the scene in the Memphis brothel from *Sanctuary*, which is reprinted here under the title "Uncle Bud and the Three Madams," is certainly more Dickensian than frontier. There is a subdued humor, sometimes shading into pathos, in the treatment of some of the Negro characters and in their dialogue. And there is an irony ranging from that in the scene in *Sanctuary* where Miss Reba, the madam, in offended decency keeps telling Temple, "Lie down and cover up your nekkidness," while the girl talks with Benbow, to that in the magnificently sustained monologue of Jason at the end of *The Sound and the Fury*.

In any case, humor in Faulkner's work is never exploited for its own sake. It is regularly used as an index, as a lead, to other effects. The humor in itself may be striking, but Faulkner is not a humorist in the sense, say, that Mark Twain is. His humor is but one perspective on the material and it is never a final perspective, as we can see from such an example as the episode of "Spotted Horses." Nothing could be more wide of the point than the remark in Maxwell Geismar's essay on Faulkner to the effect that Faulkner in *The Hamlet* "seems now to accept the antics of his provincial morons, to enjoy the chronicle of their low-grade behavior; he submerges himself in their clownish degradation." All the critic seems to find in Mink Snopes' victim with his life-long devotion to the memory of his dead wife, and Ratliff with his good heart and ironical mind and quiet wisdom, is comic "descendants of the gangling and giggling Wash Jones."

The Poor White. The above remark leads us to the not uncommon misconception about the role of the poor white in Faulkner's work. It is true that the Snopeses are poor whites, descendants of bushwhackers (and therefore outside society, as the bushwhacker was outside society, had no "side" in the Civil War but tried to make a good thing of it), and it is true that Snopesism represents a special kind of villainy and degradation, the form that the pure doctrine of exploitation and degradation takes in the society of which Faulkner writes, but any careful reader realizes that a Snopes is not to be equated with a poor white. For instance, the book most fully about the poor white, *As I Lay Dying,* is full of sympathy and poetry. There are a hundred touches like that in Cash's soliloquy about the phonograph: "I reckon it's a good thing we aint got ere a one of them. I reckon I wouldn't never get no work done a-tall for listening to it. I dont know if a little music aint about the nicest thing a fellow can have. Seems like when he comes in tired of a night, it aint nothing could rest him like having a little music played and him resting." Or like the long section toward the middle of the book devoted to Addie Bundren, a section which is full of eloquence like that of this paragraph: "And then he died. He did not know he was dead. I would lie by him in the dark, hearing the dark land talking of God's love and His beauty and His sin; hearing the dark voicelessness in which the words are the deeds, and the other words that are not deeds, that are just the gaps in peoples' lacks, coming down like the cries of geese out of the wild darkness in the old terrible nights, fumbling at the deeds like orphans to whom are pointed out in a crowd two faces and told,

That is your father, your mother." Do these passages indicate a relish in the "antics of his provincial morons"?

The whole of *As I Lay Dying* is based on the heroic effort of the Bundren family to fulfill the promise to the dead mother, to take her body to Jefferson; and the fact that Anse Bundren, after the heroic effort has been completed, immediately gets him a new wife, the "duck-shaped woman" with the "hard-looking pop-eyes," does not negate the heroism of the effort nor the poetry and feeling which give flesh to the book. We are told by one critic that "what should have been the drama of the Bundrens thus becomes in the end a sort of brutal farce," and that we are "unable to feel the tragedy because the author has refused to accept the Bundrens, as he did accept the Compsons, as tragic." Rather, I should say, the Bundrens may come off a little better than the latter-day Compsons, the whining mother, the promiscuous Caddy, the ineffectual Quentin, and the rest. The Bundrens, at least, are capable of the heroic effort, and the promise is fulfilled. What the conclusion indicates is that even such a fellow as Anse Bundren (who is not typical of his family, by the way), in the grip of an idea, in terms of promise or code, is capable of rising out of his ordinary level; Anse falls back at the end, but only after the prop of the idea and obligation have been removed. And we may recall that even the "gangling and giggling Wash Jones" has always been capable of some kind of obscure dream and aspiration (his very attachment to Sutpen indicates that), and that in the end he achieves dignity and manhood.

The final and incontrovertible evidence that Snopes is not to be equated with poor whites comes in *The Hamlet* (though actually most of the characters in the book, though they may be poor, are not strictly speaking, "poor whites" at all, but rather what uninstructed reviewers choose to call by that label). The point of the book is the assault made on a solid community of plain, hard-working small farmers by Snopeses and Snopesism. Ratliff is not rich, but he is not Flem Snopes. And if the corruption of Snopesism does penetrate into the community, there is not one here who can be compared in degradation and vileness to Jason of *The Sound and the Fury*, the Compson who has embraced Snopesism. In fact, Popeye and Flem, Faulkner's best advertised villains, cannot, for vileness and ultimate meanness, touch Jason.

The Negro. In one of Faulkner's books it is said that every white child is born crucified on a black cross. Remarks like this have led to a gross misconception of the place of the Negro in Faulkner's work, to the notion that Faulkner "hates" Negroes. For instance, we find Maxwell Geismar exclaiming what a "strange inversion" it is to take the Negro, who is the "tragic consequence," and to exhibit him as the "evil cause" of the failure of the old order in the South.

This is a misreading of the text. It is slavery, not the Negro, which is defined, quite flatly, as the curse, over and over again, and the Negro is the black cross in so far as he is the embodiment of the curse, the reminder of the guilt, the incarnation of the problem. That is the basic point. But now and then, as a kind of tangential irony, we have the notion, not of the burden of the white on the black, but of the burden of the black on the white, the weight of obligation, inefficiency, and so on, as well as the weight of guilt (the notion we find in the old story of the plantation mistress who, after the Civil War, said: "Mr. Lincoln thought he was emancipating those slaves, but he was really emancipating me.").

For instance, we get hints of this notion in "Red Leaves"; one of the Indians, sweating in the chase of the runaway Negro who is to be killed for the Man's funeral, says, "Damn that Negro," and the other Indian replies, "Yao. When have they ever been anything but a trial and a care to us?" But the black cross is, fundamentally, the weight of the white man's guilt, the white man who now sells salves and potions "to bleach the pigment and straighten the hair of Negroes that they might resemble the very race which for two hundred years had held them in bondage and from which for another hundred years not even a bloody civil war would have set them completely free." The curse is still operative, as the crime is still compounded.

The actual role of the Negro in Faulkner's fiction is consistently one of pathos or heroism. It is not merely, as has been suggested more than once, that Faulkner condescends to the good and faithful servant, the "white folks' nigger." There are figures like Dilsey, but they are not as impressive as the Negro in "Red Leaves" or Sam Fathers, who, with the bear, is the hero of "The Bear." The fugitive, who gains in the course of the former story a shadowy symbolic significance, is told in the end by one of the Indians who overtake him, "You ran well. Do not be ashamed," and when he walks among the Indians, he is "the tallest there, his high, close, mud-caked head looming above them all." And Sam Fathers is the fountainhead of the wisdom which Ike McCaslin finally gains, and the repository of the virtues which are central for Faulkner—"an old man, son of a Negro slave and an Indian king, inheritor on the one hand of the long chronicle of a people who had learned humility through suffering and learned pride through the endurance which survived suffering, and on the other side the chronicle of a people even longer in the land than the first, yet who now existed there only in the solitary brotherhood of an old and childless Negro's alien blood and the wild and invincible spirit of an old bear."

Even Christmas, in *Light in August*, though he is sometimes spoken of as a villain, is a mixture of heroism and pathos. He is the lost, suffering, enduring creature (the figure like Sam Fathers, the tall convict of *The Wild Palms*, or Dilsey in *The Sound and the Fury*), and even the murder he commits at the end is a fumbling attempt to define his manhood, is an attempt to break out of the iron ring of mechanism, to lift himself out of "nature," for the woman whom he kills has become a figure of the horror of the human which has surrendered the human attributes. (We may compare Christmas to Mink Snopes in *The Hamlet* in this respect: Mink, mean and vicious as he is, kills out of a kind of warped and confused pride, and by this affirmation is set off against his kinsman Flem, whose only values are those of pure Snopesism.)

Even such a brief comment on the Negro in Faulkner's work cannot close without this passage from "The Bear":

"Because they will endure. They are better than we are. Stronger than we are. Their vices are vices aped from white men or that white men and bondage have taught them: improvidence and intemperance and evasion—not laziness: evasion: of what white men had set them to, not for their aggrandizement or even comfort but his own—" and McCaslin

"All right. Go on: Promiscuity. Violence. Instability and lack of control. Inability to distinguish between mine and thine—" and he

"How distinguish when for two hundred years mine did not even exist for them?" and McCaslin

"All right. Go on. And their virtues—" and he

"Yes. Their own. Endurance—" and McCaslin

"So have mules:" and he

"—and pity and tolerance and forbearance and fidelity and love of children—" and McCaslin

"So have dogs:" and he

"—whether their own or not or black or not. And more: what they got not only from white people but not even despite white people because they had it already from the old free fathers a longer time free than us because we have never been free—"

And there is the single comment under Dilsey's name in the annotated genealogy of the Compsons which Faulkner has prepared for the present volume: "They endured."

Technique. There are excellent comments on this subject by Cowley, Conrad Aiken, Warren Beck, Joseph Warren Beach, and Alfred Kazin, but the subject has not been fully explored. One difficulty is that Faulkner is an incorrigible and restless experimenter, is peculiarly sensitive to the expressive possibilities of shifts in technique and has not developed (like Hemingway or Katherine Anne Porter—lyric rather than dramatic writers, artists with a great deal of self-certainty) in a straight line.

Provisionally, we may distinguish in Faulkner's work three basic methods of handling a narrative. One is best typified in *Sanctuary,* where there is a tightly organized plot, a crisp, laconic style, an objective presentation of character—an impersonal method. Another is best typified by *As I Lay Dying* or *The Sound and the Fury,* where each character unfolds in his own language or flow of being before us—a dramatic method in that the author does not obtrude, but a method which makes the subjective reference of character the medium of presentation. Another is best typified by "Was," "The Bear," or the story of the tall convict in *The Wild Palms*, where the organization of the narrative is episodic and the sense of a voice, a narrator's presence (though not necessarily a narrator in the formal sense), is almost constantly felt—a method in which the medium is ultimately a "voice" as index to sensibility. The assumptions underlying these methods, and the relations among them, would provide a study.

Cowley's emphasis on the unity of Faulkner's work, the fact that all the novels and stories are to be taken as aspects of a single, large design, is very important. It is important, for one thing, in regard to the handling of character. A character, Sutpen, for instance, may appear in various perspectives, so that from book to book we move toward a final definition much as in actual life we move toward the definition of a person. The same principle applies to event, as Conrad Aiken has pointed out, the principle of the spiral method which takes the reader over and over the same event from a different altitude, as it were, and a different angle. In relation to both character and event this method, once it is understood by the reader, makes for a kind of realism and a kind of suspense (in the formal not the factual sense) not common in fiction.

The emphasis on the unity of Faulkner's work may, however, lead to an underrating of the degree of organization within individual works. Cowley is right in pointing out the structural defect in *Light in August*, but he may be putting too much emphasis on the over-all unity and not enough on the organization of the individual work when he says that *The Hamlet* tends to resolve into a "series of episodes resembling beads on a string." I think that in that novel we have a type of organization in which the thematic rather than the narrative emphasis is the basic principle, and once we grasp that fact the unity of the individual work may come clear. In fact, the whole subject of the principle of thematic organization in the novels and long stories, "The Bear," for instance, needs investigation. In pieces which seem disjointed, or which seem to have the mere tale-teller's improvisations, we may sometimes discover the true unity if we think of the line of meaning, the symbolic ordering, and surrender ourselves to the tale-teller's "voice." And it may be useful at times to recall the distinction between the formal, forensic realism of Ibsen as opposed to the fluid, suggestive realism of Chekhov.

Symbol and Image. Cowley and O'Donnell have given acute readings of the main symbolic outline of Faulkner's fiction, but no one has yet devoted himself to the study of symbolic motifs which, though not major, are nevertheless extremely instructive. For instance, the images of the hunt, the flight, the pursuit, such as we have in "Red Leaves," *The Wild Palms*, the episode of Peter Grimm in *Light in August*, "The Bear," "Delta Autumn," "Was," and (especially in the hordes of moving Negroes) in *The Unvanquished*. Or there is the important symbolic relationship between man and earth. Or there is the contrast between images of compulsion and images of will or freedom. Or there is the device of what we might call the frozen moment, the arrested action which becomes symbolic, as in the moment when, in "An Odor of Verbena" (from *The Unvanquished*), Drusilla offers the pistols to the hero.

Polarity. To what extent does Faulkner work in terms of polarities, oppositions, paradoxes, inversions of roles? How much does he employ a line of concealed (or open) dialectic progression as a principle for his fiction? The study of these questions may lead to the discovery of principles of organization in his work not yet defined by criticism.

The study of Faulkner is the most challenging single task in contemporary American literature for criticism to undertake. Here is a novelist who, in mass of work, in scope of material, in range of effect, in reportorial accuracy and symbolic subtlety, in philosophical weight, can be put beside the masters of our own past literature. Yet this accomplishment has been effected in what almost amounts to critical isolation and silence, and when the silence has been broken it has usually been broken by someone (sometimes one of our better critics) whose reading has been hasty, whose analysis unscholarly and whose judgments superficial. The picture of Faulkner presented to the public by such criticism is a combination of Thomas Nelson Page, a fascist and a psychopath, gnawing his nails. Of course, this picture is usually accompanied by a grudging remark about genius.

Cowley's book, for its intelligence, sensitivity, and sobriety in the introduction, and for the ingenuity and judgment exhibited in the selections, would be valuable at any time. But it is especially valuable at this time. Perhaps it can mark a turning point in Faulkner's reputation. That will be of slight service to Faulkner, who, as much as any writer of our place and time, can rest in confidence. He can afford to wait. But can we?

From *The New Republic,* Vol. CXV (August 12, 1946), pp. 176–180; and (August 26, 1946), pp. 234–237. Reprinted by permission of the author and editors.

IRVING HOWE

Sherwood Anderson: An American as Artist

[1951]

"For all my egotism," wrote Sherwood Anderson at the end of his life, "I know I am but a minor figure." This self-estimate is both accurate and sincere: it comes, in the *Memoirs,* directly after an eager tribute to those writers of the past whom Anderson most admired. Yet it was characteristic of his feeling for the creative life that even when he was most humble about his work he was proud to be doing it. In some ways the minor artist needs the buttress of pride more than the major one: he must believe that his career, in its fragmentary achievement no less than its integrity of conduct, is intrinsically worthy. This pride—the pride which permits the minor artist to place himself in fraternal relation to past greatness even as he realizes the limitations of his own work—Anderson had.

The pity of it was, however, that in his last years he found it so hard to preserve that pride. How graciously a culture accepts its minor artists is one gauge of its health. A secure culture, organically related to its own past and yet forever modulating it, will quickly assimilate the minor artist's vision and will honor and bolster him during his lifetime. But American culture—committed as it is to a highly competitive ethic, a systematic suspicion of the past, and an uneasy depreciation of the frankly minor work—could hardly bolster Anderson once his imagination had begun to falter. At first it overvalued him, perhaps even turned his head, and then it ignored him as if he were unobtrusively dead; but on neither occasion could it fortify his taste or direct him with affectionate severity to what was best in his work. It was a culture with a depressingly short memory and it behaved as if that short memory were its outstanding virtue; in its frenetic quest for novelty it was always searching for new heroes to elevate, always discarding artists as if they were bankrupts defeated by stronger rivals (its most favored author, Ernest Hemingway, saw literature as a vast boxing tournament), and always rediscovering artists who should never have been forgotten. In so discontinuous a culture a writer like Anderson, who had only a slight capacity for detachment or self-protection, was certain to be wounded as he had once been praised. It is for this reason, though hardly for this reason alone, that his literary career seems representative of the effort so many Americans have made to become artists.

It was the pattern of Anderson's life that he had always to resume it as if from a fresh: he could not enjoy the kind of organic growth that an artist, or any other human being, should enjoy. For a man like Anderson, who drew so heavily from each immediate phase of the *Zeitgeist* because he could draw so little from anything else, each inevitable change in that *Zeitgeist* could only mean personal dislocation and crisis. The new beginning, with guilt or error or failure forgiven, is a typical daydream of Americans, a people convinced of its indestructible innocence or at least of the eternal possibility of a painless redemption; the new beginning, with the hero returning from fiasco to a wife-mother or mistress-mother whom he serenely expects to be waiting for him, is a pervasive theme in Anderson's books; and the new beginning, each time somewhat further stripped of innocence, is a recurrent fact in Anderson's life. That it was necessary and perhaps unavoidable in his life explains much about the fragmentary nature of his achievement.

It is here that the absence of an ample sense of tradition exacts its price— tradition not as a fashionable catalogue of great names or titles, but as the whole of those inherited resources by which a writer profits, often quite unconsciously, from the efforts of the masters who have preceded him. In a *Partisan Review* symposium in 1939 Anderson was asked whether as a writer he was aware of a "usable past." His answer was a self-portrait in miniature: "I am afraid I do not know what you mean by 'usable past.' . . . I am afraid that my difficulty in trying to answer these questions is that I spend little time thinking of either past or future. It is my passionate desire to live in the NOW. Mine is not a critical mind." And even when he did acknowledge a relationship to the past, it was usually to cite an heroic writer's resistance against society rather than to comment on a complication of thought, an enrichment of theme, a mastery of language. As Lionel Trilling has remarked, "His awareness of the past was limited, perhaps by his fighting faith in the 'modern,' and this, in a modern, is always a danger"— particularly, one might add, when it is the dubious modern of the "Chicago Renaissance."

In the ingenuousness with which he articulated his creed of the artist as a folk-inspired amateur and in the insistence with which he rehearsed, through a variety of symbolic guises, his liberation from the bourgeois world, Anderson made of his life a culture-legend which often overshadowed his work. This legend soon became a model of the struggle for articulation—or rather the struggle for identity through a cathartic articulation—in which so many untutored but gifted young American writers invariably engaged. Just as Anderson always found it necessary to erect elaborate barriers against the world from which he had escaped in 1912, so they wrote to purge themselves, again and again, of its corruptions, its barbarisms, and its constrictions. That world, however, was not easily shaken off and it showed its ultimate power over 'American writers in their compulsive need to expend a high proportion of their energy in denying it. For Anderson and for others like him, writing was at least as much a means by which to forge a personal identity as it was an objective discipline of the imagination. No wonder so many of the writers who came after Anderson, both Thomas Wolfe the individual and the innumerable facsimile Thomas Wolfes, recognized in their lives one or another variant of his legend. Anderson seemed the archetype of all those writers who were trying to raise themselves to art by sheer emotion and sheer will, who suspected intellect as a cosmopolitan snare that would destroy their gift for divining America's mystic essence, and who abominated the society which had formed them but knew no counterpoise of value by which to escape its moral dominion.

It is in terms of his legend, and the needs which impelled him to advance it, that we can best understand Anderson's literary stances and stratagems. Consider, for one, his persistent assumption of innocence or what, in another context, has been called the credo of defenselessness: that literary approach to complex situations and ideas which insists on discounting their complexity in the name of creative passion. After a time, no doubt, Anderson did exploit his innocence, perhaps because he sensed that there are situations in which defenselessness frankly acknowledged is the only possible defense. But can one doubt that his stance of innocence was originally an authentic response to a cultural situation he could not cope with, a situation which led him to elaborate his personal legend of the Liberated Artist? Or consider, again, the vague mysticism which creeps into some, though not the best, of his work. No doubt, after a while he turned to it in laziness, using a gaseous filler to occupy the vacuum left by failures of his imagination. But can one doubt that at one time his mysticism was a genuine reflection of the artist's awe before the disordered multiplicity of outer things and inner relations?

Between the legend he made for himself and the pattern of deprivation which weaves through his life there was, of course, a tie of complex interdependence. Without the deprivation there would have been no need for the legend, and without the legend no way to overcome—or evade—the deprivation. In one strand of his work, the lesser strand, legend and deprivation can be seen reinforcing each other. This is the Anderson of the political mindlessness of *Marching Men,* the emasculated sexuality of *Many Marriages,* the folk clichés of *Dark Laughter;* the Anderson who took to cultural fashion the way other novelists take to drink; who staked everything on enthusiasm and sentiment and in their absence tried awkwardly to simulate them; who saw the artist's life as an unambiguous struggle of defiant rectitude against commercial contamination; who was forever concerned with a search for freedom but lacked the spiritual rigor to define that freedom in terms of the scope and tension it had had for the great writers of the past. And this, finally, is the Anderson of whom Lionel Trilling's severe characterization is, alas, true: the Anderson whose "affirmation of life by love, passion and freedom had, paradoxically enough, the effect of quite negating life, making it grey, empty, and devoid of meaning. We are quite used to hearing that this is what excessive intellection can do; we are not so often warned that emotion . . . can be similarly destructive."

In one sentence of a letter he wrote to his brother Karl in 1931, this Anderson reached his most complete and succinct self-expression: "I hardly know what I can teach except anti-success." His whole literary life had been a long, gnarled yet not unheroic struggle to teach "anti-success"; but though it would never cease to be indispensable, this teaching was never quite enough, if only because in Anderson's over-simple terms it could not provide a sufficiently resilient barrier to the world of "success."

There are critics and readers for whom this is the *only* Anderson. They acknowledge the pathos and sincerity of his effort but see it merely as another instance of the incompleteness and truncation so pervasive in American culture. This is a view which becomes virtually mandatory once Anderson is considered in the terms he himself occasionally proposed: as a prophet and visionary. Read for moral explication, as a guide to life, his work must seem unsatisfactory; it simply does not tell us enough. But there is another, more fruitful way of reading his work: as the expression of a sensitive witness to the national experience and as the achievement of a story teller who created a small body of fiction unique in American writing for the lyrical purity of its feeling. So regarded, his best work becomes a durable part of the American literary structure.

Unquestionably durable is Anderson's testimony on the most dramatic social development in American life, the transition from an agrarian to an industrial society. No novelist, no historian has portrayed this segment of American experience with an intimacy and poignancy superior to Anderson's in *Poor White* and in his stories; no other American writer has so thoroughly communicated the sense of that historical moment when the native sweetness had not yet been lost to our life, when the nation fumbled on the verge of outwardness and began to stir from provinciality but had not yet toughened into imperial assurance. In the shabby crevices of this world Anderson discovered the lonely and deformed souls who would never be noticed by official society. In the craftsmen of the towns, whom history had passed by and left stricken and helpless, he found concealed reserves of feeling, of muted torment and love. More than most of his contemporaries among American writers, Anderson insisted that frustration and deprivation were at the base of American life, but he did so in order to credit the unused emotional resources, the unmeasured potentials that were also there. For years he bore a literary grudge against Sinclair Lewis because he suspected that beneath the brilliance of satire Lewis was selling his people short.

Anderson's America was not the powerhouse of willful myth-makers, not a sounding-board for autoerotic effusions, not even the air-conditioned nightmare of fashionable rejection—it was a social memory uniquely tender and vulnerable. This was an America to which even the most disaffected of urban intellectuals could admit an allegiance, an America not yet committed to power and accumulation. That Anderson's critique of capitalism from the standpoint of craftsmanship soon seemed naïve and inadequate hardly mattered; what evoked one's affection was the feeling behind that critique, a feeling perhaps available to all conditions of society but most deeply rooted in that epoch of American life which, at least in retrospect, suggests something of the quality of adolescence.

It is precisely this quality of adolescence, whether taken as an independent emotional datum or as a reflection of an historical moment, which has caused most of the uncertainties and difficulties in our response to Anderson's work. Though the depiction of adolescent traumas is a recurrent theme in American literature, adolescence itself is an area of experience toward which Americans remain conspicuously uneasy. They suspect, even as they remember with yearning, its flow of unsorted emotion. In their commitment to an ethos of visible achievement and status, they fear the tenderness of adolescence as an emotion which may deflect them from their ambitions or expose them to the world's ridicule. And those of us who resist this dominant ethos often find that the constricting role of resistance is itself a block to affective largesse. The height of American wisdom is to search for something called maturity—and it is the prevalence of this search in our national life which most definitively indicates the absence of genuine maturity.

With such conditioning attitudes, we must necessarily respond in terms of bedeviled ambiguity to a writer like Anderson. Almost always we categorize him as a writer who moved us greatly in adolescence but now lacks the power to affect us in maturity—as if it were quite safe to assume that our adolescent responses were so patently invalid and unworthy of selective preservation, or as if we could safely compartmentalize our lives, simply discarding in adulthood what we were in our youth. When we use the tag of adolescence to dismiss Anderson's work we forget that even in our first reading his stories appealed to our sense of "oldness" rather than immaturity, that often enough it was in those stories that we were first touched by forebodings of decay and loss. By falsely reducing adolescence to the merely callow and sentimental, we evade the real problem posed by Anderson's work, which is to discriminate between feeling realized and feeling forced or simulated. And when we say—this is the favorite gambit of hostile critics—that Anderson's work deals not with reality but with adolescent gropings, we ignore the reality of those very gropings; we ignore, as well, the fact that from these gropings none of us is or should be exempt. Alfred Kazin has put this matter well:

> When we think of the many who have written more sharply than [Anderson], who have not been content to rest on the expression of dismay, the air of grief, we tend to grow dubious about his significance. What has he done but prepare isolated histories of the puzzled and the bewildered? Perhaps they are not enough, but it is also true that there has always been something of ourselves that we have seen in them, some moment in our lives that was illuminated by theirs.

The gropings in Anderson's work are never in themselves to be condemned. Anderson himself once wrote a chilling rebuke to those who so dismiss him: "I don't think it matters much, all this calling a man muddler, groper etc. . . . the very man who throws such words as these knows in his heart that he is also facing a wall." Anderson's work becomes objectionable only when he ceases to grope, ceases to extend his curiosity and affection; only when he begins to imitate and unwittingly caricature the eagerness and openness of his best writing. The critic's job then becomes one of discriminating between that part of Anderson's work in which callowness and sentimentality frequently corrupt his achievement and that more durable part in which adolescence comes through in a radiant comeliness, a sweet surge of affectivity. Once such a distinction is made there can be no question about the value of *Winesburg* and *Poor White,* of "Death in the Woods" and "The Man Who Became a Woman."

It now becomes possible to consider the question that must suggest itself to every student of Anderson's career: what should he have done after his brief burst of fertility, after *Winesburg* and *The Triumph of the Egg?* The critical point of his career came at about 1923, the year when both *Horses and Men* and *Many Marriages* were published. *Horses and Men* was the last sustained expression of his most successful native manner, and *Many Marriages* the beginning of his disastrous venture into Lawrencian precincts. Among Anderson's friends and critics there have been two opinions about the crisis he then faced. For his Chicago friends and a few of his critics Anderson was essentially a folk or sectional writer who did his best work in the Midwest and was bewildered and contaminated by the cosmopolitan East. For his New York friends and most of his critics Anderson was a writer of undisciplined talent who, after a few creative years, desperately needed a sustaining vision of life and an organized knowledge of craft.

Abstractly, either of these estimates of Anderson, if they led to a consistent course of action, might have helped him avoid his debacles. Had he deliberately restricted himself to the short forms in which his talent was most at home, to those subjects he knew surpassingly well, and to a program of selective and sparse publication, he might have continued producing first-rate stories in the *Winesburg* manner. Had he made a herculean effort to educate himself to the complexities of modern life and thought, to use his mind at its full potential, and to relate himself actively to the great tradition of the novel, he might just possibly have become an interesting social novelist. But in actuality neither of these choices was available to him.

Anderson's Chicago friends ignore the fact that he was "contaminated" by cosmopolitanism before he left the Midwest; the whole bent of his literary life was toward the big city, toward the aggressively modern. He could not retreat to some memory of the past or region of the present because both memory and region were in process of dissolution; in modern America there was not even the marginal place for Anderson's Ohio that there was for Faulkner's Mississippi. Had he persisted in the *Winesburg* manner he might have left a greater body of successful work than he actually did, but the fact is that all the pressures of both his environment and his own ambition drove him to abandon that manner.

Still less practical was the other proposed course. By 1923 Anderson was a man in his late forties who had gone through the most painful struggles merely to become a writer and had at last won praise to an extent he could hardly have anticipated. The kind of transformation which might have made him a highly conscious artist would have been possible only under the urging and guidance of an authoritative body of literary opinion. But it was precisely this opinion which was missing from American life: the culture of the 1920's was itself beset by the weaknesses that would soon cripple Anderson. (Scott Fitzgerald, for example, wrote that *Many Marriages* was Anderson's best book!) To have urged, in these circumstances, that Anderson attempt a total self-transformation would merely have been an oblique way of suggesting that he stop writing. It was his tragedy that after the early 1920's he was trapped between two worlds: he could find sustenance neither in the deep kinships of the folk bard nor in the demanding traditions of the sophisticated artist.

If, for the biographer, Anderson's career must seem a dramatic instance of a gifted writer impoverished by a constricting culture, the critic can rest his final attention on that small segment of Anderson's work in which he overcame those constrictions. Precious as it would be at any time, that segment assumes a particular value in our present cultural situation.

There is a sense in which it may be said that Anderson has not had an appreciable influence on American writing. To be sure, there are Steinbeck and Saroyan who have brought to extremity the inferior aspects of his work. And there is Hemingway who repudiated Anderson in the name of craft but still owes him many debts. But while Steinbeck and Saroyan could enlarge on his occasional sentimentalism and Hemingway could tighten and rigidify his style, no American writer has yet been able to realize that strain of lyrical and nostalgic feeling which in Anderson's best work reminds one of another and greater poet of tenderness, Turgeniev. At his best Anderson creates a world of authentic sentiment, and while part of the meaning of his career is that sentiment is not enough for a writer, the careers of those who follow him—those who swerve to Steinbeck's sentimentality or Hemingway's toughness—illustrate how rare genuine sentiment still is in our literature.

During the last two decades our dominant writing has been shaped by the Hemingway manner. Our literature has been characterized by crude and violent action, speech distorted into stylized bravado, an aggressive scorn of the mind, and a fearful retreat from direct emotion. Too often it has seemed a mere reflection of the tendency in modern society to see life stripped of emotional inwardness, and men as mere objects. That this vision is often expressed with great skill is also characteristic of a culture which can do the most wretched things in the most efficient way.

By comparison Anderson's work must seem almost anachronistic, for no one can deny that our present world is closer to Hemingway than to Anderson. What can we make of a writer in whom there sometimes still runs freely and sweetly an affection for all things sentient?

But surely there is, there should be a place in our culture, even if only a minor one, for Sherwood Anderson. His faults, his failures and defeats can hardly be ignored: he was almost always limited in moral sensibility and social perspective. Yet there were a few moments when he spoke, as almost no one else among American writers, with the voice of love.

From *Sherwood Anderson* by Irving Howe (American Men of Letters Series), pp. 243–256. Copyright 1951 by William Sloane Associates. Reprinted by permission of the author and William Sloane Associates.

MALCOLM COWLEY
John Dos Passos: The Poet and the World
[1932-1936]

JOHN DOS PASSOS[1] is in reality two novelists. One of them is a late-Romantic, an individualist, an esthete moving about the world in a portable ivory tower; the other is a collectivist, a radical historian of the class struggle. These two authors have collaborated in all his books, but the first had the larger share in *Three Soldiers* and *Manhattan Transfer*. The second, in his more convincing fashion, has written most of *The 42nd Parallel* and almost all of *1919*. The difference between the late-Romantic and the radical Dos Passos is important not only in his own career: it also helps to explain the recent course of American fiction.

The late-Romantic tendency in his novels goes back to his years in college. After graduating from a good preparatory school, Dos Passos entered Harvard in 1912, at the beginning of a period which was later known as that of the Harvard esthetes. I have described this period elsewhere, in reviewing the poems of E. E. Cummings, but I did not discuss the ideas which underlay its picturesque manifestations, its mixture of incense, patchouli and gin, its erudition displayed before barroom mirrors, its dreams in the Cambridge subway of laurel-crowned Thessalian dancers. The esthetes themselves were not philosophers; they did not seek to define their attitude; but most of them would have subscribed to the following propositions:

That the cultivation and expression of his own sensibility are the only justifiable ends for a poet.

That originality is his principal virtue.

That society is hostile, stupid and unmanageable: it is the world of the philistines, from which it is the poet's duty and privilege to remain aloof.

That the poet is always misunderstood by the world. He should, in fact, deliberately make himself misunderstandable, for the greater glory of art.

That he triumphs over the world, at moments, by mystically including it

---

[1] *1919*, by John Dos Passos. *The Big Money*, by John Dos Passos. New York: Harcourt, Brace & Company, 1932, 1936. (The complete trilogy by John Dos Passos, made up of *The 42nd Parallel*, *1919*, and *The Big Money*, was later published under the collective title, *U. S. A.*, in 1937. [Editor's note.])

within himself: these are his moments of *ecstasy*, to be provoked by any means in his power—alcohol, drugs, madness or saintliness, venery, suicide.

That art, the undying expression of such moments, exists apart from the world; it is the poet's revenge on society.

That the past has more dignity than the present.

There are a dozen other propositions which might be added to this unwritten manifesto, but the ideas I have listed were those most generally held, and they are sufficient to explain the intellectual atmosphere of the young men who read *The Hill of Dreams,* and argued about St. Thomas in Boston bars, and contributed to *The Harvard Monthly.* The attitude was not confined to one college and one magazine. It was often embodied in *The Dial,* which for some years was almost a postgraduate edition of *The Monthly;* it existed in earlier publications like *The Yellow Book* and *La Revue Blanche;* it has a history, in fact, almost as long as that of the upper middle class under capitalism. For the last half-century it has furnished the intellectual background of poems and essays without number. It would seem to preclude, in its adherents, the objectivity that is generally associated with good fiction; yet the esthetes themselves sometimes wrote novels, as did their predecessors all over the world. Such novels, in fact, are still being published, and favorably criticised: "Mr. Zed has written the absorbing story of a talented musician tortured by the petty atmosphere of the society in which he is forced to live. His wife, whom the author portrays with witty malice, prevents him from breaking away. After an unhappy love affair and the failure of his artistic hopes, he commits suicide. . . ."

Such is the plot forever embroidered in the type of fiction that ought to be known as the art novel. There are two essential characters, two antagonists, the Poet and the World. The Poet—who may also be a painter, a violinist, an inventor, an architect or a Centaur—is generally to be identified with the author of the novel, or at least with the novelist's ideal picture of himself. He tries to assert his individuality in despite of the World, which is stupid, unmanageable and usually victorious. Sometimes the Poet triumphs, but the art novelists seem to realize, as a class, that the sort of hero they describe is likely to be defeated in the sort of society which he must face. This society is rarely presented in accurate terms. So little is it endowed with reality, so great is the author's solicitude for the Poet, that we are surprised to see him vanquished by such a shadowy opponent. It is as if we were watching motion pictures in the darkhouse of his mind. There are dream pictures, nightmare pictures; at last the walls crash in and the Poet disappears without ever knowing what it was all about; he dies by his own hand, leaving behind him the memory of his ecstatic moments and the bitter story of his failure, now published as a revenge on the world of the philistines.

The art novel has many variations. Often the World is embodied in the

Poet's wife, whose social ambitions are the immediate cause of his defeat. Or the wife may be painted in attractive colors: she is married to a mediocre Poet who finally and reluctantly accepts her guidance, abandons his vain struggle for self-expression, and finds that mediocrity has its own consolations, its country clubs and business triumphs—this is the form in which the art novel is offered to readers of *The Saturday Evening Post*. Or again the Poet may be a woman who fights for the same ambitions, under the same difficulties, as her male prototypes. The scene of the struggle may be a town on the Minnesota prairies, an English rectory, an apartment on Washington Square or Beacon Hill; but always the characters are the same; the Poet and the World continue their fatal conflict; the Poet has all our sympathies. And the novelists who use this plot for the thousandth time are precisely those who believe that originality is a writer's chief virtue.

Many are unconscious of this dilemma. The story rises so immediately out of their lives, bursts upon them with such freshness, that they never recognize it as a family tale. Others deliberately face the problem and try to compensate for the staleness of the plot by the originality of their treatment. They experiment with new methods of story-telling—one of which, the stream of consciousness, seems peculiarly fitted to novels of this type. Perhaps they invest their characters with new significance, and rob them of any real significance, by making them symbolic. They adopt new manners, poetic, mystical, learned, witty, allusive or obfuscatory; and often, in token of their original talent, they invent new words and new ways of punctuating simple declarative sentences. Not all their ingenuity is wasted. Sometimes they make valuable discoveries; a few of the art novels, like *The Hill of Dreams*, are among the minor masterpieces of late-Romantic literature; and a very few, like *A Portrait of the Artist as a Young Man*, are masterpieces pure and simple.

Dos Passos' early books are neither masterpieces nor are they pure examples of the art novel. The world was always real to him, painfully real; it was never veiled with mysticism and his characters were rarely symbolic. Yet consider the plot of a novel like *Three Soldiers*. A talented young musician, during the War, finds that his sensibilities are being outraged, his aspirations crushed, by society as embodied in the American army. He deserts after the Armistice and begins to write a great orchestral poem. When the military police come to arrest him, the sheets of music flutter one by one into the spring breeze; and we are made to feel that the destruction of this symphony, this ecstatic song choked off and dispersed on the wind, is the real tragedy of the War. Some years later, in writing *Manhattan Transfer*, Don Passos seemed to be undertaking a novel of a different type, one which tried to render the color and movement of a whole city; but the book, as it proceeds, becomes the story of Jimmy Herf (the Poet) and Ellen Thatcher (the Poet's wife), and the Poet is once again frustrated by the World: he leaves a Greenwich Village party after a last drink of gin and walks out alone, bareheaded, into the dawn. It is obvious, however, that a new conflict has been superimposed on the old one: the social ideas of the novelist are now at war with his personal emotions, which remain those of *The Dial* and *The Harvard Monthly*. Even in 1919, this second conflict persists, but less acutely; the emotional values themselves are changing, to accord with the ideas; and the book as a whole belongs to a new category.

1919 is distinguished, first of all, by the very size of the project its author has undertaken. A long book in itself, containing 473 pages, it is merely the second chapter, as it were, of a novel which will compare in length with *Ulysses*, perhaps even with *Remembrance of Things Past*. Like the latter, it is a historical novel dealing with the yesterday that still exists in the author's memory. It might almost be called a news novel, since it uses newspaper headlines to suggest the flow of events, and tells the story of its characters in reportorial fashion. But its chief distinction lies in the author's emphasis. He is not recounting the tragedy of bewildered John Smith, the rise of ambitious Mary Jones, the efforts of sensitive Richard Robinson to maintain his ideals against the blundering malice of society. Such episodes recur in this novel, but they are seen in perspective. The real hero of *The 42nd Parallel* and *1919* is society itself, American society as embodied in forty or fifty representative characters who drift along with it, struggle to change its course, or merely to find a secure footing—perhaps they build a raft of wreckage, grow fat on the refuse floating about them; perhaps they go under in some obscure eddy— while always the current sweeps them onward toward new social horizons. In this sense, Dos Passos has written the first American collective novel.

The principal characters are brought forward one at a time; the story of each is told in bare, straightforward prose. Thus, J. Ward Moorehouse, born in Wilmington, Delaware, begins his business career in a real-estate office. He writes songs, marries and divorces a rich woman, works for a newspaper in Pittsburgh—at the end of fifty-seven pages he is a successful public-relations counselor embarked on a campaign to reconcile labor and capital at the expense of labor. Joe and Janey Williams are the children of a tugboat captain from Washington, D. C.; Janey studies shorthand; Joe plays baseball, enlists in the navy, deserts after a brawl and becomes a merchant seaman. Eleanor Stoddard is a poor Chicago girl who works at Marshall Field's; she learns how to speak French to her customers and order waiters about "with a crisp little refined moneyed voice." All these characters, first introduced in *The 42nd Parallel*, reappear in *1919*, where they are joined by others: Richard Ellsworth Savage, a Kent School boy who goes to Harvard and writes poetry; Daughter, a warm-hearted flapper from Dallas, Texas; Ben Compton, a spectacled Jew from Brooklyn who becomes a Wobbly. Gradually their careers draw closer together, till finally all of them are caught up in the War.

"This whole goddam war's a gold brick," says Joe Williams. "It ain't on the level, it's crooked from A to Z. No matter how it comes out, fellows like us get the s——y end of the stick, see? Well, what I say is all bets is off . . . every man go to hell in his own way . . . and three strikes is out, see?" Three strikes is out for Joe, when his skull is cracked in a saloon brawl at St. Nazaire, on Armistice night. Daughter is killed in an airplane accident; she provoked it herself in a fit of hysteria after being jilted by Dick Savage—who for his part survives as the shell of a man, all the best of him having died when he decided to join the army and make a career for himself and let his pacifist sentiments go hang. Benny Compton gets ten years in Atlanta prison as a conscientious objector. Everybody in the novel suffers from the War and finds his own way of going to hell—everybody except the people without bowels, the empty people like Eleanor Stoddard and J. Ward Moorehouse, who stuff themselves with the proper sentiments and make the right contacts.

The great events that preceded and followed the Armistice are reflected in the lives of all these people; but Dos Passos has other methods, too, for rendering the sweep of history. In particular he has three technical devices which he uses both to broaden the scope of the novel and to give it a formal unity. The first of these consists of what he calls "Newsreels," a combination of newspaper headlines, stock-market reports, official communiqués and words from popular songs. The Newsreels effectively perform their function in the book, that of giving dates and atmospheres, but in themselves, judged as writing, they are not successful. The second device is a series of nine biographies interspersed through the text. Here are the lives, briefly told, of three middle-class rebels, Jack Reed, Randolph Bourne and Paxton Hibben; of three men of power, Roosevelt, Wilson and J. P. Morgan; and of three proletarian heroes. All these are successful both in themselves and in relation to the novel as a whole; and the passage dealing with the Wobbly martyr, Wesley Everest, is as powerful as anything Dos Passos has ever written.

The "Camera Eye," which is the third device, introduces more complicated standards of judgment. It consists in the memories of another character, presumably the author, who has adventures similar to those of his characters, but describes them in a different style, one which suggests Dos Passos' earlier books. The "Camera Eye" gives us photographs rich in emotional detail:

Ponte Decimo   in Ponte Decimo ambulances were parked in a moonlit square of bleak stone working-people's houses   hoarfrost covered everything   in the little bar the Successful Story Writer taught us to drink cognac and maraschino half and half
havanuzzerone
it turned out he was not writing what he felt he wanted to be writing   What can you tell them at home about the war?   it turned out he was not wanting what he wrote he wanted to be feeling cognac and maraschino   was no longer young

(It made us damn sore we greedy for what we felt we wanted tell 'em all they lied
see new towns go to Genoa)   havanuzzerone?   it turned out that he wished he
was a naked brown shepherd boy sitting on a hillside playing a flute in the sunlight

Exactly the same episode, so it happens, is described in Dos Passos' other
manner, his prose manner, during the course of a chapter dealing with Dick
Savage:

That night they parked the convoy in the main square of a godforsaken little
burg on the outskirts of Genoa. They went with Sheldrake to have a drink in a bar
and found themselves drinking with the Saturday Evening Post correspondent,
who soon began to get tight and to say how he envied them their good looks and
their sanguine youth and idealism. Steve picked him up about everything and argued bitterly that youth was the lousiest time in your life, and that he ought to be
goddam glad he was forty years old and able to write about the war instead of
fighting in it.

The relative merit of these two passages, as writing, is not an important
question. The first is a good enough piece of impressionism, with undertones
of E. E. Cummings and Gertrude Stein. The style of the second passage, except for a certain conversational quality, is almost colorless; it happens to be
the most effective way of recording a particular series of words and actions;
it aspires to no other virtue. The first passage might add something to a book
in which, the plot being hackneyed or inconsequential, the emphasis had to
be placed on the writing, but *1919* is not a novel of that sort. Again, the Camera Eye may justify itself in the next volume of this trilogy—or tetralogy—by
assuming a closer relation to the story and binding together the different
groups of characters; but in that case, I hope the style of it will change. So far
it has been an element of disunity, a survival of the art novel in the midst of
a different type of writing, and one in which Dos Passos excels.

He is, indeed, one of the few writers in whose case an equation can accurately and easily be drawn between social beliefs and artistic accomplishments.
When he writes individualistically, with backward glances toward Imagism,
Vorticism and the Insurrection of the Word, his prose is sentimental and
without real distinction. When he writes as a social rebel, he writes not flaw-
lessly by any means, but with conviction, power and a sense of depth, of striking through surfaces to the real forces beneath them. This last book, in which
his political ideas have given shape to his emotions, and only the Camera Eye
remains as a vestige of his earlier attitude, is not only the best of all his novels;
it is, I believe, a landmark in American fiction.

II

Four years ago in reviewing *1919*, the second volume of John Dos Passos'
trilogy, I tried to define two types of fiction that have been especially promi-

nent since the War. An *art novel,* I said, was one that dealt with the opposition between a creatively gifted individual and the community surrounding him—in brief, between the Poet and the World. Usually in books of this type the Poet gets all the attention; he is described admiringly, tenderly, and yet we learn that he is nagged and broken and often, in the end, driven to suicide by an implacably stupid World. Dos Passos' earlier novels had applied this formula, but *The 42nd Parallel* and *1919* belonged to a second category: they were *collective novels,* whose real hero was American society at large, and this fact helped to explain their greater breadth and vigor. I added, however, that certain elements in these later books—and notably the autobiographical passages called the "Camera Eye"—suggested the art novel and therefore seemed out of place.

But after reviewing *The Big Money* and rereading the trilogy as a whole, it seems to me that this judgment has to be partly revised. I no longer believe that the art novel is a "bad" type of fiction (though the philosophy behind it is a bad philosophy for our times), nor do I believe that the collective novel is necessarily a "good" type (though it has advantages for writers trying to present our period of crisis). With more and more collective novels published every year, it is beginning to be obvious that the form in itself does not solve the writer's problems. Indeed, it raises new problems and creates new disadvantages. The collective novelist is tempted to overemphasize the blindness and impotence of individuals caught in the rip tides of history. He is obliged to devote less space to each of his characters, to relate their adventures more hastily, with the result that he always seems to be approaching them from the outside. I can see now that the Camera Eye is a device adopted by Dos Passos in order to supply the "inwardness" that is lacking in his general narrative.

I can see too that although the device is borrowed from the art novel—and indeed is a series of interior monologues resembling parts of Joyce's *Ulysses*—it is not in the least alien to the general plan of the trilogy. For the truth is that the art novel and the collective novel as conceived by Dos Passos are not in fundamental opposition: they are like the two sides of a coin. In the art novel, the emphasis is on the individual, in the collective novel it is on society as a whole; but in both we get the impression that society is stupid and all-powerful and fundamentally evil. Individuals ought to oppose it, but if they do so they are doomed. If, on the other hand, they reconcile themselves with society and try to get ahead in it, then they are damned foerver, damned to be empty, shrill, destructive insects like Dick Savage and Eleanor Stoddard and J. Ward Moorehouse.

In an earlier novel, *Manhattan Transfer,* there is a paragraph that states one of Dos Passos' basic perceptions. Ellen Herf, having divorced the hero, decides to marry a rich politician whom she does not love:

Through dinner she felt a gradual icy coldness stealing through her like novo-caine. She had made up her mind. It seemed as if she had set the photograph of herself in her own place, forever frozen into a single gesture. . . . Everything about her seemed to be growing hard and enameled, the air bluestreaked with ciga-rette smoke was turning to glass.

She had made up her mind. . . . Sometimes in reading Dos Passos it seems that not the nature of the decision but the mere fact of having reached it is the unforgivable offense. Dick Savage the ambulance driver decided not to be a pacifist, not to escape into neutral Spain, and from that moment he is forever frozen into a single gesture of selfishness and dissipation. Don Stevens the radical newspaper correspondent decides to be a good Communist, to obey party orders, and immediately he is stricken with the same paralysis of the heart. We have come a long way from the strong-willed heroes of the early nineteenth century—the English heroes, sons of Dick Whittington, who ad-mired the world of their day and climbed to the top of it implacably; the French heroes like Julien Sorel and Rastignac and Monte Cristo who despised their world and yet learned how to press its buttons and pull its levers. To Dos Passos the world seems so vicious that any compromise with its standards turns a hero into a villain. The only characters he seems to like instinctively are those who know they are beaten, but still grit their teeth and try to hold on. That is the story of Jimmy Herf in *Manhattan Transfer;* to some extent it is also the story of Mary French and her father and Joe Askew, almost the only admirable characters in *The Big Money.* And the same lesson of dogged, courageous impotence is pointed by the Camera Eye, especially in the admi-rable passage where the author remembers the execution of Sacco and Van-zetti:

America,our nation has been beaten by strangers who have turned our language inside out who have taken the clean words our fathers spoke and made them slimy and foul

their hired men sit on the judge's bench they sit back with their feet on the tables under the dome of the State House they are ignorant of our beliefs they have the dollars the guns the armed forces the power-plants . . .

all right we are two nations

"The hired men with guns stand ready to shoot," he says in another pas-sage, this one dealing with his visit to the striking miners in Kentucky. "We have only words against POWER SUPERPOWER." And these words that serve as our only weapons against the machine guns and tear gas of the invaders, these words of the vanquished nation are only that America in developing from pioneer democracy into monopoly capitalism has followed a road that leads toward sterility and slavery. Our world is evil, and yet we are powerless to change or direct it. The sensitive individual should cling to his own standards, and yet he is certain to go under. Thus, the final message of Dos Passos' three collective novels is similar to that of his earlier novels dealing with maladjusted artists. Thus, for all the vigor of *1919* and *The Big Money*, they leave us wondering whether the author hasn't overstated his case. For all their scope and richness, they fail to express one side of contemporary life—the will to struggle ahead, the comradeship in struggle, the consciousness of new men and new forces continually rising. Although we may be for the moment a beaten nation, the fight is not over.

From *The New Republic*, Vol. LXX (April 27, 1932), pp. 303–305; and Vol. LXXXVIII (September 9, 1936), p. 34. Reprinted by permission.

ROBERT CANTWELL

Sinclair Lewis

[1936]

WITH some fifteen novels to his credit at the age of fifty, together with enough short stories to fill several more volumes, Sinclair Lewis stands out as the most prolific author of his generation, with the mournful exception of Upton Sinclair. It is almost the worst thing you can say about him. For although Lewis has written at least two first-rate novels, and created a dozen powerful characters, and produced half-a-hundred masterly satirical sketches scattered throughout these books—as well as added new words to the language and popularized, more than anybody else, a new and skeptical slant on American life—he has also turned out as much journalistic rubbish as any good novelist has signed his name to, and he has written novels so shallow and dull they would have wrecked any reputation except his own.

He has, in fact, been one of the most plunging and erratic writers in our literary history; unpredictability, waywardness, unevenness are his distinguishing characteristics, as a brooding inconclusiveness is the mark of Sherwood Anderson. He has written the best novel of American business in *Babbitt*, only to make up for it by writing the worst in *Work of Art* and adding half-a-dozen wretched *Saturday Evening Post* stories on the same subject to the bargain. He has written the sharpest parodies of the lush, rococo, euphemistic sales-talk of American business life that we have, but he has also weighed down his novels with a heavy burden of unreal and exaggerated jargon, palmed off as common speech, with unfunny topical jokes, passed on as native humor, and the weight of that dated mockery grows heavier every year.

But Lewis has not only been the most uneven of American novelists; he has also been one of the most ambitious. There is an architectural symmetry in the order of the books that followed *Main Street*. Unlike his contemporaries, who seem always to have been improvising in the sequence of their work, Lewis apparently recognized a conscious program for his writing simultaneously with his recognition of his power, and seems to have driven toward its realization with something of the high-pressure intensity he has satirized so often. Where Dreiser gives the impression of having brooded, with a sort of ponderous aimlessness, over whatever lay close at hand, forever turning aside,

494

distracted by every incidental issue, and where Anderson and Vachel Lindsay, more than any of the others, were blown about in the cross-currents of American life until they were saturated with its apparently patternless variety, Lewis visualized on the strength of *Main Street* a cycle of novels comparable at least in scope to those of Zola and Balzac.

It was a spacious and inclusive project, bolder than anything an American novelist had tried to do, signalizing a final break with that narrowness of outlook which, exemplified in a thousand old swimming-hole sentimentalities, pathetic regionalisms and phony family dilemmas, had become almost the sole driving force of American fiction. And even now, when the limitations and shortcomings of that imaginative exploration are more apparent than its freshness and originality, it is still a little breath-taking to consider the broad outlines of the work that Lewis laid out for himself, to see that he planned nothing less than a catalogue of the interwoven worlds of American society, the small towns and cities, the worlds of business, of science, of religion, of education, and eventually the worlds of labor and professional politics, working it out at a time when the shabby, optimistic, patriotic smugness of the American literary tradition—the tradition of Henry Van Dyke that, significantly, he attacked in his Nobel Prize address—still imprisoned the imaginations of so many of his contemporaries.

Lewis had a line on American society, and tenacity, if not much flexibility and resourcefulness, in following it. But more than that he had a sense of the physical variety and the cultural monotony of the country, an easy familiarity with the small towns and square cities, the real-estate developments and restricted residential areas, the small business men, the country doctors, the religious fakers, the clubwomen, the county officeholders, the village atheists and single-taxers, the schoolteachers, librarians, the windbags of the lower income groups, the crazy professors and the maddened, hyperthyroid, high-pressure salesmen—the main types of middle-class and lower-middle-class provincial society, conspicuous now because he has identified them so thoroughly. He had a grasp of these people and their environments, together with a sense of the country as a whole, where so many of his generation had nothing but an oppressed conviction of its emptiness or a dread of its rawness.

Only Vachel Lindsay and Upton Sinclair had seen so much of the country, in the elementary geographical sense of the term. Lewis had never taken any of the wild and pathetic zigzag journeys of Lindsay, dropping in on miners and hill-billies and reading poems for his supper, nor had he spent a season in the hell of the stockyards, as did Upton Sinclair, his first guide, at the beginning of a career no less extraordinary. But he had knocked around at an impressive variety of jobs after he left Yale in 1904—he had been a janitor in Upton Sinclair's Helicon Hall, a soda jerk, a reporter on *The San Francisco Bulletin*—which was probably, under Fremont Older in the days before his capitulation, the best paper in the country to be a reporter on—a ghost writer for Jack London and an editor, in Washington, of a magazine for the deaf; he had taken the grand cruise of his generation on a cattle boat to England and had hitchhiked through the Middle West. He had traveled over the face of the country and, although within pretty narrow limits, up and down through its social strata. And although his first four books were hack jobs, the native experiences he had packed away were too powerful to be satisfied with evocations of the joys of a stenographer's work, or of the wisdom of picturesque and homely old folks, or of an aristocratic Eastern girl made wholesome by contact with the great West—the substance of *The Job*, *The Innocents* and *Free Air*. Even as hack work those books are bad. They seem to tremble with some internal explosive disgust; in a way they are like the bad jokes and stale opinions that Babbitt and his friends take refuge in at their parties, when they dare not express even a little of what is going on in their minds, lest they betray their hatred of their environments, their boredom, their thwarted desire for change.

Apparently Lewis thought at the beginning of his career that the muse could be embraced and laid aside at will, and that she would not take her revenge by addling the wits of her ravisher—at least his first books prove nothing except that he did not believe the writing of fiction demanded a writer's full energy and his deepest understanding. That implicit irresponsibility has been his greatest limitation as a novelist and the source of much of the unevenness of his work. Even the broad project mentioned above—the cycle of novels following *Main Street*—is a vision of an imaginative survey of American life such as a glorified and super-competent hack writer might conceive: a writer, that is, who thought of his writing, not in terms of its momentary inspirations and the pressure of living that played through him and upon him, but in terms of the accomplishment of a foreknown task; who thought of a novel of business, of religion, of science, as if he believed he could turn his art to any subject, regardless of how much it meant to him and how close to his heart it lay; who felt that it lay within his power to "collect material" without becoming emotionally entangled in it or acting in response to what it implied. T. K. Whipple, who has written the only searching study of Lewis that we have, has compared his attitude in studying American society with that of a Red Indian stalking through the land of his enemies—it is a good description, for it suggests his wariness and vigilance, the surface accuracy of his observation, what can be called the heartlessness of his approach, and above all his enforced detachment from the scene he viewed and the solitary and personal basis of his satire.

Now that the scandals that attended the publications of Lewis' books have been forgotten, the outlines of the world he created are clearer. On re-examination that world seems in a more advanced state of decay and disintegration than Lewis' first critics were willing to admit—it is, as Whipple has said, a city of the dead, in which the dead are above all determined that no one shall live. After *Main Street* his characters were still the long-winded, provincial, narrow-visioned old folks, the dreamy and timid job-holders, the clerks and salesmen and doctors—with here and there a workman from the semi-independent crafts—who figured in his first books and were all dominated by those strange, self-satisfied, self-possessed, jovially witless bankers and business men who loom so large in Lewis' world. But where such characters had been harmless and happy in the early novels, they were now vindictive, spiteful, vaguely threatening in their inertia and immobility. Before the War Lewis had written of their provincialism as if it were a source of serenity, however its expression might rasp on the sensibilities of the cultivated; for the provincials and the innocents themselves, it was an insulation against the cares of the world and not without its own homely poetry and wisdom.

But with *Main Street* that provincialism was identified as an evil force, destructive not only to the Carol Kennicotts and Eric Valborgs, to Martin Arrowsmith and Paul Reisling—it was also poisoning the lives of those who clung to it and triumphed and, when their guards were down for a moment, were seen to be bewildered, distressed, clinging desperately to their appearance of smugness because they had nothing else to cling to. The problem of *Main Street* might have been "how much of Gopher Prairie's eleven miles of cement walk" was "made out of the tombstones of John Keatses"—but the message of *Babbitt, Arrowsmith, Elmer Gantry,* however Lewis might deny that it was his intention to preach it, was simply that American society was death to any disinterested effort, to any human tolerance, almost to any human sympathy; that it was regimented within an inch of its intellectual life; that any deviation from its norm of self-seeking, money-grubbing, career-making, throat-cutting, treachery, slander, blackmailing, was instantly punished with exile and disgrace; that spontaneity or generous emotions or a freedom from calculation, among the calculating wolves of business, amounted to suicide of a long-drawn-out and painful kind. Lewis drew a revolutionary picture of American middle-class life without coming to revolutionary conclusions about it, unlike Upton Sinclair, who leaped to revolutionary conclusions and then filled in the picture; he recognized the mechanics of capitalist control, and satirized them, without challenging the ends to which they were applied or visualizing any alternative except an escape—for those sensitive souls enlightened enough to be aware of their horror—into reverie and day-dreaming.

The moral atmosphere, with exceptions that will be noted, grew thicker and more poisonous with each succeeding book. Carol Kennicott's sensibilities were outraged by Gopher Prairie, and she was revolted by the hypocrisy and narrowness she found there, but the enemies she faced were largely passive—

inertia, sluggishness and sullenness, the dominance of petrified prejudice. In comparison with *Babbitt* and the books that followed it, this is an almost pastoral view of life. The difference is not only in the greater violence of the later books, the general strike that interrupts *Babbitt* midway, the flare of melodrama in Reisling's attempt to murder his wife, the corruption and blackmail that accompany Babbitt's business career. It is rather in the cagey watchfulness with which Babbitt's friends of the service clubs bear down on each other for every deviation from their class line, and it is nowhere better dramatized than in the sequence that follows Reisling's tragedy—when Babbitt, shaken by it, develops an intermittent sort of tolerance, the others, particularly the sinister Virgil Gunch, get their knives ready for him at once, and the high point of the book, perhaps the highest point of Lewis' writing, is the realization that they are ready to spring, like the stronger wolves on a crippled member of the pack, at the first sign of Babbitt's confusion and dismay.

Yet even Babbitt's sacrifices for the good opinion of such prosperous thugs is nothing compared with the desperation of Angus Duer, in *Arrowsmith*, who tries to cut the throat of a watchman who has inadvertently threatened his career, and the indifference that Carol Kennicott faced in Gopher Prairie is nothing compared with the sustained enmity and malice that Arrowsmith faces in Wheatsylvania. The enemy—the provincial, conforming, suspicious enemy—is no longer merely passive and mocking; it has become aggressive, strident, criminal; it turns to blackmail and violence; it is ready to frame and destroy anyone who even raises questions that it cannot answer. And by the time *It Can't Happen Here* was written, Lewis' picture of the world was such that the violence with which the book is filled had become obsessive and perverse, divorced from any purpose and uncontrolled by any aim, an eruption of cruelty and horror and little more.

Spaced unevenly between the works in which this panorama of social damnation is drawn are those books of Lewis' that even his acquiescent critics usually overlook: *Mantrap, The Trail of the Hawk, Work of Art, Ann Vickers, Dodsworth*, the grotesque short stories that he wrote for *The Saturday Evening Post* and that seem particularly bad because there is so much evidence that Lewis knew so much better when he wrote them. He has never been a fastidious writer—he has a gift for slogans, a talent for mimicry, a kind of tormented delight in some of the cruder commonplaces of American speech, but he has always manipulated his people awkwardly to make them demonstrate what he wanted them to reveal about society, and his works have always been weakened, even in their moments of gravity, by a tumultuous and slapstick humor that seems less an expression of emotion than of a desire to escape it. As his career has developed he has relied more and more on his ability to capture the perishable local color of American life, the blaring and raucous Babbittry that surrounds his people, the pep-talks, the idiot drooling of advertisers and go-getters, instead of the indefinite but still sustained and consequential conflicts of Carol and her husband, of Babbitt and his friends—but this material, which was used in *Main Street* to show what a character who could not stomach it was up against, began to be used in the novels that followed almost for its own sake, until with *The Man Who Knew Coolidge* there was scarcely anything else in the book.

But precisely because Lewis has attached so little fundamental importance to such outpourings as Dr. Pickerbaugh's health sermons, or Chum Frinkley's poems, his increasing insistence on material of this sort is all the more clearly a sign of imaginative indecision and doubt. And how, after having so clearly shown the mechanics of American business control in *Babbitt,* and the psychological ravages of it, could he have drawn so unrealistic a figure of a millionaire as Dodsworth, or so romantic a business man as the Ora Weagle of *Work of Art?* In his best books Lewis had told us that the pursuit of wealth— or even a career in a business-dominated society—was a fierce and scrambling affair that killed its victims and crippled its victors; now he presented an industrialist whose unaccountable naïveté persisted (although he collected secret reports on the dissipations of his employees), and a starry-eyed, well-meaning hotel manager whose poetic dreams revolved around the creation of more elaborate comforts for the exhausted Babbitts who could afford them— presented without art, without irony, at best with a kind of curdled romanticism that gave an impression of spleen and exasperation on the part of their author. With these books Lewis' explorations into American society stopped. His characters had become idealizations of the Babbitts he had previously condemned; his satire had degenerated to a kind of stylized mockery, closer in spirit to George Ade's *Fables in Slang* or to some of Mencken's less purposeful buffoonery than to the realities of American life—or it had become so broad and farcical that it had lost its point, just as, in his antifascist novel, his fascists were presented as so weird and unearthly that no practicing strikebreakers, vigilantes, lynchers, anti-Semites, jingoes or acquiescent journalists need feel an instant's identification with them.

But with all this acknowledged, the positive contribution of Lewis' novels remains—and, in one sense, if books like *Dodsworth, Work of Art,* or *Ann Vickers* seem so shallow, it is in large part because Lewis himself has made us conscious in his best work of the native realities that are absent in them. In his best books he has caught, better than anybody else, the desultory, inhibited, half-sad and half-contented middle-class life of the Middle West, a life of spiritless conflicts and drives in the country, of social gatherings as nerve-racking and exhausting as final examinations, of interminable business plots and fears of ruin, of frightened infidelities, limitless ambitions, of forced enthusiasms and false simplicities—a life hedged in behind social barriers set by

the least enlightened members of the community and existing under a dictatorship that is no less powerful for being masked and unadmitted by those
who bow to it. And even in his worst books Lewis has always been able to
summon up some neglected, recognizable corner of the country—the run-
down, red-leather hotel lobbies of *Work of Art,* the formaldehyde, oiled-floor,
civil-service stench of public buildings in *Ann Vickers*—with such graphic
power that he has always seemed to be setting the stage for some more momentous drama than he has ever shown taking place.

That effect may be the result of his inability clearly to imagine any antagonist capable of sustained struggle with the rulers of his city of the dead. He is
more aware of the monstrous extent of the stables that must be cleaned than
he is of the possibility of any Hercules ever cleaning them; and when he pictures people who are pitted against their environments he usually shows them
struggling without much hope of victory, without allies, and often with in-
grown doubts as to whether or not they are on the right side. And most often,
when their feeble feints establish the strength of the enemy, they merely sub-
side into that outward acquiescence and inward rebellion that is the death of
drama—so Carol Kennicott, defeated in Gopher Prairie, dreams of a grass hut
over some tropical river bank; Babbitt hungers for some wild woodland spirit
as he awakens into the steel world of Zenith; Ora Weagle plans gigantic and
flawless super-hotels as he fires the help of a run-down Florida boarding house,
and these vague aspirations to escape their own environments are presented
by Lewis as conferring some secret distinction on the people who hold them.

In denying that he is a satirist Lewis has said that he is a romantic, in much
the same sense that these characters of his are romantics, and that he has re-
belled against American society because it has none of the picturesque feudal
remains that he associated with a rich and stable culture. But his characters
are not romantic rebels committed to struggle. They are self-dramatists whose
imaginations flower from their evasions of conflict—they are always posing
before themselves and others, not in order to fulfill a consistent Byronic rôle,
and to take the responsibility for it, but in order to conceal their true reactions
and to hide the concerns that oppress them. They are always in the camp of
their enemies; they cannot forget themselves for a moment, lest they reveal
the depths of their revulsion. They dramatize themselves in order to endure
the demands of a society that they have no hope of bettering and whose reality they cannot face, and they imagine themselves in all kinds of rôles—except the ones they actually occupy—because they cannot get through their
days without the help of such fantasy.

So the final testimony of Lewis' novels always seems a little grimmer than
he apparently intended it to be, and never so grim as when he envisions the
rebels and aspiring spirits who front the resolute conformists. He never comes
so close to giving a clinical description of psychic breakdown as when he

shows his characters making their peace with the world. It was a mistake of his critics to see in these novels evidence of that intellectual awakening and skeptical self-criticism which has become known as America's coming-of-age. For Lewis is the historian of America's catastrophic going-to-pieces—or at least of the going-to-pieces of her middle class—with no remedy to offer for the decline that he records; and he has dramatized the process of disintegration, as well as his own dilemma, in the outlines of his novels, in the progress of his characters, and sometimes, and most painfully, in the lapses of taste and precision that periodically weaken the structure of his prose.

From *The New Republic*, Vol. LXXXVIII (October 21, 1936), pp. 298–301. Reprinted by permission.

E. K. BROWN
Willa Cather
[1946]

BEFORE the year ends, Willa Cather will be seventy.[1] Lately her fiction has been of less concern to critics than it was ten years ago, and even then was of less concern than in the second and third decades of the century. It is among the gross abuses of much recent American criticism—I mean, of the criticism which mirrors the time, has influence, is widely quoted, and passes into anthologies—to discuss books primarily as illustrations or turning points of social and aesthetic tendencies, rather than as entities delightful and significant in themselves, made so by a beauty of craftsmanship and depth of vision. A well-read critic will find it very easy, even if he has little or no perception of depth and beauty, to discuss a book in the current fashion; he has no need to find his way into the core of the book, to discover its inmost principle, the source of its unity, warmth, and color; instead he may pontificate upon qualities he has known in a hundred other books, and about whose worth he has long ago made up his mind and closed it.

It is by no means easy to relate Miss Cather's fiction to the vogue of technical stunts and of psychoanalytical explorations which distinguished the Nineteen-twenties, and it is scarcely easier to relate it to the ill-digested massive sociological inquiries which bloated so much of the fiction of the Nineteen-thirties. There are relations. It was amid the technical enthusiasms of the Twenties that Miss Cather developed a new method of narration and a new use of setting, shaking off all the heavinesses and dulnesses of the traditional novel as she had formerly conceived it and as most of her contemporaries continued to practise it. Her fiction, too, has its sociology: she broke off her history of the decay of the small Mid-Western town just where Sinclair Lewis began his. Between *A Lost Lady* and *Main Street* there are many threads of relationship, and there are almost as many between *One of Ours* and *Babbitt*. No novelist has seen with a more discerning eye the role the railroad plays in the social and ethical life of the Western town. Still, the fullest understanding of such relationships would carry one but a very small distance towards the rare essence of Miss Cather's fiction. This may be apprehended not by the

[1] Written in 1946. Willa Cather died on April 24, 1947. (Editor's note.)

critic who is forever remembering what her contemporaries have been thinking and devising, but only if one will forget the characteristics of the historical moment in which she happened to write and look long and directly at
what she actually has written. Before the historical moment is wholly left behind there is, however, one fact to be noted—her strong, conscious, and rapidly increasing aversion from it.

Ten years ago, in the prefatory note to *Not Under Forty*, Miss Cather remarked that "the world broke in two in 1922 or thereabouts," confessed that
she was among those who had remained on the far side of the chasm, and
warned all under forty that the expressions of her mind could scarcely interest
them. 1922 is the year of *Ulysses* and *The Waste Land*, and in method and
temper these works are a world apart from the serenity and lucidity of her
fiction. But her estrangement from the modern world, particularly the modern American world, is much more than literary. When she spoke of 1922 I
doubt that she was primarily remembering Joyce or T. S. Eliot; indeed, I
should not be surprised to hear that she was not thinking of them at all. She
was certainly thinking much more painfully of changes closer to the actual
fabric of living in America. In her memorial portrait of Mrs. James T. Fields,
the widow of the great Boston publisher, she evokes the old house in Charles
Street, where she had so often sat at tea with the tireless hostess and Sarah
Orne Jewett, amid so many relics of what was most distinguished in English
and American arts and letters and song in the last century, and where conversation continued to have that fusion of fragrance with substance which
was a mark of the older time when people could still linger like Dr. Johnson
and have their talk out, and when into that talk they distilled suggestions of
their deepest thoughts and most considered feelings. That house in Charles
Street has, she says, given way to a garage. "Perhaps," she suggests, "the garage and all it stands for represent the only real development and have altogether taken the place of things formerly cherished on that spot." The garage is her real enemy, not *Ulysses*. In "Coming, Aphrodite!" a short story
written not long before 1922, and expressing with delicate truth what Greenwich Village was like when it was the true home of poetry and art, there is a
deeply felt picture of Washington Square in the spring, the grass "blindingly
green," the fountain alive again after its winter arrest, and through the Arch
a vista of "the young poplars with their bright sticky leaves, and the Brevoort
glistening in its spring coat of paint, and shining horses and carriages," and
marring all, the portent of "an automobile, misshapen and sullen, like an ugly
threat in a stream of things that were bright and beautiful and alive."

In 1922 Miss Cather must have been at work upon *A Lost Lady*, which
came out in the following year. In it and in *One of Ours*, which actually appeared in 1922, the ruling mood is one new to her fiction. She had always
been critical of that aspect of American life for which the garage was to be so

bountiful a fulfilment, although it was not until she wrote these novels that she went in fear of it. Standardized, money-minded, complacently respectable folk, devoted to mechanical things, or spiritual things mechanically apprehended, had always fared ill in her fiction. In one of the most biting of her short stories, "A Gold Slipper," she had exhibited lightly but firmly the core of emptiness in a pillar of Pittsburgh (a city she knew well from her years of reporting and teaching), a coal-dealer, member of the Presbytery of the First Church, and despiser of all living things. In his premature old age he goes to his office every week-end because there is no other place in the whole round of his life that interests him, and turns over his will and his insurance policies. He had laid his finger upon reality only once, when a great singer, out of devilment, left a gold slipper in his Pullman when she withdrew after a futile conversation to her drawing room. He had made nothing of her at the time except that she was a nuisance and that he was glad to have told her some brief home truths about herself and her art, but after a while he was pleased that he had not thrown the slipper away, and could turn it over in his hands between readings of the will and the policies. "The Black Hawk boys," Miss Cather wrote in *My Antonia,* "looked forward to marrying the Black Hawk girls, and living in a brand-new little house, with best chairs that must not be sat upon and hand-painted china that must not be used." But this contemptible half-dead world of the prairie town was no real danger to heroic or distinguished character; the vigorous, beautiful, dynamic Scandinavian and Slavic girls from the surrounding farms had the future in their keeping; if they had a rough time so long as they served in the town, one made a fortune in the Klondike, another as the leading *couturière* in San Francisco; and Antonia herself, the finest of all, had a dozen magnificent children, and ruled over a vast and fertile farm. The townsfolk of Black Hawk were impotent creatures, and in the end they did not matter. In *The Song of the Lark,* the same confidence appeared. Thea Kronborg appreciated that the characteristic townsfolk of Moonstone were her natural enemies; she accepted, while she was still young, as the inevitable lot of great talent, that she should find disapproval and envy among even her own brothers and sisters. But Moonstone could not delay her in her course; it could irritate and grieve her, but that was all. Toward 1922, Miss Cather came to feel that such confidence was misplaced. Black Hawk and Moonstone and pillars of the Presbytery of the First Church in Pittsburgh were much more powerful than she had supposed; it was they who determined the future. In *One of Ours* she fights the new and appalling conviction, and there is a roughness in the texture of the novel. In *A Lost Lady* she has the perception under control: the shaping idea which imparts so admirable a unity to the book, and allows it to be written with such a tension of restrained resentment and regret, is the contrast between a dying way of life which is spacious and noble and a new way which is petty and crude. The figure that primarily represents the old way has a grandeur that had not been within her reach before, a poetic beauty. In old Captain Forrester Archbishop Latour is already implicit.

A Lost Lady is one of the books on which Miss Cather's survival will depend, by which it will be assured. For all their vigor and truth, the earlier novels suffer from what Henry James criticised in Arnold Bennett and the other realistic novelists of the first decade of the century, an excess of saturation in material detail, a failure to make the figure in the carpet the true centre. In her essay on "The Novel Démeublé" Miss Cather is as critical of saturation as James had been. The novelist, she says, is to suggest rather than to state, is to aim primarily at that kind of effect which is given by a bare stage and a handful of characters coming into impacts which disclose nothing but their essential selves. *A Lost Lady* is the first of her novels to be wholly uncluttered. In *My Antonia* she had adopted the relaxed form of the memoir, and in introducing it had emphasized how casually the memoir grew, how capriciously it took its dimensions. The memoir is supposed to be Jim Burden's; he is a busy New York lawyer, but still a Nebraskan in spirit, who has occupied himself at long intervals over many years during long trips by train in evoking Antonia and his own youth, now one aspect, now another. "I didn't take time to arrange it," he says in the introductory note, "I simply wrote down pretty much all that her name recalls to me. I suppose that is hasn't any form." *My Antonia* is not at all the insufferably garrulous book to which these warnings point; but material details do heap together in it, and for whole chapters the figure in the carpet is partly obscured and by the reader forgotten. The structure of *The Song of the Lark* is perfectly conventional; in this respect, even in its radically revised form, it does not differ from a Dreiser novel. Thea Kronborg's states of mind, the slow and difficult development of her great voice along with her growth, harsh and rough, as a great personality, are at the centre of the book; but they do not strictly govern the choice of material, and they do not always mesh with the incidents in the narrative. It is a massive work, and it communicates an impression of perfect truth, but it is somewhat cluttered; it lags, especially in the urban chapters; the controlling idea does not always control. With *O Pioneers!* the case is not very different.

In comparison with these novels, so massive, so firmly stamped with material truth, *A Lost Lady* seems very slight, even attenuated. But in essential substance, it is richer than any of Miss Cather's books that preceded and, in force of feeling as well as in the exhibition of the figure in its particular carpet, vastly their superior. It was Antonia's greatness that she could "leave images in the mind that did not fade—that grew stronger with time." It is a large part of her creator's greatness to do the same. *Shadows on the Rock* was to be a sequence of such memorable images; they are already beautifully strong and frequent in *A Lost Lady*. When I took up the novel recently it was ten years since I had read it, but I could turn at once to a number of the images which had kept all their original strength during that time and had also gathered a depth of increasing meaning. The chief of these images is in the second part of the seventh chapter. Young Niel Herbert goes through the fields near Sweet Water in the summer dawn to pick a bouquet of roses and lay it outside the shuttered French windows of Mrs. Forrester's bedroom. "As he bent to place the flowers on the sill, he heard from within a woman's soft laughter; impatient, indulgent, teasing, eager. Then another laugh, very different, a man's. And it was fat and lazy,—ended in something like a yawn." In an instant, the gleaming candor of the dawn and of the boy's innocent idealism is blotted out. The style has not yet acquired the full beauty of surface which makes every page of the historical novels a radiant thing; it has not yet the glow or the firmness of contour; but only the shortcoming in style—a merely relative shortcoming, for Miss Cather was already writing as well as any contemporary novelist—prevents one from saying that this half-chapter could go unchanged into *Madame Bovary,* which is one of her principal admirations as it must be with anyone who cherishes the art of fiction without being the victim of sectarian prejudice. *A Lost Lady* is full of symbolic images abounding with suggestion and with beauty. In place of the elaborate descriptions of the earlier novels—one could find his way in the dark from the depot at Moonstone to the Kronborg parsonage, and then out by the sandhills and by the grove of the Kohlers—stand such golden moments arrested forever in their force and beauty.

Yet *A Lost Lady* is not of Miss Cather's very best. It has a grave intellectual weakness, a weakness of vision. Her pioneers will not quite bear the weight she assigns to them. The tone in which she always refers to Captain Forrester's powerful friends who travel back and forth on the Burlington in their private cars and break the trip at Sweet Water—railroad-builders, financiers, founders of great department stores like Marshall Field—arouses some uneasiness. It is a simple thing to grant that men in the habit of great affairs, men for whom the breaking of new ground is the breath of life, "great-hearted adventurers," are of another and higher kind than small-town shysters, vulgarians, and gossips. But Miss Cather presses us to do much more than grant this; she asks us to believe that as a group, by definition, her builders and founders have a spiritual breadth, a heroic wisdom, for which it is difficult indeed to extort our assent. One cannot long escape the feeling that she has built them up somewhat artificially out of a need to annihilate the petty present. In *One of Ours* the hero, Claude Wheeler, remarks that "no battlefield or shattered country was ever as ugly as this world would be if men like his brother Bayliss controlled it altogether." It is easy to agree, and Bayliss is of the same gross stuff as Ivy Peters, the shyster and gossip who rules the last phase of *A Lost Lady.* Still, the countervailing characters in these novels—those who represent the splendors of the Western past, and must do so for there is no other past except the almost unknown aboriginal for the area these novels picture—are not grand enough for their role. Even Captain Forrester, impressive as he is by his silences, his fixities, his genial calm, is not quite grand enough.

The hunger for a glorious past in the West appeared early in Miss Cather's writing, and is its deepest emotional motive. There is a curiously moving chapter in *My Antonia* where the Scandinavian and Slavic girls ask to hear the tale of Coronado and his search for the Seven Golden Cities, and find in the thought that the Spanish adventurers have been in Nebraska the source of a new radiance in the wheat fields and the sunset. This is a reworking of a beautiful sketch, "The Enchanted Bluff," still uncollected. In *The Song of the Lark* the most formative of all Thea Kronborg's experiences, far more significant than any contact she ever had with a person—the experience which lent wings to her spirit and so to her voice—was a summer in Arizona when she lay every day at the mouth of one of the caves in a village of the "ancient people," the Cliff-Dwellers. To be from the West would no longer mean to her being from Moonstone; it would mean being from the region of the builders of those caves. "The Cliff-Dwellers had lengthened her past. She had older and higher obligations." She grew to meet them. In *The Professor's House,* the small Mid-Western college town with its petty professorial rivalries and the bright superficialities of academic families suddenly vanishes. In the most melodramatic strangeness of structure in all Miss Cather's fiction, the long narrative from Tom Outland's notebook breaks in upon the pace of life in the town, with its tale of the mesas. Tom Outland had taken from the Indians of the Southwest just what Thea Kronborg had taken: "I had read of filial piety in the Latin poets," he wrote, "and I knew that was what I felt for this place." The old Indian civilization turns to ridicule the new house which has been built, with its elaborate bathrooms and, of course, its garage, from the prize money the professor received for the many-volumed work on the Spanish adventurers, which was the best part of his life. He finds that he does not care to move into his new house: the bleak old house, with the creaking stairs leading to the uncomfortable attic where the great feat of imaginative reconstruction had taken place, is far more akin to his spirit. It is not so absurdly unlike what the Cliff-Dwellers had made.

The old Southwest had ruled in Miss Cather's imagination since the time of her earliest novels; but she had shied away from it in the conviction that it was eminently a subject for a Catholic to realize. In the end, she could not be content with using it merely as a background. In *Death Comes for the Archbishop* it is the core of the work. Here Indian villages, the exploits of the Spanish adventurers and missionaries, the coming of a new layer of high civilization with the French priests, and the small but true contribution of the best of the great-hearted adventurers of Anglo-Saxon blood, men like Kit

Carson, are set before us as on a frieze. *Death Comes for the Archbishop* is her great book, the most beautiful achievement of her imagination; in it at last her craftsmanship and her vision are in relation, and that relation is complete. The length of her unconscious preparation to write it had served her well indeed.

Miss Cather had always understood that a person's relation to a place might be as valuable to him, and as decisive in his growth or retardation, as any relation he might have with other persons. What happens in one place could not have taken from Moonstone or from Chicago what the villages of the Cliff-Dwellers gave her. But in the earlier novels the landscape did not impinge upon the reader with the vitality that distinguishes it in *Death Comes for the Archbishop*. Much to his own surprise, Archbishop Latour decides against returning to his native Auvergne to pass the years of his retirement and preparation for death. The ties of his family, the promise of fine architecture on every side, and of the scholarly associations of which through his long years in Santa Fe he had been deprived, were, he found, less powerful than the atmosphere of New Mexico. When he wakens in the early morning at Santa Fe, the southwestern air communicates to him a conviction of eternal youth, of energy, of ever-possible spiritual growth. A response of this kind might have been a part of *My Antonia* or of *The Song of the Lark,* but at the time when she wrote these novels Miss Cather could not have found such language as she uses in conveying the quality of the atmosphere at Santa Fe. "His first consciousness was a sense of the light dry wind blowing in through the windows, with the fragrance of hot sun and sage-brush and sweet clover. . . . Something soft and wild and free that whispered to the ear on the pillow, lightened the heart, softly, softly picked the lock, slid the bolts, and released the spirit of man into the wind, into the blue and gold, into the morning, into the morning!" Her craftsmanship in language, her sense of a true economy, her command of rhythms individual without being eccentric, had never before reached such a delicate sureness. It is the language which makes the impressions of the New Mexico landscape superior to any presentation of setting in the earlier books. She had borne the memories of this landscape in her mind for a long time, and at last she had the words to convey them in simple, perfect strength.

The same sure delicacy marks her manipulation of character and incident, a richer material than she had ever before worked in, more varied, more intense, and at times more heroic. The deliberate and often ponderous movement in the earlier narratives is now replaced by a movement wonderfully quick and light, beautifully appropriate to the atmosphere. In the structure what might easily have become solid masses, comparable with long reaches in the earlier novels, is broken up by brief tales inset with an apparent casualness which recalls the ingenuous narrative manner of Cervantes or Smollett.

Everything in *Death Comes for the Archbishop* is from the past, but it is not all from the same past, and in this lies much of the great formal beauty and almost as much of the great emotional effect of the novel. The framework belongs to the mid-nineteenth century when two priests from a quiet town in Auvergne who had worked not too happily along the Ohio, set out to revive the Catholic faith and discipline in the Southwest. In their missionary travels throughout the immense diocese they made fragmentary acquaintance with a far older past—the sixteenth century when the Spanish Franciscans first entered the region coming up from the see of Durango, and the slightly later time when their successors, isolated and often degenerate, gave individual twists to the gospel and the priestly estate. It is in the tales of this older past, picked up by the French priests in their wanderings, that Miss Cather's narrative art is most remarkable. She was always an admirable writer of short stories, and shortly after the appearance of *Death Comes for the Archbishop* her mastery of shorter media came to its height in the *nouvelles* of *Obscure Destinies*, particularly in the moving "Old Mrs. Harris." Her manner in the tales inset in *Death Comes for the Archbishop* is even more accomplished. It is the manner appropriate to the older and better kind of hagiography, simple, concrete, unemphatic, concentrated. The tale of the bold and evil friar who ruled on the crag at Acoma is among the perfect short narratives, suggestive, swimming in the atmosphere of the time and the place, without a touch of false exaggeration or falser complexity. At every turn in the story, the setting is alive, almost overpoweringly sensible. The friar and his clerical guests at dinner and the servant whom he kills say next to nothing, but we catch them in their characterizing attitudes and know them as human beings. The height of Miss Cather's success is in the pages which follow the death and evoke a silence and immobility as thick and ominous as Conrad with his more lavish methods could suggest. With the simplest of means, which are also the most difficult, she has accomplished a triumph.

The method of *Death Comes for the Archbishop* was used again, with minor changes, in *Shadows on the Rock*. In a letter to Wilbur L. Cross, Miss Cather defined with a preciseness unusual for her in speaking of her own work the subtle effect at which she aimed in her novel of French Canada at the end of the seventeenth century. "I . . . tried to develop it into a prose composition not too conclusive, not too definite: a series of pictures remembered rather than experienced; a kind of thinking, a mental complexion inherited, left over from the past, lacking in robustness, and full of pious resignation." The Indians and Spaniards who had given such vigorous color to *Death Comes for the Archbishop* have no equivalent in the later novel. Nor has it the peculiar depth given to *Death Comes for the Archbishop* by the inset tales of a remoter past.

Shadows on the Rock is a novel of the north. The great rock of Quebec in all its grayness is the eternal antagonist supported by the endless Canadian winter and the untouched wastes. But on the rock, stronger than its strength, the spirit of European civilization preserves its precarious life: this is a novel of survivals, a series of pictures illustrating the will of a highly civilized people to preserve its civilization. To maintain French cookery through the six or seven frozen months—not to subsist on frozen meat or coarse fare, but to have vegetables growing in the cellar and fowls laid away in lard—becomes not only significant but in its way heroic. On uncommonly cold nights little Cécile Auclair, taking her dead mother's place as head of the household before she was in her teens, would throw off the covers and stir her chilly legs to cover the parsley. Her father would call out: *"Qu'est-ce que tu fais, petite?"* The sleepy voice would reply: *"Papa, j'ai peur pour le persil."* It had not frozen in her mother's time, it should not freeze in hers. Euclide Auclair's household, a particle of Louis XIV's Paris accidentally transported to Quebec, is cherished by not only those who live in it but all sorts of people, even by Monseigneur Laval, because they find in the food and the furniture and in the spirit of the critical enlightened apothecary something that appeals to their nostalgia and promises the continuance in the colony of what they admired in the distant and at times incredible capital. The light cheerful quality of the Auclairs, father and daughter, is beautifully balanced by such grim figures as Laval with his terrifying features, his formidable language, and his immense disappointments, and Jeanne Le Ber, recluse of Montreal, won for a religious life by no less a person than the Venerable Marguerite Bourgeoys. Laval comes before us ringing the cathedral bell at every hour all through the long night before All Souls', a punctual reminder to all on the rock of the force by which it is ruled and linked with Europe. The recluse, living in her bare rooms inset in the cathedral, worn to nothing by her devotions, is an evidence that in French Canada God is already served as He had been in the deserts of Egypt in the early centuries of Christianity, that the great cold of the Montreal winter cannot alter in one iota the creed the French had planted with the lilies. Light and dark shadows are so juxtaposed that in the novel as a whole there is an image of life in its variety and promise.

It is far too little to say of *Shadows on the Rock* that it is the best novel drawn from the rich material of Canadian history. Beside it William Kirby's *Golden Dog* is clumsy and external, Charles G. D. Roberts's *Forge in the Forest* conventional, and Gilbert Parker's *Seats of the Mighty* merely facile. Nor would any historical novels written by French Canadians sustain a comparison with Miss Cather's craftsmanship and vision. Still, if *Shadows on the Rock* is perfect in the beauty of structure and style, if the author's sense of relevance is unfailing, if the mood of nostalgic charm is perfectly conveyed, it is a novel with but little dramatic incident, and the personages are figures in a legend rather than living characters. These are indeed but shadows! The shortcomings in drama and in vitality of character are quite deliberate, the coloring in the sequence of pictures is intentionally faint, for the book was to be an equivalent in prose of a fresco by Puvis de Chavannes. No more graceful book has been accomplished in our time.

Shadows on the Rock was followed by a collection of three *nouvelles*, *Obscure Destinies*. From the appearance of *One of Ours*, Miss Cather had avoided the massiveness of the full-length novel; in everything she has written since the crucial year 1922 the literal dimensions have been relatively brief, and the method has been that of the tale or *nouvelle*, or of the short novel with shorter works inset. Nowhere does her discrimination show more finely than in *Obscure Destinies* or in *My Mortal Enemy*, that somewhat earlier work in which the same method was tried out. In the *nouvelle* she finds sufficient space to work in the symbols and pictures on which she has come more and more to depend, and to allow an occasional incident to flow into a dramatic scene, and yet has no need to make of a character a complex personality. In "Old Mrs. Harris," she exhibits in their essence the powers that in her later years she has most wished to exercise, the power of picture, the power of symbol, the power of structure, the power of style. In it also her vision of the aged, defeated, lonely, and unhappy comes to its clearest and most moving expression.

What Miss Cather has published since the appearance of *Obscure Destinies* in 1932—it has been remarkably little—has revealed no new kinds of power or charm, nor has it ever quite matched the work of the preceding decade, which will more and more be recognized as the time in which her craftsmanship and her vision attained their height. *Lucy Gayheart*, in which she returned to her own Middle West, is slight, not as *A Lost Lady* is slight but with the slightness of minor work, although the last part is, for feeling and form, comparable with almost anything in *A Lost Lady*. *Sapphira and the Slave Girl*, more nearly a successor to the historical novels, evokes Virginia before the Civil War, the Virginia of which she heard tales when she was growing up near Winchester, in a series of quiet pictures which have the charm but not the depth of those in *Death Comes for the Archbishop* or *Shadows on the Rock*. It came out six years ago, and since then Miss Cather has been silent.

While she is still among us, although her work must be nearly over, if the time for a formal and considered estimate has perhaps not yet arrived, we may yet see her fiction in sufficient perspective to tell her on the occasion of her seventieth anniversary something of what her craftsmanship and vision mean to us. What we have gained by her craftsmanship is, above all, a beautiful lightening of the novel form. From George Eliot's time down to ours, the load upon the novel form has been steadily increasing until in works such as *The Financier* and *The World of William Clissold*—to choose examples from novelists who have recently died—the form broke beneath the stress. I suppose that for popular fiction of a semi-serious sort, and for fiction which aspires to distinction without fully attaining it, the characteristic formula during the past fifteen years or so has been the memoir of a crowded life, abounding in rather crude sexual experience and with somewhat hasty reflections on education, industry, and the social system, and coming to a climax in a melodramatic ethical regeneration or else in an equally melodramatic recognition of life's futility. Examples of such fiction, written for the day, or at best for the decade, will be in everyone's mind. In most of them, character and story are mere props and are handled with an almost unbelievable clumsiness; structure and tone are scarcely considered; and in style the model appears to be the manner of the more lively foreign correspondents. Against such a degradation of the art of fiction to mere journalism, Miss Cather's craftsmanship stands out with an alien definiteness and firmness of beauty.

Her vision is of essences. In her earlier novels the essential subject, a state of mind or of feeling, was enveloped in the massiveness of the conventional modern realist novel. It was there, but it was muffled. Then Miss Cather saw that if she abandoned the devices of massive realism, if she depended upon picture and symbol and style, she could disengage her essential subject, and make it tell upon the reader with a greater directness and power, help it to remain uncluttered in his mind. The things that pass, the things that merely adhere to states of mind and feeling, she began to use with a severe economy. Her fiction became a kind of symbolism, with the depths and suggestions that belong to symbolist art, and with the devotion to a music of style and structure for which the great literary symbolists strove, Pater and Moore and the later James. Over their work hers has the advantage that her vision was never eccentric, disproportioned, or perverse. What she cares for in humanity and in nature many sensitive and cultivated people have cared for in every time. There could be not better assurance that her fiction will endure and that some of the novels and tales will interpret us to a later day. At seventy, it may be a satisfaction to her that she has written not for the day or the decade but for the long future, and that in a time when most of those works which usurp the leading places in our book reviews will have nothing to say, *My Antonia* (despite its passages of excessive detail), *A Lost Lady, Death Comes for the Archbishop, Shadows on the Rock,* and *Obscure Destinies* will be the sources of pleasure and the subjects of thought.

From *The Yale Review,* copyright Yale University Press, Vol. XXXVI (September, 1946), pp. 77–92. Reprinted by permission of the author and editors.

FRANCIS FERGUSSON

Eugene O'Neill

[1930]

AFTER Eugene O'Neill had spent several years traveling about the country with his father, James O'Neill, who was playing in *The Count of Monte Cristo,* and a few more bumming all over the world, he fell ill; and while recovering in a sanatorium, decided he wanted to write plays. His first plays, written while he was studying under Professor Baker at Harvard, and working with the young Provincetown Playhouse, are the product of his romantic youth and a desire to write for the stage. They are not complicated by the anxiety about his own soul which gets in his way later, and, more clearly than his later work, they show the real nature of his vocation to the stage. The first published volume, *Thirst,* is now repudiated. Mr. Barrett Clark, whose book on O'Neill contains all the available information about his life and the origins of his plays, says that the plays collected under this title are similar to those in the earliest preserved collection, *The Moon of the Caribbees,* though cruder.

The first thing that strikes one on reading the latter collection is the over-emphatic language. The characters, usually the crew of a tramp steamer, communicate almost entirely in profanity. Mr. Clark, who once made the crossing on a cattle-boat, testifies that the dialogue is not inaccurate; but the more educated people in the later plays, while not so profane, also seem to be laboring to express the inexpressible, and achieving a similar flatness. I conclude that the fault is with the dramatist rather than with his material. This conclusion is borne out by the fact that, except in the "atmospheric" play, *The Moon of the Caribbees,* the author remains on a level with his characters. We are required to accept people with ineffable sorrows or longings as carrying the main burden of the play. And the plots and situations are built on a similar assumption of a vast emotion which cannot be put into words.

I understand that O'Neill has never liked *In the Zone;* but it seems to differ from the other plays in the volume we are discussing, chiefly in having a neater and more self-conscious technique. It may be that O'Neill thinks that this interferes with its sincerity; or it may be that I do him an injustice. The crew of a tramp steamer crossing the submarine-infested zone, is nervously on the watch for spies. What a spy would be doing there is never satisfactorily

explained. This does not prevent the men, in search of a scapegoat, from sus-
pecting Smitty. This character is a recurrent figure in the early plays: a melancholy and solitary hobo "of the higher type." Someone discovers him reading
a batch of letters one night; they tie him up in spite of his screams, and investigate. But instead of the telegrams from the Kaiser which they expected, they
find letters from Smitty's lady-love, who rejected him years ago because he
drank. One dried rose falls to the floor. At this sudden revelation of hidden
sorrow the rough sailors, whose hearts are really of gold, are abashed and
conscience-stricken.

   This plot, which, however absurd it may sound in the telling never fails to
move an audience, is really as helplessly bombastic as the language; a language of childish superlatives which are always trying to imply more than
they succeed in stating. I take it that the essence of melodrama is to accept
emotions uncritically; which, in the writing, amounts to assuming or suggesting emotions that are never realized either in language or action. Melodrama
in this sense is a constant quality in O'Neill's work. It disfigures his middle
period, when his feeling for a character is out of all proportion to that character's importance to the play, as well as his later period, when his attempt to
deal with his own unattached emotion takes the unhappy form of a passion
for some large idea. In fact it seems that O'Neill typically resorts to the stage,
not to represent emotions through which he has already passed; which have
been criticised and digested, and so may be arranged in patterns to form works
of art: he resorts to the stage to convey a protest, the *first* cry of the wounded
human being. His fundamental feeling for the stage, so clearly shown in these
first plays, is not that of the artist, but of the melodramatist: the seeker after
sensational effect.

   Nevertheless, his naïve belief in emotion is related to a priceless quality,
which one may call histrionic sincerity, the essence of mummery. Every
dramatist as well as every actor depends for his power over his audience on
his own belief in what he is trying to put on the stage, whether it be an emotion, a character, or a situation. An audience is extremely malleable. It may
be swayed by suggestion, hypnotized by the concentration of the stage figure.
This complete concentration, which would be wrecked by a wakeful critical
faculty or a touch of humor at the wrong time, O'Neill possesses in a very
high degree. It is the secret of his success; and when it is joined to an interest
in a character, it produces his best scenes.

II

   After O'Neill had exhausted the vein of mood and atmosphere derived
from his early experiences of bumming, he ceased to write melodrama for its
own sake, and developed an interest in people he had known or heard about.
His next plays begin with an interest in a character or characters. O'Neill thus

explains the origin of *Beyond the Horizon,* the earliest play of this type to be preserved: "I think the real life experience from which the idea of *Beyond the Horizon* sprang was this: On the British tramp steamer on which I made a voyage as ordinary seaman, Buenos Aires to New York, there was a Norwegian A. B. and we became quite good friends. The great sorrow and mistake of his life, he used to grumble, was that as a boy he had left the small paternal farm to run away to sea. He had been at sea twenty years, and had never gone home once in that time. . . . Yet he cursed the sea and the life it had led him—affectionately. . . . I thought, 'What if he had stayed on the farm, with his instincts? What would have happened?' . . . And from that point I started to think of a more intellectual, civilized type . . . a man who would have my Norwegian's inborn craving for the sea's unrest, only in him it would be diluted into a vague, intangible wanderlust. . . . He would throw away his instinctive dream and accept the thraldom of the farm for— why, for almost any nice, little poetical craving—the romance of sex, say." Though we do not have O'Neill's account of the origins of most of his plays, I should say, from internal evidences, that *Gold, Anna Christie, Diff'rent, All God's Chillun Got Wings,* and perhaps *Desire Under the Elms,* started from a similar interest in a character, which was sometimes real, sometimes partly or entirely imaginary. I shall look at *All God's Chillun* as typical of this group. It shows his most characteristic failings as well as some of his very best results.

The first scene shows Ella, a white girl, and Jim, a sensitive little negro boy, having a childish love affair in their native slum. This scene, unnecessary for the main theme of the play, is typical of O'Neill. Its only possible relevance is as psychological and sociological background, for the important information is duplicated later. I shall have more to say later about O'Neill's use of this type of realism. Meanwhile observe that the realism of the dialogue and the natural history of the stage full of children (which, I may say, is extremely difficult to do practically), are complicated by a kind of symbolism or super-realism of the set. The scene is a street-corner, one street being full of black faces and negro tunes, the other street full of white faces and their tunes. Aside from the sloppiness of leaving so much to the carpenter and the régisseur (which I shall also mention later), it may be doubted whether realism with a superimposed symbolism of this kind is ever a success. Even Ibsen, with his Wild Ducks and his sea-ladies, has the greatest difficulty in making it seem anything but artificial, and Mr. O'Neill hasn't a tenth of his skill.

Ella falls in with tough companions and gradually degenerates, while Jim painfully acquires education and starts to study Law. Ella, disillusioned with her own kind, marries Jim in a moment of depression, as the only "white" man she knows. There is a good "symbolistic" scene showing the newly married couple emerging from the church between rows of hostile faces, white on one side and black on the other. And then the real drama begins: the struggle in Jim between his love for Ella and his ambition to succeed in the world; the struggle in Ella between her love for Jim and her hatred of him as the cause of her exile from her own people. The point of conflict is Jim's career: for his self-respect he needs to become a lawyer, while Ella, who has never really accepted Jim as her husband, needs to preserve her spiritual ascendancy by preventing him from passing his examinations. Tied together by their love and by their solitude, they alternately take refuge in each other's arms and fight for mastery or vengeance. The scenes throughout this middle part of the play, in spite of their inadequate language, are deeply convincing. But at the end they both give up: Jim agrees to play a little boy to Ella's little girl. In effect, they cease to strive for an adult relation of husband and wife and accept a childish one.

Now if the previous scenes mean anything, this conclusion marks a degeneration on both their parts. But O'Neill, under the necessity of ending his play, asks us to accept it as a hard won *Verklärung:*

Jim—Forgive me, God—and make me worthy! . . . Let this fire of burning suffering purify me of selfishness and make me worthy of the child you send me for the woman you take away!
Ella—Honey, Honey, I'll play right up to the gates of heaven with you!

What is the reason for this extraordinary failure of O'Neill's to master his material? Between the untidy and unnecessary first scene and the bathetic and evasive finale, there are several scenes of really tragic significance. Beginning with a person, and proceeding with that complete concentration on the stage figure which I described above, O'Neill sometimes sees his people so deeply that they acquire overtones of universal import. One may sometimes feel Jim and Ella, through their excellent concreteness, as every pair of exiles in love, and their story as realizing certain profound truths about the relation between a man, his work, and his wife. But these jewels are so rare, and are embedded in such a disheartening matrix of psychology, bathos, and cheap symbolism that they seem not only accidental but misunderstood when they appear. And the end finally persuades one that the author wrought better than he knew. He turns away from his tragic vision, and all is lost.

But did he ever have a tragic vision? The finale, so wrong for the middle scenes, is not inconsistent with the characters. The reason it jars is that it belies the point of view from which their struggles were seen as having a dignity and a significance beyond themselves. It might be appropriate in some terrible comedy, but the characters are not seen as in any sense comic figures. In fact, they are not seen "as" anything: if they at times reveal heights and depths, that is an accident, for O'Neill's relation to them is personal. They are for him friends and enemies, other individuals in an anarchical universe, not parts of any larger vision. He is prepared to echo their cry, "Can such things be?" It is all very well for a character in a play to demonstrate this emotion, but when an author shows it it means that he has not digested his material to the point where it becomes suitable for a work of art. Interested in his people's psychology, yes: hence the filling in of naturalistic background in scene 1; but interested in the esthetic value of their dignity, no: and hence no possible ending for their story. O'Neill is right when he says, "Life doesn't end, one experience is but the birth of another. Violent death is seldom the solution of anything, in life or in fiction. It is too often a makeshift device. . . ." Life doesn't end, but a work of art does; a work of art is a bounded whole, and O'Neill's unsatisfying endings are a proof that his interest in his people is not the disinterested and final one of the artist, but the developing and tentative one of a man among men.

But O'Neill's power of convincing an audience is vastly aided by the fact that his belief in his characters is so purely naturalistic. Where there is no publicly established convention, the only way to make a character acceptable is to establish him naturalistically. An audience will believe in a character who used to play on a certain street-corner in Harlem, and whose father was in the coal business, but it will not believe in one who can only be identified by the qualities of his soul, and toward whom it is invited to adopt no personal attitude. The limitations of this type of realism have been admirably studied by Virginia Woolf, in her essay, *Mr. Bennett and Mrs. Brown*. It has this inestimable advantage of being publicly understood, but the most that can be said for it as an art form is that it may, as in this play of O'Neill's, lead to the accidental discovery of a few muddy diamonds. O'Neill himself has never been satisfied with it; he has never called himself a realist: we have seen that even in these plays of his middle period he resorts to symbolism. And finally he abandons his interest in character altogether and attempts to enunciate general ideas.

III

Beginning perhaps with *The Hairy Ape*, and continuing through *The Fountain, The Great God Brown, Marco Millions, Lazarus Laughed*, and *Dynamo*, Mr. O'Neill's character studies are interspersed with, and finally superseded by, plays in which the author shows no interest in the concrete, and assumes the rôle of prophet. It is as though he had ceased to interrogate his acquaintances about which course he is to expect of "Life," and had begun to interrogate Nietzsche and other nineteenth-century philosophers. About the prophecies themselves Mr. Clark says the last word: "If O'Neill were a genuinely original thinker, or even a brilliant spokesman for the ideas of a brilliant thinker, we might argue as to whether we should be the losers if he were to give up writing plays altogether, but his ideas as contributions to contemporary thought are negligible; they are at best slightly varied forms of what we have all been reading during the past decade or so." Lazarus' Nietzschean exclamation is typical: "Men are also unimportant! . . . Man remains! Man slowly arises from the past of the race of men that was his tomb of death! For Man death is not! Man, Son of God's Laughter, is!" O'Neill is not a thinker, and we need not attempt to investigate his thought any further. It is true that Lazarus sounds a little like O'Neill's own fundamental cry, that "life goes on"—implying, perhaps, some confusion between pessimism and the unhappy ending, which would affect his ability to write plays; moreover, it is doubtful whether Lazarus' generalized and rather hysterical optimism could ever be realized in live characters; but the question which concerns us more nearly, in our attempt to understand O'Neill as a playwright, is not so much the quality of the thought as the relation between the thought, the author, and the play.

O'Neill, we find, is more interested in affirming his ideas than in representing the experience in which they are implied. The example of Elizabethan drama seems to prove that an unsatisfying philosophy may underlie a great play. But there the play is the thing, and the philosophy may at most be deduced from it as from a direct experience of life. In *Lazarus Laughed,* on the other hand, there is little or no play at all, for Caligula, the anti-Lazarus, is no more credible than Lazarus himself, and their conflicts fail entirely to move us. The burden of the play is carried by two elements: by Lazarus' philosophical arias, and by spectacular effects of crowd movements and colored lights. About the first of these, enough has been said. With regard to the element of spectacle, Reinhardt has shown us what can be achieved in this line, especially in his production of Büchner's *Danton.* Gordon Craig has hailed these departures as first steps toward a new form, his hypothetical "pure art of the theatre." As a form, it is related to the seventeenth-century masque, and the modern revue. It seems to mean a dissolution of the classic partnership of actor and author, to which we owe most great drama, in favor of a third figure, the régisseur. A good régisseur may of course get artistically satisfying effects with well-trained crowds and carefully calculated light and sound effects—too often at the author's expense. When an author resorts to it, it usually means that he has ceased to be interested in mastering the medium of the stage. This is certainly true in *Lazarus Laughed:* the stage becomes O'Neill's lifeless megaphone. Nothing stands between the audience and O'Neill, shouting his views. For his relation to his ideas, in these prophetic plays, is the same as his relation to his characters in his middle period: they are emotionally significant to him, they play a part in his equilibrium as a man. Attaining no vision outside himself, his plays remain attached to him by his eternal immaturity.

We are not surprised to find, therefore, that his audience is often more interested in the author than in his play: "It is salvation the agnostic playwright is seeking. One might trace his life like one of those dry southwestern roads where the Penitente Brothers have laid down the dead man they are are carrying." O'Neill's plays are crosses. Follow the road he travels and you will often hear the sound of flagellation. Look and you will often see that the whip is brought down by a tormented soul on his own back. But flowers grow on this desert track, and the mountains and the sunset lie *Beyond the Horizon*. The very imperfection which connects the author with his play also connects the author with his audience. The one quality which his admirers agree in stressing is his sincerity. We have seen that he believes in his own mood in his early plays, and in the personal reality of his characters in his middle period, while in his latest plays he is in earnest in asserting some Nietzschean war-cry. As a person, he is sincerely interested in figuring out his life, and perhaps in attaining a stable point of view—though unconsciously. He has in fact never attained it. He has managed to recognize his emotional demands, but he has not reached the further heroism of accepting what becomes of them: of describing them with reference to some independent reality. He has a sense of human needs, but none of human destiny. He offers us the act of seeking, but no disinterested contemplation; himself, therefore, rather than his work. Only the dead cease to change; but by discipline it is sometimes possible to produce a work complete and independent of the suffering individual. O'Neill's failings may all be ascribed to the fact that he has never found any such discipline.

IV

I do not intend, in this essay, to enquire directly to what extent O'Neill's failure to find a discipline through which to realize his talent is due to his own shortcomings, and to what extent to "conditions" beyond his control. A slight acquaintance with modern drama since Ibsen shows one how difficult it is to write plays of artistic as distinguished from sentimental or sociological interest. But to tackle the general question of O'Neill as a modern dramatist —and an American—would involve questions which I am not competent to treat. It seems more profitable to compare briefly O'Neill's career with those of two other American playwrights, George Kelly and E. E. Cummings, who followed very different paths to the stage, in the hope that some sense of O'Neill's place in the contemporary scene may emerge by implication.

O'Neill began to work about the time of the 1912 Renaissance. He belongs with Mencken, Sherwood Anderson, and Theodore Dreiser (who was in advance of his time). This was the generation that raised the hue and cry about Puritanism. They were, as a group, impatient of tradition and convention, and their great discovery was their emotional needs. They were more interested in man's emotions than in a map of them; therefore, more interested in the man than his work. Most of them wrote fiction—a genre which is much better suited to this temperament than the stage; but they also gave birth to the Little Theatre, and O'Neill, whose first plays were produced by the Provincetown, is in many ways a Little Theatre product. This movement seems never to have had anything more positive than a dissatisfaction with Broadway, and an ambition. It was a revolt against narrow commercialism; it asserted that the theatre was an art; but, having no standards and no technique, it remained somewhat ineffectual in its new freedom.

George Kelly on the other hand is a product of the commercial, which is also the professional stage. He began as a vaudeville actor and presently he was writing his own skits. He stood behind the scenes with a stop-watch, and if the audience did not laugh soon enough, he rewrote the act. From vaudeville he graduated to the three-act comedy, and finally to the drama. His experience proves that a certain sense of craftsmanship is not incompatible with Broadway, rare though it is there: having set himself the comparatively modest problem of making the *honnête* Babbitts laugh, he was rewarded by the natural discipline which an actual audience and a particular stage can give. Assuming the viewpoint of "common sense" where O'Neill urges some large idea; accepting the realistic set and the realistic dialogue which he found publicly established, where O'Neill was always making strange demands on the carpenter and the electrician, Kelly's work was that of the artist: to master and refine a given medium to the point where it can be made to realize his vision. While O'Neill's freedom has resulted in a complete loss of bearings, so that he has of late almost ceased to be a dramatist, Kelly has bequeathed us several comedies which are complete, and refer to nothing outside themselves. If they are rather trivial, and if there are signs that his home-folks, having moved to more expensive suburbs and learned to drink gin, are no longer to be satisfied with his neat little interiors, the fault is not with his method, which was after all the method of Shakespeare and Molière. Kelly seems to have encountered the limitations of the theatre as it exists with us here and now. It is doubtful whether a method, which depends upon an acceptance of the existing theatre, would ever prove the solution for a man of O'Neill's potential dimensions.

If the Little Theatre, in its revolt against commercialism, forfeited incidentally the discipline of the craftsman which a Kelly could work out for himself on Broadway, it never showed the slightest tendency to develop its own standards and its own conventions. A play with a "kick" has remained its ideal. We have seen that the personality of the author or the agony of some unassimilated "character" can satisfy its cravings for drama better than a formal and autonomous play.

E. E. Cummings, however, was a poet before he tried to write for the stage. That is to say, he had trained himself—with what success I shall not attempt to say: his method rather than his results concern us here—to see his material as an artist. His play, *Him,* is evidently more "autobiographical" than any of O'Neill's and yet the characters at least of Him and Me are acceptable as parts of the pattern of the play without reference to the author. Without trying to judge the merit of the play as a whole, I should say that the scenes between Him and Me have all the qualities we have failed to find in O'Neill's work. The characters, the rhythm, and the sense of the stage are all of a piece, whereas in O'Neill's plays we find realistic dialogue, symbolistic settings, and characters which are unamenable to any pattern or underlying rhythm. In a real writer for the stage, language, character, and the sound and movement of the stage, spring from the same root conception. A Molière dialogue implies the stage empty save for a few spectators, a little furniture, and the actors; it implies a rhythm derived from the pantomime of the "Commedia dell'Arte," and a certain relation between actor and audience. A Cummings dialogue implies a brief light interval between "blackouts," a certain rhythm derived from the vaudeville act, and an audience which good-humoredly challenges the performer to "put his stuff across." Cummings' work, in fact, has style. His solitary discipline has enabled him to work in stage terms, disinterestedly, and with a mastery which O'Neill, for all his experience, has never attained.

But Cummings, unlike Kelly, is an artist of the theatre without either theatre or audience. I have said that his style was derived from vaudeville, but no vaudeville actor could manage a speech of Him's and no vaudeville audience could understand his play. In spite of his very authentic feeling for the stage, and in spite of his ingenious and courageous effort to dramatize his very lack of connection with a live stage and audience (so neatly of a piece with the "stunt" feeling of his vaudeville style), Cummings' first play remains mere closet drama. It was in fact produced at O'Neill's native theatre; but the Provincetown's crowd of Greenwich Villagers, just the thing to relish a revival of *In the Zone* and *Moon of the Caribbees,* were at a loss to deal with *Him.* Cummings does not belong at the Provincetown. So far he does not seem to belong anywhere. But O'Neill indubitably belongs at the Provincetown, at the Guild, in the suburbs of London, in Berlin, and in Little Theatres all over the English-speaking world. The man O'Neill is very close to a vast audience.

From *The Hound and Horn,* Vol. III (January–March, 1930), pp. 145–160. Reprinted by permission.

STARK YOUNG

American Drama in Production

MOURNING BECOMES ELECTRA
Eugene O'Neill[1]

[1931]

To HEAR the bare story, shortly told, of this new O'Neill play, with all its crimes and murders, may easily bring a flouting smile or recall Mrs. Malaprop's announcement of Sir Lucius' and Bob Acres' duel: "So, so, here's fine work, here's fine suicide, parricide, and simulation going on in the fields!" The same thing could be said of *Hamlet* or *King Lear* or *Oedipus King*, of course, but this is sure to be the line the jibes will take from such of the play's critics as are unfriendly or impatient or incapable. As to the length of the event, the actual performance at the Guild could be considerably shortened by going faster in many places; the length of the play itself is for the most part organic with both its meaning and its effect. As to the depressing effects of the play, we will come to that later.

The title, as we see, intends to dispose at the start of the relation of *Mourning Becomes Electra* to the Greek drama. The story of the house of Atreus was set down by Homer, Pindar, Aeschylus, Sophocles, Euripides and diverse Greek writers whose works are not extant. From this house shadowed by an ancient curse, Agamemnon, brother of Menelaus, goes forth to the war at Troy. His wife Clytaemnestra, the sister of Helen, during her husband's absence takes for her paramour Aegisthos and shares the government of Argos with him. In due time Agamemnon, having at the god's behest sacrificed his daughter Iphigenia and bringing with him Cassandra, Priam's daughter, returns, and is murdered by Clytaemnestra and her lover. Electra, his daughter, is shamed and degraded and prays for the return of her brother Orestes, long ago sent out of the country by his mother and now become a man. Orestes returns, kills Clytaemnestra and Aegisthos. He is pursued by the Erinyes, and only after wandering and agony and a vindication of himself before the tribunal of Athena's Areopagos is he cleansed of his sin.

[1] *Mourning Becomes Electra*, a trilogy: *Homecoming, The Hunted, The Haunted,* by Eugene O'Neill. Guild Theatre, New York City. October 26, 1931.

Mourning Becomes Electra begins with the mother and daughter, Christine and Lavinia, waiting, there in this house of the Mannons, the return of Ezra Mannon from the war, which with Lee's surrender is almost over. A thread of romance is introduced between, on the one side, Hazel and Peter, a brother and sister, and, on the other, the son, Orin, and Lavinia. Meanwhile Captain Brant comes to call; he pays a certain court to Lavinia, and she, acting on a cue from the hired man, who has been on the place these sixty years, traps him into admitting that he is the son of one of the Mannons who had seduced a Canadian maid-servant and been driven from home by his father, Lavinia's grandfather. She has all her data straight now. She has suspected her mother, followed her to New York, where Christine has pretended to go because of her own father's illness but has in fact been meeting Adam Brant. Lavinia has written her father and her brother, hinting at the town gossip about her mother. We learn that Captain Brant had returned to avenge his mother but instead had fallen passionately in love with Christine, who loves him as passionately as she hates her husband. From this point the play moves on, with the father's hatred of the son, who returns it, the son's adoration of his mother, the daughter's and the mother's antagonism, the daughter's and the father's devotion, to Christine's murder of her husband with the poison sent by Brant and substituted for the medicine prescribed against his heart trouble. Part One of the plays ends here. Orin returns, after an illness from a wound in the head. Christine tries to protect herself in her son's mind against the plots of Lavinia. Lavinia, in the room where her father's body lies, convinces Orin with the facts; they trail Christine to Brant's ship, where she has gone to warn him against Orin. Orin shoots Brant. Christine next day kills herself. Brother and sister take a long voyage to China, stop at the southern isles, come home again. Substitutions have taken place, Lavinia has grown like her mother, Orin more like his father. Meanwhile his old affair with Hazel, encouraged at last by Lavinia, who now wants to marry Peter, is canceled; he finds himself making an incestuous proposal to Lavinia and is repulsed by her. He shoots himself. In the end Lavinia, speaking words of love to Peter, finds Adam's name on her lips. She breaks with Peter, orders the blinds of her house nailed shut, and goes into the house, to live there till her death. Justice has been done, the Mannon dead will be there and she will be there.

So bare an account serves the plot a little, but can give scant indication of the direct speeches and actions heavily charged with the burden and meaning of the scenes; nor does it convey the power and direct arrangement of some of them, that, for example, of the brother and sister at Brant's cabin, where the mere visual elements convey as much as the words. The chanty with which this scene opens, the song and the singer's drunkenness, the lonely ship in the dusk, establishing as it does the mood of longing, futility, land chains and the sea's invitation and memory, is a fine idea and greatly enriches the scene's texture, though the performance did not fully establish the current or motive.

It will be obvious that the American dramatist, as the Greek did, used a well-known outline which he could fill in to his purpose. Obviously, too, Ezra Mannon is Agamemnon, Captain Brant Aegisthos, Christine Clytaemnestra, Lavinia Electra, and Orin Orestes. But to dismiss the matter by saying that Mr. O'Neill has merely repeated the classic story in modern terms is off the track. Let it go at that and you will miss even the really classic elements in the play and get only the Greek side of it that is self-evident and that would be easy for any dramatist.

The story itself follows the Greek plays up to the middle of the third division of the play, and here the incest motive, the death of Orin and the transference of the whole situation and dramatic conclusion to the sister depart from Aeschylus, Sophocles and Euripides. The blood motive in the lover, Adam Brant's relation to the family, is an addition. The old hired man, the confidant, parallels to some extent a Greek device, familiar to us, however, in countless plays. The townspeople and workmen are now and again a kind of chorus. Many of the shadings and themes are from the older plays; for an example, the servant's line in Aeschylus,

I see the dead are killing one who lives

which underlies one of the new play's main themes. The death of the lover, as in Aeschylus and Euripides, not as in Sophocles, comes before that of the mother, which throws the stress where the O'Neill play needs it. The division of the play into three parts is of course like the trilogy of the Greek dramatists. On the other hand, the dividing line is much less distinct in *Mourning Becomes Electra;* the final curtain of the first part, for example, falls, it is true, on Mannon's death, as in Aeschylus it does on Agamemnon's, but there is not the same effect of totality because of the stress put on Lavinia; in *Agamemnon* Electra does not even appear.

The magnificent theme that there is something in the dead that we cannot placate falsely is in the Greek plays and in the O'Neill play. The end of the play is by imaginative insight Greek in spirit: Lavinia goes into the house, the blinds are closed forever, the stage is silent, the door shut, the exaltation is there, the completion, the tragic certainty. Finally, the peculiar kind of suspense employed in the play is Greek. The playwright has learned the adult suspense of the classics as compared with the adolescent sense of it, hit off happily enough at times, that reigns in the romantic drama of the North. Classic suspense does not depend on a mere crude strain, wondering how things will turn out, however entertaining and often dramatic that effect may be. The classic suspense has even a biological defense: you know that in life you will come to death, but just how the course of all your living will shade and fulfill itself you do not know, and you are borne up by an animal will to survive, a passionate participation, an absorbed contemplation of the course, till the last moment completes itself. In the classic form where the outcome is already known, lies the highest order of suspense. Knowing how things will end, you are left free to watch what qualities and what light will appear in their progression toward their due and necessary finish. You hang on what development, what procession exactly of logic, ecstasy or fate, will ensue with them, what threads of beautiful or dark will come into their human fabric.

It is interesting in our confused and feministic epoch that this new employment of the theme gives the play to Electra. Nowhere in Greek does this happen. From Sophocles there survives what must be only a section of a trilogy, the *Electra;* and though so much of the torment and waiting has been hers, Electra is at the end let off with a betrothal to Orestes' faithful Horatio, Pylades, and the forebodings and remorse rise in Orestes only, who has struck the death blow on his mother. In Euripides' *Electra* the conclusion is the forebodings of Orestes and the marriage of Electra to Pylades; in his *Orestes* Electra cleaves to her brother, who is in a violent neurotic sickness, quite modernly indicated; they are both in danger from the State for their action, and the whole situation is solved with a trivial and silly dénouement, gods from the machine, killings and abductions, wholly undramatic and redeemed, in so far as it is redeemed, only by Euripides' dialectic and poetic glamor. In Aeschylus, Electra appears only in the middle of the trilogy; the central hero is the royal line, Agamemnon and Orestes.

Along with these more accessible and manifest likes and dislikes, there are numerous points about Mr. O'Neill's play that so far at least as the Greek original goes, are variations or additions. The most brilliant of these is the incest motive, coming toward the last of the play. (We must recall Shelley's remark that of all tragic motives incest is the most powerful, since it brings the passions most violently into play.) For Orestes the gray forms at the back, invisible at first to all but himself, are the Erinyes, the Furies who will avenge the crime he has committed within his own blood. They are the daughters of night, and when they have been appeased, their other selves, the Eumenides, the Gentle Ones, will pass by and leave him peace. For Orin Mannon there comes the sudden form of his desire: incest: the realization and admission of what it has all been about all along, his feelings toward his father, toward his mother, toward Brant, toward Lavinia. This recognition of his obsession is his avenging Erinyes. The mother in *Mourning Becomes Electra* is not killed by her son but takes her own life; his essential murder of his mother turns in his mind with a terror more modern but no less destroying; his mind storms with the Furies—"thoughts that accuse each other," as Cicero, writing in the sophistication of four centuries later, defined them. In such details alone might rest the argument that Eugene O'Neill, placing a Greek theme in the middle of the last century, has written the most modern of all his plays.

It is not wholly the Guild's fault if there is no overwhelming performance in *Mourning Becomes Electra*. The casting of such a play is very difficult, and doubly so in the absence of any training in our theatre that would prepare actors for the requirements of such parts. The best performances came in the scenes between the mother and son, where Mme. Nazimova's sense of theatre and her fluid response combined with Mr. Earle Larimore's simple and right attack on his part, were truly convincing, and in the scene between husband and wife, where Mr. Lee Baker gave a wholly right impersonation and the exact dramatic value for the play. Mr. Erskine Sanford turns out admirably in two character parts, the village doctor and the old workman who takes a bet on braving the ghost in the house. Miss Alice Brady had the rôle of all rôles in the play most difficult. Her performance of this modern Electra was sincere, and was sustained at times not only by a sort of tour-de-force achievement, but with real physical power, voice and all. In a few scenes she was pathetic as well, clear and moving, and her beauty most impressive. No doubt there was some instruction from the author himself as to keeping the face like a mask, rigid and motionless, as if fate itself were living there in this passionate and resolute being. As for the Greek of that intention, we must recall that in the Attic theatre the mask for Electra was very likely one of tortured lines, that the Greek theatre changed masks if need be from one scene to another, and that the Greek actor in the part could avail himself of gesture, dance movement, and a thorough training in voice, meter, speech, and singing. Realistically—that is to say in life—such rigidity never occurs except as a sign of disease. Esthetically it belongs only in the midst of a general stylistic whole, as in the Greek drama or the Chinese theatre that Mei Lan-fang brought to us. Technically it is immensely difficult, and derives not from an actual rigidity at all. Rigidity, masklike to the utmost, if you will, is a form of rhythm, as silence exists with a rhythm, when perceptible. It is unfair to bring so great an artist as Mei Lan-fang into the argument, but he gave us the whole model for such a problem in acting—the eyes constantly moving, the head imperceptibly in motion, supported by a complete and often almost invisible rhythm of the body, the emotions precise and compelling because of their very abstraction. Miss Brady's performance had several unforgetable moments. On the whole it moved gravely and in a manner remarkably well sustained just below the surface of the motives set for her by the dramatist; but her performance by failing both the darkness and the exaltation of the part often made only oppressive and unvaried what should have been burning and unconquerably alive and dominating. When we come right down to it, however, the best acting in the play is Mr. Earle Larimore's. In all his scenes up to the very last part, where he mouths too much and makes faces instead of a more intense concentration on his effects, he comes off first. In the scenes with his mother especially, he surpassed everybody else in the company; he conveyed to us the dramatist's meanings completely, without implying that the character himself was conscious of them; and by a certain emotional humility before the moment in which he shared, he came out securely right.

Out of Mr. Robert Edmond Jones' curtain and four settings, the rooms and the ship seem to me adequate without any haunting of the imagination, the front of the house dramatically right save for the lighting toward the rear, unnecessarily cruel to the actors. Mr. Philip Moeller's directing was admirable all through for its taste and evenness, its clear movement and fine placing of the scene. Its one fault was its tempo. There can be no doubt that Mr. O'Neill's play suffers greatly and will be accused of pretentiousness where it is wholly sincere and direct, in the first section especially, by the slowness with which the speeches are taken. Very often the effect is only that of a bourgeois respect for something to be taken as important. If it is the Greek spirit that is sought, the answer is that the Greek reading of lines was certainly formal but not necessarily slow; the chances are, in fact, that in the Greek theatre the cues were taken closely in order to keep the music going. And the Greeks had the advantage of music, dancing, and a great declamatory style, the lack of which will have to be balanced by anything rather than this obvious spacing and pausing and trend toward monotone, a great deal of which anyway proceeds only from a theoretical stage New England.

The two gifts that Eugene O'Neill up to now has displayed are for feeling and for dramatic image. His plays have often conveyed a poignancy that is unique in the modern drama, you felt that whatever was put down was at the dramatist's own expense, he paid out of himself as he went. His great theatre gift has been in the creation of images that speak for themselves, such for instance as the tittering of the Great Khan's ladies-in-waiting at the western Marco Polo, the dynamo in the play by the same name, and another, images so vivid that their mere repetition in people's talk makes the play sound better and more complete than it ever was. Sometimes this dramatic image spreads to the scope of a dramatic pattern that is the whole sum of the play. This happened not in more recent and elaborate plays, such as *Strange Interlude,* but in at least two of the earlier, *The Emperor Jones* and *The Hairy Ape,* where the whole plot was like an expanded sentence. In *Mourning Becomes Electra* Mr. O'Neill comes now into the full stretch of clear narrative design. He discovers that in expressive pattern lies the possibility of all that

parallels life, a form on which fall infinite shadings and details, as the light
with its inexhaustible nuances and elements appears on a wall. He has come
to what is so rare in Northern art, an understanding of repetition and variation on the same design, as contrasted with matter that is less deep or subtle,
though expressed with lively surprise, variety or novelty. It is a new and
definite state in his development.

None of the old tagging appears in this play, no scientific terms that can be
mistaken for psychological finalities. The feeling of Orin toward his father,
for example, or of the daughter toward him, is not labeled. They are motives
contrived to speak for themselves, and no specious explanation appears to be
offered. The lapses in taste, as regards the writing itself, the trite jargon or
the pushing of a situation to an obvious extreme, have vanished. The interest
in shocking the bourgeois, not always lacking hitherto, has matured into the
desire only to put in the truth. On the other hand the feeling remains. If not
always as lyric as before, it has spread out into a more impersonal and dis-
tributed but no less passionate element in the play. The novelties and causes,
masks, labor, sex, and asides, devices, are not in evidence, or rather have
moved inward whatever there was in them beyond sheer theatrical effectiveness. Through most of its length the play moves steadily. The uncertainty in
progression, comparative only, appears in the final scenes. This is a modern
difficulty, due to the fact that the matter turns inward, where the Greeks, in
contrast, had the advantage of robust and sure outward symbols, tribunals,
ceremonial processions, and the forms of music and dance.

As to the depressing element of *Mourning Becomes Electra,* I have only to
say that this play seems to me above anything else exhilarating. I trust I will
not be thought pedantic when I say that what depresses me in the theatre is
when the author dabbles in what is deep, enters where he has no right to be,
and is glib about what he does not even taste the savor of. I need take no
example, the stage is full of such. In *Mourning Becomes Electra* the end is
fulfilled; Lavinia follows her direction, the completion of herself and her own
inevitable satisfaction are seen. It may be that here life, as the Greek proverb
said, wails as to a tomb. There may be other ways to manage, Rotarian healthy
thoughts, exercise, good sense, saving the situation, leaving us more cheerful, marching on; but what of that? It is another situation that would be
saved. There is a line of Leopardi's where he speaks of "my delight and my
Erinyes"; and once, thinking of the eternal silence, he hears the wind among
the trees and goes comparing the infinite silence to that voice, and remembers
the eternal, and the dead seasons, and the present and living, and the sound of
it, *e il suon di lei.* In this immensity his thought drowns, and shipwreck is
sweet to him in such a sea. When the play ended, and the last Mannon was
gone into the house, the door shut, I felt in a full, lovely sense that the

Erinyes were appeased, and that the Eumenides, the Gentle Ones, passed over the stage.

From *The New Republic*, Vol. LXVIII (November 11, 1931), pp. 352–355. Reprinted by permission. Later included in Mr. Young's volume of dramatic essays and reviews, *Immortal Shadows* (Charles Scribner's Sons, 1948).

STREET SCENE

Elmer Rice[1]

[1929]

IN A dry season, when so many theatres are closed and not a few managers have given up the game for the nonce and gone off to sunny beaches and Hollywood, Mr. Elmer Rice's *Street Scene* has come to many people as a treat, an excellent play, a worthy entertainment; and there is no need to throw any blight over the flower of their enthusiasm. In the realm of the blind, following the Spanish proverb, let the one-eyed be king; we may cheer *Street Scene* and wish it well.

In a setting by Mr. Jo Mielziner, cleverly realistic without being foolishly so and photographic without idle intrusions of dusty neighborhood detail from Ninth Avenue, where the play is laid, we see the story unwind itself entertainingly, with an amiable pace and plenty of time for the talk of the apartment house people as they go in and out, with engaging colors drawn from the contact of diverse nationalities, Jews, Germans, Irish, Italians and 100 per cent Americans, and with a due complaisance and tidy willingness to please. There is a genuinely expert economy in the way in which the life of the Maurrant family is conveyed to us, and an economy of means that is even finer in the portrait of the wife's career, this doomed Anna Maurrant, whose husband is brutal and indifferent in his treatment of her, is given to drink, is full of principles and ideas of what a family should be and what his own has got to be, he'll see to that.

The inmates of the apartment house, then, go in and out, linger about the doorstep in the stifling summer heat, sit at their windows, gossip of their children and each other, of the little husband on the third floor who acts as if he were having the baby instead of his thin little wife, of the Hildebrand family whose head has disappeared and who are about to be dispossessed. And through the whole texture of conversation they weave the thread of this pale woman's tragedy on the second floor, the visits of the milk collector

[1] *Street Scene*, by Elmer Rice. The Playhouse Theater, New York City. January 10, 1929.

that they have all observed, the spreading scandal about Mrs. Maurrant. Idly and emptily they are doing her to death, but it is all a part of the day's chatter and the neighborhood news. We see Rose, her daughter, and the married suitor, who wants to take her from the job in his office and set her up in an apartment and a place on the stage; we see Maurrant himself, a member of the stage-hands' union, a drinker, sullen and bullying. Meanwhile, Mrs. Jones has something to say about everything, takes her husband, George, to task, and her dog, Queenie, to walk, and professes complete ease of mind about her children, one of whom is a hulking thug and the other almost a tart.

From that on, the play takes its course, clearly foreseen. The baby is born upstairs, Mrs. Maurrant tends the mother all night, she is even more brutally treated by her suspicious husband; he says he is going out of town with a show, her daughter is at the funeral of a member of the firm she works for, and Mrs. Maurrant asks the milk collector—cleverly portrayed by the author as by no means attractive and so more indicative of the woman's despair—to come up to her rooms. The husband returns, kills the lover, and mortally wounds the wife, and after a long search is caught by the police. Rose, his daughter, refuses the attentions of the married suitor, and at the last does not accept the love of the Jewish student; she goes away for her own life, with her own ideas about one's dependence on something within oneself and reflections on the history of her father and mother in the light of that theory.

All this time, as a kind of matrix for the story, people have been passing, an ingenious assemblage of types and interests, curiosities of the town, vignettes of Manhattan, incidents of a day, and so on and so on, rendered with an amiable and accurate diversity that carries matters pleasantly along. And in the apartment house itself the well-edited sayings of the different persons and races accompany this drab pageantry and sweet genre.

Mr. Rice's directing is good. Among the many players necessary for this *monde* of the West Side, Miss Mary Servoss, as the tragic central figure of the woman who is killed, gives a performance that is always convincing, and that, while she is on the stage, lifts the scenes to something like pathos and point. Miss Erin O'Brien Moore, as her daughter, Rose, has to surmount many platitudinous approaches to the character, and speeches that are without imagination or reality, but plays well; she presents a young image that our eyes easily believe in, and a sincere and simple rendering of the character, so far as is possible with the lines. She illustrates, however, one melancholy point that may as well be aired now as any other time, and this is in the matter of clothes. In play after play on Broadway, where there is a young creature whose muted life is in some factory, slum or dingy, tragic neighborhood, we see these young ladies whose rôles are leading ones—the other players may be as mussy as you like and as photographic as the actor or the author chooses

—walking about in their trim little frocks and perfect shoes, simple but smartly turned out, and, however modest, taking no chances at lessening the drawing power of their pretty looks. American girls, however poor, may have, if you like, a trick of looking smart, what with the sales and all, but there is a *chic* higher up and more costly that fools nobody with pretenses of humility, and it is the pale cast of this thought that makes so absurd the picture of these leading young ladies in drab plays; and makes us ponder the problem of sincerity in art. Miss Beulah Bondi's Mrs. Jones is excellent playing.

So much for *Street Scene,* then, which on one plane of consideration is pleasantly entertaining. On another plane, where you take the play seriously and where you ask yourself whether for an instant you have believed in any single bit of it, either as art, with its sting of surprise and creation, or as life, with its reality, *Street Scene* is only rubbish, or very close to rubbish. For me, who was not bored with it as an evening's theatre, it is something less than rubbish, theatrical rubbish, in that curious, baffling way that the stage provides. The presence of living beings in the rôles engages us, and gives a certain plausibility to whatever takes place, and a certain actuality to any character whatever. But is it possible that anyone who could understand the values of the first act of *Anna Christie,* for example, or a play of Chekhov's, could fail to see that the last act in *Street Scene*—to take the most evident letdown—is empty and made up? The girl has found her mother shot, seen blood, at the hospital she has seen her mother die without speaking, she has seen her father caught and torn and bleeding, the Jewish boy, who loves her so much, offers to leave everything and go away with her, and she stands there making a little speech about dependence on one's self, and so on and so on, while nurses with perambulators have appeared and various persons come prowling around at the scene of a murder, and the obvious life goes on, amusing remarks from odd characters, and the rest of it—obliging journalism in sum. It must be a very elementary principle that the essential idea of a work of art goes through it, and that the themes and conceptions to be expressed must lie inherently in the substance of it, and that they are to be expressed in creation, not in superimposed sentiments.

Must we gloomily conclude that what most human beings like in the theatre is a farrago of living matter with the sting taken out of it? If this Anna Maurrant's life and death really bit into us, cost us something, instead of providing a mere thrill and the comfort of pseudo-thought afterward, would we not wreck the stage for rage when we see how little this matter has stung the dramatist? One of the ways we know a work of art is by the cost of its unity in kind, in the same way that the soul within him, determining his form as he comes into the world, prevents a man's having the bulk, strength and peace of an elephant. One of the ways we can tell an artist is by the extent to which reality puts the fear of God into him; a painter of no worth will paint you anything from Napoleon crossing the Alps to an old mill in Vermont, but a real painter trembles before the mere character of human hands and the problem of their conversion into the unity that is his style. Is it any wonder that Ingres, in his despair at the success of the second-rate, threatened to paint an Allegory of Mediocrities?

On a milder level of discourse, we may say that the acting in *Street Scene* furnishes a good instance of one of the problems in the art. For the most part the company at the Playhouse is made up of people who fit the characters ready-made. An Italian plays an Italian, a Jewess a Jewess, and so on, though the roster of names is mostly shining Anglo-Saxon—but that is nothing new in the theatre. In the hurry and pressure of things there is little time to discover or train actors, perhaps; and perhaps the need for actuality in this particular piece led the casting toward these ready-made types. The result is that there is a good deal of entertainment in *Street Scene* that comes from watching these actual people as we might see them on Ninth Avenue, but very little interest in watching them as actors. They are mostly neither bad nor good. Their looks are better than their acting, and they seem better than what they say. As a minor by-product of the perplexity induced by such a situation, I have no idea whether the player written down as Mr. James M. Qualen, whose janitor, Olsen, seems to me the best performance of the evening, is only a Nordic of that ilk, chosen for his type, or a capital actor.

From *The New Republic*, Vol. LVII (January 30, 1929), pp. 296–298. Reprinted by permission.

WINTERSET

Maxwell Anderson[1]

[1935]

I HAD intended from the start to see Mr. Maxwell Anderson's *Winterset* again; and a second visit, as was always manifest, merely enlarges the first impression. The purpose of a work of art is to arouse our response to its content; the ideal means employed will be that which will bring forth the fullest of responses. In the case of *Winterset* the means is, of course, a poetic medium of expression. But there is also a list of characters unusually clear and firm in their outline, and raised far beyond the limits of our familiar stage. These varieties of character are further intensified, each in itself, so that they strike one against another at a high level, or on an intense plane. All

[1] *Winterset,* by Maxwell Anderson. Martin Beck Theatre, New York City. September 25, 1935.

these people are seen in a tremendous—and genuinely created—perspective: the judge haunted by a sentence he passed, the son of the victim haunted by his father's innocence, and divers others driven forward by forces within the years. This uncommonly strong element of perspective in the play relates it further, in some elusive sense, to the poetic medium. The alternating resistance and advance of metrical form appears doubly right in the conveyance of this check and impulse, memory and passion, fateful past and power of life, that the characters' lives proceed upon.

Discussion of the use of poetry in drama will always be likely to end in confusion. To some persons the mere term implies the great and deep, to others the soft and pretty. To some—this notion is more nearly ineradicable—great intellectual conceptions appear in prose; we go to poetry for a beautiful and moving expression of concepts already known to us. This is but partially true. The successful poetic expression of a concept is likely to be the first complete expression of it, since in such a case the concept in full is expressed in terms of the complete human being and the human being in terms of the concept. One of the great descriptions of poetry is Dante's saying that poetry is the loving use of wisdom. In praising the poetic style we must not say that our present American drama may be too austere or stark. The proper word is barren (or arid, or merely journalistic).

It gets nowhere to say, as Mr. Richard Watts, Jr., did in the *Herald Tribune* of a fortnight back, that "the state of dramatic poetry being what it is, the playwright who relies on the quality of his conception rather than on the turn of his phrases is most likely to qualify as a master of a great lyric mood." Conception is inseparable from expression. The playwright who relies on the turn of a phrase, except in so far as that phrase is organic and necessary to the conception, writes not only bad drama, he writes bad poetry. The defects in *Winterset*, in the last act especially, are not due to the fact that the poetic form is being employed, but rather to the fact that the poetry is bad, bad either *per se* or bad in relation to the scene—it comes to the same thing.

Mr. Watts says also that "recognized lyric forms are clearly no more adapted to the use of drama these days than they are to other types of current narrative and, since they were originally devised for other days, it is not easy to employ their archaic mannerisms in the service of authentic and convincing dramatic speech." You may almost as well say recognized human forms are with difficulty suited to acting. A poet-playwright will, naturally, in so far as he is successful, use only such poetic forms as express his content. But much of any content belongs to centuries, not decades. And recognized lyric forms do not necessarily imply archaic mannerisms.

"The last fifteen minutes of the play strike me as dull and unfortunate, chiefly because Mr. Anderson appears to be presenting a defeatist argument on behalf of the beauties of compromise in modern life, and although that message of his may have its practical virtues it does not exactly express a poetic subject." For my part, I thought merely that Mr. Anderson got himself rather far afield with some handsome semi-Irish-poetical, often extraneous and willful, lines and cadences, and thus crippled the effect. At any rate, it is true that there is no such thing as a non-poetic subject. The possibilities, near and far, of any subject will depend on the artist undertaking it. "I fear," says Mr. Watts, of the last quarter-hour, "that the slightly muddy confusion of the play's ideas may hurt the poetic drama in so far as it suggests that lyricism and hard-headed contemplation have difficulty in getting along together in the theatre." Suggesting difficulty in art hurts nothing; it intimidates fools; it raises the level of the enterprise.

Whatever confusion there may be does not arise from lyricism and contemplation finding it hard to get along together in the theatre; the confusion arises from the writing not having absorbed or expressed the thought with completeness sufficient to include the writer's full self, brain, emotions, and so on. As a matter of fact, all theatrical expression of thought includes immediately a certain lyricism. Contemplation in itself—if there be such a thing —will not project itself into the audience. Nor will the audience contemplate what it can acquire no feeling for.

Speaking practically, on our American theatre's behalf, the greatest compliment we could pay a poetic play is to say it does no harm to poetic drama's chances. In spite of its defects, and in spite of the threats in the last act to do so, *Winterset* does not harm the cause of poetic drama. In its best moments we are aware of the poetic medium only as a matter of heightened respiration on our part. The lines hint of intensified feeling and thought, and of words with all the emphasis of passionate life repeated. At its worst we have only verses that are sucking a sugar-teat in the Muses' nursery. In such of Mr. Anderson's verse the images appear to be a hangover of the period when Stephen Phillips' cadences were petals of blown roses on the grass. In such cases, Mr. Anderson, both as poet and playwright, needs to get away, not so much from traditional forms in poetry as from a merely traditional use of them regardless of their content.

It is true, of course, that on Broadway one must be completely successful, tossing off with facility what the greatest artists might retreat from in despair. *Winterset* is fair enough melodrama at bottom, which is saying a good deal. Why should we expect, also, that a playwright should, almost single-handed, produce a completely successful poetic drama? I should rather say that *Winterset* is not only and easily the most important play of this season, but also the most notable effort in the poetic dramatic medium that up to now we have had in the American theatre.

From *The New Republic*, Vol. LXXXIV (November 6, 1935), p. 365. Reprinted by permission.

JOSEPH WOOD KRUTCH
Two American Playwrights

THE AUSTERITY OF GEORGE KELLY

[1933]

GEORGE KELLY is something of an anomaly in the contemporary theatre. Two of his plays have enjoyed phenomenal runs on Broadway and one of the two won the Pulitzer prize besides. Yet neither of these is as characteristic of the author as others less successful, and it would not be rash to wager that neither is as close to Mr. Kelly's own heart as one or two which the public has classed as failures. Both of his "hits"—*The Show-Off* and *Craig's Wife*— richly deserved their popularity. Both were soundly constructed and both were based upon shrewd and honest observation, but each had, in addition, the advantage of belonging to a familiar and popular genre. The first, with a blustering Babbitt for a hero, was a recognizable addition to the growing literature of native satire. The second, which drew at full length the portrait of a hard woman in whom the virtue of being a good housekeeper had become a vice, was typically "modern" in a slightly different way. It illustrated admirably that tendency to "transvaluate values" which Ibsen had introduced into the theatre and which, in a somewhat popularized form, one will discover in such typical plays of the recent past as *The Silver Cord* and *Rain*. No wonder that Mr. Kelly was set down as a dramatist working in a current tradition and sufficiently of Broadway to find ready acceptance. No wonder, also, that his public was somewhat *froissé* by the increasing bitterness of *Daisy Mayme* or that it should have been frankly bewildered by the almost mystical tone of *Behold the Bridegroom*. Mr. Kelly refused to stay put and was determined to accentuate those aspects of his attitude which were the least familiar and the least acceptable to his audience. He was saying with a calm and cold emphasis: "Make no mistake. I am not of Broadway."

With his latest work in mind it is easy to look back over the earlier plays and to catch in their text ominous hints of this more stern and acrid tone. Even in *The Show-Off* there are moments when a certain unexpected bitterness rises momentarily to the surface, as when, for example, the harassed

535

mother hears the remark that her daughter must lie on the bed she has made
and replies quite simply: "It's often not the people who make the beds who
have to lie on them. It's someone else." A few moments later the observation
has been forgotten in the flow of pure fun, but for an instant there has found
expression something in the author which would be cynicism if it were not
too sternly moralistic to be quite that. Indeed, the whole character of this
mother adds to the play an element quite foreign to its dominant tone, for
she is a sort of chorus supplying disillusioned comment, prophesying woe,
and refusing to enter fully into the easy joy of the rest when good fortune
solves all their difficulties.

Even more significant is the one-act play, *Smarty's Party,* written long before, during the five years when Mr. Kelly was appearing in vaudeville in
playlets of his own composition. Here the story is that of a vulgar adventuress
who entangles a young man supposed to be very wealthy, who comes to his
supposed mother to enjoy her moment of triumph, and who then is crushed
with the information that her victim is not really that woman's son at all.
Here Mr. Kelly first delineates with cruel expertness the vulgarity of the adventuress and then, with a kind of savage delight, destroys her utterly. Thus
the pattern of the play is exactly the same as the pattern of *Craig's Wife,*
where another evil woman is analyzed at full length before the author, with
an almost sadistic fury, plunges her into a special circle of hell so arranged
that her vice will constitute the means by which she is tortured. The heroine
of *Smarty's Party* wanted money and got poverty; Craig's wife loved her
home so much that she found herself homeless at last.

One cannot help observing that Mr. Kelly's three most bitterly excoriated
characters—namely, the two just mentioned and one to be discussed later—
are all women. There is in him, therefore, a strain of what one is tempted
to call misogyny, but it is not certain that the term would be exactly accurate.
He does not seem to be saying that women as a sex are worse than men. He
is only saying instead, "Lilies that fester smell far worse than weeds," and the
key to his temperament is a particular kind of austerity which goes commonly
under the name of puritanism. Vulgarity offends him, not only esthetically
but morally as well, and the kind of meanness which he sees most commonly
in men and women strikes him always as a sort of vulgarity of the soul. He
despises it with a certain cold fury, and his desire is the puritanical desire to
see a crushing justice meted out to it. Others may feel that to understand all
is to pardon all, but to the puritan that saying is incomprehensible nonsense.
To understand all is to hate all—if that "all" be hateful. Each of his most
striking heroine-victims is understood with a cruel clarity, but none is pardoned and none, be it noted also, is reformed and then rewarded. All three
are cast out instead into outer—and utter—darkness.

It was *Craig's Wife* produced in October, 1925, which won the Pulitzer prize. The next year Kelly produced without great success another acrid study of family life called *Daisy Mayme*, but it is *Behold the Bridegroom* (1928) which represents Mr. Kelly's most determined and most nearly successful effort to break completely away from the themes and methods of the contemporary stage in order to give full expression to his underlying attitude.

All of Mr. Kelly's other plays are richly overlaid with local color. The immediate effectiveness of all depends in large part upon skillful mimicry and upon the literal realism with which he pictures middle-class American life. Here, however, he departs from his accustomed milieu. Manners are more elegant, characters more self-consciously analytic, and the whole style is more formally literary. But the effect is only to disengage more completely the essential moral problem and to make the discussion of it quite clearly the only *raison d'être* of the play. Again the hero—if she can be called that—is a woman, but this time her sin is that vulgarity which results from the indulgence of a too facile and too shallow emotional nature. She is smart, sophisticated, and charming. She has moved gracefully from one love affair to another and thinks that she has demonstrated by her success how completely the intelligence may dispense with those simple rules of puritan morality which are never far from Mr. Kelly's mind. But the moment comes when she realizes that she really loves for the first time in her life. And her creator seizes the opportunity to destroy her as he had destroyed Craig's wife. She looks into the bridegroom's eyes, reads there his contempt, and then dies, not so much because of that contempt as because she has realized at last her own emptiness.

Probably most persons were made a little uncomfortable by the mercilessness with which justice was visited upon Mr. Kelly's earlier heroines. Some have even suggested that a more knowing playwright would not have pushed retribution so far as to swing the sympathy of the audience round in the direction of its victim. But it is no mere dramaturgic mistake which is responsible for Mr. Kelly's relentlessness either in the case of *Craig's Wife* or in the case of *Behold the Bridegroom*. He must have known very well that the public would not judge the heroine of the latter play so harshly as he did, that there is, as a matter of fact, no sin which this public is more ready to forgive—in fiction at least—than the sin of light love. Indeed, the romantic-sentimental tradition makes it almost the necessary prelude to a grand passion. But Mr. Kelly would not compromise here with his puritan conscience or make any effort to hide his contempt for contemporary morality. His heroine had wasted her capacities on cheap loves, she was not ready when the bridegroom came, and she had forfeited all right to the thing whose value she had come to understand only when it was too late. Hence she awakes, not to be saved, but only in order that she may realize what she has lost. Only thus can the puritan sense of justice be served, for the damned must be given one glimpse of paradise before they are plunged into hell forever.

No other play by Mr. Kelly—indeed, few contemporary plays by any author whatsoever—has, in certain respects, a finer literary quality than this one has. There is a passionate sincerity in the conception and a beautiful clarity in the dialogue which raise it far above the level of merely successful dramatic writing. The author seems to be struggling to free himself from the limitations of mere naturalism, and very nearly succeeds, by his passion and his coherence, in raising it to the level of quasi-poetic tragedy. Yet the fact remains that the play was commercially a failure and, what is more important, that all the respect which one feels for it does not prevent certain objections from arising in the mind of either the spectator or the reader.

One is, to put it briefly, neither quite convinced nor quite sure that one ought to be. "Men have died from time to time and worms have eaten them, but not for love." This we have upon the authority of one of Shakespeare's heroines, and it may be urged against the conclusion which Mr. Kelly has given to his play, but the most serious of my doubts are not of this naturalistic kind. I can accept the physical features of his conclusion and I can respect the moral sincerity which has enabled him to develop an almost pietistic thesis without falling into mere priggishness on the one hand or into rant on the other, but I honestly doubt that nature is constructed upon any plan so in accord with a puritan sense of moral fitness. Perhaps a spoiled and empty woman should die of self-contempt when she sees herself; perhaps she should feel herself forever unworthy of love if she chances at last to meet it; but I doubt that she would actually feel so or that there is anything to be gained by trying to make her. We forgive ourselves more easily and it is as well that we should. Artists and moralists both love to contemplate the irreparable—it helps the one to be dramatic and it helps the other to satisfy his sense of justice. But nature is more compliant. Time cannot be called back, and what has been physically destroyed cannot be found again, but nothing else is irretrievably lost and there are no sins that ought not and cannot be forgiven.

Mr. Kelly has been silent since he produced *Maggie the Magnificent* in November, 1929.[1] In this latest of his plays he returned to the middle-class milieu and the more realistic manner. But here again he is concerned with integrity of character as it is brought out in the contrast between the disorderly soul of an uncultivated mother and the efficient determination of a daughter who lifts herself by her own efforts above the vulgarity amidst

---

[1] A new play, *Reflected Glory,* was produced in 1936; another, *The Deep Mrs. Sykes,* in 1945; a third, *The Fatal Weakness,* in 1946. George Kelly's principal earlier plays were produced as follows: *The Torchbearers* in 1921, *The Show-Off* in 1923, *Craig's Wife* in 1925, *Daisy Mayme* in 1926, *Behold the Bridegroom* in 1927, *Maggie the Magnificent* in 1929, *Philip Goes Forth* in 1931. (Editor's note, 1950.)

which she grew up. But Mr. Kelly seems incapable of making either men or women as likable as they ought to be. There is in the characters whom he admires something stiff and prim and priggish which chills the beholder and seems to suggest that the author hates what is cheap and common with such an all-absorbing fury that he has become incapable of exercising his critical judgment upon anyone who escapes the one vice he cannot forgive. The "bridegroom" in the previous play was not intended to be repellently self-righteous, but there was a suggestion of repellent self-righteousness in him. Similarly, the Maggie of this piece is actually a good deal less than magnificent. She is neat, orderly, assured, decent, and correct, but only Mr. Kelly would admire her with warmth. We are expected to feel in her an austere nobility, but we actually feel a kind of spinsterish frigidity, and we cannot rejoice as we should in her triumph because we cannot sympathize warmly enough with her essentially negative aspirations.

This suggests, I think, the key to the mystery surrounding the fact that Mr. Kelly's most characteristic and most seriously meant plays do not quite achieve the success that they seem at times about to reach. There is a touch of coldness in his nature, a certain stubborn negativeness in his moral attitude, which lays a blight upon his plays. Essentially they are rather dour and frost-bitten, rather bleak at the very moments when a grave beauty ought to emerge. He wants, like Milton, to express the grandeur of puritanism, but he is somehow earthbound and cannot entirely escape from a certain unlovely rigidity. There is too much realism, too much prose, where a kind of ecstasy is called for. When a puritan is also a poet, the result can be magnificent, but Mr. Kelly is not quite poet enough. He commands respect but he cannot quite inspire a genuine enthusiasm.

From *The Nation*, Vol. CXXXVII (August 30, 1933), pp. 240–242. Reprinted by permission of the author.

THE DRAMATIC VARIETY OF SIDNEY HOWARD

[1933]

THE theatrical season which began in the fall of 1924 was made remarkable by the appearance of two very original plays from the pens of little-known playwrights. The first was *What Price Glory?* by the Messrs. Anderson and Stallings, the other *They Knew What They Wanted,* by Sidney Howard. In many respects the two were different enough, but they were commonly mentioned together for the very good reason that they were the first thoroughly successful efforts to express in dramatic form a realistic attitude marked by certain novel features. All three of the authors were fresh from their experiences in the Great War, and the fact may very well have had something to do with the tone of the plays, but the best way to describe them would be, perhaps, to say that both were essentially serious without being in the slightest degree "high-brow."

This in itself was a kind of novelty. The "new American drama" written by the "experimental playwrights" who had grown up around the Provincetown Playhouse and the Washington Square Company had been very self-conscious and very much under foreign influences. Sometimes it tended to be a kind of neo-Ibsen problem play, sometimes it was "arty" in much less substantial ways, but it was very much inclined to think of itself as a thing apart, as the product of a "movement" if not actually of a cult. Mr. Howard, on the other hand, had somehow managed to escape from all that. The Theatre Guild produced his play for a general public which found it highly acceptable, and one way to define the fact that he was a new kind of "new playwright" would be to say that he was writing for the commercial theatre. But to say that is to imply something much more important than the fact itself. It is to imply that he had thoroughly assimilated the attitude of the generation which had been busy rebelling against the long lingering Victorianism of our theatre, and that, without arguing or explaining, he could assume it as the point of view from which men and women were to be presented. The "new drama" had lost its self-conscious newness. It was taking itself and asking that it be taken as a matter of course.

Underlying the play was a moral attitude which a Victorian would certainly have found incomprehensible and which an anti-Victorian would certainly have made it his chief business to expound. The heroine is the mother of an illegitimate child conceived on the eve of her marriage to a kindly old man whom she does not love; the hero is this kindly old man, who discovers the wrong which has been done him but who ends by accepting the child because a child was what he really wanted. What an opportunity—entirely neglected by Mr. Howard—to expound a paradoxical morality, to define Love, to explain the Case for the Unmarried Mother, and, in general, épater les bourgeois! But the explanation supplied by Mr. Howard for these events is not intellectual at all. They become understandable and acceptable purely in terms of the characters; convincing and satisfactory as a series of concrete situations which work themselves out in that way. The play, in other words, is not a play about ideas but a play about men and women, and the same may be said of all its author's best work. Behind that work may of necessity lie a point of view and a philosophy; but the concrete situation and the concrete persons who find themselves in it always come first. They are not invented to illustrate a thesis. The thesis, if any, is discovered by the audience—and I suspect by the author as well—by contemplating them.

They Knew What They Wanted was Mr. Howard's third play. He had come from California and the University of California to spend one year in Professor Baker's class. After that he had served in the ambulance corps on the western front during the early days of the war and as a captain in the flying service after the United States became involved. He had also collaborated on a book of reporting, *The Labor Spy,* and produced *Swords* (1922) and *Bewitched* (1924)—the latter in collaboration with Edward Sheldon. The first of these plays was a romantic melodrama with more than a suggestion of pastiche; the second a romance rather poetic than realistic. Both achieved a certain *succès d'estime* without attracting any large audience, and both were apprentice work for a man who found himself as a dramatist in *They Knew What They Wanted.*

Since the latter was produced—and won the Pulitzer prize—Mr. Howard has had nine plays on Broadway. The themes of the nine show a variety which would probably be impossible for a playwright who did not, like him, find his inspiration in the concrete situation, and they have met a variety of fates—ranging all the way from flat failure like that which attended *Half Gods* to the triumphant success won by *Ned McCobb's Daughter* (1926), *The Silver Cord* (1926), and *The Late Christopher Bean* (1932). In the meanwhile he has also found time for a very successful career as a writer in Hollywood, and, as an active member of the Willard Straight Post of the American Legion, to help that post be a thorn in the side of the national organization.[1]

All this suggests the energy and vigor which are so characteristic of his work. Being enthusiastic and impulsive rather than primarily reflective, he is both prolific and not the best judge of his own work. Indeed, the public has been more right than he, and his finest plays since his first success have been the other successes, *Ned McCobb's Daughter, The Silver Cord,* and *The Late Christopher Bean.* Moreover, each is, despite the variety of moods and materials, like *They Knew What They Wanted* in that the author has devoted himself in each to the task of presenting concrete situations and concrete characters. He has, to be sure, a conspicuous gift for achieving a clear, straightforward dramatic construction; he has also been lucky in having a series of excellent actors—Pauline Lord, Richard Bennett, Alfred Lunt, Laura Hope Crewes, and Walter Connolly—for his best pieces. But essentially their effectiveness has been due to the fact that they were less comments on contemporary life than presentations of it. One never knows what Mr. How-

---

[1] Sidney Howard died on August 23, 1939. His principal plays were: *Swords* (1921), *They Knew What They Wanted* (1925), *Lucky Sam McCarver* (1926), *Ned McCobb's Daughter* (1926), *The Silver Cord* (1927), *Half Gods* (1930), *Alien Corn* (1933), *The Late Christopher Bean* (after René Fauchois, 1933), *Dodsworth* (after Sinclair Lewis, 1934), *Yellow Jack* (with Paul de Kruif, 1934), *Paths of Glory* (after Humphrey Cobb, 1935), *The Ghost of Yankee Doodle* (1938). (Editor's note, 1950.)

ard is going to say. With him, one sometimes feels, a conviction is an enthusiasm and, like any other enthusiasm, likely to disappear as soon as it has emerged. But one is always sure that the situations will be dramatic, the characters vivid, and the motives understandable.

The Silver Cord is the only one of his plays which develops in accordance with a rationalistic formula. It deals quite explicitly with a mother complex, and the most dogmatic Freudian would find nothing to disagree with. Yet Mr. Howard is known to have quarreled violently with the Theatre Guild because its directors insisted upon discussing it in Freudian terms, and the fact is significant of his temperamental antipathy to intellectual formulas, of his impatience with anybody's ideas even though they happen to be also his own. Last year he was one of those writers who signed the manifesto in favor of William Z. Foster. Put that fact alongside the further facts that he rushed into the war as soon as possible and then, once it was over, helped organize the obstreperous Willard Straight Post of the American Legion. Together they give you the picture of a man who loves a row, or, rather, who loves a joyous participation in dramatic events. That also is the man who writes the plays. In them the clash of creeds and temperaments interests him for his own sake. He can take sides enthusiastically but he can also change them. He is, whether he knows it or not, pretty certain to be on the side most likely to precipitate a dramatic crisis and pretty likely, in his plays, to see to it that one takes place. Being also a man of intelligence, his attitude is usually intelligible and his crisis significant. But it is the happening which interests him and the happening which interests his audience.

Under the circumstances it would obviously be useless to inquire what his leading ideas are. He is not, like Mr. Kelly, primarily a moralist. Neither is he, like Mr. O'Neill, a writer of tragedy, nor, like Mr. Behrman, a consistent writer of comedy. He can expound Freudianism in The Silver Cord, approach tragedy in They Knew What They Wanted, declaim rather intemperately in Half Gods, and achieve a serene comedy in The Late Christopher Bean. But none is more characteristic of him than the rest. Neither is there anything common to them all except the vigor of the characterization plus a certain robust delight in the conflict for its own sake. Their unity, therefore, is only the unity of a temperament, and the only way to describe what kind of plays Mr. Howard writes is to describe what sort of man he reveals himself to be.

To witness one of his plays is to experience the same sort of exhilarating pleasure that one gets from the society of an active man with quick and vigorous perceptions. One is plunged at once into a series of happenings and made to share the wholehearted interest of a writer who throws himself into everything with an unreserved enthusiasm. The characters are observed with extraordinary intentness and set down in sharp bold strokes. Something of the author's own decisiveness is communicated to them, and the dialogue has something of the crisp clarity of his own speech. Subtlety of a kind is by no means absent and poetry of a kind is also present. But the subtlety does not exhibit itself as hair-splitting and the poetry is neither rhapsodical nor dreamy. The men and women are plain people with their feet on the ground; the scene, some very definite corner of our particular America. Obviously Mr. Howard hates any sort of artistic pretentiousness as much as he hates intellectual dogmas. He is determined to exercise his subtlety in the accurate observation of familiar things, to find his poetry in the loves and hates of people who may be distinguished by the strength and the clarity of their passions but who remain, nevertheless, essentially familiar types.

His is, therefore, a daylight world, in which common sense is still the standard by which everything is judged. An epigram may flash forth here and there, but in no other way does he ever permit himself to approach a conventionally literary style. There are no Orphic utterances, no purple patches, no evocation of what the more esoteric devotees of the drama call "moods." Nothing ever eludes the spectator, nothing ever seems vaguely to mean more than it says. But what it does unmistakably say is enough for anyone capable of sharing Mr. Howard's very active pleasure in straightforward passions and straightforward events. His plays are not highbrow plays because their author is not a highbrow, and they teach no doctrine because he is not a doctrinaire. Essentially tough-minded, he is interested in facts and out of them he builds his plays. It is for that reason, no doubt, that the captain of aviation never wrote a patriotic play nor the supporter of Mr. Foster a communistic one. He took part in a war and some day he may, conceivably, help along a revolution. But it would be safe to wager that he will never either preach loyalty to the flag or write a treatise on dialectic materialism.

Writers who are intelligent without being "intellectual," and artistic without being in any sense "arty," frequently get from critics somewhat less consideration than they deserve. They are too clear to require explaining and too popular to need defense. Your critic, accordingly, all too frequently prefers to discourse at more length upon the merits of those persons whose excellences are less evident. But the fact remains that Mr. Howard's plays are among the best ever written in America. They have, in addition, probably had more influence upon dramatic writing than can ever be directly measured. Mr. Howard stands very near to the head of the list of those who rescued the popular drama from that sentimentality which for some reason continued to be considered indispensable there long after it had disappeared from most serious writing in other forms.

From *The Nation*, Vol. CXXXVII (September 13, 1933), pp. 294–295. Reprinted by permission of the author.

NEWTON ARVIN
Individualism and the American Writer
[1931]

THE artist, it cannot be too clearly understood," says Arthur Symons in his book on the symbolist movement, "has no more part in society than a monk in domestic life." The dogma of literary individualism has never been phrased more simply or more grotesquely; and, as Mr. Symons belongs to a generation now pretty completely superseded, it is no longer fashionable to say the thing in just these terms, or to appeal to such authority as his for support. But the spirit behind his epigram is a spirit that still operates not only in British but in American letters. Even sentimental estheticism, though the cut of its clothes is no longer in the mode of the nineties, has by no means disappeared; and, on a less fatuous level, the doctrine of irresponsibility—in more forms than one, of course—is virtually the prevailing gospel. The breach between our writers and our society could hardly be wider: one gets a measure of it by trying to imagine a contemporary poet or novelist of distinction occupying the kind of official post—an ambassadorship, a professorship, the editorship of a prosperous magazine or newspaper—which, fifty and sixty years ago, was one of the natural rewards of literary celebrity. This sort of thing is now a joke, and a stale joke at that. Yet there is intrinsically nothing funny in the conception of a writer's rôle in society as responsible to the point of officialdom; and many things are more unlikely than that we shall return to it in the course of events. Meanwhile, and for excellent reasons, the literary life in America is the scene of a sweeping separatism: the typical American writer is as tightly shut up in his own domain, and as jealous of his prerogatives, as one of the Free Cities of the late Middle Ages. Is this in the very nature of things, or is it a passing circumstance?

To ask such a question is to go, at once, below or beyond the purely literary terrain. It is to pose the whole problem of individuality and its life history. But it is to pose the problem in a form to which writers neither *as* writers nor as human beings can afford to be indifferent. There is really no more acute, no more concrete, no more pressingly personal a problem, at the moment, than this. Is our familiar individualism, our conception of ourselves as "simple, separate persons," equivalent any longer to the achievement of a sound individuality? "Trust thyself": does every heart still vibrate to that "iron

544

string"? Specifically, can American writers hope to develop fully as individuals while divorcing themselves not only from society as a whole but from any class or group within society? With what group or class, indeed, *can* they ally themselves? Is the alternative to literary individualism the surrender to a merely political movement, or, worse still, to some form of repressive standardization? Are there now no supra-personal purposes with which a writer can affiliate himself?

Our answers to such questions will be really satisfactory only if, in giving them, we are able to look back upon the road we have come on. For the story of American letters is the story of the blossoming, the fruition, and the corruption of exactly the individualism that is now on trial. It is far from being a new thing: it is a many times more than twice-told tale. In its origins it was a fruitful principle because it corresponded to a historical reality, to a historical reality that is now part of our past. In short, American writers have always belonged to the middle class, and not only in the literal sense of being born in it: they have belonged to the middle class spiritually, and their self-reliance, their self-expression, their self-consciousness have expressed the sociological individualism of their class heritage. It is no accident that, emblematically at least, at the very gateway of American literature should stand two autobiographies: no accident that Jonathan Edwards should have written his "Personal Narrative" or Franklin the story of his life. Nothing was more natural than that Edwards and Franklin should have taken themselves as subjects; between them, they span the whole reach, upward and downward, of the individualist principle; they are the sacred and profane extremes of one spirit— Edwards, with his Calvinistic particularism, his intense introspectiveness, his spiritual egoism; Franklin, with his complete system of self-help, his enlightened careerism, his pragmatic worship of frugality and diligence. Neither man can be imagined in a precapitalist order. Only one essential note in our national chorus remained to be struck, and that was the secessionist note of the frontier; when Fenimore Cooper created the character of Leatherstocking, the embodiment of backwoods resourcefulness, independence, and idiosyncracy, the ensemble was complete.

Complete, that is, psychologically. In a literary sense, American individualism was not to reach its apogee until the generation which filled in the twenty or thirty years before the Civil War. These years witnessed, from a cultural point of view, the historic culmination of the principle of self-reliance: during these years that principle, because it rationalized the true needs of society, had a genuine spiritual authority. It was a period, in short, when our special form of individualism could really be reconciled with the deeper-lying claims of individuality; when a man could achieve distinction as a person without going much beyond the limits of self-reliance. This is, of course, what accounts for the literary pre-eminence, in the age, of Emerson ("Accept your genius and say what you think"), of Thoreau ("I would rather sit on a pumpkin and have it all to myself than be crowded on a velvet cushion"), and of Whitman ("I will effuse egotism"). In these three men our individualism, on its brighter side, attained its classic meridian. There was of course, even then, a darker side; there were men for whom the gospel of self-help—or the habit of estrangement, which is a form it may always take—proved to be the path toward confusion, morbidity, and a kind of impotence; and Poe, Hawthorne, and Melville, men of the richest endowments, paid a tragic price for sitting on pumpkins and effusing egotism. Their careers suggest that the principle, from the artist's point of view, is at best a precarious one; and that its spiritual fruitfulness is exhausted almost before it is realized.

The sequel of the Civil War demonstrated the exhaustion at least of its youthful energies. The triumph of economic irresponsibility, in the feverish burgeoning of big business after the war, coincided with the corruption of individualism as a cultural motive. Two things happened: on the one hand, the writers of secondary talents watered down and deodorized the old contumacy until it became reconcilable with the mildest heresies and even with a conformity in which neither self-reliance nor self-expression had breathing-space; on the other hand, the writers of genius, incapable of such surrender, went still farther along the path taken by Poe, Hawthorne, and Melville. To turn from Emerson to G. W. Curtis, from Thoreau to John Muir, from Whitman to Burroughs, is to turn, as if in a single life-span, from Moses to Zedekiah. The contrast is instructive enough, yet it is less eloquent than the spectacle offered by the higher careers of Henry James, Mark Twain, and Henry Adams. Hawthorne's theme of estrangement, the Ishmaelite theme that obsessed Melville, were driven by Henry James to a formulation still more extreme; and expatriation, the frankest form of desertion, became both his literary munition and his personal fate. With Mark Twain the Fenimore Cooper wheel came full circle: the old, heroic anarchism of the backwoods is travestied, in its decay, by Mark Twain's vacillation between a servile conformity and the puerile philosophy of self-interest outlined in "What Is Man?" ("From his cradle to his grave a man never does a single thing which has any *first and foremost* object but one—to secure peace of mind, spiritual comfort *for himself*.") For Mark Twain the outcome was, not Emerson's and Whitman's "fatalistic optimism," but an equally fatalistic pessimism; and Henry Adams, who had a truer sense of the limits of self-interest, but whose social impotence and personal isolation were still more thoroughgoing, stands very close to Mark Twain as our first consistent preacher of futility.

II

By the turn of the century the old class basis of American literature was rapidly entering upon the cycle of erosion, subsidence, and re-emergence. It was still true that American writers belonged personally to the middle classes, but the old bond between literary expression and the middle-class philosophy had been broken once for all; and henceforth there seemed to be only the choice between a loyalism that was the negation of individuality and a repudiation that too generally left its heresiarchs high and dry. For a fresh alignment of a positive sort the time was not yet ripe; and by the second decade of the century we found ourselves in the midst of an individualistic revolt which superficially seemed to appeal to the authority of Emerson, Thoreau, and Whitman, but which, unlike theirs, was radically personal and anti-social. It had been anticipated, a few years before, by the Nietzschean egoism of Jack London and the antinomianism of Dreiser; and it was to mingle the elements of misanthropy, transcendentalism, anarchism, and high aspiration in bewildering proportions. The new individualism ran the whole gamut from the Menckenian-Cabellian praise of aristocracy to Anderson's primitivism and O'Neill's romantic affirmations, from Lewis' exposure of the standardized bourgeois to Van Wyck Brooks' subtle studies in frustration. In the perspective of history, the high colors in which this generation dealt will doubtless show like the hues in the clouds that surround a setting sun. It was the last chapter of one volume, not the first of a new one; and of this essential belatedness the patriarchal gravity, the chilly sagacity of such poets as Robinson and Frost are but convenient measures.

The vitality of that movement was naturally still shorter-lived than the "Emersonian June" itself had been. The hopeless sterility of a pure individualism at this moment in history could hardly be more dramatically demonstrated than by the collapse of the Menckenian boom in our own "reconstruction" after the war. The men who led it, of course, still survive, but they have subsided either into silence or into a bewilderment that masks itself variously; and their juniors, for the most part, have drawn the moral from their experience in either one of two disastrous but natural ways. One group, the heirs of Poe, Hawthorne, and Melville, have retreated, in their despair of finding solid ground on which to build a personal life, to an explicit philosophy of negation; and pitched here and there on the sands of the Waste Land one descries the tents, black as Tamburlaine's on the third day of a siege, of Jeffers and MacLeish, of Krutch and Aiken, of Hemingway and Faulkner. The other group, less honest emotionally, but intellectually more impressive, has taken refuge from the high winds of individualism in the shelter of some archaic code, religious, authoritarian, or sociological: humanism, neo-Thomism, Alexandrianism, royalism, or agrarianism. Both the negativists and the authoritarians betray all the symptoms of corruption: both shine with the phosphorescence of decay; but the latter have at least the logic that goes with positive loyalties.

For the necessary answers to the questions we began with are becoming clearer and clearer to middle-class intellectuals; they have long been clear to our handful of working-class writers. That it is not possible for a writer to develop a rich individuality and remain loyal to an individualist society in its later stages—this was the discovery of the Menckenian generation. All questions of humanitarian sentiment aside, that generation discovered that to co-operate with an inhumane system is to be personally corrupted and demoralized. The experience of the last decade has shown, though the proof was hardly needed, that mere nonconformity leads nowhere but to barrenness. If individuality means anything, as distinguished from individualism, it means the achievement, personally, of a many-sided unity, a rich and complicated integration; and in an individualistic economy it is not possible for anyone, certainly not for a writer, either to develop freely on all sides or to unify his personal life in the only fruitful way—that is, by organizing it with reference to a significant purpose. It is the paradox of individuality that it is meaningless without its social pole: neither the variety nor the centrality that go to make it up can be described except with constant (though of course not exclusive) reference to a group. Now that American writers, consciously or unconsciously, have made their final break with the middle class, it should be obvious that, unless they prefer a bleak or an elegant futility, they can turn in but one direction, to the proletariat. By identifying their interests with the life and needs of that class they can at once enrich and unify their own lives in the one way now historically open to them. Far from being a merely political or sociological affiliation, this joining of forces with the working class is chiefly important, even now, and certainly in the long run, on psychological and cultural grounds. It is a question, for the writer, not of sentiment or quixotism, but of self-preservation. Our literary history is the true argument, and this it would be idle to labor further.

How many things this may mean as time goes on, there is no space to say here; and indeed it would be both presumptuous and irrelevant, in this connection, to undertake to say them. One must grant that the case for a proletarian literature is not always cogently stated or wisely defended—any more than the case against it. One must insist that to adopt the proletarian point of view does not mean, for a novelist, to deal solely with economic conflicts, or, for a poet, to be a voice only for protest, momentous as both things are and *implicit* as they are bound to be. That a truly proletarian literature, for us in America at least, would mean a break with the mood of self-pity, with the cult of romantic separatism, with sickly subjectivism and melodramatic misanthropy— this much is almost too clear to deserve stating. But the duty of the critic is certainly not to file an order for a particular sort of fiction or poetry before the event; his duty is to clarify, as best he can, the circumstances in which fiction and poetry must take shape, and to rationalize their manifestations when they arrive. For the moment the important thing is that American criticism should define its position: in the midst of so much confusion, so much wasted effort, so much hesitation, this will itself be an advance.

From *The Nation*, Vol. CXXXIII (October 14, 1931), pp. 391–393. Reprinted by permission of the author and editors.

PHILIP RAHV

The Cult of Experience in American Writing

[1940]

EVERY attentive reader of Henry James remembers that highly dramatic scene in *The Ambassadors*—a scene singled out by its author as giving away the "whole case" of his novel—in which Lambert Strether, the elderly New England gentleman who had come to Paris on a mission of business and duty, proclaims his conversion to the doctrine of experience. Caught in the spell of Paris, the discovery of whose grace and form is marked for him by a kind of meaning and intensity that can be likened only to the raptures of a mystic vision, Strether feels moved to renounce publicly the morality of abstention he had brought with him from Woollett, Mass. And that mellow Sunday afternoon, as he mingles with the charming guests assembled in the garden of the sculptor Gloriani, the spell of the world capital of civilization is so strong upon the sensitive old man that he trembles with happiness and zeal. It is then that he communicates to little Bilham his newly acquired piety towards life and the fruits thereof. The worst mistake one can make, he admonishes his youthful interlocutor, is not to live all one can.—"It doesn't so much matter what you do in particular so long as you have your life. If you haven't had that what *have* you had? . . . Live, live!"

To an imaginative European, who is unfamiliar with the prohibitive American past and with the long-standing American habit of playing hide and seek with experience, Strether's pronouncement in favor of sheer life may well seem so commonplace as hardly to be worth the loving concentration of a major novelist. While the idea that one should "live" one's life came to James as a revelation, to the contemporary European novelists this idea had long been a completely assimilated and natural assumption; experience to them was the medium in which they tested and created values, whereas to him it represented something more than that—romance, reality, civilization, a self-propelling, autonomous value inexhaustibly alluring in its own right. This attitude to experience in James is often overlooked by readers who are excessively impressed (or depressed?) by his oblique methods and effects of remoteness and ambiguity. Actually, from the standpoint of the history of the national letters, the lesson taught by James in *The Ambassadors,* as in many

550

of his other books, must be understood as no less than a revolutionary appeal. It is a veritable declaration of the rights of man—not, to be sure, of the rights of the public, of the political man, but of the rights of the private man, of the rights of personality, whose openness to experience provides the sole effective guaranty of its development.

Strether's appeal, in curiously elaborated, varied, as well as ambivalent forms, pervades all of James's work; and for purposes of critical symbolisation it might well be regarded as the compositional key to the whole modern movement in American writing. No literature, it might be said, takes on the qualities of a truly national body of expression unless it is possessed by a basic theme and unifying principle of its own. Thus the German creative mind has in the main been actuated by philosophical interests, the French by the highest ambitions of the intelligence unrestrained by system or dogma, the Russian by the passionately candid questioning and shaping of values. And since Whitman and James the American creative mind, seizing at last upon what had long been denied to it, has found the terms and objects of its activity in the urge toward and immersion in experience. It is this search for experience, conducted on diverse and often conflicting levels of consciousness, which has been the dominant, quintessential theme of the characteristic American literary productions—from *Leaves of Grass* to *Winesburg, Ohio* and beyond; and the more typically American the writer—a figure like Thomas Wolfe is a patent example—the more deeply does it engulf him.

More adequately, I believe, than any other factor that could be cited, it is this preoccupation that accounts for some of the striking peculiarities of modern American writing: its unique indifference, for instance, to the larger cultural aims implicit in the esthetic rendering of experience—to theories of value, to the wit of the speculative and problematical, and to ideas generally. In his own peculiar way even an artist as supremely aware as James—who was the analyst of fine consciences but scarcely of fine minds—shared this indifference. The intellectual is the only character missing in the American novel, which contains everything except ideas. But what are ideas? At best judgments of reality and at worst substitutes for it. The American novelist's conversion to reality, however, has been so belated that he cannot but be baffled by judgments and vexed by substitutes.

The American novel exhibits a singular pattern consisting, on the one hand, of a disinclination to thought and, on the other, of an intense predilection for the real: and the real it conceives as a vast phenomenology swept by waves of sensation and feeling. In this welter there is little room for the intellect, which in the unconscious belief of many imaginative Americans is naturally impervious, if not actually inimical, to reality. Consider the literary qualities of Ernest Hemingway, for example. There is nothing Hemingway despises more than experience of a make-believe, vague, or frigid nature, but in order to safeguard himself against the counterfeit he consistently avoids drawing upon the more abstract resources of the mind, he snubs the thinking man and mostly confines himself to the depiction of life on its physical levels. Of course, his extraordinary mastery of the sensuous element amply compensates for whatever losses he may sustain in other spheres. But Hemingway is only a particular instance. Other writers, less gifted and not so self-sufficiently and incisively one-sided as he is, have through this same creative psychology come to grief. Under its conditioning some of them have produced work so limited to the recording of the immediately apparent and unmistakably and recurrently real that it can truly be said of them that their art ends exactly where it should begin.

"How can one make the best of one's life?" André Malraux asks in one of his novels. "By converting as wide a range of experience as possible into conscious thought." It is precisely this reply which is alien to the typical American artist, who is so utterly absorbed in experience that he is often satisfied to let it "write its own ticket"—to carry him to its own chance or casual destination.

II

The disunity of American literature, its polar division into above and below or highbrow and lowbrow writing, has been noted more than once. Whitman and James, who form a kind of fatal antipodes, have repeatedly served as the standard examples of this dissociation. There is one sense, however, in which the contrast between these two arch-typical Americans might be said to have been overdrawn. There is, after all, a common ground on which they finally, though perhaps briefly, meet—an essential Americanism subsuming them both that is best defined by their mutual affirmation of experience. True, what one affirmed the other was apt to negate; still it is not in their attitude to experience as such that the difference between them becomes crucial but rather in their contradictory conceptions of what constitutes experience. One sought its ideal manifestations in America, the other in Europe. Whitman, plunging with characteristic heedlessness into the turbulent, formless life of the frontier and of the big cities, accepted experience in its total ungraded state, whereas James, insisting on a precise scrutiny of its origins and conditions, was endlessly discriminatory, thus carrying forward his ascetic inheritance into the very act of reaching out for the charms and felicities of the great European world. But the important thing to keep in mind here is that this plebeian and patrician are historically associated in the radical enterprise of subverting, each from his own end, the puritan code of stark utility in the conduct of life and in releasing the long compressed springs of experience in the national letters. In this sense, Whitman and James are the true initiators of the American line of modernity.

If a positive approach to experience is the touchstone of the modern, a negative approach is the touchstone of the classic in American writing. The literature of early America is a sacred rather than a profane literature. Immaculately spiritual at the top and local and anecdotal at the bottom, it is essentially, as the genteel literary historian Barrett Wendell accurately noted, a "record of the national inexperience" marked by "an instinctive disregard of actual fact." For this reason it largely left untouched the two chief experiential media—the novel and the drama. Brockden Brown, Cooper, Hawthorne, and Melville were "romancers" rather than novelists. They were incapable of apprehending the vitally new principle of realism by virtue of which the art of fiction in Europe was in their time rapidly evolving toward an hitherto inconceivable condition of objectivity and familiarity with existence. Not until James did a fiction-writer appear in America who was able to sympathize with and hence to take advantage of the methods of Thackeray, Balzac, and Turgenev. Since the principle of realism presupposes a thoroughly secularized relationship between the ego and experience, Hawthorne and Melville could not possibly have apprehended it. Though not religious men themselves, they were nevertheless held in bondage by ancestral conscience and dogma, they were still living in the afterglow of a religious faith that drove the ego, on its external side, to aggrandize itself by accumulating practical sanctions while scourging and inhibiting its intimate side. In Hawthorne the absent or suppressed experience reappears in the shape of spectral beings whose function is to warn, repel, and fascinate. And the unutterable confusion that reigns in some of Melville's narratives (*Pierre, Mardi*), and which no amount of critical labor has succeeded in clearing up, is primarily due to his inability either to come to terms with experience or else wholly and finally to reject it.

Despite the featureless innocence and moral-enthusiastic air of the old American books, there is in some of them a peculiar virulence, a feeling of discord that does not easily fit in with the general tone of the classic age. In such worthies as Irving, Cooper, Bryant, Longfellow, Whittier, and Lowell there is scarcely anything more than meets the eye, but in Poe, Hawthorne, and Melville there is an incandescent symbolism, a meaning within meaning, the vitality of which is perhaps only now being rightly appreciated. D. H. Lawrence was close to the truth when he spoke of what serpents they were, of the "inner diabolism of their underconsciousness." Hawthorne, "that blue-eyed darling," as well as Poe and Melville, insisted on a subversive vision of human nature at the same time as cultivated Americans were everywhere relishing the orations of Emerson who, as James put it, was helping them "to take a picturesque view of one's internal possibilities and to find in the landscape of the soul all sorts of fine sunrise and moonlight effects." Each of these three creative men displays a healthy resistance to the sentimentality and vague idealism of his contemporaries; and along with this resistance they display morbid qualities that, aside from any specific biographical factors, might perhaps be accounted for by the contradiction between the poverty of the experience provided by the society they lived in and the high development of their moral, intellectual, and affective natures—though in Poe's case there is no need to put any stress on his moral character. And the curious thing is that whatever faults their work shows are reversed in later American literature, the weaknesses of which are not to be traced to poverty of experience but to an inability to encompass it on a significant level.

The dilemma that confronted these early writers chiefly manifests itself in their frequent failure to integrate the inner and outer elements of their world so that they might stand witness for each other by way of the organic linkage of object and symbol, act and meaning. For that is the linkage of art without which its structure cannot stand. Lawrence thought that *Moby Dick* is profound *beyond* human feeling—which in a sense says as much against the book as for it. Its further defects are dispersion, a divided mind: its real and transcendental elements do not fully interpenetrate, the creative tension between them is more fortuitous than organic. In *The Scarlet Letter* as in a few of his shorter fictions, and to a degree in *The Blithedale Romance,* Hawthorne was able to achieve an imaginative order that otherwise eluded him. A good deal of his writing, despite his gift for precise observation, consists of phantasy unsupported by the conviction of reality.

Many changes had to take place in America before its spiritual and material levels could fuse in a work of art in a more or less satisfactory manner. Whitman was already in the position to vivify his democratic ethos by an appeal to the physical features of the country, such as the grandeur and variety of its geography, and to the infinite detail of common lives and occupations. And James, too, though sometimes forced to resort to makeshift situations, was on the whole successful in setting up a lively and significant exchange between the moral and empiric elements of his subject-matter. Though he was, in a sense, implicitly bound all his life by the morality of Hawthorne, James none the less perceived what the guilt-tossed psyche of the author of *The Marble Faun* prevented him from seeing—that it is not the man trusting himself to experience but the one fleeing from it who suffers the "beast in the jungle" to rend him.

The Transcendentalist movement is peculiar in that it expresses the native tradition of inexperience in its particulars and the revolutionary urge to experience in its generalities. (Perhaps that is what Van Wyck Brooks meant when, long before prostrating himself at his shrine, he wrote that Emerson was habitually abstract where he should be concrete, and vice versa.) On a purely theoretical plane, in ways curiously inverted and idealistic, the cult of experience is patently prefigured in Emerson's doctrine of the uniqueness and infinitude, as well as in Thoreau's equally steep estimate, of the private man.

American culture was then unprepared for anything more drastic than an affirmation of experience in theory alone, and even the theory was modulated in a semi-clerical fashion so as not to set it in too open an opposition to the dogmatic faith that, despite the decay of its theology, still prevailed in the ethical sphere. No wonder, then, that Transcendentalism declared itself most clearly and dramatically in the form of the essay—a form in which one can preach without practicing.

Isolation was the price Whitman and James were compelled to pay for their break with the tradition of inexperience. James was protected somewhat by his social tone and expatriate interests, but Whitman suffered the full penalty of his iconoclasm. W. D. Howells survived by assuming the role of mediator between the old and the new. But it was not until the twentieth century that the urge to experience at last overwhelmed and decisively transformed literary art.

III

Personal liberation from social taboos and conventions was the war-cry of the group of writers that came to the fore in the second decade of the century. They employed a variety of means to formulate and press home this program. Dreiser's tough-minded though somewhat arid naturalism, Anderson's softer and spottier method of articulating the protest of shut-in people, Lewis' satires of Main Street, Cabell's florid celebrations of pleasure, Edna Millay's emotional expansiveness, Mencken's worldly wisdom and assaults on the provincial pieties, the early Van Wyck Brooks's high-minded though bitter evocations of the inhibited past, his ideal of creative self-fulfilment—all these were weapons brought to bear by the party of rebellion in the struggle to gain free access to experience. And the secret of energy in that struggle seems to have been the longing for what was then called "sexual freedom"; for at the time Americans seeking emancipation were engaged in a truly elemental discovery of sex whose literary expression on some levels, as Randolph Bourne remarked, easily turned into "caricatures of desire." The novel, the poem, the play—all contributed to the development of a complete symptomatology of sexual frustration and release. In retrospect much of this literature seems but a naïve inversion of the dear old American innocence, a turning inside out of inbred fear and reticence, but the qualities one likes about it are its positiveness of statement, its zeal, and its pathos of the limited view.

The concept of experience was then still an undifferentiated whole. But as the desire for personal liberation, even if only from the less compulsive social pressures, was partly gratified and the tone of the literary revival changed from eagerness to disdain, the sense of totality gradually wore itself out. Since the 1920's a process of atomization of experience has forced each of its spokesmen into a separate groove from which he can step out only at the risk of utterly disorienting himself. Thus, to cite some random examples, poetic technique became the special experience of Ezra Pound, language that of Gertrude Stein, the concrete object was appropriated by W. C. Williams, super-American phenomena by Sandburg and related nationalists, Kenneth Burke experienced ideas (which is by no means the same as thinking them), Archibald MacLeish experienced public attitudes, F. Scott Fitzgerald the glamor of the very rich, Hemingway death and virile sports, and so on and so forth. Finally Thomas Wolfe plunged into a chaotic recapitulation of the cult of experience as a whole, traversing it in all directions and ending nowhere.

Though the crisis of the 1930's arrested somewhat the progress of the experiential mode, it nevertheless managed to put its stamp on the entire social-revolutionary literature of the decade. A comparison of European and American left-wing writing of the same period will at once show that whereas Europeans like Malraux and Silone enter deeply into the meaning of political ideas and beliefs, Americans touch only superficially on such matters, as actually their interest is fixed almost exclusively on the class war as an experience which, to them at least, is new and exciting. They succeed in representing incidents of oppression and revolt, as well as sentimental conversions, but conversions of the heart and mind they merely sketch in on the surface or imply in a gratuitous fashion. (What does a radical novel like *The Grapes of Wrath* contain, from an ideological point of view, that agitational journalism cannot communicate with equal heat and facility? Surely its vogue cannot be explained by its radicalism. Its real attraction for the millions who read it lies elsewhere—perhaps in its vivid recreation of a "slice of life" so horrendously unfamiliar that it can be made to yield an exotic interest.) The sympathy of these presumably political writers with the revolutionary cause is often genuine, yet their understanding of its inner movement, intricate problems, and doctrinal and strategic motives is so deficient as to call into question their competence to deal with political material. In the complete works of the so-called proletarian school you will not find a single viable portrait of the Marxist intellectual or of any character in the revolutionary drama who, conscious of his historical role, is not a mere automaton of spontaneous class force or impulse. What really happened in the 1930's is that due to certain events the public aspects of experience appeared more meaningful than its private aspects, and literature responded accordingly. But the subject of political art is *history,* which stands in the same relation to experience as fiction to biography: and just as surely as failure to generalize the biographical element thwarts the aspirant to fiction, so the ambition of the literary Left to create a political art was thwarted by its failure to lift experience to the level of history.[1]

----

[1] For the benefit of those people who habitually pause to insist on what they call "strictly literary values," I might add that by "history" in this connection I do not mean

Experience is the main but by no means the total substance of literature. The part experience plays in the esthetic sphere might well be compared to the part that the materialist conception of history assigns to economy. Experience, in the sense of this analogy, is the substructure of literature above which there rises a superstructure of values, ideas, and judgments—in a word, of the multiple forms of consciousness. But this base and summit are not stationary: they continually act and react upon each other.

It is precisely this superstructural level which is seldom reached by the typical American writer of the modern era. Most of the well-known reputations will bear out my point. Whether you approach a poet like Ezra Pound or novelists like Steinbeck and Faulkner, what is at once noticeable is the uneven, and at times quite distorted, development of the various elements that constitute literary talent. What is so exasperating about Pound's poetry, for example, is its peculiar combination of a finished technique (his special share in the distribution of experience) with amateurish and irresponsible ideas. It could be maintained that for sheer creative power Faulkner is hardly excelled by any living novelist, yet who would seriously compare him to Mann or Joyce? The diversity and intensity of the experience represented in his narratives cannot make up for their lack of order, of a self-illuminating structure, and for their irksome obscurity of value and meaning.[2] One might naturally counter this criticism by stating that though Faulkner rarely or never sets forth values directly, they none the less exist in his work by implication. Yes, but implications incoherently expressed are no better than mystifications, and nowadays it is values that we can least afford to take on faith. Moreover, in a more startling manner perhaps than any of his contemporaries, Faulkner illustrates the tendency of the experiential mode, if pursued to its utmost extreme, to turn into its opposite through unconscious self-parody. In Faulkner the excess, the systematic inflation of the horrible is such a parody of experience. In Thomas Wolfe the same effect is produced by his swollen rhetoric and by his compulsion to repeat himself—and repetition is an obvious form of parody. This repetition-compulsion has plagued a good many American writers. Its first and most conspicuous victim, of course, was Whitman, who also occasionally slipped into unintentional parodies of himself.

Yet there is a positive side to the primacy of experience in late American literature. For this primacy has conferred certain benefits upon it, of which none is more bracing than its relative immunity from abstraction and other-

---

"history-books" or anything resembling what is known as the "historical novel" or drama. A political art would succeed in lifting experience to the level of history if its perception of life—any life—were organised around a perspective relating the artist's sense of the *society* of the dead to his sense of the *society* of the living and the yet unborn.

[2] His recent novel, *The Hamlet,* includes so many imaginative marvels that one is appalled by the ease with which it nevertheless runs aground.

worldliness. The stream of life, unimpeded by the rocks and sands of ideology, flows through it freely. If inept in coping with the general, it particularizes not at all badly; and the assumptions of sanctity that so many European artists seem to require as a kind of guaranty of their professional standing are not readily conceded in the lighter and clearer American atmosphere. "Whatever may have been the case in years gone by," Whitman wrote in 1888, "the true use for the imaginative faculty of modern times is to give ultimate vivification to facts, to science, and to common lives, endowing them with glows and glories and final illustriousness which belong to every real thing, and to real things only." As this statement was intended as a prophecy, it is worth noting that while the radiant endowments that Whitman speaks of—the "glows and glories and final illustriousness"—have not been granted, the desired and predicted vivification of facts, science, and common lives has in a measure been realized, though in the process Whitman's democratic faith has as often been belied as confirmed.

IV

It is not the mere recoil from the inhibitions of puritan and neo-puritan times that instigated the American search for experience. Behind it is the extreme individualism of a country without a long past to brood on, whose bourgeois spirit had not worn itself out and been debased in a severe struggle against an old culture so tenacious as to retain the power on occasion to fascinate and render impotent even its predestined enemies. Moreover, in contrast to the derangements that have continually shaken Europe, life in the United States has been relatively fortunate and prosperous. It is possible to speak of American history as a "successful" history. Within the limits of the capitalist order—and until the present period the objective basis for a different social order simply did not exist here—the American people have been able to find definitive solutions for the great historical problems that faced them. Thus both the Revolutionary and Civil War were complete actions that once and for all abolished the antagonisms which had initially caused the breakdowns of national equilibrium. In Europe similar actions have usually led to festering compromises that in the end reproduced the same conflicts in other forms.

It is plain that in America there has really been no urgent need for high intellectual productivity. Indeed, the American intelligentsia developed very slowly as a semi-independent grouping; and what is equally important, for more than a century now and especially since 1865, it has been kept at a distance from the machinery of social and political power.[3] What this means is that insofar as it has been deprived of certain opportunities, it has also been

[3] The situation in this respect has changed considerably during the last decade. The New Deal government is the first administration since the early days of the Republic that has shown any disposition to avail itself of the particular gifts of the intelligentsia.

sheltered and pampered. There was no occasion or necessity for the intervention of the intellectuals—it was not mentality that society needed most in order to keep its affairs in order. On the whole the intellectuals were left free to cultivate private interests, and, once the moral and esthetic ban on certain types of exertion had been removed, uninterruptedly to solicit individual experience. It is this lack of a sense of extremity and many-sided involvement which explains the peculiar shallowness of a good deal of American literary expression. If some conditions of insecurity have been known to retard and disarm the mind, so have some conditions of security. The question is not whether Americans have suffered less than Europeans, but of the quality of whatever suffering and happiness have fallen to their lot.

The consequence of all this has been that American literature has tended to make too much of private life, to impose on it, to scour it for meanings that it cannot always legitimately yield. Henry James was the first to make a cause, if not a fetish, of personal relations; and the justice of his case, despite his vaunted divergence from the pioneer type, is that of a pioneer too, for while Americans generally were still engaged in "gathering in the preparations and necessities" he resolved to seek out the "amenities and consummations." Furthermore, by exploiting in a fashion altogether his own the contingencies of private life that fell within his scope, he was able to dramatize the relation of the new world to the old, thus driving the wedge of historical consciousness into the very heart of the theme of experience. Later not a few attempts were made to combine experience with consciousness, to achieve the balance of thought and being characteristic of the great traditions of European art. But except for certain narratives of James, I know of very little American fiction which can unqualifiedly be said to have attained this end.

Since the decline of the regime of gentility many admirable works have been produced, but in the main it is the quantity of felt life comprised in them that satisfies, not their quality of belief or interpretative range. In poetry there is evidence of more distinct gains, perhaps because the medium has reached that late stage in its evolution when its chance of survival depends on its capacity to absorb ideas. The modern poetic styles—metaphysical and symbolist—depend on a conjunction of feeling and idea. But, generally speaking, bare experience is still the *Leitmotif* of the American writer, though the literary depression of recent years tends to show that this theme is virtually exhausted. At bottom it was the theme of the individual transplanted from an old culture taking inventory of himself and of his new surroundings. This inventory, this initial recognition and experiencing of oneself and one's surroundings, is all but complete now, and those who persist in going on with it are doing so out of mere routine and inertia.

The creative power of the cult of experience is almost spent, but what lies beyond it is still unclear. One thing, however, is certain: whereas in the past, throughout the nineteenth and well into the twentieth century, the nature of American literary life was largely determined by national forces, now it is international forces that have begun to exert a dominant influence. And in the long run it is in the terms of this historic change that the future course of American writing will define itself.

From *The Partisan Review*, Vol. VII (November–December, 1940), pp. 412–424. Reprinted by permission of the author and editors. This essay, in an expanded form, has been included in the author's volume of critical essays, *Image and Idea* (New Directions, 1949).

F. W. DUPEE
The Americanism of Van Wyck Brooks
[1939]

NEW ENGLAND has given to the United States its most literate body of native tradition, and educated Americans, regardless of their particular backgrounds, are always tending to become spiritual New Englanders. If the Yankee tradition is no longer very much alive, so much the worse for educated Americans.

Of this type of native mind Van Wyck Brooks is an excellent example. It is true that years ago, as the spokesman of an American city culture which was then just emerging in its strength, Brooks made a great effort to master the spiritual New Englander in himself. He did not quite carry it off; his Yankee alter ego has since taken entire possession of him. It is now clear that he has always owed to the older tradition a great many of his qualities—the restraint and conscience that have marked all his work; the taste for arduous scholarship; the rather elaborate prose which is the conscious register of his highly-organized individuality; but above all the air of unworldliness, of consecration, which comes perhaps from his allegiance to the New England principle of intensive cultivation. "The great thing is to be saturated with something," Henry James, another spiritual New Englander, used to maintain. Brooks has saturated himself with the problems of art and society in the United States. And it was another tendency of the rhapsodic Yankee strain to turn everybody—novelists, philosophers, critics, historians, naturalists—into poets; Brooks, too, admirable though he has been as a scholar and social critic, has always at bottom worked and thought in the manner commonly ascribed to poets. Like them he tends to see all experience in the light of a single overmastering situation. In his case the great situation, the *donnée,* is associated with the vicissitudes of creative inspiration in the United States, with the difficulty of realizing oneself, not only as an artist in America, but as an American artist. The effort to reconcile art and society in terms of our national experience has dominated all his work, both the early and the late, and has given an otherwise episodic career an urgent inner consistency.

II

By working very hard a single important piece of territory a writer may earn, at the very least, the reputation of being a "phenomenon." This has been

the case with Brooks, yet it has always been hard to say just what kind of phenomenon he is. During the years when aestheticism was the prevailing literary
creed, he used to be called, rather invidiously, a sociologist. But as sociology
came to seem to us less alien, less of a mystery, it was decided that Brooks's
social insights were the by-products of a temperament primarily ethical. People pointed to his *Freeman* essays, which showed that when hard-pressed by
disappointments, as he appears to have been during the post-war years, he
was capable of taking up a position of reproachful righteousness barely distinguishable from that of the New Humanists, whom he had always assailed.
Let us see to what extent these various distinctions were justified. Morality,
it is true, is the socialism of the individualist, who seeks to extend to society
at large the codes that have come to govern people in their individual relationships. Brooks has been as consistently an individualist as he has been consistently preoccupied with the larger questions of society. But in deriving his
ethical ideas from the new psychology of the Unconscious, he broke in part
with the philosophy of traditional moral individualists. Like them he continued to conceive society by analogy with the structure of the human personality, but instead of picturing personality as a complex of higher and lower
selves, as a Plato or an Arnold—moralists even in their psychology—normally
pictured it, Brooks saw in it the Freudian pattern of repression and sublimation. This pattern, modified as much by vestiges in him of the old ethical severity as by elements of modern materialism, he extended to social experience.
Thus, the United States was to him a case of "atrophied personality," a "prodigious welter of unconscious life" which it was the task of the new intelligentsia to bring to consciousness.

In America where the middle class, filling·the whole picture, had made
life as precarious for specialized types of individuality as it had made it safe
for the more standard varieties, it was natural that a critic like Brooks should
seize upon the new psychology, apply its insights to American writers of the
past, and preach its ethic of self-fulfillment to the writers of the present. His
criticism had therefore its intimate connection with his time and place, a connection that we shall presently consider in detail. But let us first look at
Brooks's criticism in its more technical aspects. His generation was making a
great point of the importance of being "creative," a slogan which Brooks translated into his own medium, developing a criticism that had many of the qualities of imaginative literature. In form it was eloquent, concentrated, boldly
thematic; and it carried the biographical method to a higher point of development than it had yet reached in America. In a sense Brooks's approach is
merely a variant of methods employed by Sainte-Beuve and Taine, but it has
acquired a special character through the intensity both of his individualism
and of his preoccupation with psychology. The questions of culture at large
he approaches in terms of leading individuals; the work of single writers he

considers in the light of their biography. Thus *The Ordeal of Mark Twain, The Pilgrimage of Henry James* and *The Life of Emerson* are all attempts to characterize entire cultural periods through the experience of leading individuals; and even *The Flowering of New England*, as someone has said, is not so much a history as a composite biography. The biographical method is commonly used to cast light on the work of literature. With Brooks, this procedure is usually reversed. When he appeals to the work it is in order to confirm some theory about the man. Literature gets dissolved into biography in such a way that the work itself with its four walls and established furniture as given by its author is often quite lost to view. And this is true concerning his treatment of the intellectual as well as the structural properties of literature. For all his vital interest in the New England tradition, he has never made it very clear just what transcendentalism, considered as a philosophy, really was. And surely it is a paradox of his career that he should have been so warm in his championship of the artist, yet so cold to the work of art, so ready to proclaim America's intellectual poverty, yet in practice so indifferent to ideas.

There have been many instances where Brooks's critical methods involved no particular difficulties. The literary portraits in "Our Poets" were certainly not lacking in a vivid aesthetic concreteness, nor were they demonstrably inconsistent with the actual work of the authors concerned. But other books, notably the *Pilgrimage* and the *Ordeal,* have been deplored because the accomplishment of James and Mark Twain was so largely ignored or distorted. Let us consider these objections, taking up first *The Pilgrimage of Henry James.* This book testifies to Brooks's ability to say things of value and to raise important issues even when in his main argument he appears most mistaken. For the picture of James that emerges from the *Pilgrimage* is a deduction rather from Brooks's general theory of literary nationalism than from the novels themselves, the latter having a complex irony which Brooks fails to take into account and which in the end seriously undermines his thesis. Yet it is curious that in this case Brooks *did* examine the novels, and one concludes, not that his method is necessarily faulty in itself, but that he possesses in any case a strongly metaphysical cast of mind. To the sober scholar in him there is yoked a visionary and the two have some trouble pulling together in harmony. A myth-maker on one side of his nature, he sometimes strikes us as being himself that very poet-prophet, that reincarnated Whitman, which he once had the habit of invoking; but on the other side he is a sceptic, a critic, and an historian. Of the effects of this ambivalence there is further evidence in *The Ordeal of Mark Twain.* The general thesis here is much sounder than that of the *Pilgrimage;* and in addition to having been a pioneer in the attempt to fuse the historical and Freudian perspectives, the *Ordeal* was a splendid example of closely-textured argument, analytical wit and the restrained use of local color. It would be hard indeed to forget its picture of Mark Twain,

"that shorn Samson, led about by a little child, who in the profound som-
nolence of her spirit, was simply going through the motions of an inherited
domestic piety." Nevertheless the *Ordeal* is full of difficulties. It is one thing
to muckrake a period, as Brooks here so effectively muckrakes the genteel era,
pointing out its stultifying effects on a writer of genius; but it is another thing
again to assume that in happier conditions your writer would have been a
Tolstoy. That is more or less what Brooks does assume, with the result that the
historical Mark Twain is everywhere dogged by the shadow of an ideal or
potential or Unconscious Mark Twain, a kind of spectral elder brother whose
brooding presence is an eternal reproof to the mere author of *Huckleberry
Finn*. In addition to being highly speculative, Brooks's approach has the disadvantage of diverting him from what Mark Twain really achieved through
the cultivation, however fragmentary, of his richly plebeian sensibility. This
achievement it was left to Ernest Hemingway and other practicing artists to
discover for themselves.

III

Brooks's habit of using the materials of history and biography to construct
didactic myths, literary lessons in the shape of parables, was probably the
effect of the period in which he came to maturity and of what he was trying to
accomplish in that period. Throughout the years of industrial revolution following the Civil War, writers in America had been consigned, some of them
to a limbo of servility, others to virtual oblivion, depending on whether they
accepted or embraced the prevailing standards of that iron age. But when
Brooks's first volume appeared, in 1909, the old exploitative phalanx of American society had been for some years breaking up. There was a great increase
of radical consciousness on the part of the working classes, and intellectuals
had taken advantage of the general ferment to assert once more the claims of
the individual. For the first time since the 1850's, there came into existence a
body of professionals sufficiently independent, militant and cohesive to be
called an intelligentsia. It had in a sense been the creation of the radical movement; it therefore applied itself to politics, in turn, and evolved a special type
in the shape of the muckraker. But this was only the first phase in the career
of the new intelligentsia. Later on, in Brooks's generation, a reaction set in
against social reformism, which had so plainly missed its mark, and writers
turned from politics to literature. The "artist" supplanted the muckraker as the
standard intellectual type; consciousness of self was cultivated in place of
class consciousness; and writers set out to express and assert and fulfill themselves. Thus the old subjective ethos of romanticism, freshly implemented by
modern psychology, was reborn in America some sixty years after the decline
of Emersonianism.

Nothing was more remarkable in Brooks than the flair for assimilation and synthesis which permitted him to bring to focus in his criticism all the chief tendencies of those decades. For Brooks, in the long run, art and politics were to seem two separate universes; but his early criticism embodied a notable attempt to bring the two into a better relation and so to combine the ideals of the muckrakers with those of his own primarily aesthetic generation. The actual political content of his criticism was vague and shifting; yet whenever he attempted a definite formulation it became clear that he regarded socialism as a pre-condition of the "creative life" in America. In many respects his early writings provided the United States with its closest parallel to the social-democratic literatures then flourishing in Europe.

Nevertheless Brooks was at heart a psychologist and he was to keep the morality of self-fulfillment squarely in the center of his work. Nor did his socialist convictions in the long run prevent him from conceiving art as a process essentially self-contained, commanding an area of experience to all purposes special and separate. He seems to have taken over from Carlyle and Ruskin the "organic" view of society while rejecting the faith in authoritarian institutions that usually goes with it. The mysticism inherent in this view conflicted all along the line with the scientific perspectives of socialism, forcing upon him a kind of unsystematic dualism. Concerning the relation of politics to literature he tended to conceive the first as a function of a material world, the second as an enterprise connected with a world of the spirit. But Brooks did not exploit the music of antinomies to the extent that it has been exploited by a Thomas Mann, and in practice his dualism merely meant that in his opinion intellectuals ought to keep out of politics. They had, he assured them, a special mission, which was to "articulate the whole life of the people" by supplying the United States with new myths and new values. To this role he advised them to apply themselves with the fervor of a consecrated minority, a priesthood, as he said, or a hierarchy. It was an age that made much of seers and cosmic vocations. Writers were looking for prophets—particularly among themselves. Every nation, every social group, considered itself to have a "special mission." If Brooks was akin to Ruskin and Arnold, he was a Ruskin or an Arnold brought up to date: the *culture* which they had advocated as social medicine, he endeavored to implement in terms of an *organized intelligentsia*. For it was an age, too, of heightened crisis and organized struggle in the field of social relations.

In his preoccupation with the intelligentsia there was a considerable value. More than anyone else, unless it was Randolph Bourne, he grasped the importance to America of the emergence of such a body. He understood what it could mean to the labor movement, and he knew, too, that its absence had for half a century inflicted great hardship on American artists, leaving them solitary and exposed in the arena of a hostile society. It was on the new intelligentsia, then, that Brooks set his hopes for the country's future, to them that

he addressed his case histories in literary frustration, his essays in diagnosis
and prescription, in short the whole of that prodigious anatomy of the creative
life which took shape in his early writings. When, eventually, he ceased to
exhort the intellectuals, he lost at the same time a good share of his intellectual
vitality.

In view of his socialist professions it is curious that Brooks came to concentrate so exclusively on conditions in a single country. He appears to have
felt that in Europe the abuses of capitalism had been somewhat mitigated by
the social-democratic movement, a movement whose success he was inclined
to attribute to the efforts of literary critics. The United States, on the other
hand, was a full-blown capitalist nation which possessed only the weak beginnings of a critical culture. We must develop such a culture if we were ever to
experience a genuine social transformation. It was by some such reasoning as
this that Brooks tended to justify his exclusive concern with the United States,
his tendency to idealize Europe, his habit of ascribing to literary culture the
decisive role in reformist politics.

Proceeding always by the rule of opposites, he thought of the United States
as the antithesis of Europe in respect to the quality, the unity and the social
use-value of its culture. French culture, he pretended, had at the touch of
Montaigne fallen together like a single organism. But America had lacked
such a master-spirit. Here there had always existed, between literature and
experience, theory and practice, a profound cleavage which had affected for
the worse both our intellectual and our daily life, condemning the first to
impotent idealism and the second to stark materialism. From the beginning
the Highbrow and the Lowbrow had divided things between them. An
effective middle tradition had failed to appear. In default of the spiritual
checks which such a tradition might have exercised, Big Business had got
firmly into the saddle and the Acquisitive Life had prevailed over the Creative
Life. And with the optimism of a latter-day Whitman—the optimism of a
generation pioneering in social aesthetics (they used indeed to declare that
social reform constituted the new American "frontier") as their fathers had
pioneered in industry—Brooks foresaw a culture which should replace the
obsolete hegemony of New England, and represent the country in all its racial,
class and sectional complexity.

IV

It is true that on the programmatic side Brooks's early writings were in-
fected with the extravagance that is common to the "organic" conception of
society. French critics, we have reason to believe, would be the first to dis-
claim any super-unity in the culture supposedly begotten by Montaigne. As
for America: its intractable minorities and far-flung regions have offered to the
literary nationalist a problem so stubborn that it refuses to be solved short of

a social reconstruction more profound than any envisaged by Brooks. But on the critical side his work, attracting to it all the severity of a mind divided between poles of scepticism and faith, was of a trenchancy and cleverness rare in American writing. Our culture did actually suffer, as he maintained, from a split personality which expressed itself in various idealistic chivalries on the one hand, and on the other in a plebeian vigor, unlighted by consciousness. Surely, considering the provocation, Brooks was justified in preaching a bold scepticism. "It is of no use," he told the patriots of his day, "to go off in a corner with American literature . . . in a sulky, private sort of way, taking it for granted that if we give up world values we are entitled to our own little domestic rights and wrongs, criticism being out of place by the fireside." Not that Brooks was the only cosmopolitan critic of American letters; but where the New Humanists, for example, took as their standard of comparison the achievements of some remote Periclean or Racinian age, Brooks looked to the European literature of his time. Moreover, in his account of the Genteel Tradition as "the culture of an age of pioneering, the reflex of the spirit of material enterprise," as in a whole range of similar insights, he went far towards situating the country's cultural problems in a concrete atmosphere of social and economic forces. In the long run, however, the value of his early work seems mainly to lie in the skill and courage with which he isolated the data of intellectual maturity in America. In his hands the Highbrow-Lowbrow antithesis served rather as a descriptive than as an analytical tool. And what he really produced was a kind of symptomology sprinkled with clues and half-clues, with partial explanations, with portents adduced as causes and causes in the guise of portents. The materialist in him was always coming into conflict with the "organic" visionary, the social historian with the psychologist. Accustomed to conceiving matter and spirit in the shape of an antithesis, he never attained a stable view of cultural phenomena; and his lack of clarity on this point caused his criticism to veer back and forth between extremes of free will and determinism, so that while it seemed to him at times that the single writer might change the world unaided, at other times it appeared that one was very much at history's mercy. And psychology came to dominate his thought to the extent that he ended by giving the impression that he wanted to fasten upon American writers a cultural inferiority complex. It was probably this impression rather than simply the severity of his critiques that would help to bring him into partial eclipse in later years. His work would presently appear to belong neither to literary criticism nor to realistic social analysis. When he had finished trying to reconcile politics and literature, mysticism and science, he would be left with an ideology as diffuse as that of an Emerson or a Whitman; and he would seem, like them, to belong to some more primitive stage of American society, the intellectual disorder of whose prophets signified a lack of urgent pressures in the age itself. Even Gide and Mann, accomplished dialecticians and great writers, have not really achieved "universality" in our time: they have merely undergone a series of significant conversions. And Brooks, endeavoring to embrace the Whole, ended by losing touch with its parts; his sensibility acquired a certain abstractness; and in time he was to seem almost the type of that Liberal critic whom Eliot from one angle, and Mencken from another, were to assail with so much effectiveness.

V

The fate of Brooks's ideas was to receive a kind of summing-up, concentrated and dramatic, in the brief career of the *Seven Arts* review. Appearing in the fall of 1916, *The Seven Arts* had Brooks as its chief spokesman; his theme was the necessity of a national literature for an America made acutely conscious of its individuality by the war in Europe. But a year later, America having entered the war, *The Seven Arts* showed a growing distaste for the struggle and was obliged to cease publication. Meanwhile Randolph Bourne had all but replaced Brooks as spokesman, and Bourne's theme was, more and more, the social revolution. What had happened to push *The Seven Arts,* in a single year, from literary nationalism to literary revolutionism? Had we come of age in a world already too far advanced in decay? Had the United States, in attaining to the level of the great powers, likewise fallen heir to a crisis common to the entire capitalist world? This was more or less what had happened, as we can see in retrospect. Nationalism, having simply turned into a sordid imperialism, could no longer inspire a literature. Nor could the idea of the organic society survive the violent manifestations of a period of general revolution. *The Seven Arts,* in its rapid transition, was a fair register of the fact that ideas could appear viable at one moment, only to be swept the next into obsolescence.

The war had witnessed America's maturing as a world power: would we by the same token "catch up" with the elder nations in a cultural sense? To Brooks, at least, it began very shortly to appear that we would not. In America as elsewhere literature's response to war and crisis was both violent and immediate. And the centrifugal tendencies which it developed were the reverse of what Brooks had preached and anticipated. Writers who, like Bourne and Reed, shared his social idealism, were steered by its logic towards socialist theory and politics. There remained the literary majority which, in the main hostile to all politics, was split between two groups. The expatriate generation, addressing themselves to poetry and tradition, pretty much ignored America. The "Titans," who were presently to found *The American Mercury,* stayed in this country, as Mencken boldly confessed, solely to make merry at the spectacle of its foolishness. In the United States itself the aftermath of the war witnessed the definitive triumph of Bohemia over the universities- and other centers of genteel culture. Instead of merging with the Highbrow to produce a middle tradition, the Lowbrow staged a *coup d'état*. Debunking replaced the respectable profession of muckraking. The common man, whom Brooks had respected as an element in his proposed national synthesis, was now to be widely scorned as a simple moron. And if Brooks had taken issue with Dreiser on the grounds that his determinism prevented his fiction from qualifying as healthy social realism, he was now to be faced with a whole generation of Dreisers. In America, in short, there was none of the philosophical scepticism which Brooks had advocated but only the "fashionable pessimism" (as he said) of parvenu plebeians, the coarse laughter of irresponsible satirists. And among the exiles there was an atmosphere of "fashionable pedantry," reactionary metaphysics, symbolist mystification—and Brooks had never cared much for symbolism. The age of prophets and special missions had largely passed. The present age demanded of its artists and critics above all a concrete literary consciousness. Brooks was in no position either to sympathize with its aims or to fulfill its demands. The papers he wrote for the *Freeman* in the early Twenties, and indirectly the biographies of Mark Twain and Henry James, were an index to his opinion of the times. As for the opinion that came generally to be held of him: it was not long before people began to complain that "for all his apparent enthusiasm for the artist, he does not seem vitally interested in art when it appears." He fails to criticize, they said, he merely exhorts. And "the development of young artists is not achieved through exhortation." These strictures were made by Paul Rosenfeld in the mid-Twenties. They reveal the strongly experimental cast of the decade on which Brooks, with his *a priori* temper, had had the misfortune to fall.

VI

In *The Pilgrimage of Henry James* he remarked that to the expatriated author of *The Ambassadors* Europe had remained "a fairy tale to the end." This was scarcely just to James but it showed the high value which Brooks himself, in 1925, still placed on the critical spirit. The years that followed were to witness his rapid retreat from this position.

In 1920 he had published *The Ordeal of Mark Twain*, which was followed some years later by the *Pilgrimage*, and then after a long interval by *The Life of Emerson*. These books, which, together with the *Freeman* papers, constitute a transition between the earlier and later works, show Brooks in the process of trying to thrash his way out of the isolation in which he has landed. Someone has compared the three biographies to the phases of the Hegelian dialectic, that of Mark Twain being the "thesis," that of Henry James the "antithesis" and that of Emerson the "synthesis." But note that this is a dialectic that opens out towards the past. Brooks is intent not only upon making studies in literary frustration, not only upon furnishing the Twenties with didactic parables (there is reason to think that the *Ordeal*, with its stress upon

Mark Twain's immature pessimism, was aimed at the Menckenites, as the *Pilgrimage*, elaborating on the expatriate sensibility, is directed at Eliot's generation), but he is also intent upon discovering the ideal American writer. He finds him at last in the man of old Concord, the "barbaric sage" as W. C. Brownell had called him. And from the rediscovery of Emerson there follows a transfiguration of Emerson's entire society. Brooks has found the key to American literature; he begins to write a cultural history in several volumes, the first of which turns out to be a chronicle, charming as literature, largely fabulous as history, of the creative life in New England. The present has failed us, it is evil; doesn't the past, then, by the law of contraries become good? The modern world has proven to be sadly incoherent; let us seek the organic virtues in the little pre-metropolitan half-agrarian universe of Concord and Boston. It was a Springtime culture and Spring is always virtuous. And if anyone feels disposed to remind us of "world values," let us reply that "we are entitled to our own little domestic rights and wrongs, criticism being out of place by the fireside."

Prefigured in the closing chapters of the *Pilgrimage* (it was Brooks, one feels, much more than it was James who longed to take passage for America), his nostalgia begins to affect his style and the very structure of his work. The pointed, argumentative, and analytical manner gives way to a prose of anecdote and local color, a blur of sensuous matter, a dreamlike pastiche of remembered quotations. And one sees that Brooks has affixed to his camera a soft-focus filter.

A comparison of the early and later work reveals, then, an astonishing reversal of opinion in respect to the achievement of New England. "An age of rude, vague, boisterous, dyspeptic causes" was the way he had formerly characterized that time. Its puritanism he had described as "a noble chivalry to which provinciality was almost a condition." Its Ripleys and Danas and Alcotts had seemed "a queer miasmatical group of lunar phenomena." Longfellow had been "an expurgated German student," whom it was foolish to approach critically. And Hawthorne for all his charm had felt life "rather as a phantom than as a man." But already in *The Life of Emerson* Hawthorne has become "a reminder as it were of some vast Cimmerian universe . . . a real Sphinx, with a subterranean self buried fathoms deep in the desert sand." What has happened is that Hawthorne has altered not so much in kind as in scale; he has been blown up to enormous stature in order that he may play the Prince of Darkness to Emerson's Son of Light in a kind of veiled cosmological allegory that runs all through the *Life*. And if Hawthorne, once a little less than a man, is capable of becoming something only short of a god, we can imagine how it will be with Emerson. As New England's chief intelligence Emerson had always figured to Brooks as the personification of a tradition shot through with false sublimities and seriously deficient in experience of life. For

Emerson were reserved the most caustic phrases in *America's Coming-of-Age*. "A strange fine ventriloquism . . . a continual falsetto . . . abstract at the wrong times and concrete at the wrong times . . . he could write page after page about a poet or painter without one intelligibly apt utterance . . . he was not interested in human life; he cared nothing for emotion, possessing so little himself . . . all the qualities of the typical baccalaureate sermon." And so on. But compare this portrait with the estimate of Emerson's virtues implied (for, as in the case of Hawthorne, it is only implied) in the *Life* and *The Flowering of New England*. Here the author of *Representative Men* has become a veritable embodiment of the creative spirit, a Yankee Balder. His prose evokes images of mountain streams, his passage through the New England world is accompanied by the springing up of greenery and flowers.

A few reservations are necessary if we are to see Brooks's two periods in a proper light. Needless to say he was never a debunker, even in his most militant phase, and the severity of his judgments on the New England school was plentifully sweetened with qualification. Indeed he was the writer of his generation who strove hardest to play the mediator between past and present. If he stressed the shortcomings of the Yankee tradition it was because that tradition seemed at best a sectional phenomenon and because it had come to block the growth of a larger intellectual consciousness in America. Nor can we ignore the very considerable merits of Brooks's latest work. The *Life* may seem a rather flimsy performance, but surely the *Flowering* has notable qualities. The opening chapters, dealing with the birth of the artistic spirit in a young nation, and the closing pages, describing Lowell and Holmes as characters of the Yankee twilight, cause the book to be enclosed in a frame of excellent criticism. But in the absence of any such criticism in the case of Emerson, Thoreau, Hawthorne and the rest, the frame only serves to set off a certain sponginess in the picture itself. Here, then, is a New England crowded with creative spirits but virtually bare of masterpieces, for Brooks has given up almost entirely the practice of correlating biography with literature. Here, above all, is a New England purged of conflict and contradiction, presented as an idyll of single-hearted effort; for Brooks had likewise given up the habit of correlating literary enterprise with social history. His perspective as a man of the twentieth century, his values as a socialist and an historian, have all gone by the board in the interests of an impressionistic *immediacy*. We are invited to survey the New England renaissance as if through the eyes of some actual participant, some breathless Lyceum ticket-holder of the period.

So the *Flowering* represents not so much a frank revision of Brooks's earlier judgments as a shift to a sphere where critical judgment operates only by implication. The Yankee culture has been lifted from the plane of "world values," where it shows as very small and incomplete, into an historical void where it becomes as great as you please. Indeed it is symptomatic of Brooks's present tendency that he nowhere tries to come to terms with his earlier work or to offer a reasonable explanation of the apparent disjunction between his two periods. The most he has done along these lines has been to remark, in the preface to a reissue of three early essays, that the judgments of his first period were the indiscretions of a youth bent on following an iconoclastic fashion. A fashion! So much then for the ardors, the sincerities, the hopes that went into *America's Coming-of-Age*. In dispensing with a rational view of American history it seems that he has lost the desire to make sense of his own history.

And the once-powerful critic of American life has become the chief curator of its antiquities; the oracle of the intellectuals has turned into the oracle of the book-clubs. He has accomplished his lifelong purpose of reconciling the native artist with the native society—but he has accomplished it in terms of a distant past, an imaginary past. If Europe was a fairy tale to Henry James, what has the United States become to Van Wyck Brooks?

From *The Partisan Review*, Vol. VI (Summer, 1939), pp. 69–85. Reprinted in this revised version by permission of the author and editors.

DELMORE SCHWARTZ
The Literary Dictatorship of T. S. Eliot
[1949]

WHEN we think of the character of literary dictators in the past, it is easy to see that since 1922 Eliot has occupied a position in the English-speaking world analogous to that occupied by Ben Jonson, Dryden, Pope, Samuel Johnson, Coleridge, and Matthew Arnold. It is significant that each of these dictators has been a critic as well as a poet, and we may infer from this the fact that it is necessary for them to practice both poetry and criticism.

Another characteristic is that each of these literary dictators has in some way reversed the judgments of his immediate predecessor. For example, Arnold denied that Pope and Dryden were really poets, declaring that they were merely "wit-writers." Eliot in the same way has declared that Pope and Dryden were truly poets and that Keats and Shelley, two of Arnold's favorites, were really insufficient and inadequate as poets.

One can hardly use such a term as dictatorship without suggesting unfortunate political associations. A literary dictatorship, however, is quite unlike a political one because you cannot force people to like poets or poetry, although you can persuade them. The remarkable thing about most literary dictators is that they succeeded in persuading at least one generation of readers to accept their literary taste.

When we come to Eliot's reign, we find that something has really been added: we have virtually two dictatorships from one literary dictator. Between 1922 and 1933 Eliot, in a series of unprecedented essays which were initially disguised as book reviews, evaluated the history of English poetry in one set of terms; between 1933 and 1946 he gradually reversed his whole evaluation, so that, for example, Tennyson, whom he scorned in 1922, was the object of serious and elevated commendation in 1936. In the same way Yeats, who in 1922 was said to be outside of the tradition of English poetry merely because he was Irish, was praised in the highest terms in 1933 as someone who "by a great triumph of development began to write and is still writing some of the most beautiful poetry in the language, some of the clearest, simplest, most direct." Some of the poems that Eliot refers to were written long before 1922. Thus it is almost possible to say of Eliot, "The

573

dictator has abdicated. Long live the dictator!" This is the only instance I know where anyone has abdicated and immediately succeeded to his own throne.

We can take 1922 as the approximate beginning of the first period, for in that year Eliot began to edit *The Criterion,* and *The Waste Land* was published in the first number. It was in 1921 that Eliot published the reviews in the London *Times Literary Supplement* which were later collected as three essays in *Homage to John Dryden.* In the most famous of these essays, "The Metaphysical Poets," Eliot declared that English poetry had not been the same since the death of John Donne. Dryden was a good poet, and Milton was a good poet, but their very virtues brought about a dissociation of sensibility in their successors. Since the time of Donne, according to this essay, there have been no poets in English who really enjoyed a unity of sensibility. What Eliot means by "unity of sensibility," a dubious psychological phrase, is difficult to make clear, but can perhaps best be stated by paraphrasing Eliot's remark that Donne felt his thoughts at the tips of his senses. All poets since Donne, with a few exceptional moments of unity, have permitted their thoughts and their emotions to be separated. "In the seventeenth century," says Eliot, "a dissociation of sensibility set in from which we have never recovered; this dissociation was not natural and was aggravated by the two most powerful poets of the century, Milton and Dryden. . . . The sentimental age began early in the eighteenth century and continued. Poets revolted against the ratiocinative; they thought and felt by fits unbalanced. . . . In one or two passages of Shelley's 'Triumph of Life' and Keats' second 'Hyperion' there are traces of struggle toward unification of sensibility. But Keats and Shelley died, and Tennyson and Browning ruminated." The poets prior to Dryden and Milton, however, "are more mature . . . and were better than later poets of certainly not less literary ability."

By 1934 Eliot had fruitfully contradicted, modified or qualified practically all the literary and critical judgments implicit in this essay. He had praised not only Tennyson and Yeats, but also Wordsworth and Coleridge, who were more or less rejected in 1921. In 1937, when questioned during a radio interview on the British Broadcasting Company about what he regarded as great poetry, he replied that Wordsworth's "Independence and Resolution" and Coleridge's "Ode on Dejection" were probably "touchstones of greatness." This is a far cry from what Eliot said in 1922 and what has been echoed a countless number of times by critics who have been influenced by Eliot.

And yet I do not mean to imply in the least that Eliot is merely contradictory. It is true that no one could have guessed, by reading his essay on "The Metaphysical Poets" in 1922, that by 1937 he would admire Wordsworth and Coleridge very much and cite them, rather than Donne, as "touchstones of greatness." Nor could anyone have guessed or suspected that he would praise Byron and Kipling, among other unlikely possibilities. But on the other hand, there is a real unity in back of all of these seemingly contradictory judgments. One basis of this unity is the admiration for Dante which obviously began when Eliot was still an undergraduate. If we understand Eliot's gradual and profound re-reading of Dante, then we can see how at one point, fascinated by one aspect of Dante, he would be likely to salute Donne, while at a later stage it would be natural for him to admire the characteristic directness and clarity of the poems by Wordsworth and Coleridge which he cited as touchstones of what is great in poetry. If we examine these poems carefully, we can see that in the most direct way they resemble the very beginning of *The Divine Comedy*.

And here, too, we can find at least one explanation of the distaste Eliot has expressed at various times for the poetry of Milton. It was in 1933 at Columbia that Eliot, by using what we may call the method of invidious comparison, compared Milton to Dante, although the two poets are not really comparable. Since Milton was a dedicated, self-conscious literary artist who decided to write an epic poem which would be like other epic poems and which would be a national epic, it seems clear to me that the true comparison would be to Virgil. How, then, are we to explain Eliot's dispraise of Milton?

We have as possibilities all sorts of unconvincing explanations: for example, it is said that Eliot depreciates Milton because Milton was anti-authoritarian in religious matters, while Eliot himself is nothing if not authoritarian,—an explanation which might be based upon Eliot's remark that "Milton's celestial and infernal regions are large but insufficiently furnished apartments, filled by heavy conversation; and one remarks about the Puritan mythology its thinness." But this is clearly not a sufficient explanation, since we know that Ezra Pound expressed an equal dislike of Milton, and no one can suppose that Ezra Pound's literary opinions were influenced by Anglo-Catholicism.

Another possible explanation is that Milton is not the kind of poet that Eliot himself desired to be, and there is, as everyone knows, a natural tendency upon the part of a poet who writes criticism to try to justify and praise in his criticism what he attempts to accomplish in his poetry. Thus Eliot criticizes Milton and reduces his importance by saying that "the very greatest poets set you before real men talking, carry you on in real events, moving." In the same essay in which Eliot makes this remark he says, "There is a large class of persons, including some who appear in print as critics, who regard any censure upon a great poet as a breach of the peace, as an act of wanton iconoclasm, or even hoodlumism. The kind of derogatory criticism that I have to make upon Milton is not intended for such persons, who cannot understand that it is more important, in some vital respects, to be a good poet than to be a great poet." This sounds to me as if Mr. Eliot were protesting far too much.

Milton is a crucial instance, because Milton is the one poet for whom Eliot expresses a distaste in both his revaluations of English poetry. Let us take the sentence I have just quoted. In the same essay Eliot says, "It must be admitted that Milton is a very 'great' poet indeed." We have then to determine, if we can, the difference between being a "very great poet" and being "one of the very greatest," and since Eliot puts the term "great" in quotation marks as if it were a dubious one, it would not be strange if a man from Mars decided that some infinitesimal hair-splitting were involved, or that Eliot, like Milton, had found darkness visible, for surely there is a kind of darkness in distinguishing between "very great" and "the very greatest."

II

What standards were involved in Eliot's initial evaluation of the history of English poetry and his subsequent revaluation?

They can be named in a summary and incomplete way as follows: first, actuality; second, honesty (closely connected with actuality); third, the purification and maintenance of the English language; fourth, the dramatic sense, which I shall try to define in a moment; fifth, the quality of the versification.

Needless to say, this list is not by any means exhaustive and obviously each of these sought-for qualities overlaps and interconnects with the others. For example, the sense of the actual is necessary to a poet's being dramatic; a sensitivity to the manifold possibilities of versification cannot really be separated from a desire to purify, maintain and sustain the English language.

Let me now try briefly to define and illustrate each of these qualities as they manifest themselves in Eliot's criticism of English poetry. First, the sense of the actual, which is perhaps the most difficult of all to define, since whenever we attempt to define anything, we must do so by referring to the actual and perhaps by merely pointing to it.

An illustration, not from Eliot himself, but from James Joyce, who in so many ways is profoundly close to Eliot as an author, may be useful. A would-be novelist came to Joyce with the manuscript of a novel she had just finished, telling Joyce that she would like his opinion of the novel and saying that only one other person had read the book, the porter of the hotel in which she was living. "What did the porter say?" Joyce inquired. "He objected to only one episode," replied the female novelist. "The episode in which the lover finds the locket of his beloved while walking in the woods, picks it up, and kisses it passionately." "What was the porter's objection?" said Joyce. "He said," she replied, "that before kissing the locket passionately, the lover should have rubbed it against his coat to get the dirt off it." "Go back," said Joyce, "to that porter. There is nothing I can tell you that he does not already know." This too is not as complete a pointing to the actual as one might wish, since the actual might be misunderstood to mean only that which is sordid, only that which the muckraker concerns himself with, while Eliot has in mind the actuality of human emotion and human nobility as well.

Moreover, Eliot makes it clear that a sense of the actual is really incomplete and warped without a sense of the past, that sense of the past which, he says, is indispensable to "anyone who wants to continue to be a poet after his twenty-fifth year." But we must be careful not to misunderstand Eliot's con‑ cern with a sense of the past as mere nostalgia for the days when knighthood was in flower. It is the past as actual, as an actual part of the present, which concerns Eliot. And one must have a strong sense of actuality in order to know just what of the past is alive in the present and what is merely a monument or a souvenir. Without a sense of the past, one's sense of the actual is likely to be confused with an obsessive pursuit of what is degraded, or idiosyncratic, or transitory, or brand-new. This is the dead-end of the naturalistic novelist who supposes that the slum is somehow more real than the library. Conversely, a sense of the actual enables one to understand the past itself as something which was not by any means Arcadian. Perhaps one can go so far as to say that one cannot have much of a sense of the past without a sense of the actual or much of a sense of the actual without a sense of the past. Thus, to use an example which can stand for much that is characteristic of Eliot, if one looks at a church, one does not really see very much of what one is looking at if one does not have both a sense of the actual, a sense of the past, and a sense of the past *as* actual in the present.

Let me turn now to a few instances of how Eliot uses the criterion of actuality in his criticism. Blake is praised because one of his poems expresses "the naked observation" and another "the naked insight":

> But most through midnight streets I hear
> How the youthful harlot's curse
> Blasts the newborn infant's ear
> And blights with plagues the marriage hearse.

In the same essay, which was written in 1920, Blake is praised because he possesses the peculiar honesty which, according to Eliot, is peculiar to all great poetry, an honesty which is to be found, Eliot says, in Homer, Aeschylus, and Dante, and an honesty which is, he adds, in a world too frightened to be honest, curiously terrifying, an honesty against which the whole world con-spires because it is unpleasant. Here we can see how closely connected in Eliot's mind are the sense of the actual and the ability of a poet to be honest.

Now let us take a negative instance, that of Swinburne. Swinburne for

Eliot is a poet whose real virtue was his verbalism, his use of words for their own sake. "In the verse of Swinburne the object (or we might say the actual) has ceased to exist. . . ." Swinburne, says Eliot, dwelt exclusively and consistently among words divorced from any reference to objects and actualities, and this kind of poetry is compared not only with that of Campion, which has both a beauty of language and a reference to actuality, but also with "the language which is more important to us . . . that which is struggling to digest new objects . . . new feelings, new aspects, as, for instance, the prose of James Joyce or the earlier Conrad."

There is another important negative instance. Eliot speaks of the images in the plays of Beaumont and Fletcher as "cut and slightly withered flowers stuck in the sand" in comparison with the images of Shakespeare, Donne, Webster, and Middleton, which have, he says, "tentacular roots" which reach down to "the deepest terrors and desires." In the same way, Tennyson is praised for his great technical skill but the quotations which Eliot cites, in 1936 when he reverses his judgment of Tennyson, are praised partly because they are descriptions of a particular time and place.

Now, to return for a moment to my general subject, we can see here the underlying unity which is involved in Eliot's revision of his first evaluation of English poetry. For in praising Blake as one who was unpleasantly honest and full of naked observations and insights, Eliot said that such honesty could not exist apart from great technical skill. In his first evaluation Eliot had praised Tennyson for his technical skill but dismissed him as one who merely ruminated. When Eliot came to revise his judgment of Tennyson in 1936, his revision was consequent upon a study of Tennyson's versification, which led him to see how that poet's great technical skill did in fact, at times, enable him to render the actual and not merely ruminate upon it. Thus, in a sense, Eliot is consistent throughout; the reason that a revision has been necessary is that Eliot was burdened by preconceptions which belonged to the period in which he was writing, and perhaps he had simply not read sufficiently in some of the poets he dismissed.

So too with the poetry of Milton, although I do not think that here it is a question of insufficient reading. When Eliot says in depreciation of some of Milton's poems that they are conventional, artificial, and enamelled, he is objecting to the absence of the actual, as we see further in the same essay when he says that "the greatest poets set you before real men talking, carry you on in real events, moving." It seems to me likely enough that by now Eliot has perceived beneath the perhaps artificial and certainly grandiloquent surface of Milton's language precisely that peculiar honesty about the essential strength or sickness of the human soul which he found in Dante, Shakespeare, Blake, and other of the very greatest poets. I should think that this desirable revision of opinion may also have come about as a result of the de-

velopment of Eliot's own writing during recent years. When Eliot spoke of
Milton at Columbia in 1933, he said that "Samson Agonistes" is not really a
dramatic poem but rather an extended lyric. In the *Four Quartets,* there are
many indications that the kind of experience Milton deals with in "Samson
Agonistes"—Samson, shorn, blind and chained to the wheel, and Milton
himself blind and chained to old age—will be more understandable to the
poet and critic who writes:

> The poetry does not matter.
> It was not (to start again) what one had expected.
> What was to be the value of the long looked forward to,
> Long hoped for calm, the autumnal serenity
> And the wisdom of age?

And who writes later in the same group of poems:

> Since our concern was speech, and speech impelled us
>   To purify the dialect of the tribe
>   And urge the mind to aftersight and foresight,
> Let me disclose the gifts reserved for age
>   To set a crown upon your lifetime's effort.
>   First, the cold friction of expiring sense
> Without enchantment, offering no promise,
>   But bitter tastelessness of shadow fruit
>   As body and soul begin to fall asunder.
> Second, the conscious impotence of rage
>   At human folly, and the laceration
>   Of laughter at what ceases to amuse.
> And last, the rending pain of re-enactment
>   Of all that you have done, and been; the shame
>   Of motives late revealed, and the awareness
> Of things ill done and done to others' harm
>   Which once we took for exercise of virtue.
>   Then fools' approval stings, and honor stains.

It seems to me that the poet who wrote these lines cannot fail to recognize
at last both the spiritual grandeur of "Samson Agonistes" and also the concern
with speech, the effort to purify the dialect of the tribe, and urge the mind to
aftersight and foresight, which is characteristic of that great poem.

In thus supposing that Eliot's experience of the last decade will lead him to
a new recognition and admiration of Milton, it seems to me that I am illustrating another aspect of the sense of the actual.[1] It is actuality itself, the

---

[1] Mr. Eliot's later revaluation of Milton appeared in his lecture before the British
Academy in 1947 and was published in the *Proceedings of the British Academy* in that
year; reprinted in *The Sewanee Review,* Vol. LVI (April–June, 1948), pp. 185–209. (Editor's note, 1950.)

actuality of middle age approaching old age, which leads to a deeper understanding of Milton's major poetry, most of which, after all, was written in
middle or old age.

III

Let us return now to the other touchstones, or criteria, of poetic genuine-
ness.

Honesty is perhaps a shorthand term for a willingness to face the reality
of one's emotions. Thomas Middleton is given what seems to me virtually
fabulous praise by being said to have created in *The Changeling*, "an eternal tragedy, as permanent as *Oedipus* or *Antony and Cleopatra* . . . the
tragedy of the unmoral nature suddenly trapped in the inexorable toils of
morality. . . . A play which has a profound and permanent moral value
and horror." Thus we can see how a poet's honesty is, in fact, very often a
concern with morality, with the actuality of morality. Yet this moralism must
be distinguished carefully from that overt didacticism which has spoiled the
work of many great artists such as Tolstoy and resulted in the censorship of
more than one masterpiece. Notice I have said the actuality of morality
rather than simply morality as such. A further elucidation is to be found in
Eliot's discussion of Hamlet, a character who suffered, says Eliot, from "the
intense feeling, ecstatic or terrible, without an object or exceeding its object,
which every person of sensibility has known. . . . The ordinary person
puts such feelings to sleep, or trims down his feelings to fit the business world.
The artist keeps them alive. . . ." In *Hamlet* Shakespeare "tackled a problem
that proved too much for him. Why he attempted it at all, is an insoluble
puzzle; under the compulsion of what experience he attempted to express the
inexpressibly horrible, we cannot ever know." To conclude that *Hamlet* is a
failure, as Eliot does, though it is the most read, performed, and studied of all
plays, seems to me to have a curious notion of success. To enquire as to why
Shakespeare wrote the play at all is strange in view of what Eliot says about
the artist's effort to deal with emotions which are ecstatic, terrible, and inexpressibly horrifying. But I am not concerned so much with the wrongness of
Eliot's judgment, in an essay written as early as 1919, as with the relation of
these remarks to the honesty of the poet and the actuality of moral existence,
to which these remarks point. The poet's honesty, and thus his morality, consists in his ability to face the ecstasy and the terror of his emotions, his desires,
his fears, his aspirations, and his failure to realize his and other human beings'
moral allegiances. Thus the morality of the poet consists not in teaching other
human beings how to behave, but in facing the deepest emotional and moral
realities in his poems, and in this way making it possible for his readers to confront the total reality of their existence, physical, emotional, moral and religious.

As Eliot says in one of his poems, "Mankind cannot bear very much reality," and Eliot looks always for those qualities in a poem which are likely to help the reader to see reality, if not to bear it.

IV

Eliot's theory of the nature and history of English poetry as stated in 1921 can be summarized as follows: "The metaphysical poets possessed a mind and sensibility which could devour *any* kind of experience." (Here, in passing, we may question whether any poet can devour any or all kinds of experience, and further whether such a poet as Wordsworth was not capable of taking hold of certain kinds of experience which the metaphysical poets know little or nothing about.)

Eliot continues by saying that Milton and Dryden were so powerful— "performed certain poetic functions so magnificently that the magnitude of the effect conceals the absence of others." The language of poetry improved from that time forward, says Eliot, but "the feeling became more crude." In the metaphysical poets and their predecessors, "there is a direct sensuous apprehension of thought, or a recreation of thought into feeling," and there is also a kind of intellectual wit, as Eliot observes in his companion essay on Andrew Marvell. But in Collins, Gray, Wordsworth, Shelley, Tennyson, Browning, Hardy, Yeats, and practically every poet since the time of Donne, there is missing that capacity of the mind, that wholeness of sensibility which makes it possible to say of Donne that "a thought was to him an experience," while Tennyson and Browning "merely ruminated"—"they are poets and they think; but they do not feel their thought as immediately as the odor of a rose." When Eliot adds Hardy to this list because he was a modern English-man and Yeats because he was Irish, it seems to me that we may justifiably say that seldom have so many poets been depreciated or dismissed in so few pages. Yet, extreme and sectarian as this view is, it depends nonetheless upon a profound sense of the nature of poetry. We can see what this sense comes to when Eliot says that "those critics who tell poets to look into their hearts and write do not tell them to look deep enough. . . . Racine and Donne looked into a great deal more than the heart. One must look into the cerebral cortex, the nervous system, and the digestive tracts."

V

The third of the standards with which Eliot has criticized poetry is language as such. This is connected, as we would expect, with the remarks I have just quoted, for Eliot says, that "in French poetry, for example, the two greatest masters of diction are also the two greatest psychologists, the most curious ex-plorers of the soul." In English poetry, however, Eliot finds that two of the greatest masters of diction are Milton and Dryden and they triumph, he says, "by a dazzling disregard of the human soul." Here again there is an underlying consistency in the operation of Eliot's mind, for what he is saying of Dryden and Milton is close to what he had said in 1920 of Swinburne as being purely verbal, of using language really divorced from any reference to objects. And it should be noted that only by a very strong sense of the actual can we distinguish between poetry which explores the human soul and poetry which is largely verbal. There is an intermediate mode: poetry whose chief aim is that of incantation, of inducing a certain state of emotion. The two instances Eliot cites are Poe and Mallarmé in an essay written in French in 1926 and never translated into English.

The essence of Eliot's concern with language in itself is perhaps best formulated in the following quotation: "The poetry of a people takes its life from the people's speech and in turn gives life to it; it represents its highest point of consciousness, its greatest power, and its most delicate sensibility." If we take this concern with language in isolation it might seem that the chief purpose of poetry is to maintain and purify the language, and indeed Eliot's praise of Dryden often seems to be bestowed on that poet merely because he effected a reformation in the use of language, rather than for his intrinsic qualities. Throughout Eliot's own poetry there are references to the difficulties and trials of anyone who attempts to use language carefully. In "The Love Song of J. Alfred Prufrock," the protagonist resents the fact that he is formulated in a phrase; in "Sweeney Agonistes" one character says "I gotta use words when I talk to you." In *The Waste Land* each human being is said to be isolated from all other human beings, to be in a prison, the prison of the self, hearing only aethereal rumors of the external world. There are many other instances but perhaps a quotation from the *Four Quartets* is the most explicit of all:

> So here I am, in the middle way, having had twenty years—
> Twenty years largely wasted, the years of *l'entre deux guerres*—
> Trying to learn to use words, and every attempt
> Is a wholly new start, and a different kind of failure
> Because one has only learnt to get the better of words
> For the thing one no longer has to say, or the way in which
> One is no longer disposed to say it. . . .

Throughout Eliot's criticism the quality of the poet's language and its effect upon the future of the English language has always concerned Eliot very much. I think we can say that never before has criticism been so conscious of all that can happen to language, how easily it can be debased, and how marvelously it can be elevated and made to illuminate the most difficult and delicate areas of experience.

VI

The fourth criterion is the dramatic sense, and Eliot maintains that all great poetry is dramatic. However, there is perhaps some confusion here, since Eliot means by dramatic the attitudes and emotions of a human being in a given situation. But when he comes to apply this broad definition, he is often influenced by his own love of Elizabethan drama, where the term, dramatic, narrows itself to the specific theatrical sense of the word, a sense in which it must be distinguished from meaning any human being's attitudes in any situation. This shift in meaning makes it possible for Eliot to say that Milton is not dramatic. For if we stick to the broad definition of the term, then, obviously, what could be more dramatic than the attitudes of Lucifer in "Paradise Lost," or the attitudes of Samson in "Samson Agonistes"? Again, if we accept Eliot's broad definition, then perhaps we must say that the "Elegy in a Country Churchyard" is just as dramatic, *qua* dramatic, as *Hamlet*. I do not mean to say that Eliot's emphasis upon the dramatic in poetry is not justified and fruitful to a certain extent; for example, there is a sense in which we can say that Gray's Elegy is less dramatic than, let us say, Donne's "The Funeral," which might be taken as a kind of elegy. My point is that Eliot sometimes uses this criterion of the dramatic to enforce prejudices about poetry which he does not like for other reasons.

We come, finally, to the question of versification. It is here that Eliot has been most influenced by his own poetic practice. For at one time or another he has enunciated practically every possible theory of what the nature of versification is. In a late essay on the poetry of Yeats he says that blank verse cannot be written in the 20th century because it still retains its period quality. The period presumably is the Elizabethan one, and such a statement is belied by the fact that not only has some of Eliot's best poetry been written in blank verse, but such a statement disregards the triumphs of blank verse, the inexhaustible variety of this form of versification to be found in Milton, Wordsworth, in Keats' "Hyperion," in certain poems of Tennyson which Eliot himself has praised precisely for their technical mastery of blank verse, and in Browning. Many other instances could be mentioned. Eliot's fundamental concern has been, however, with what he calls the "auditory imagination," "the feeling for syllable and rhythm, penetrating far below the conscious levels of thought and feeling, invigorating every word; sinking to the most primitive and forgotten, returning to the origin and bringing something back; seeking the beginning and the end." This should suggest that underneath the contradictory statements about the possibilities of versification which run throughout Eliot's criticism, there is a powerful intuition of how various, unpredictable, and profound are the possibilities of language when it is versified. The quotation I have just cited should suggest certainly that Eliot has found versification a means of raising to the surface of consciousness much that is otherwise concealed. We ought to remember Goethe's remark about Wordsworth, which is quoted by Matthew Arnold in his essay on Wordsworth: that Wordsworth was deficient as a poet because he knew too well the reason he chose every word and line. This paradoxical remark is not based upon a belief that the poet ought to be irrational and spontaneous, but, I think, based upon the sense that through rhythm the poet drew upon depths of being which could not be deliberately or consciously tapped. And let us remember that Goethe and Arnold were in no sense exponents of surrealism.

If we examine Eliot's scrutiny of English versification from the time of Marlowe to the time of Hardy and Yeats, and are not seduced into glib and futile logic-chopping, we come upon a theory of the nature of versification which seems to do justice to the many different things that Eliot has said about it. Namely, the theory that the essence of metre and thus of versification is any repetitive pattern of words, and the endless arguments about versification from Campion to Amy Lowell and the Free Verse movement are caused by the curious feeling that some *one* repetitive pattern, or kind of pattern, is the only true method of versification.

It will doubtless have been obvious by now that in a summary and incomplete way I have been attempting to make systematic the work of a critic who far from proceeding in terms of system or of *a priori* conceptions or of philosophical theory as to the nature of poetry has, on the contrary, developed the body of his work in the course of writing book-reviews, and essays inspired by a particular occasion. Indeed, Eliot has deplored the fact that he often had to write criticism when he wanted to write poetry, and it is certainly true that he did not always choose the subjects of his criticism. Yet it is likely that, to proceed in this way, at the mercy of accident, editorial whim, and his own intuitive sense of what he really felt about poetry, was probably the only way in which much of Eliot's criticism could have come into being.

VII

Let me now try to place Eliot's criticism in terms of a classification which was first suggested by the late Irving Babbitt, and I believe misused by him. Babbitt speaks of impressionistic criticism, scientific criticism, neo-classic criticism, and a fourth kind to which he gives no name, except to quote Abraham Lincoln's epigram about how you can't fool all the people all the time: a kind of criticism which is sometimes called the test of time or the verdict of posterity. This fourth kind presents many difficulties, including the fact that the posterity of the past, the only posterity we know about, has changed its mind so often, at different times preferring Dryden's *All for Love* to Shakespeare's *Antony and Cleopatra*, not to dwell upon such sad and brutal facts as that most of Sophocles' ninety plays have disappeared, and thus evaded the test of time and the fickleness of posterity, or such another dismaying piece of information as the fact that the Romans thought Ennius, whose work has almost entirely disappeared, was a far better epic poet than Virgil. Or again, let us remember that when the Mohammedans burnt the great library at Alexandria, they destroyed survival in time as a literary criterion and a basis for literary criticism.

Babbitt's other three kinds of criticism are also, I think, inadequate classifications. For example, when Babbitt speaks of scientific criticism, what he really means is historical criticism, since he cites Taine as its leading exponent. What we ought to distinguish and emphasize is the purpose which each kind of critic has in mind when he takes hold of a literary work. The neoclassic critic looks in the new literary work for the specific characteristics which he has found in masterpieces of the past, and consequently he denounces Shakespeare because he did not write like Sophocles. Thus, Voltaire condemns Shakespeare as a barbarian because he does not write like Racine. The historical critic is interested in the causes, social and biographical, of the literary work rather than in the work itself. The impressionistic critic is interested in the effects of the literary work upon himself as a delicate and rare sensibility rather than in the work as an objective and social phenomenon. The historical critic goes in back of the work to its causes; the impressionistic critic is concerned with himself rather than with the work itself; to use Pater's unfortunately immortal phrase, he wants to burn with a hard gemlike flame before the work of art, usually neglecting, in his concern with being inflamed, to distinguish and discriminate carefully between the objects which excite him. Eliot's criticism fits none of these classifications, although it is to be regretted that there has not been more of the historical critic in him. He has proceeded, as I have said, by intuition and by seeking out what most interested him from time to time. Yet, at his best he has been what I would like to call the classic kind of critic, the critic who is expert precisely because he depends upon the quality of his own experience, while, at the same time being aware that the more experience of literature he has, the more expert he becomes. There are no substitutes for experience, a platitude which is ignored invariably by the neo-classic critic, whose essential effort is to deduce from classics of the past a ready-made formula for judging any new work. Eliot's classicism at its best is illustrated when he says that if a truly classic work were written in our time, it would not be recognized as such by most of us. It would seem so monstrous, so queer and horrifying. This remark was made in 1933, when a good deal of James Joyce's *Finnegans Wake* had appeared and had been greeted by Eliot in the following terms: "We can't have much more of this sort of thing." Eliot has since changed his mind about this work, and though I do not know whether he considers it truly classical, certainly he admires it very much, and in this shift from dismay and perplexity to admiration we can see how the truly classical critic, the true expert, depends upon experience, and permits experience to correct his errors in appreciation. Experience is thus for the expert, or classical critic, not only the great teacher but the best textbook. Eliot, in revising his initial revaluation of English poetry, has permitted experience to teach him as no theory and no authority possibly could.

Having reviewed this long and complex critical career, we come finally to the question of what conclusions we can draw and what lessons we can gain from it. It seems to me that we have reached a point in our knowledge of the history of taste, the history of literary reputation, and literary judgment, where we can clearly mark out some of the most important dangers and pitfalls involved in any kind of literary criticism. Is it not clear that the kind of action and reaction which characterizes so good a critic as Eliot may very well be the expense of spirit in a waste of false discrimination? Is it necessary, in order to praise poets A, B, and C, to condemn poets D, E, F, G, H, and the rest of the alphabet? Perhaps it is necessary, but if we think concretely of the really shocking blunders in taste which prevail throughout literary history, then perhaps the very consciousness of these blunders can help us to arrive at a point of view in which there is no mere seesaw of praise and rejection. When Dr. Johnson declared that "Lycidas" was a worthless literary production, when Turgenev said that Dostoevsky was a "morbid mediocrity" and announced that he was very bored by the first volume of *War and Peace*, when Tolstoy ridiculed Shakespeare's *King Lear*, and asserted that his own masterpieces were worthless because they could not hold the attention of peasants; or when, for that matter, Shakespeare lost his popularity with Elizabethan audiences because Beaumont and Fletcher seemed to be able to turn out the same kind of thing in a slicker style—but it is unnecessary to continue with what might be an endless catalogue. The point is that the more we know about the history of literary reputation and literary opinion, the more conscious we are of how unjust and how stupid even the greatest critics can be, the more likely we are to avoid such errors in our own experience of literature. The matter is not merely a question of the reader's welfare; the creative writer himself is crucially involved, for just as we may suppose that Shakespeare turned to romantic comedy when his popularity declined, so too it seems likely enough that the failure of *Moby Dick* and *Pierre* reduced Melville to a silence and inactivity from which he emerged now and again for thirty years with short novels which suggest how much more he might have done, given his unquestionable genius, had his greatest work received the recognition it deserved at the time it appeared instead of some thirty years after Melville's death. Thus it does not seem to me to be claiming too much for literary criticism when one declares that upon the goodness, the consciousness, and the justice of literary criticism the very existence of great works sometimes depends, not to speak of the existence of great poets, nor to dwell too much upon mighty poets in their misery dead. I should add at this point that it is only by a knowledge of the literary past that contemporary critical practice can be of much use in preventing new neglect, stupidity, unjustified admiration, and unwarranted blindness. Two of the best poets of the 19th century, Gerard Manley Hopkins and Emily Dickinson, went to their graves with hardly any external recognition; it is quite possible that they did not really know that they had written good poetry. At present Hopkins and Emily Dickinson are much admired but only at the expense of Wordsworth and Hardy. By reviewing Eliot's critical career we can envisage a point of view which will free our scrutiny of literature from many of the sins of the past, while at the same time illuminating anew all that we have inherited from the past. And we can, I think, see how it might be desirable to have no literary dictators.

From *The Partisan Review*, Volume XVI (February, 1949), pp. 119–137, where it appeared as a "shortened version of a lecture given at the English Graduate Union of Columbia University on April 6, 1947." Reprinted in this revised version by permission of the author and editors.

RICHARD CHASE
An Approach to Melville
[1947]

LET's say that Melville was in certain demonstrable ways an artist, that he succeeded in writing certain great books. This will keep us from being too preoccupied with the Heroic Failure, the Inspired but Frustrated American—the Wounded Titan who lies athwart the vision of so many writers on Melville. Finally, of course, we must consider Melville as the Wounded Titan: one part of his personality *is* like Ahab, the Hero with the wound and the harpoon, and like Pierre, the Hero with the wound and the pen-turned-into-a-pistol. But if we see Melville's works as a whole, a total concept of personality begins to emerge and of this totality Ahab and Pierre represent only one of several parts, one person in a multiple personality which also includes Pip, Ahab's cabin boy; Bartleby, in the short story called "Bartleby the Scrivener"; Benito Cereno; Bulkington in *Moby Dick,* Jack Chase in *White Jacket,* the Confidence Man, and Billy Budd.

Our assumption that Melville was an artist cannot be fully explored so long as we make up our minds about Melville's books from the facts of his life, concluding, because he failed in certain ways, that *therefore* his books are all magnificent botches. It is easy to misrepresent these American creators and culture heroes who crack up in a riptide of alcohol or in an apocalypse of chromium and splintered glass or against the battering-ram head of the White Whale. Melville had his crack-up, in his own Victorian way; and that is our strongest image of him. But we owe it to any writer whom we profess to admire to try the experiment of looking at his books objectively. To begin, nevertheless, with the wounded Hero.

THE MAIMED MAN IN THE GLEN

Typee, Melville's first novel, is not just the young author's South Sea adventure story, separate in method and meaning from the later "philosophical" novels (which in any case are not philosophical in any strict sense of the word, but, rather, symbolic and allegorical). It contains many of the themes which Melville was later to develop. The most striking is what we may call The Maimed Man in the Glen. The hero of the story, who has injured his leg, languishes on a tropical island in the deep, secluded valley of the Typees, a tribe of Polynesians. The valley is a soporific paradise, a utopia for Archaists and Doasyoulikes. Yet there is something menacing or guilty about it. The natives are friendly to the hero and even worship him, as a glamorous object from a distant land. But they are firm in their refusal to let him leave the valley. He begins to suspect them of cannibalism. But glossing over these fears, the hero allows himself to fall into a narcissistic reverie, as monotonous and opiate as the procession of the days and nights. He oscillates between sickness and health, pain and pleasure. He is "unmanned" by the "mysterious disease" in his leg, which he is unable to cure. He is, as we come gradually to realize, symbolically castrated.

In *Mardi* (a fantastic travelogue which can be loosely compared with *Gulliver's Travels*) we discover a young king named Donjalolo. An ancient taboo forces him to spend his life within the dark, narrow defile which encloses his kingdom. Like his ancestors, he must "bury himself forever in this fatal glen." He rapidly changes from a young man of great energy and promise to an effeminate exquisite who flatters his senses with incense and languid maidens and who, to escape the oppressive libidinal intensity of the sun, passes back and forth every day between the House of the Morning and the House of the Afternoon, two dark temples constructed with phallic gigantism out of stone.

Ahab is one of these Maimed Men. He is castrated by his whalebone leg, as Melville makes apparent in the chapter called "Ahab's Leg." The central figure of *Pierre* (the novel which followed *Moby Dick*, in 1852) suffers from an Oedipus complex; he is another of these heroes—in *Pierre* Melville makes use of etymology in the names of his characters, as Joyce was later to do: Pierre Glendinning means "the stone which dwells in the glen." In *The Confidence Man*, "a kind of invalid Titan" emerges from a "cavernous old gorge" and strikes down a smooth-talking peddler for selling a phony medicine called the Samaritan Pain Dissuader. All of Melville's wounded heroes have affinities with the saint and the savior—with Christ; with Adonis; with the magician; with the *shaman*, whom primitive peoples worship because of the *mana* he has acquired through his neurotic behavior. But in Melville the fate of these heroes, as we see from Ahab and Pierre, is that they rush headlong into violent action, betraying whatever is creative within them and submitting themselves to everything that is mechanical, corrupting, repressive, and death-wishing. In doing so they kill themselves and all whose fate is in their hands. They are the Tragic Suicides. But they are only a part of a larger personality.

THE DIVINE INERT

The Divine Inert, as Melville says in *Moby Dick*, are "God's true princes of the Empire . . . a choice hidden handful "who are as superior to the

Tragic Suicides as the Tragic Suicides are to "the dead level of the mass." They are figures whose withdrawal from the world has been uncompromising and complete and who have gained the spiritual illumination which comes from dying out of life without dying into death. Pip, the Negro cabin boy, has been "mystically illumined" by the terrifying ordeal of being lost overboard: he sees "God's foot upon the treadle of the loom." He is saved from the sea, but he does not emerge from the depths of his own unconscious. To Ahab, Pip now seems "holy." And Ahab banishes Pip from the deck, saying that there is something in him "which I feel too curing to my malady"; he fears that somehow, without meaning to, Pip will dissuade him from the inexorable hunt after the whale.

Bartleby is another of the Divine Inert. An industrious scrivener who works in a Wall Street law office, he gradually becomes a schizophrenic, cutting himself off from the commercial world about him, saying little whenever he is addressed except "I should prefer not to," and inspiring his philistine employer with a sense of religious awe. Bartleby regresses into the shadows of his childhood as relentlessly as Ahab drives himself into outward action against the whale. He dies curled up like a child, a prisoner in the Tombs. "Benito Cereno" is also a story about a man cut off from the world and living in the twilight of consciousness. In this story Melville dramatizes the psychic plight of the Divine Inert by showing us a Spanish sea captain who has been subjected to the will of a mutinous band of slaves aboard a ship off the coast of South America. He is terrorized into a spiritual illumination, a fact which eludes the honest but obtuse Yankee captain, Amasa Delano. The Yankee captain saves Don Benito bodily but fails to grasp the implications of his spiritual plight.

THE HANDSOME SAILOR

The aspects of personality we have noticed so far are not mutually exclusive; there is much of Pip in Ahab, for example. The Handsome Sailor encompasses and reconciles both the Suicide and the Divine Inert, a kind of synthesis which the dialectic of personality produces out of thesis and antithesis. Yet the figure of the Handsome Sailor remains so inadequately objectified in Melville's books that it cannot fully serve as a synthesis; it is a direction, a motion, as well as an objective reality. At the beginning of *Billy Budd* the Handsome Sailor is pictured as a gigantic Negro wearing a Scotch Highland bonnet with a tartan band—the symbol, as we shall see, of the Promethean Light or the humanizing Intelligence. He is attended by a retinue of fellow sailors, an "assortment of tribes and complexions." Surrounding the superior figure, they move along the Liverpool docks as the lesser light of a constellation move with the central star. The tribes and complexions, Melville seems to be saying, have chosen to live with the Handsome

Sailor rather than, as they do in *Moby Dick,* die with the master who hurls them at the White Whale.

In *Moby Dick,* the Handsome Sailor is Bulkington—the man from the Southern mountains, with "noble shoulders and a chest like a coffer-dam"— who stands at the helm of the Pequod on the Christmas night when she "thrusts her vindictive bows" into the cold Atlantic. But Bulkington disappears from the story, with only a brief farewell from the author: "Take heart, O Bulkington. . . . Up from the spray of thy ocean-perishing—straight up, leaps thy apotheosis!" He must in fact disappear from the story if the story is to go on. Otherwise he would have done what Jack Chase, the Handsome Sailor of *White Jacket,* was driven to do: countermand the orders of the captain and save the ship. Together with Billy Budd these are Melville's Handsome Sailors. We do not see much of them (with the exception of Billy Budd, but he is too complex a problem to consider here). They are direction, force, potentiality rather than completed forms. They are the stuff and energy of an heroic American personality in the act of setting forth toward fulfillment—the Titanic body of America stirring out of the uncreated Night and passing ponderously into motion and consciousness.

PROMETHEUS

"Prometheus" is the name we may give to the total personality which encompasses the Suicide, the Divine Inert, and the Handsome Sailor. The Suicide is a false Prometheus, false because of the blind violence to which he is driven by his neurosis. The Divine Inert is also a false Prometheus because his compact with death and the unconscious is irrevocable. The Promethean man is he who has attained the spiritual illumination of the Divine Inert without losing the capacity for action of the Suicide but whose action is creative—whose action, that is, takes the direction of the Handsome Sailor. To put it another way, he is a man who is able to use the rhythms of life and death toward creative ends.

WITHDRAWAL AND RETURN

Melville symbolizes the rhythms of life and death in several ways. In these pages I can hardly do more than set them down: sea *vs.* land, valley *vs.* mountain, stasis *vs.* motion, time *vs.* space, narcissism *vs.* genius, dark *vs.* light, night *vs.* day, and so on. In his *Study of History,* Toynbee has subsumed these rhythms under the general idea of "Withdrawal and Return." Briefly, Withdrawal and Return may be described as the passage of the ego from the objective world into the unconscious and back to the outer world. This spiritual transit is the highest manifestation of the basic rhythms of the universe: the alternation of night and day, of death and life, the change of the seasons, the cycle of vegetation. The transit is not automatically productive in the higher

RICHARD CHASE

forms of life. It succeeds only when the organism emerges on the returning beat of the rhythm transfigured by the ordeal of the journey and in possession of revived potency and "illumination." Withdrawal and Return is symbolized in a great many mythical themes—for example, awakening after a deep, deathlike sleep the folk-heroes who are beheaded or otherwise injured and magically restored; the death and rebirth of the savior-gods (Christ, Attis, Adonis, Osiris); the banishment and return of heroes like Oedipus; the ordeal of the Arthurian knights in their search for the grail. Toynbee's point, and Melville seems to be making approximately the same point, is that all creativity, whether individual or social, proceeds from individuals who can uncompromisingly embark on the transit of Withdrawal and Return and who, so to speak, can ride out the rhythms without coming into conflict with them.

The Divine Inert fail because they respond only to the first beat of the rhythm.

The Tragic Suicides fail because they allow themselves to be caught and mangled between beats. Theirs is the complex personality which demands to withdraw from the world in preparation for the ordeal of heroic accomplishment on the returning beat of the rhythm. But they are unable to countermand the demonic energy generated by their conflicts which prohibits a decisive withdrawal and goads them into violence and negation. As Freud pointed out, the repetitive rhythms of human activity are either creative postponements of death or they are short-cuts to self-destruction. For Ahab and Pierre, they are the latter. The Hero who cannot "withdraw" when the economy of his personality demands that he should, must finally withdraw by committing suicide.

In the figure of the Handsome Sailor we see personality in the act of emerging from the dark night of the soul—the giant Negro with the emblem of Light on his forehead. The particular facts of his future are unknown. But his eventual apotheosis is assured, for he has been able to ally himself with the spiritual transit.

AHAB AND THE WHALE

But of course the picture is only half complete. So far we have man and we have man transfigured into Prometheus or, to put it another way, we have man a fragment and man complete. There must be an Adversary, a God and Father—a Zeus in opposition to whom Prometheus undergoes his ordeal. Melville almost always regards God as the enemy of man. Moby Dick is God incarnate in the Mechanical Brute, the huge mindless hulk which "god-bullies" the Pequod. He is the challenge which God hurls at man, hoping that in the fight with the whale, man will "unman" himself—that is, undergo transfiguration, not into the image of Prometheus, but into the image of the

Beast-Machine. This is precisely what happens to Ahab and it is what constitutes his falseness. Like the true Promethean guardian of humanity, Ahab can shout defiantly at his "fiery father" that "in the midst of the personified impersonal, a personality stands here." Yet caught in the final violence of the whale hunt, Ahab is transfigured into the "impersonal," into the mechanical monster with blood on his brain. He knows well enough what is happening and what is at stake. The idea of the false Prometheus obsesses him. In the machinelike operations of the ship's carpenter and blacksmith he sees himself, caught in the iron hand of his own death-wishing will power, which makes such ready and fatal use of the mechanical techniques of tyranny in general and the whale hunt in particular. He has an almost hallucinatory awareness of an apotheosis looming up behind the blacksmith. The blacksmith is making a new whalebone leg for Ahab, and Ahab, addressing him ironically as "Prometheus," says,

I'll order a complete man after a desirable pattern. Imprimis, fifty feet high in his socks; then, chest modeled after the Thames Tunnel; then, legs with roots to 'em, to stay in one place; then, arms three feet through at the wrist; no heart at all, brass forehead, and about a quarter of an acre of fine brains; and let me see—shall I order eyes to see outwards? No, but put a skylight on top of his head to illuminate inwards.

It is the abortive transfiguration of Ahab himself, the master of the ship and all the tribes and complexions aboard.

In Melville, then, God manifests Himself as Death, as whatever unmans man. The incarnate Adversary is at once tantalizing and murderous. Man is tempted to forsake the creative Promethean ethos and to imitate the lure of God. Ahab fails because he imitates what is bestial and godlike and thereby fails to imitate what is pre-eminently human. For the rhythm of life out of which issues the Promethean *élan,* he substitutes the mechanical, death-wishing rhythm of the three final onslaughts against the Whale.

As for the comprehensive and pervasive meaning of *Moby Dick,* D. H. Lawrence seems to me to have been right (in his *Classic American Literature*). Melville's theme is the apocalypse and doom of civilization, the whole world hustled to extinction by an American master, the spectacular spiritual-intellectual-emotional failure of the great Prometheus of the West.

PIERRE

The theme of *Pierre* is incest and parricide. Pierre Glendinning, an aristocratic and promising youth, has made a god of his dead father. In the shrine of his heart "reposes the perfect marble form of his departed father; without blemish, unclouded, snow-white, serene." With his proud, handsome, willful mother Pierre enjoys a blissful adolescence. He falls in love with Lucy

Tartan, a pure and lovely girl. But then the dark lady of the story enters: Isabel, the daughter of Pierre's father by an illicit intercourse. Overcome with feelings of guilt, Pierre forms an incestuous attachment with Isabel. They flee to New York. Pierre tries to write a great novel. His mother dies. Lucy joins Pierre and Isabel. The two central projects of Pierre's life—his novel and a happy, productive relationship with Isabel—are both impossible to accomplish, given Pierre's temperament, capabilities, and the social system which he cannot escape even in Bohemian New York. Yet he drives towards his goal with all the mad zeal of Ahab. The whole thing ends quickly when Pierre shoots his cousin, Glendinning Stanly, who has been trying to rescue Lucy. Pierre and Isabel take poison and die in a prison cell. Lucy dies of the shock.

In many ways *Pierre* is a preposterous novel, full of clumsy melodrama and downright bad prose. But there is seldom any doubt that it was written by a great man. And through the murk we can see the scaffolding of an ambitious if imperfect allegory—so ambitious that *Pierre* can be compared with *Finnegans Wake*. *Pierre* has usually been thought of as an unsatisfactory Romantic-period *Hamlet*. But the allegory, once we have spotted it, makes the book far more impressive than that. I shall have to set down the elements of this allegory very dogmatically. As in reading Joyce, we have to recognize several levels of meaning at once. Lucy Tartan, as her first name indicates, is Light or the Promethean fire (thus the symbolism of the tartan bonnet on the head of the giant Negro, mentioned above). Isabel represents Night, Darkness, or the Unconscious. Pierre oscillates between these two figures: they are the opposite poles of the rhythm of Withdrawal and Return; they are less real women than two aspects of Pierre's mother. Pierre means "stone" —that is, he is the Earth alternating between day and night; and he is the human clay to whom "Lucy" gives the creative intelligence and to whom "Isabel" gives the spiritual experience of withdrawal. Caught in a cruel dilemma between the two, Pierre drives on toward the seductive bait of the Annihilating God: the snow-white marble form of his father—Death.

The book has other levels of meaning. For example, there is a kind of aesthetic allegory in which Lucy is the visual principle, Isabel is the auditory principle, and Pierre is Experience or Matter seeking to be transfigured into Art. Again, Lucy is Space and Isabel Time.

ALLEGORY

At one point in *Pierre* the youthful hero burns a portrait of his father, making a kind of ritualistic sacrifice. This ritual symbolizes the function of allegory in Melville's novels. As Melville writes in his essay on Hawthorne, a morally profound work of art is one which "beginning with the hollow follies and affectations of the world—all vanities and empty theories and forms are, one after another, and by admirably graduated, growing comprehensiveness, thrown into the allegorical fire." Allegory is the fire which consumes the Father—that is, every hypostatization of experience which inhibits creativity and destroys personality. Allegory is itself an hypostatization; it meets the "hollow follies" on their own ground. But it does so without losing the Promethean fire and so is able to defeat the "follies," leaving the field to "the all-engendering heart of man."

THE IMAGE OF NARCISSUS

This is important in Melville. It is sometimes touched on in *Moby Dick*; it is the theme of the short story called "The Bell Tower." In *Pierre,* the hero reflects that his cousin Glendinning Stanly, whom he shoots, is "the finest part of Pierre." The shooting of Stanly is part of the hero's suicide (etymologically Pierre Glendinning and Glendinning Stanly—for "stone field"—are virtually the same name). Nearly everyone in *Pierre* is a relative of the hero; even Lucy comes to New York as his "cousin." His mother is himself "translated into another sex." Like a child, Pierre "dabbles in the vomit of his loathed identity." The deaths of Pierre's father and mother, of Lucy, of Isabel, and of his cousin are planetary catastrophes involved in Earth's general suicide. The whole Ptolemaic universe is a mocking hypostatization of the young Titan's ego.

THE CONFIDENCE MAN

No account of Melville can afford to ignore or underestimate *The Confidence Man*. To begin with, it is a great book (and almost unobtainable in America). It is not at all a chaotic cry of despair but a buoyant, energetic piece of writing, on the whole free of Melville's often clumsy rhetoric. It is even a finished work, if read in the light of Melville's over-all themes; by no means is it a fragment, broken off in a fit of neurotic nihilism, as some writers have dramatically proclaimed. *The Confidence Man* (like *Israel Potter*) is a book of folklore. It is a wonderfully perceptive study of the American character, done at the folklore level, where character is clear and vulnerable. Many of the characters can be found in Constance Rourke's *American Humor:* the Yankee peddler, the Negro, the frontiersman, and so on. Also, the confidence man, peddling phony wares to his compatriots on a Mississippi river boat, is another false Prometheus, Prometheus in a loud American suit. He is a do-gooder, a Progressive in fact, and an emotional-intellectual-spiritual cutpurse. The ironical joke about him is that among other things he sells an Omni-Balsamic Reinvigorator—the life-principle of Promethean *élan*, patented and bottled.

THE LARGER VIEW

Melville's books have enough energy, coherence, and intelligence to justify our calling the author an artist. At the present stage of Melville criticism that is the important fact. Certainly it is wrong to discuss Melville as a great progressive, an heroic democrat, a culture hero, a noble heart, or a prophet of the good society apart from Melville as an artist—as so many liberal or progressive critics have been content to do. To do this is to make Melville a lesser man than he was, and to repeat the old heresy about art not being connected with life and morals.

Melville's moral intelligence must not be underestimated either. It is wrong to allow our liberal political scruples to keep us from fully understanding Melville's idea of the Heroic American. Is this Heroic American "undemocratic?" Perhaps and perhaps not. The important point is that Melville does not discount the resources of personality. Melville's Promethean Hero is no vaporous or irresponsible extravagance of the Romantic Age. He is elementary psychology for American moralists.

From *The Partisan Review*, Vol. XIV (May–June, 1947), pp. 285–294. Reprinted by permission of the author and editors. The "approach" to Melville proposed in this essay has been developed in Mr. Chase's book *Herman Melville* (New York: The Macmillan Company, 1949).

ALFRED KAZIN

William James and Henry James: "Our Passion is Our Task"

[1943]

. . . This method of narration by interminable elaboration of suggestive reference (I don't know what to call it, but you know what I mean) goes agin the grain
of all my own impulses in writing; and yet in spite of it all, there is a brilliancy
and cleanness of effect, and in this book especially a high-toned social atmosphere
that are unique and extraordinary. . . . But why won't you, just to please Brother,
sit down and write a new book, with no twilight or mustiness in the plot, with
great vigor and decisiveness in the action, no fencing in the dialogue, no psychological commentaries, and absolute straightness in the style? . . .

I mean . . . to try to produce some uncanny form of thing, in fiction, that will
gratify you, as Brother—but let me say, dear William, that I shall greatly be humiliated, if you *do* like it, and thereby lump it, in your affection, with things of the
current age, that I have heard you express admiration for and that I would sooner
descend to a dishonored grave than have written. . . . I'm always sorry when I
hear of your reading anything of mine, and always hope you won't—you seem to
me so constitutionally unable to "enjoy" it. . . . How far apart and to what different ends we have had to work out (very naturally and properly!) our respective
intellectual lives.

THUS William James to Henry James on the publication of *The Golden
Bowl* in 1905, and the latter's unusually sharp reply to the older brother whom
he adored—and could barely read. There is always a certain irony in honoring
the Jameses together: they could never fully honor or, after a certain point,
really understand each other. This was a fact both recognized and that
William openly enjoyed. They were always seeking to gratify each other, "as
Brother," for the Jameses loved each other as frankly as they insisted on their
differences and delighted in each other's careers. Perhaps never as in the
James family was so little envy or indifference brought to so many conflicting
intellectual ambitions, and rarely has so much fraternity been conferred on

so little mutual understanding. How deeply the elder James delighted in his genius sons, though he could only, from his vast intimacy with God, look down on both science and art as frivolously incomplete! How ready William always was to read each of Henry's essays and novels as it came along, how quick with eager brotherly praise, how ready to define Henry's subtlest triumphs and to miss them! How much Henry stood in awe of William, showered him with adulation, professed himself a "pragmatist," and resented it when William forgot to send even a technical monograph!

Their devotion to each other was deep; their essential antipathy of spirit went deeper still. But antipathy is not the word: there was only a kind of loving non-recognition. Parallel as they were in their studies of human consciousness, in raising to an ideal end the supreme operativeness and moral certainty of an individual "center of revelation," they could only smile to each other across the grooves in which each had his temperament. Henry at least knew his failure to recognize the design unfolded in William's empiricism, where William so genially slid over the symbolic design stamped on Henry's every effort, praised him for his "high-toned social atmosphere," patronized him, and missed that need to *use* the novel as a creed of perfection that cut Henry's career off from the Anglo-American fiction of his generation. Henry was an isolated figure even in the philosophic James household, where William was its reigning heir, the versatile young naturalist who spoke in his father's hearty voice even when he revolted against his father's theology, the naturalist in a scientific era whose interests drew him everywhere. William could at least follow Henry's works and comment on them (he commented on everything)—praise the early style or deplore the later, admire a character and confer a judgment. When William's first book, the great *Psychology,* appeared in 1890, Henry could only fidget in embarrassment and complain that he was too absorbed properly to appreciate "your mighty and magnificent book, which requires a stretch of leisure and an absence of 'crisis' in one's own egotistical little existence." Or, later, say of *The Pluralistic Universe* that he had read it "with enchantment, with pride, and almost with comprehension. It may sustain and inspire you a little to know that I'm *with* you, all along the line. . . . Thank the powers—that is, thank *yours*—for a relevant and assimilable and referable philosophy . . . your present volume seems to me exquisitely and adorably cumulative. . . ."

There it was: William's thought was always "adorable," but Henry was too absorbed. Henry had always been absorbed, where William's mind opened out to all the world, from his father's notations on Swedenborg to psychical research, from Kant to William Jennings Bryan: Henry was absorbed in making novels. William tried to be an artist and a chemist, went to Brazil with Agassiz to collect fishes, took an M. D. between periods of almost suicidal depression, debated endlessly with his opponents and loved them all, learned psychology by teaching it, wrote letters to all the cranks about their manias, gravitated into philosophy, fought against imperialism; Henry went on making novels. He made novels as he had made his first critical essays; his famous "impressions" and the enduring myth of England he kept from his childhood reading in *Punch*: by storing and molding what he had, and by never taking in anything he would not use. They had tried to make a lawyer out of him, they tried to teach him some elementary facts of science; Henry went on collecting impressions—impressions of Italy and of the pictures he found in Italy (Emerson loved these), impressions of Newport, Paris, Geneva and Saratoga; impressions of the mourned cousin, Mary Temple, whose face was the face of Milly Theale, Maggie Verver and Isabel Archer. The only culture he had was literature and pictures, and the only literature he sought was the nineteenth-century novel—he did not care much even for poetry; but he had a mission and his mind and life composed a single order of desire: he made novels.

To the other Jameses Henry was always the mysterious child who sat quietly alone, dreaming pictures and studying novels, and always bewilderingly content with his own mind. He adhered to nothing but his own taste; he had no "message," no positive belief or apparent need of one. William, on the other hand, was racked until he could find an ontology as plastic as life and true of every last thing in it; and he ran excitedly through all the disciplines, rejecting, disputing, extracting, until he could square the "irreducible facts" with the highest fact of his own nature. To Henry he might have said what their father had said to Emerson: "Oh, you man without a handle! shall one never be able to help himself out of you, according to his needs, and be dependent only upon your fitful tippings-up?" William always needed a handle; and he could use one only by reacting against something. What he principally reacted against was his father. Henry drew from the elder James by enclosing himself in the independence the father preached; he did not react against his father's theology, he ignored it. William, however, was too much like his father in combativeness and vivacious curiosity to reproduce anything but his temperament. Nothing could have seemed more boring to him than his father's metaphysics, poetic as many elements in it were. The elder James had escaped the dreariness of Calvinism—its belief in a kind of haphazard criminality of human nature—by nailing the human mind and will to the dreariness of a perpetual mysticism. The world was now joy, where Calvin's had been the fear of fate; but the only release allowed man was submission; the only hope a projected drowning in God. Utopian socialist though he fancied himself, he saw the natural world only as a lens on supernatural truth. Thought was reduced to the labored ecstasy of extracting mystic "secrets"; man lived in an unremitting effort at revelation.

Nothing was more alien to William than any belief which bound man to something not in his particular nature and experience. In his biological theory of mind the mind was not a mere faculty, as the soul was not a region; it was an effect and transmission of consciousness, purposive by definition; the endlessly probing antennae of the whole human organism, it was what it did. All of a man's life was engaged in his thought or spoke or hid in it; the mind did not "receive" ideas, it shaped them in seeking adaptability; it sought ends. Yet what was so significant in William's psychology, often condemned as "literary," was that it buttressed in moral terms a theory of knowledge. Though he was almost the first American to establish psychological studies in the laboratory, he was always impatient with laboratory psychology and a mere corpus of data. What he was getting at, as in his pragmatism, was not only a more elastic sense of reality, a more honest and imaginative perception that all life and thought begin in discrete individuals and are shaped by their differences, but a need to show that what was not a real experience to an individual had no existence that one could name and take account of.

To the merely bookish, who would rather intone their knowledge than be shaped by it; to the merely devout, who would rather worship their God than be transformed by Him; to the formal logicians and contented monists, for whom the world's radical disorder and depth are so easily sacrificed, William James has always seemed loose or even vulgar because he preached that an idea has meaning only as it is expressed in action and experience. That he was so misunderstood is partly James's own fault, since he *would* speak of "the cash-value" of an idea in his characteristic attempt to reach the minds even of those for whom cash-value was the main value. But that he continues to be misunderstood is largely the fault of our personal culture, since the rarest thing in it is still the *active* moral imagination. For what James was leading to in his pragmatism—once it had served as a theory of knowledge—was moral in the most burning sense of conduct, moral in the enduring sense of the use a human life is put to. Tell me, he seemed always to be saying to those who were so content with ideas rather than with thinking, with thinking rather than realization, what is it you *experience*, what is it that is changed in you or by you, when you have achieved your certainty or knowledge? What is it you live by, appreciably, when you have proved that something is true? James knew well enough, and could formulate the ends and satisfactions of his opponents better than many of them could; but that was only incidental to his essential aim. Knowledge is for men that they may live—and men may live for ideal ends. So is the monist happy in his all-enveloping unity, the rationalist in his ideal symmetry, the mystic in his visions. And all of these exist, said James: all of these must be taken into our account of the human experience and the demands of our nature. But do not confuse, he went on, your individual need of certainty with the illusion that some supra-human order is ascertained by it; do not confuse your use of reason—and delight in it—with the illusion that what cannot be named or verified by rationalism does not exist.

To say this is not to forget how treacherous James's ideal of the provisional can be, and that he is particularly dissatisfying when he leaves us at the borders of metaphysics. He triumphed by disproving all the cults and systems which ignored the shaping power of man's individuality, by threshing his way through pre-scientific myths and post-scientific arrogance. But like so many American naturalistic thinkers, he took a certain necessary definition of the good life for granted (or confused it with the Elysian fields of the Harvard Department of Philosophy?); whereas it is the unrelenting consciousness of it that is most lacking. Yet what is most important here is that the great particular for him, as for all the Jameses, was the human self, and that out of it they made all their universals (though it is always a question what Henry's universals were). For the elder James the center of existence was the self that seeks to know God and to be sublimated in Him; William's theory of knowledge began with the knowing mind that *initiates* the ideas to which the test of experience is to be applied; Henry found his technical—and moral—triumph in the central Jamesian intelligence which sifts the experiences of all the other characters and organizes them. This, had William not so clearly pined for Stevenson when he read Henry's novels, he might have recognized as Henry's "handle." For in an age when all the materials through which William was running so eagerly demanded large positive answers, wholesale reconstructions and a world view, Henry had quietly and stubbornly reproduced his father's mystical integrity in the radiance of the observing self—in a prose which was more and more attuned to the most spontaneous music of the mind. The novel for him was to be *histoire morale,* a branch of history that sought the close textures and hidden lights of painting; but the highest morality was not so much in the story as in the exercise of the creative principle behind it.

That devotion to a creative principle was the great epic of Henry's integrity, as everything he ever sought or wrote was a commentary on it. In most writers their works exemplify their ambition; Henry's were about his ambition, as they were, in one sense, only his ambition written large. Just as William's vision always came back to a loose sea of empiricism in which man could hold on only to his own plurality, so Henry's was to define and to fill out the moral history of composition. His theory of art was not preparatory to a manipulation of experience; it *was* his experience. His interest was fixed on writing about the symbolic devotion of writing, as so many of his stories were of writers (but only of depressed or unsuccessful writers: there was no "dramatic process" in the surface of success). And the central Jamesian intelligence, in all his disguises as "the foreground observer," "the center of revelation," the artist planning his effects, the critic "remounting the stream of composition," was always sifting and commenting in turn. "The private history of any sincere work," he wrote once, "looms large with its own completeness"; the artist was his symbol of man's sincerity in operation. He studied his novels endlessly as he wrote them, corrected them endlessly when they were published, wrote prefaces in which he summarized the history of their composition, defined his every intent and use of means, speculated on the general principles they illustrated, and at the end, as he hinted to Grace Norton, might have written a preface to the prefaces, commenting on *them* in turn. The figure in the carpet was woven out of honor, not secrecy: out of so self-driven an integrity, as out of the intense interior life of his characters, there could be grasped the central fact of the effort, the search, the aura of devotion, that gave meaning to the artist's life and form to his work. And always the thread remained firmly in the artist's hand, pulling it back to himself—the story of Henry James was the story of Henry James writing his novels.

Life for both always returned to the central self. Significantly, it was always the richness of their personal nature that distinguished all the Jameses, and the overflow of life in them that gave them their vascular styles. Ralph Barton Perry says of the elder James that he felt his visions so intensely, and had so many together, that he had to get them all out at once. The elder James was always running over, laughing at himself for it, and never stopped running over. Like William, he had so many possible thoughts about so many things; and he had the James exuberance (the seed *was* Irish) that always ran so high in them despite (or in protest against) the family neurosis. Superficially, of course, no two styles would seem to be so different as William's and Henry's: the one so careful to sound spontaneous, the other so spontaneously labored; the one so informal in its wisdom, flinging witticisms, philosophical jargon, homeliness and hearty German abstractions about with a seeming carelessness, protesting doubt at every point, yet probing with angelic friendliness into all the blocks around the human mind; the other so *made* a style, solemnly and deliciously musical, reverberating with all the echoes of all the books Henry had ever read, forever sliding into cozy French idioms, shyly offering the commonest spoken expressions in quotation marks—Henry always sought to be friendly. Yet both were great spoken styles, intimate and with an immense range of tone: the only difference being that William talked to friendly Harvard seniors and Henry addressed some ideally patient friend. What no one has ever said enough about Henry's style, of course, is that it was the family style at its most intense: like all the Jameses, he wrote straight out of amplitude. He gushed and he purred, but there was always the James motor power behind him, their insatiable need to seize and define everything in range. And more, there was that "blague and benignity" in his style, as Ezra Pound named it: the tricky interior changes of pace, the slow mandarin whisperings, the adjectives that opened all vistas for him like great bronze doors, the wonderful tone *soundings* he could make with words, and covering them all, always his deceiving gentleness, the ceremonial diffidence, and his sudden barbs and winks.

To think of their styles is to be aware of the great and radiant innocence that was in all the Jameses, an innocence of personal spirit if hardly of moral perception. Financially secure, encouraged by their father to be different and uncontrolled, even to be without a profession, both ranged at will in what was still the household age of modern thought—a period when the security of their society encouraged those first studies in the naturalism of the psyche, and a voracious interior life. The only revolution either could envision was in new ways of knowing; and it is significant that William led the way to "the stream of consciousness." They all had the natural outpouring that came with innocence, the innocence that trusted in all the data of their enquiry, took the social forms for granted, and based life upon the integrity of the observing self. "In self-trust are all the virtues comprehended." It was the last and the best of Emerson in their culture, in all its lovable trust in individuality. Just as the elder James's theology committed man, as it were, to be a recording angel, to seek the necessary revelation and inscribe it, so they were all recording angels, as William said of Henry that under all his "rich sea-weeds" and "rigid barnacles and things" he cared only for making novels. Life was here and now, in all that system of relations between minds in which experience immediately consists; man *studied* it. The highest aim, of course, was to be an author. But there is no very great sense of revolt in any of them (compare them with the Adamses), no sense of that deeper radicalism, or metaphysical despair, which is uncontained even by pluralism and is not mollified by the individual creatingness.

Yet in a time like our own, when men are so peculiarly lost in themselves because they are so lost from each other, the Jamesian integrity is the very rock of comfort. We can take no social form for granted; we cannot possess or be possessed by those explorations in human consciousness which only parallel —or at best reveal—our quest for security. Our enforced sense of evil has nothing so creative in it as their innocence; and their legacy is still most precious for its symbolic integrity, its trust in mind, its superiority to our "failure of nerve." Even Henry James's greatest contributions to human pleasure and self-comprehension, or his insistence on the integrity of a work of art, are less important now than the emblem his pride raises before us. Even William's full devotion to realism, his imaginative projection of complexity, are less important to us now than the respect he breeds in us for all the forms of reality and our necessary understanding of them. And it is this which is now most visible in them and most important to us: the bounteousness of their feeling for life and the intensity of their respect for it. They both worked in that period of modern history when the trust of man in his power to know was at its highest, when the revolution of modern political democracy, science and materialism carried along even those who were skeptical of the idea of progress. But if we feel at times that they are geater than their thought, more beautiful than the books that contain them, it is because they burned with that indestructible zeal which we need so badly to recover—the zeal that cries that life does have a meaning: we seek to *be*.

In "The Middle Years," one of those exquisite stories in which Henry James was always writing out the lesson of his own loneliness and neglect in the story of the celebrated writer neglected and misunderstood by those nearest him, the writer cries on his deathbed: "It *is* glory—to have been tested, to have had our little quality, and cast our spell." "You're a great success!" his young attendant assures him. And Dencombe replies, wearily, but with mounting exaltation: "We work in the dark—we do what we can—we give what we have. Our doubt is our passion, and our passion is our task."

From *The New Republic*, Vol. CVIII (February 15, 1943), pp. 216–218. Reprinted in this revised version by permission of the author and editors.

PART V

Modern Criticism: Its Problems, Methods, and Prospects

T. S. ELIOT
Experiment in Criticism

[1929]

THERE is no department of literature in which it is more difficult to establish a distinction between "traditional" and "experimental" work than literary criticism. For here both words may be taken in two senses. By traditional criticism we may mean that which follows the same methods, aims at the same ends, and expresses much the same state of mind as the criticism of the preceding generation. Or we may mean something quite different; a criticism which has a definite theory of the meaning and value of the term "tradition," and which may be experimental in reverting to masters who have been forgotten. And as for "experiment" one may mean the more original work of the present generation, or else the work of critics who are pushing into new fields of inquiry, or enlarging the scope of criticism with other kinds of knowledge. To use the word "experimental" in the first sense would be invidious, for it would cover all the critical work of our time which one considers to have merit. For it is obvious that every generation has a new point of view, and is self-conscious in the critic; his work is twofold: to interpret the past to the present, and to judge the present in the light of the past. We have to see literature through our own temperament in order to see it at all, though our vision is always partial and our judgment always prejudiced; no generation, and no individual, can appreciate every dead author and every past period; universal good taste is never realized. In this way, all criticism is experimental, just as the mode of life of every generation is an experiment. It is only in my second sense, therefore, that it is worth while to talk of experimental criticism; only by considering what critics today may be deliberately attempting some kind of critical work which has not been deliberately attempted before.

In order to make clear exactly what there is that is new in contemporary critical writing I shall have to go back a hundred years. We may say, roughly, that modern criticism begins with the work of the French critic Sainte-Beuve, that is to say about the year 1826. Before him, Coleridge had attempted a new type of criticism, a type which is in some respects more allied to what is now called esthetics than to literary criticism. But from the Renaissance through the eighteenth century literary criticism had been confined to two narrow, and closely related, types. One was a type which has always existed and I hope always will, for it can always have very great value; it may be called practical notes on the art of writing by practitioners, parallel to the treatises on painting which have been left us by Leonardo da Vinci and others. Such notes are of the greatest value to other artists, particularly when studied in conjunction with the author's own work. Two classical examples in English are the Elizabethan treatises on rhymed and unrhymed verse written by Thomas Campion and Samuel Daniel. The prefaces and essays of Dryden, the prefaces of Corneille, are of the same type but on a larger scale and engage wider issues. But at the same time there is a large body of criticism, a considerable quantity in English and still more in French, written by men who were professionally critics rather than creative writers; the most famous critic of this sort is of course Boileau. This type of critic was primarily the *arbiter of taste,* and his task was to praise and condemn the work of his contemporaries, and especially to lay down the laws of good writing. These laws were supposed to be drawn from the practice, but still more from the theory, of the ancients. Aristotle was highly respected; but in practice this type of criticism was usually far from following the profound insight of Aristotle, and confined itself to translating, imitating, and plagiarizing Horace's *Art of Poetry.* At its best, it confirmed and maintained permanent standards of good writing; at its worst, it was a mere sequence of precepts. In general, French criticism was more theoretic and, as in La Harpe, more desiccated; the normal English type was nearer to plain good sense, as in Johnson's *Lives of the Poets;* though interesting theory, usually on specific literary types such as the drama, is found in authors like Thomas Rymer and Daniel Webb in the seventeenth and eighteenth centuries.

It is worth delaying for a moment to point out one of the qualities of seventeenth- and eighteenth-century literary criticism, which gives it enduring value and at the same time marks it off from more modern criticism. We are apt to think of this older criticism as dry and formal, and as setting up classical molds in which no living literature could be shaped. But we should remember in its favor that this criticism recognized literature as literature, and not another thing. Literature was something distinct from philosophy and psychology and every other study; and its purpose was to give a refined pleasure to persons of sufficient leisure and breeding. If the older critics had not taken for granted that literature was something primarily to be enjoyed, they could not have occupied themselves so sedulously with laying down rules of what was right to enjoy. This seems a very commonplace remark, and no distinction; but if you compare the criticism of those two centuries with that of the nineteenth, you will see that the latter does not take this simple truth wholly for granted. Literature is often treated by the critic rather as a means for eliciting truth or acquiring knowledge. If the critic is of a more philosophic or religious mind, he will look for the expression of philosophic or religious intuition in the work of the author criticised; if he is of a more realistic turn, he will look to literature as material for the discovery of psychological truths, or as documents illustrating social history. Even in the mouths of Walter Pater and his disciples, the phrase "art for art's sake" means something very different from the sense in which literature was literature for literature's sake up to the latter part of the eighteenth century. If you read carefully the famous epilogue to Pater's *Studies in the Renaissance* you will see that "art for art's sake" means nothing less than art as a substitute for everything else, and as a purveyor of emotions and sensations which belong to life rather than to art. To distinguish clearly between these two attitudes, that of art for art's sake and that of the eighteenth century, does require a strong effort of imagination. But the former doctrine would have been unintelligible to the earlier age. For the earlier period, art and literature were not substitutes for religion or philosophy or morals or politics, any more than for dueling or love-making: they were special and limited adornments of life. On each side there is a profit and a loss. We have gained perhaps a deeper insight, now and then; whether we enjoy literature any more keenly than our ancestors I do not know; but I think we should return again and again to the critical writings of the seventeenth and eighteenth centuries, to remind ourselves of that simple truth that literature is primarily literature, a means of refined and intellectual pleasure.

How, we ask immediately, did human beings ever come to abandon so simple and satisfying a limitation of criticism? The change comes about incidentally to a larger change, which may be described as the growth of the historical attitude. But this change—to which I shall return in a moment—is preceded, so far as literary criticism is concerned—by a freakish phenomenon, by a book written by one of the wisest and most foolish men of his time and perhaps the most extraordinary; a book which is itself one of the wisest and silliest, the most exciting and most exasperating book of criticism ever written—the *Biographia Literaria* of Coleridge. There, if you like, was "experiment in criticism," everything in fact except the power of sticking to the point—a power noticeably absent from Coleridge's ill-regulated life. Coleridge was one of the most learned men of his time, and no man of his time had wider interests except Goethe; and one of the first things that strikes us about his book, besides its uncommon diffuseness, is the novel variety of knowledge which he brings to bear on literary criticism. Much of his knowledge, as of the romantic German philosophers, does not seem to us today particularly worth having, but it was held to be valuable then; and we owe to Coleridge as much as to anybody our enjoyment of the doubtful benefits of German Idealism. His book naturally contains specimens of several types of criticism; its impulse, of course, was a defense of the new—or as the newspapers of our time would say, "modernist"—poetry of Wordsworth; and as such belongs to the type of technical notes of a craftsman; but when Coleridge started on anything, it could lead to almost everything else. He had not the historical point of view, but by the catholicity of his literary lore, and his ability for sudden and illuminating comparisons drawn from poetry of different ages and different languages, he anticipated some of the most useful accomplishments of the historical method. But one thing that Coleridge did effect for literary criticism is this. He brought out clearly the relation of literary criticism to that branch of philosophy which has flourished amazingly under the name of esthetics; and, following German writers whom he had studied, he puts the criticism of literature in its place as merely one department of the theoretic study of the Fine Arts in general. His fine discrimination of Fancy and Imagination cannot be held as permanent, for terms and relations change; but it remains one of the important texts for all who would consider the nature of poetic imagination. And he establishes literary criticism as a part of philosophy: or, to put it more moderately, he made it necessary for the "literary critic" to acquaint himself with general philosophy and metaphysics.

Biographia Literaria appeared in 1817; the activities of Charles Augustin Sainte-Beuve may be said to begin about 1826. Coleridge and Sainte-Beuve have very little in common—as little, that is, as two men who were both great critics could have in common. And Sainte-Beuve would not have been a great critic solely on the ground of what is new and experimental in his work. He had a very French intelligence and good taste which enabled him to share the ideals and sympathies of the great French writers of every time; there was much in him of the eighteenth century, a good deal even of the seventeenth. There were many gaps, certainly, in his appreciations, both of his contemporaries and of his predecessors; but he had that essential critical quality of imagination which made it possible for him to grasp literature as a whole. Where he differed from previous French critics was in his implicit conception of literature, not only as a body of writings to be enjoyed, but as a process of change in history, and as a part of the study of history. The notion that literary values are relative to literary periods, that the literature of a period is primarily an expression and a symptom of the time, is so natural to us now that we can hardly detach our minds from it. We can hardly conceive that the degree and kind of self-consciousness which we have could ever not have been. How much criticism of contemporary literature is taken up with discussing whether, and in what degree, this book or novel or poem is expressive of our mentality, of the personality of our age; and how often our critics seemed to be interested rather in inquiring what we (including themselves) are like, than with the book, novel, or poem as a work of art! This is an extreme, but the extreme of a tendency which began, in criticism, a good hundred years ago. Sainte-Beuve was not, like Coleridge, a metaphysician; he is indeed more modern and more skeptical; but he was the first interesting historian in criticism. And it is by no means irrelevant that he began his career with the study of medicine; he is not only an historian but a biologist in criticism.

It is, I think, interesting to turn to some good recent piece of literary criticism, and underline some of the assumptions of knowledge and theory which you would not find in criticism of two hundred years ago. Mr. Herbert Read's lucid little primer, *Phases of English Poetry,* will do for our purpose. On the second page he tells us that his is an inquiry into the evolution of poetry, and speaks presently of English poetry as a "living and developing organism." Even these few words should give a hint of the extent to which the critical apparatus has changed with the general changes in scientific and historical conceptions, when a literary critic can treat his audience to terms like "evolution" and "living organism" with the assurance of their being immediately apprehended. He is taking for granted certain vague but universal biological ideas. A little later he informs us that "the beginning of this study belongs to anthropology." Now, a great deal of work has had to be done by a great many people, and already more or less popularized, before a critic of literature can talk in this way. The work of Bastian, Tylor, Mannhardt, Durkheim, Lévy-Bruhl, Frazer, Miss Harrison, and many others has gone before. And a great deal of purely literary investigation has been made too, before anyone can talk of the evolution of poetry. Mr. Read begins by studying the origins of ballad poetry. It would not have been possible for him to do so without a great deal of work done in the later nineteenth century and the early twentieth; for example, by Professor Child of Harvard, Professor Gummere of Haverford, Professor Gaston Paris of the Sorbonne, and Professor W. P. Ker of London. Such studies in ballad poetry, and in all the heretofore unexplored ages of literature, have fostered in us the sense of flux and evolution, the sense of the relation of the poetry of each period to the civilization of the period, and also have tended slightly to *level* literary values. It was W. P. Ker, who perhaps knew the whole history of European poetry better than any man of his time, who said that in literature there were no Dark Ages. And in the next paragraph to the one which I have just quoted, Mr. Read observes that in theories of the origin of poetry we "go right back to the origin of speech." Even to make so simple a remark as this requires the work of another group of scientists: the philologists. The modern critic must have some acquaintance with them too—with the work of such contemporary philologists as Professor Jespersen of Copenhagen.

There are other branches of knowledge (or at least of science) some acquaintance with which you take for granted in any applicant whom you may employ as literary critic. Especially, of course, psychology, particularly analytical psychology. All of the studies I have mentioned, and more, do themselves touch the edges, and handle some of the problems, of criticism; so conversely the critic is distinguished first by the current notions which he shares with all educated or half-educated persons, such as the notion of evolution, and by the number and variety of sciences of which he has to know a little. And he has to know them, not in order to do their work for them, but to collaborate— and also in order that he may know where to stop. We require much general knowledge in order to see the limits of our particular ignorance.

Now although Sainte-Beuve did not have the equipment which we expect of our contemporaries, he had a great deal of the method, and very typically the state of mind which results from such a method at our stage of history. The awareness of the process of time has obscured the frontiers between litera-ture and everything else. If you read the earlier critics, such as Dryden, you find the problems of literature comparatively simple ones. For Dryden and his contemporaries there were the Greek and Latin classics, a solid block of accepted canon, and there were their contemporaries, that is to say, English literature from Shakespeare and French literature from Malherbe; and they spent a good deal of their time in discussing whether the moderns, as they called themselves, had any literary virtues not surpassed by the ancients. Their estimate of the classics was not complicated by worrying about serpent and mistletoe cults, or the finances of the Athenian government. And between the ancients and Shakespeare and Malherbe there was nothing much to think about. They had really a great deal more faith in themselves than we have. They were certainly not bothered about "the future." It often seems to me that all our concern of it, which Mr. Shaw and Mr. Wells used to enjoy, are tokens of a profound pessimism. We hardly have time to get any fun out of what is being written now, so concerned are we about the quality of what may be written fifty years hence. Even Mr. Read's chapter on "Modern Poetry" seems to be as much engrossed by the puzzle of what poetry will be as by the puzzle of what it is. This kind of doubt seems to me to continue the doubt of Sainte-Beuve and Renan. Sainte-Beuve wrote a book of seven volumes on that re-markable French religious movement of the seventeenth century known as "Port Royal," and on that remarkable group of religious people of whom the most famous is Pascal. It is the masterpiece on that subject. It comes to no con-clusion. It ends with the words: "He who had it most at heart to know his object, whose ambition was most engaged in seizing it, whose pride was most alert to paint it—how powerless he feels, and how far beneath his task, on the day when, seeing it almost finished and the result obtained, he feels his exalta-tion sink, feels himself overcome by faintness and inevitable disgust, and per-ceives in his turn that he too is only a fleeting illusion in the midst of the in-finite illusory flux!" Sainte-Beuve was a modern critic for this reason: he was a man of restless curiosity about life, society, civilization, and all the problems which the study of history arouses. He studied these things through literature, because that was the center of his interests; and he never lost his literary sensi-bility in his investigation of problems reaching far beyond literature. But he was an historian, a sociologist (in the best sense of that word) and a moralist. He is a typical modern critic in that he found himself obliged to brood over the larger and darker problems which, in the modern world, lie behind the specific problems of literature.

The criticism of literature has by no means been absorbed in something else, as alchemy into chemistry. The core of the matter is still there, though the ramifications are endless, and the task of the critic is indeed hard. But there is still a valid distinction to be drawn between those modern critics who would make literature a substitute for a definite philosophy and theology, and thus promulgate, in an inverted form, the old gospel of art for art's sake, and those who would try to keep the distinctions clear, while admitting that the study of the one leads to the other, and that the possession of clear literary standards must imply the possession of clear moral standards. The various attempts to find the fundamental axioms behind both good literature and good life are among the most interesting "experiments" of criticism in our time.

The most considerable of such attempts so far is that which is known under the name of Humanism, and which owes its origin chiefly to the work of Professor Babbitt of Harvard. Mr. Babbitt, who is one of the most learned men of our time, is to some extent a disciple of Sainte-Beuve. There is no one living who knows more intimately (among many other things) the whole history of literary criticism. In his own writings, criticism of literature has been a means of criticising every aspect of modern society. He is a scholar of classical education, and classical tastes. He is keenly aware of the fact that the weaknesses of modern literature are symptoms of the weaknesses of modern civilization, and he has set himself with immense patience and perseverance to analyze these weaknesses. His conclusions may be read in his two most recent books, *Rousseau and Romanticism,* an account and a theory of the deterioration of taste since the early eighteenth century, and a book of still wider scope, *Democracy and Leadership.* As a moralist and as an Anglo-Saxon, he has on one side more in common with Matthew Arnold than with Sainte-Beuve. The tendency of the "humanist" in France is rather to diagnose, without prescribing a remedy; witness two recent books of brilliant literary and social criticism by M. Julien Benda, *Belphégor* and *La Trahison des clercs;* the Anglo-Saxon finds it intolerable to diagnose a disease without prescribing a remedy. Mr. Babbitt, like Arnold and Sainte-Beuve, finds that the decay of religious dogma has inflicted grave injury on society; like Arnold and Sainte-Beuve, he refuses to accept the remedy of returning to religious dogma; like Arnold and unlike Sainte-Beuve, he proposes another remedy, a theory of positive ethics based on human experiment, on the needs and capacities of the human as human, without reference to revelation or to supernatural authority or aid.

I do not propose, in this brief account, to discuss Mr. Babbitt's positive contribution, or the points at which I agree or disagree. I only want to call at-

tention to a most important movement which is primarily, or in its inception,
a movement within literary criticism, and of which a great deal more will be
heard. It is significant because it shows that the modern literary critic must
be an "experimenter" outside of what you might at first consider his own
province; and as evidence that nowadays there is no literary problem which
does not lead us irresistibly to larger problems. There is one weakness, or
rather danger, of literary criticism which perceives the inevitable continuation
of literary questions into general questions, which I might as well point out,
because otherwise you will see it for yourselves and attach too much importance to it. The danger is that when a critic has grasped these vital moral
problems which rise out of literary criticism, he may lose his detachment and
submerge his sensibility. He may become too much a servant of his mind and
conscience; he may be too impatient with contemporary literature, having
pigeonholed it under one or another of the modern social maladies; and may
demand edification at once, when appreciation of genius and accomplishment
should come first. When he upholds "classicism" and denounces "romanticism" he is likely to give the impression that we should write like Sophocles
or Racine; that everything contemporary is "romantic" and therefore not worth
talking about. He makes us suspect that if a truly great, original classical work
of imagination were to be written today, no one would like it. There will always be romantic people to admire romantic work; but we wonder whether
the classicists would certainly know a classical work when it came. But these
qualifications should not lead us to reject the humanist's theories: they should
only lead us to apply them for ourselves.

Mr. Ramon Fernandez is a younger critic who has also taken the word
humanism for his device, though his humanism, arrived at independently in
France, is of a rather different brand from that which has arisen in America.
His humanism has this in common: that it is also a development from literary
criticism, and that it is also an attempt to arrive at a positive ethics while rejecting any revealed religion or supernatural authority. His first volume of
essays, *Messages,* has been translated into English. It is important I think not
so much by its achievement—for indeed the author has still a great many
tangled knots in his style, which is cumbered by a good deal of philosophical
and psychological terminology—as by its new attempt. Mr. Fernandez is less
encyclopedic, less concerned with the past. He pores steadily over contemporaries and over the nineteenth century, and is more devoted to the study of
special individuals, such as Montaigne, than to the study of the general course
of literary history. Like the American humanists, he ponders over "classicism"
and "romanticism"; but he wishes to be flexible, and is anxious to distinguish
the essentials of classicism (which he finds, for instance, in George Eliot)
from its appearances at any particular time. His theory is one which I do not
wholly understand, and which has not yet been fully expounded, and prob-

ably not yet fully developed: but he illustrates, as clearly as the American humanists, the new experimental method of dealing with literary problems as moral problems, and the attempt to find guidance in conduct out of statement in literature—especially from the great novelists, and particularly, for he is a close student of English literature, from George Eliot and George Meredith. (In any case, his essay on Marcel Proust, the French novelist, in the volume mentioned, is a masterpiece of his particular method.) He is, in general, less the sociologist and more the individual psychologist. And from the best of his essays on novelists one draws this conclusion: that if we should exclude from literary criticism all but purely literary considerations, there would not only be very little to talk about, but actually we should be left without even literary appreciation. This is true of our appreciation of ancient authors but still more obviously of our appreciation of modern authors. For the same expansion of interest which has been imposed upon the modern critic has been imposed, or at least has been assumed, by the modern imaginative writer. We cannot write a purely literary criticism of George Eliot, for instance, unless it is admittedly a very imperfect criticism: for as the interests of the author were wide, so must be those of the critic.

I have tried to show that the tendency throughout a whole epoch to the present moment has been to widen the scope of criticism and increase the demands made upon the critic. This development might be traced in terms of the development of human self-consciousness, but that is a general philosophical question beyond the margin of this paper. There is along with this expansion a compensating tendency. As the number of sciences multiply, of sciences that is which have a bearing upon criticism, so we ask ourselves first whether there is still any justification for literary criticism at all, or whether we should not merely allow the subject to be absorbed gently into exacter sciences which will each annex some side of criticism. Just as in the history of philosophy, we find many subjects surrendered from time to time by philosophy, now to mathematics and physics, now to biology and psychology; until there seems to be almost nothing left to philosophize about. I think that the answer is clear: that so long as literature is literature, so long will there be a place for criticism of it—for criticism, that is, on the same basis as that on which the literature itself is made. For so long as poetry and fiction and such things are written, its first purpose must always be what it always has been—to give a peculiar kind of pleasure which has something constant in it throughout the ages, however difficult and various our explanations of that pleasure may be. The task of criticism will be, accordingly, not only to expand its borders but to clarify its center, and the insistency of the latter need grows with that of the former. Two hundred years ago, when it was taken for granted that one knew well enough what literature was, and it was not the number of other things which it is always now seeming to be, terms could be used more freely and carelessly without close definition. Now, there is an urgent need for experiment in criticism of a new kind, which will consist largely in a logical and dialectical study of the terms used. My own interest in these problems has been fostered partly by dissatisfaction with the *meaning* of my own statements in criticism, and partly by dissatisfaction with the terminology of the Humanists. In literary criticism we are constantly using terms which we cannot define, and defining other things by them. We are constantly using terms which have an *intension* and an *extension* which do not quite fit; theoretically they ought to be made to fit; but if they cannot, then some other way must be found of dealing with them so that we may know at every moment what we mean. I will take a very simple example with which I have been dealing myself: the possibility of defining "metaphysical poetry." Here is a term which has a whole history of meanings down to the present time, all of which must be recognized, although it cannot have all of them at once. The term means on the one hand a certain group of English poets in the seventeenth century. On the other hand it must have an intensive meaning, must stand for a peculiar whole of qualities which is exemplified by the several poets. The ordinary critical method would be to define what "metaphysical poetry" means to you in the abstract, fit as many poets to it as well as you can, and reject the rest. Or else, you take the poets who have been held to be "metaphysical," and find out what they have in common. The odd thing is that by doing the sum, so to speak, in two different ways, you get two different results. A larger problem in the same kind of definition is that of "classicism" and "romanticism." Everyone who writes about these two abstractions believes that he knows what the words mean; actually they mean something a little different for each observer, and merely mean to mean the same things. In this way you have material for endless wrangling with no conclusion, which is not satisfactory. Such problems involve, of course, both logic and the theory of knowledge and psychology; there is no one, perhaps, more concerned with them than Mr. I. A. Richards, the author of *Principles of Literary Criticism* and *Practical Criticism*.

There is good cause for believing—apart from the obvious assertion that every generation must criticize for itself—that literary criticism, far from being exhausted, has hardly begun its work. On the other hand, I am more than skeptical of the old superstition that criticism and "creative writing" never flourish in the same age: that is a generalization drawn from a superficial inspection of some past ages. "Creative writing" can look after itself; and certainly it will be none the better for suppressing the critical curiosity. And in any case, the times which we have lived in seem to me, on the false antithesis mentioned, rather "creative" than "critical." (The current superstition that our epoch is Alexandrine, decadent, or "disillusioned" is parallel; there are no "disillusioned ages," only disillusioned individuals; and our time is just as deluded as any other.) The present age has been, rather, uncritical, and partly for economic causes. The "critic" has been chiefly the reviewer, that is to say, the hurried amateur wage-slave. I am aware of the danger that the types of criticism in which I am interested may become too professional and technical. What I hope for is the collaboration of critics of various special training, and perhaps the pooling and sorting of their contributions by men who will be neither specialists nor amateurs.

From *The Bookman*, Vol. LXX (November, 1929), pp. 225–233. Reprinted by permission of the author and editor. The essay has not been collected by the author in his books. It was included in *Tradition and Experiment in Present-Day Literature* (London: Oxford University Press–Humphrey Milford, 1929), pp. 198–215.

Religion and Literature
[1935]

WHAT I have to say is largely in support of the following propositions: Literary criticism should be completed by criticism from a definite ethical and theological standpoint. In so far as in any age there is common agreement on ethical and theological matters, so far can literary criticism be substantive. In ages like our own, in which there is no such common agreement, it is the more necessary for Christian readers to scrutinize their reading, especially of works of imagination, with explicit ethical and theological standards. The "greatness" of literature cannot be determined solely by literary standards; though we must remember that whether it is literature or not can be determined only by literary standards.[1]

We have tacitly assumed, for some centuries past, that there is *no* relation between literature and theology. This is not to deny that literature—I mean, again, primarily works of imagination—has been, is, and probably always will be judged by some moral standards. But moral judgments of literary works are made only according to the moral code accepted by each generation, whether it lives according to that code or not. In any age which accepts some precise Christian theology, the common code may be fairly orthodox: though even in such periods the common code may exalt such concepts as "honour," "glory" or "revenge" to a position quite intolerable to Christianity. The dramatic ethics of the Elizabethan Age offers an interesting study. But when the common code is detached from its theological background, and is consequently

---

[1] As an example of literary criticism given greater significance by theological interests, I would call attention to Theodor Haecker: *Virgil* (Sheed and Ward).

more and more merely a matter of habit, it is exposed both to prejudice and to change. At such times morals are open to being altered *by* literature; so that we find in practice that what is "objectionable" in literature is merely what the present generation is not used to. It is a commonplace that what shocks one generation is accepted quite calmly by the next. This adaptability to change of moral standards is sometimes greeted with satisfaction as an evidence of human perfectibility: whereas it is only evidence of what unsubstantial foundations people's moral judgments have.

I am not concerned here with religious literature but with the application of our religion to the criticism of any literature. It may be as well, however, to distinguish first what I consider to be the three senses in which we can speak of "religious literature." The first is that of which we say that it is religious "literature" in the same way that we speak of "historical literature" or of "scientific literature." I mean that we can treat the Authorized translation of the Bible, or the works of Jeremy Taylor, as literature, in the same way that we treat the historical writing of Clarendon or of Gibbon—our two great English historians—as literature; or Bradley's *Logic*, or Buffon's *Natural History*. All of these writers were men who, incidentally to their religious, or historical, or philosophic purpose, had a gift of language which makes them delightful to read to all those who can enjoy language well written, even if they are unconcerned with the objects which the writers had in view. And I would add that though a scientific, or historical, or theological, or philosophic work which is also "literature," may become superannuated as anything but literature, yet it is not likely to be "literature" unless it had its scientific or other value for its own time. While I acknowledge the legitimacy of this enjoyment, I am more acutely aware of its abuse. The persons who enjoy these writings *solely* because of their literary merit are essentially parasites; and we know that parasites, when they become too numerous, are pests. I could easily fulminate for a whole hour against the men of letters who have gone into ecstasies over "the Bible as literature," the Bible as "the noblest monument of English prose." Those who talk of the Bible as a "monument of English prose" are merely admiring it as a monument over the grave of Christianity. I must try to avoid the by-paths of my discourse: it is enough to suggest that just as the work of Clarendon, or Gibbon, or Buffon, or Bradley would be of inferior literary value if it were insignificant as history, science, and philosophy respectively, so the Bible has had a *literary* influence upon English literature *not* because it has been considered as literature, but because it has been considered as the report of the Word of God. And the fact that men of letters now discuss it as "literature" probably indicates the *end* of its "literary" influence.

The second kind of relation of religion to literature is that which is found in what is called "religious" or "devotional" poetry. Now what is the usual attitude of the lover of poetry—and I mean the person who is a genuine and first-hand enjoyer and appreciator of poetry, not the person who follows the admirations of others—towards this department of poetry? I believe, all that may be implied in his calling it a *department.* He believes, not always explicitly, that when you qualify poetry as "religious" you are indicating very clear limitations. For the great majority of people who love poetry, *"religious* poetry" is a variety of *minor* poetry: the religious poet is not a poet who is treating the whole subject matter of poetry in a religious spirit, but a poet who is dealing with a confined part of this subject matter: who is leaving out what men consider their major passions, and thereby confessing his ignorance of them. I think that this is the real attitude of most poetry lovers towards such poets as Vaughan, or Southwell, or Grashaw, or George Herbert, or Gerard Hopkins.

But what is more, I am ready to admit that up to a point these critics are right. For there is a kind of poetry, such as most of the work of the authors I have mentioned, which is the product of a special religious awareness, which may exist without the general awareness which we expect of the major poet. In some poets, or in some of their works, this general awareness may have existed; but the preliminary steps which represent it may have been suppressed, and only the end-product presented. Between these, and those in which the religious or devotional genius represents the *special* and limited awareness, it may be very difficult to discriminate. I do not pretend to offer Vaughan, or Southwell, or George Herbert, or Hopkins as major poets: I feel sure that the first three, at least, are poets of this limited awareness. They are not great religious poets in the sense in which Dante, or Corneille, or Racine, even in those of their plays which do not touch upon Christian themes, are great Christian religious poets. Or even in the sense in which Villon and Baudelaire, with all their imperfections and delinquencies, are Christian poets. Since the time of Chaucer, Christian poetry (in the sense in which I shall mean it) has been limited in England almost exclusively to minor poetry.

I repeat that when I am considering Religion and Literature, I speak of these things only to make clear that I am not concerned primarily with Religious Literature. I am concerned with what should be the relation between Religion and all Literature. Therefore the third type of "religious literature" may be more quickly passed over. I mean the literary works of men who are sincerely desirous of forwarding the cause of religion: that which may come under the heading of Propaganda. I am thinking, of course, of such delightful fiction as Mr. Chesterton's *Man Who Was Thursday,* or his *Father Brown.* No one admires and enjoys these things more than I do; I would only remark that when the same effect is aimed at by zealous persons of less talent than Mr. Chesterton the effect is negative. But my point is that such writings do not enter into any serious consideration of the relation of Religion and Literature: because they are conscious operations in a world in which it is assumed that Religion and Literature are not related. It is a conscious and limited relating. What I want is a literature which should be *un*consciously, rather than deliberately and defiantly, Christian: because the work of Mr. Chesterton has its point from appearing in a world which is definitely not Christian.

I am convinced that we fail to realize how completely, and yet how irrationally, we separate our literary from our religious judgments. If there could be a complete separation, perhaps it might not matter: but the separation is not, and never can be, complete. If we exemplify literature by the novel—for the novel is the form in which literature affects the greatest number—we may remark this gradual secularization of literature during at least the last three hundred years. Bunyan, and to some extent Defoe, had moral purposes: the former is beyond suspicion, the latter may be suspect. But since Defoe the secularization of the novel has been continuous. There have been three chief phases. In the first, the novel took the Faith, in its contemporary version, for granted, and omitted it from its picture of life. Fielding, Dickens, and Thackeray belong to this phase. In the second, it doubted, worried about, or contested the Faith. To this phase belong George Eliot, George Meredith, and Thomas Hardy. To the third phase, in which we are living, belong nearly all contemporary novelists except Mr. James Joyce. It is the phase of those who have never heard the Christian Faith spoken of as anything but an anachronism.

Now, do people in general hold a definite opinion, that is to say religious or anti-religious; and do they read novels, or poetry for that matter, with a separate compartment of their minds? The common ground between religion and fiction is behaviour. Our religion imposes our ethics, our judgment and criticism of ourselves, and our behaviour toward our fellow men. The fiction that we read affects our behaviour towards our fellow men, affects our patterns of ourselves. When we read of human beings behaving in certain ways, with the approval of the author, who gives his benediction to this behaviour by his attitude toward the result of the behaviour arranged by himself, we can be influenced towards behaving in the same way.[2] When the contemporary novelist is an individual thinking for himself in isolation, he may have something important to offer to those who are able to receive it. He who is alone may speak to the individual. But the majority of novelists are persons drifting in the stream, only a little faster. They have some sensitiveness, but little intellect.

We are expected to be broadminded about literature, to put aside prejudice or conviction, and to look at fiction as fiction and at drama as drama. With what is inaccurately called "censorship" in this country—with what is much

[2] Here and later I am indebted to Montgomery Belgion. *The Human Parrot* (chapter on "The Irresponsible Propagandist").

more difficult to cope with than an official censorship, because it represents the opinions of individuals in an irresponsible democracy, I have very little sympathy; partly because it so often suppresses the wrong books, and partly because it is little more effective than Prohibition of Liquor; partly because it is one manifestation of the desire that state control should take the place of decent domestic influence; and wholly because it acts only from custom and habit, not from decided theological and moral principles. Incidentally, it gives people a false sense of security in leading them to believe that books which are *not* suppressed are harmless. Whether there *is* such a thing as a harmless book I am not sure: but there very likely are books so utterly unreadable as to be incapable of injuring anybody. But it is certain that a book is not harmless merely because no one is consciously offended by it. And if we, as readers, keep our religious and moral convictions in one compartment, and take our reading merely for entertainment, or on a higher plane, for aesthetic pleasure, I would point out that the author, whatever his conscious intentions in writing, in practice recognizes no such distinctions. The author of a work of imagination is trying to affect us wholly, as human beings, whether he knows it or not; and we are affected by it, as human beings, whether we intend to be or not. I suppose that everything we eat has some other effect upon us than merely the pleasure of taste and mastication; it affects us during the process of assimilation and digestion; and I believe that exactly the same is true of anything we read.

The fact that what we read does not concern merely something called our *literary taste,* but that it affects directly, though only amongst many other influences, the whole of what we are, is best elicited, I think, by a conscientious examination of the history of our individual literary education. Consider the adolescent reading of any person with some literary sensibility. Everyone, I believe, who is at all sensible to the seductions of poetry, can remember some moment in youth when he or she was completely carried away by the work of one poet. Very likely he was carried away by several poets, one after the other. The reason for this passing infatuation is not merely that our sensibility to poetry is keener in adolescence than in maturity. What happens is a kind of inundation, of invasion of the undeveloped personality, the empty (swept and garnished) room, by the stronger personality of the poet. The same thing may happen at a later age to persons who have not done much reading. One author takes complete possession of us for a time; then another; and finally they begin to affect each other in our mind. We weigh one against another; we see that each has qualities absent from others, and qualities incompatible with the qualities of others: we begin to be, in fact, critical; and it is our growing critical power which protects us from excessive possession by any one literary personality. The good critic—and we should all try to be critics, and not leave criticism to the fellows who write reviews in the papers—is the man who, to a keen and abiding sensibility, joins wide and increasingly discriminating reading. Wide reading is not valuable as a kind of hoarding, an accumulation of knowledge, or what sometimes is meant by the term "a well-stocked mind." It is valuable because in the process of being affected by one powerful personality after another, we cease to be dominated by any one, or by any small number. The very different views of life, cohabiting in our minds, affect each other, and our own personality asserts itself and gives each a place in some arrangement peculiar to ourself.

It is simply not true that works of fiction, prose or verse, that is to say works depicting the actions, thoughts and words and passions of imaginary human beings, *directly* extend our knowledge of life. Direct knowledge of life is knowledge directly in relation to ourselves, it is our knowledge of *how* people behave in general, of *what* they are like in general, in so far as that part of life in which we ourselves have participated gives us material for generalization. Knowledge of life obtained through fiction is only possible by another stage of self-consciousness. That is to say, it can only be a knowledge of other people's knowledge of life, not of life itself. So far as we are taken up with the happenings in any novel in the same way in which we are taken up with what happens under our eyes, we are acquiring at least as much falsehood as truth. But when we are developed enough to say: "This is the view of life of a person who was a good observer within his limits, Dickens, or Thackeray, or George Eliot, or Balzac; but he looked at it in a different way from me, because he was a different man; he even selected rather different things to look at, or the same things in a different order of importance, because he was a different man; so what I am looking at is the world as seen by a particular mind"—then we are in a position to gain something from reading fiction. We are learning *something* about life from these authors direct, just as we learn something from the reading of history direct; but these authors are only really helping us when we can see, and allow for, their differences from ourselves.

Now what we get, as we gradually grow up and read more and more, and read a greater diversity of authors, is a variety of views of life. But what people commonly assume, I suspect, is that we gain this experience of other men's views of life only by "improving reading." This, it is supposed, is a reward we get by applying ourselves to Shakespeare, and Dante, and Goethe, and Emerson, and Carlyle, and dozens of other respectable writers. The rest of our reading for amusement is merely killing time. But I incline to come to the alarming conclusion that it is just the literature that we read for "amusement," or "purely for pleasure" that may have the greatest, and least suspected influence upon us. It is the literature which we read with the least effort that can have the easiest and most insidious influence upon us. Hence it is that the influence of popular novelists, and of popular plays of contemporary life, requires to be scrutinized most closely. And it is chiefly *contemporary* literature that the majority of people ever read in this attitude of "purely for pleasure," of pure passivity.

The relation of what I have been saying to the subject announced for my discourse should now be a little more apparent. Though we may read literature merely for pleasure, of "entertainment" or of "aesthetic enjoyment," this reading never affects simply a sort of special sense: it affects us as entire human beings; it affects our moral and religious existence. And I say that while individual modern writers of eminence can be improving, contemporary literature as a whole tends to be degrading. And that even the effect of the better writers, in an age like ours, may be degrading to some readers; for we must remember that what a writer does to people is not necessarily what he intends to do. It may be only what people are capable of having done to them. People exercise an unconscious selection, in being influenced. A writer like D. H. Lawrence may be in his effect either beneficial or pernicious. I am not even sure that I have not had some pernicious influence myself.

At this point I anticipate a rejoinder from the liberal-minded, from all those who are convinced that if everybody says what he thinks, and does what he likes, things will somehow, by some automatic compensation and adjustment, come right in the end. "Let everything be tried," they say, "and if it is a mistake, then we shall learn by experience." This argument might have some value, if we were always the same generation upon earth; or if, as we know to be not the case, people ever learned much from the experience of their elders. These liberals are convinced that only by what is called unrestrained individualism, will truth ever emerge. Ideas, views of life, they think, issue distinct from independent heads, and in consequence of their knocking violently against each other, the fittest survive, and truth rises triumphant. Anyone who dissents from this view must be either a mediaevalist, wishful only to set back the clock, or else a fascist, and probably both.

If the mass of contemporary authors were really individualists, every one of them inspired Blakes, each with his separate vision, and if the mass of the contemporary public were really a mass of *individuals* there might be something to be said for this attitude. But this is not, and never has been, and never will be. It is not only that the reading individual to-day (or at any day) is not enough an individual to be able to absorb all the "views of life" of all the authors pressed upon us by the publishers' advertisements and reviewers, and to be able to arrive at wisdom by considering one against another. It is that the contemporary authors are not individuals enough either. It is not that the world of separate individuals of the liberal democrat is undesirable; it is simply that this world does not exist. For the reader of contemporary literature is not, like the reader of the established great literature of all time, exposing himself to the influence of divers and contradictory personalities; he is exposing himself to a mass movement of writers who, each of them, think that they have something individually to offer, but are really all working together in the same direction. And there never was a time, I believe, when the reading public was so large, or so helplessly exposed to the influences of its own time. There never was a time, I believe, when those who read at all, read so many more books by living authors than books by dead authors; there never was a time so completely parochial, so shut off from the past. There may be too many publishers; there are certainly too many books published; and the journals ever incite the reader to "keep up" with what is being published. Individualistic democracy has come to high tide: and it is more difficult to-day to be an individual than it ever was before.

Within itself, modern literature has perfectly valid distinctions of good and bad, better and worse; and I do not wish to suggest that I confound Mr. Bernard Shaw with Mr. Noel Coward, Mrs. Woolf with Miss Mannin. On the other hand, I should like it to be clear that I am not defending a "high"-brow against a "low"-brow literature. What I do wish to affirm is that the whole of modern literature is corrupted by what I call Secularism, that it is simply unaware of, simply cannot understand the meaning of, the primacy of the supernatural over the natural life: of something which I assume to be our primary concern.

I do not want to give the impression that I have delivered a mere fretful jeremiad against contemporary literature. Assuming a common attitude between you, or some of you, and myself, the question is not so much, what is to be done about it? as, how should we behave towards it?

I have suggested that the liberal attitude towards literature will not work. Even if the writers who make their attempt to impose their "view of life" upon us were really distinct individuals, even if we as readers were distinct individuals, what would be the result? It would be, surely, that each reader would be impressed, in his reading, merely by what he was previously prepared to be impressed by; he would follow the "line of least resistance," and there would be no assurance that he would be made a better man. For literary judgment we need to be acutely aware of two things at once: of "what we like," and of "what we *ought* to like." Few people are honest enough to know either. The first means knowing what we really feel: very few know that. The second involves understanding our shortcomings; for we do not really know what we ought to like unless we also know why we ought to like it, which involves knowing why we don't yet like it. It is not enough to understand what we ought to be, unless we know what we are; and we do not understand what we are, unless we know what we ought to be. The two forms of self-consciousness, knowing what we are and what we ought to be, must go together.

It is our business, as readers of literature, to know what we like. It is our business, as Christians, *as well as* readers of literature, to know what we ought to like. It is our business as honest men not to assume that whatever we like is what we ought to like; and it is our business as honest Christians not to assume that we do like what we ought to like. And the last thing I would wish for would be the existence of two literatures, one for Christian consumption and the other for the pagan world. What I believe to be incumbent upon all Christians is the duty of maintaining consciously certain standards and criteria of criticism over and above those applied by the rest of the world; and that by these criteria and standards everything that we read must be tested. We must remember that the greater part of our current reading matter is written for us by people who have no real belief in a supernatural order, though some of it may be written by people with individual notions of a supernatural order which are not ours. And the greater part of our reading matter is coming to be written by people who not only have no such belief, but are even ignorant of the fact that there are still people in the world so "backward" or so "eccentric" as to continue to believe. So long as we are conscious of the gulf fixed between ourselves and the greater part of contemporary literature, we are more or less protected from being harmed by it, and are in a position to extract from it what good it has to offer us.

There are a very large number of people in the world to-day who believe that all ills are fundamentally economic. Some believe that various specific economic changes alone would be enough to set the world right; others demand more or less drastic changes in the social as well, changes chiefly of two opposed types. These changes demanded, and in some places carried out, are alike in one respect, that they hold the assumptions of what I call Secularism: they concern themselves only with changes of a temporal, material, and external nature; they concern themselves with morals only of a collective nature. In an exposition of one such new faith I read the following words:

> In our morality the one single test of any moral question is whether it impedes or destroys in any way the power of the individual to serve the State. [The individual] must answer the questions: "Does this action injure the nation? Does it injure other members of the nation? Does it injure my ability to serve the nation?" And if the answer is clear on all those questions, the individual has absolute liberty to do as he will.

Now I do not deny that this is a kind of morality, and that it is capable of great good within limits; but I think that we should all repudiate a morality which had no higher ideal to set before us than that. It represents, of course, one of the violent reactions we are witnessing, against the view that the community is solely for the benefit of the individual; but it is equally a gospel of this world, and of this world alone. My complaint against modern literature is of the same kind. It is not that modern literature is in the ordinary sense "immoral" or even "amoral"; and in any case to prefer that charge would not be enough. It is simply that it repudiates, or is wholly ignorant of, our most fundamental and important beliefs; and that in consequence its tendency is to encourage its readers to get what they can out of life while it lasts, to miss no "experience" that presents itself, and to sacrifice themselves, if they make any sacrifice at all, only for the sake of tangible benefits to others in this world either now or in the future. We shall certainly continue to read the best of its kind, of what our time provides; but we must tirelessly criticize it according to our own principles, and not merely according to the principles admitted by the writers and by the critics who discuss it in the public press.

From *Essays Ancient and Modern* by T. S. Eliot, pp. 93–112. Copyright, 1932, 1936, by Harcourt, Brace and Company, Inc. Reprinted by permission of the publishers. First published in *Faith that Illuminates,* ed. by V. A. Demant (London: Centenary Press, 1935), pp. 29–54.

From Poe to Valéry
[1948]

WHAT I attempt here is not a judicial estimate of Edgar Allan Poe; I am not trying to decide his rank as a poet or to isolate his essential originality. Poe is indeed a stumbling block for the judicial critic. If we examine his work in detail, we seem to find in it nothing but slipshod writing, puerile thinking unsupported by wide reading or profound scholarship, haphazard experiments in various types of writing, chiefly under pressure of financial need, without perfection in any detail. This would not be just. But if, instead of regarding his work analytically, we take a distant view of it as a whole, we see a mass of unique shape and impressive size to which the eye constantly returns. Poe's influence is equally puzzling. In France the influence of his poetry and of his poetic theories has been immense. In England and America it seems almost negligible. Can we point to any poet whose style appears to have been formed by a study of Poe? The only one whose name immediately suggests itself is— Edward Lear. And yet one cannot be sure that one's own writing has *not* been influenced by Poe. I can name positively certain poets whose work has influenced me, I can name others whose work, I am sure, has not; there may be still others of whose influence I am unaware, but whose influence I might be brought to acknowledge; but about Poe I shall never be sure. He wrote very few poems, and of those only half a dozen have had a great success: but those few are as well known to as large a number of people, are as well remembered by everybody, as any poems ever written. And some of his tales have had an important influence upon authors, and in types of writing where such influence would hardly be expected.

I shall here make no attempt to explain the enigma. At most, this is a contribution to the study of his influence; and an elucidation, partial as it may be, of one cause of Poe's importance in the light of that influence. I am trying to look at him, for a moment, as nearly as I can, through the eyes of three French poets, Baudelaire, Mallarmé and especially Paul Valéry. The sequence is itself important. These three French poets represent the beginning, the middle and the end of a particular tradition in poetry. Mallarmé once told a friend of mine that he came to Paris because he wanted to know Baudelaire; that he had once seen him at a bookstall on a quai, but had not had the courage to accost him. As for Valéry, we know from the first letter to Mallarmé, written when he was hardly more than a boy, of his discipleship of the elder poet; and we know of his devotion to Mallarmé until Mallarmé's death. Here are three literary generations, representing almost exactly a century of French poetry. Of course, these are poets very different from each other; of course, the literary progeny of Baudelaire was numerous and important, and there are other lines of descent from him. But I think we can trace the development and descent of one particular theory of the nature of poetry through these three poets and it is a theory which takes its origin in the theory, still more than in the practice, of Edgar Poe. And the impression we get of the influence of Poe is the more impressive, because of the fact that Mallarmé, and Valéry in turn, did not merely derive from Poe through Baudelaire: each of them subjected himself to that influence directly, and has left convincing evidence of the value which he attached to the theory and practice of Poe himself. Now, we all of us like to believe that we understand our own poets better than any foreigner can do; but I think we should be prepared to entertain the possibility that these Frenchmen have seen something in Poe that English-speaking readers have missed.

My subject, then, is not simply Poe but Poe's effect upon three French poets, representing three successive generations; and my purpose is also to approach an understanding of a peculiar attitude towards poetry, by the poets themselves, which is perhaps the most interesting, possibly the most characteristic, and certainly the most original development of the esthetic of verse made in that period as a whole. It is all the more worthy of examination if, as I incline to believe, this attitude towards poetry represents a phase which has come to an end with the death of Valéry. For our study of it should help towards the understanding of whatever it may be that our generation and the next will find to take its place.

Before concerning myself with Poe as he appeared in the eyes of these French poets, I think it as well to present my own impression of his status among American and English readers and critics; for, if I am wrong, you may have to criticise what I say of his influence in France with my errors in mind. It does not seem to me unfair to say that Poe has been regarded as a minor, or secondary, follower of the Romantic Movement: a successor to the so-called "Gothic" novelists in his fiction, and a follower of Byron and Shelley in his verse. This however is to place him in the English tradition; and there certainly he does not belong. English readers sometimes account for that in Poe which is outside of any English tradition, by saying that it is American; but this does not seem to me wholly true either, especially when we consider the other American writers of his own and an earlier generation. There is a certain flavour of provinciality about his work in a sense in which Whitman is not in the least provincial: it is the provinciality of the person who is not at home where he belongs, but cannot get to anywhere else. Poe is a kind of displaced European; he is attracted to Paris, to Italy and to Spain, to places which he could endow with romantic gloom and grandeur. Although his ambit of movement hardly extended beyond the limits of Richmond and Boston longitudinally, and neither east nor west of these centres, he seems a wanderer with no fixed abode. There can be few authors of such eminence who have drawn so little from their own roots, who have been so isolated from any surroundings.

I believe the view of Poe taken by the ordinary cultivated English or American reader is something like this: Poe is the author of a few, a very few short poems which enchanted him for a time when he was a boy, and which do somehow stick in the memory. I do not think that he re-reads these poems, unless he turns to them in the pages of an anthology; his enjoyment of them is rather the memory of an enjoyment which he may for a moment recapture. They seem to him to belong to a particular period when his interest in poetry had just awakened. Certain images, and still more certain rhythms, abide with him. This reader also remembers certain of the tales—not very many—and holds the opinion that "The Gold Bug" was quite good for its time, but that detective fiction has made great strides since then. And he may sometimes contrast him with Whitman, having frequently re-read Whitman, but not Poe.

As for the prose, it is recognised that Poe's tales had great influence upon some types of popular fiction. So far as detective fiction is concerned, nearly everything can be traced to two authors: Poe and Wilkie Collins. The two influences sometimes concur, but are also responsible for two different types of detective. The efficient professional policeman originates with Collins, the brilliant and eccentric amateur with Poe. Conan Doyle owes much to Poe, and not merely to Monsieur Dupin of "The Murders in the Rue Morgue." Sherlock Holmes was deceiving Watson when he told him that he had bought his Stradivarius violin for a few shillings at a second-hand shop in the Tottenham Court Road. He found that violin in the ruins of the house of Usher. There is a close similarity between the musical exercises of Holmes and those of Roderick Usher: those wild and irregular improvisations which, although on one occasion they sent Watson off to sleep, must have been excruciating to any ear trained to music. It seems to me probable that the romances of improbable and incredible adventure of Rider Haggard found their inspiration in Poe—and Haggard himself had imitators enough. I think it equally likely that H. G. Wells, in his early romances of scientific exploration and invention, owed much to the stimulus of some of Poe's narratives—"Gordon Pym," or "A Descent into the Maelstrom" for example, or "The Facts in the Case of Monsieur Valdemar." The compilation of evidence I leave to those who are interested to pursue the enquiry. But I fear that nowadays too few readers open *She* or *The War of the Worlds* or *The Time Machine;* fewer still are capable of being thrilled by their predecessors.

What strikes me first, as a general difference between the way in which the French poets whom I have cited took Poe, and the way of American and English critics of equivalent authority, is the attitude of the former towards Poe's *oeuvre,* towards his work as a whole. Anglo-Saxon critics are, I think, more inclined to make separate judgments of the different parts of an author's work. We regard Poe as a man who dabbled in verse and in several kinds of prose, without settling down to make a thoroughly good job of any one *genre.* These French readers were impressed by the variety of form of expression, because they found, or thought they found, an essential unity; while admitting, if necessary, that much of the work is fragmentary or occasional, owing to circumstances of poverty, frailty and vicissitude, they nevertheless take him as an author of such seriousness that his work must be grasped as a whole. This represents partly a difference between two kinds of critical mind; but we must claim, for our own view, that it is supported by our awareness of the blemishes and imperfections of Poe's actual writing. It is worth while to illustrate these faults, as they strike an English-speaking reader.

Poe had, to an exceptional degree, the feeling for the incantatory element in poetry, of that which may, in the most nearly literal sense, be called "the magic of verse." His versification is not, like that of the greatest masters of prosody, of the kind which yields a richer melody, through study and long habituation, to the maturing sensibility of the reader returning to it at times throughout his life. Its effect is immediate and undeveloping; it is probably much the same for the sensitive schoolboy and for the ripe mind and cultivated ear. In this unchanging immediacy, it partakes perhaps more of the character of very good *verse* than of poetry—but that is to start a hare which I have no intention of following here, for it is, I am sure, "poetry" and not "verse." It has the effect of an incantation which, because of its very crudity, stirs the feelings at a deep and almost primitive level. But, in his choice of the word which has the right *sound,* Poe is by no means careful that it should have also the right *sense.* I will give one comparison of uses of the same word by Poe and by Tennyson—who, of all English poets since Milton, had probably the most accurate and fastidious appreciation of the sound of syllables. In Poe's "Ulalume"—to my mind one of his most successful, as well as typical, poems—we find the lines

> It was night in the lonesome October
> Of my most immemorial year.

Immemorial, according to the Oxford Dictionary, means: "that is beyond memory or out of mind; ancient beyond memory or record: extremely old." None of these meanings seems applicable to this use of the word by Poe. The year was not beyond memory—the speaker remembers one incident in it very well; at the conclusion he even remembers a funeral in the same place just a year earlier. The line of Tennyson, equally well known, and justly admired because the sound of the line responds so well to the sound which the poet wishes to evoke, may already have come to mind:

> The moan of doves in immemorial elms.

Here *immemorial,* besides having the most felicitous sound value, is exactly the word for trees so old that no one knows just how old they are.

Poetry, of different kinds, may be said to range from that in which the attention of the reader is directed primarily to the sound, to that in which it is directed primarily to the sense. With the former kind, the sense may be apprehended almost unconsciously; with the latter kind—at these two extremes —it is the sound, of the operation of which upon us we are unconscious. But, with either type, sound and sense must cooperate; in even the most purely incantatory poem, the dictionary meaning of words cannot be disregarded with impunity.

An irresponsibility towards the meaning of words is not infrequent with Poe. "The Raven" is, I think, far from being Poe's best poem; though, partly because of the analysis which the author gives in "The Philosophy of Composition," it is the best known.

> In there stepped a stately Raven of the saintly days of yore.

Since there is nothing particularly saintly about the raven, if indeed the ominous bird is not wholly the reverse, there can be no point in referring his origin to a period of saintliness, even if such a period can be assumed to have existed. We have just heard the raven described as *stately;* but we are told presently that he is *ungainly,* an attribute hardly to be reconciled, without a good deal of explanation, with *stateliness.* Several words in the poem seem to be inserted either merely to fill out the line to the required measure, or for the sake of a rhyme. The bird is addressed as "no craven" quite needlessly, except for the pressing need of a rhyme to "raven"—a surrender to the exigencies of rhyme with which I am sure Malherbe would have had no patience. And there is not always even such schoolboy justification as this: to say that the lamplight "gloated o'er" the sofa cushions is a freak of fancy which, even were it relevant to have a little gloating going on somewhere, would appear forced.

Imperfections in "The Raven" such as these—and one could give others— may serve to explain why "The Philosophy of Composition," the essay in which Poe professes to reveal his method in composing "The Raven"—has not been taken so seriously in England or America as in France. It is difficult for us to read that essay without reflecting, that if Poe plotted out his poem with such calculation, he might have taken a little more pains over it: the result hardly does credit to the method. Therefore we are likely to draw the conclusion that Poe in analysing his poem was practising either a hoax, or a piece of self-deception in setting down the way in which he wanted to think that he had written it. Hence the essay has not been taken so seriously as it deserves.

Poe's other essays in poetic esthetic deserve consideration also. No poet, when he writes his own *art poétique,* should hope to do much more than ex- plain, rationalise, defend or prepare the way for his own practice: that is, for writing his own kind of poetry. He may think that he is establishing laws for all poetry; but what he has to say that is worth saying has its immediate rela- tion to the way in which he himself writes or wants to write: though it may well be equally valid to his immediate juniors, and extremely helpful to them. We are only safe in finding, in his writing about poetry, principles valid for any poetry, so long as we check what he says by the kind of poetry he writes. Poe has a remarkable passage about the impossibility of writing a long poem— for a long poem, he holds, is at best a series of short poems strung together. What we have to bear in mind is that he himself was incapable of writing a long poem. He could conceive only a poem which was a single simple effect: for him, the whole of a poem had to be in one mood. Yet it is only in a poem of some length that a variety of moods can be expressed; for a variety of moods requires a number of different themes or subjects, related either in themselves or in the mind of the poet. These parts can form a whole which is more than the sum of the parts; a whole such that the pleasure we derive from the read- ing of any part is enhanced by our grasp of the whole. It follows also that in a long poem some parts may be deliberately planned to be less "poetic" than others: these passages may show no lustre when extracted, but may be intended to elicit, by contrast, the significance of other parts, and to unite them into a whole more significant than any of the parts. A long poem may gain by the widest possible variations of intensity. But Poe wanted a poem to be of the first intensity throughout: it is questionable whether he could have appreciated the more philosophical passages in Dante's *Purgatorio*. What Poe had said has proved in the past of great comfort to other poets equally incapable of the long poem; and we must recognize that the question of the possibility of writing a long poem is not simply that of the strength and staying power of the individual poet, but may have to do with the conditions of the age in which he finds himself. And what Poe has to say on the subject is illuminating, in helping us to understand the point of view of poets for whom the long poem is impossible.

The fact that for Poe a poem had to be the expression of a single mood— it would here be too long an excursus to try to demonstrate that "The Bells," as a deliberate exercise in several moods, is as much a poem of one mood as any of Poe's—this fact can better be understand as a manifestation of a more fundamental weakness. Here, what I have to say I put forward only tentatively: but it is a view which I should like to launch in order to see what becomes of it. My account may go to explain, also, why the work of Poe has for many readers appealed at a particular phase of their growth, at the period of life when they were just emerging from childhood. That Poe had a powerful intellect is undeniable: but it seems to me the intellect of a highly gifted young person before puberty. The forms which his lively curiosity takes are those in which a pre-adolescent mentality delights: wonders of nature and of mechanics and of the supernatural, cryptograms and cyphers, puzzles and labyrinths, mechanical chess-players and wild flights of speculation. The variety and ardour of his curiosity delight and dazzle; yet in the end the eccentricity and lack of coherence of his interests tire. There is just that lacking which gives dignity to the mature man: a consistent view of life. An attitude can be mature and consistent, and yet be highly sceptical: but Poe was no sceptic. He appears to yield himself completely to the idea of the moment: the effect is, that all of his ideas seem to be *entertained* rather than believed. What is lacking is not brain power, but that maturity of intellect which comes only with the maturing of the man as a whole, the development and coordination of his various emotions. I am not concerned with any possible psychological or pathological explanation: it is enough for my purpose to record that the work of Poe is such as I should expect of a man of very exceptional mind and sensibility, whose emotional development has been in some respect arrested at an early age. His most vivid imaginative realisations are the realisation of a dream: significantly, the ladies in his poems and tales are always ladies lost, or ladies vanishing before they can be embraced. Even in "The Haunted Palace," where the subject appears to be his own weakness of alcoholism, the disaster has no moral significance; it is treated impersonally as an isolated phenomenon; it has not behind it the terrific forces of such lines as those of François Villon when he speaks of his own fallen state.

Having said as much as this about Poe, I must proceed to enquire what it was that three great French poets found in his work to admire, which we have not found. We must first take account of the fact that none of these poets knew the English language very well. Baudelaire must have read a certain amount of English and American poetry: he certainly borrows from Gray, and apparently from Emerson. He was never familiar with England, and there is no reason to believe that he spoke the language at all well. As for Mallarmé, he taught English and there is convincing evidence of his imperfect knowledge, for he committed himself to writing a kind of guide to the use of the language. An examination of this curious treatise, and the strange phrases which he gives under the impression that they are familiar English proverbs, should dispel any rumour of Mallarmé's English scholarship. As for Valéry, I never heard him speak a word of English, even in England. I do not know what he had read in our language: Valéry's second language, the influence of which is perceptible in some of his verse, was Italian.

It is certainly possible, in reading something in a language imperfectly understood, for the reader to find what is not there; and when the reader is himself a man of genius, the foreign poem read may, by a happy accident, elicit something important from the depths of his own mind, which he attributes to what he reads. And it is true that in translating Poe's prose into French, Baudelaire effected a striking improvement: he transformed what is often a slipshod and a shoddy English prose into admirable French. Mallarmé, who translated a number of Poe's poems into French prose, effected a similar improvement: but on the other hand, the rhythms, in which we find so much of the originality of Poe, are lost. The evidence that the French overrated Poe because of their imperfect knowledge of English remains accordingly purely negative: we can venture no farther than saying that they were not disturbed by weaknesses of which we are very much aware. It does not account for their high opinion of Poe's *thought*, for the value which they attached to his philosophical and critical exercises. To understand that we must look elsewhere.

We must, at this point, avoid the error of assuming that Baudelaire, Mallarmé and Valéry all responded to Poe in exactly the same way. They are great poets, and they are each very different from the other; furthermore, they represent, as I have reminded you, three different generations. It is with Valéry that I am here chiefly concerned. I therefore say only that Baudelaire, to judge by his introduction to his translation of the tales and essays, was the most concerned with the personality of the man. With the accuracy of his portrait I am not concerned: the point is that in Poe, in his life, his isolation and his worldly failure, Baudelaire found the prototype of le poète maudit, the poet as the outcast of society—the type which was to realise itself, in different ways, in Verlaine and Rimbaud, the type of which Baudelaire saw himself as a distinguished example. This nineteenth-century archetype, le poète maudit, the rebel against society and against middle-class morality (a rebel who descends of course from the continental myth of the figure of Byron) corresponds to a particular social situation. But, in the course of an introduction which is primarily a sketch of the man Poe and his biography, Baudelaire lets fall one remark indicative of an esthetic that brings us to Valéry:

> He believed [says Baudelaire], true poet that he was, that the goal of poetry is of the same nature as its principle, and that it should have nothing in view but itself.

"A poem does not say something—it is something": that doctrine has been held in more recent times.

The interest for Mallarmé is rather in the technique of verse, though Poe's is, as Mallarmé recognises, a kind of versification which does not lend itself to use in the French language. But when we come to Valéry, it is neither the man nor the poetry, but the theory of poetry, that engages his attention. In a very early letter to Mallarmé, written when he was a very young man, introducing himself to the elder poet, he says: "I prize the theories of Poe, so profound and so insidiously learned; I believe in the omnipotence of rhythm, and especially in the suggestive phrase." But I base my opinion, not primarily upon this credo of a very young man, but upon Valéry's subsequent theory and practice. In the same way that Valéry's poetry, and his essays on the art of poetry, are two aspects of the same interest of his mind and complement each other, so for Valéry the poetry of Poe is inseparable from Poe's poetic theories.

This brings me to the point of considering the meaning of the term "la poésie pure": the French phrase has a connotation of discussion and argument which is not altogether rendered by the term "pure poetry."

All poetry may be said to start from the emotions experienced by human beings in their relations to themselves, to each other, to divine beings, and to the world about them; it is therefore concerned also with thought and action, which emotion brings about, and out of which emotion arises. But, at however primitive a stage of expression and appreciation, the function of poetry can never be simply to arouse these same emotions in the audience of the poet. You remember the account of Alexander's feast in the famous ode of Dryden. If the conqueror of Asia was actually transported with the violent emotions which the bard Timotheus, by skilfully varying his music, is said to have aroused in him, then the great Alexander was at the moment suffering from automatism induced by alcohol poisoning, and was in that state completely incapable of appreciating musical or poetic art. In the earliest poetry, or in the most rudimentary enjoyment of poetry, the attention of the listener is directed upon the subject matter; the effect of the poetic art is felt, without the listener being wholly conscious of this art. With the development of the consciousness of language, there is another stage, at which the auditor, who may by that time have become the reader, is aware of a double interest in a story for its own sake, and in the way in which it is told: that is to say, he becomes aware of style. Then we may take a delight in discrimination between the ways in which different poets will handle the same subject: an appreciation not merely of better or worse, but of differences between styles which are equally admired. At a third stage of development, the subject may recede to the background: instead of being the purpose of the poem, it becomes simply a necessary means for the realisation of the poem. At this stage the reader or listener may become as nearly indifferent to the subject matter as the primitive listener was to the style. A complete unconsciousness or indifference to the style at the beginning, or to the subject matter at the end, would however take us outside of poetry altogether: for a complete unconsciousness of anything but subject matter would mean that for that listener poetry had not yet appeared; a complete unconsciousness of anything but style would mean that poetry had vanished.

This process of increasing self-consciousness—or, we may say, of increasing consciousness of language—has as its theoretical goal what we may call *la poésie pure*. I believe it to be a goal that can never be reached, because I think that poetry is only poetry so long as it preserves some "impurity" in this sense: that is to say, so long as the subject matter is valued for its own sake. The Abbé Brémond, if I have understood him, maintains that while the element of *la poésie pure* is necessary to make a poem a poem, no poem can consist of *la poésie pure* solely. But what has happened in the case of Valéry is a change of attitude toward the subject matter. We must be careful to avoid saying that the subject matter becomes "less important." It has rather a different kind of importance: it is important as *means*: the *end* is the poem. The subject exists for the poem, not the poem for the subject. A poem may employ several subjects, combining them in a particular way; and it may be meaningless to ask "What is the subject of the poem?" From the union of several subjects there appears, not another subject, but the poem.

Here I should like to point out the difference between a theory of poetry propounded by a student of esthetics, and the same theory as held by a poet. It is one thing when it is simply an account of how the poet writes, without knowing it, and another thing when the poet himself writes consciously according to that theory. In affecting writing, the theory becomes a different thing from what it was merely as an explanation of how the poet writes. And Valéry was a poet who wrote very consciously and deliberately indeed: per-

haps, at his best, not wholly under the guidance of theory; but his theorising
certainly affected the kind of poetry that he wrote. He was the most self-
conscious of all poets.

To the extreme self-consciousness of Valéry must be added another trait:
his extreme scepticism. It might be thought that such a man, without belief in
anything which could be the subject of poetry, would find refuge in a doctrine of "art for art's sake." But Valéry was much too sceptical to believe even
in art. It is significant, the number of times that he describes something he
has written as an *ébauche*—a rough draft. He had ceased to believe in *ends,*
and was only interested in *processes.* It often seems as if he had continued to
write poetry, simply because he was interested in the introspective observation
of himself engaged in writing it: one has only to read the several essays—
sometimes indeed more exciting than his verse, because one suspects that he
was more excited in writing them—in which he records his observations.
There is a revealing remark in *Variété V,* the last of his books of collected
papers: "As for myself, who am, I confess, much more concerned with the
formation or the fabrication of works of art than with the works themselves,"
and, a little later in the same volume: "In my opinion the most authentic
philosophy is not in the objects of reflection, so much as in the very act of
thought and its manipulation."

Here we have, brought to their culmination by Valéry, two notions which
can be traced back to Poe. There is first the doctrine, elicited from Poe by
Baudelaire, which I have already quoted: "A poem should have nothing in
view but itself"; second the notion that the composition of a poem should be
as conscious and deliberate as possible, that the poet should observe himself in
the act of composition—and this, in a mind as sceptical as Valéry's, leads to
the conclusion, so paradoxically inconsistent with the other, that the act of
composition is more interesting than the poem which results from it.

First, there is the "purity" of Poe's poetry. In the sense in which we speak
of "purity of language" Poe's poetry is very far from pure, for I have commented upon Poe's carelessness and unscrupulousness in the use of words. But
in the sense of *la poésie pure,* that kind of purity came easily to Poe. The subject is little, the treatment is everything. He did not have to achieve purity by
a process of purification, for his material was already tenuous. Second, there is
that defect in Poe to which I alluded when I said that he did not appear to
believe, but rather to entertain, theories. And here again, with Poe and Valéry,
extremes meet, the immature mind playing with ideas because it had not developed to the point of convictions, and the very adult mind playing with
ideas because it was too sceptical to hold convictions. It is by this contrast,
I think, that we can account for Valéry's admiration for "Eureka"—that cosmological fantasy which makes no deep impression upon most of us, because
we are aware of Poe's lack of qualification in philosophy, theology or natural

science, but which Valéry, after Baudelaire, esteemed highly as a "prose poem." Finally, there is the astonishing result of Poe's analysis of the composition of "The Raven." It does not matter whether "The Philosophy of Composition" is a hoax, or a piece of self-deception, or a more or less accurate record of Poe's calculations in writing the poem; what matters is that it suggested to Valéry a method and an occupation—that of observing himself write. Of course, a greater than Poe had already studied the poetic process. In the *Biographia Literaria* Coleridge is concerned primarily, of course, with the poetry of Wordsworth; and he did not pursue his philosophical enquiries concurrently with the writing of his poetry; but he does anticipate the question which fascinated Valéry: "What am I doing when I write a poem?" Yet Poe's "Philosophy of Composition" is a *mise au point* of the question which gives it capital importance in relation to this process which ends with Valéry. For the penetration of the poetic by the introspective critical activity is carried to the limit by Valéry, the limit at which the latter begins to destroy the former. M. Louis Bolle, in his admirable study of this poet, observes pertinently: "This intellectual narcissism is not alien to the poet, even though he does not explain the whole of his work: 'why not conceive as a work of art the production of a work of art?' "

Now, as I think I have already hinted, I believe that the *art poétique* of which we find the germ in Poe, and which bore fruit in the work of Valéry, has gone as far as it can go. I do not believe that this esthetic can be of any help to later poets. What will take its place I do not know. An esthetic which merely contradicted it would not do. To insist on the all-importance of subject-matter, to insist that the poet should be spontaneous and irreflective, that he should depend upon inspiration and neglect technique, would be a lapse from what is in any case a highly civilised attitude to a barbarous one. We should have to have an esthetic which somehow comprehended and transcended that of Poe and Valéry. This question does not greatly exercise my mind, since I think that the poet's theories should arise out of his practice rather than his practice out of his theories. But I recognise first that within this tradition from Poe to Valéry are some of those modern poems which I most admire and enjoy; second, I think that the tradition itself represents the most interesting development of poetic consciousness anywhere in that same hundred years; and finally I value this exploration of certain poetic possibilities for its own sake, as we believe that all possibilities should be explored. And I find that by trying to look at Poe through the eyes of Baudelaire, Mallarmé and most of all Valéry, I become more thoroughly convinced of his importance, of the importance of his *work* as a whole. And, as for the future: it is a tenable hypothesis that this advance of self-consciousness, the extreme awareness of and concern for language which we find in Valéry, is something which must ulti-

mately break down, owing to an increasing strain against which the human
mind and nerves will rebel; just as, it may be maintained, the indefinite elaboration of scientific discovery and invention, and of political and social machinery, may reach a point at which there will be an irresistible revulsion of
humanity and a readiness to accept the most primitive hardships rather than
carry any longer the burden of modern civilisation. Upon that I hold no fixed
opinion: I leave it to your consideration.

JOHN CROWE RANSOM
Criticism as Pure Speculation[1]

[1941]

A CHASM, perhaps an abyss, separates the critic and the esthetician ordinarily, if the books in the library are evidence. But the authority of criticism depends on its coming to terms with esthetics, and the authority of literary esthetics depends on its coming to terms with criticism.

When we inquire into the "intent of the critic," we mean: the intent of the generalized critic, or critic as such. We will concede that any professional critic is familiar with the technical practices of poets so long as these are conventional, and is expert in judging when they perform them badly. We expect a critical discourse to cover that much, but we know that more is required. The most famous poets of our time, for example, make wide departures from conventional practices: how are they to be judged? Innovations in poetry, or even conventions when pressed to their logical limits, cause the ordinary critic to despair. They cause the good critic to review his esthetic principles; perhaps to reformulate his esthetic principles. He tries the poem against his best philosophical conception of the peculiar character that a poem should have.

Mr. T. S. Eliot is an extraordinarily sensitive critic. But when he discusses the so-called "metaphysical" poetry, he surprises us by refusing to study the so-called "conceit" which is its reputed basis; he observes instead that the metaphysical poets of the seventeenth century are more like their immediate predecessors than the latter are like the eighteenth and nineteenth century poets, and then he goes into a very broad philosophical comparison between two whole "periods" or types of poetry. I think it has come to be understood that his comparison is unsound; it has not proved workable enough to assist critics who have otherwise borrowed liberally from his critical principles. (It contains the famous dictum about the "sensibility" of the earlier poets, it im-

---

[1] This essay was presented as a lecture at Princeton University in the winter of 1940–41 in a series of four lectures entitled *The Intent of the Critic*. The other participants were Edmund Wilson, Norman Foerster, and W. H. Auden. The first two paragraphs, referring to the local occasion of the discussion, have here been condensed into the present first paragraph by the editor, with the author's permission.

putes to them a remarkable ability to "feel their thought," and to have a kind of "experience" in which the feeling cannot be differentiated from the thinking.) Now there is scarcely another critic equal to Eliot at distinguishing the practices of two poets who are closely related. He is supreme as a comparative critic when the relation in question is delicate and subtle; that is, when it is a matter of close perception and not a radical difference in kind. But this line of criticism never goes far enough. In Eliot's own range of criticism the line does not always answer. He is forced by discontinuities in the poetic tradition into sweeping theories that have to do with esthetics, the philosophy of poetry; and his own philosophy probably seems to us insufficient, the philosophy of the literary man.

The intent of the critic may well be, then, first to read his poem sensitively, and make comparative judgments about its technical practice, or, as we might say, to emulate Eliot. Beyond that, it is to read and remark the poem knowingly; that is, with an esthetician's understanding of what a poem generically "is."

Before I venture, with inadequate argument, to describe what I take to be the correct understanding of poetry, I would like to describe two other understandings which, though widely professed, seem to me misunderstandings. First, there is a smart and belletristic theory of poetry which may be called "psychologistic." Then there is an altogether staid and commonplace theory which is moralistic. Of these in their order.

II

It could easily be argued about either of these untenable conceptions of poetry that it is an act of despair to which critics resort who cannot find for the discourse of poetry any precise differentia to remove it from the category of science. Psychologistic critics hold that poetry is addressed primarily to the feelings and motor impulses; they remind us frequently of its contrast with the coldness, the unemotionality, of science, which is supposed to address itself to the pure cognitive mind. Mr. Richards came out spectacularly for the doctrine, and furnished it with detail of the greatest ingenuity. He very nearly severed the dependence of poetic effect upon any standard of objective knowledge or belief. But the feelings and impulses which he represented as gratified by the poem were too tiny and numerous to be named. He never identified them; they seemed not so much psychological as infra-psychological. His was an esoteric poetic: it could not be disproved. But neither could it be proved, and I think it is safe at this distance to say that eventually his readers, and Richards himself, lost interest in it as being an improvisation, much too unrelated to the public sense of a poetic experience.

With other critics psychologism of some sort is an old story, and one that will probably never cease to be told. For, now that all of us know about psychology, there must always be persons on hand precisely conditioned to declare that poetry is an emotional discourse indulged in resentment and compensation for science, the bleak cognitive discourse in its purity. It becomes less a form of knowledge than a form of "expression." The critics are willing to surrender the honor of objectivity to science if they may have the luxury of subjectivity for poetry. Science will scarcely object. But one or two things have to be said about that. In every experience, even in science, there is feeling. No discourse can sustain itself without interest, which is feeling. The interest, or the feeling, is like an automatic index to the human value of the proceeding—which would not otherwise proceed. Mr. Eliseo Vivas is an esthetician who might be thought to reside in the camp of the enemy, for his affiliations are positivist; yet in a recent essay he writes about the "passion" which sustains the heroic labors of the scientist as one bigger and more intense than is given to most men.

I do not mean to differ with that judgment at all in remarking that we might very well let the passions and the feelings take care of themselves; it is precisely what we do in our pursuit of science. The thing to attend to is the object to which they attach. As between two similar musical phrases, or between two similar lines of poetry, we may often defy the most proficient psychologist to distinguish the one feeling-response from the other; unless we permit him to say at long last that one is the kind of response that would be made to the first line, and the other is the kind of response that would be made to the second line. But that is to do, after much wasted motion, what I have just suggested: to attend to the poetic object and let the feelings take care of themselves. It is their business to "respond." There may be a feeling correlative with the minutest alteration in an object, and adequate to it, but we shall hardly know. What we do know is that the feelings are grossly inarticulate if we try to abstract them and take their testimony in their own language. Since it is not the intent of the critic to be inarticulate, his discriminations must be among the objects. We understand this so well intuitively that the critic seems to us in possession of some esoteric knowledge, some magical insight, if he appears to be intelligent elsewhere and yet refers confidently to the "tone" or "quality" or "value" of the feeling he discovers in a given line. Probably he is bluffing. The distinctness resides in the cognitive or "semantical" objects denoted by the words. When Richards bewilders us by reporting affective and motor disturbances that are too tiny for definition, and other critics by reporting disturbances that are too massive and gross, we cannot fail to grow suspicious of this whole way of insight as incompetent.

Eliot has a special version of psychologistic theory which looks extremely fertile, though it is broad and nebulous as his psychologistic terms require it to be. He likes to regard the poem as a structure of emotion and feeling. But the emotion is singular, there being only one emotion per poem, or at least per passage: it is the central emotion or big emotion which attaches to the main theme or situation. The feeling is plural. The emotion combines with many feelings; these are our little responses to the single words and phrases, and he does not think of them as being parts of the central emotion or even related to it. The terminology is greatly at fault, or we should recognize at once, I think, a principle that might prove very valuable. I would not answer for the conduct of a technical philosopher in assessing this theory; he might throw it away, out of patience with its jargon. But a lay philosopher who respects his Eliot and reads with all his sympathy might salvage a good thing from it, though I have not heard of anyone doing so. He would try to escape from the affective terms, and translate Eliot into more intelligible language. Eliot would be saying in effect that a poem has a central logic or situation or "para-phrasable core" to which an appropriate interest doubtless attaches, and that in this respect the poem is like a discourse of science behind which lies the sufficient passion. But he would be saying at the same time, and this is the important thing, that the poem has also a context of lively local details to which other and independent interests attach; and that in this respect it is unlike the discourse of science. For the detail of scientific discourse intends never to be independent of the thesis (either objectively or affectively) but always functional, and subordinate to the realization of the thesis. To say that is to approach to a structural understanding of poetry, and to the kind of un-derstanding that I wish presently to urge.

III

As for the moralistic understanding of poetry, it is sometimes the specific moralists, men with moral axes to grind, and incidentally men of unassailable public position, who cherish that; they have a "use" for poetry. But not ex-clusively, for we may find it held also by critics who are more spontaneous and innocent: apparently they fall back upon it because it attributes some special character to poetry, which otherwise refuses to yield up to them a character. The moral interest is so much more frequent in poetry than in sci-ence that they decide to offer its moralism as a differentia.

This conception of poetry is of the greatest antiquity—it antedates the evolution of close esthetic philosophy, and persists beside it too. Plato some-times spoke of poetry in this light—perhaps because it was recommended to him in this light—but nearly always scornfully. In the *Gorgias,* and other dialogues, he represents the poets as moralizing, and that is only what he, in the person of Socrates, is doing at the very moment, and given to doing; but he considers the moralizing of poets as mere "rhetoric," or popular philosophy, and unworthy of the accomplished moralist who is the real or technical philos-opher. Plato understood very well that the poet does not conduct a technical or an original discourse like that of the scientist—and the term includes here the moral philosopher—and that close and effective moralizing is scarcely to be had from him. It is not within the poet's power to offer that if his intention is to offer poetry; for the poetry and the morality are so far from being identical that they interfere a little with each other.

Few famous estheticians in the history of philosophy have cared to bother with the moralistic conception; many critics have, in all periods. Just now we have at least two schools of moralistic critics contending for the official possession of poetry. One is the Neo-Humanist, and Mr. Foerster has identified himself with that. The other is the Marxist, and I believe it is represented in some degree and shade by Mr. Wilson, possibly by Mr. Auden. I have myself taken profit from the discussions by both schools, but recently I have taken more—I suppose this is because I was brought up in a scholastic discipline rather like the Neo-Humanist—from the writings of the Marxist critics. One of the differences is that the Neo-Humanists believe in the "respectable" virtues, but the Marxists believe that respectability is the greatest of vices, and equate respectable with "genteel." That is a very striking difference, and I think it is also profound.

But I do not wish to be impertinent; I can respect both these moralities, and appropriate moral values from both. The thing I wish to argue is not the comparative merits of the different moralities by which poetry is judged, but their equal inadequacy to the reading of the poet's intention. The moralistic critics wish to isolate and discuss the "ideology" or theme or paraphrase of the poem and not the poem itself. But even to the practitioners themselves, if they are sophisticated, comes sometimes the apprehension that this is moral rather than literary criticism. I have not seen the papers of my colleagues in this discussion, for that was against the rules, but it is reported to me that both Mr. Wilson and Mr. Foerster concede in explicit words that criticism has both the moral and the esthetic branches; Mr. Wilson may call them the "social" and esthetic branches. And they would hold the critical profession responsible for both branches. Under these circumstances the critics cease to be mere moralists and become dualists; that is better. My feeling about such a position would be that the moral criticism we shall have with us always, and have had always, and that it is easy—comparatively speaking—and that what is hard, and needed, and indeed more and more urgent after all the failures of poetic understanding, is a better esthetic criticism. This is the branch which is all but invariably neglected by the wise but morally zealous critics; they tend to forget their dual responsibility. I think I should go so far as to think that, in strictness, the business of the literary critic is exclusively with an esthetic criticism. The business of the moralist will naturally, and properly, be with something else.

If we have the patience to read for a little while in the anthology, paying some respect to the varieties of substance actually in the poems, we cannot logically attribute ethical character by definition to poetry; for that character is not universal in the poems. And if we have any faith in a community of character among the several arts, we are stopped quickly from risking such a definition for art at large. To claim a moral content for most of sculpture, painting, music, or architecture, is to plan something dialectically very round-about and subtle, or else to be so arbitrary as to invite instant exposure. I should think the former alternative is impractical, and the latter, if it is not stupid, is masochistic.

The moralistic critics are likely to retort upon their accusers by accusing them in turn of the vapid doctrine known as Art for Art's Sake. And with frequent justice; but again we are likely to receive the impression that it is just because Art for Art's Sake, the historic doctrine, proved empty, and availed them so little esthetically, like all the other doctrines that came into default, that they have fled to their moralism. Moralism does at least impute to poetry a positive substance, as Art for Art's Sake does not. It asserts an autonomy for art, which is excellent; but autonomy to do what? Only to be itself, and to reduce its interpreters to a tautology? With its English adherents in the 'nineties the doctrine seemed to make only a negative requirement of art, that is, that it should be anti-Victorian as we should say today, a little bit naughty and immoral perhaps, otherwise at least non-moral, or carefully squeezed dry of moral substance. An excellent example of how two doctrines, inadequate equally but in opposite senses, may keep themselves alive by abhorring each other's errors.

It is highly probable that the poem considers an ethical situation, and there is no reason why it should repel this from its consideration. But, if I may say so without being accused of verbal trifling, the poetic consideration of the ethical situation is not the same as the ethical consideration of it. The straight ethical consideration would be prose; it would be an act of interested science, or an act of practical will. The poetic consideration, according to Schopenhauer, is the objectification of this act of will; that is, it is our contemplation and not our exercise of will, and therefore qualitatively a very different experience; knowledge without desire. That doctrine also seems too negative and indeterminate. I will put the point as I see it in another way. It should be a comfort to the moralist that there is ordinarily a moral composure in the poem, as if the poet had long known good and evil, and made his moral choice between them once and for all. Art is post-ethical rather than unethical. In the poem there is an increment of meaning which is neither the ethical content nor opposed to the ethical content. The poetic experience would have to stop for the poet who is developing it, or for the reader who is following it, if the situation which is being poetically treated should turn back into a situation to be morally determined; if, for example, the situation were not a familiar one, and one to which we had habituated our moral wills; for it would rouse the moral will again to action, and make the poetic treatment impossible under its heat. Art is more cool than hot, and a moral fervor is as disastrous to it as a burst of passion itself. We have seen Marxists recently so revolted by Shakespeare's addiction to royal or noble *personae* that they cannot obtain esthetic experience from the plays; all they get is moral agitation. In another art, we know, and doubtless we approve, the scruple of the college authorities in not permitting the "department of fine arts" to direct the collegians in painting in the nude. Doctor Hanns Sachs, successor to Freud, in a recent number of his *American Imago,* gives a story from a French author as follows:

He tells that one evening strolling along the streets of Paris he noticed a row of slot machines which for a small coin showed pictures of women in full or partial undress. He observed the leering interest with which men of all kind and description, well dressed and shabby, boys and old men, enjoyed the peep show. He remarked that they all avoided one of these machines, and wondering what uninteresting pictures it might show, he put his penny in the slot. To his great astonishment the generally shunned picture turned out to be the Venus of Medici. Now he begins to ponder: Why does nobody get excited about her? She is decidedly feminine and not less naked than the others which hold such strong fascination for everybody. Finally he finds a satisfactory answer: They fight shy of her because she is beautiful.

And Doctor Sachs, though in his own variety of jargon, makes a number of wise observations about the psychic conditions precedent to the difficult apprehension of beauty. The experience called beauty is beyond the powerful ethical will precisely as it is beyond the animal passion, and indeed these last two are competitive, and coordinate. Under the urgency of either we are incapable of appreciating the statue or understanding the poem.

IV

The ostensible substance of the poem may be anything at all which words may signify: an ethical situation, a passion, a train of thought, a flower or landscape, a thing. This substance receives its poetic increment. It might be safer to say it receives some subtle and mysterious alteration under poetic treatment, but I will risk the cruder formula: the ostensible substance is increased by an x, which is an increment. The poem actually continues to contain its ostensible substance, which is not fatally diminished from its prose state: that is its logical core, or paraphrase. The rest of the poem is x, which we are to find.

We feel the working of this simple formula when we approach a poetry with our strictest logic, provided we can find deliverance from certain inhibiting philosophical prepossessions into which we have been conditioned by the critics we have had to read. Here is Lady Macbeth planning a murder with her husband:

> When Duncan is asleep—
> Whereto the rather shall his hard day's journey
> Soundly invite him—his two chamberlains
> Will I with wine and wassail so convince,
> That memory, the warder of the brain,
> Shall be a fume, and the receipt of reason
> A limbec only; when in swinish sleep
> Their drenched natures lie as in a death,
> What cannot you and I perform upon
> The unguarded Duncan? what not put upon
> His spongy officers, who shall bear the guilt
> Of our great quell?

It is easy to produce the prose argument or paraphrase of this speech; it has one upon which we shall all agree. But the passage is more than its argument. Any detail, with this speaker, seems capable of being expanded in some direction which is not that of the argument. For example, Lady Macbeth says she will make the chamberlains drunk so that they will not remember their charge, nor keep their wits about them. But it is indifferent to this argument whether memory according to the old psychology is located at the gateway to the brain, whether it is to be disintegrated into fume as of alcohol, and whether the whole receptacle of the mind is to be turned into a still. These are additions to the argument both energetic and irrelevant—though they do not quite stop or obscure the argument. From the point of view of the philosopher they are excursions into particularity. They give, in spite of the argument, which would seem to be perfectly self-sufficient, a sense of the real density and contingency of the world in which arguments and plans have to be pursued. They bring out the private character which the items of an argument can really assume if we look at them. This character spreads out in planes at right angles to the course of the argument, and in effect gives to the discourse another dimension, not present in a perfectly logical prose. We are expected to have sufficient judgment not to let this local character take us too far or keep us too long from the argument.

All this would seem commonplace remark, I am convinced, but for those philosophically timid critics who are afraid to think that the poetic increment is local and irrelevant, and that poetry cannot achieve its own virtue and keep undiminished the virtues of prose at the same time. But I will go a little further in the hope of removing the sense of strangeness in the analysis. I will offer a figurative definition of a poem.

A poem is, so to speak, a democratic state, whereas a prose discourse—mathematical, scientific, ethical, or practical and vernacular—is a totalitarian state. The intention of a democratic state is to perform the work of state as effectively as it can perform it, subject to one reservation of conscience: that it will not despoil its members, the citizens, of the free exercise of their own private and independent characters. But the totalitarian state is interested solely in being effective, and regards the citizens as no citizens at all; that is, regards them as functional members whose existence is totally defined by their allotted contributions to its ends; it has no use for their private characters, and therefore no provision for them. I indicate of course the extreme or polar opposition between two polities without denying that a polity may come to us rather mixed up.

In this trope the operation of the state as a whole represents of course the logical paraphrase or argument of the poem. The private character of the citizens represents the particularity asserted by the parts in the poem. And this last is our x.

For many years I had seen—as what serious observer has not—that a poem as a discourse differentiated itself from prose by its particularity, yet not to the point of sacrificing its logical cogency or universality. But I could get no further. I could not see how real particularity could get into a universal. The object of esthetic studies became for me a kind of discourse, or a kind of natural configuration, which like any other discourse or configuration claimed universality, but which consisted actually, and notoriously, of particularity. The poem was concrete, yet universal, and in spite of Hegel I could not see how the two properties could be identified as forming in a single unit the "concrete universal." It is usual, I believe, for persons at this stage to assert that somehow the apparent diffuseness or particularity in the poem gets itself taken up or "assimilated" into the logic, to produce a marvellous kind of unity called a "higher unity," to which ordinary discourse is not eligible. The belief is that the "idea" or theme proves itself in poetry to be even more dominating than in prose by overcoming much more energetic resistance than usual on the part of the materials, and the resistance, as attested in the local development of detail, is therefore set not to the debit but to the credit of the unifying power of the poetic spirit. A unity of that kind is one which philosophers less audacious and more factual than Hegel would be loath to claim. Critics incline to call it, rather esoterically, an "imaginative" rather than a logical unity, but one supposes they mean a mystical, an ineffable, unity. I for one could neither grasp it nor deny it. I believe that is not an uncommon situation for poetic analysts to find themselves in.

It occurred to me at last that the solution might be very easy if looked for without what the positivists call "metaphysical prepossessions." Suppose the logical substance remained there all the time, and was in no way specially remarkable, while the particularity came in by accretion, so that the poem turned out partly universal, and partly particular, but with respect to different parts. I began to remark the dimensions of a poem, or other work of art. The poem was not a mere moment in time, nor a mere point in space. It was sizeable, like a house. Apparently it had a "plan," or a central frame of logic, but it had also a huge wealth of local detail, which sometimes fitted the plan functionally or served it, and sometimes only subsisted comfortably under it; in either case the house stood up. But it was the political way of thinking which gave me the first analogy which seemed valid. The poem was like a democratic state, in action, and observed both macroscopically and micro-scopically.

The house occurred also, and provided what seems to be a more negotiable trope under which to construe the poem. A poem is a *logical structure* having a *local texture*. These terms have been actually though not systematically em-ployed in literary criticism. To my imagination they are architectural. The walls of my room are obviously structural; the beams and boards have a func-tion; so does the plaster, which is the visible aspect of the final wall. The plaster might have remained naked, aspiring to no character, and purely func-tional. But actually it has been painted, receiving color; or it has been papered, receiving color and design, though these have no structural value; and perhaps it has been hung with tapestry, or with paintings, for "decoration." The paint, the paper, the tapestry are texture. It is logically unrelated to structure. But I indicate only a few of the textural possibilities in architecture. There are not fewer of them in poetry.

The intent of the good critic becomes therefore to examine and define the poem with respect to its structure and its texture. If he has nothing to say about its texture he has nothing to say about it specifically as a poem, but is treating it only insofar as it is prose.

I do not mean to say that the good critic will necessarily employ my terms.

V

Many critics today are writing analytically and with close intelligence, in whatever terms, about the logical substance or structure of the poem, and its increment of irrelevant local substance or texture. I believe that the under-standing of the ideal critic has to go even further than that. The final desidera-tum is an ontological insight, nothing less. I am committed by my title to a representation of criticism as, in the last resort, a speculative exercise. But my secret committal was to speculative in the complete sense of—ontological.

There is nothing especially speculative or ontological in reciting, or even ap-praising, the logical substance of the poem. This is its prose core—its science perhaps, or its ethics if it seems to have an ideology. Speculative interest asserts itself principally when we ask why we want the logical substance to be com-pounded with the local substance, the good lean structure with a great volume of texture that does not function. It is the same thing as asking why we want the poem to be what it is.

It has been a rule, having the fewest exceptions, for estheticians and great philosophers to direct their speculations by the way of overstating and over-valuing the logical substance. They are impressed by the apparent obedience of material nature, whether in fact or in art, to definable form or "law" imposed upon it. They like to suppose that in poetry, as in chemistry, everything that figures in the discourse means to be functional, and that the poem is imperfect in the degree that it contains items, whether by accident or intention, which manifest a private independence. It is a bias with which we are entirely familiar, and reflects the extent to which our philosophy hitherto has been impressed by the successes of science in formulating laws which would "govern" their objects. Probably I am here reading the state of mind of yesterday rather than of today. Nevertheless we know it. The world-view which ultimately forms itself in the mind so biassed is that of a world which is rational and intelligible. The view is sanguine, and naïve. Hegel's world-view, I think it is agreed, was a subtle version of this, and if so, it was what determined his view of art. He seemed to make the handsomest concession to realism by offering to knowledge a kind of universal which was not restricted to the usual abstracted aspects of the material, but included all aspects, and was a concrete universal. The concreteness in Hegel's handling was not honestly, or at any rate not fairly, defended. It was always represented as being in process of pointing up and helping out the universality. He could look at a work of art and report all its substance as almost assimilated to a ruling "idea." But at least Hegel seemed to distinguish what looked like two ultimate sorts of substance there, and stated the central esthetic problem as the problem of relating them. And his writings about art are speculative in the sense that he regarded the work of art not as of great intrinsic value necessarily, but as an object-lesson or discipline in the understanding of the world-process, and as its symbol.

I think of two ways of construing poetry with respect to its ultimate purpose; of which the one is not very handsome nor speculatively interesting, and the other will appear somewhat severe.

The first construction would picture the poet as a sort of epicure, and the poem as something on the order of a Christmas pudding, stuffed with what dainties it will hold. The pastry alone, or it may be the cake, will not serve; the stuffing is wanted too. The values of the poem would be intrinsic, or immediate, and they would include not only the value of the structure but also the incidental values to be found in the texture. If we exchange the pudding for a house, they would include not only the value of the house itself but also the value of the furnishings. In saying intrinsic or immediate, I mean that the poet is fond of the precise objects denoted by the words, and writes the poem for the reason that he likes to dwell upon them. In talking about the main value and the incidental values I mean to recognize the fact that the latter engage the affections just as truly as the former. Poetic discourse therefore would be more agreeable than prose to the epicure or the literally acquisi-

tive man; for prose has but a single value, being about one thing only; its parts
have no values of their own, but only instrumental values, which might be
reckoned as fractions of the single value proportionate to their contributions to
it. The prose is one-valued and the poem is many-valued. Indeed there will
certainly be poems whose texture contains many precious objects, and aggre-
gates a greater value than the structure.

So there would be a comfortable and apparently eligible view that poetry
improves on prose because it is a richer diet. It causes five or six pleasures to
appear, five or six good things, where one had been before; an alluring consideration for robustious, full-blooded, bourgeois souls. The view will account
for much of the poem, if necessary. But it does not account for all of it, and
sometimes it accounts for less than at other times.

The most impressive reason for the bolder view of art, the speculative one,
is the existence of the "pure," or "abstractionist," or non-representational works
of art; though these will probably occur to us in other arts than poetry. There
is at least one art, music, whose works are all of this sort. Tones are not words,
they have no direct semantical function, and by themselves they mean nothing. But they combine to make brilliant phrases, harmonies, and compositions.
In these compositions it is probable that the distinction between structure or
functional content, on the one hand, and texture or local variation and departure, on the other, is even more determinate than in an impure art like
poetry. The world of tones seems perfectly inhuman and impracticable; there
is no specific field of experience "about which" music is telling us. Yet we
know that music is powerfully affective. I take my own musical feelings, and
those attested by other audients, as the sufficient index to some overwhelming
human importance which the musical object has for us. At the same time it
would be useless to ask the feelings precisely what they felt; we must ask the
critic. The safest policy is to take the simplest construction, and try to impro-
vise as little fiction as possible. Music is not music, I think, until we grasp its
effects both in structure and in texture. As we grow in musical understanding
the structures become always more elaborate and sustained, and the texture
which interrupts them and sometimes imperils them becomes more bold and
unpredictable. We can agree in saying about the works of music that these
are musical structures, and they are richly textured; we can identify these
elements, and perhaps precisely. To what then do our feelings respond? To
music as structural composition itself; to music as manifesting the structural
principles of the world; to modes of structure which we feel to be ontologically
possible, or even probable. Schopenhauer construed music very much in that
sense. Probably it will occur to us that musical compositions bear close analogy
therefore to operations in pure mathematics. The mathematicians confess that
their constructions are "non-existential"; meaning, as I take it, that the constructions testify with assurance only to the structural principles, in the light

of which they are possible but may not be actual, or if they are actual may not be useful. This would define the mathematical operations as speculative: as motivated by an interest so generalized and so elemental that no word short of ontological will describe it.

But if music and mathematics have this much in common, they differ sharply in their respective world-views or ontological biases. That of music, with its prodigious display of texture, seems the better informed about the nature of the world, the more realistic, the less naïve. Perhaps the difference is between two ontological educations. But I should be inclined to imagine it as rising back of that point: in two ontological temperaments.

There are also, operating a little less successfully so far as the indexical evidences would indicate, the abstractionist paintings, of many schools, and perhaps also works of sculpture; and there is architecture. These arts have tried to abandon direct representational intention almost as heroically as music. They exist in their own materials and indicate no other specific materials; structures of color, light, space, stone—the cheapest of materials. They too can symbolize nothing of value unless it is structure or composition itself. But that is precisely the act which denotes will and intelligence; which becomes the act of fuller intelligence if it carefully accompanies its structures with their material textures; for then it understands better the ontological nature of materials.

Returning to the poetry. It is not all poems, and not even all "powerful" poems, having high index-ratings, whose semantical meanings contain situations important in themselves or objects precious in themselves. There may be little correlation between the single value of the poem and the aggregate value of its contents—just as there is no such correlation whatever in music. The "effect" of the poem may be astonishingly disproportionate to our interest in its materials. It is true, of course, that there is no art employing materials of equal richness with poetry, and that it is beyond the capacity of poetry to employ indifferent materials. The words used in poetry are the words the race has already formed, and naturally they call attention to things and events that have been thought to be worth attending to. But I suggest that any poetry which is "technically" notable is in part a work of abstractionist art, concentrating upon the structure and the texture, and the structure-texture relation, out of a pure speculative interest.

At the end of *Love's Labour's Lost* occurs a little diversion which seems proportionately far more effective than that laborious play as a whole. The play is over, but Armado stops the principals before they disperse to offer them a show:

ARMADO.   But, most esteemed greatness, will you hear the dialogue that the two learned men have compiled in praise of the owl and the cuckoo? It should have followed in the end of our show.

KING.   Call them forth quickly; we will do so.
ARMADO.   Holla! approach.
Re-enter Holofernes, etc.

This side is Hiems, Winter, this Ver, the Spring; the one maintained
by the owl, the other by the cuckoo. Ver, begin.

THE SONG

SPRING.   When daisies pied and violets blue
          And lady-smocks all silver-white
          And cuckoo-buds of yellow hue
          Do paint the meadows with delight,
          The cuckoo then, on every tree,
          Mocks married men; for thus sings he,
                    Cuckoo;
          Cuckoo, cuckoo: O word of fear,
          Unpleasing to a married ear!

          When shepherds pipe on oaten straws,
          And merry larks are ploughmen's clocks,
          When turtles tread, and rooks, and daws,
          And maidens bleach their summer smocks,
          The cuckoo then, on every tree,
          Mocks married men; for thus sings he,
                    Cuckoo;
          Cuckoo, cuckoo: O word of fear,
          Unpleasing to a married ear!

WINTER.   When icicles hang by the wall,
          And Dick the shepherd blows his nail,
          And Tom bears logs into the hall,
          And milk comes frozen home in pail,
          When blood is nipp'd and ways be foul,
          Then nightly sings the staring owl,
                    Tu-who;
          Tu-whit, tu-who, a merry note,
          While greasy Joan doth keel the pot.

          When all aloud the wind doth blow,
          And coughing drowns the parson's saw,
          And birds sit brooding in the snow,
          And Marian's nose looks red and raw,
          When roasted crabs hiss in the bowl,
          Then nightly sings the staring owl,
                    Tu-who;
          Tu-whit, tu-who, a merry note,
          While greasy Joan doth keel the pot.

ARMADO.   The words of Mercury are harsh after the songs of Apollo.
You that way,—we this way. (*Exeunt.*)

The feeling-index registers such strong approval of this episode that a critic
with ambition is obliged to account for it. He can scarcely account for it in
terms of the weight of its contents severally.

At first glance Shakespeare has provided only a pleasant little caricature of
the old-fashioned (to us, medieval) debate between personified characters. It is
easygoing, like nonsense; no labor is lost here. Each party speaks two stanzas
and concludes both stanzas with the refrain about his bird, the cuckoo or the
owl. There is no generalized argument, or dialectic proper. Each argues by
citing his characteristic exhibits. In the first stanza Spring cites some flowers;
in the second stanza, some business by country persons, with interpolation of
some birds that make love. Winter in both his stanzas cites the country business of the season. In the refrain the cuckoo, Spring's symbol, is used to refer
the love-making to more than the birds; and this repeats itself, though it is
naughty. The owl is only a nominal symbol for Winter, an "emblem" that is
not very emblematic, but the refrain manages another reference to the kitchen,
and repeats itself, as if Winter's pleasure focussed in the kitchen.

In this poem texture is not very brilliant, but it eclipses structure. The argument, we would say in academic language, is concerned with "the relative advantages of Spring and Winter." The only logical determinateness this structure has is the good coordination of the items cited by Spring as being really
items peculiar to Spring, and of the Winter items as peculiar to Winter. The
symbolic refrains look like summary or master items, but they seem to be a
little more than summary and in fact to mean a little more than they say. The
argument is trifling on the whole, and the texture from the point of view of
felt human importance lacks decided energy; both which observations are to be
made, and most precisely, of how many famous lyrics, especially those before
that earnest and self-conscious nineteenth century! The value of the poem is
greater than the value of its parts: that is what the critic is up against.

Unquestionably it is possible to assemble very fine structures out of ordinary
materials. The good critic will study the poet's technique, in confidence that
here the structural principles will be discovered at home. In this study he will
find as much range for his activities as he desires.

Especially must he study the metrics, and their implications for structural
composition. In this poem I think the critic ought to make good capital of the
contrast between the amateurishness of the pleasant discourse as meaning and
the hard determinate form of it phonetically. The meter on the whole is out of
relation to the meaning of the poem, or to anything else specifically; it is a
musical material of low grade, but plastic and only slightly resistant material,
and its presence in every poem is that of an abstractionist element that belongs
to the art.

And here I will suggest another analogy, this one between Shakespeare's poem and some ordinary specimen of painting. It does not matter how old-fashioned or representational the painting is, we shall all, if we are instructed in the tradition of this art, require it to exhibit along with its represented object an abstract design in terms of pure physical balance or symmetry. We sense rather than measure the success of this design, but it is as if we had drawn a horizontal axis and a vertical axis through the center of the picture, and required the painted masses to balance with respect to each of these two axes. This is an over-simple statement of a structural requirement by which the same details function in two worlds that are different, and that do not correlate with each other. If the painting is of the Holy Family, we might say that this object has a drama, or an economy, of its own, but that the physical masses which compose it must enter also into another economy, that of abstract design; and that the value of any unit mass for the one economy bears no relation to its value for the other. The painting is of great ontological interest because it embodies this special dimension of abstract form. And turning to the poem, we should find that its represented "meaning" is analogous to the represented object in the painting, while its meter is analogous to the pure design.

A number of fascinating speculative considerations must follow upon this discovery. They will have to do with the most fundamental laws of this world's structure. They will be profoundly ontological, though I do not mean they must be ontological in some recondite sense; ontological in such a homely and compelling sense that perhaps a child might intuit the principles which the critic will arrive at analytically, and with much labor.

I must stop at this point, since I am desired not so much to anticipate the critic as to present him. In conclusion I will remark that the critic will doubtless work empirically, and set up his philosophy only as the drift of his findings will compel him. But ultimately he will be compelled. He will have to subscribe to an ontology. If he is a sound critic his ontology will be that of his poets; and what is that? I suggest that the poetic world-view is Aristotelian and "realistic" rather than Platonic and "idealistic." He cannot follow the poets and still conceive himself as inhabiting the rational or "tidy" universe that is supposed by the scientists.

From *The Intent of the Critic* edited, with an Introduction, by Donald A. Stauffer, pp. 91–124. Copyright, 1941, by Princeton University Press. Reprinted by permission of the author and publishers.

HARRY LEVIN

Literature as an Institution

[1946]

I. THE CONTRIBUTION OF TAINE

"LITERATURE is the expression of society, as speech is the expression of man." In this aphorism the Vicomte de Bonald summed up one of the bitter lessons that the French Revolution had taught the world. With the opening year of the nineteenth century, and the return of the Emigration, coincided a two-volume study by Madame de Staël: *De la Littérature considérée dans ses rapports avec les institutions sociales.* This was not the first time, of course, that some relationship had been glimpsed. Renaissance humanism, fighting out the invidious quarrel between ancient and modern literatures, had concluded that each was the unique creation of its period, and had adumbrated a historical point of view. Romantic nationalism, seeking to undermine the prestige of the neo-classic school and to revive the native traditions of various countries, was now elaborating a series of geographical comparisons. It was left for Hippolyte Taine—in the vanguard of a third intellectual movement, scientific positivism —to formulate a sociological approach. To the historical and geographical factors, the occasional efforts of earlier critics to discuss literature in terms of "moment" and "race," he added a third conception, which completed and finally eclipsed them. "Milieu," as he conceived it, is the link between literary criticism and the social sciences. Thus Taine raised a host of new problems by settling an old one.

When Taine's history of English literature appeared, it smelled—to a contemporary reader, Amiel—like the exhalations from a laboratory. To that sensitive Swiss idealist, it conveyed a whiff of "the literature of the future in the American style," of "the death of poetry flayed and anatomized by science." This "intrusion of technology into literature," as Amiel was shrewd enough to observe, is a responsibility which Taine shares with Balzac and Stendhal. As Taine self-consciously remarked, "From the novel to criticism and from criticism to the novel, the distance at present is not very great." Taine's critical theory is grounded upon the practice of the realists, while their novels are nothing if not critical. His recognition of the social forces behind literature coincides with their resolution to embody those forces in their works. The first to acknowledge Stendhal as a master, he welcomed Flaubert as a colleague and lived to find Zola among his disciples. "When M. Taine studies Balzac," Zola acknowledged, "he does exactly what Balzac himself does when he studies Père Grandet." There is no better way to bridge the distance between criticism and the novel, or to scrutinize the presuppositions of modern literature, than by a brief reconsideration of Taine's critical method.

A tougher-minded reader than Amiel, Flaubert, noted in 1864 that—whatever the *Histoire de la littérature anglaise* left unsettled—it got rid of the uncritical notion that books dropped like meteorites from the sky. The social basis of art might thereafter be overlooked, but it could hardly be disputed. Any lingering belief in poetic inspiration could hardly withstand the higher criticism that had disposed of spontaneous generation and was disposing of divine revelation. When Renan, proclaiming his disbelief in mysteries, depicted Jesus as the son of man and analyzed the origins of Christianity, then Taine could depict genius as the outgrowth of environment and analyze the origins of literature. On the whole, though critics have deplored the crudity of his analyses and scholars have challenged the accuracy of his facts, his working hypothesis has won acceptance. He has become the stock example of a rigorous determinist—especially for those who think determinism is a modern version of fatalism. Taine's determinism, however, is simply an intensive application of the intellectual curiosity of his age. It is no philosopher's attempt to encroach upon the freedom of the artist's will; it is simply a historian's consciousness of what the past has already determined.

As for Taine's rigor, a more thoroughgoing historical materialist, George Plekhanov, has gone so far as to accuse him of arrant idealism. A recent artist-philosopher, Jean-Paul Sartre, describes Taine's empiricism as an unsuccessful effort to set up a realistic system of metaphysics. Actually his position is that of most realists, so outrageous to their early readers and so tame to later critics. His method explained too much to satisfy his contemporaries; it has not explained enough to satisfy ours. Confronted with the provocative statement, "Vice and virtue are products like vitriol and sugar," we are not shocked by the audacity that reduces moral issues to chemical formulae; we are amused at the naïveté that undertakes to solve them both by a single equation. Taine's introduction to his history of English literature, which abounds in dogmas of this sort, is rather a manifesto than a methodology. If, reading on, we expect the history to practice what the introduction preaches, we are amiably disappointed. Each successive author is more freely individualized. How does Taine's all-determining scheme meet its severest test? With Shakespeare, he explains, after canvassing the material factors, "all comes from within—I mean from his soul and his genius; circumstances and externals have contributed but little to his development."

The loophole that enables Taine to avoid the strict consequences of his three determinants is a fourth—a loose system of psychology. Psychology takes over where sociology has given up, and the sociologist has shown surprisingly little interest in classes or institutions. He has viewed history as a parade of influential individuals, themselves the creatures of historical influences. To understand their achievements is "a problem in psychological mechanics." The psychologist must disclose their ruling passions; he must hit upon that magnificent obsession, that "master faculty" which conditions have created within the soul of every great man. Let us not be put off by the circular logic, the mechanical apparatus, and the scientific jargon: Taine, conscientious child of his temperament and time, was an ardent individualist. His theory of character owes quite as much to Balzac as his theory of environment owes to Stendhal. Had it been the other way around, had he combined Stendhal's psychological insight with Balzac's sociological outlook, he might have been a better critic. His portrait of Balzac, for better or worse, is as monomaniacal as Balzac's portrait of Grandet.

Psychology is a knife, Dostoevsky warns us, which cuts two ways. We may look for a man in his books, or we may look to the man for the explanation of his books. Taine's is the more dangerous way: to deduce the qualities of a work from a presupposition about the author. The whole *Comédie humaine* follows from the consideration that Balzac was a business man, and Livy's history is what you might expect from a writer who was really an orator. This mode of critical characterization must perforce be limited to a few broad strokes, much too exaggerated and impressionistic to be compared with the detailed nuances of Sainte-Beuve's portraiture. Most of Taine's figures bear a strong family likeness. He is most adroit at bringing out the generic traits of English literature: the response to nature, the puritan strain, the fact—in short—that it was written by Englishmen. He himself, true to his theories, remains an intransigent Frenchman, and his history—to the point where he abandons Tennyson for Musset and recrosses the channel—remains a traveler's survey of a foreign culture. Why, in spite of all temptations to interpret other cultures, should Taine have been attracted to England?

Taine's critical faculties were conditioned not by science but by romanticism, and who was Taine to repudiate his own conditioning? Madame de Staël had been drawn to Germany, and Melchior de Vogué would soon be seeking the Russian soul, but English was for most Frenchmen the typically romantic literature. France had been the Bastille of classicism, while Britain had never been enslaved to the rules; untamed nature, in Saxon garb, resisted the shackles of Norman constraint. It took very little perception of the technique of English poetry for Taine to prefer blank verse to Alexandrines. Form, as he construed it, was a body of artificial restrictions which inhibited free expression, and which English men of letters had somehow succeeded in doing without. One might almost say that they had developed a literature of pure content. "Not in Greece, nor in Italy, nor in Spain, nor in France," said Taine, "has an art been seen which tried so boldly to express the soul and the most intimate depths of the soul, the reality and the whole reality." What seemed to him so unprecedented is, on closer scrutiny, a complex tradition. Elizabethan drama is so much more baroque than the succinct tragedies of Racine that Taine missed its pattern altogether, and believed he was facing a chaos of first-hand and unconstrained realities. His impressions were those of Fielding's barber Partridge at the play, wholly taken in by theatrical make-believe, naïvely mistaking the actors for the characters they represent, quixotically confusing literature with life.

2. SOCIOLOGICAL CRITICISM AND SOCIAL CRITICS

Remembering Lamb's essay on the artificiality of Restoration comedy, we cannot share Taine's facile assumption that the English stage received and retained "the exact imprint of the century and the nation." We cannot accept this free translation of Hamlet's impulse to give "the very age and body of the time his form and pressure." We can admit that Taine was less of a critic than a historian, but we cannot forgive him for being such an uncritical historian. His professed willingness to trade quantities of charters for the letters of Saint Paul or the memoirs of Cellini does not indicate a literary taste; it merely states a preference for human documents as against constitutional documents. In exploiting literature for purposes of historical documentation, Taine uncovered a new mine of priceless source material. But he never learned the difference between ore and craftsmanship. In his *Philosophie de l'art,* to be sure, he could no longer sidestep esthetic and technical discussion. He was forced to concede that art could be idealistic as well as realistic, and to place Greek sculpture at a farther remove from reality than Flemish painting. This concession allowed him to turn his back on the sculpture, and to reconstruct, with a freer hand than ever, the moment, the race, and the milieu of ancient Greece.

The serious objection to environmentalism is that it failed to distinguish, not between one personality and another, but between personality and art. It encouraged scholars to write literary histories which, as Ferdinand Brunetière pointed out, were nothing but chronological dictionaries of literary biography. It discouraged the realization, which Brunetière called the evolution of *genres,* that literary technique had a history of its own. It advanced a brilliant generalization, and established—as first-rate ideas will do in second-rate minds—a rule of thumb. The incidental and qualified extent to which books epitomize their epoch may vary from one example to the next. Taine's successors made no allowances for the permutations of form; rather they industrialized his process for extracting the contents of the books. The prevailing aim of literary historiography, under the sponsorship of Gustave Lanson in France and other professors elsewhere, has been a kind of illustrated supplement to history. Academic research has concentrated so heavily on the backgrounds of literature that the foreground has been almost obliterated.

Meanwhile Taine's influence has been felt in the wider areas of criticism, and here it has been subordinated to political ends. Taine himself was bitterly anti-political. He did not realize the importance of ideas until he had lost faith in his own: originally he had been a proponent of the doctrines of the *philosophes*, which he blamed in his later studies, *Les Origines de la France contemporaine*, for instigating the revolution of 1789. It was a Danish critic, closely associated with Ibsen, Nietzsche, and the controversies of the eighties, who broadened the range and narrowed the tendency of literary history. For politics, and for literature too, Georg Brandes had more feeling than Taine. A cosmopolitan liberal, deeply suspicious of the ascendancy of Prussia, he found a touchstone for the romanticists in their struggles or compromises with clerical reaction and the authority of the state. Byron and Heine were his urbane prophets, the Schlegels were renegades, and the revolution of 1848 was the anticlimax toward which his *Main Currents of Nineteenth Century Literature* moved. Where a book had been an end-product to Taine, to Brandes it was continuing force, and the critic's function was to chart its repercussions.

Both aspects have been duly stressed in the critical interpretation of American writers—their reactions to their environment and their contributions to the liberal tradition. Our foremost literary historian, V. L. Parrington, extended and modified Taine's formula to fit our problems, dramatizing New England puritanism from the standpoint of western populism, and pitting a heroic Jefferson against a sinister Hamilton. His title, *Main Currents in American Thought*, conveyed a fraternal salute to Brandes, and denoted an additional qualification. Parrington got around Taine's difficulty—the difficulty of using imaginative writers as historical sources—by drawing upon the moralists and the publicists. His chapters on Roger Williams and John Marshall are ample and rewarding; his accounts of Poe and Henry James are so trivial that they might better have been omitted. The latest period is inevitably the hardest and his last volume is posthumous and fragmentary, but it seems to mark an increasing conflict between artistic and political standards. Granville Hicks, going over the same ground, was able to resolve that conflict by the simple device of discarding artistic standards.

Mr. Hicks, if he still adheres to his somewhat elusive conception of *The Great Tradition*, is a Marxist critic in the sense that Parrington was a Jeffersonian critic. The choice between them is largely a matter of political standards. Jeffersonianism, naturally the most favorable climate in which to discuss American literature, has been taken in vain so often that it has begun to resist definition. Marxism, by redefining milieu in economic terms, has presented a more rigorous theory of historical causation than Taine's and a more ruthless canon of political allegiance than Brandes'. It has introduced criticism to a sociological system which is highly illuminating and a social doctrine which is highly controversial. It has tightened the relations between literature and life by oversimplifying them beyond recognition. In this respect Karl Marx, as he occasionally confessed, was no Marxist: he repeatedly cautioned his followers against expecting the arts to show a neat conformity with his views. Perhaps if he had written his projected study of Balzac, he would have bequeathed them a critical method. For lack of one, they took what was available. Marxist criticism superimposed its socialistic doctrine on the deterministic method, and judged according to Marx what it had interpreted according to Taine.

Extension and modification have added their corollary to Taine's method: the relations between literature and society are reciprocal. Literature is not only the effect of social causes; it is also the cause of social effects. The critic may investigate its causes, as Taine tried to do; or he may, like Brandes and others, be more interested in its effects. So long as he is correlating works of art with trends of history, his function is relatively clear. It becomes less clear as he encounters his contemporaries, and as the issues become more immediate. He is then concerned, no longer with a secure past, but with a problematic future. An insecure present may commit him to some special partisanship, Marxist or otherwise, and incline him to judge each new work by its possible effect—whether it will advance or hinder his party's program. Since art can be a weapon, among other things, it will be judged in the heat of the battle by its polemical possibilities. We need not deny the relevance or significance of such judgments; we need only recognize that they carry us beyond the limits of esthetic questions into the field of moral values. There are times when criticism cannot conveniently stop at the border. Whenever there are boundary disputes, questions involving propaganda or regulation, we may be called upon to go afield. We shall be safe while we are aware that virtue and beauty are as intimately related as beauty and truth, and as eternally distinct.

3. THE RÔLE OF CONVENTION[1]

It was as if Taine had discovered that the earth was round, without realizing that another continent lay between Europe and Asia. The distance was longer, the route more devious, than sociological criticism had anticipated. Not that the intervening territory was unexplored; but those who had explored it most thoroughly were isolationists. Those who were most familiar with the techniques and traditions of literature were least conscious of its social responsibilities. Most of them were writers themselves, lacking in critical method perhaps,

---

[1] Mr. Levin's discussion of convention is further developed in another essay, "Notes on Convention," included in *Perspectives of Criticism,* edited by Harry Levin and published by the Harvard University Press, Cambridge, 1950. (Editor's note, 1950.)

yet possessing the very skills and insights that the methodologists lacked. A few were philosophers, striving—on the high plane of idealism—toward a historical synthesis of the arts. Their concept of expressive form, inherited by the esthetic of Croce from the literary history of Francesco de Sanctis, resembles the "organic principle" that Anglo-American criticism inherits from the theory of Coleridge, the preaching of Emerson, and the practice of Thoreau. By whichever name, it is too sensitive an instrument to be used effectively, except by acute critics on acknowledged masterpieces. With cruder material, in unskilled hands, its insistence on the uniqueness of each work of art and its acceptance of the artist at his own evaluation dissolve into esthetic impressionism and romantic hero-worship.

While this school is responsible for many admirable critiques, it has never produced that "new criticism" which the late J. E. Spingarn tried vainly to define. Conceiving art as the fullest expression of individuality, it has disregarded the more analytic approaches. Taine's school, though less discriminating, has been more influential, because it conceives art as a collective expression of society. The fallacy in this conception—we have already seen—is to equate art with society, to assume a one-to-one correspondence between a book and its subject-matter, to accept the literature of an age as a complete and exact replica of the age itself. One way or another, literature is bound to tell the truth; but it has told the whole truth very seldom, and nothing but the truth hardly ever; some things are bound to be left out, and others to be exaggerated in the telling. Sins of omission can usually be traced to some restriction in the artist's freedom of speech, his range of experience, or his control of his medium. Sins of commission are inherent in the nature of his materials. The literary historian must reckon with these changing degrees of restriction and exaggeration. Literary history, if it is to be accurate, must be always correcting its aim.

To mention one conspicuous case, the relations between the sexes have received a vast—possibly a disproportionate—amount of attention from writers. From their miscellaneous and contradictory testimony it would be rash to infer very much, without allowing for the artistic taboos of one period or the exhibitionism of another. An enterprising sociologist, by measuring the exposed portions of the human figure in various paintings, has arrived at a quantitative historical index of comparative sensuality. What inference could not be drawn, by some future sciolist, from the preponderance of detective stories on the shelves of our circulating libraries? Those volumes testify, for us, to the colorless comfort of their readers' lives. We are aware, because we are not dependent on literary evidence, that ours is no unparalleled epoch of domestic crime—of utterly ineffectual police, of criminals who bear all the earmarks of innocence, and of detectives whose nonchalance is only equalled by their erudition. These, we are smugly aware, have not much more significance than the counters of a complicated game. Nevertheless, it is disturbing to imagine what literal-minded critics may deduce when the rules of the game have been forgotten. It suggests that we ourselves may be misreading other books through our ignorance of the lost conventions on which they hinge.

Convention may be described as a necessary difference between art and life. Some differences, strictly speaking, may be quite unnecessary: deliberate sallies of the imagination, unconscious effects of miscalculation or misunderstanding. But art must also differ from life for technical reasons: limitations of form, difficulties of expression. The artist, powerless to overcome these obstacles by himself, must have the assistance of his audience. They must agree to take certain formalities and assumptions for granted, to take the word for the deed or the shading for the shadow. The result of their unspoken agreement is a compromise between the possibilities of life and the exigencies of art. Goethe might have been speaking of convention when he said, *"In der Beschränkung zeigt sich erst der Meister."*[2] Limitation has often been a source of new forms, and difficulty—as the defenders of rhyme have argued, from Samuel Daniel to Paul Valéry—has prompted poets to their most felicitous expressions. Without some sort of conventionalization art could hardly exist. It exists by making virtues of necessities; after the necessities disappear, we forget the conventions. After perspective is invented, we misjudge the primitives; after scenery is set up, we challenge the unities. And Taine, forgetting that feminine roles were played by boys, is appalled at finding masculine traits in Elizabethan heroines.

His former classmate, Francisque Sarcey, who became—through forty years of playgoing—the most practical of critics, might have supplied the needed correction for Taine's theories. "It is inadequate to repeat that the theater is a representation of human life," Sarcey had learned. "It would be a more precise definition to say that dramatic art is the sum of conventions, universal or local, eternal or temporary, which help—when human life is represented on the stage—to give a public the illusion of truth." This illusion may be sustained in the novel more easily than on the stage; but it is still an illusion, as Maupassant frankly admitted. Although drama may be the most conventional of literary forms, and fiction the least, even fiction is not entirely free. Even Proust, the most unconventional of novelists, must resort to the convention of eavesdropping in order to sustain the needs of first-person narrative. We need not condone such melodramatic stratagems; we can observe that the modern novel has endeavored to get along without them; upon fuller consideration we may even conclude that the whole modern movement of realism, technically considered, is an endeavor to emancipate literature from the sway of conventions.

² "The true master first reveals himself when he works under limitations."

4. TOWARD AN INSTITUTIONAL METHOD

This provisional conclusion would explain why literary historians, under the influence of realism, have slighted literary form. In their impatience to lay bare the so-called content of a work, they have missed a more revealing characteristic: the way the artist handles the appropriate conventions. Whether it is possible, or even desirable, to eliminate artifice from art—that is one of the largest questions that criticism must face. But realistic novelists who declare their intentions of transcribing life have an obvious advantage over realistic critics who expect every book to be a literal transcript. Stendhal, when he declares that "a novel is a mirror riding along a highway," is in a position to fulfil his picaresque intention. When Taine echoes this precept, defining the novel as "a kind of portable mirror which can be conveyed everywhere, and which is most convenient for reflecting all aspects of nature and life," he puts the mirror before the horse. He is then embarrassed to discover so few reflections of the *ancien régime* in French novels of the eighteenth century. His revulsion from neo-classical generalities and his preference for descriptive details carry him back across the channel, from Marmontel and Crébillon *fils* to Fielding and Smollett. Some mirrors, Taine finally discovered, are less reliable than others.

The metaphor of the mirror held up to nature, the idea that literature reflects life, was mentioned by Plato only to be rejected. By the time of Cicero it was already a commonplace of criticism. It was applied by the ancients to comedy, the original vehicle of realism; later it became a byword for artistic didacticism, for the medieval zeal to see vice exposed and virtue emulated. When Shakespeare invoked it, he had a definite purpose which those who quote him commonly ignore. Hamlet is not merely describing a play, he is exhorting the players. His advice is a critique of bad acting as well as an apology for the theater, a protest against unnatural conventions as well as a plea for realism. Like modern critics who derive their metaphors from photography, he implies a further comparison with more conventionalized modes of art— particularly with painting. To hold up a photograph or a mirror, as it were, is to compare the "abstract and brief chronicles of the time" with the distorted journeywork that "imitated humanity so abominably." Art should be a reflection of life, we are advised, not a distortion—as it has all too frequently been. Criticism, in assuming that art invariably reflects and forgetting that it frequently distorts, wafts us through the looking-glass into a sphere of its own, where everything is clear and cool, logical and literal, and more surrealistic than real.

In questioning the attempts of scholars to utilize Shakespeare as the mirror of his time, Professor Stoll has reminded them that their business is to separate historical fact from literary illusion, to distinguish the object from its reflected image. Literature, instead of reflecting life, refracts it. Our task, in any given case, is to determine the angle of refraction. Since the angle depends upon the density of the medium, it is always shifting, and the task is never easy. We are aided today, however, by a more flexible and accurate kind of critical apparatus than Taine was able to employ. An acquaintance with artistic conventions, which can best be acquired through comparative studies in technique, should complement an awareness of social backgrounds. "Literature is complementary to life." This formula of Lanson's is broad enough to include the important proviso that there is room in the world of art for ideals and projects, fantasies and anxieties, which do not ordinarily find a habitation in the world of reality. But, in recognizing that literature adds something to life or that it subtracts something from life, we must not overlook the most important consideration of all—that literature is at all times an intrinsic part of life. It is, if we can work out the implications of Leslie Stephen's phrase, "a particular function of the whole social organism."

The organic character of this relationship has been most explicitly formulated by a statesman and historian, Prosper de Barante. Writing of the ideas behind the French revolution while they were still fresh in men's minds, his comprehension of their political interplay was broader than Taine's. "In the absence of regular institutions," wrote Barante, "literature became one." The truth, though it has long been obscured by a welter of personalities and technicalities, is that literature has always been an institution. Like other institutions, the church or the law, it cherishes a unique phase of human experience and controls a special body of precedents and devices; it tends to incorporate a self-perpetuating discipline, while responding to the main currents of each succeeding period; it is continually accessible to all the impulses of life at large, but it must translate them into its own terms and adapt them to its peculiar forms. Once we have grasped this fact, we begin to perceive how art may belong to society and yet be autonomous within its own limits, and are no longer puzzled by the apparent polarity of social and formal criticism. These, in the last analysis, are complementary frames of reference whereby we may discriminate the complexities of a work of art. In multiplying these discriminations between external impulses and internal peculiarities—in other words, between the effects of environment and convention—our ultimate justification is to understand the vital process to which they are both indispensable.

To consider the novel as an institution, then, imposes no dogma, exacts no sacrifice, and excludes none of the critical methods that have proved illuminating in the past. If it tends to subordinate the writer's personality to his achievement, it requires no further apology, for criticism has long been unduly subordinated to biography. The tendency of the romanticists to live their writings and write their lives, and the consequent success of their critics as biographers, did much to justify this subordination; but even Sainte-Beuve's "natural history of souls," though it unified and clarified an author's works by fitting them into the pattern of his career, was too ready to dismiss their purely artistic qualities as "rhetoric." More recently the doctrines of Freud, while imposing a topheavy vocabulary upon the discussion of art, have been used to corroborate and systematize the sporadic intuitions of artists; but the psychologists, like the sociologists, have been more interested in utilizing books for documentary purposes than in exploring their intrinsic nature. Meanwhile, on the popular level, the confusion between a novelist and his novels has been consciously exploited. A series of novelized biographies, calling itself *Le Roman des grandes existences,* invites the common reader to proceed from "the prodigious life of Balzac" through "the mournful life of Baudelaire" to "the wise and merry life of Montaigne."

If fiction has seldom been discussed on a plane commensurate with its achievements, it is because we are too often sidetracked by personalities. If, with Henry James, we recognize the novelist's intention as a figure in a carpet, we must recognize that he is guided by his material, his training, his commission, by the size and shape of his loom, and by his imagination to the extent that it accepts and masters those elements. Psychology—illuminating as it has been—has treated literature too often as a record of personal idiosyncrasies, too seldom as the basis of a collective consciousness. Yet it is on that basis that the greatest writers have functioned. Their originality has been an ability to "seize on the public mind," in Bagehot's opinion; conventions have changed and styles have developed as lesser writers caught "the traditional rhythm of an age." The irreducible element of individual talent would seem to play the same role in the evolution of *genres* that natural selection plays in the origin of species. Amid the mutations of modern individualism, we may very conceivably have overstressed the private aspects of writing. One convenience of the institutional method is that it gives due credit to the never-ending collaboration between writer and public. It sees no reason to ignore what is relevant in the psychological prepossessions of the craftsman, and it knows that he is ultimately to be judged by the technical resources of his craftsmanship; but it attains its clearest and most comprehensive scope by centering on his craft—on his social status and his historical function as participant in a skilled group and a living tradition.

When Edgar Quinet announced a course at the Collège de France in *La Littérature et les institutions comparées de l'Europe méridionelle,* he was requested by Guizot's ministry to omit the word "institutions" and to limit himself to purely literary discussion. When he replied that this would be impossible, his course was suspended, and his further efforts went directly into those reform agitations which culminated in the democratic revolution of the following year, 1848. Thereby proceeding from sociological to social criticism, he demonstrated anew what French critics and novelists have understood particu-

larly well—the dynamic interaction between ideas and events. In a time which
has seen that demonstration repeated on so vast a scale, the institutional forces
that impinge upon literature are self-evident. The responsibilities that literature owes to itself, and the special allegiance it exacts from us, should also become apparent when we conceive it as an institution in its own right. The
misleading dichotomy between substance and form, which permits literary
historians, like Parrington, to dismiss "belletristic philandering," and esthetic
impressionists, like Mr. R. P. Blackmur, to dispose of "separable content,"
should disappear as soon as abstract categories are dropped and concrete relations are taken up. And the jurisdictional conflict between truth and beauty
should dissolve when esthetics discovers the truth about beauty; when criticism becomes—as Bacon intended, and Renan and Sainte-Beuve remembered,
and all too many other critics have forgotten—the science of art.

From *Accent*, Vol. VI (Spring, 1946), pp. 159–
168. Reprinted by permission of the author and
editors.

KENNETH BURKE
Psychology and Form
[1925]

IT IS not until the fourth scene of the first act that Hamlet confronts the ghost of his father. As soon as the situation has been made clear, the audience has been, consciously or unconsciously, waiting for this ghost to appear, while in the fourth scene this moment has been definitely promised. For earlier in the play Hamlet had arranged to come to the platform at night with Horatio to meet the ghost, and it is now night, he is with Horatio and Marcellus, and they are standing on the platform. Hamlet asks Horatio the hour.

> HOR. I think it lacks of twelve.
> MAR. No, it is struck.
> HOR. Indeed? I heard it not: then it draws near the season
>   Wherein the spirit held his wont to walk.

Promptly hereafter there is a sound off-stage. "A flourish of trumpets, and ordnance shot off within." Hamlet's friends have established the hour as twelve. It is time for the ghost. Sounds off-stage, and of course it is not the ghost. It is, rather, the sound of the king's carousal, for the king "keeps wassail." A tricky and useful detail. We have been waiting for a ghost, and get, startlingly, a blare of trumpets. And, once the trumpets are silent, we feel how desolate are these three men waiting for a ghost, on a bare "platform," feel it by this sudden juxtaposition of an imagined scene of lights and merriment. But the trumpets announcing a carousal have suggested a subject of conversation. In the darkness Hamlet discusses the excessive drinking of his countrymen. He points out that it tends to harm their reputation abroad, since, he argues, this one showy vice makes their virtues "in the general censure take corruption." And for this reason, although he himself is a native of this place, he does not approve of the custom. Indeed, there in the gloom he is talking very intelligently on these matters, and Horatio answers, "Look, my Lord, it comes." All this time we had been waiting for a ghost, and it comes at the one moment which was not pointing towards it. This ghost, so assiduously prepared for, is yet a surprise. And now that the ghost has come, we are waiting

667

for something further. Program: a speech from Hamlet. Hamlet must confront
the ghost. Here again Shakespeare can feed well upon the use of contrast for
his effects. Hamlet has just been talking in a sober, rather argumentative manner—but now the flood-gates are unloosed:

> Angels and ministers of grace defend us!
> Be thou a spirit of health or goblin damn'd,
> Bring with thee airs from heaven or blasts from hell . . .

and the transition from the matter-of-fact to the grandiose, the full-throated
and full-voweled, is a second burst of trumpets, perhaps more effective than
the first, since it is the rich fulfillment of a promise. Yet this satisfaction in turn
becomes an allurement, an itch for further developments. At first desiring
solely to see Hamlet confront the ghost, we now want Hamlet to learn from
the ghost the details of the murder—which are, however, with shrewdness
and husbandry, reserved for "Scene V—Another part of the Platform."

I have gone into this scene at some length, since it illustrates so perfectly the
relationship between psychology and form, and so aptly indicates how the one
is to be defined in terms of the other. That is, the psychology here is not the
psychology of the *hero*, but the psychology of the *audience*. And by that distinction, form would be the psychology of the audience. Or, seen from another
angle, form is the creation of an appetite in the mind of the auditor, and the
adequate satisfying of that appetite. This satisfaction—so complicated is the
human mechanism—at times involves a temporary set of frustrations, but in
the end these frustrations prove to be simply a more involved kind of satisfaction, and furthermore serve to make the satisfaction of fulfillment more intense. If, in a work of art, the poet says something, let us say, about a meeting,
writes in such a way that we desire to observe that meeting, and then, if he
places that meeting before us—that is form. While obviously, that is also the
psychology of the audience, since it involves desires and their appeasements.

The seeming breach between form and subject-matter, between technique
and psychology, which has taken place in the last century is the result, it seems
to me, of scientific criteria being unconsciously introduced into matters of
purely esthetic judgment. The flourishing of science has been so vigorous that
we have not yet had time to make a spiritual readjustment adequate to the
changes in our resources of material and knowledge. There are disorders of
the social system which are caused solely by our undigested wealth (the basic
disorder being, perhaps, the phenomenon of overproduction: to remedy this,
instead of having all workers employed on half time, we have half working
full time and the other half idle, so that whereas overproduction could be the
greatest reward of applied science, it has been, up to now, the most menacing
condition our modern civilization has had to face). It would be absurd to
suppose that such social disorders would not be paralleled by disorders of cul-

ture and taste, especially since science is so pronouncedly a spiritual factor. So that we are, owing to the sudden wealth science has thrown upon us, all *nouveaux-riches* in matters of culture, and most poignantly in that field where lack of native firmness is most readily exposed, in matters of esthetic judgment.

One of the most striking derangements of taste which science has temporarily thrown upon us involves the understanding of psychology in art. Psychology has become a body of information (which is precisely what psychology in science should be, or must be). And similarly, in art, we tend to look for psychology as the purveying of information. Thus, a contemporary writer has objected to Joyce's *Ulysses* on the ground that there are more psychoanalytic data available in Freud. (How much more drastically he might, by the same system, have destroyed Homer's *Odyssey!*) To his objection it was answered that one might, similarly, denounce Cézanne's trees in favor of state forestry bulletins. Yet are not Cézanne's landscapes themselves tainted with the psychology of information? Has he not, by perception, *pointed out* how one object lies against another, *indicated* what takes place between two colors (which is the psychology of science, and is less successful in the medium of art than in that of science, since in art such processes are at best implicit, whereas in science they are so readily made explicit)? Is Cézanne not, to that extent, a state forestry bulletin, except that he tells what goes on in the eye instead of on the tree? And do not the true values of his work lie elsewhere—and precisely in what I distinguish as the psychology of form?

Thus, the great influx of information has led the artist also to lay his emphasis on the giving of information—with the result that art tends more and more to substitute the psychology of the hero (the subject) for the psychology of the audience. Under such an attitude, when form is preserved it is preserved as an annex, a luxury, or, as some feel, a downright affectation. It remains, though sluggish, like the human appendix, for occasional demands are still made upon it; but its true vigor is gone, since it is no longer organically required. Proposition: The hypertrophy of the psychology of information is accompanied by the corresponding atrophy of the psychology of form.

In information, the matter is intrinsically interesting. And by intrinsically interesting I do not necessarily mean intrinsically valuable, as witness the intrinsic interest of backyard gossip or the most casual newspaper items. In art, at least the art of the great ages (Aeschylus, Shakespeare, Racine), the matter is interesting by means of an extrinsic use, a function. Consider, for instance, the speech of Mark Antony, the "Brutus is an honourable man." Imagine in the same place a very competently developed thesis on human conduct, with statistics, intelligence tests, definitions; imagine it as the finest thing of the sort ever written, and as really being at the roots of an understanding of Brutus. Obviously, the play would simply stop until Antony had finished. For in the case of Antony's speech, the value lies in the fact that his words are shaping the future of the audience's desires, not the desires of the Roman populace, but the desires of the pit. This is the psychology of form as distinguished from the psychology of information.

The distinction is, of course, absolutely true only in its nonexistent extremes. Hamlet's advice to the players, for instance, has little of the quality which distinguishes Antony's speech. It is, rather, intrinsically interesting, although one could very easily prove how the play would benefit by some such delay at this point, and that anything which made this delay possible without violating the consistency of the subject would have, in this, its formal justification. It would, furthermore, be absurd to rule intrinsic interest out of literature. I wish simply to have it restored to its properly minor position, seen as merely one out of many possible elements of style. Goethe's prose, often poorly imagined or neutral in its line-for-line texture, especially in the treatment of romantic episode—perhaps he felt that the romantic episode in itself was enough?—is strengthened into a style possessing affirmative virtues by his rich use of aphorism. But this is, after all, but one of many possible facets of appeal. In some places, notably in *Wilhelm Meisters Lehrjahre* when Wilhelm's friends disclose the documents they have been collecting about his life unbeknown to him, the aphorisms are almost rousing in their efficacy, since they involve the story. But as a rule the appeal of aphorism is intrinsic: that is, it satisfies without being functionally related to the context.[1] Also, to return to the matter of Hamlet, it must be observed that the style in this passage is no mere "information-giving" style; in its alacrity, its development, it really makes this one fragment into a kind of miniature plot.

One reason why music can stand repetition so much more sturdily than correspondingly good prose is because music, of all the arts, is by its nature least suited to the psychology of information, and has remained closer to the psychology of form. Here form cannot atrophy. Every dissonant chord cries for its solution, and whether the musician resolves or refuses to resolve this dissonance into the chord which the body cries for, he is dealing in human appetites. Correspondingly good prose, however, more prone to the temptations of pure information, cannot so much bear repetition since the esthetic value of information is lost once that information is imparted. If one returns to such a work again it is purely because, in the chaos of modern life, he has been able to forget it. With a desire, on the other hand, its recovery is as agreeable as its discovery. One can memorize the dialogue between Hamlet and Guildenstern, where Hamlet gives Guildenstern the pipe to play

---

[1] Similarly, the epigram of Racine is "pure art," because it usually serves to formulate or clarify some situation within the play itself. In Goethe the epigram is most often of independent validity, as in *Die Wahlverwandtschaften,* where the ideas of Ottilie's diary are obviously carried over boldly from the author's notebook. In Shakespeare we have the union of extrinsic and intrinsic epigram, the epigram growing out of its context and yet valuable independent of its context.

on. For, once the speech is known, its repetition adds a new element to compensate for the loss of novelty. We cannot take a recurrent pleasure in the new (in information) but we can in the natural (in form). Already, at the moment when Hamlet is holding out the pipe to Guildenstern and asking him to play upon it, we "gloat over" Hamlet's triumphal descent upon Guildenstern, when, after Guildenstern has, under increasing embarrassment, protested three times that he cannot play the instrument, Hamlet launches the retort for which all this was preparation:

Why, look you now, how unworthy a thing you make of me. You would play upon me, you would seem to know my stops; you would pluck out the heart of my mystery; you would sound me from my lowest note to the top of my compass; and there is much music, excellent voice, in this little organ, yet cannot you make it speak. 'Sblood, do you think I am easier to be played on than a pipe? Call me what instrument you will, though you can fret me, you cannot play upon me.[2]

In the opening lines we hear the promise of the close, and thus feel the emotional curve even more keenly than at first reading. Whereas in most modern art this element is underemphasized. It gives us the gossip of a plot, a plot which too often has for its value the mere fact that we do not know its outcome.[3]

Music, then, fitted less than any other art for imparting information, deals minutely in frustrations and fulfillments of desire,[4] and for that reason more often gives us those curves of emotion which, because they are natural, can bear repetition without loss. It is for this reason that music, like folk tales, is most capable of lulling us to sleep. A lullaby is a melody which comes quickly to rest, where the obstacles are easily overcome—and this is precisely the parallel to those waking dreams of struggle and conquest which (especially during childhood) we permit ourselves when falling asleep or when trying to induce sleep. Folk tales are just such waking dreams. Thus it is right that art should be called a "waking dream." The only difficulty with this definition (indicated by Charles Baudouin in his *Psychoanalysis and Aesthetics,* a very valuable study of Verhaeren) is that today we understand it to mean art as a

[2] One might indicate still further appropriateness here. As Hamlet finishes his speech, Polonius enters, and Hamlet turns to him, "God bless you, sir!" Thus, the plot is continued (for Polonius is always the promise of action) and a full stop is avoided: the embarrassment laid upon Rosencrantz and Guildenstern is not laid upon the audience.

[3] Yet modern music has gone far in the attempt to renounce this aspect of itself. Its dissonances become static, demanding no particular resolution. And whereas an unfinished modulation by a classic musician occasions positive dissatisfaction, the refusal to resolve a dissonance in modern music does not dissatisfy us, but irritates or stimulates. Thus, "energy" takes the place of style.

[4] Suspense is the least complex kind of anticipation, as surprise is the least complex kind of fulfillment.

waking dream for the artist. Modern criticism, and psychoanalysis in particular, is too prone to define the essence of art in terms of the artist's weaknesses. It is, rather, the audience which dreams, while the artist oversees the conditions which determine this dream. He is the manipulator of blood, brains, heart, and bowels which, while we sleep, dictate the mold of our desires. This is, of course, the real meaning of artistic felicity—an exaltation at the correctness of the procedure, so that we enjoy the steady march of doom in a Racinian tragedy with exactly the same equipment as that which produces our delight with Benedick's "Peace! I'll stop your mouth. (*Kisses her*)" which terminates the imbroglio of *Much Ado About Nothing*.

The methods of maintaining interest which are most natural to the psychology of information (as it is applied to works of pure art) are surprise and suspense. The method most natural to the psychology of form is eloquence. For this reason the great ages of Aeschylus, Shakespeare, and Racine, dealing as they did with material which was more or less a matter of common knowledge so that the broad outlines of the plot were known in advance (while it is the broad outlines which are usually exploited to secure surprise and suspense), developed formal excellence, or eloquence, as the basis of appeal in their work.

Not that there is any difference in kind between the classic method and the method of the cheapest contemporary melodrama. The drama, more than any other form, must never lose sight of its audience: here the failure to satisfy the proper requirements is most disastrous. And since certain contemporary work is successful, it follows that rudimentary laws of composition are being complied with. The distinction is one of intensity rather than of kind. The contemporary audience hears the lines of a play or novel with the same equipment as it brings to reading the lines of its daily paper. It is content to have facts placed before it in some more or less adequate sequence. Eloquence is the minimizing of this interest in fact, *per se,* so that the "more or less adequate sequence" of their presentation must be relied on to a much greater extent. Thus, those elements of surprise and suspense are subtilized, carried down into the writing of a line or a sentence, until in all its smallest details the work bristles with disclosures, contrasts, restatements with a difference, ellipses, images, aphorism, volume, sound-values, in short all that complex wealth of minutiae which in their line-for-line aspect we call style and in their broader outlines we call form.

As a striking instance of a modern play with potentialities in which the intensity of eloquence is missing, I might cite a recent success, Capek's *R. U. R.* Here, in a melodrama which was often astonishing in the rightness of its technical procedure, when the author was finished he had written nothing but the scenario for a play by Shakespeare. It was a play in which the author produced time and again the opportunity, the demand, for eloquence, only to move on. (At other times, the most successful moments, he utilized the modern discovery of silence, writing moments wherein words could not possibly serve but to detract from the effect: this we might call the "flowering" of information.) The Adam and Eve scene of the last act, a "commission" which the Shakespeare of the comedies would have loved to fill, was in the verbal barrenness of Capek's play something shameless to the point of blushing. The Robot, turned human, prompted by the dawn of love to see his first sunrise, or hear the first bird-call, and forced merely to say, "Oh, see the sunrise," or, "Hear the pretty birds"—here one could do nothing but wring his hands at the absence of that esthetic mold which produced the overslung "speeches" of *Romeo and Juliet.*

Suspense is the concern over the possible outcome of some specific detail of plot rather than for general qualities. Thus, "Will A marry B or C?" is suspense. In *Macbeth,* the turn from the murder scene to the porter scene is a much less literal channel of development. Here the presence of one quality calls forth the demand for another, rather than one tangible incident of plot awaking an interest in some other possible tangible incident of plot. To illustrate more fully, if an author managed over a certain number of his pages to produce a feeling of sultriness, or oppression, in the reader, this would unconsciously awaken in the reader the desire for a cold, fresh north wind—and thus some aspect of a north wind would be effective if called forth by some aspect of stuffiness. A good example of this is to be found in a contemporary poem, T. S. Eliot's *The Waste Land,* where the vulgar, oppressively trivial conversation in the public house calls forth in the poet a memory of a line from Shakespeare. These slobs in a public house, after a desolately low-visioned conversation, are now forced by closing time to leave the saloon. They say good-night. And suddenly the poet, feeling his release, drops into another good-night, a good-night with *désinvolture,* a good-night out of what was, within the conditions of the poem at least, a graceful and irrecoverable past.

> "Well that Sunday Albert was home, they had a hot gammon,
>   And they asked me in to dinner, to get the beauty of it hot"—
>   [at this point the bartender interrupts: it is closing time]
> "Goonight Bill. Goonight Lou. Goonight May. Goonight. Ta ta.
>   Goonight. Goonight.
>   Good-night, ladies, good-night, sweet ladies, good-night, good-night."

There is much more to be said on these lines, which I have shortened somewhat in quotation to make my issue clearer. But I simply wish to point out here that this transition is a bold juxtaposition of one quality created by another, an association in ideas which, if not logical, is nevertheless emotionally natural. In the case of *Macbeth,* similarly, it would be absurd to say that the audience, after the murder scene, wants a porter scene. But the audience does want the quality which this porter particularizes. The dramatist might, conceivably, have introduced some entirely different character or event in this place, provided only that the event produced the same quality of relationship and contrast (grotesque seriousness followed by grotesque buffoonery). One of the most beautiful and satisfactory "forms" of this sort is to be found in Baudelaire's "Femmes Damnées," where the poet, after describing the business of a Lesbian seduction, turns to the full oratory of his apostrophe:

> Descendez, descendez, lamentables victimes,
> Descendez le chemin de l'enfer éternel . . .

while the stylistic efficacy of this transition contains a richness which transcends all moral (or unmoral) sophistication: the efficacy of appropriateness, of exactly the natural curve in treatment. Here is morality even for the godless, since it is a morality of art, being justified, if for no other reason, by its paralleling of that staleness, that disquieting loss of purpose, which must have followed the procedure of the two characters, the *femmes damnées* themselves, a remorse which, perhaps only physical in its origin, nevertheless becomes psychic.[5]

But to return, we have made three terms synonymous: form, psychology, and eloquence. And eloquence thereby becomes the essence of art, while pity, tragedy, sweetness, humor, in short all the emotions which we experience in life proper, as non-artists, are simply the material on which eloquence may feed. The arousing of pity, for instance, is not the central purpose of art, although it may be an adjunct of artistic effectiveness. One can feel pity much more keenly at the sight of some actual misfortune—and it would be a great mistake to see art merely as a weak representation of some actual experience.[6] That artists today are content to write under such an esthetic accounts in part for the inferior position which art holds in the community. Art, at least in the great periods when it has flowered, was the conversion, or transcendence, of emotion into eloquence, and was thus a factor added to life. I am reminded of St. Augustine's caricature of the theatre: that whereas we do not dare to wish people unhappy, we do want to feel sorry for them, and therefore turn

[5] As another aspect of the same subject, I could cite many examples from the fairy tale. Consider, for instance, when the hero is to spend the night in a bewitched castle. Obviously, as darkness descends, weird adventures must befall him. His bed rides him through the castle; two halves of a man challenge him to a game of nine-pins played with thigh bones and skulls. Or entirely different incidents may serve instead of these. The quality comes first, the particularization follows.

[6] Could not the Greek public's resistance to Euripides be accounted for in the fact that he, of the three great writers of Greek tragedy, betrayed his art, was guilty of esthetic impiety, in that he paid more attention to the arousing of emotion *per se* than to the sublimation of emotion into eloquence?

to plays so that we can feel sorry although no real misery is involved. One might apply the parallel interpretation to the modern delight in happy endings, and say that we turn to art to indulge our humanitarianism in a well-wishing which we do not permit ourselves towards our actual neighbors. Surely the catharsis of art is more complicated than this, and more reputable.

Eloquence itself, as I hope to have established in the instance from *Hamlet* which I have analyzed, is no mere plaster added to a framework of more stable qualities. Eloquence is simply the end of art, and is thus its essence. Even the poorest is eloquent, but in a poor way, with less intensity, until this aspect is obscured by others fattening upon its leanness. Eloquence is not showiness; it is, rather, the result of that desire in the artist to make a work perfect by adapting it in every minute detail to the racial appetites.

The distinction between the psychology of information and the psychology of form involves a definition of esthetic truth. It is here precisely, to combat the deflection which the strength of science has caused to our tastes, that we must examine the essential breach between scientific and artistic truth. Truth in art is not the discovery of facts, not an addition to human knowledge in the scientific sense of the word.[7] It is, rather, the exercise of human propriety, the formulation of symbols which rigidify our sense of poise and rhythm. Artistic truth is the externalization of taste.[8] I sometimes wonder, for instance, whether the "artificial" speech of John Lyly might perhaps be "truer" than the revelations of Dostoevsky. Certainly at its best, in its feeling for a statement which returns upon itself, which attempts the systole to a diastole, it *could* be much truer than Dostoevsky.[9] And if it is not, it fails not through a mistake of Lyly's

[7] One of the most striking examples of the encroachment of scientific truth into art is the doctrine of "truth by distortion," whereby one aspect of an object is suppressed the better to emphasize some other aspect; this is, obviously, an attempt to *indicate* by art some fact of knowledge, to make some implicit aspect of an object as explicit as one can by means of the comparatively dumb method of art (dumb, that is, as compared to the perfect ease with which science can indicate its discoveries). Yet science has already made discoveries in the realm of this "factual truth," this "truth by distortion" which must put to shame any artist who relies on such matter for his effects. Consider, for instance, the motion-picture of a man vaulting. By photographing this process very rapidly, and running the reel very slowly, one has upon the screen the most striking set of factual truths to aid in our understanding of an athlete vaulting. Here, at our leisure, we can observe the contortions of four legs, a head, and a butt. This squirming thing we saw upon the screen showed us an infinity of factual truths anent the balances of an athlete vaulting. We can, from this, observe the marvelous system of balancing which the body provides for itself in the adjustments of moving. Yet, so far as the esthetic truth is concerned, this on the screen was not an athlete, but a squirming thing, a horror, displaying every fact of vaulting except the exhilaration of the act itself.

[8] The procedure of science involves the elimination of taste, employing as a substitute the corrective norm of a pragmatic test, the empirical experiment, which is entirely intellectual. Those who oppose the "intellectualism" of critics like Matthew Arnold are involved in an hilarious blunder, for Arnold's entire approach to the appreciation of art is through delicacies of taste intensified to the extent almost of squeamishness.

[9] As for instance, the "conceit" of Endymion's awakening, when he forgets his own name, yet recalls that of his beloved.

esthetic, but because Lyly was a man poor in character whereas Dostoevsky was rich and complex. When Swift, making the women of Brobdingnag enormous, deduces from this discrepancy between their size and Gulliver's that Gulliver could sit astride their nipples, he has written something which is esthetically true, which is, if I may be pardoned, profoundly "proper," as correct in its Euclidean deduction as any corollary in geometry. Given the companions of Ulysses in the cave of Polyphemus, it is true that they would escape clinging to the bellies of the herd let out to pasture. St. Ambrose, detailing the habits of God's creatures, and drawing from them moral maxims for the good of mankind, St. Ambrose in his limping natural history rich in scientific inaccuracies that are at the very heart of emotional rightness, St. Ambrose writes "Of night-birds, especially the nightingale which hatches her eggs by song; of the owl, the bat, and the cock at cock-crow; in what these may apply to the guidance of our habits," and in the sheer rightness of that program there is the truth of art. In introducing this talk of night-birds, after many pages devoted to other of God's creatures, he says:

What now! While we have been talking, you will notice how the birds of night have already started fluttering about you, and, in this same fact of warning us to leave off with our discussion, suggest thereby a further topic—

and this seems to me to contain the best wisdom of which the human frame is capable, an address, a discourse, which can make our material life seem blatant almost to the point of despair. And when the cock crows, and the thief abandons his traps, and the sun lights up, and we are in every way called back to God by the well-meaning admonition of this bird, here the very blindnesses of religion become the deepest truths of art.

From *Counter-Statement* by Kenneth Burke, pp. 38–56. Copyright, 1931. Reprinted by permission of Harcourt, Brace and Company, Inc., and the author. Originally published in *The Dial*, Vol. LXXIX (July, 1925), pp. 34–46.

LIONEL TRILLING
Freud and Literature
[1940-1947]

THE Freudian psychology is the only systematic account of the human mind which, in point of subtlety and complexity, of interest and tragic power, deserves to stand beside the chaotic mass of psychological insights which literature has accumulated through the centuries. To pass from the reading of a great literary work to a treatise of academic psychology is to pass from one order of perception to another, but the human nature of the Freudian psychology is exactly the stuff upon which the poet has always exercised his art. It is therefore not surprising that the psychoanalytical theory has had a great effect upon literature. Yet the relationship is reciprocal, and the effect of Freud upon literature has been no greater than the effect of literature upon Freud. When, on the occasion of the celebration of his seventieth birthday, Freud was greeted as the "discoverer of the unconscious," he corrected the speaker and disclaimed the title. "The poets and philosophers before me discovered the unconscious," he said. "What I discovered was the scientific method by which the unconscious can be studied."

A lack of specific evidence prevents us from considering the particular literary "influences" upon the founder of psychoanalysis; and, besides, when we think of the men who so clearly anticipated many of Freud's own ideas—Schopenhauer and Nietzsche, for example—and then learn that he did not read their works until after he had formulated his own theories, we must see that particular influences cannot be in question here but that what we must deal with is nothing less than a whole *Zeitgeist,* a direction of thought. For psychoanalysis is one of the culminations of the Romanticist literature of the nineteenth century. If there is perhaps a contradiction in the idea of a science standing upon the shoulders of a literature which avows itself inimical to science in so many ways, the contradiction will be resolved if we remember that this literature, despite its avowals, was itself scientific in at least the sense of being passionately devoted to a research into the self.

In showing the connection between Freud and this Romanticist tradition, it is difficult to know where to begin, but there might be a certain aptness in starting even back of the tradition, as far back as 1762 with Diderot's *Ra-*

meau's Nephew. At any rate, certain men at the heart of nineteenth-century thought were agreed in finding a peculiar importance in this brilliant little work: Goethe translated it, Marx admired it, Hegel—as Marx reminded Engels in the letter which announced that he was sending the book as a gift— praised and expounded it at length, Shaw was impressed by it, and Freud himself, as we know from a quotation in his *Introductory Lectures,* read it with the pleasure of agreement.

The dialogue takes place between Diderot himself and a nephew of the famous composer. The protagonist, the younger Rameau, is a despised, outcast, shameless fellow; Hegel calls him the "disintegrated consciousness" and credits him with great wit, for it is he who breaks down all the normal social values and makes new combinations with the pieces. As for Diderot, the deuteragonist, he is what Hegel calls the "honest consciousness," and Hegel considers him reasonable, decent, and dull. It is quite clear that the author does not despise his Rameau and does not mean us to. Rameau is lustful and greedy, arrogant yet self-abasing, perceptive yet "wrong," like a child. Still, Diderot seems actually to be giving the fellow a kind of superiority over himself, as though Rameau represents the elements which, dangerous but wholly necessary, lie beneath the reasonable decorum of social life. It would perhaps be pressing too far to find in Rameau Freud's *id* and in Diderot Freud's *ego;* yet the connection does suggest itself; and at least we have here the perception which is to be the common characteristic of both Freud and Romanticism, the perception of the hidden element of human nature and of the opposition between the hidden and the visible. We have too the bold perception of just what lies hidden: "If the little savage [i.e., the child] were left to himself, if he preserved all his foolishness and combined the violent passions of a man of thirty with the lack of reason of a child in the cradle, he'd wring his father's neck and go to bed with his mother."

From the self-exposure of Rameau to Rousseau's account of his own childhood is no great step; society might ignore or reject the idea of the "immorality" which lies concealed in the beginning of the career of the "good" man, just as it might turn away from Blake struggling to expound a psychology which would include the forces beneath the propriety of social man in general, but the idea of the hidden thing went forward to become one of the dominant notions of the age. The hidden element takes many forms and it is not necessarily "dark" and "bad"; for Blake the "bad" was the good, while for Wordsworth and Burke what was hidden and unconscious was wisdom and power, which work in despite of the conscious intellect.

The mind has become far less simple; the devotion to the various forms of autobiography—itself an important fact in the tradition—provides abundant examples of the change that has taken place. Poets, making poetry by what seems to them almost a freshly discovered faculty, find that this new power may be conspired against by other agencies of the mind and even deprived of its freedom; the names of Wordsworth, Coleridge, and Arnold at once occur to us again, and Freud quotes Schiller on the danger to the poet that lies in the merely analytical reason. And it is not only the poets who are threatened; educated and sensitive people throughout Europe become aware of the depredations that reason might make upon the affective life, as in the classic instance of John Stuart Mill.

We must also take into account the preoccupation—it began in the eighteenth century, or even in the seventeenth—with children, women, peasants, and savages, whose mental life, it is felt, is less overlaid than that of the educated adult male by the proprieties of social habit. With this preoccupation goes a concern with education and personal development, so consonant with the historical and evolutionary bias of the time. And we must certainly note the revolution in morals which took place at the instance (we might almost say) of the *Bildungsroman,* for in the novels fathered by *Wilhelm Meister* we get the almost complete identification of author and hero and of the reader with both, and this identification almost inevitably suggests a leniency of moral judgment. The autobiographical novel has a further influence upon the moral sensibility by its exploitation of all the modulations of motive and by its hinting that we may not judge a man by any single moment in his life without taking into account the determining past and the expiating and fulfilling future.

It is difficult to know how to go on, for the further we look the more literary affinities to Freud we find, and even if we limit ourselves to bibliography we can at best be incomplete. Yet we must mention the sexual revolution that was being demanded—by Shelley, for example, by the Schlegel of *Lucinde,* by George Sand, and later and more critically by Ibsen; the belief in the sexual origin of art, baldly stated by Tieck, more subtly by Schopenhauer; the investigation of sexual maladjustment by Stendhal, whose observations on erotic feeling seem to us distinctly Freudian. Again and again we see the effective, utilitarian ego being relegated to an inferior position and a plea being made on behalf of the anarchic and self-indulgent *id.* We find the energetic exploitation of the idea of the mind as a divisible thing, one part of which can contemplate and mock the other. It is not a far remove from this to Dostoevski's brilliant instances of ambivalent feeling. Novalis brings in the preoccupation with the death wish, and this is linked on the one hand with sleep and on the other hand with the perception of the perverse, self-destroying impulses, which in turn leads us to that fascination by the horrible which we find in Shelley, Poe, and Baudelaire. And always there is the profound interest in the dream—"Our dreams," said Gérard de Nerval, "are a second life"—

and in the nature of metaphor, which reaches its climax in Rimbaud and the later Symbolists, metaphor becoming less and less communicative as it approaches the relative autonomy of the dream life.

But perhaps we must stop to ask, since these are the components of the *Zeitgeist* from which Freud himself developed, whether it can be said that Freud did indeed produce a wide literary effect. What is it that Freud added that the tendency of literature itself would not have developed without him? If we were looking for a writer who showed the Freudian influence, Proust would perhaps come to mind as readily as anyone else; the very title of his novel, in French more than in English, suggests an enterprise of psychoanalysis and scarcely less so does his method—the investigation of sleep, of sexual deviation, of the way of association, the almost obsessive interest in metaphor; at these and at many other points the "influence" might be shown. Yet I believe it is true that Proust did not read Freud. Or again, exegesis of *The Waste Land* often reads remarkably like the psychoanalytic interpretation of a dream, yet we know that Eliot's methods were prepared for him not by Freud but by other poets.

Nevertheless, it is of course true that Freud's influence on literature has been very great. Much of it is so pervasive that its extent is scarcely to be determined; in one form or another, frequently in perversions or absurd simplifications, it has been infused into our life and become a component of our culture of which it is now hard to be specifically aware. In biography its first effect was sensational but not fortunate. The early Freudian biographers were for the most part Guildensterns who seemed to know the pipes but could not pluck out the heart of the mystery, and the same condemnation applies to the early Freudian critics. But in recent years, with the acclimatization of psychoanalysis and the increased sense of its refinements and complexity, criticism has derived from the Freudian system much that is of great value, most notably the license and the injunction to read the work of literature with a lively sense of its latent and ambiguous meanings, as if it were, as indeed it is, a being no less alive and contradictory than the man who created it. And this new response to the literary work has had a corrective effect upon our conception of biography. The literary critic or biographer who makes use of the Freudian theory is no less threatened by the dangers of theoretical systematization than he was in the early days, but he is likely to be more aware of these dangers; and I think it is true to say that now the motive of his interpretation is not that of exposing the secret shame of the writer and limiting the meaning of his work, but, on the contrary, that of finding grounds for sympathy with the writer and for increasing the possible significances of the work.

The names of the creative writers who have been more or less Freudian in tone or assumption would of course be legion. Only a relatively small number, however, have made serious use of the Freudian ideas. Freud himself seems to have thought this was as it should be: he is said to have expected very little of the works that were sent to him by writers with inscriptions of gratitude for all they had learned from him. The Surrealists have, with a certain inconsistency, depended upon Freud for the "scientific" sanction of their program. Kafka, with an apparent awareness of what he was doing, has explored the Freudian conceptions of guilt and punishment, of the dream, and of the fear of the father. Thomas Mann, whose tendency, as he himself says, was always in the direction of Freud's interests, has been most susceptible to the Freudian anthropology, finding a special charm in the theories of myths and magical practices. James Joyce, with his interest in the numerous states of receding consciousness, with his use of words as things and of words which point to more than one thing, with his pervading sense of the interrelation and interpenetration of all things, and, not least important, his treatment of familial themes, has perhaps most thoroughly and consciously exploited Freud's ideas.

II

It will be clear enough how much of Freud's thought has significant affinity with the anti-rationalist element of the Romanticist tradition. But we must see with no less distinctness how much of his system is militantly rationalistic. Thomas Mann is at fault when, in his first essay on Freud, he makes it seem that the "Apollonian," the rationalistic, side of psychoanalysis is, while certainly important and wholly admirable, somehow secondary and even accidental. He gives us a Freud who is committed to the "night side" of life. Not at all: the rationalistic element of Freud is foremost; before everything else he is positivistic. If the interpreter of dreams came to medical science through Goethe, as he tells us he did, he entered not by way of the *Walpurgisnacht* but by the essay which played so important a part in the lives of so many scientists of the nineteenth century, the famous disquisition on Nature.

This correction is needed not only for accuracy but also for any understanding of Freud's attitude to art. And for that understanding we must see how intense is the passion with which Freud believes that positivistic rationalism, in its golden-age pre-Revolutionary purity, is the very form and pattern of intellectual virtue. The aim of psychoanalysis, he says, is the control of the night side of life. It is "to strengthen the ego, to make it more independent of the super-ego, to widen its field of vision, and so to extend the organization of the *id*." "Where *id* was,"—that is, where all the irrational, non-logical, pleasure-seeking dark forces were—"there shall ego be,"—that is, intelligence and control. "It is," he concludes, with a reminiscence of Faust, "reclamation work, like the draining of the Zuyder Zee." This passage is quoted by Mann when, in taking up the subject of Freud a second time, he does indeed speak of

Freud's positivistic program; but even here the bias induced by Mann's artistic interest in the "night side" prevents him from giving the other aspect of Freud its due emphasis. Freud would never have accepted the role which Mann seems to give him as the legitimizer of the myth and the dark irrational ways of the mind. If Freud discovered the darkness for science he never endorsed it. On the contrary, his rationalism supports all the ideas of the Enlightenment that deny validity to myth or religion; he holds to a simple materialism, to a simple determinism, to a rather limited sort of epistemology. No great scientist of our day has thundered so articulately and so fiercely against all those who would sophisticate with metaphysics the scientific principles that were good enough for the nineteenth century. Conceptualism or pragmatism are anathema to him through the greater part of his intellectual career, and this, when we consider the nature of his own brilliant scientific methods, has surely an element of paradox in it.

From his rationalistic positivism comes much of Freud's strength and what weakness he has. The strength is the fine, clear tenacity of his positive aims, the goal of therapy, the desire to bring to men a decent measure of earthly happiness. But upon the rationalism must also be placed the blame for the often naïve scientific principles which characterize his early thought—they are later much modified—and which consist largely of claiming for his theories a perfect correspondence with an external reality, a position which, for those who admire Freud and especially for those who take seriously his views on art, is troublesome in the extreme.

Now Freud has, I believe, much to tell us about art, but whatever is suggestive in him is not likely to be found in those of his works in which he deals expressly with art itself. Freud is not insensitive to art—on the contrary —nor does he ever intend to speak of it with contempt. Indeed, he speaks of it with a real tenderness and counts it one of the true charms of the good life. Of artists, especially of writers, he speaks with admiration and even a kind of awe, though perhaps what he most appreciates in literature are specific emotional insights and observations; as we have noted, he speaks of literary men, because they have understood the part played in life by the hidden motives, as the precursors and coadjutors of his own science.

And yet eventually Freud speaks of art with what we must indeed call contempt. Art, he tells us, is a "substitute gratification," and as such is "an illusion in contrast to reality." Unlike most illusions, however, art is "almost always harmless and beneficent" for the reason that "it does not seek to be anything but an illusion. Save in the case of a few people who are, one might say, obsessed by Art, it never dares make any attack on the realm of reality." One of its chief functions is to serve as a "narcotic." It shares the characteristics of the dream, whose element of distortion Freud calls a "sort of inner dishonesty." As for the artist, he is virtually in the same category with the neurotic. "By such separation of imagination and intellectual capacity," Freud says of the hero of a novel, "he is destined to be a poet or a neurotic, and he belongs to that race of beings whose realm is not of this world."

Now there is nothing in the logic of psychoanalytical thought which requires Freud to have these opinions. But there is a great deal in the practice of the psychoanalytical therapy which makes it understandable that Freud, unprotected by an adequate philosophy, should be tempted to take the line he does. The analytical therapy deals with illusion. The patient comes to the physician to be cured, let us say, of a fear of walking in the street. The fear is real enough, there is no illusion on that score, and it produces all the physical symptoms of a more rational fear, the sweating palms, pounding heart, and shortened breath. But the patient knows that there is no cause for the fear, or rather that there is, as he says, no "real cause": there are no machine guns, man traps, or tigers in the street. The physician knows, however, that there is indeed a "real" cause for the fear, though it has nothing at all to do with what is or is not in the street; the cause is within the patient, and the process of the therapy will be to discover, by gradual steps, what this real cause is and so free the patient from its effects.

Now the patient in coming to the physician, and the physician in accepting the patient, make a tacit compact about reality; for their purpose they agree to the limited reality by which we get our living, win our loves, catch our trains and our colds. The therapy will undertake to train the patient in proper ways of coping with this reality. The patient, of course, has been dealing with this reality all along, but in the wrong way. For Freud there are two ways of dealing with external reality. One is practical, effective, positive; this is the way of the conscious self, of the ego which must be made independent of the super-ego and extend its organization over the *id*, and it is the right way. The antithetical way may be called, for our purpose now, the "fictional" way. Instead of doing something about, or to, external reality, the individual who uses this way does something to, or about, his affective states. The most common and "normal" example of this is daydreaming, in which we give ourselves a certain pleasure by imagining our difficulties solved or our desires gratified. Then, too, as Freud discovered, sleeping dreams are, in much more complicated ways, and even though quite unpleasant, at the service of this same "fictional" activity. And in ways yet more complicated and yet more unpleasant, the actual neurosis from which our patient suffers deals with an external reality which the mind considers still more unpleasant than the painful neurosis itself.

For Freud as psychoanalytic practitioner there are, we may say, the polar extremes of reality and illusion. Reality is an honorific word, and it means what is *there*; illusion is a pejorative word, and it means a response to what is *not there*. The didactic nature of a course of psychoanalysis no doubt requires a certain firm crudeness in making the distinction; it is after all aimed not at theoretical refinement but at practical effectiveness. The polar extremes are practical reality and neurotic illusion, the latter judged by the former. This, no doubt, is as it should be; the patient is not being trained in metaphysics and epistemology.

This practical assumption is not Freud's only view of the mind in its relation to reality. Indeed what may be called the essentially Freudian view assumes that the mind, for good as well as bad, helps create its reality by selection and evaluation. In this view, reality is malleable and subject to creation; it is not static but is rather a series of situations which are dealt with in their own terms. But beside this conception of the mind stands the conception which arises from Freud's therapeutic-practical assumptions; in this view, the mind deals with a reality which is quite fixed and static, a reality that is wholly "given" and not (to use a phrase of Dewey's) "taken." In his epistemological utterances, Freud insists on this second view, although it is not easy to see why he should do so. For the reality to which he wishes to reconcile the neurotic patient is, after all, a "taken" and not a "given" reality. It is the reality of social life and of value, conceived and maintained by the human mind and will. Love, morality, honor, esteem—these are the components of a created reality. If we are to call art an illusion then we must call most of the activities and satisfactions of the ego illusions; Freud, of course, has no desire to call them that.

What, then, is the difference between, on the one hand, the dream and the neurosis, and, on the other hand, art? That they have certain common elements is of course clear; that unconscious processes are at work in both would be denied by no poet or critic; they share too, though in different degrees, the element of fantasy. But there is a vital difference between them which Charles Lamb saw so clearly in his defense of the sanity of true genius: "The . . . poet dreams being awake. He is not possessed by his subject but he has dominion over it."

That is the whole difference: the poet is in command of his fantasy, while it is exactly the mark of the neurotic that he is possessed by his fantasy. And there is a further difference which Lamb states; speaking of the poet's relation to reality (he calls it Nature), he says, "He is beautifully loyal to that sovereign directress, even when he appears most to betray her"; the illusions of art are made to serve the purpose of a closer and truer relation with reality. Jacques Barzun, in an acute and sympathetic discussion of Freud, puts the matter well: "A good analogy between art and *dreaming* has led him to a false one between art and *sleeping*. But the difference between a work of art and a dream is precisely this, that the work of art *leads us back to the outer reality by taking account of it*." Freud's assumption of the almost exclusively hedonistic nature and purpose of art bar him from the perception of this.

Of the distinction that must be made between the artist and the neurotic Freud is of course aware; he tells us that the artist is not like the neurotic in that he knows how to find a way back from the world of imagination and "once more get a firm foothold in reality." This however seems to mean no more than that reality is to be dealt with when the artist suspends the practice of his art; and at least once when Freud speaks of art dealing with reality he actually means the rewards that a successful artist can win. He does not deny to art its function and its usefulness; it has a therapeutic effect in releasing mental tension; it serves the cultural purpose of acting as a "substitute gratification" to reconcile men to the sacrifices they have made for culture's sake; it promotes the social sharing of highly valued emotional experiences; and it recalls men to their cultural ideals. This is not everything that some of us would find that art does, yet even this is a good deal for a "narcotic" to do.

III

I started by saying that Freud's ideas could tell us something about art, but so far I have done little more than try to show that Freud's very conception of art is inadequate. Perhaps, then, the suggestiveness lies in the application of the analytic method to specific works of art or to the artist himself? I do not think so, and it is only fair to say that Freud himself was aware both of the limits and the limitations of psychoanalysis in art, even though he does not always in practice submit to the former or admit the latter.

Freud has, for example, no desire to encroach upon the artist's autonomy; he does not wish us to read his monograph on Leonardo and then say of the "Madonna of the Rocks" that it is a fine example of homosexual, autoerotic painting. If he asserts that in investigation the "psychiatrist cannot yield to the author," he immediately insists that the "author cannot yield to the psychiatrist," and he warns the latter not to "coarsen everything" by using for all human manifestations the "substantially useless and awkward terms" of clinical procedure. He admits, even while asserting that the sense of beauty probably derives from sexual feeling, that psychoanalysis "has less to say about beauty than about most other things." He confesses to a theoretical indifference to the form of art and restricts himself to its content. Tone, feeling, style, and the modification that part makes upon part he does not consider. "The layman," he says, "may expect perhaps too much from analysis . . . for it must be admitted that it throws no light upon the two problems which probably interest him the most. It can do nothing toward elucidating the nature of the artistic gift, nor can it explain the means by which the artist works—artistic technique."

What, then, does Freud believe that the analytical method can do? Two things: explain the "inner meanings" of the work of art and explain the temperament of the artist as man.

A famous example of the method is the attempt to solve the "problem" of *Hamlet* as suggested by Freud and as carried out by Dr. Ernest Jones, his early and distinguished follower. Dr. Jones's monograph is a work of painstaking scholarship and of really masterly ingenuity. The research undertakes not only the clearing up of the mystery of Hamlet's character, but also the discovery of "the clue to much of the deeper workings of Shakespeare's mind." Part of the mystery in question is of course why Hamlet, after he had so definitely resolved to do so, did not avenge upon his hated uncle his father's death. But there is another mystery to the play—what Freud calls "the mystery of its effect," its magical appeal that draws so much interest toward it. Recalling the many failures to solve the riddle of the play's charm, he wonders if we are to be driven to the conclusion "that its magical appeal rests solely upon the impressive thoughts in it and the splendor of its language." Freud believes that we can find a source of power beyond this.

We remember that Freud has told us that the meaning of a dream is its intention, and we may assume that the meaning of a drama is its intention, too. The Jones research undertakes to discover what it was that Shakespeare intended to say about Hamlet. It finds that the intention was wrapped by the author in a dreamlike obscurity because it touched so deeply both his personal life and the moral life of the world; what Shakespeare intended to say is that Hamlet cannot act because he is incapacitated by the guilt he feels at his unconscious attachment to his mother. There is, I think, nothing to be quarreled with in the statement that there is an Oedipus situation in *Hamlet;* and if psychoanalysis has indeed added a new point of interest to the play, that is to its credit.[1] And, just so, there is no reason to quarrel with Freud's conclusion when he undertakes to give us the meaning of *King Lear* by a tortuous tracing of the mythological implications of the theme of the three caskets, of the relation of the caskets to the Norns, the Fates, and the Graces, of the connection of these triadic females with Lear's daughters, of the transmogrification of the death goddess into the love goddess and the identification of Cordelia with both, all to the conclusion that the meaning of *King Lear* is to be found in the tragic refusal of an old man to "renounce love, choose death, and make friends with the necessity of dying." There is something both beautiful and suggestive in this, but it is not *the* meaning of *King Lear* any more than the Oedipus motive is *the* meaning of *Hamlet.*

It is not here a question of the validity of the evidence, though that is of

---

[1] However, A. C. Bradley, in his discussion of Hamlet (*Shakespearean Tragedy*), states clearly the intense sexual disgust which Hamlet feels and which, for Bradley, helps account for his uncertain purpose; and Bradley was anticipated in this view by Löning. It is well known, and Dover Wilson has lately emphasized the point, that to an Elizabethan audience Hamlet's mother was not merely tasteless, as to a modern audience she seems, in hurrying to marry Claudius, but actually adulterous in marrying him at all because he was, as her brother-in-law, within the forbidden degrees.

course important. We must rather object to the conclusions of Freud and Dr. Jones on the ground that their proponents do not have an adequate conception of what an artistic meaning is. There is no single meaning to any work of art; this is true not merely because it is better that it should be true, that is, because it makes art a richer thing, but because historical and personal experience show it to be true. Changes in historical context and in personal mood change the meaning of a work and indicate to us that artistic understanding is not a question of fact but of value. Even if the author's intention were, as it cannot be, precisely determinable, the meaning of a work cannot lie in the author's intention alone. It must also lie in its effect. We can say of a volcanic eruption on an inhabited island that it "means terrible suffering," but if the island is uninhabited or easily evacuated it means something else. In short, the audience partly determines the meaning of the work. But although Freud sees something of this when he says that in addition to the author's intention we must take into account the mystery of *Hamlet's* effect, he nevertheless goes on to speak as if, historically, *Hamlet's* effect had been single and brought about solely by the "magical" power of the Oedipus motive to which, unconsciously, we so violently respond. Yet there was, we know, a period when *Hamlet* was relatively in eclipse, and it has always been scandalously true of the French, a people not without filial feeling, that they have been somewhat indifferent to the "magical appeal" of *Hamlet*.

I do not think that anything I have said about the inadequacies of the Freudian method of interpretation limits the number of ways we can deal with a work of art. Bacon remarked that experiment may twist nature on the rack to wring out its secrets, and criticism may use any instruments upon a work of art to find its meanings. The elements of art are not limited to the world of art. They reach into life, and whatever extraneous knowledge of them we gain—for example, by research into the historical context of the work—may quicken our feelings for the work itself and even enter legitimately into those feelings. Then, too, anything we may learn about the artist himself may be enriching and legitimate. But one research into the mind of the artist is simply not practicable, however legitimate it may theoretically be. That is, the investigation of his unconscious intention as it exists apart from the work itself. Criticism understands that the artist's statement of his conscious intention, though it is sometimes useful, cannot finally determine meaning. How much less can we know from his unconscious intention considered as something apart from the whole work? Surely very little can be called conclusive or scientific. For, as Freud himself points out, we are not in a position to question the artist; we must apply the technique of dream analysis to his symbols, but, as Freud says with some heat, those people do not understand his theory who think that a dream may be interpreted without the dreamer's free association with the multitudinous details of his dream.

We have so far ignored the aspect of the method which finds the solution to the "mystery" of such a play as *Hamlet* in the temperament of Shakespeare himself and then illuminates the mystery of Shakespeare's temperament by means of the solved mystery of the play. Here it will be amusing to remember that by 1935 Freud had become converted to the theory that it was not Shakespeare of Stratford but the Earl of Oxford who wrote the plays, thus invalidating the important bit of evidence that Shakespeare's father died shortly before the composition of *Hamlet*. This is destructive enough to Dr. Jones's argument, but the evidence from which Dr. Jones draws conclusions about literature fails on grounds more relevant to literature itself. For when Dr. Jones, by means of his analysis of *Hamlet*, takes us into "the deeper workings of Shakespeare's mind," he does so with a perfect confidence that he knows what *Hamlet* is and what its relation to Shakespeare is. It is, he tells us, Shakespeare's "chief masterpiece," so far superior to all his other works that it may be placed on "an entirely separate level." And then, having established his ground on an entirely subjective literary judgment, Dr. Jones goes on to tell us that *Hamlet* "probably expresses the core of Shakespeare's philosophy and outlook as no other work of his does." That is, all the contradictory or complicating or modifying testimony of the other plays is dismissed on the basis of Dr. Jones's acceptance of the peculiar position which, he believes, *Hamlet* occupies in the Shakespeare canon. And it is upon this quite inadmissible judgment that Dr. Jones bases his argument: "It may be expected *therefore* that anything which will give us the key to the inner meaning of the play will *necessarily* give us the clue to much of the deeper workings of Shakespeare's mind." (The italics are mine.)

I should be sorry if it appeared that I am trying to say that psychoanalysis can have nothing to do with literature. I am sure that the opposite is so. For example, the whole notion of rich ambiguity in literature, of the interplay between the apparent meaning and the latent—not "hidden"—meaning, has been reinforced by the Freudian concepts, perhaps even received its first impetus from them. Of late years, the more perceptive psychoanalysts have surrendered the early pretensions of their teachers to deal "scientifically" with literature. That is all to the good, and when a study as modest and precise as Dr. Franz Alexander's essay on *Henry IV* comes along, an essay which pretends not to "solve" but only to illuminate the subject, we have something worth having. Dr. Alexander undertakes nothing more than to say that in the development of Prince Hal we see the classic struggle of the ego to come to normal adjustment, beginning with the rebellion against the father, going on to the conquest of the super-ego (Hotspur, with his rigid notions of honor and glory), then to the conquests of the *id* (Falstaff, with his anarchic self-indulgence), then to the identification with the father (the crown scene) and the assumption of mature responsibility. An analysis of this sort is not momentous and not exclusive of other meanings; perhaps it does no more than point up and formulate what we all have already seen. It has the tact to *accept* the play and does not, like Dr. Jones's study of *Hamlet,* search for a "hidden motive" and a "deeper working," which implies that there is a reality to which the play stands in the relation that a dream stands to the wish that generates it and from which it is separable; it is this reality, this "deeper working," which, according to Dr. Jones, produced the play. But *Hamlet* is not merely the product of Shakespeare's thought, it is the very instrument of his thought, and if meaning is intention, Shakespeare did not intend the Oedipus motive or anything less than *Hamlet;* if meaning is effect then it is *Hamlet* which affects us, not the Oedipus motive. *Coriolanus* also deals, and very terribly, with the Oedipus motive, but the effect of the one drama is very different from the effect of the other.

IV

If, then, we can accept neither Freud's conception of the place of art in life nor his application of the analytical method, what is it that he contributes to our understanding of art or to its practice? In my opinion, what he contributes outweighs his errors; it is of the greatest importance, and it lies in no specific statement that he makes about art but is, rather, implicit in his whole conception of the mind.

For, of all mental systems, the Freudian psychology is the one which makes poetry indigenous to the very constitution of the mind. Indeed, the mind, as Freud sees it, is in the greater part of its tendency exactly a poetry-making organ. This puts the case too strongly, no doubt, for it seems to make the working of the unconscious mind equivalent to poetry itself, forgetting that between the unconscious mind and the finished poem there supervene the social intention and the formal control of the conscious mind. Yet the statement has at least the virtue of counterbalancing the belief, so commonly expressed or implied, that the very opposite is true, and that poetry is a kind of beneficent aberration of the mind's right course.

Freud has not merely naturalized poetry; he has discovered its status as a pioneer settler, and he sees it as a method of thought. Often enough he tries to show how, as a method of thought, it is unreliable and ineffective for conquering reality; yet he himself is forced to use it in the very shaping of his own science, as when he speaks of the topography of the mind and tells us with a kind of defiant apology that the metaphors of space relationship which he is using are really most inexact since the mind is not a thing of space at all, but that there is no other way of conceiving the difficult idea except by metaphor. In the eighteenth century Vico spoke of the metaphorical, imagistic language of the early stages of culture; it was left to Freud to discover how, in a scientific age, we still feel and think in figurative formations, and to create, what psychoanalysis is, a science of tropes, of metaphor and its variants, synecdoche and metonymy.

Freud showed, too, how the mind, in one of its parts, could work without logic, yet not without that directing purpose, that control of intent from which, perhaps it might be said, logic springs. For the unconscious mind works without the syntactical conjunctions which are logic's essence. It recognipes no *because,* no *therefore,* no *but;* such ideas as similarity, agreement, and community are expressed in dreams imagistically by compressing the elements into a unity. The unconscious mind in its struggle with the conscious always turns from the general to the concrete and finds the tangible trifle more congenial than the large abstraction. Freud discovered in the very organization of the mind those mechanisms by which art makes its effects, such devices as the condensations of meanings and the displacement of accent.

All this is perhaps obvious enough and, though I should like to develop it in proportion both to its importance and to the space I have given to disagreement with Freud, I will not press it further. For there are two other elements in Freud's thought which, in conclusion, I should like to introduce as of great weight in their bearing on art.

Of these, one is a specific idea which, in the middle of his career (1920), Freud put forward in his essay *Beyond the Pleasure Principle.* The essay itself is a speculative attempt to solve a perplexing problem in clinical analysis, but its relevance to literature is inescapable, as Freud sees well enough, even though his perception of its critical importance is not sufficiently strong to make him revise his earlier views of the nature and function of art. The idea is one which stands besides Aristotle's notion of the catharsis, in part to supplement, in part to modify it.

Freud has come upon certain facts which are not to be reconciled with his earlier theory of the dream. According to this theory, all dreams, even the unpleasant ones, could be understood upon analysis to have the intention of fulfilling the dreamer's wishes. They are in the service of what Freud calls the pleasure principle, which is opposed to the reality principle. It is, of course, this explanation of the dream which had so largely conditioned Freud's theory of art. But now there is thrust upon him the necessity for reconsidering the theory of the dream, for it was found that in cases of war neurosis—what we once called shellshock—the patient, with the utmost anguish, recurred in his dreams to the very situation, distressing as it was, which had precipitated his neurosis. It seemed impossible to interpret these dreams by any assumption of a hedonistic intent. Nor did there seem to be the usual amount of distortion in them: the patient recurred to the terrible initiatory situation with great literalness. And the same pattern of psychic behavior could be observed in the play of children; there were some games which, far from fulfilling wishes, seemed to concentrate upon the representation of those aspects of the child's life which were most unpleasant and threatening to his happiness.

To explain such mental activities Freud evolved a theory for which he at first refused to claim much but to which, with the years, he attached an increasing importance. He first makes the assumption that there is indeed in the psychic life a repetition-compulsion which goes beyond the pleasure principle. Such a compulsion cannot be meaningless, it must have an intent. And that intent, Freud comes to believe, is exactly and literally the developing of fear. "These dreams," he says, "are attempts at restoring control of the stimuli by developing apprehension, the pretermission of which caused the traumatic neurosis." The dream, that is, is the effort to reconstruct the bad situation in order that the failure to meet it may be recouped; in these dreams there is no obscured intent to evade but only an attempt to meet the situation, to make a new effort of control. And in the play of children it seems to be that "the child repeats even the unpleasant experiences because through his own activity he gains a far more thorough mastery of the strong impression than was possible by mere passive experience."

Freud, at this point, can scarcely help being put in mind of tragic drama; nevertheless, he does not wish to believe that this effort to come to mental grips with a situation is involved in the attraction of tragedy. He is, we might say, under the influence of the Aristotelian tragic theory which emphasizes a qualified hedonism through suffering. But the pleasure involved in tragedy is perhaps an ambiguous one; and sometimes we must feel that the famous sense of cathartic resolution is perhaps the result of glossing over terror with beautiful language rather than an evacuation of it. And sometimes the terror even bursts through the language to stand stark and isolated from the play, as does Oedipus's sightless and bleeding face. At any rate, the Aristotelian theory does not deny another function for tragedy (and for comedy, too) which is suggested by Freud's theory of the traumatic neurosis—what might be called the mithridatic function, by which tragedy is used as the homeopathic administration of pain to inure ourselves to the greater pain which life will force upon us. There is in the cathartic theory of tragedy, as it is usually understood, a conception of tragedy's function which is too negative and which inadequately suggests the sense of active mastery which tragedy can give.

In the same essay in which he sets forth the conception of the mind embracing its own pain for some vital purpose, Freud also expresses a provisional assent to the idea (earlier stated, as he reminds us, by Schopenhauer) that there is perhaps a human drive which makes of death the final and desired goal. The death instinct is a conception that is rejected by many of even the most thoroughgoing Freudian theorists (as, in his last book, Freud mildly noted); the late Otto Fenichel in his authoritative work on the neurosis argues cogently against it. Yet even if we reject the theory as not fitting the facts in any operatively useful way, we still cannot miss its grandeur, its ultimate tragic courage in acquiescence to fate. The idea of the reality principle and the idea of the death instinct form the crown of Freud's broader speculation on the life of man. Their quality of grim poetry is characteristic of Freud's system and the ideas it generates for him.

And as much as anything else that Freud gives to literature, this quality of his thought is important. Although the artist is never finally determined in his work by the intellectual systems about him, he cannot avoid their influence; and it can be said of various competing systems that some hold more promise for the artist than others. When, for example, we think of the simple humanitarian optimism which, for two decades, has been so pervasive, we must see that not only has it been politically and philosophically inadequate, but also that it implies, by the smallness of its view of the varieties of human possibility, a kind of check on the creative faculties. In Freud's view of life no such limitation is implied. To be sure, certain elements of his system seem hostile to the usual notions of man's dignity. Like every great critic of human nature —and Freud is that—he finds in human pride the ultimate cause of human wretchedness, and he takes pleasure in knowing that his ideas stand with those of Copernicus and Darwin in making pride more difficult to maintain. Yet the Freudian man is, I venture to think, a creature of far more dignity and far more interest than the man which any other modern system has been able to conceive. Despite popular belief to the contrary, man, as Freud conceives him, is not to be understood by any simple formula (such as sex) but is rather an inextricable tangle of culture and biology. And not being simple, he is not simply good; he has, as Freud says somewhere, a kind of hell within him from which rise everlastingly the impulses which threaten his civilization. He has the faculty of imagining for himself more in the way of pleasure and satisfaction than he can possibly achieve. Everything that he gains he pays for in more than equal coin; compromise and the compounding with defeat constitute his best way of getting through the world. His best qualities are the result of a struggle whose outcome is tragic. Yet he is a creature of love; it is Freud's sharpest criticism of the Adlerian psychology that to aggression it gives everything and to love nothing at all.

One is always aware in reading Freud how little cynicism there is in his thought. His desire for man is only that he should be human, and to this end his science is devoted. No view of life to which the artist responds can insure the quality of his work, but the poetic qualities of Freud's own principles, which are so clearly in the line of the classic tragic realism, suggest that this is a view which does not narrow and simplify the human world for the artist but on the contrary opens and complicates it.

From *The Liberal Imagination* by Lionel Trilling. Viking Press. Copyright, 1950, by Lionel Trilling. Reprinted by permission of the author and publishers. Originally published as "The Legacy of Sigmund Freud: Literary and Aesthetic" in *The Kenyon Review,* Vol. II (Spring, 1940), pp. 152–173; and, in a revised version, as "Freud and Literature" in *Horizon* (London), Vol. XVI (September, 1947), pp. 182–200.

EDMUND WILSON

Marxism and Literature

[1937]

1. LET us begin with Marx and Engels. What was the role assigned to literature and art in the system of Dialectical Materialism? This role was much less cut-and-dried than is nowadays often supposed. Marx and Engels conceived the forms of human society in any given country and epoch as growing out of the methods of production which prevailed at that place and time; and out of the relations involved in the social forms arose a "superstructure" of higher activities such as politics, law, religion, philosophy, literature and art. These activities were not, as is sometimes assumed, wholly explicable in terms of economics. They showed the mold, in ways direct or indirect, of the social configuration below them, but each was working to get away from its roots in the social classes and to constitute a professional group, with its own discipline and its own standards of value, which cut across class lines. These departments "all react upon one another and upon the economic base. It is not the case that the economic situation is the sole active cause and everything else only a passive effect. But there is a reciprocal interaction within a fundamental economic necessity, which in the last instance always asserts itself" (Engels to Hans Starkenburg, January 25, 1894). So that the art of a great artistic period may reach a point of vitality and vision where it can influence the life of the period down to its very economic foundations. Simply, it must cease to flourish with the social system which made it possible by providing the artist with training and leisure, even though the artist himself may have been working for the destruction of that system.

2. Marx and Engels, unlike some of their followers, never attempted to furnish social-economic formulas by which the validity of works of art might be tested. They had grown up in the sunset of Goethe before the great age of German literature was over, and they had both set out in their youth to be poets; they responded to imaginative work, first of all, on its artistic merits. They could ridicule a trashy writer like Eugène Sue for what they regarded as his *petit bourgeois* remedies for the miseries of contemporary society (*The*

Holy Family); they could become bitter about Ferdinand Freiligrath, who had deserted the Communist League and turned nationalist in 1870 (Marx to Engels, August 22, 1870). And Marx could even make similar jibes at Heine when he thought that the latter had stooped to truckling to the authorities or when he read the expressions of piety in his will (Marx to Engels, December 21, 1866 and May 8, 1856). But Marx's daughter tells us that her father loved Heine "as much as his work and was very indulgent of his political shortcomings. He used to say that the poets were originals, who must be allowed to go their own way, and that one shouldn't apply to them the same standards as to ordinary people." It was not characteristic of Marx and Engels to judge literature—that is, literature of power and distinction—in terms of its purely political tendencies. In fact, Engels always warned the socialist novelists against the dangers of *Tendenz-Literatur* (Engels to Minna Kautsky, November 26, 1885; and to Margaret Harkness, April 1888). In writing to Minna Kautsky about one of her novels, he tells her that the personalities of her hero and heroine have been dissolved in the principles they represent. "You evidently," he says, "felt the need of publicly taking sides in this book, of proclaiming your opinions of the world. . . . But I believe that the tendency should arise from the situation and the action themselves without being explicitly formulated, and that the poet is not under the obligation to furnish the reader with a ready-made historical solution for the future of the conflict which he describes." When Ferdinand Lassalle sent Marx and Engels his poetic tragedy, *Franz von Sickingen,* and invited them to criticize it, Marx replied that, "setting aside any purely critical attitude toward the work," it had on a first reading affected him powerfully—characteristically adding that upon persons of a more emotional nature it would doubtless produce an even stronger effect; and Engels wrote that he had read it twice and had been moved by it so profoundly that he had been obliged to lay it aside in order to arrive at any critical perspective. It was only after pulling themselves together and making some purely literary observations that they were able to proceed to discuss, from their special historical point of view, the period with which the drama dealt and to show how Lassalle's own political position had led him to mistake the role of his hero. Aeschylus Marx loved for his grandeur and for the defiance of Zeus by Prometheus; Goethe they both immensely admired: Engels wrote of him as a "colossal" and "universal" genius whose career had been marred by an admixture in his character of the philistine and the courtier (*German Socialism in Verse and Prose*); Shakespeare Marx knew by heart and was extremely fond of quoting, but never—despite the long, learned and ridiculous essays which have appeared in the Soviet magazine, *International Literature*—attempted to draw from his plays any general social moral. So far, indeed, was Marx from having worked out a systematic explanation of the relation of art to social arrangements that he could assert, apropos of

Greek art, in his *Introduction to the Critique of Political Economy*, that "certain periods of highest development of art stand in no direct connection with the general development of society, nor with the material basis and the skeleton structure of its organization."

3. With Marx and Engels there is not yet any tendency to specialize art as a "weapon." They were both too much under the influence of the ideal of the many-sided man of the Renaissance, of the "complete" man, who, like Leonardo, had been painter, mathematician and engineer, or, like Machiavelli, poet, historian and strategist, before the division of labor had had the effect of splitting up human nature and limiting everyone to some single function (Engels' preface to his *Dialectic and Nature*). But with Lenin we come to a Marxist who is specialized himself as an organizer and fighter. Like most Russians, Lenin was sensitive to music; but Gorky tells us that on one occasion, after listening to Beethoven's Appassionata Sonata and exclaiming that he "would like to listen to it every day: it is marvelous superhuman music —I always think with pride . . . what marvelous things human beings can do," he screwed up his eyes and smiled sadly and added: "But I can't listen to music too often. It affects your nerves, makes you want to say stupid, nice things, and stroke the heads of people who could create such beauty while living in this vile hell. And now you mustn't stroke anyone's head—you might get your hand bitten off." Yet he was fond of fiction, poetry and the theater, and by no means doctrinaire in his tastes. Krupskaya tells how, on a visit to a Youth Commune, he asked the young people, "What do you read? Do you read Pushkin?" " 'Oh, no!' someone blurted out. 'He was a bourgeois. Mayakovsky for us.' Ilyitch smiled. 'I think Pushkin is better.' " Gorky says that one day he found Lenin with *War and Peace* lying on the table: " 'Yes, Tolstoy. I wanted to read over the scene of the hunt, then remembered that I had to write a comrade. Absolutely no time for reading.' . . . Smiling and screwing up his eyes, he stretched himself deliciously in his armchair and, lowering his voice, added quickly, 'What a colossus, eh? What a marvelously developed brain! Here's an artist for you, sir. And do you know something still more amazing? You couldn't find a genuine *muzhik* in literature till this count came upon the scene.' " In his very acute essays on Tolstoy, he deals with him much as Engels deals with Goethe—with tremendous admiration for Tolstoy's genius, but with an analysis of his non-resistance and mysticism in terms not, it is interesting to note, of the psychology of the landed nobility, but of the patriarchal peasantry with whom Tolstoy had identified himself. And Lenin's attitude toward Gorky was much like that of Marx toward Heine. He suggests in one of his letters that Gorky would be helpful as a journalist on the side of the Bolsheviks, but adds that he mustn't be bothered if he is busy writing a book.

4. Trotsky is a literary man as Lenin never was, and he published in 1924 a most remarkable little study called *Literature and Revolution*. In this book he tried to illuminate the problems which were arising for Russian writers with the new society of the Revolution. And he was obliged to come to grips with a question with which Marx and Engels had not been much concerned—the question of what Mr. James T. Farrell in his book, *A Note on Literary Criticism*, one of the few sensible recent writings on this subject, calls "the carry-over value" of literature. Marx had assumed the value of Shakespeare and the Greeks and more or less left it at that. But what, the writers in Russia were now asking, was to be the value of the literature and art of the ages of barbarism and oppression in the dawn of socialist freedom? What in particular was to be the status of the culture of that bourgeois society from which socialism had just emerged and of which it still bore the unforgotten scars? Would there be a new proletarian literature, with new language, new style, new form, to give expression to the emotions and ideas of the new proletarian dictatorship? There had been in Russia a group called the Proletcult, which aimed at monopolizing the control of Soviet literature; but Lenin had discouraged and opposed it, insisting that proletarian culture was not something which could be produced synthetically and by official dictation of policy, but only by natural evolution as a "development of those reserves of knowledge which society worked for under the oppression of capitalism, of the landlords, of the officials." Now, in *Literature and Revolution*, Trotsky asserted that "such terms as 'proletarian literature' and 'proletarian culture' are dangerous, because they erroneously compress the culture of the future into the narrow limits of the present day." In a position to observe from his Marxist point of view the effects on a national literature of the dispossession of a dominant class, he was able to see the unexpected ways in which the presentments of life of the novelists, the feelings and images of the poets, the standards themselves of the critics, were turning out to be determined by their attitudes toward the social-economic crisis. But he did not believe in a proletarian culture which would displace the bourgeois one. The bourgeois literature of the French Revolution had ripened under the old regime; but the illiterate proletariat and peasantry of Russia had had no chance to produce a culture, nor would there be time for them to do so in the future, because the proletarian dictatorship was not to last: it was to be only a transition phase and to lead the way to "a culture which is above classes and which will be the first truly human culture." In the meantime, the new socialist literature would grow directly out of that which had already been produced during the domination of the bourgeoisie. Communism, Trotsky said, had as yet no artistic culture; it had only a political culture.

5. All this seems to us reasonable enough. But, reasonable and cultured as Trotsky is, ready as he is to admit that "one cannot always go by the principles of Marxism in deciding whether to accept or reject a work of art," that such a work "should be judged in the first place by its own law—that is, by the law of art," there is none the less in the whole situation something which is alien to us. We are not accustomed, in our quarter of the world, either to having the government attempt to control literature and art or to having literary and artistic movements try to identify themselves with the government. Yet Russia, since the Revolution, has had a whole series of cultural groups which have attempted to dominate literature either with or without the authority of the government; and Trotsky himself, in his official position, even in combating these tendencies, cannot avoid passing censure and pinning ribbons. Sympathizers with the Soviet regime used to assume that this state of affairs was inseparable from the realization of socialism: that its evils would be easily outgrown and that in any case it was a great thing to have the government take so lively an interest in culture. I believe that this view was mistaken. Under the Tsar, imaginative literature in Russia played a role which was probably different from any role it had ever played in the life of any other nation. Political and social criticism, pursued and driven underground by the censorship, was forced to incorporate itself in the dramatic imagery of fiction. This was certainly one of the principal reasons for the greatness during the nineteenth century of the Russian theater and novel, for the mastery by the Russian writers—from Pushkin's time to Tolstoy's—of the art of implication. In the 'fifties and 'sixties, the stories of Turgenev, which seem mild enough to us today, were capable of exciting the most passionate controversies—and even, in the case of *A Sportsman's Sketches,* causing the dismissal of the censor who had passed it—because each was regarded as a political message. Ever since the Revolution, literature and politics in Russia have remained inextricable. But after the Revolution the intelligentsia themselves were in power; and it became plain that in the altered situation the identification of literature with politics was liable to terrible abuses. Lenin and Trotsky, Lunacharsky and Gorky, worked sincerely to keep literature free; but they had at the same time, from the years of Tsardom, a keen sense of the possibility of art as an instrument of propaganda. Lenin took a special interest in the moving pictures from the propaganda point of view; and the first Soviet films, by Eisenstein and Pudovkin, were masterpieces of implication, as the old novels and plays had been. But Lenin died; Trotsky was exiled; Lunacharsky died. The administration of Stalin, unliterary and uncultivated himself, slipped into depending more and more on literature as a means of manipulating a people of whom, before the Revolution, 70 or 80 per cent had been illiterate and who could hardly be expected to be critical of what they read. Gorky seems to have exerted what influence he could in the direction of liberalism: to him was due, no doubt, the liquidation of RAPP, the latest device for the monopoly of culture, and the opening of the Soviet canon to the best contemporary foreign writing and the classics. But though this made possible more freedom of form and a wider range of reading, it could not, under the dictatorship of Stalin, either stimulate or release a living literature. Where no political opposition was possible, there was possible no political criticism; and in Russia political questions involve vitally the fate of society. What reality can there be for the Russians, the most socially-minded writers on earth, in a freedom purely "esthetic"? Even the fine melodramatic themes of the post-revolutionary cinema and theater, with their real emotion and moral conviction, have been replaced by simple trash not very far removed from Hollywood, or by dramatized exemplifications of the latest "directive" of Stalin which open the night after the speech that has announced the directive. The recent damning of the music of Shostakovich on the ground that the commissars were unable to hum it seems a withdrawal from the liberal position. And it is probable that the death of Gorky, as well as the imprisonment of Bukharin and Radek, have removed the last brakes from a precipitate descent, in the artistic as well as the political field, into a nightmare of informing and repression. The practice of deliberate falsification of social and political history which began at the time of the Stalin-Trotsky crisis and which has now attained proportions so fantastic that the government does not seem to hesitate to pass the sponge every month or so over everything that the people have previously been told and to present them with a new and contradictory version of their history, their duty, and the characters and careers of their leaders—this practice cannot fail in the end to corrupt every department of intellectual life, till the serious, the humane, the clear-seeing must simply, if they can, remain silent.

6. Thus Marxism in Russia for the moment has run itself into a blind alley —or rather, it has been put down a well. The Soviets seem hardly at the present time to have retained even the Marxist political culture, even in its cruder forms—so that we are relieved from the authority of Russia as we are deprived of her inspiration. To what conclusions shall we come, then, at this time of day about Marxism and literature—basing our views not even necessarily upon texts from the Marxist Fathers, but upon ordinary commonsense? Well, first of all, that we can go even further than Trotsky in one of the dicta I have quoted above and declare that Marxism by itself can tell us nothing whatever about the goodness or badness of a work of art. A man may be an excellent Marxist, but if he lacks imagination and taste he will be unable to make the choice between a good and an inferior book both of which are ideologically unexceptionable. What Marxism *can* do, however, is throw a great deal of light on the origins and social significance of works of art. The study of literature in its relation to society is as old as Herder—and even Vico. Coleridge had flashes of insight into the connection between literary and social phenomena, as when he saw the Greek state in the Greek sentence and the individualism of the English in the short separate statements of Chaucer's Prologue. But the

great bourgeois master of this kind of criticism was Taine, with his *race* and *moment* and *milieu;* yet Taine, for all his scientific professions, responded artistically to literary art, and responded so vividly that his summings-up of writers and re-creations of periods sometimes rival or surpass their subjects. Marx and Engels further deepened this study of literature in relation to its social background by demonstrating for the first time inescapably the importance of economic systems. But if Marx and Engels and Lenin and Trotsky are worth listening to on the subject of books, it is not merely because they created Marxism, but also because they were capable of literary appreciation.

7. Yet the man who tries to apply Marxist principles without real understanding of literature is liable to go horribly wrong. For one thing, it is usually true in works of the highest order that the purport is not a simple message, but a complex vision of things, which itself is not explicit but implicit; and the reader who does not grasp them artistically, but is merely looking for simple social morals, is certain to be hopelessly confused. Especially will he be confused if the author *does* draw an explicit moral which is the opposite of or has nothing to do with his real purport. Friedrich Engels, in the letter to Margaret Harkness already referred to above, in warning her that the more the novelist allows his political ideas to "remain hidden, the better it is for the work of art," says that Balzac, with his reactionary opinions, is worth a thousand of Zola, with all his democratic ones. (Balzac was one of the great literary admirations of both Engels and Marx, the latter of whom had planned to write a book on him.) Engels points out that Balzac himself was, or believed himself to be, a legitimist engaged in deploring the decline of high society; but that actually "his irony is never more bitter, his satire never more trenchant, than when he is showing us these aristocrats . . . for whom he felt so profound a sympathy," and that "the only men of whom he speaks with undissimulated admiration are his most determined political adversaries, the republican heroes of the Cloître-Saint-Merri, the men who at that period (1830–1836) truly represented the popular masses." Nor does it matter necessarily in a work of art whether the characters are shown engaged in a conflict which illustrates the larger conflicts of society or in one which from that point of view is trivial. In art—it is quite obvious in music, but it is also true in literature—a sort of law of moral interchangeability prevails: we may transpose the the actions and the sentiments that move us into terms of whatever we do or are ourselves. Real genius of moral insight is a motor which will start any engine. When Proust, in his wonderful chapter on the death of the novelist Bergotte, speaks of those moral obligations which impose themselves in spite of everything and which seem to come through to humanity from some source outside its wretched self (obligations "invisible only to fools—and are they really to them?"), he is describing a kind of duty which he felt only in connec-

tion with the literary work which he performed in his dark and fetid room; yet he speaks for every moral, esthetic or intellectual passion which holds the expediencies of the world in contempt. And the hero of Thornton Wilder's *Heaven's My Destination,* the traveling salesman who tries to save souls in the smoking car and writes Bible texts on hotel blotters, is something more than a symptom of Thornton Wilder's religious tendencies: he is the type of all saints who begin absurdly; and Wilder's story would be as true of the socialist Upton Sinclair as of the Christian George Brush. Nor does it necessarily matter, for the moral effect of a work of literature, whether the forces of bravery or virtue with which we identify ourselves are victorious or vanquished in the end. In Hemingway's story *The Undefeated,* the old bullfighter who figures as the hero is actually humiliated and killed, but his courage has itself been a victory. It is true, as I. Kashkin, the Soviet critic, has said, that Hemingway has written much about decadence, but in order to write tellingly about death you have to have the principle of life, and those that have it will make it felt in spite of everything.

8. The Leftist critic with no literary competence is always trying to measure works of literature by tests which have no validity in that field. And one of his favorite occupations is giving specific directions and working out diagrams for the construction of ideal Marxist books. Such formulas are of course perfectly futile. The rules observed in any given school of art become apparent, not before but after, the actual works of art have been produced. As we were reminded by Burton Rascoe at the time of the Humanist controversy, the esthetic laws involved in Greek tragedy were not formulated by Aristotle until at least half a century after Euripides and Sophocles were dead. And the behavior of the Marxist critics has been precisely like that of the Humanists. The Humanists knew down to the last comma what they wanted a work of literature to be, but they never—with the possible exception, when pressed, of *The Bridge of San Luis Rey,* about which they had, however, hesitations— were able to find any contemporary work which fitted their specifications. The Marxists did just the same thing. In an article called "The Crisis in Criticism" in the *New Masses* of February 1933, Granville Hicks drew up a list of requirements which the ideal Marxist work of literature must meet. The primary function of such a work, he asserted, must be to "lead the proletarian reader to recognize his role in the class struggle"—and it must therefore (1) "directly or indirectly show the effects of the class struggle"; (2) "the author must be able to make the reader feel that he is participating in the lives described"; and, finally, (3) the author's point of view must "be that of the vanguard of the proletariat; he should be, or should try to make himself, a member of the proletariat." This formula, he says, "gives us . . . a standard by which to recognize the perfect Marxian novel"—and adds "no novel as yet

written perfectly conforms to our demands." But the doctrine of "socialist real-ism" promulgated at the Soviet Writers' Congress of August 1934 was only an attempt on a larger scale to legislate masterpieces into existence—a kind of attempt which always indicates sterility on the part of those who engage in it, and which always actually works, if it has any effect at all, to legislate existing good literature *out of* existence and to discourage the production of any more. The prescribers for the literature of the future usually cherish some great figure of the past whom they regard as having fulfilled their conditions and whom they are always bringing forward to demonstrate the inferiority of the literature of the present. As there has never existed a great writer who really had anything in common with these critics' conception of literature, they are obliged to provide imaginary versions of what their ideal great writers are like. The Humanists had Sophocles and Shakespeare; the socialist realists had Tol-stoy. Yet it is certain that if Tolstoy had had to live up to the objectives and prohibitions which the socialist realists proposed he could never have written a chapter; and that if Babbitt and More had been able to enforce against Shakespeare their moral and esthetic injunctions he would never have written a line. The misrepresentation of Sophocles, which has involved even a tam-pering with his text in the interests not merely of Humanism but of academic classicism in general, has been one of the scandalous absurdities of scholarship. The Communist critical movement in America, which had for its chief spokes-man Mr. Hicks, tended to identify their ideal with the work of John Dos Passos. In order to make this possible, it was necessary to invent an imaginary Dos Passos. This ideal Dos Passos was a Communist, who wrote stories about the proletariat, at a time when the real Dos Passos was engaged in bringing out a long novel about the effects of the capitalist system on the American middle-class and had announced himself—in the *New Republic* in 1930—politically a "middle-class liberal." The ideal Dos Passos was something like Gorky without the mustache—Gorky, in the meantime, having himself un-gone some transmogrification at the hands of Soviet publicity—and this myth was maintained until the Communist critics were finally compelled to re-pudiate it, not because they had acquired new light on Dos Passos, the novelist and dramatist, but because of his attitude toward events in Russia.

9. The object of these formulas for the future, as may be seen from the above quotations from Mr. Hicks, is to make of art an effective instrument in the class struggle. And we must deal with the dogma that "art is a weapon." It is true that art may be a weapon; but in the case of some of the greatest works of art, some of those which have the longest carry-over value, it is difficult to see that any important part of this value is due to their direct functioning as weapons. The *Divine Comedy,* in its political aspect, is a weapon for Henry of Luxemburg, whom Dante—with his medieval internationalism and his

lack of sympathy for the nationalistic instincts which were impelling the Italians of his time to get away from their Austrian emperors—was so passionately
eager to impose on his countrymen. Today we may say with Carducci that we
would as soon see the crown of his "good Frederick" rolling in Olona vale:
"Jove perishes; the poet's hymn remains." And, though Shakespeare's *Henry
IV* and *Henry V* are weapons for Elizabethan imperialism, their real center is
not Prince Hal but Falstaff; and Falstaff is the father of *Hamlet* and of all
Shakespeare's tragic heroes, who, if they illustrate any social moral—the
moral, perhaps, that Renaissance princes, supreme in their little worlds, may go
to pieces in all kinds of terrible ways for lack of a larger social organism to re-
strain them—do so evidently without Shakespeare's being aware of it. If these
works may be spoken of as weapons at all, they are weapons in the more general struggle of modern European man emerging from the Middle Ages and
striving to understand his world and himself—a function for which "weapon"
is hardly the right word. The truth is that there is short-range and long-range
literature. Long-range literature attempts to sum up wide areas and long periods of human experience, or to extract from them general laws; short-range
literature preaches and pamphleteers with the view to an immediate effect.
A good deal of the recent confusion of our writers in the Leftist camp has been
due to their not understanding, or being unable to make up their minds,
whether they are aiming at long-range or short-range writing.

10. This brings us to the question of what sort of periods are most favorable
for works of art. One finds an assumption on the Left that revolutionary or
pre-revolutionary periods are apt to produce new and vital forms of literature.
This, of course, is very far from the truth in the case of periods of actual revolution. The more highly developed forms of literature require leisure and a
certain amount of stability; and during a period of revolution the writer is
usually deprived of both. The literature of the French Revolution consisted of
the orations of Danton, the journalism of Camille Desmoulins and the few political poems that André Chenier had a chance to write before he was guillo-
tined. The literature of the Russian Revolution was the political writing of
Lenin and Trotsky, and Alexander Blok's poem, *The Twelve,* almost the last
fruit of his genius before it was nipped by the wind of the storm. As for pre-
revolutionary periods in which the new forces are fermenting, they *may* be
great periods for literature—as the eighteenth century was in France and the
nineteenth century in Russia (though here there was a decadence after 1905).
But the conditions that make possible the masterpieces are apparently not produced by the impending revolutions, but by the phenomenon of literary technique, already highly developed, in the hands of a writer who has had the
support of long-enduring institutions. He may reflect an age of transition, but
it will not necessarily be true that his face is set squarely in the direction of

the future. The germs of the Renaissance are in Dante and the longing for a better world in Virgil, but neither Dante nor Virgil can in any real sense be described as a revolutionary writer: they sum up or write elegies for ages that are passing. The social organisms that give structure to their thought—the Roman Empire and the Catholic Church—are already showing signs of decay. It is impossible, therefore, to identify the highest creative work in art with the most active moments of creative social change. The writer who is seriously intent on producing long-range works of literature should, from the point of view of his own special personal interests, thank his stars if there is no violent revolution going on in his own country in his time. He may disapprove of the society he is writing about, but if it were disrupted by an actual upheaval he would probably not be able to write.

11. But what about "proletarian literature" as an accompaniment of the social revolution? In the earlier days of the Communist regime in Russia, one used to hear about Russian authors who, in the effort to eliminate from their writings any vestige of the bourgeois point of view, had reduced their vocabulary and syntax to what they regarded as an A B C of essentials—with the result of becoming more unintelligible to the proletarian audience at whom they were aiming than if they had been Symbolist poets. (Indeed, the futurist poet Mayakovsky has since that time become a part of the Soviet canon.) Later on, as I have said, Soviet culture followed the road that Trotsky recommended: it began building again on the classics and on the bourgeois culture of other countries and on able revolutionary Russian writers who had learned their trade before the Revolution. "Soviet publishers"—I quote from the Russian edition of *International Literature,* issue 2 of 1936—"are bringing out Hemingway and Proust not merely in order to demonstrate 'bourgeois decay.' Every genuine work of art—and such are the productions of Hemingway and Proust—enriches the writer's knowledge of life and heightens his esthetic sensibility and his emotional culture—in a word, it figures, in the broad sense, as a factor of educational value. Liberated socialist humanity inherits all that is beautiful, elevating and sustaining in the culture of previous ages." The truth is that the talk in Soviet Russia about proletarian literature and art has resulted from the persistance of the same situation which led Tolstoy under the old regime to put on the muzhik's blouse and to go in for carpentry, cobbling and plowing: the difficulty experienced by an educated minority, who were only about 20 per cent of the people, in getting in touch with the illiterate majority. In America the situation is quite different. The percentage of illiterates in this country is only something like 4 per cent; and there is relatively little difficulty of communication between different social groups. Our development away from England, and from the old world generally, in this respect—in the direction of the democratization of our idiom—is demon-

strated clearly in H. L. Mencken's *The American Language;* and if it is a
question of either the use for high literature of the language of the people or
the expression of the dignity and importance of the ordinary man, the country
which has produced *Leaves of Grass* and *Huckleberry Finn* has certainly
nothing to learn from Russia. We had created during our pioneering period
a literature of the common man's escape, not only from feudal Europe, but
also from bourgeois society, many years before the Russian masses were beginning to write their names. There has been a section of our recent American literature of the last fifteen years or so—the period of the boom and the
depression—which has dealt with our industrial and rural life from the point
of view of the factory hand and the poor farmer under conditions which were
forcing him to fight for his life, and this has been called proletarian literature;
but it has been accompanied by books on the white-collar worker, the store-
keeper, the well-to-do merchant, the scientist and the millionaire in situations
equally disastrous or degrading. And this whole movement of critical and
imaginative writing—though with some stimulus, certainly, from Russia—
had come quite naturally out of our literature of the past. It is curious to observe that one of the best of the recent strike novels, *The Land of Plenty* by
Robert Cantwell, himself a Westerner and a former mill worker, owes a good
deal to Henry James.

12. Yet when all these things have been said, all the questions have not
been answered. All that has been said has been said of the past; and Marxism
is something new in the world: it is a philosophical system which leads directly to programs of action. Has there ever appeared before in literature such
a phenomenon as M. André Malraux, who alternates between attempts,
sometimes brilliant, to write long-range fiction on revolutionary themes, and
exploits of aviation for the cause of revolution in Spain? Here creative political action and the more complex kind of imaginative writing have united at
least to the extent that they have arisen from the same vision of history and
have been included in the career of one man. The Marxist vision of Lenin—
Vincent Sheean has said it first—has in its completeness and its compelling
force a good deal in common with the vision of Dante; but, partly realized
by Lenin during his lifetime and still potent for some years after his death, it
was a creation, not of literary art, but of actual social engineering. It is society
itself, says Trotsky, which under communism becomes the work of art. The
first attempts at this art will be inexpert and they will have refractory material
to work with; and the philosophy of the Marxist dialectic involves idealistic
and mythological elements which have led too often to social religion rather
than to social art. Yet the human imagination has already come to conceive
the possibility of re-creating human society; and how can we doubt that, as it
acquires the power, it must emerge from what will seem by comparison the

revolutionary "underground" of art as we have always known it up to now and deal with the materials of actual life in ways which we cannot now even foresee? This is to speak in terms of centuries, of ages; but, in practicing and prizing literature, we must not be unaware of the first efforts of the human spirit to transcend literature itself.

From *The Triple Thinkers* by Edmund Wilson. First published in 1938, by Harcourt, Brace and Company, Inc.; and in a revised edition by the Oxford University Press, 1948, from which the essay is here reproduced by permission of the author and publishers. First published in *The Atlantic Monthly*, Volume CLX (December, 1937), pp. 741–750.

WILLIAM PHILLIPS and
PHILIP RAHV

Private Experience and Public Philosophy

[1936]

THAT "free individual interpretation" and "private experience" are essential to poetry is one postulate that few critics have cared to question. Also, for the most part they agree that the greatness of a poem is in some way related to the outlook or public philosophy of the poet. But here the argument begins. For what is "private" to one group is "public" to another, and frequently it is claimed that a harmonious marriage of the two is impossible because ultimately they are incompatible. Thus compartmentalized, experience and philosophy are pitted against each other. T. S. Eliot, who embodies the contradictions as well as the achievements of his period, sees the necessity for both elements while contending they are incompatible. The two quotations are from "Poetry and Propaganda," written in 1930:

> Yet we can hardly doubt that the "truest" philosophy is the best material for the greatest poet; so that the poet must be rated in the end both by the philosophy he realizes in his poetry and by the fullness and adequacy of the realization.

> There is a gulf, and I think an impassable one, between the intuitions of the poets as such, and any particular philosophy, or even any philosophical direction rather than any other.

The position Eliot takes in this essay and his eclectic conclusions betray a rudderless philosophy of value; that is, a notion that no one philosophy is true and that any "profound" philosophy may be held and used by poets. Sharing this notion, poets during the last few decades felt relieved of responsibility for their ideas. Experience—personal, ever more unique experience—became the touchstone of poetry. Today the problem looms again: as poets pass from one intellectual climate into another public philosophy and private experience are put up as the horns of a poetic dilemma. Suspension among a variety of beliefs, with the consequent gyrations into formal experiments, is

706

no longer acceptable to those who have taken a definite attitude toward the world we live in. How to communicate this attitude, even while maintaining the integrity of personal experience, is one of the major problems of the poet in this age.

We are convinced that behind many of the attacks on revolutionary poetry lurks the notion of the contradiction we have just discussed. What else will account for the charge that the philosophy of social revolution strait-jackets the poet's experience, leaving no room for the play of his imagination and the unique quality of his personal emotions? We are led to believe that the revolutionary poet is a mere puppet pulled by the strings of sociology and politics, and that his talent is spent on the linguistic decoration of a closed order of beliefs. Naturally, such poetry is regarded as a violent break with tradition—a noble medium reduced to the service of menial utilitarian ends.

If, however, theory is at bottom no more than history generalizing about itself, then let us check the indictment against the poetic objects involved. You could easily fit this theory to a body of anonymous poetry, inasmuch as all the poems, expressing an impersonal public philosophy, would prove to be essentially identical. But except for ideological direction, what is there in common between Fearing and Schneider, either in method, intention, or feeling? And though both Gregory and Aragon move within the Marxian orbit, in his actual verse-texture Gregory is as far away from Aragon as he is from Allen Tate. The fact is that revolutionary poetry teems with personal tonalities, and is composed of many strains and tendencies. It is true, of course, that the work of a small scattered group of "leftists," poaching on the fringes of revolutionary poetry, does illustrate in several ways the charges of impersonality and barren publicism. But it is just as dishonest to identify this group with revolutionary poetry in its representative aspects as it would be for a Marxist to identify the criticism of T. S. Eliot with that of William Lyon Phelps for the sole reason that from a strictly political point of view both are anti-communist. Caught in the wiles of literalism, the infantile "leftists" have equated the weapon of art with the art of weapons, with the result that they are not writing poetry but clichéd slogans and stale manifestoes. Yet the critics of the right hardly excel in this respect, for in their own field they too have accepted this monstrous equation. Fundamentally it involves the same faulty understanding of Marxism, though one group accepts it and the other rejects it.

If we were to explore all the corners of the creative problem implied in this controversy, we should hear its echoes in the philosophic question concerning the relation of the ego to the objective world. Or, granting that poetry is an objective body of poems, having continuity and a social status, what is the relation of poetry to the individual poet? Assume a contradiction between a public philosophy and the private experience of the poet and what you get is poetic solipsism, whereby the history and tradition of poetry are dissolved in the acid of uniqueness. A contradiction arises between the poet and the objective meanings of the poetry that has been written, and the only reality remaining to him is his own work. French poetry of post-symbolist days and the writing of the *transition* school actually approached this state. In Paul Valéry's essay, "A Foreword," we observe the process of ideas by means of which any given poetry purges itself of all else, even of other poetry:

> . . . One can say that the greatest . . . of the versified works which have come down to us belong to the didactic or historical order.

> Finally, toward the middle of the nineteenth century, French literature saw the birth of a remarkable ambition—that of isolating poetry from every essence other than its own.

> I mean to say that our tendency . . . toward a beauty always more independent of all *subjects,* and free from sentimental vulgar interest . . . was leading to an almost inhuman state.

This inhuman state was the dead end, though much important poetry steered clear of it.

It would be almost gratuitous to recall that Shakespeare was soaked in prevailing "Elizabethan" attitudes, and that Dante did not seek poetic pastures fenced off from Catholic philosophy. It is only in times like the present, when opposing philosophies battle for power and art is compelled to choose between several public viewpoints, that the presence of social thought in poetry is questioned. The choice before him makes the writer aware of the implications of his work in other fields of discourse and action; it shows him how his private experience illustrates and confirms one public philosophy rather than another. He does not choose between freedom and bondage, but between freedom within one frame and freedom within another. Homer was not free to write from the outlook of Goethe, and many poets today reject the "freedom" to see through the eyes of Robinson Jeffers, for example. Whether a poet has consciously or unconsciously taken to a set of beliefs is irrelevant if we are concerned with objective social effects. In facing the task of creation, however, the distinction may be crucial. In this decade many of our most important poets are pitching their writing in a revolutionary key. But since this is in defiance of habitual attitudes, the poet must consciously adjust his medium to his philosophy. At this point a host of creative questions take on new meaning, because the way the adjustment is made has much to do with the quality of the poem.

Consider the question of theme. Unfortunately many misguided enthusiasts of revolution, effacing their own experience, take for their subject-matter the

public philosophy as such, or attempt to adorn with rhetorical language conventionalized patterns of feeling and action. What they don't see is that these
patterns are, in the final analysis, just as impersonal as the philosophy itself.
Hence we get poems that are really editorial write-ups, a kind of "reality" on
parade from which the deeper spiritual and emotional insights are necessarily
banished. If there is to be an ever-fresh balance between the accent of the
poet and the attitude he shares with other people, he must understand the
connection between what is *real* to him as an individual and what is *real* to
him as a partisan of some given philosophy.

Too often reality is thought of as a pictorial essence, or invoked as a platonic idea. Both the kind of poetry which is a series of snapshots and the kind
which is pure generalization fail to convey the full human meaning of the
subject. Experience as such, abstracted from the social situation that bore and
reared it, is merely a fake short-cut to a desperate originality; and philosophy
divested of the *genius loci,* no matter how nobly declaimed, is like a pedant
preaching in meter. To see oneself truly is to see oneself in relation to the
larger social issue, and to see the larger social issue truly is to see oneself in it.

Of course, to talk about a philosophy without considering its validity would
be like talking about international diplomacy without reference to the concrete interests of nations. We have argued that there is no contradiction between philosophy and experience, but patently such a contradiction is inevitable if the philosophy is false. It was necessary for Eliot to pervert the
testimony of his early poems before he could enter credibly into the sanctum
of theology. On the other hand, poets like Verlaine, Rimbaud, and Crane
accepted no philosophies within their reach, for their experience denied its
validity. But today poets are being drawn to an interpretation of the world
which is but a broader generalization of the evidence inherent in their own
material. No honest and typical experience of our age can exclude a sense of
the organized vulgarity and corruption of modern society. The movement of
history has again made possible the much desired integration of the poet's
conception with the leading ideas of his time.

This necessary integration is being achieved by those revolutionary poets
who have been most aware that their revolt is esthetic as well as social, and
that as such it is a revolt within the tradition of poetry rather than against it.
In the work of Horace Gregory, Kenneth Fearing, and a number of younger
poets—who make up the representative school of revolutionary poetry in this
country—we observe the emergence of a basic symbolism of rejection and
aspiration marking the development of the medium to articulate in its own
terms a new hope and a valiant effort. On this ground they have come in
conflict with a counter-symbolism of barricades and flag-waving lifted from
the surface of events. Those following the line of least resistance grasp these
precipitant and standardized emblems as substitutes for the living tissue of the

thing itself. In their own right such emblems may exercise a certain appeal for naïve readers, yet they remain a means of evading poetic endeavor. No matter what color it runs to, centrally heated rhetoric stifles the spirit. It is only when the poet, sustained by an objective world-view, tempers his symbols in the fires of his own imagination, that he is able to achieve that intensity and truth which is poetry.

From *Poetry: A Magazine of Verse*, Vol. XLVIII
(May, 1936), pp. 98–105. Reprinted by permission.

R. S. CRANE

I. A. Richards on the Art of Interpretation

[1949]

No ONE in our time has written more voluminously than Mr. I. A. Richards on the difficulties that confront the interpreter of philosophical and literary texts, and no one has been more widely credited with the discovery of new principles and techniques by the aid of which, once they are fully elaborated, we may attain, in his own words, to "levels of intelligence in interpretation higher than those yet reached." The books which are cited in support of these high claims, from *The Meaning of Meaning* and *Principles of Literary Criticism* through *Mencius on the Mind* to *The Philosophy of Rhetoric, Interpretation in Teaching,* and *How To Read a Page,* constitute, indeed, an impressive series of disquisitions on what were once called the Liberal Arts, which cannot be neglected by those curious about contemporary developments in intellectual criticism and exegesis. Their originality is undeniable; what is not so certain—and it is into this that I propose to inquire—is whether they have anything substantial to contribute, in the way either of general concepts or of particular methods, which would justify the confidence of Mr. Richards' admirers that he has succeeded in putting the old art of interpreting texts on not only a new but a greatly improved basis.

Although he has written a great many pages in explanation of his doctrine, the doctrine itself is comparatively simple. Let us note two facts, to begin with, concerning the manner in which, according to him, correct thought about both the meaning of texts and the meaning of the meaning of texts must be derived. The two facts are closely related, and they are—as will become evident later—at once postulates of the right method of inquiry into both these questions and necessary consequences of the application of this method to the problems it allows or compels us to pose. In the first place, as Mr. Richards constantly reminds us, there is no thinking about anything that does not proceed inevitably by sorting and analogy. "Thinking," he remarks, "is radically metaphoric. Linkage by analogy is its constituent law or principle, its causal nexus. . . . To think of anything is to take it *as* of a sort." Nor is this true only of the "fluid" discourse which, because of its relaxation of definition, is nearly related to poetry. Recognition of likes and discrimination of unlikes is the universal mode of generalization, and "Mathematics and the sciences, so often praised, and rightly, for the training in Logic they provide, are the leisurely, analyzed, explicitly recorded developments of the very same processes that, well or ill, operate in the main mode of metaphor." "To think of anything is to take it *as* of a sort." To think of the interpretation of discourse, as of discourse itself and of language in general, is, therefore, to think of it in terms of some fundamental analogy, some context or causal nexus with our past experience, by which the words we employ in the inquiry may be made to yield useful generalizations.

But—and this is the second postulate—since the end of our inquiry is knowledge, the only analogy which will serve our purpose is one that exhibits meaning and the meaning of meaning as instances of a sort of thing that in some sense can be pointed to rather than as instances merely of the theorist's attitudes or desires. We must endeavor, in other words, to rid our thinking about the subject from the fictions which have obscured it in the speculations of our predecessors, and to this end we must fashion our language in speaking of it as nearly as possible according to the pattern of natural science. And this means that we must dispense systematically with all terms which men have employed in the vain attempt to say *what* meaning or discourse is or *why* it is so and so, and confine ourselves to the terms we use to say *how* something behaves.

For science, which is simply our most elaborate way of *pointing* to things systematically, tells us and can tell us nothing about the nature of things in any *ultimate* sense. It can never answer any questions of the form: *What* is so and so? It can only tell us *how* so and so behaves. And it does not attempt to do more than this. Nor, indeed, can more than this be done. Those ancient, deeply troubling, formulations that begin with "What" and "Why" prove, when we examine them, to be not questions at all; but requests—for emotional satisfaction. They indicate our desire not for knowledge but for assurance, a point which appears clearly when we look into the "How" of questions and requests, of knowledge and desire.

The only meaningful way, then, in which we can talk about meaning is in terms of some analogy to the local motion of natural objects considered as a temporal sequence of events linked merely by efficient causes. It is a revealing fact that the terms and metaphors (in Mr. Richards' sense of the word) that recur most frequently in the key positions of his analysis are those designated by such expressions as "action," "motion," "behavior," "event." Thus thought "in the widest sense" is "any event in the mind"; "our knowledge is a reaction in us to something"; and the principles of Basic English—a language the theory of which recognizes no categories other than action and reaction—are "the oldest and most indubitable of all" (though at the same time the most modern and scientific) precisely because they represent "what we and our pre-human ancestors know most about," namely, how to perform those movements by which we maintain our vulnerable bodies in a world of "hard, moving, impenetrable and excarnificatory objects." The method of the inquiry is thus determined in a way strictly appropriate to the findings it seeks to obtain; and it will consequently occasion no surprise to the reader to learn from *The Philosophy of Rhetoric* that for Mr. Richards the true theory of interpretation—as distinguished from the superficial or erroneous theories of the past, which have been content with "bad analogies" based on unanswerable questions—not only has some affinities with physics but is "obviously a branch of biology."

It is at this point that the beautiful simplicity of Mr. Richards' scheme shines most clearly through the sophisticated diction and tortuous movement of the prose in which it is explained. Like the early Greek physicists who accounted for all things by means of one or two pairs of contrary terms such as the dense and the rare or Love and Strife, he has found a way of reducing the whole problem of reading texts, even the most elaborately organized ones, to no more than two closely related distinctions, the one primarily psychological, the other (in the broadest sense of the term) linguistic. Meaning, he argues, is a kind of event which occurs whenever these two pairs of contraries mingle in the experience of any sensible creature, whether animal or human being, and there is no variety of meaning, at whatever level of intelligence or education, that cannot be adequately understood by considering it as an instance of this sort of behavior. Pavlov's dog hearing a bell from a distant part of the mansion and thereupon rushing incontinently to the dining-room; a man expecting a flame when he hears the scratch of a match; a scientist in the laboratory observing an instrument and writing down a formula in his notebook; a scholar expounding a passage in Plato—the only principles we need to interpret any of these example of what Mr. Richards calls the universal "sign-situation" are, first, the fact that any response of an organism to a stimulus from its environment involves at once, though in varying proportions on different occasions, an appropriation of the stimulus and a reaction against it, and, second, the circumstance that any awareness the organism may have of the relation between the felt impression and its antecedents or consequences in the environment or in the organism itself is a resultant of the interaction of the immediate experience with remembered experiences of like character in the past. Whether dog or scholar, we are all merely organisms living and functioning in the midst of things, capable of responding both to stimuli from without and to motions or feelings from within; and when we do respond, whether the result is to submit ourselves to things or to assert our purposes emotively with respect to them, the process is invariably one in which something taken as a sign is referred to something, real or fictitious, taken as a thing, by means of the co-operation in our minds of the present occasion with parallel or analogous events remembered from our past.

We need not ask why this is so; it is enough that we are so constituted that whenever a sign (as the sound of the dinner-bell or the occurrence of a puzzling word or construction in a text) is presented to our mind at a particular moment and in a particular set of circumstances, it acts upon us, through a kind of metaphoric attraction of like to like, by calling up the missing parts of the "context" of things or actions with which it has been linked in our previous experience. The meaning of any sign is thus the missing parts of its contexts; it is the "delegated efficacy" which any symbol acquires through its peculiar ability to serve as a substitute "exerting the powers of what is not there." We can have no sign-situation—no act of thinking or interpretation— of which this linking, by analogy, of past and present is not the essential feature; but it is obvious, given our nature as organisms in a world of things, that the process by which signs function as meanings may vary widely from time to time according as the major pull in the experience comes from the world of external objects to which the sign is being referred or from the needs and desires of the organism demanding emotional satisfaction. We may use signs or react to them, in other words, either in terms of their reference to objects or in terms of the effects in emotion and attitude which the reference produces; in the one case the mind is subjected to things, in the other it moulds things to its own purposes and passions. No thought is possible in which the rivalry of the two functions is not to be discerned; however completely we teach our reactions to correspond with external states of affairs, the disturbing factor of the organism is always present.

The theory of discourse which Mr. Richards constructs by analogy with his account of the natural sign-situation is inevitably a theory in which the essential parts of any written composition—-its meanings or our perceptions of its meanings—are treated as discrete events involving the co-operation or rivalry of "contexts." The term "context," as he points out, must here be understood in a double sense.

(1) A word, like any other sign, gets whatever meaning it has through belonging to a recurrent group of events, which may be called its context. Thus a word's context, *in this sense,* is a certain recurrent pattern of *past* groups of events, and to say that its meaning depends upon its context would be to point to the process by which it has acquired its meaning. (2) In another, though a connected sense, a word's context is *the words which surround it in the utterance,* and the other *contemporaneous signs* which govern its interpretation. . . . For clarity we may distinguish the second sort of context by calling it the *setting.*

Whenever, in short, we use words to make a statement, or what looks like a statement, about anything, we are taking part in a process of analogical interaction between the "setting" in which our words are placed and the various "contexts"—there may be an indefinite number of them—which have surrounded the words in their past careers. A meaning is always an instance of a sort, its efficacy dependent upon a perceived likeness between present and former occasions—that is what is meant by the dictum that all thinking is radically metaphoric; and when the former occasions have been particularly numerous and conflicting, it is obvious that the pull of divergent possible interpretations upon the new "setting" must be severe. In his chapter on the meanings of the word "definite" in *Interpretation in Teaching*, Mr. Richards gives some striking examples, from the "protocols" of his students, of the force of these opposing attractions, but there is every reason to suppose that they operate more or less constantly in the literary prose of more expert writers. It is only rarely, indeed—and chiefly in the vocabulary of the rigorously limited laboratory sciences—that the "contexts" determining the meanings of terms approach a state of uniformity which allows us to say that the words and sentences in a passage "mean what they mean absolutely and unconditionally." The function of definition in the sciences is precisely to effect such a control over the interaction of contexts for the specific purpose in hand, but it is seldom, outside "the relatively *simple* fields of the sciences," that an equivalent control is possible, or even desirable.

Argument is a peculiar, specialized use of language to which it has not yet accommodated itself. To put it more strictly, the logical use of words, with single constant senses that are the same for each recurrence, maintained unchanged through a series of sentence manipulations, is an extremely artificial sort of behaviour to which our minds do not lend themselves until after a long and severe training. It is no more like our usual ways of talking than the goosestep is like our strolling gait. And the fluidity, the incessant delicate variation in the meaning of our words, which is a hindrance to explicit argument, is the virtue of language for our other purposes.

It is an error, consequently, to suppose that "if a passage means one thing it cannot at the same time mean another and an incompatible thing." The different contexts or types of context which supply the meaning for a single utterance are in constant rivalry one with another, with the result that we should "expect ambiguity to the widest extent and of the subtlest kinds nearly everywhere, and of course we find it."

The problem of the interaction of contexts is inseparable, for Mr. Richards, from the larger question, arising from the double character of all organic behavior, of the differences and connections among "the various aims of discourse, the purposes for which we speak or write." It is characteristic that here again, abandoning as unfruitful the traditional attempt to differentiate kinds of writing in terms of subject-matter, method, or end, he reduces the problem to a distinction, by analogy with the facts of the universal sign-situation, among "the functions of language." The fundamental opposition thus derived

—familiar to all his readers since the *Principles of Literary Criticism*—is that between "pure scientific impersonal or neutral statement," in which words are used to point to things, and "emotive utterance which expresses and evokes states of feeling." The theory of discourse, thus, must take account of all the complicated ways in which emotional attitude may be combined with reference and reference distorted by attitude; it must be prepared to distinguish clearly the varieties of "statement, full and explicit, or condensed (by abstraction, ambiguity or implication, the hint, the aposiopesis); statement literal or direct, and indirect (by metaphor, simile, comparison, parallel, etc.); suasion, open (from cajolery) or concealed (either as mere statement or as mere ornament) and so on." And the principle which unifies the extremes is still the same principle of the interinanimation of contexts on which, as we have seen, all significances depend.

From Pavlov's dog responding meaningfully to the sound of the dinner-bell to the writer or reader of a prose masterpiece successfully contending with the divergent attractions of linguistic contexts and functions, the transition is thus perfectly clear: to understand the behavior of the one is to know by simple analogy all the truth that can be found out about the behavior of the other. The statement of that truth in words which must themselves necessarily exemplify it constitutes the scientific or theoretical aspect of the philosophy of interpretation. But interpretation, like any sort of animal response, exists only as event, so that to interpret a particular text is to function in a sign-situation in no way different in kind from those precipitated by the sound of the dinner-bell or the scratch of the match, but of course immensely more complicated in the number of co-operating and conflicting stimuli, whether contexts or settings, that are brought to bear on the mind of the interpreter. It is here, in Mr. Richards' argument, that we abandon, at least momentarily, the simplicities of theory for the paradoxes and duplicities of practice. It would seem, on the one hand, that, since interpretation is a natural process, nature herself, assisted by a kind of exercise similar to that which gives strength to the muscles, could well be trusted to make us all at least reasonably good interpreters of books. And this, indeed, is largely true. We are all born, Mr. Richards assures us, with a "natural skill in interpretation"—a skill that need not wait upon training in principles to be "inexplicably, unimaginably and all-but-triumphantly, successful already." Let us then avoid, in education, anything that will interfere with the working of the instinctive dialectic by which, as in all our thinking, we recognize likes and discriminate unlikes as a normal result of the process of contextual interaction. Yet nothing is more evident, we are also told (and the students' "protocols" quoted by Mr. Richards bear out the point), than that the natural skill in interpretation, when it is brought to bear on the words of a particular text, too often becomes confused and fails. An art of interpretation is therefore needed which will start with the "uncanny powers" we have already developed and help us develop them a little further.

For the outlines of such an art Mr. Richards reverts to the distinctions of the medieval trivium. "Less by design than from the nature, history and life of its subject," he says in the introduction to *Interpretation in Teaching*, "this treatise has grown into three parts which correspond roughly to ancient provinces of thought. Rhetoric, Grammar and Logic—the first three liberal Arts, the three ways to intelligence and a command of the mind that met in the Trivium, meet here again." What is needed is precisely the training they are fitted to give, a training now almost entirely lacking in the curriculum; but such a training can be fruitful, can lead to better interpretations, only if Rhetoric, Grammar, and Logic are taught to students not as sciences but as arts, and as arts, moreover, which have in common, for all their differences in emphasis, the basic problems of the sign-situation.

For improvement of the natural skill in interpretation, however, even the minimum of theoretical analysis to which the arts are thus reduced is of little direct importance. The difficulty is not that our students are ignorant of principles; it is rather that they do not know "how to distinguish and meet the varying modes of language *in practice*." Our only sure reliance, therefore, must be the art of the teacher who, though he himself is an expert in the theory of meaning, takes care not to interfere with the natural growth of his pupils by imposing ideas upon them but contents himself with inventing occasions for self-discovery and with devising exercises which will bring his students to an awareness of their failures through comparison with the failures or only partial successes of others. The essential character of the method, as Mr. Richards expounds and illustrates it, is that of a free dialectic working on passages or sentences through exhibition of the contexts of their words or through construction of parallels between them and other passages or sentences. Controls are no doubt necessary, but they take the form not of explicit criteria for determining when a proper adjustment has been made between context and setting but rather of collections of the chief contexts of key words, such as "grammar" or "definite" or "is," or of translations into the vocabulary of Basic English.

The spirit of the procedure Mr. Richards recommends is well exemplified in his own "interpretation," in chapter xvii of *Interpretation in Teaching*, of a sentence from John Stuart Mill's *Inaugural Address at St. Andrews*. The problem is how we know what the pronoun·'their' refers to in the last clause of the following: "Even as mere languages, no modern European language is so valuable a discipline to the intellect as those of Greece and Rome, on account of their regular and complicated structure."

How do we know what 'their' refers to? If we wrote 'their irregular and oversimple structure' the sentence would in several minor ways not mean the same, but most of Mill's main point would be preserved—only 'their' would have been switched over then to modern European languages, not to Greek and Latin. And equally it would be the context [i.e., our knowledge of the recurrent group of past events in which 'irregular' and 'simple' have referred to the structure of modern languages] which told us how to read it. . . . With the setting he is not likely to misread, for we know that Greek and Latin will be thought to be more regular and complicated than modern languages—whatever the facts in the matter, and the assumptions, as to the sorts of regularity and complication involved may be. Moreover, 'regular,' at least, in such an occurrence as this, seems a word of praise [i.e., to have an emotive context] and so goes with 'valuable.' This joins with the setting to bar out the possibility that Mill (as others have sometimes thought) was thinking that the less regular a language the harder the task of learning it and therefore the better the discipline. There is an articulation between 'regular' and 'complicated,' which was lost by my rephrasing, 'their irregular and over-simple structure.' Mill's full point is 'though complicated yet regular.' And this articulation shows us that Mill is thinking of a certain sort of discipline which he expects from Greek and Latin.

It will no doubt have occurred to many readers that the problem of the reference of "their" in Mill's sentence—if problem it be—could have been solved much more expeditiously than it is solved here by the traditional devices of grammatical analysis. Mr. Richards seems to be aware of the objection, but he readily dismisses it as already outlawed by the original assumptions and analogies on which his system is erected:

This kind of analysis of the factors in interpretation can I believe usefully take the place of formal grammatical parsing. Parsing gave exercise in it incidentally, and had value as far as it did; but, in itself, it is an unnatural and distracting antic. This other sort of interpretative study follows closely the actual processes that take place in composition; parsing does not. No one asks, or should ask, himself in writing, 'What does this dependent phrase qualify?' We do all inquire, all the time we are writing, about the consiliences and the articulations of the meanings of the parts with one another; or, if we don't, we can very easily be made to.

It should be clear from what has gone before why he thinks this a completely cogent answer. For if the only questions that can give us the truth about things are questions concerning *how* something behaves, then obviously we are merely troubling our mind with fictions and seeking emotional assurance rather than knowledge if we permit ourselves, whether in writing something of our own or in reading the work of others, to put such queries as *"What does this dependent phrase qualify?"* The antic is indeed both unnatural and distracting—unnatural since it is an arbitrary intrusion into the process of contextual interaction, and distracting since it tends to mingle emotive with referential words. What we can know—and to know this is precisely the end of the art of interpretation—is *how* we have become aware, in so far as we have been successful in our reading, of *how* the words in a particular passage "behave."

Such, in its broad outlines, is the new art of interpreting prose, and of teaching the interpretation of prose, which Mr. Richards would have us substitute for the pre-scientific or magic-mongering systems of the past. His success in winning support for his proposals has been, as we all know, very considerable; and the secret is not hard to find. He has had the great advantage of knowing how to deal with perennial issues in a thoroughly modern style. In an age of faith in biology, he has contrived to frame the problems of literature, with rare consistency, in terms of primordial organic processes; in an age convinced beyond any in the past that the key to all philosophic mysteries, and to most of our practical difficulties as well, is to be found in the study of words, he has effected a remarkable renovation of the liberal arts by substituting for their traditional distinctions and devices a universal theory of signs. The natural appeal of his doctrine, moreover, has been greatly enhanced by the assured, not to say dogmatic, manner of its delivery. Nothing is more distinctive of his exposition, in all his many books, than the "damnatory clauses" in which, as Macaulay said of the Benthamites, his creed abounds "far beyond any theological symbol with which we are acquainted." "I neither am," he has said, "nor hope to be a scholar"; but this modesty has not prevented him from exposing, with his usual vigor of expression, the trivialities, the confusions, the absurdities, the false problems and unnecessary mysteries, the gross evasions of the most interesting issues, which have characterized, almost without exception, the efforts of scholars in the past to deal with the meaning of texts. It is no wonder that, armed with such credentials, he has succeeded in convincing a wide public that only now at last, in this crucial matter of literary interpretation, have our eyes been opened to the reality of things, our first principles properly established, and the one true method of procedure clearly revealed.

It behooves us, therefore, if we are to form an independent judgment of a system so alluring in its modernity, so imposing in its dogmatic rigor, to look a little more closely both at the first principles upon which it is founded and at the practical consequences which appear to flow inevitably from them.

It is obvious, first of all, that Mr. Richards' consideration of discourse is organized about three fundamental terms—the venerable triad which has served countless writers on logic, grammar, and rhetoric since Plato and Aristotle: the words in which texts are composed, the ideas or thoughts they symbolize, and the "real" things or events to which their words and statements refer. This triple distinction is the basis of the famous triangle of meaning first presented in *The Meaning of Meaning* and since then employed consistently in all his linguistic or rhetorical arguments. There is nothing in this fact by itself, of course, that is in any way unique: how else, indeed, could we say anything intelligible about any human discourse save by reference to the subject-matter dealt with in its statements, the doctrines or beliefs set forth concerning this subject-matter, and the words by which these doctrines are expressed? Everything turns, therefore, on the manner in which, in any given theory of discourse or interpretation, the three indispensable factors are related to each other as organizing principles of the discussion. There are only two major possibilities: on the one hand, we may recognize that, since the three terms are in themselves, apart from any use we make of them, completely equivocal words, the literal senses we give to them and the relations constructed among these senses may legitimately vary from context to context, so that our treatment of words or of thought or of subject-matter may be quite distinct according as we are concerned, let us say, with the analysis of poems, or of rhetorical compositions, or of philosophical arguments. Or, on the other hand, we may prefer once for all to fix the relation of words, thoughts, and things in a single pattern, determined by a fundamental analogy, which will henceforth persist throughout our consideration of individual problems as a device by which the particularities of our subject-matter may be resolved into a set of simple universal laws. Now the choice as between these two primary modes of procedure is obviously one that cannot be avoided by any writer who proposes to treat of the problem of interpretation, and once made it just as obviously entails consequences which, if the resulting analysis is self-consistent, must be expected to manifest themselves even in the least details of the system. And the essential point is that the choice itself—however deplorable the fact may seem—is a choice that involves, for the theorist of discourse, simply a decision as to the way in which he intends to use his own words—whether, on the one hand, to mark off sharp distinctions of meaning, so that no one distinguishable aspect of an object is resolved into anything else, or, on the other hand, to make possible a reduction of such distinctions in the interest of a simple unified truth. The choice is therefore independent of the nature of things, except as the nature of things may be held responsible for the necessity of such a choice; and it is logically prior to any true conclusions that may be reached about characteristics of writings which can be attributed to them only through use of the particular mode of definition and argument that has been selected.

Mr. Richards, it need hardly be said, has chosen the second rather than the first of these two ways of dealing with words, thoughts, and things as basic factors in the interpretation of discourse. He has chosen to fix the meanings

and relations of his three central terms prior to his use of them in any particular inquiries; and he has chosen to fix them by means of a fundamental
analogy or "metaphor" (in his sense of that word) which takes various forms
in his writings, but is perhaps best represented by the parallel, in *The Meaning of Meaning,* of Pavlov and his dog.

   The basis of that metaphor, it will be recalled, is a situation involving two
distinct elements, one of which—the dog moving toward the dining-room—is
biological strictly, and the other of which—Pavlov conditioning the dog so
that it will perform this action whenever the dinner-bell rings—is biological
only in an indirect and unimportant sense, its essential character being that
of an interference by human art with the processes of nature. From each of
these elements Mr. Richards derives one of the two basic distinctions of his
scheme: from the motions of the dog considered as an organism capable both
of attending to things outside itself and of responding to stimuli from within,
he takes the distinction which emerges on the level of human speech as the
contrast of emotive and referential language or of fluid and rigid discourse;
from the purposive actions of Pavlov so connecting food and the sound of the
dinner-bell in the reflexes of the dog that, whenever the bell is heard, a
motion is set up toward the usual place of food, he borrows the distinction,
central to the art of interpretation as he conceives it, between linguistic "contexts" and "settings." The device whereby he brings the two elements of the
analogy together in his system involves taking the sound of the dinner-bell as
at once a sign of the previous situations, arranged by Pavlov, in which it had
been connected with food, and as a stimulus to biological reactions on the
part of the dog when it is again heard. When symbols are interpreted thus,
the terms of the original triad of words, thoughts, and things fall into a characteristically simple pattern: the only problem we need consider is that of the
function of individual words as the medium by which, in the uninterrupted
flow of experience, human thought is shaped by reference either to things
(considered always as "sorts") or to fictions that take the place of things. In
this function words may obviously become important instruments for manipulating thoughts to one or another of the two purposes, given by the biological
part of the analogy, for which symbols may be employed—to point to things
or to express our own emotions; but the ways in which they work are determined by things in the sense of the contexts of past events, whether involving
things or thoughts, in which they have been used. The processes of nature,
of meaning and of intention are thus separable only dialectically, as a consequence of our acquired ability to discriminate signs; no independent consideration of any of the three is possible, and hence no independent analysis,
such as has been attempted by writers in the past, of words as applied to
things or to ideas or to words or of ideas in relation to their objects or of

objects in relation to other objects; rather all the problems tend to merge into one, which can only be examined with profit—that is, as a problem of things rather than merely of thought or words—by considering how particular words "behave" with respect to each other and to the things and thoughts they bring before our minds.

It is this radical unification of the whole traditional analysis in terms of the "behavior" of individual words that impels Mr. Richards to dismiss, with such telling effect, not only the notion that any art or methodology is involved in his firsthand dealings with language, but likewise all the various systems of grammar, logic, and rhetoric in which previous writers—more concerned, in his view, with theories than with applications—have developed principles for an analysis of the structural aspects of discourse or for a particularized consideration of its various kinds. Preoccupied as he is with inducing a heightened awareness of individual sign-situations by comparisons of words, he has nothing to offer but a universal method for the reading of texts—a method without any devices for discriminating differences in subject-matter or in method or in intention in the sense of the specific ends, peculiar to the given work, to which means have been rationally adapted by the author.

The causes of this curious dialectical asceticism will perhaps become clear if we revert to the analogy in the light of which Mr. Richards' system has been constructed. The difficulty is not, of course, that the facts upon which one half of the metaphor is based involve nothing more exalted than the natural motions of a dog; readers of Plato, at all events, will not have forgotten the excellent use which Socrates makes of this same animal in the *Republic* when it is a question of determining what virtues are appropriate to the guardians of the state. And there is surely no reason why an analysis of argument, more nearly adequate than any Mr. Richards gives us for the explanation of structural characteristics in prose, could not be developed from postulates as strictly biological as his. The proof, if proof were needed, is afforded by the recent work of John Dewey, *Logic: The Theory of Inquiry*. The condition of such a development, as Mr. Dewey shows, is simply the recognition that organic behavior is typically sequential; that, as appears plainly in such "unified and continuous" animal responses as hunting and stalking prey, it is not merely "a succession and compounding of independent discrete reflex-art units" but a kind of elementary problem-solving with direction and cumulative force. If this is granted, and if we assume a continuity of evolution from animal forms and activities to those of man, then, given the potentiality, on the human level, of a cultural environment and of reflective thought, we need no other principles whereby to justify, in purely naturalistic terms, a fairly elaborate analysis of intellectual discourse as an art of fitting logical means to consequences in the solution of problems. Mr. Richards, however, although he can insist that the theory of interpretation is obviously a branch of biology, is not free to push the biological part of his metaphor as far as this; the dog is not simply a dog, it is Pavlov's dog; and this being the case, its contribution to the explanation of language is necessarily limited to those aspects of its natural behavior which are adequately described—to borrow Mr. Dewey's phrase—as "simply a succession of isolated and independent units of excitation-reaction," or, in other words, as discrete events considered apart from any possible sequence of actions in which they function as means to an intelligible end. To the extent, therefore, that the problem of discourse and of the interpretation of discourse is determined by this part of Mr. Richard's analogy, the most we can expect in the way of principles is a simple pair of contraries applicable only to particular words.

The relation of means and consequences, however, is clearly implied in the part of the metaphor which concerns Pavlov, and the beginnings at least of an analysis of intellectual method, relevant to many kinds of prose literature, might easily have been derived by considering what is involved when a scientist selects one experiment rather than another as more directly conducive to a specific end. Needless to say, it is not this aspect of Pavlov that interests Mr. Richards, but rather two more limited aspects, one of which has to do with the results of his acts of conditioning as these appear in the subsequent operations of the dog whenever the dinner-bell rings, and the other of which relates to the processes and immediate intentions of the experiment itself. From the first comes the idea of the interaction of "contexts" and "settings" which is, for Mr. Richards, the essence of "meaning" interpreted as a natural event solely in terms of its efficient cause. But it is still necessary to account for the contexts themselves which determine materially the behavior of signs whenever these occur in a novel setting; and since, when the problem is transferred to the level of human discourse, there can be no longer a Pavlov conditioning our reflexes, some substitute, less external in a literal sense to the individual organism but still in a way external, must evidently be discovered for the function he performs as experimenter in the original situation. That substitute is, in the first place, the long history of contextual interactions, in other men and in our past lives, which we call our cultural and linguistic inheritance. By this, as represented, for example, in the vast proliferation of meanings contained in the *Oxford English Dictionary* or in Mr. Richards' lists, we are all controlled, much as Pavlov's dog was controlled, in each of our uses or interpretations of any of the words we write or read, so that ambiguity—i.e., the intrusion into a particular setting of many contexts—is an ever-present and never entirely soluble problem. But what has been conditioned may also, to a certain extent at least, be reconditioned; and if Pavlov persists in Mr. Richards' account of language and discourse as the more or less external control exercised over our words and thoughts by past associations of words with things, he also re-emerges, especially in practical treatises like *In-*

terpretation in Teaching, in the person of the teacher who sets his pupils exercises in verbal comparisons and translations to the end of heightening their awareness of how words behave in relation to other words and to things and ideas. He is the enlightened teacher, but he is also that most valuable instrument of the enlightened teacher, Basic English—a language that contributes to our understanding of both things and words by reducing the vocabulary of English to those words which are closest to things inasmuch as their primary contexts are the organic motions of putting and taking, giving and getting, pointing and feeling; a language, moreover, that enables us to cope more efficiently with the problem of ambiguity by increasing still farther that disproportion between the finiteness of words and the infiniteness of things from which ambiguity arises!

It would be unfair to say of the procedure Mr. Richards recommends for the practice and teaching of interpretation that it consists merely of a technique of lexicographical exercise without other ends than the exercise itself. The ends are there, and they are stated variously as understanding, as intelligence, as heightened awareness, as intellectual discernment, as insight, as self-discovery, as improvement of our command of all the interconnections of thought, non-verbal as well as verbal. Yet, however distinct these aims may appear in statements of them taken out of their context in Mr. Richards' system, it is evident, when we recall the basic principles of that system, that they are all ends as nearly identifiable with the means devised for their realization as was Pavlov's awareness of the behavior of his dog with the experiment he conducted for the sake of inducing that behavior. What Mr. Richards gives us, in short, in following out this aspect of his analogy, is simply a set of experimental devices for bringing about in the reader a sharpened consciousness of linguistic particulars as sorts of universal motions.

To go beyond this either by traveling the biological road taken by Mr. Dewey or by developing the implications of Pavlov as the artist in experiments would entail the elaboration of a general scheme of analysis applicable to particular texts in such a way that the particularity of their structure rather than the universality of their material constituents would become the center of attention. He is restrained, however, from adopting either of these courses by the peculiar character of the metaphor from which his whole method springs. It is a metaphor resting on what is clearly a constructed situation, partly natural and partly artificial, with the two elements so related that any full development of one of them is immediately checked or interfered with by some trait in the other. In the end, for Mr. Richards, it is nature which exerts the stronger dialectical pull, and it does so by virtue of the skeptical implications for our understanding of the terms of philosophy and the arts contained in his biological distinction between pointing and feeling, with its equivalent in the linguistic contrast of referential and emotive words. We have seen that this distinction underlies his doubts about the scientific meaningfulness of any other questions than those which ask *how* something behaves, and so deprives him from the start of all explanatory resources except such as are furnished by his very limited conception of the efficient cause. We have seen how it leads him to posit, as the ideal mode of interpretation, a procedure which, unlike the unnatural and distracting antic of parsing, follows closely the actual processes of composition as these should be if not as they are. And we may suggest that the strong suspicion of previous theories of criticism and interpretation which runs throughout his works, and which confirms him in his preference for a method so nearly universal that it seems to him no method at all, gains much of its force from precisely this bias in favor of one rather than the other of the two components, not quite perfectly fused, of the original metaphor.

The method is a universal one, but it *is* a method, and as such it is only fair to judge it, finally, in terms of its consequences apart from the somewhat arbitrarily constructed first principles by which it is validated theoretically. And first of all, as we have noted so often, there is a whole range of problems —real problems, too, since they force themselves on us, independently of any theories of interpretation, whenever we attempt to understand a text as a whole or to compare two writings on the same subject—for the solution of which his scheme provides no apparatus whatever. Thus we are constantly tempted to ask, in reading prose works of any distinction, on what principles the words or sentences are ordered in this or that passage, or why the parts of the argument are arranged as they are, or how we may account for the author's insistence on certain aspects of his problem and his neglect of other aspects which, in the writings of his predecessors or successors, have usually been given a prominent place. In order to find answers to such questions we obviously need devices which will enable us to discover a writer's basic terms, not merely as so many frequently recurrent words, but rather as the fundamental scheme of concepts by means of which his problem is stated and the parts and order of his argument determined; we need principles by which, once the terms have been established, possible modes of working with them may be distinguished; and we need other principles, involving still more particularized discriminations of ends and means, in the light of which the peculiar structural characteristics of individual works may be understood and appreciated. It is evident that no such principles or devices are to be looked for anywhere in Mr. Richards' many publications. He speaks much of purposes in writing, but what he has in mind are the universal purposes, or linguistic "functions," common to the sophisticated author and the simplest biological organism, not those which differentiate writers as voluntary agents. He writes books which expound, as we have seen, a highly characteristic

system of thought; but nowhere in these books does he provide means whereby
the system may be understood in its distinctive outlines or whereby we may
progress, in our reading of his books, beyond what is stated in separate paragraphs and sentences.

It is to these, indeed—the significant wholes to which his method tends to
reduce all literature—that he systematically endeavors to confine our attention. For the Richardian interpreter of discourse there can be only one problem, and whether that problem is stated generally as the interaction of contexts and settings or is specified as ambiguity or metaphor or confusion of
statement and definition, it is clearly one which can be adequately posed and
solved in terms of isolated statements considered apart from the total artistic
or logical structure of the works in which they appear. For the problem is
really one of the universal behavior of words as determined by events which
in any strict sense are extra-literary, and a solution is possible just as soon as
we have enough of the immediate setting of the word before us to permit an
estimate of what various contexts have been at work. Thus—to adapt an example from *Basic Rules of Reason*—it is not necessary to read the whole of
the *Preface to the "Lyrical Ballads"* in order to deal with the question of what
is meant by "poetry" in Wordsworth's assertion that "poetry is the look on the
face of science"; instead we have only to recognize that the problem turns
essentially on the meaning of "is," that "is" may have different meanings according as the sentences in which it occurs are definitions of words or statements about the things of which the word is the name, that if we compare
the saying of Wordsworth with other sayings about "poetry" (Mr. Richards
gives a good many of them) we see that it is more like a statement than a
definition, and that as such, separated from a definition, it may have as many
senses as Wordsworth or we ourselves at any time have attached to the word.

All this, granted the way in which the problem is stated, is no doubt true,
and there is clearly abundant justification in the circumstance for Mr. Richards' insistence on our need of a "better apparatus for controlling the senses of
our words." A twofold difficulty, however, immediately confronts us. On the
one hand, even if we allow that the question of Wordsworth's meaning in the
sentence quoted can be intelligibly discussed in terms of that sentence alone
plus the "contexts" of its words, there is nothing, so far as one can see, in the
"better apparatus" Mr. Richards gives us—neither in his lists of the senses of
"is" or of "poetry" nor in his directions for translation exercises into Basic
English—that can do anything more than heighten our awareness of the
problem. And, on the other hand, if we are seriously interested in discovering
Wordsworth's intention rather than simply in playing a new and somewhat
complicated linguistic game, and if consequently we insist on considering the
question not in the vacuum of a single sentence but in the total context,

highly particularized as it is, of Wordsworth's argument and method in the *Preface*, then we are already provided, in various of the devices afforded by traditional dialectic, with much of the apparatus we need. For the problem of ambiguity is not, as many of Mr. Richards' disciples suppose, a new one; and if the problem is what we have always thought it to be, the means of dealing with it available to us in (say) the first book of the *Topics* would still seem adequate to most of our uses. It is not easy, therefore, to escape the suspicion that what is at issue for Mr. Richards is not the question of ambiguity, in the usual meaning, at all; that his concern is less with solutions that make sense of difficult texts in their authors' terms than with the discovery or manufacture of problems by which linguistic wonder may be excited, and that that method is best, accordingly, which so restricts its means of solution that what emerges from any act of interpretation is not so much understanding of the author as increased insight into our own marvelous but somewhat confused minds.

There would be no objection to this were it not that the reading of a book in any sense that involves doing justice to the distinctive intentions of its author is rendered impossible thereby. For the essence of Mr. Richards' method, so far as it assumes a positive character at all, is translation; and what inevitably happens when that technique is applied to a writer of any intellectual sophistication or systematic integrity will be plain to whoever meditates on the strange fate of John Stuart Mill in chapter xvii of *Interpretation in Teaching*. But translation in the mode exhibited in this chapter is innocent enough when compared to the fundamental distortion necessarily undergone by any writer who philosophizes in other categories than action and reaction when his statements are subjected to the Procrustean dialectic of Basic English—a language whose key terms have been selected in explicit opposition to most of the varied ways of dealing with the problem of words, ideas, and things to be found in the important prose writers of the past.

It is at this point that the question of method and the practical consequences thereof rejoins the question of principles. For if it be indeed true, as has been occasionally insinuated by followers of Mr. Richards, that his is a theory that ends all theories except itself and the better thought about language we may look for in the future, then the objections we have brought against his program for the reform of interpretation are not only irrelevant but philosophically unsound—expressions of our wishes that carry over into a new age the fictions and magic-charged concepts of the past. Our examination of Mr. Richards' views will perhaps have been justified if it has revealed the essential circularity of all such retorts. For what is the force of an appeal to the nature of things against rival doctrines of language or discourse when that nature itself has been determined by a decision, prior to any inquiry, to identify reality only with what can be signified in a particular fixed relationship among three equivocal words? And what is there to compel an abandonment of the distinctions of traditional grammar or logic in an argument which derives all its negative cogency from a metaphor so admirably adapted to the end of destroying such distinctions as that upon which Mr. Richards' system is based?

From *Ethics*, Vol. LIX, No. 2, Part I, (January, 1949), pp. 112–126. Reprinted by permission of the author and editors.

CLEANTH BROOKS
Irony as a Principle of Structure
[1949]

ONE can sum up modern poetic technique by calling it the rediscovery of metaphor and the full commitment to metaphor. The poet can legitimately step out into the universal only by first going through the narrow door of the particular. The poet does not select an abstract theme and then embellish it with concrete details. On the contrary, he must establish the details, must abide by the details, and through his realization of the details attain to whatever general meaning he can attain. The meaning must issue from the particulars; it must not seem to be arbitrarily forced upon the particulars. Thus, our conventional habits of language have to be reversed when we come to deal with poetry. For here it is the tail that wags the dog. Better still, here it is the tail of the kite—the tail that makes the kite fly—the tail that renders the kite more than a frame of paper blown crazily down the wind.

The tail of the kite, it is true, seems to negate the kite's function: it weights down something made to rise; and in the same way, the concrete particulars with which the poet loads himself seem to deny the universal to which he aspires. The poet wants to "say" something. Why, then, doesn't he say it directly and forthrightly? Why is he willing to say it only through his metaphors? Through his metaphors, he risks saying it partially and obscurely, and risks not saying it at all. But the risk must be taken, for direct statement leads to abstraction and threatens to take us out of poetry altogether.

The commitment to metaphor thus implies, with respect to general theme, a principle of indirection. With respect to particular images and statements, it implies a principle of organic relationship. That is, the poem is not a collection of beautiful or "poetic" images. If there really existed objects which were somehow intrinsically "poetic," still the mere assemblage of these would not give us a poem. For in that case, one might arrange bouquets of these poetic images and thus create poems by formula. But the elements of a poem are related to each other, not as blossoms juxtaposed in a bouquet, but as the blossoms are related to the other parts of a growing plant. The beauty of the poem is the flowering of the whole plant, and needs the stalk, the leaf, and the hidden roots.

If this figure seems somewhat highflown, let us borrow an analogy from another art: the poem is like a little drama. The total effect proceeds from all the elements in the drama, and in a good poem, as in a good drama, there is no waste motion and there are no superfluous parts.

In coming to see that the parts of a poem are related to each other organically, and related to the total theme indirectly, we have come to see the importance of *context*. The memorable verses in poetry—even those which seem somehow intrinsically "poetic"—show on inspection that they derive their poetic quality from their relation to a particular context. We may, it is true, be tempted to say that Shakespeare's "Ripeness is all" is poetic because it is a sublime thought, or because it possesses simple eloquence; but that is to forget the context in which the passage appears. The proof that this is so becomes obvious when we contemplate such unpoetic lines as "vitality is all," "serenity is all," "maturity is all,"—statements whose philosophical import in the abstract is about as defensible as that of "ripeness is all." Indeed, the commonplace word "never" repeated five times becomes one of the most poignant lines in *Lear*, but it becomes so because of the supporting context. Even the "meaning" of any particular item is modified by the context. For what is said is said in a particular situation and by a particular dramatic character.

The last instances adduced can be most properly regarded as instances of "loading" from the context. The context endows the particular word or image or statement with significance. Images so charged become symbols; statements so charged become dramatic utterances. But there is another way in which to look at the impact of the context upon the part. The part is modified by the pressure of the context.

Now the *obvious* warping of a statement by the context we characterize as "ironical." To take the simplest instance, we say "this is a fine state of affairs," and in certain contexts the statement means quite the opposite of what it purports to say literally. This is sarcasm, the most obvious kind of irony. Here a complete reversal of meaning is effected: effected by the context, and pointed, probably, by the tone of voice. But the modification can be most important even though it falls far short of sarcastic reversal, and it need not be underlined by the tone of voice at all. The tone of irony can be effected by the skillful disposition of the context. Gray's *Elegy* will furnish an obvious example.

> Can storied urn or animated bust
> Back to its mansion call the fleeting breath?
> Can Honour's voice provoke the silent dust,
> Or Flatt'ry soothe the dull cold ear of death?

In its context, the question is obviously rhetorical. The answer has been implied in the characterization of the breath as fleeting and of the ear of death as dull and cold. The form is that of a question, but the manner in which the question has been asked shows that it is no true question at all.

These are obvious instances of irony, and even on this level, much more poetry is ironical than the reader may be disposed to think. Many of Hardy's poems and nearly all of Housman's, for example, reveal irony quite as definite and overt as this. Lest these examples, however, seem to specialize irony in the direction of the sardonic, the reader ought to be reminded that irony, even in its obvious and conventionally recognized forms, comprises a wide variety of modes: tragic irony, self-irony, playful, arch, mocking, or gentle irony, etc. The body of poetry which may be said to contain irony in the ordinary senses of the term stretches from *Lear,* on the one hand, to "Cupid and Campaspe Played," on the other.

What indeed would be a statement wholly devoid of an ironic potential—a statement that did not show any qualification of the context? One is forced to offer statements like "Two plus two equals four," or "The square on the hypotenuse of a right triangle is equal to the sum of the squares on the two sides." The meaning of these statements is unqualified by any context; if they are true, they are equally true in any possible context.[1] These statements are properly abstract, and their terms are pure denotations. (If "two" or "four" actually happened to have connotations for the fancifully minded, the connotations would be quite irrelevant: they do not participate in the meaningful structure of the statement.)

But connotations are important in poetry and do enter significantly into the structure of meaning which is the poem. Moreover, I should claim also—as a corollary of the foregoing proposition—that poems never contain abstract statements. That is, any "statement" made in the poem bears the pressure of the context and has its meaning modified by the context. In other words, the statements made—including those which appear to be philosophical generalizations—are to be read as if they were speeches in a drama. Their relevance, their propriety, their rhetorical force, even their meaning, cannot be divorced from the context in which they are imbedded.

The principle I state may seem a very obvious one, but I think that it is nonetheless very important. It may throw some light upon the importance of

[1] This is not to say, of course, that such statements are not related to a particular "universe of discourse." They are indeed, as are all statements of whatever kind. But I distinguish here between "context" and "universe of discourse." "Two plus two equals four" is not dependent on a special dramatic context in the way in which a "statement" made in a poem is. Compare "two plus two equals four" and the same "statement" as contained in Housman's poem:

> —To think that two and two are four
>   And neither five nor three
> The heart of man has long been sore
>   And long 'tis like to be.

the term *irony* in modern criticism. As one who has certainly tended to over-use the term *irony* and perhaps, on occasion, has abused the term, I am closely concerned here. But I want to make quite clear what that concern is: it is not to justify the term *irony* as such, but rather to indicate why modern critics are so often tempted to use it. We have doubtless stretched the term too much, but it has been almost the only term available by which to point to a general and important aspect of poetry.

Consider this example: The speaker in Matthew Arnold's "Dover Beach" states that the world, "which seems to lie before us like a land of dreams . . . hath really neither joy nor love nor light. . . ." For some readers the statement will seem an obvious truism. (The hero of a typical Hemingway short story or novel, for example, will say this, though of course in a rather different idiom.) For other readers, however, the statement will seem false, or at least highly questionable. In any case, if we try to "prove" the proposition, we shall raise some very perplexing metaphysical questions, and in doing so, we shall certainly also move away from the problems of the poem and, finally, from a justification of the poem. For the lines are to be justified in the poem in terms of the context: the speaker is standing beside his loved one, looking out of the window on the calm sea, listening to the long withdrawing roar of the ebbing tide, and aware of the beautiful delusion of moonlight which "blanches" the whole scene. The "truth" of the statement, and of the poem itself, in which it is imbedded, will be validated, not by a majority report of the association of sociologists, or a committee of physical scientists, or of a congress of meta-physicians who are willing to stamp the statement as proved. How is the statement to be validated? We shall probably not be able to do better than to apply T. S. Eliot's test: does the statement seem to be that which the mind of the reader can accept as coherent, mature, and founded on the facts of ex-perience? But when we raise such a question, we are driven to consider the poem as drama. We raise such further questions as these: Does the speaker seem carried away with his own emotions? Does he seem to oversimplify the situation? Or does he, on the other hand, seem to have won to a kind of detachment and objectivity? In other words, we are forced to raise the ques-tion as to whether the statement grows properly out of a context; whether it acknowledges the pressures of the context; whether it is "ironical"—or merely callow, glib, and sentimental.

I have suggested elsewhere that the poem which meets Eliot's test comes to the same thing as I. A. Richards' "poetry of synthesis"—that is, a poetry which does not leave out what is apparently hostile to its dominant tone, and which, because it is able to fuse the irrelevant and discordant, has come to terms with itself and is invulnerable to irony. Irony, then, in this further sense, is not only an acknowledgment of the pressures of a context. Invulnera-bility to irony is the stability of a context in which the internal pressures balance and mutually support each other. The stability is like that of the arch: the very forces which are calculated to drag the stones to the ground actually provide the principle of support—a principle in which thrust and counterthrust become the means of stability.

In many poems the pressures of the context emerge in obvious ironies. Marvell's "To His Coy Mistress" or Raleigh's "Nymph's Reply" or even Gray's "Elegy" reveal themselves as ironical, even to readers who use irony strictly in the conventional sense.

But can other poems be subsumed under this general principle, and do they show a comparable basic structure? The test case would seem to be presented by the lyric, and particularly the simple lyric. Consider, for example, one of Shakespeare's songs:

> Who is Silvia: what is she
>   That all our swains commend her?
> Holy, fair, and wise is she;
>   The heavens such grace did lend her,
> That she might admired be.
>
> Is she kind as she is fair?
>   For beauty lives with kindness.
> Love doth to her eyes repair,
>   To help him of his blindness,
> And, being help'd, inhabits there.
>
> Then to Silvia let us sing,
>   That Silvia is excelling;
> She excels each mortal thing
>   Upon the dull earth dwelling:
> To her let us garlands bring.

On one level the song attempts to answer the question "Who is Silvia?" and the answer given makes her something of an angel and something of a goddess. She excels each mortal thing "Upon the dull earth dwelling." Silvia herself, of course, dwells upon that dull earth, though it is presumably her own brightness which makes it dull by comparison. (The dull earth, for example, yields bright garlands which the swains are bringing to her.) Why does she excel each mortal thing? Because of her virtues ("Holy, fair, and wise is she"), and these are a celestial gift. She is heaven's darling ("The heavens such grace did lend her").

Grace, I suppose, refers to grace of movement, and some readers will insist that we leave it at that. But since Silvia's other virtues include holiness and wisdom, and since her grace has been lent from above, I do not think that we can quite shut out the theological overtones. Shakespeare's audience would have found it even more difficult to do so. At any rate, it is interesting to see what happens if we are aware of these overtones. We get a delightful richness, and we also get something very close to irony.

The motive for the bestowal of grace—that she might admired be—is oddly untheological. But what follows is odder still, for the love that "doth to her eyes repair" is not, as we might expect, Christian "charity" but the little pagan god Cupid ("Love doth to her eyes repair, / To help him of his blindness.") But if Cupid lives in her eyes, then the second line of the stanza takes on another layer of meaning. "For beauty lives with kindness" becomes not merely a kind of charming platitude—actually often denied in human experience. (The Petrarchan lover, for example, as Shakespeare well knew, frequently found a beautiful and *cruel* mistress.) The second line, in this context, means also that the love god lives with the kind Silvia, and indeed has taken these eyes that sparkle with kindness for his own.

Is the mixture of pagan myth and Christian theology, then, an unthinking confusion into which the poet has blundered, or is it something wittily combined? It is certainly not a confusion, and if blundered into unconsciously, it is a happy mistake. But I do not mean to press the issue of the poet's self-consciousness (and with it, the implication of a kind of playful irony). Suffice it to say that the song is charming and delightful, and that the mingling of elements is proper to a poem which is a deft and light-fingered attempt to suggest the quality of divinity with which lovers perennially endow maidens who are finally mortal. The touch is light, there is a lyric grace, but the tone is complex, nonetheless.

I shall be prepared, however, to have this last example thrown out of court since Shakespeare, for all his universality, was a contemporary of the metaphysical poets, and may have incorporated more of their ironic complexity than is necessary or normal. One can draw more innocent and therefore more convincing examples from Wordsworth's Lucy poems.

> She dwelt among the untrodden ways
>   Beside the springs of Dove,
> A maid whom there were none to praise
>   And very few to love;
>
> A violet by a mossy stone
>   Half hidden from the eye!
> Fair as a star, when only one
>   Is shining in the sky.
>
> She lived unknown, and few could know
>   When Lucy ceased to be;
> But she is in her grave, and, oh,
>   The difference to me.

Which is Lucy really like—the violet or the star? The context in general seems to support the violet comparison. The violet, beautiful but almost unnoticed, already half hidden from the eye, is now, as the poem ends, completely hidden in its grave, with none but the poet to grieve for its loss. The star comparison may seem only vaguely relevant—a conventional and here a somewhat anomalous compliment. Actually, it is not difficult to justify the star comparison: to her lover's eyes, she is the solitary star. She has no rivals, nor would the idea of rivalry, in her unselfconscious simplicity, occur to her.

The violet and the star thus balance each other and between themselves define the situation: Lucy was, from the viewpoint of the great world, unnoticed, shy, modest, and half hidden from the eye, but from the standpoint of her lover, she is the single star, completely dominating that world, not arrogantly like the sun, but sweetly and modestly, like the star. The implicit contrast is that so often developed ironically by John Donne in his poems where the lovers, who amount to nothing in the eyes of the world, become, in their own eyes, each the other's world—as in "The Good-Morrow," where their love makes "one little room an everywhere," or as in "The Canonization," where the lovers drive into the mirrors of each other's eyes the "towns, countries, courts"—which make up the great world; and thus find that world in themselves. It is easy to imagine how Donne would have exploited the contrast between the violet and the star, accentuating it, developing the irony, showing how the violet was really like its antithesis, the star, etc.

Now one does not want to enter an Act of Uniformity against the poets. Wordsworth is entitled to his method of simple juxtaposition with no underscoring of the ironical contrast. But it is worth noting that the contrast with its ironic potential is there in his poem. It is there in nearly all of Wordsworth's successful lyrics. It is certainly to be found in "A slumber did my spirit seal."

> A slumber did my spirit seal;
>   I had no human fears:
> She seemed a thing that could not feel
>   The touch of earthly years.
>
> No motion has she now, no force;
>   She neither hears nor sees,
> Rolled round in earth's diurnal course,
>   With rocks, and stones, and trees.

The lover's insensitivity to the claims of mortality is interpreted as a lethargy of spirit—a strange slumber. Thus the "human fears" that he lacked are apparently the fears normal to human beings. But the phrase has a certain pliability. It could mean fears *for* the loved one as a mortal human being; and the lines that follow tend to warp the phrase in this direction: it does not occur to the lover that he needs to fear for one who cannot be touched by "earthly years." We need not argue that Wordsworth is consciously using a witty device, a purposed ambiguity; nor need we conclude that he is confused. It is enough to see that Wordsworth has developed, quite "normally," let us say, a context calculated to pull "human fears" in opposed directions, and that the slightest pressure of attention on the part of the reader precipitates an ironical effect.

As we move into the second stanza, the potential irony almost becomes overt. If the slumber has sealed the lover's spirit, a slumber, immersed in which he thought it impossible that his loved one could perish, so too a slumber has now definitely sealed *her* spirit: "No motion has she now, no force; / She neither hears nor sees." It is evident that it is her unnatural slumber that has waked him out of his. It is curious to speculate on what Donne or Marvell would have made of this.

Wordsworth, however, still does not choose to exploit the contrast as such. Instead, he attempts to suggest something of the lover's agonized shock at the loved one's present lack of motion—of his response to her utter and horrible inertness. And how shall he suggest this? He chooses to suggest it, not by saying that she lies as quiet as marble or as a lump of clay; on the contrary, he attempts to suggest it by imagining her in violent motion—violent, but imposed motion, the same motion indeed which the very stones share, whirled about as they are in earth's diurnal course. Why does the image convey so powerfully the sense of something inert and helpless? Part of the effect, of course, resides in the fact that a dead lifelessness is suggested more sharply by an object's being whirled about by something else than by an image of the object in repose. But there are other matters which are at work here: the sense of the girl's falling back into the clutter of things, companioned by things chained like a tree to one particular spot, or by things completely inanimate, like rocks and stones. Here, of course, the concluding figure leans upon the suggestion made in the first stanza, that the girl once seemed something not subject to earthly limitations at all. But surely, the image of the whirl itself is important in its suggestion of something meaningless—motion that mechanically repeats itself. And there is one further element: the girl, who to her lover seemed a thing that could not feel the touch of earthly years, is caught up helplessly into the empty whirl of the earth which measures and makes time. She is touched by and held by earthly time in its most powerful and horrible image. The last figure thus seems to me to summarize the poem—to offer to almost every facet of meaning suggested in the earlier lines a concurring and resolving image which meets and accepts and reduces each item to its place in the total unity.

Wordsworth, as we have observed above, does not choose to point up specifically the ironical contrast between the speaker's former slumber and the loved one's present slumber. But there is one ironical contrast which he does stress: this is the contrast between the two senses in which the girl becomes insulated against the "touch of earthly years." In the first stanza, she "could not feel / The touch of earthly years" because she seemed divine and immortal. But in the second stanza, now in her grave, she still does not "feel the touch of earthly years," for, like the rocks and stones, she feels nothing at all. It is true that Wordsworth does not repeat the verb "feels"; instead he writes "She neither *hears* nor *sees*." But the contrast, though not commented upon directly by any device of verbal wit, is there nonetheless, and is bound to make itself felt in any sensitive reading of the poem. The statement of the first stanza has been literally realized in the second, but its meaning has been ironically reversed.

Ought we, then, to apply the term *ironical* to Wordsworth's poem? Not necessarily. I am trying to account for my temptation to call such a poem ironical—not to justify my yielding to the temptation—least of all to insist that others so transgress. Moreover, Wordsworth's poem seems to me admirable, and I entertain no notion that it might have been more admirable still had John Donne written it rather than William Wordsworth. I shall be content if I can make a much more modest point: namely, that since both Wordsworth and Donne are poets, their work has at basis a similar structure, and that the dynamic structure—the pattern of thrust and counterthrust—which we associate with Donne has its counterpart in Wordsworth. In the work of both men, the relation between part and part is organic, which means that each part modifies and is modified by the whole.

Yet to intimate that there are potential ironies in Wordsworth's lyric may seem to distort it. After all, is it not simple and spontaneous? With these terms we encounter two of the critical catchwords of the nineteenth century, even as *ironical* is in danger of becoming a catchword of our own period. Are the terms *simple* and *ironical* mutually exclusive? What after all do we mean by *simple* or by *spontaneous*? We may mean that the poem came to the poet easily and even spontaneously: very complex poems may—indeed have—come just this way. Or the poem may seem in its effect on the reader a simple and spontaneous utterance: some poems of great complexity possess this quality. What is likely to cause trouble here is the intrusion of a special theory of composition. It is fairly represented as an intrusion since a theory as to how a poem is written is being allowed to dictate to us how the poem is to be read. There is no harm in thinking of Wordsworth's poem as simple and spontaneous unless these terms deny complexities that actually exist in the poem, and unless they justify us in reading the poem with only half our minds. A slumber ought not to seal the *reader's* spirit as he reads this poem, or any other poem.

I have argued that irony, taken as the acknowledgment of the pressures of context, is to be found in poetry of every period and even in simple lyrical poetry. But in the poetry of our own time, this pressure reveals itself strikingly. A great deal of modern poetry does use irony as its special and perhaps its characteristic strategy. For this there are reasons, and compelling reasons. To cite only a few of these reasons: there is the breakdown of a common symbolism; there is the general scepticism as to universals; not least important, there is the depletion and corruption of the very language itself, by advertising and by the mass-produced arts of radio, the moving picture, and pulp fiction. The modern poet has the task of rehabilitating a tired and drained language so that it can convey meanings once more with force and with exactitude. This task of qualifying and modifying language is perennial; but it is imposed on the modern poet as a special burden. Those critics who attribute the use of ironic techniques to the poet's own bloodless sophistication and tired scepticism would be better advised to refer these vices to his potential readers, a public corrupted by Hollywood and the Book of the Month Club. For the modern poet is not addressing simple primitives but a public sophisticated by commercial art.

At any rate, to the honor of the modern poet be it said that he has frequently succeeded in using his ironic techniques to win through to clarity and passion. Randall Jarrell's "Eighth Air Force" represents a success of this sort.

> If, in an odd angle of the hutment,
> A puppy laps the water from a can
> Of flowers, and the drunk sergeant shaving
> Whistles O Paradiso!—shall I say that man
> Is not as men have said: a wolf to man?
>
> The other murderers troop in yawning;
> Three of them play Pitch, one sleeps, and one
> Lies counting missions, lies there sweating
> Till even his heart beats: One; One; One.
> O murderers! . . . Still, this is how it's done:
>
> This is a war. . . . But since these play, before they die,
> Like puppies with their puppy; since, a man,
> I did as these have done, but did not die—
> I will content the people as I can
> And give up these to them: Behold the man!
>
> I have suffered, in a dream, because of him,
> Many things; for this last saviour, man,
> I have lied as I lie now. But what is lying?

Men wash their hands, in blood, as best they can:
I find no fault in this just man.

There are no superfluous parts, no dead or empty details. The airmen in their hutment are casual enough and honest enough to be convincing. The raw building is domesticated: there are the flowers in water from which the mascot, a puppy, laps. There is the drunken sergeant, whistling an opera aria as he shaves. These "murderers," as the poet is casually to call the airmen in the next stanza, display a touching regard for the human values. How, then, can one say that man is a wolf to man, since these men "play before they die, like puppies with their puppy." But the casual presence of the puppy in the hutment allows us to take the stanza both ways, for the dog is a kind of tamed and domesticated wolf, and his presence may prove on the contrary that the hutment is the wolf den. After all, the timber wolf plays with its puppies.

The second stanza takes the theme to a perfectly explicit conclusion. If three of the men play pitch, and one is asleep, at least one man is awake and counts himself and his companions murderers. But his unvoiced cry "O murderers" is met, countered, and dismissed with the next two lines: ". . . Still this is how it's done: / This is a war. . . ."

The note of casuistry and cynical apology prepares for a brilliant and rich resolving image, the image of Pontius Pilate, which is announced specifically in the third stanza:

I will content the people as I can
And give up these to them: behold the man!

Yet if Pilate, as he is first presented, is a jesting Pilate, who asks "What is truth?" it is a bitter and grieving Pilate who concludes the poem. It is the integrity of Man himself that is at stake. Is man a cruel animal, a wolf, or is he the last savior, the Christ of our secular religion of humanity?

The Pontius Pilate metaphor, as the poet uses it, becomes a device for tremendous concentration. For the speaker (presumably the young airman who cried "O murderers") is himself the confessed murderer under judgment, and also the Pilate who judges, and, at least as a representative of man, the savior whom the mob would condemn. He is even Pilate's better nature, his wife, for the lines "I have suffered, in a dream, because of him, / Many things" is merely a rearrangement of Matthew 27:19, the speech of Pilate's wife to her husband. But this last item is more than a reminiscence of the scriptural scene. It reinforces the speaker's present dilemma. The modern has had high hopes for man; are the hopes merely a dream? Is man incorrigible, merely a cruel beast? The speaker's present torture springs from that hope and from his reluctance to dismiss it as an empty dream. This Pilate is even harder-pressed than was the Roman magistrate. For he must convince himself of this last savior's innocence. But he has lied for him before. He will lie for him now.

> Men wash their hands in blood, as best they can:
> I find no fault in this just man.

What is the meaning of "Men wash their hands in blood, as best they can"? It can mean: Since my own hands are bloody, I have no right to condemn the rest. It can mean: I know that man can love justice, even though his hands are bloody, for there is blood on mine. It can mean: Men are essentially decent: they try to keep their hands clean even if they have only blood in which to wash them.

None of these meanings cancels out the others. All are relevant, and each meaning contributes to the total meaning. Indeed, there is not a facet of significance which does not receive illumination from the figure.

Some of Jarrell's weaker poems seem weak to me because they lean too heavily upon this concept of the goodness of man. In some of them, his approach to the theme is too direct. But in this poem, the affirmation of man's essential justness by a Pilate who contents the people as he washes his hands in blood seems to me to supply every qualification that is required. The sense of self-guilt, the yearning to believe in man's justness, the knowledge of the difficulty of so believing—all work to render accurately and dramatically the total situation.

It is easy at this point to misapprehend the function of irony. We can say that Jarrell's irony pares his theme down to acceptable dimensions. The theme of man's goodness has here been so qualified that the poet himself does not really believe in it. But this is not what I am trying to say. We do not ask a poet to bring his poem into line with our personal beliefs—still less to flatter our personal beliefs. What we do ask is that the poem dramatize the situation so accurately, so honestly, with such fidelity to the total situation that it is no longer a question of our beliefs, but of our participation in the poetic experience. At his best, Jarrell manages to bring us, by an act of imagination, to the most penetrating insight. Participating in that insight, we doubtless become better citizens. (One of the "uses" of poetry, I should agree, is to make us better citizens.) But poetry is not the eloquent rendition of the citizen's creed. It is not even the accurate rendition of his creed. Poetry must carry us beyond the abstract creed into the very matrix out of which, and from which, our creeds are abstracted. That is what "The Eighth Air Force" does. That is what, I am convinced, all good poetry does.

For the theme in a genuine poem does not confront us as abstraction—that is, as one man's generalization from the relevant particulars. Finding its proper symbol, defined and refined by the participating metaphors, the theme becomes a part of the reality in which we live—an insight, rooted in and growing out of concrete experience, many-sided, three-dimensional. Even the resistance to generalization has its part in this process—even the drag of the particulars away from the universal—even the tension of opposing themes—play their parts. The kite properly loaded, tension maintained along the kite string, rises steadily *against* the thrust of the wind.

Published in this form for the first time by permission of the author.

RANDALL JARRELL
The End of the Line
[1942]

WHAT has impressed everyone about modernist poetry is its *differentness*. The familiar and rather touching "I like poetry—but not modern poetry" is only another way of noticing what almost all criticism has emphasized: that modernist poetry is a revolutionary departure from the romantic poetry of the preceding century. Less far-reaching changes would have seemed a revolutionary disaster to "conventional" poets, critics, and readers, who were satisfied with romantic poetry; a revolutionary improvement to more "advanced" poets and critics, who disliked romanticism with the fervor of converts. *Romantic* once again, after almost two centuries, became a term of simple derogation; correspondingly, there grew up a rather blank cult of the "classical," and poets like Eliot hinted that poets like Pound might be the new classicism for which all had been waiting.

All this seems to me partially true, essentially false. The change from romantic poetry was evolutionary, not revolutionary: the modernists were a universe away from the great-grandfathers they admired; they *were* their fathers, only more so. I want to sketch this evolution. But if the reader understands me to be using *romantic* as an unfavorably weighted term, most of what I say will be distorted. Some of the tendencies of romanticism are bad; some of the better tendencies, exaggerated enough, are bad; but a great deal of the best poetry I know is romantic. Of course, one can say almost that about any of the larger movements into which critics divide English poetry; and one might say even better things about the "classical tradition" in English poetry, if there were one. (It is not strange that any real movement, compared to this wax monster, comes off nowhere; but it is strange that anyone should take the comparison for a real one.) If I pay more attention to unfortunate or exaggerated romantic tendencies, it is because these are the most characteristic: the "good" tendencies of movements are far more alike than the "bad" ones, and a proof that two movements are essentially similar needs to show that they share each other's vices.

Modernist poetry—the poetry of Pound, Eliot, Crane, Tate, Stevens, Cummings, MacLeish, et cetera—appears to be and is generally considered to be a violent break with romanticism; it is actually, I believe, an extension of romanticism, an end product in which most of the tendencies of romanticism have been carried to their limits. Romanticism—whether considered as the product of a whole culture or, in isolation, as a purely literary phenomenon—is necessarily a process of extension, a vector; it presupposes a constant experimentalism, the indefinite attainment of "originality," generation after generation, primarily by the novel extrapolation of previously exploited processes. (Neo-classicism, in theory at least, is a static system.) All these romantic tendencies are exploited to their limits; and the movement which carries out this final exploitation, apparently so different from earlier stages of the same process, is what we call modernism. Then, at last, romanticism is confronted with an impasse, a critical point, a genuinely novel situation that it can meet successfully only by contriving genuinely novel means—that is, means which are not romantic; the romantic means have already been exhausted. Until these new means are found, romanticism operates by repeating its last modernist successes or by reverting to its earlier stages; but its normal development has ended, and—the momentum that gave it most of its attraction gone—it becomes a relatively eclectic system, much closer to neo-classicism than it has hitherto been. (A few of these last romanticists resort to odd varieties of neo-classicism.) If this account seems unlikely to the reader, let me remind him that a similar course of development is extremely plain in modern music.

A good many factors combine to conceal the essentially romantic character of modernist poetry. (1) A great quantitative change looks like a qualitative one: for instance, the attenuation or breaking-up of form characteristic of romanticism will not be recognized or tolerated by the average romantic when it reaches its limit in modernist poetry. (2) The violent contrast between the modernist limits of romantic tendencies and the earlier stages of these tendencies, practiced belatedly and eclectically by "conventional" poets, is an important source of confusion. (3) Most of the best modern criticism of poetry is extremely anti-romantic—a poet's criticism is frequently not a reflection of but a compensation for his own poetry; and this change in theory has helped to hide the lack of any essential change in practice. (4) Modernist poems, while possessing some romantic tendencies in hypertrophied forms, often lack others so spectacularly that the reader disregards those they still possess; and these remaining tendencies may be too common for him to be conscious of them as specifically romantic. (Most of the romantic qualities that poetry has specialized in since 1800 seem to the average reader "normal" or "poetic," what poetry inescapably is.) (5) Romanticism holds in solution contradictory tendencies which, isolated and exaggerated in modernism, look startlingly opposed both to each other and to the earlier stages of romanticism. (6) Both modernist and conventional critics have been unable to see the fundamental similarities between modernist and romantic poetry because they were unwilling to see anything but differences: these were to the former a final recommendation, and to the latter a final condemnation.

We can understand modernist poetry better by noticing where and how it began. The English poetry that we call *fin de siècle*—the most important tendency of its time—was a limit of one easily recognizable extension of romanticism. These "decadent" poets were strongle influenced by Baudelaire, Verlaine, and similar French poets. Rimbaud, Laforgue, and Corbière—who had already written "modern" poetry—had no influence on them. Why? Because a section of French poetry was developing a third of a century ahead of English poetry: Rimbaud wrote typically modernist poetry in the 1870's; in the '90's a surrealist play, Jarry's *Ubu Roi*, scared the young Yeats into crying: "After us the Savage God!" France, without England's industrial advantages and enormous colonial profits, had had little of the Victorian prosperity which slowed up the economic and political rate of change in England—had still less of that complacent mercantile Christianity the French dismissed as "English hypocrisy." And—if we stick to a part of the culture, literature—the rate of change could be greater in France because romanticism was more of a surface phenomenon there. English poetry was not *ready* to be influenced by French modernism for many years. Meanwhile there were two movements particularly suited to criticism. Accompanying the triumph of prose naturalism there was a prosy, realistic, rather limited reaction against "decadent" poetry (it included Robinson, Frost, Masters, Masefield, some of the Georgians, etc.). The other movement, Imagism, carried three or four romantic tendencies to their limits with the perfection of a mathematical demonstration.

French modernist poetry first influenced poetry in English through Americans who, lacking a determining or confining tradition of their own, were particularly accessible and susceptible: Pound and Eliot (like Picasso, Stravinsky, and Joyce) were in some sense expatriates in both space and time. They imported modernism into English rather more deliberately and openly than Wordsworth and Coleridge had imported romanticism; but all Pound's early advice to poets could be summed up in a sentence half of which is pure Wordsworth: Write like prose, like speech—and *read French poetry!* The work of this most influential of modern poets, Ezra Pound, is a recapitulation of the development of our poetry from late romanticism to modernism. His early work is a sort of anthology of romantic sources: Browning, early Yeats, the *fin de siècle* poets, Villon and the troubadours (in translations or imitations that remind one of Swinburne's and Rossetti's), Heine. *His* variety of imagism is partly a return to the fresh beginnings of romantic practices, from their diluted and perfunctory ends; partly an extension to their limits of some of the most characteristic obsessions of romanticism—for instance, its passion for "pure" poetry, for putting everything in terms of sensation and emotion,

with logic and generalizations excluded; and partly an adaptation of the
exotic procedures of Chinese poetry, those silks that swathe a homely heart.
When Pound first wrote poems that are modernist in every sense of the word,
their general "feel" is reminiscent of what one might call a lowest common
denominator of Corbière, Laforgue, and Rimbaud; but Heine had by no
means disappeared; and the original Cantos I and II, gone now, were still
full of Browning. But if Eliot was willing to base his form on Browning's
(the dramatic monologue is primarily a departure from the norm of ordinary
poetry; but in modernist poetry this departure *itself becomes the norm*), he
had no interest in Browning's content and manner; in even his earliest poems
one is seeing romanticism through Laforgue, and one can reconstruct this
romanticism, in the pure form in which it had once existed, only from Eliot's
remarks about his early feelings for Rossetti and Swinburne. . . . All during
this time the Irish expatriate Joyce was making his way from late-romantic
lyrics (in verse, though there is much that is similar in his early prose) to the
modernist poetry (in prose) that crops up here and there in *Ulysses,* and that
is everywhere in *Finnegans Wake.*

But it would take fifty or a hundred pages to write about this development
in terms of specific poets. One can indicate the resemblances of romanticism
and modernism more briefly, by making a list of some of the general characteristics of modernist poetry:

(1) A pronounced experimentalism: "originality" is everyone's aim, and
novel techniques are as much prized as new scientific discoveries. Eliot states
it with surprising naïveté: "It is exactly as wasteful for a poet to do what has
been done already as for a biologist to rediscover Mendel's discoveries."
(2) External formlessness, internal disorganization: these are justified either
as the disorganization necessary to express a disorganized age or as new and
more complex forms of organization. Language is deliberately disorganized,
meter becomes irregular or disappears; the rhythmical flow of verse is broken
up into a jerky half-prose *collage* or *montage.* (3) Heightened emotional intensity; violence of every sort. (4) Obscurity, inaccessibility: logic, both for
structure and for texture, is neglected; without this for a ground the masses
of the illogical or a-logical lose much of their effectiveness. The poet's peculiar
erudition and allusiveness (compare the Alexandrian poet Lycophron) consciously restrict his audience to a small, highly specialized group; the poet is
a specialist like everyone else. He intimidates or overawes the public by an
attitude one may paraphrase as: "The poet's cultivation and sensibility are of
a different order from those of his readers; even if he tried to talk down to
them—and why should he try?—he would talk about things they have never
heard of, in ways they will never understand." But he did not despair of their
understanding a slap in the face. (5) A lack of restraint or proportion: all
tendencies are forced to their limits, even contradictory tendencies—and not
merely in the same movement but, frequently, in the same poet or the same

poem. Some modernist poetry puts an unparalleled emphasis on texture, connotation, violently "interesting" language (attained partly by an extension of
romantic principles, partly by a more violent rhetoric based on sixteenth and
seventeenth century practices); but there has never before been such prosaic
poetry—conversational-colloquial verse without even a pretense at meter.
(6) A great emphasis on details—on parts, not wholes. Poetry is essentially
lyric: the rare narrative or expository poem is a half-fortuitous collocation of
lyric details. Poetry exploits particulars and avoids and condemns generalizations. (7) A typically romantic preoccupation with sensation, perceptual
nuances. (8) A preoccupation with the unconscious, dreams, the stream of
consciousness, the irrational: this *surréaliste* emphasis might better have been
called *sousréaliste*. (9) Irony of every type: Byronic, Laforguian, dryly metaphysical, or helplessly sentimental. Poetry rejects a great deal, accepts a little,
and is embarrassed by that little. (10) *Fauve* or neo-primitive elements. (11)
Modernist poets, though they may write about the ordinary life of the time,
are removed from it, have highly specialized relations with it. The poet's
naturalism is employed as indictment, as justification for his own isolation;
prosaic and sordid details become important as what writers like Wallace
Stevens and William Carlos Williams somewhat primitively think of as the
anti-poetic. Contemporary life is condemned, patronized, or treated as a dis-
graceful aberration or special case, compared to the past; the poet hangs out
the window of the Ivory Tower making severe but obscure remarks about
what is happening below—he accepts the universe with several (thin) volumes of reservations. What was happening below was bad enough; the poet
could characterize it, truthfully enough, with comparative forms of all those
adjectives that Goethe and Arnold had applied to their ages. But its disasters,
at least, were of unprecedented grandeur; it was, after all, "the very world,
which is the world/ Of all of us,—the place where, in the end,/ We find our
happiness or not at all"; and the poet's rejection or patronizing acceptance of
it on his own terms—and, sometimes, what terms they were!—hurt his poetry
more than he would have believed. (12) Individualism, isolation, alienation.
The poet is not only different from society, he is as different as possible from
other poets; all this differentness is exploited to the limit—is used as subject-
matter, even. Each poet develops an elaborate, "personalized," bureaucratized
machinery of effect; *refine your singularities* is everybody's maxim. (13)
These poets, typically, dislike and condemn science, industrialism, humanitarianism, "progress," the main tendencies of Western development; they
want to trade the present for a somewhat idealized past, to turn from a scientific, commercial, and political world-view to one that is literary, theological,
and personal.

   This complex of qualities is essentially romantic, and the poetry that exhibits it is the culminating point of romanticism.

It is the end of the line. Poets can go back and repeat the ride; they can settle in attractive, atavistic colonies along the railroad; they can repudiate the whole system, *à la* Yvor Winters, for some neo-classical donkey-caravan of their own. But Modernism As We Knew It—the most successful and influential body of poetry of this century—is dead. Compare a 1940 issue of *Poetry* with a 1930 issue. Who could have believed that modernism would collapse so fast? Only someone who realized that modernism is a limit which it is impossible to exceed. How can poems be written that are more violent, more disorganized, more obscure, more—supply your own adjective—than those that have already been written? But if modernism could go no further, it was equally difficult for it to stay where it was: how could a movement completely dynamic in character, as "progressive" as the science and industrialism it accompanied, manage to become static or retrogressive without going to pieces? Among modernist poets, from 1910 to 1925, there was the same feeling of confident excitement, of an individual but irregularly cooperative experimentalism, of revolutionary discoveries just around the corner, that one regularly sees at certain stages in the development of a science; they had ahead of them the same Manifest Destiny that poets have behind them today. Today, for the poet, there is an embarrassment of choices: young poets can choose—do choose—to write anything from surrealism to imitations of Robert Bridges; the only thing they have no choice about is making their own choice. The Muse, forsaking her sterner laws, says to everyone: "Do what you will." Originality can no longer be recognized by, and condemned or applauded for, its obvious experimentalism; the age offers to the poet a fairly heartless eclecticism or a fairly solitary individuality. He can avoid being swept along by the current—there is no current; he can congratulate himself on this, and see behind him, glittering in the distance of time, all those bright streams sweeping people on to the wildest of excesses, the unlikeliest of triumphs.

For a long time society and poetry have been developing in the same direction, have been carrying certain tendencies to their limits: how could anyone fail to realize that the excesses of modernist poetry are the necessary concomitants of the excesses of late-capitalist society? (An example too pure and too absurd even for allegory is Robinson Jeffers, who must prefer a hawk to a man, a stone to a hawk, because of an individualism so exaggerated that it contemptuously rejects affections, obligations, relations of any kind whatsoever, and sets up as a nostalgically-awaited goal the war of all against all. Old Rocky Face, perched on his sea crag, is the last of *laissez faire*; Free Economic Man at the end of his rope.) How much the modernist poets disliked their society, and how much they resembled it! How often they contradicted its letter and duplicated its spirit! They rushed, side by side with their society, to the limits of all tendencies. When, at the beginning of the '30's, these limits were reached, what became of these individualists? They turned toward anything collective: toward Catholicism, communism, distributism, social credit, agrarianism; they wrote neo-classical criticism or verse; they wrote political (Marxist or fellow-traveller) criticism or verse; they stopped writing; and when they read the verse of someone like E. E. Cummings, as it pushed on into the heart of that last undiscovered continent, *e. e. cummings,* they thought of this moral impossibility, this living fossil, with a sort of awed and incredulous revulsion.

I have no space to write of later developments. Auden was so influential because his poetry was the only novel and successful reaction away from modernism; and a few years later Dylan Thomas was so influential—in England—because his poetry was the only novel and successful reaction away from Auden. But his semi-surrealist experimentalism could be as good as it was, and as influential as it was, only in a country whose poets had never carried modernism to the limits of its possibilities. No one can understand these English developments if he forgets that, while we were having the modernism of Pound, Stevens, Williams, Moore, Eliot, Tate, Crane, Cummings, and all the rest, England was having the modernism of the Sitwells.

I am afraid that my hypothesis about romanticism and modernism, without the mass of evidence that can make a theory plausible, or the tangle of extensions and incidental insights that can make it charming, may seem improbable or unpleasant to some of my readers. It is intended to be partial: I have not written about the hard or dry or "classical" tendencies of some modern verse—what Empson and Marianne Moore have in common, for instance; and I have not listed the differences between modernism and romanticism that everybody has seen and stated. But I hope that nobody will dislike my article because he thinks it an attack on romanticism or modernism. This has been description, not indictment. Burke said that you can't indict a whole people, and I hope I am not such a fool as to indict a century and a half of a world. Besides, so far as its poetry is concerned, it was wonderful. Wordsworth and Blake and Heine, Baudelaire and Corbière, Hardy and Yeats and Rilke—the names crowd in; and there are dozens more. That some of these poets were, sometimes, as strange as they were wonderful; that some of their successors were, alas, rather stranger: all this is as true as it is obvious. But the "classical" prejudice which hints that these poets were somehow deceived and misguided as (say) Dryden and Valéry were not, seems every year more grotesque. One repeats to oneself, *Whom God deceives is well deceived,* and concludes that if these poets were not classical, so much the worse for classicism.

From *The Nation,* Vol. CLIV (February 21, 1942), pp. 222–228. Reprinted in this revised version by permission of the author and editors.

WILLIAM BARRETT

The End of Modern Literature: Existentialism and Crisis

[1949]

WE ARE told that this is the century when man has become for the first time fully and thoroughly problematic to himself. If so, it would only seem natural that literature too should be posed as a new and extreme kind of problem for literary men. Natural and inevitable too, that this problem should be raised particularly by the French, whose literature, whatever its rank, has always been the most programmatic of all literatures, and the most self-consciously attached to critical theory. For some time now French critics have been talking about a "crisis" in their literature. "Crisis" is a violent word, and there has possibly been some over-dramatization in its use; but there can be no doubt about the seriousness of the situation that has evoked this word: French literature suggests a countryside overrun by generations of industrious cultivators until the point of diminishing returns seems reached, where the soil continues to yield crops only after exacting very much more drastic methods of cultivation and ever more painful labor. By the turn of the century some traditional genres already looked exhausted, and recently some French writers have been declaring that the language itself (so much narrower in its range of effects than our protean English) demands new means of expression. American literature is very far from reaching this stage, and perhaps we are wrong to bother our heads at all with asking any extreme or ultimate questions of literature; we are primitives and perhaps for the time being we shall do better to remain such; but if we do choose to think about the problem of literature as a total one, then we can learn much from seeing this problem raised within the French context, which may very well represent the extreme state toward which modern literature, so long as it still remembers its ambitions, is tending everywhere in the world.

The background of Sartre's book[1] is this continuing crisis in French literature. But he is also beset by another and much more urgent crisis—the condition of French and European society after the Second World War—which penetrates so much of European life now that it places the writer in a precarious relation even to his craft. It is very useful to us to have a writer like

[1] *What Is Literature?* By Jean-Paul Sartre. Philosophical Library.

Sartre confront this double crisis. By this time it seems clear that he is not, nor is likely to become, a great writer: clever, enormously, furiously energetic, he does not possess the authentic gifts of a really first-rate creative talent. But in the present case this may be no disadvantage: a greater writer, for whom literature itself might never become a question, might be less sensitive to the historic forces that now push the literary man into such an odd and difficult place in the world. And what we can always count on in Sartre is the pro-digious intelligence (however it may miscarry in details) with which he plunges into any problem. Sartre divides the problem of literature into three questions: *What is writing? Why write? For whom does one write?* These questions themselves breathe the air of crisis, for they are not the kinds of question that enter the writer's head during his periods of fertility and over-flow; they become urgent and sometimes paralyzing for him only when he has descended into the pits of silence, anguish, artistic nihilism; when he exists on the margins of literature where language itself seems to become impossible. But since the writer cannot exist without descending from time to time into these waste places, these are questions that cannot be shirked, and it is better to raise and try to answer them whenever we can than to wait till the heavy silence descends and makes their answer seem hopeless.

Coming out of this double crisis in the French situation, Sartre's book is really a revolutionary one, though he himself gives the rather odd impression of not quite grasping the real revolution he announces. He hardly presents us any radically new theory of literature: most of Sartre's views had their antecedents in the Marxist theorizing of the 'thirties, though he gives them a new philosophical color. The revolutionary import of Sartre's message lies in his complete acceptance of the conditions under which, it appears, the writer may soon have to work, even though to accept these conditions may imply a radical break with the whole tradition of literature in France. Thus his book is revolutionary as a symptom of what is happening to literature, cul-ture, and human society in this epoch—and not only in France.

Sartre attempts to give a historical answer to the three questions that divide his book by reviewing the conditions of author, public, and society during the major periods of French literature. This history is sketched in large rapid strokes: the seventeenth, eighteenth, nineteenth or bourgeois century; the present period (the situation of the writer in 1947) and Sartre's hope for the future. Inevitably the treatment of history shows more of the influence of Marx and Hegel than of Existentialism. Sartre has obviously profited a good deal from a sympathetic reading of Hegel, but the Hegelian apparatus often seems unnecessary and cumbrous, and his use of it an exuberant but self-indulgent practice of virtuosity. The influence of Marxism shows itself in an-other direction: it actually forms Sartre's judgments of taste at certain points. Thus he undervalues the literature of the seventeenth century because it was aristocratic, actually preferring the comedies of Beaumarchais, which belong to the more democratic eighteenth century, to those of Molière, and going so far as to describe Molière's *Le Misanthrope* as a comedy dealing only with the trivial subject of manners. The trouble is not that Sartre lacks taste —the whole book is evidence of his passionate addiction to literature—but that, as usual, he is driven too furiously by his ideas into the violation of perceptible fact—here the perceptible facts of taste. The result is that the brilliance of his insights on the past is often spoiled by extreme and doctrinaire judgments.

This lack of critical balance has its most serious consequences when Sartre is dealing with the bourgeois literature of the nineteenth century. Here Sartre's judgments are obviously colored by his passionate hatred of the bourgeois class itself, and in this respect he reveals the state of mind of France, and indeed of all Europe, where the bourgeoisie is so discredited that the unpleasant associations of the word reflect back on the whole century of civilization dominated by that class. We in America who have not yet had to live through the ruin of that class are still permitted another point of view: as bourgeois civilization—in France, England, and elsewhere—disappears, it is possible to regret its passing and to question very seriously the superiority of the culture that is replacing it. Though Sartre makes some telling points against bourgeois literature, they are usually directed at its weakest side and hardly do justice to its main bulk of significant work. Sartre's error is the familiar one of seeking to convert political and social sympathies too directly into literary judgment, so that he accepts much too simply and wholeheartedly the plebeian or populist taste embedded in the Marxist mind. In general, it can be said of Sartre that he has come to Marxism too late, that he has not lived through it and beyond it, so that he still sees political and cultural realities under the too drastic Marxist simplifications. The facts, however, are always more complex. Flaubert, to take one example, has always been a target for Sartre, and in this book Sartre attempts to justify his severity by citing long passages from Flaubert's letters that express an aristocratic hatred of the mob. This is all very well; but then we are suddenly reminded of the human complications of literary composition when we recall that Flaubert, despite his correspondence, has produced in the few pages of *Un Coeur Simple* a more profound and sympathetic picture of the poor than in all the thousand pages of Sartre's recent trilogy. And if we are going to insist at all on the social role of literature, we may as well remember that it was the bourgeois epoch which first produced the conception of a literature embracing the whole of society in a single understanding vision.

All this brings us now to the core of Sartre's message, which is of course his now well-known concept of *littérature engagée*, where we will also be dealing with some of the hazy notions left in the American mind by the "social-consciousness" of the 'thirties. ("Engaged literature," by the way, is a piece of linguistic nonsense that the translator might have spared us; if some of the literal force of the French is to be kept, he might have rendered it as "enlisted literature," which is the connotation to French ears; but, all told, "engagement" is probably best done into English as *commitment*.) Sartre complains that he has been misunderstood, but despite all his efforts in this book his idea of commitment still remains somewhat unclear. He has still not dealt adequately with the kinds and degrees of commitment, nor with the question of the necessary *artistic* detachment that must accompany the writer's *human* commitments. It is easy to be sympathetic to the causes that prompt Sartre's doctrine. The most eloquent pages in this book are those on the French experience under the German occupation, which make it quite clear that after such experiences the writer could no longer immure himself in an aestheticism for which neither concentration camps, executioners, nor victims would exist. We can very well accept the decisive force of such experiences for the young men of Sartre's generation. But then, can this experience be generalized for the writer everywhere and allowed to circumscribe his material, methods, and attitudes?

The point is, again, that the writer's involvement is a more complicated matter than Sartre allows. Commitment may work on various levels and in various degrees: the detached writer sometimes turns out to be the most committed at a deeper level, and the most blatantly committed writer to have only a transitory connection with the deeper issues of history, society, and literary tradition. Proust complains in one of his letters of the criticism (made after the first volumes of his novel had already appeared and been acclaimed) that his was the work of a snob, showing no recognition of social (by which was meant socialist) ideas. The criticism was in fact just, in the sense that the socialist ideology plays no role at all in the work of Proust. Yet, by some curious irony of detachment not at all unusual in works of art, *A La Recherche du Temps Perdu* is a profounder study of the breakdown of a social class than anything given us by proletarian or "social realist" literature. No modern writer seems to offer us a more fanatical example of detachment than Joyce. Certainly, during the seventeen years in which he was composing his last work, withdrawn from the ideological battles of the 'twenties and 'thirties, he seemed a curiously eccentric and private figure. Yet the appearance of *Finnegans Wake* in 1939 coincided portentously with the outbreak of a War that seemed the destruction of the whole civilization so laboriously embedded in Joyce's pages, and by some miracle of literary creation the book seemed to sum up a whole epoch. Was Joyce a committed writer? It depends, of course, on what kinds of commitment one has in mind. Joyce was committed in the deepest sense to the fact of human language, and consequently to the whole literary tradition in which he was working; he drew deeply upon the modern consciousness in matters like anthropology and psychoanalysis; and beyond all these, he had a human commitment, which became also the writer's deepest message, to the most primitive and universal emotions of familial life. In the face of such formidable commitments, the absence of a political ideology looks like a rather superficial deficiency in Joyce. The examples could be multiplied, but the point that emerges from them is already clear: we demand of the writer a commitment to his time in the sense that his work incorporate contemporary mind and feeling at their deepest levels; but to exist deeply in one's time is not the same as to exist in the spotlight, to pass oneself off as a political leader or sage, and to lose oneself in all the more violently public currents. Withdrawal and silence may open to the writer resources that reflect his time at a profounder level than those works which—in their insistence on being relevant, committed, or conscripted—are only a step beyond the daily newspaper. Some of Sartre's recent work gives the impression of a man writing with the Zeitgeist breathing hotly down his neck.

In the broad human sense, no doubt, Sartre is in the right direction. His doctrine is an insistence upon the reintegration of literature into life, against the idea of the priesthood of letters that germinated during the whole of the nineteenth century to come to full and final bloom in Flaubert and the symbolists. Mallarmé put it perfectly when he said, "Everything exists in order to get into a book," willing to countenance the inversion of existence that would subordinate the man to the writer. Our own period hardly permits this attitude: we have to insist that the writer is a man, that he never leaves humanity, and that, living in his period, he has political opinions like everybody else. But expecting the writer to be a citizen, we should not also expect that the literary profession gives him any special privileges of trespass into politics. Politics is usually considered fair game for everybody, and literary men have sometimes been the worst offenders, confusing their vaguest feelings with facts, their rhetoric with logic, and their will to belong with moral heroism. Sartre's own forays into politics show a good deal of this naïveté and confusion. It is time we recognized that there is such a thing as "literary" politics, to be taken no more seriously than "literary" philosophizing, "literary" psychology, and the rest of these adulterated products. During the 'thirties, of course, "literary" politics was the universal pastime; the mood of the period was some excuse, but that period has now passed, and literary men and fellow-travelers ought to be told that politics is a special discipline, with its own data and rules, concerning which one ought occasionally to think before one talks.

But the real revolution that Sartre announces for literature is not a matter chiefly of politics. He hardly states this revolution in so many words; we glimpse it only if we measure his theory by his practice, taking the present book along with his novels and plays, which are, after all, his deliberate at-

tempts to realize his own projects for literature; and only too if we read a
little between the lines in the present work, observing the writers to whom he
makes most frequent and essential reference. Sartre once said that Dos Passos
was the greatest modern novelist; in the present work his admiration for
American writers is more cautious than in the past, but we notice repeated
reference to Richard Wright as a great writer. This is entirely natural, for
Wright's books, dealing with the Negro question in America, satisfy Sartre's
demand that literature be directed at changing the fundamental conditions
of social existence. The highbrow critic in America is likely to settle on altogether different names in any fundamental literary discussion: Joyce or
Eliot or Proust are the names that remind us of the possible ambitions of literature. Sartre, however, is interested in a very practical program for literature, and his point would seem to be effectively this: that in the crisis of exhaustion, or threatened exhaustion, in which French literature now seems to
find itself, the way out may be just to propose the second-rate as an ideal.
Perhaps, being second-rate, it is something within reach, and therefore a
thoroughly practicable goal for literature. In the sense that his book represents
a deliberate abnegation from the great ambitions of modern literature, Sartre
is in effect announcing the end of a whole literary period.

For the fact is that the one thing that distinguishes modern literature as a
whole from the literature of previous periods is its extraordinary, and perhaps
even overweening, ambition. We are now at the mid-point of the century,
and looking back on the half-century of writers who will eventually give their
names to the period, we seem to see them in retrospect as belonging almost to
a vanished culture, so different were the conditions of their existence from
those of the period into which we are now entering. If they inherited the
nineteenth-century view of the writer as a separate and anointed being, a
kind of priest, they were able to hold on to this role only with the tensions of
an irony that provided it with a new human content. Proust, Joyce, Mann
and the others, all exist in the full plenitude of a tradition, of which they
sought to lose no part, so that their work in its richness already carries the
seeds of disorder and dissolution. Probably a moment like this in literary history could not be prolonged any further. Sartre's is perhaps the first conscious
announcement that the conditions of literature must return to a lower and
less ambitious level; but even if the program did not become conscious, the
attitude has already begun to prevail generally. We are now able to understand our surprise at the evolution of Sartre's career. The discrepancy between the very abstract and involved philosophy and the rudimentary and
plodding fiction is no longer a puzzle. It was something of a shock, after the
intellectual sophistication and complexity of *L'être et le néant,* to descend
upon the first volume of Sartre's trilogy, not because his creative gifts were
lacking but because he was willing to aim so low in the novel. But all this

now turns out to have been intentional: the deliberate aiming at the second-rate is part of Sartre's program for literature. The committed writer disdains the creation of masterpieces, and even the very concept of the masterpiece, with whatever silence, exile, or cunning it may exact, no longer seems to have any connection with that act of writing that aims essentially at making an impact, just as one might strike a blow or fire a pistol.

Sartre is therefore entirely consistent with himself when he proposes that the writer neglect none of the mass media, like radio and cinema, available in this period. He notes with satisfaction that the modern writer is able to reach a much vaster audience than his predecessor of the nineteenth century: for Sartre this is the great opportunity in the present situation. It is true that he also observes the other side of the coin—that when Gide, for example, becomes known through the cinema to thousands who have not read him, the writer also becomes inseparable from the face of Michele Morgan—but he fails to consider what will happen if this process continues unchecked. The cultural process in modern society (which, whatever its form of economy, is everywhere becoming a mass society) is precisely this watering down of content as the writer reaches larger masses of people, and usually not through his own written word but through the mechanical image that an advanced technology substitutes for the printed page. Sartre accepts the process, in fact seeks to assist it; for in his view the writer should aim essentially at addressing the concrete collectivity, which is the total mass of mankind, and eventually this mass is a classless society. This is as utopian as most of Sartre's politics; but programs—and a program for literature is no exception—should deal with present possibilities, and the contemporary writer who seeks to reach this mass audience will inevitably find himself rejecting his own essential difficulties, his complications and subtleties, and indeed the very limitations of personality that have in the past defined his most authentic themes. Here again we have nothing less than a proposal to put an end to modern literature. For the qualities that define modern literature have been in great part the result of a desperate effort to preserve itself by a deliberate escape from a mass audience.

It would be a mistake, however, to discount too easily Sartre's attitudes toward literature as simply the result of his own unhappy will to have a political vocation. We would be right in part, but we would be wrong to forget the more significant question why the writer today should be so furiously haunted by the need to search for such a vocation. Sartre's position might be very different without the large and vocal presence of the Communists upon the French scene: the writer of La Nausée, in becoming the leader of a school, has had to sacrifice himself to the public figure who is drawn into competition with the Communists and has had consequently to offer a message emphasizing more and more the "positive" and social role of literature. It is very significant, thus, that the discussion of the present situation of the writer in 1947, with which this book concludes, should be in large part an unequivocal attack upon communism as a moral and intellectual phenomenon (a section which, along with his destruction of the literary theories of surrealism, represents Sartre at his polemic best); but it is even more significant of the ambiguous situation of the French writer now that Sartre's anticommunism on the political level has been so very much less equivocal. Communism and communist ideology do not play the same role in America; but in this respect the French situation may not be so much different as simply in advance of our own, and what we must be prepared for all over the world is a literature produced under the conditions of a mass society, whatever may be the political regime imposed upon this mass base. The end of modern literature, however, does not mean the end of literature. We may regret the passing of a period, but lamentation cannot become the content of a critical doctrine. In the new period which we are now entering the literary medium may discover new forms and adventures for itself: for one thing, the social process in which the writer is now caught up may put an end to his famous alienation in our time, and a literature with very different possibilities may result. Unfortunately all this is still very much in the future, while right now I do not think there can be much doubt that these new conditions are producing, and will probably produce for some time, a literature that is plainly inferior to the old.

From *The Partisan Review*, Vol. XVI (September, 1949), pp. 942–950. Reprinted by permission of the author and editors.

STANLEY EDGAR HYMAN

Attempts at an Integration

[1948]

I: THE IDEAL CRITIC

IF WE could, hypothetically, construct an ideal modern literary critic out of plastics and light metals, his method would be a synthesis of every practical technique or procedure used by his flesh-and-blood colleagues. From all the rival approaches he would borrow as much as could be used in a synthesis without distorting the whole, he would balance one bias or excess or over-specialization against another so that both canceled out, and he was left with only neutral elements adaptable to his own purposes. From Edmund Wilson he would take the function of translation or interpretation, of explaining the work's paraphrasable content, and augment it with the greater concern for poetic and formal values found, say, in the early interpretative criticism of Ezra Pound. From Yvor Winters he would borrow the emphasis on evaluation and comparative judgment, as well as Winters's refusal to be intimidated by conventional opinions in his judgments, rather than the judgments themselves. He could use T. S. Eliot's passionate concern with grounding literature in a tradition although his tradition would probably look more like V. F. Parrington's, and he could also use Eliot's functional relationship between poetry and criticism. From Van Wyck Brooks our ideal critic would take the biographical method of the early books, and the general concern with the cultural climate of a writer. Constance Rourke would contribute her emphasis on the folk background of a work, as well as her insistence that this tradition tends to be one of form rather than content, and abstract rather than realistic. Maud Bodkin's psychoanalytic method would go into the synthesis, augmented by theories and procedures from Gestalt, revisionist Freudian, and other psychologies; as would Christopher Caudwell's Marxist method, modified by Plekhanov's historical relativism, Alick West's detailed concern with specific texts, and many insights from other sociologies.

Our ideal critic would adopt Caroline Spurgeon's conscientious scholarship, going to John Livingston Lowes's lengths and extending the results with

the imaginative rashness of G. Wilson Knight; as well as Armstrong's preoccupation with the image cluster as a unit of special poetic significance.
From R. P. Blackmur he would take the technique of hard work and research, the preoccupation with language and diction, and the insistence on
the high importance of art and the symbolic imagination. William Empson
would furnish his exploration of categories and ambiguities, his close and
ingenious textual reading, and his general concern with the significance of
literary forms. From I. A. Richards our ideal critic would borrow the concern
with communication, techniques of interpretation, and the experimental
method; from Kenneth Burke, the concern with symbolic action, techniques
of integration within a framework of dramatism, and the introspective
method. Other critics would furnish still other elements to the synthesis:
Jane Harrison's ritual anthropology and Margaret Schlauch's linguistics;
Herbert Read's sympathetic attention to every new current of thought and
every youthful artist; the balanced concern with the totality of the work of
the *Scrutiny* group; F. O. Matthiessen's subtle correlations between the sociological and the aesthetic; Francis Fergusson's use of the ritual drama and
William Troy's use of the ritual myth; the focus on poetic structure of John
Crowe Ransom, Allen Tate, Cleanth Brooks, and Robert Penn Warren; and
much else from others. Finally, the ideal critic would be a neo-Aristotelian,
scrupulously inducing from poetic practice, as well as a neo-Coleridgean,
frankly deducing from philosophic concepts.

At the same time our ideal critic would discard from all these critics those
features of their practice that seemed to him irrelevant, worthless, or private
to them, stripping from the neutral and objective method their special obsessions, preoccupations, and weaknesses. He would have no use for Wilson's
superficiality or dealings in second-hand ideas or impatience with form. He
would not want Winters's obsessive morality, nor his semantically meaningless dogmatism with no basis for judgment given, nor his bad temper, nor
his high percentage of error. In adopting Eliot's concern with tradition, he
would husk it of its religious and political bias, and in adopting Eliot's organic continuity between the poetic and critical function, he would maintain
criticism's independence and integrity. Rejecting Brooks's *a priori* assumptions
and contempt for imaginative literature, the ideal critic would not use his
biographical method as a Procrustean bed for writers, or as an excuse for
escaping from the work to the personality, or as a way of dispensing sweetness and light at a literary tea. In taking over Miss Rourke's method, he
would steer clear of both the "folksy" and the "*völkisch*," and would operate
from a far wider learning than hers. Miss Bodkin's mystic and religious emphasis would be discarded (along with Jung's Nazi racialism and blood-and-
soil irrationalism, which she avoided); as would Caudwell's bias against psychoanalysis, guilt about poetry, class debunking, absolutism, and preference

for generalities rather than texts. Both Freud and Marx would be used with as sharp a sense as theirs, and a sharper sense than their followers', of the limitations of their approaches applied to literature. Our ideal critic would operate from the same sharp awareness of the limits of scholarship, the area where it must shade over into criticism to be fulfilled, and he would adopt neither Miss Spurgeon's timidity about following through on conclusions nor her personal mysticism. He would probably find not very much to reject in Blackmur, Empson, Richards, and Burke, but could probably get along without the traces of preciousness in the first, the occasional overelaboration of the second, the blind alley of Basic English in the third, and the anachronistic resistance to progress in the fourth. From the other critics he drew on he would make similar scrapings, and in most cases would probably find more to scrape away than to keep. Even Aristotle and Coleridge would not be entirely to his purpose.

This ideal integration of all of modern critical method into one supermethod could not be on the analogy of stew, with everything thrown at random into the pot, but would have to be on the analogy of construction, with the structure built up according to an orderly plan on some foundation or around some skeleton framework. What, then, would that foundation, framework, or basis be? The most enthusiastic candidate for the job is Marxism, whose spokesmen have regularly insisted that dialectical materialism is an integrative frame able to encompass and use the newest advances in all fields of knowledge, and in fact must do so to function. This was undoubtedly true of Marx and Engels, who drew enthusiastically on immense accumulations of knowledge in every area, and adapted to new developments so elastically that Engels remarked: "With each epoch-making discovery in the department of natural science, materialism has been obliged to change its form." It is also to a large extent true of Caudwell, who insists in the Introduction to *Illusion and Reality:* "But physics, anthropology, history, biology, philosophy and psychology are also products of society, and therefore a sound sociology would enable the art critic to employ criteria drawn from these fields without falling into eclecticism or confusing art with psychology or politics." Later Marxists, however, with the exception of a few isolated figures like Caudwell, have lacked the elasticity and scrupulousness of Marx and Engels, as well as their learning and brilliance, so that Marxism in practice has hardly made good its claim as an all-embracing integrative system. Most contemporary Marxist thinkers, in fact, would toss the greater part of our ideal critical method out the window immediately as "decadent" frippery.

Few other individual methods or disciplines are even formulated so as to embrace other approaches, and where they are sciences or near-sciences, like psychology and anthropology, or clearly demarcated fields, like scholarship or biography, they obviously could not invade other territories without automatically losing their special character. Clearly, the basis for an ideal critical integration would have to be a literary or philosophic concept (it should be obvious from the foregoing that when Marxism sets itself up as a giant integrative frame, it is not in its aspect as a sociology but in its aspect as a philosophic *Weltanschauung*). Without aspiring to solve the problem off-hand, we might note a few possible bases for such a synthesis. One would be the concept of Organicism, the organic unity of the human personality, Richards's continuity of experience, in terms of which all these critical approaches could be unified as dealing with related aspects of human behavior: man as poet, man as reader, the family man, the social man, man communicating, and so on. Another, avoiding the nominalism inherent in the first, would be Social Activity, organizing the various approaches as relational aspects with different groups, inherent in the work of art. Others would include: Burke's metaphor of Dramatism, with its pentad of act, scene, agent, agency, and purpose, treating the other approaches as emphases on one term or another, conflicting and co-operating like characters in a play; Empson's concept of Ambiguity extended, with all other approaches as further ambiguities of meaning in the words of the poem; or even Blackmur's doctrine of Hard Work, equated with Burke's Use All There Is to Use, as simply the rather disorganized organizing principle of investigating every possible line of significance.

In our ideal critic we would assume not only the use of all the fruitful methods of modern criticism on some organizing base, but necessarily all the abilities and special aptitudes behind them, a fearful assumption of personal capacity, as well as the requisite learning in all these areas, and the requisite flexibility of focus. Our ideal critic would not only have to *do* more than any actual critic, he would have to *know* more, *range* farther, and *be* more (as well as *write* better, certainly). The classification of critics in this book has been largely by method; noting other possible classifications that cut across this one on the bias should suggest how much else is involved. Thus classification by focus would have: Blackmur the specialist in words, Miss Spurgeon in images, Empson in forms, Burke in the totality of a man's work, and so forth. Classification by learning would have: Eliot the man knowing literature temporarily out of fashion, Caudwell the man knowing modern science, Brooks the man knowing minor writers of the period, Miss Bodkin knowing the classics, and so on. Classification by attribute (which has been necessarily assumed as underlying the method) would have: Empson the keen reader, Burke the intelligence shooting sparks, Richards the patient teacher, Blackmur and Miss Spurgeon (in different senses) the painstaking workers. (It might be pointed out here that Blackmur's hard work, which has been treated throughout as a method, is much more definitely a personal attribute. It has been classified as a method only because it seems both essential and transmissible: any critic can and must do hard work, in the sense in which he cannot or need not at all set himself to becoming an intelligence shooting sparks.)

The last problem that our ideal critic would have to face, and the most overwhelming of all, is that each of the methods developed by modern critics is only in a first preliminary stage of exploration, and at one time or another all of their originators have had to recognize that they have only scratched the surface and will hardly be able to do more in their lifetimes. Each method is capable of almost limitless extension and ramification, and our harried ideal critic would have not only to use them all, but to proliferate each of them enormously, solving the problems and adjusting to the perspectives confronting each method in isolation. . . . He would have to do it all himself, too. Each of our modern critics needs disciples, a school to carry on, apply, and extend his work; but the difficulty is that in so far as the disciples are themselves brilliant and creative (and the problem if they are not is obvious), they inevitably tend to go off in their own directions—as in the case of Richards's star pupil, Empson—and in turn to need disciples of their own, Blackmur, Fergusson, Slochower, and Cowley are all to some extent applying Burke's method to other literary problems and texts, but at the same time they are in business for themselves, and they will be efficient disciples in inverse proportion to how original, creative, and ultimately valuable to criticism they are. Only in the world inhabited by our ideal critic do people use a method with exactly the same aims and in exactly the same fashion as its originator. In the real world of criticism there is probably nothing we would want less.

To sum up, our ideal critic would extend his whole integrated method just as far as its individual component methods are capable of extension in isolation. He would, in short, do everything possible with a work of literature. For a brief lyric, as can be imagined, this would result in a tome of several volumes; for a more elaborate work, a long poem, play, or novel, it would obviously be a life study. Our ideal critic, however, has an infinity of time, and we might take advantage of his patience to note at random some of the things he would do with a poem, without attempting to assign any temporal or hierarchical priorities. He would tell what the poem is about, that is, translate its paraphrasable content as far as possible (considering the economy inherent in the work of art, this in itself should bulk much larger than the work). He would relate it to its sources and analogues in earlier literature, place it fully in a tradition, and compare it at length with contemporary and earlier works both within and outside of the tradition. He would analyze it exhaustively in terms of any available biographical information about its author: his mind, life, and personality; his family, amatory, and marital relations; his occupation, his childhood, his social relations, his physical appearance and habits. He would find its folk sources and analogues, and investigate the author's dependence on his native folk tradition, the poem's surface texture of folk speech and characteristics, and its deeper polarization in the patterns of timeless primitive ritual. He would interpret it psychologically as an expression of the author's deepest wishes and fears, in terms of complexes, repressions, sublimations, and compensations, as an expression of the archetypal patterns of collective experience, as an expression of behavioral, neurological, and endocrinological phenomena, and as an expression of the socially conditioned patterns of the author's personality and character structure; he would relate it to comparable manifestations in primitives, psychotics, children, and even animals; he would explore its organization in terms of clusters of imagery related in unconscious associations, in terms of structure functioning as psychological ritual, and in terms of the *Gestalt* configurations of its totality and their relation to other configurations.

He would interpret the poem socially as a complex and interacting reflection of the poet's social class, status, and occupation; analyze it in terms of the productive relations of his time and nation and their related climate of ideas, and the climate of ideas transcending those productive relations and going backward or forward to others; and he would discuss the social and political attitudes the poem advocates, states, or implies. He would turn all the vast resources of literary scholarship on it, or utilize all that had already been done, and follow the conclusions through with a quite unscholarly courage and imagination. He would explore at the greatest length possible its diction and the relevant ambiguous possibilities of meaning and relations in the significant words; its images and symbols and all their relevant suggestions; its formal pattern or patterns and their function and effects; its formal or informal sound-devices, rhythmic structure, and other musical effects; and its larger patterns of movement and organization; as well as the interrelationships of all the foregoing. He would study all the things outside the poem to which it makes reference and interpret it in their light. He would explore and categorize the key attitude that arises out of the interrelationship of the poem's content and form, note the implications of that category, and discuss the poem comparatively with contemporary and earlier literary expressions of the same category in different terms. Our ideal critic would investigate the whole problem of what the poem communicates, how, and to whom, using every available source of information to find out what it was meant to communicate; and then every technique, from introspection to the most objective laboratory testing, to find out what it actually does communicate, to differing individuals and groups at different times and under different circumstances. He would investigate the whole problem of symbolic action in the poem, what it does symbolically for the poet, what it does symbolically for the reader, what the relationship is between these two actions, and how it functions within the larger symbolic structure of the total development of the author's writing, or even larger symbolic movements, like a literary age. He would discuss a vast number of other problems involved in the poem, far too many to be even listed, from ultimate philosophic and ethical questions like the beliefs and ideas reflected by the poem and the values it affirms, and their relation to beliefs and values (or their absence) in the reader and the cultural context; to such minutiae as the poem's title and any unusual features of typography, spelling, or punctuation. He would place the poem in the development of the author's writing from every angle (for which purpose, naturally, he would be familiar with everything else the author wrote), confront the problem of the circumstances under which it arose, and discuss the unique features of its style and its unique reflections of a mind and personality. Finally, on the basis of all this analysis, our ideal critic would subjectively evaluate the poem and its parts aesthetically in relation to aim, scope and validity of aim, and degree of accomplishment, place its value in terms of comparable works by the same poet and others, estimate its present and future significance and popularity, assign praise or blame, and, if he cared to, advise the reader or writer or both about it. If he were so inclined, he could go on and discuss his data and opinions in relation to the data and opinions of other critics, ideal or not. He would then wipe his brow, take a deep breath, and tackle another poem.

II: THE ACTUAL CRITIC

Our ideal critic is of course nonsense, although perhaps useful nonsense as a Platonic archetype. Let us demolish him and return to the real world and the practical human possibilities of the individual. A substantial and quite impressive amount of integration is possible in the work of one rounded man using a number of methods and disciplines. At one time or another Kenneth Burke has done almost everything in the repertoire of modern criticism, and generally a number of things in conjunction. This has been only less true of Richards, Empson, and Blackmur; they have not synthesized quite so much, and they have tended, particularly Blackmur, to do only one thing at a time, whichever the work under discussion seemed particularly to call for. These are our best critics, and their individual and shifting integrations tend to be enormously successful. Their formula for avoiding the endless labors of theoretical total integration is: pursuing none of their techniques to the end of the line, but merely far enough to suggest the further possibilities; and stressing at any given time only those approaches that seem most fruitful for the specific work under discussion, slighting or ignoring others temporarily less fruitful, which would then have their place in dealing with a different type of work. Even within these limitations our best critics never seem to have enough time or space to go as far as they would like, and the demand on their learning is formidable. In the future we can expect that the burden of having a working command of every field of man's knowledge applicable to literary criticism will grow increasingly difficult to bear, and eventually simply become impossible.[1] With the tremendous growth of the social sciences in particular, sooner or later knowing enough of any one of them to turn it fruitfully on literature will demand a life study, leaving no time for anything else except some acquaintance with the corpus of literature itself. The Baconian critic, taking all knowledge for his province, is our most impressive figure, but the days of the Baconian critic in an age of more and more complete specialization seem inevitably numbered.

We must, then, consider the specialist critic, the man using one highly developed method. The ones we have had are individually less impressive than the Baconians, and we tend to feel that their very specialization makes them lopsided, inevitably distorters of literature. For the most part, they are either extremely limited figures able to do only one thing well, like Edmund Wilson's paraphrases or Van Wyck Brooks's biographies; or else they are specialists in some extra-literary field: Miss Bodkin's psychoanalysis, Caudwell's Marxism, or Miss Rourke's folk material. These critics with a single developed method are most fruitful either when specializing in literature that their method is best equipped to handle, as the Cambridge school does in Greek literature, so close to its ritual origins; or when specializing in those aspects of any work of literature which their points of view can best elucidate, as psychoanalytic and Marxist critics do (or should do).

Both these types of critical specialization need something else to make them fruitful. That something must be some form of plural, co-operative or collective criticism—Eliot's hope, expressed as far back as "Experiment in Criticism" in the *Bookman*, November 1929, for "the collaboration of critics of various special training, and perhaps the pooling and sorting of their contributions by men who will be neither specialists nor amateurs." This collaborative criticism we might call the Symposium, a word that, whatever heavy-handed use it has had in the past, still carries some pleasant associations from its root meaning, a convivial drinking-party. We have had a number of published examples of the critical symposium, some of them fairly successful, some less so. They include: scholarly and reference works done by specialists, like *A Companion to Shakespeare Studies;* symposia on special topics, like *Humanism in America* and its answer, *The Critique of Humanism, Books That Changed Our Minds,* and *The Mind in Chains;* symposia on a country or a period, like *American Writers on American Literature, After the Genteel Tradition,* and *The Great Tudors;* symposia on a writer, sometimes memorial,

---

[1] Thomas Young, an English physician, optical physicist, physiologist, Egyptologist, etc., who died in 1829, is supposed to have been the last man who knew everything scientific there was to know. No one since has come forward to dispute the honor.

like *A Garland for John Donne, Herbert Read: an introduction to his work,* and *Scattering Branches: Tributes to the Memory of W. B. Yeats;* or special issues of one of the literary magazines devoted to a writer, like the *Hound & Horn* James number, the *Southern Review* Yeats number, the *Kenyon Review* Hopkins numbers, the *Quarterly Review of Literature* Valéry number, and the *Harvard Wake* Cummings number; or even periodical symposia devoted to a single work, like the *transition* series on *Finnegans Wake,* published as *Our Exagmination,* etc., or a topic, like the *Chimera* Myth and Detective Fiction numbers, or problems of varying scope, like the several issues of *Focus.* In addition, we have had a number of false symposia or anthologies compiled after the fact, assemblages of work written at different times for different purposes, like *The Question of Henry James, The Kafka Problem,* the Critics Group *Ibsen,* and others.

The chief fault with all of these, particularly the false symposia, is that they are not specialized enough: the choice of critics tends to be haphazard and overlapping, with many methods and points of view not represented at all. In some cases the fault lies in attempting to cover too much ground, so that the contributors never meet on the same subject at all, losing the chief value of the symposium, which is not in the differences of subject-matter, but in the differences of approach to the same subject-matter. A wholly successful critical symposium would have to consist in the planned and organized cooperation of specialists, with the lines of their specialties rigidly drawn on the basis of method rather than subject. (Even the *Hound & Horn* Henry James issue, one of the best of the symposia so far, assigns most of its contributors a reserve safe from poaching, "The Early Novels," "The Critical Prefaces," and so on, and in only a few cases is the specialization purely one of method, like Francis Fergusson's study of "Drama in *The Golden Bowl.*") At the same time such a symposium would of necessity encourage an increasing division of labor, men more and more clearly demarcating just what they are doing in criticism, and doing that one thing and nothing else. It would thus tend to make modern critics even more partial, limited, specialized, and fragmentary, but they would gain in depth and assurance by way of compensation, and the whole critical job would have the virtues of scope and completeness that the modern critic can rarely get except at the cost of superficiality.

What possibilities are there in practice for such a symposium criticism? First, of course, there are the literary quarterlies, in their special numbers on a man or a topic. Even granting that the planning and organization were ideal, their handicap is that they are rarely in complete control: they cannot get any critic or type of critic they want for any project and perforce have to make do with what they can get; they lack the power to impose rigid limits of subject or method on professional critics, who tend to spread out automatically, or the money to make it worth the critic's while to remain within imposed limits; their information as to just who is capable of doing what is always haphazard; they are restricted to the amount of detailed critical study their readers will put up with; and frequently they are forced to build a symposium around work already written for other purposes and fill in the cracks as best they can, sometimes in the office. A new magazine, calling itself the *Critic* or the *Symposium,* devoted to a detailed collective study of a man or a book or a poem in each issue, acquiring and training a body of specialist critics capable of doing the things it wanted done, and gaining the prestige to get independent critics to bend their work to its purposes and readers to like it, could solve some of these problems; others would still remain.[2]

Next there are the universities, which have the money and prestige for such a project and are accustomed to procedures of specialization almost identical, in scholarship of all sorts. Whether they would be likely to indulge it in so dubious an activity as criticism, either in the form of a magazine, a series of books, or even the organization of their own literature studies in such a fashion is another thing. One of the most encouraging signs is the recent publication by the press of Princeton University of several series of papers on literature and the humanities, including *The Intent of the Artist, The Intent of the Critic,* and *The Language of Poetry,* each of them a small excellent symposium by four or five specialized authorities. Another is the sponsorship, by the English Institute, of precisely such a symposium or experiment in co-operative criticism as is here described. A seminar was held at Columbia University during a week in September 1941, under the direction of Norman Holmes Pearson of Yale. Four critics spoke for an hour each on the same poem, each on a different day. The critics chosen were Horace Gregory, Lionel Trilling, Cleanth Brooks, and Frederick Pottle (a fifth critic invited, Morton Dauwen Zabel, was not able to be present). The poem chosen was Wordsworth's "Ode on Intimations of Immortality." The audience numbered almost a hundred. I was not present at the affair, but from Donald Stauffer's account of it in "Cooperative Criticism: A Letter from the Critical Front" in the *Kenyon Review,* Winter 1942, I would guess that its relative failure lay chiefly in its narrowness of range. An even more encouraging long-range sign is the existence of a few teachers in universities throughout the country (among them Professor Leonard Brown of Syracuse University, under whom I studied) whose advanced literature classes study by the symposium method, with each student tackling the work over a long period from a different viewpoint and method, and the whole organized and assembled by the teacher. Besides the quarterlies and the universities, no likely area for

[2] The closest thing to this ideal in existence is probably the English critical magazine *Scrutiny,* which certainly has both the body of co-operating talents and the requisite prestige. Its scope is too limited ever to give the complete picture, however, and its celebrated "scrutinies," or co-operative surveys, have tended to be on cultural or educational problems rather than on writers or literary works.

the critical symposium to flourish in comes to mind. A good many oral critical symposia go on over the radio and in various forums, but the nature of impromptu speaking and the demands of a mass audience tend to confine them to inevitable triviality (as a reading of the published programs of one of the best of them, Invitation to Learning, makes unhappily clear).

One of the greatest hopes for collective criticism by symposium is that it would be equipped to unravel works so complex that they have not yet been successfully dealt with by any individual critic. *Moby Dick* is the obvious example here. When Matthiessen remarked in the introduction to *American Renaissance:* "I have not yet seen in print an adequately detailed scrutiny . . . of *Moby Dick,*" he was understating badly; we have not yet had any reading that made much sense beyond the most superficial and one-dimensional. To perhaps a lesser extent this is true of every great work of literature; all readings are inadequate, and we only satisfy ourselves by an act of impromptu collective criticism, by suspending several in our mind at once. Even where we are satisfied with our reading of the work, the addition of other meanings gives it greater depth and richness. When the old-fashioned Shakespeare professor tells his class that Hamlet's line to Polonius about Ophelia: "Let her not walke i' th' Sunne," does not carry any weight unless it is seen as a complicated pun, with at least the four suggestions of the sun as a source of madness, corruption and decay, the King and his court, and the son (Hamlet), added to its explicit meaning of pregnancy by spontaneous generation, he is not suddenly enlisted in the cause of Empsonian ambiguity, but merely recognizing that no one meaning, however reasonable, quite explains the line's sense of significance and ominousness.

In so far as great works, or key spots in any work, or the bulk of serious modern literature as a special product of the divided modern mind, all have many levels of meaning, we must have a many-leveled criticism to deal with them. Essentially this means that where the work is worth the trouble, the critic going into it with any vocabulary will emerge with a meaning paraphrasable in that vocabulary. Increasingly this has been generally recognized in recent times. Charles Baudouin, in *Psychoanalysis and Aesthetics,* speaks of it as "multiple parallelism" and compares it with the polyglot Bible. Richards calls it "multiple definition" or "multiple interpretation," and it is actually . . . the subject of all his work. Burke calls it "multiple causation" and speaks of "a set of widening circles, ranging from the uniquely particularized, through placement in terms of broad cultural developments, to absolute concepts of relationship or ground." Erich Fromm is working from a similar concept in things like his palimpsest reading of Kafka in psychoanalytic, social, and religious terms, as is Harry Slochower in his psychoanalytic, social and philosophic readings of Mann and other writers. William Troy is after the same thing in his mythic, psychoanalytic, and social readings of a number of authors, as well as in his campaign to revive the medieval "four levels of meaning" or something analogous; and on a smaller scale Jack Lindsay operates similarly in his Marxist, psychoanalytic, and anthropological readings. F. C. Prescott's "multiple significance," Herbert Muller's "multiple meaning and multivalence," Donald A. Stauffer's "multiplex meanings," and Raymond Preston's "co-operative reading" all approximate it; Empson's "ambiguity" points at it, and Philip Wheelwright's "plurisignation" and Austin Warren's "concurrent multivalence" come even closer. All criticism of *Finnegans Wake* has been automatically pluralistic from the first.

Whatever this type of criticism is called, plural or multiple or many-leveled, it is clearly becoming increasingly essential. We might if we wish call it "continuum criticism" and leave a place for all possible levels of meaning on a continuum from the most completely individual, subjective, and personal (the unconscious) to the most completely social, objective, and impersonal (the historical). The addition of Jung's "racial unconscious" would bring the two ends of our continuum together in a circle. Thus we could take, say, Eliot's symbol of the Waste Land in the poem of that name, a symbol of great depth and complexity, and read it at any level we cared to insert a vocabulary: at the most intimate level, to the Freudian, it would be castration and impotence; at a more conscious level, to a post-Freudian psychology, perhaps the fear of artistic sterility; on the daily-life level, in the biographical terms of Van Wyck Brooks, the symbol of Eliot's preconversion state; on a more social level, to a critic like Parrington, the empty life of the artist or the frustration of the upper class; to Eliot himself, the irreligion of the times; in broadly historical terms, to the Marxist, the decay of capitalism; in Jungian terms, the archetypal ritual of rebirth. Similarly, the symbol of Mynheer Peeperkorn in Mann's *Magic Mountain* would range from the Oedipal father, through the forceful rival personality, to the power of agrarian capital or the Corn God; Hitler's concept of German unity in *Mein Kampf* would range from the Oedipal mother, through "in unity there is strength," to such events in history as the absorption of Austria and Czechoslovakia, and so forth. In the symbol or work of depth there are as many meanings as critics can find levels or vocabularies with which to explore; name it, in other words, and you can have it.

There is another advantage to this sort of multiple-level or plural-meaning criticism. Thinking about the fact that Italian criticism contemporary with it completely ignored the Commedia dell' Arte, and the Elizabethan criticism for a long time completely ignored Shakespeare and the Elizabethan drama, the critic sometimes gets the nightmare idea that we in our time may similarly be ignoring works and whole art forms that will ultimately prove to be of greater significance than anything with which we deal. By sampling the movies, the detective story, the radio, and the comic book, the likely fields for this great ignored art form in our time, the critic generally manages to assuage his fears. Nevertheless, the nightmare itself is significant. What is actually disturbing his peace of mind is the tremendous responsibility the individual critic carries. He is, alone and on the authority of his own knowledge, taste, and intelligence, the sole guardian of art and its magic portals. A collective or symposium criticism would have the virtue not only of establishing a multiplicity of readings and meanings, but also of giving them all a hearing, and in the last analysis of establishing some true and valid ones. It would be not only plural, but in a very real sense dialectic or dramatistic. From the interplay of many minds, even many errors, truth arises, as our wise men have known since Plato's dialogues. This synthesis of critical method is not simple multiplicity or plurality or anarchy, but a genuine dialectic contest or *agon*. From it, too, truth will arise. We may get it within the individual critic, in an integrated method, or outside the individual critic, in the group symposium, but in some form or other we must get it. And "we" here stands for the whole world, for where "truth" is at issue, we are all of necessity critics.

From *The Armed Vision: A Study in the Methods of Modern Literary Criticism* by Stanley Edgar Hyman (New York: Alfred A. Knopf, 1948), pp. 395–407, where it appears as "Conclusion: Attempts at an Integration." Reprinted by permission of the author and publisher.

R. P. BLACKMUR

A Critic's Job of Work

[1935]

CRITICISM, I take it, is the formal discourse of an amateur. When there is enough love and enough knowledge represented in the discourse it is a self-sufficient but by no means an isolated art. It witnesses constantly in its own life its interdependence with the other arts. It lays out the terms and parallels of appreciation from the outside in order to convict itself of internal intimacy; it names and arranges what it knows and loves, and searches endlessly with every fresh impulse or impression for better names and more orderly arrangements. It is only in this sense that poetry (or some other art) is a criticism of life; poetry names and arranges, and thus arrests and transfixes its subject in a form which has a life of its own forever separate but springing from the life which confronts it. Poetry is life at the remove of form and meaning; not life lived but life framed and identified. So the criticism of poetry is bound to be occupied at once with the terms and modes by which the remove was made and with the relation between—in the ambiguous stock phrase—content and form; which is to say with the establishment and appreciation of human or moral value. It will be the underlying effort of this essay to indicate approaches to criticism wherein these two problems—of form and value—will appear inextricable but not confused—like the stones in an arch or the timbers in a building.

These approaches—these we wish to eulogize—are not the only ones, nor the only good ones, nor are they complete. No approach opens on anything except from its own point of view and in terms of its own prepossessions. Let us set against each other for a time the facts of various approaches to see whether there is a residue, not of fact but of principle.

The approaches to—or the escapes from—the central work of criticism are as various as the heresies of the Christian church, and like them testify to occasional needs, fanatic emphasis, special interest, or intellectual pride, all flowing from and even the worst of them enlightening the same body of insight. Every critic like every theologian and every philosopher is a casuist in spite of himself. To escape or surmount the discontinuity of knowledge, each resorts to a particular heresy and makes it predominant and even omnivorous.[1]

For most minds, once doctrine is sighted and is held to be the completion of insight, the doctrinal mode of thinking seems the only one possible. When doctrine totters it seems it can fall only into the gulf of bewilderment; few minds risk the fall; most seize the remnants and swear the edifice remains, when doctrine becomes intolerable dogma.[2] All fall notwithstanding; for as knowledge itself is a fall from the paradise of undifferentiated sensation, so equally every formula of knowledge must fall the moment too much weight is laid upon it—the moment it becomes omnivorous and pretends to be omnipotent—the moment, in short, it is taken literally. Literal knowledge is dead knowledge; and the worst bewilderment—which is always only comparative —is better than death. Yet no form, no formula, of knowledge ought to be surrendered merely because it runs the risk in bad or desperate hands of being used literally; and similarly, in our own thinking, whether it is carried to the point of formal discourse or not, we cannot only afford, we ought scrupulously to risk the use of any concept that seems propitious or helpful in getting over gaps. Only the use should be consciously provisional, speculative, and dramatic. The end-virtue of humility comes only after a long train of humiliations; and the chief labor of humbling is the constant, resourceful restoration of ignorance.

The classic contemporary example of use and misuse is attached to the name of Freud. Freud himself has constantly emphasized the provisional, dramatic character of his speculations: they are employed as imaginative illumination, to be relied on no more and no less than the sailor relies upon his buoys and beacons.[3] But the impetus of Freud was so great that a school of literalists arose with all the mad consequence of schism and heresy and fundamentalism which have no more honorable place in the scientific than the artistic imagination. Elsewhere, from one point of view, Caesarism in Rome and Berlin is only the literalist conception of the need for a positive state. So, too, the economic insights of Marxism, merely by being taken literally in their own field, are held to affect the subject and value of the arts, where actually they offer only a limited field of interest and enliven an irrelevant purpose. It is an amusing exercise—as it refreshes the terms of bewilderment and provides a common clue to the secrets of all the modes of thinking —to restore the insights of Freud and Fascism and Marxism to the terms of

---

[1] The rashest heresy of our day and climate is that exemplified by T. S. Eliot when he postulates an orthodoxy which exists whether anyone knows it or not.

[2] Baudelaire's sonnet "Le Gouffre" dramatizes this sentiment at once as he saw it surmounted in Pascal and as it occurred insurmountably in himself.

[3] Santayana's essay "A Long Way Round to Nirvana" (in *Some Turns of Thought in Modern Philosophy*) illustrates the poetic-philosophic character of Freud's insight into death by setting up its analogue in Indian philosophy; and by his comparison only adds to the stimulus of Freud.

the Church; when the sexual drama in Freud becomes the drama of original sin, and the politics of Hitler and Lenin becomes the politics of the City of God in the sense that theology provides both the sanctions of economics and the values of culture. Controversy is in terms absolutely held, when the problems argued are falsely conceived because necessarily abstracted from "real" experience. The vital or fatal nexus is in interest and emotion and is established when the terms can be represented dramatically, almost, as it were, for their own sakes alone and with only a pious or ritualistic regard for the doctrines in which they are clothed. The simple, and fatal, example is in the glory men attach to war; the vital, but precarious example, is in the intermittent conception of free institutions and the persistent reformulation of the myth of reason. Then the doctrines do not matter; since they are taken only for what they are worth (whatever rhetorical pretensions to the contrary) as guides and props, as aids to navigation. What does matter is experience, the life represented and the value discovered, and both dramatized or enacted under the banner of doctrine. All banners are wrong-headed, but they make rallying points, free the impulse to cry out, and give meaning to the cry itself simply by making it seem appropriate.

It is on some analogue or parallel to these remarks alone that we understand and use the thought and art of those whose doctrines differ from our own. We either discount, absorb, or dominate the doctrine for the sake of the life that goes with it, for the sake of what is *formed* in the progressive act of thinking. When we do more—when we refine or elaborate the abstracted notion of form—we play a different game, which has merit of its own like chess, but which applied to the world we live in produces false dilemmas like solipsism and infant damnation. There is, taking solipsism for example, a fundamental distinction. Because of the logical doctrine prepared to support it, technical philosophers employ years[4] to get around the impasse in which it leaves them; whereas men of poetic imagination merely use it for the dramatic insight it contains—as Eliot uses it in the last section of *The Waste Land;* or as, say, everyone uses the residual mythology of the Greek religion —which its priests nevertheless used as literal sanction for blood and power.

Fortunately, there exist archetypes of unindoctrinated thinking. Let us incline our minds like reflectors to catch the light of the early Plato and the whole Montaigne. Is not the inexhaustible stimulus and fertility of the *Dialogues* and the *Essays* due as much as anything to the absence of positive doctrine? Is it not that the early Plato always holds conflicting ideas in shifting balance, presenting them in contest and evolution, with victory only the last shift? Is it not that Montaigne is always making room for another idea, and

---

[4] Santayana found it necessary to resort to his only sustained labor of dialectic, *Scepticism and Animal Faith,* which, though a beautiful monument of intellectual play, is ultimately valuable for its *incidental* moral wisdom.

implying always a third for provisional adjudicating irony? Are not the forms of both men themselves ironic, betraying in its most intimate recesses the duplicity of every thought, pointing out, so to speak, in the act of self-incrimination, and showing it not paled on a pin but in the buff life? . . . Such an approach, such an attempt at vivid questing, borrowed and no doubt adulterated by our own needs, is the only rational approach to the multiplication of doctrine and arrogant technologies which fills out the body of critical thinking. Anything else is a succumbing, not an approach; and it is surely the commonest of ironies to observe a man altogether out of his depth do his cause fatal harm merely because, having once succumbed to an idea, he thinks it necessary to stick to it. Thought is a beacon not a life-raft, and to confuse the functions is tragic. The tragic character of thought—as any perspective will show—is that it takes a rigid mold too soon; chooses destiny like a Calvinist, in infancy, instead of waiting slowly for old age, and hence for the most part works against the world, good sense, and its own object: as anyone may see by taking a perspective of any given idea of democracy, of justice, or the nature of the creative act.

Imaginative skepticism and dramatic irony—the modes of Montaigne and Plato—keep the mind athletic and the spirit on the stretch. Hence the juvenescence of The Tempest and hence, too, perhaps, the air almost of precocity in Back to Methuselah. Hence, at any rate, the sustaining power of such varied works as The Brothers Karamazoff, Cousine Bette, and The Magic Mountain. Dante, whom the faithful might take to the contrary, is yet "the chief imagination of Christendom"; he took his doctrine once and for all from the Church and from St. Thomas and used it as a foil (in the painter's sense) to give recessiveness, background, and contrast. Virgil and Aristotle, Beatrice and Bertrans de Born have in their way as much importance as St. Thomas and the Church. It was this security of reference that made Dante so much more a free spirit than were, say, Swift and Laurence Sterne. Dante had a habit (not a theory) of imagination which enabled him to dramatize with equal ardor and effect what his doctrine blessed, what it assailed, and what, at heart, it was indifferent to. Doctrine was the seed and structure of vision, and for his poems (at least to us) never more. The Divine Comedy no less than the Dialogues and the Essays is a true Speculum Mentis.

With lesser thinkers and lesser artists—and in the defective works of the greater—we have in reading, in criticising, to supply the skepticism and the irony, or, as may be, the imagination and the drama, to the degree, which cannot be complete since then we should have had no prompts, that they are lacking. We have to rub the looking-glass clear. With Hamlet, for example, we have to struggle and guess to bring the motive out of obscurity: a struggle which, aiming at the wrong end, the psychoanalysts have darkened with counsel. With Shelley we have to flesh out the Platonic Ideas, as with

Blake we have to cut away, since it cannot be dramatized, all the excrescence of doctrine. With Baudelaire we have sometimes to struggle with and sometimes to suppress the problem of belief, working out the irony implicit in either attitude. Similarly, with a writer like Pascal, in order to get the most out of him, in order to compose an artistic judgment, we must consider such an idea as that of the necessity of the wager, not solemnly as Pascal took it, but as a dramatized possibility, a savage, but provisional irony; and we need to show that the skepticisms of Montaigne and Pascal are not at all the same thing—that where one produced serenity the other produced excruciation.

Again, speaking of André Gide, we should remind ourselves not that he has been the apologist of homosexuality, not that he has become a communist, but that he is *par excellence* the French puritan chastened by the wisdom of the body, and that he has thus an acutely scrupulous ethical sensibility. It is by acknowledging the sensibility that we feel the impact of the apologetics and the political conversion. Another necessity in the apprehension of Gide might be put as the recognition of similarity in difference of the precocious small boys in Dostoevski and Gide, *e.g.*, Kolya in *Karamazoff* and young George in *The Counterfeiters:* they are small, cruel engines, all naked sensibility and no scruple, demoniacally possessed, and used to keep things going. And these in turn may remind us of another writer who had a predilection for presenting the *terrible* quality of the young intelligence: of Henry James, of the children in *The Turn of the Screw,* of *Maisie,* and all the rest, all beautifully efficient agents of dramatic judgment and action, in that they take all things seriously for themselves, with the least prejudice of preparation, candidly, with an intelligence life has not yet violated.

Such feats of agility and attention as these remarks illustrate seem facile and even commonplace, and from facile points of view there is no need to take them otherwise. Taken superficially they provide escape from the whole labor of specific understanding; or, worse, they provide an easy vault from casual interpretation to an omnivorous world-view. We might take solemnly and as of universal application the two notions of demonic possession and inviolate intelligence of Gide, Dostoievski, and James, and on that frail nexus build an unassailable theory of the sources of art, wisdom, and value; unassailable because affording only a stereotyped vision, like that of conservative capitalism, without reference in the real world. The maturity of Shakespeare and of Gertrude Stein would then be found on the same childish level.

But we need not go so far in order to draw back. The modes of Montaigne and Plato contain their own safety. Any single insight is good only at and up to a certain point of development and not beyond, which is to say that it is a provisional and tentative and highly selective approach to its field. Furthermore, no observation, no collection of observations, ever tells the whole story; there is always room for more, and at the hypothetical limit of attention and interest there will always remain, quite untouched, the thing itself. Thus the complex character—I say nothing of the value—of the remarks above reveals itself. They flow from a dramatic combination of all the skills and conventions of the thinking mind. They are commonplace only as a criticism—as an end-product or function. Like walking, criticism is a pretty nearly universal art; both require a constant intricate shifting and catching of balance; neither can be questioned much in process; and few perform either really well. For either a new terrain is fatiguing and awkward, and in our day most men prefer paved walks or some form of rapid transit—some easy theory or outmastering dogma. A good critic keeps his criticism from becoming either instinctive or vicarious, and the labor of his understanding is always specific, like the art which he examines; and he knows that the sum of his best work comes only to the pedagogy of elucidation and appreciation. He observes facts and he delights in discriminations. The object remains, and should remain, itself, only made more available and seen in a clearer light. The imagination of Dante is for us only equal to what we can know of it at a given time.

Which brings us to what, as T. S. Eliot would say,[5] I have been leading up to all the time, and what has indeed been said several times by the way. Any rational approach is valid to literature and may be properly called critical which fastens at any point upon the work itself. The utility of a given approach depends partly upon the strength of the mind making it and partly upon the recognition of the limits appropriate to it. Limits may be of scope, degree, or relevance, and may be either plainly laid out by the critic himself, or may be determined by his readers; and it is, by our argument, the latter case that commonly falls, since an active mind tends to overestimate the scope of its tools and to take as necessary those doctrinal considerations which habit has made seem instinctive. No critic is required to limit himself to a single approach, nor is he likely to be able to do so; facts cannot be exhibited without comment, and comment involves the generality of the mind. Furthermore, a consciously complex approach like that of Kenneth Burke or T. S. Eliot, by setting up parallels of reference, affords a more flexible, more available, more stimulating standard of judgment—though of course at a greater risk of prejudice—than a single approach. What produces the evil of stultification and the malice of controversy is the confused approach, when the limits are not seen because they tend to cancel each other out, and the driving power becomes emotional.

[5] . . . that when "morals cease to be a matter of tradition and orthodoxy—that is, of the habits of the community formulated, corrected, and elevated by the continuous thought and direction of the Church—and when each man is to elaborate his own, then *personality* becomes a thing of alarming importance." (*After Strange Gods.*) Thus Mr. Eliot becomes one of those viewers-with-alarm whose next step is the very hysteria of disorder they wish to escape. The hysteria of institutions is more dreadful than that of individuals.

The worse evil of fanatic falsification—of arrogant irrationality and barbarism in all its forms—arises when a body of criticism is governed by an *idée fixe*, a really exaggerated heresy, when a notion of genuine but small scope is taken literally as of universal application. This is the body of tendentious criticism where, since something is assumed proved before the evidence is in, distortion, vitiation, and absolute assertion become supreme virtues. I cannot help feeling that such writers as Maritain and Massis—no less than Nordau before them—are tendentious in this sense. But even here, in this worst order of criticism, there is a taint of legitimacy. Once we reduce, in a man like Irving Babbitt, the magnitude of application of such notions as the inner check and the higher will, which were for Babbitt paramount—that is, when we determine the limits within which he really worked—then the massive erudition and acute observation with which his work is packed become permanently available.

And there is no good to be got in objecting to and disallowing those orders of criticism which have an ulterior purpose. *Ulterior* is not in itself a pejorative, but only so when applied to an enemy. Since criticism is not autonomous—not a light but a process of elucidation—it cannot avoid discovering constantly within itself a purpose or purposes ulterior in the good sense. The danger is in not knowing what is ulterior and what is not, which is much the same as the cognate danger in the arts themselves. The arts serve purposes beyond themselves; the purposes of what they dramatize or represent at that remove from the flux which gives them order and meaning and value; and to deny those purposes is like asserting that the function of a handsaw is to hang above a bench and that to cut wood is to belittle it. But the purposes are varied and so bound in his subject that the artist cannot always design for them. The critic, if that is his bent, may concern himself with those purposes or with some one among them which obsess him; but he must be certain to distinguish between what is genuinely ulterior to the works he examines and what is merely irrelevant; and he must further not assume except within the realm of his special argument that other purposes either do not exist or are negligible or that the works may not be profitably discussed apart from ulterior purposes and as examples of dramatic possibility alone.

II

Three examples of contemporary criticism primarily concerned with the ulterior purposes of literature should, set side by side, exhibit both the defects and the unchastened virtues of that approach; though they must do so only tentatively and somewhat invidiously—with an exaggeration for effect. Each work is assumed to be a representative ornament of its kind, carrying within it the seeds of its own death and multiplication. Let us take then, with an eye sharpened by the dangers involved, Santayana's essay on Lucretius (in *Three*

Philosophical Poets), Van Wyck Brooks' *Pilgrimage of Henry James,* and Granville Hicks' *The Great Tradition.* Though that of the third is more obvious in our predicament, the urgency in the approach is equal in all three.

Santayana's essay represents a conversion or transvaluation of an actually poetic ordering of nature to the terms of a moral philosophy which, whatever its own responsibilities, is free of the special responsibility of poetry. So ably and so persuasively is it composed, his picture seems complete and to contain so much of what was important in Lucretius that *De Rerum Natura* itself can be left behind. The philosophical nature of the insight, its moral scope and defect, the influence upon it of the Democritan atom, once grasped intellectually as Santayana shows us how to grasp them, seem a good substitute for the poem and far more available. But, what Santayana remembers but does not here emphasize since it was beyond his immediate interest, there is no vicar for poetry on earth. Poetry is idiom, a special and fresh saying, and cannot for its life be said otherwise; and there is, finally, as much difference between words used about a poem and the poem as there is between words used about a painting and the painting. The gap is absolute. Yet I do not mean to suggest that Santayana's essay—that any philosophical criticism—is beside the point. It is true that the essay may be taken as a venture in philosophy for its own sake, but it is also true that it reveals a body of facts about an ulterior purpose in Lucretius' poem—doubtless the very purpose Lucretius himself would have chosen to see enhanced. If we return to the poem it will be warmer as the facts come alive in the verse. The re-conversion comes naturally in this instance in that, through idioms differently construed but equally imaginative, philosophy and poetry both buttress and express moral value. The one enacts or represents in the flesh what the other reduces to principle or raises to the ideal. The only precaution the critic of poetry need take is negative: that neither poetry nor philosophy can ever fully satisfy the other's purposes, though each may seem to do so if taken in an ulterior fashion. The relationship is mutual but not equivalent.

When we turn deliberately from Santayana on Lucretius to Van Wyck Brooks on Henry James, we turn from the consideration of the rational ulterior purposes of art to the consideration of the irrational underlying predicament of the artist himself, not only as it predicts his art and is reflected in it, but also, and in effect predominantly, as it represents the conditioning of nineteenth-century American culture. The consideration is sociological, the method of approach that of literary psychology, and the burden obsessive. The conversion is from literary to biographical values. Art is taken not as the objectification or mirroring of social experience but as a personal expression and escape-fantasy of the artist's personal life in dramatic extension. The point for emphasis is that the cultural situation of Henry James' America stultified the expression and made every escape ineffectual—even that of Europe.

This theme—the private tragedy of the unsuccessful artist—was one of Henry James' own; but James saw it as typical or universal—as a characteristic tragedy of the human spirit—illustrated, as it happened for him, against the Anglo-American background. Brooks, taking the same theme, raises it to an obsession, an omnivorous concept, under which all other themes can be subsumed. Applied to American cultural history, such obsessive thinking is suggestive in the very exaggeration of its terms, and applied to the private predicament of Henry James the man it dramatically emphasizes—uses for all and more than it is worth—an obvious conflict that tormented him. As history or as biography the book is a persuasive imaginative picture, although clearly not the only one to be seen. Used as a nexus between James the man and the novels themselves, the book has only possible relevance and cannot be held as material. *Hamlet*, by a similar argument, could be shown to be an unsuccessful expression of Shakespeare's personality. To remain useful in the field of literary criticism, Brooks' notions ought to be kept parallel to James' novels but never allowed to merge with them. The corrective, the proof of the gap, is perhaps in the great air of freedom and sway of mastery that pervades the "Prefaces" James wrote to his collected edition. For James art was enough because it molded and mirrored and valued all the life he knew. What Brooks' parallel strictures can do is to help us decide from another point of view whether to choose the values James dramatized. They cannot affect or elucidate but rather—if the gap is closed by will—obfuscate the values themselves.

In short, the order of criticism of which Brooks is a masterly exponent, and which we may call the psycho-sociological order, is primarily and in the end concerned less with the purposes, ulterior or not, of the arts than with some of the ulterior *uses* to which the arts can be appropriately put. Only what is said in the meantime, by the way—and does not depend upon the essence of argument but only accompanies it—can be applied to the arts themselves. There is nothing, it should be added, in Brooks' writings to show that he believes otherwise or would claim more; he is content with that scope and degree of value to which his method and the strength of his mind limit him; and his value is the greater and more urgent for that.

Such tacit humility, such implicit admission of contingency, are not immediate characteristics of Granville Hicks' *The Great Tradition*, though they may, so serious is his purpose, be merely virtues of which he deliberately, for the time being and in order to gain his point, deprives himself of the benefit. If this is so, however expedient his tactics may seem on the short view they will defeat him on the long. But let us examine the book on the ground of our present concern alone. Like Brooks, Hicks presents an interpretation of American literature since the Civil War, dealing with the whole body rather than single figures. Like Brooks he has a touchstone in an obsessive idea, but where we may say that Brooks *uses* his idea—as we think for more than it is

worth—we must say that Hicks is victimized by his idea to the point where
the travail of judgment is suspended and becomes the mere reiteration of formula. He judges literature as it expressed or failed to express the economic
conflict of classes sharpened by the industrial revolution, and he judges individual writers as they used or did not use an ideology resembling the Marxist analysis as prime clue to the clear representation of social drama. Thus
Howells comes off better than Henry James, and Frank Norris better than
Mark Twain, and, in our own day, Dos Passos is stuck on a thin eminence
that must alarm him.

Controversy is not here a profitable exercise, but it may be said for the
sake of the record that although every period of history presents a class struggle, some far more acute than our own, the themes of great art have seldom
lent themselves to propaganda for an economic insight, finding, as it happened, religious, moral or psychological—that is to say, interpretative—insights more appropriate impulses. If *Piers Plowman* dealt with the class struggle, *The Canterbury Tales* did not, and Hicks would be hard put, if he looked
sharp, to make out a better case of social implication in Dostoievski than in
Henry James.

What vitiates *The Great Tradition* is its tendentiousness. Nothing could
be more exciting, nothing more vital, than a book by Hicks which discovered
and examined the facts of a literature whose major theme hung on an honest
dramatic view of the class struggle—and there is indeed such a literature now
emerging from the depression. And on the other hand it would be worth
while to have Hicks sharpen his teeth on all the fraudulent or pseudo-art
which actually slanders the terms of the class and every other struggle.

The book with which he presents us performs a very different operation.
There is an initial hortatory assumption that American literature ought to represent the class struggle from a Marxist viewpoint, and that it ought thus to be
the spur and guide to political action. Proceeding, the point is either proved or
the literature dismissed and its authors slandered. Hicks is not disengaging for
emphasis and contemporary need an ulterior purpose; he is not writing criticism at all; he is writing a fanatic's history and a casuist's polemic, with the
probable result—which is what was meant by suggesting above that he had
misconceived his tactics—that he will convert no one who retains the least
love of literature or the least knowledge of the themes which engage the most
of life. It should be emphasized that there is no more quarrel with Hicks' economic insight as such than there was with the insights of Santayana and Van
Wyck Brooks. The quarrel is deeper. While it is true and good that the arts
may be used to illustrate social propaganda—though it is not a great use—you
can no more use an economic insight as your chief critical tool than you can
make much out of the Mass by submitting the doctrine of transubstantiation
to chemical analysis.

These three writers have one great formal fact in common, which they illustrate as differently as may be. They are concerned with the separable content of literature, with what may be said without consideration of its specific setting and apparition in a form; which is why, perhaps, all three leave literature so soon behind. The quantity of what can be said directly about the content alone of a given work of art is seldom great, but the least saying may be the innervation of an infinite intellectual structure, which, however valuable in itself, has for the most part only an asserted relation with the works from which it springs. The sense of continuous relationship, of sustained contact, with the works nominally in hand is rare and when found uncommonly exhilarating; it is the fine object of criticism; as it seems to put us in direct possession of the principles whereby the works move without injuring or disintegrating the body of the works themselves. This sense of intimacy by inner contact cannot arise from methods of approach which hinge on seized separable content. We have constantly—if our interest is really in literature—to prod ourselves back, to remind ourselves that there was a poem, a play, or a novel of some initial and we hope terminal concern, or we have to falsify and set up fictions[6] to the effect that no matter what we are saying we are really talking about art after all. The question must often be whether the prodding and reminding is worth the labor, whether we might not better assign the works that require it to a different category than that of criticism.

III

Similar strictures and identical precautions are necessary in thinking of other, quite different approaches to criticism, where if there are no ulterior purposes to allow for there are other no less limiting features—there are certainly such, for example, for me in thinking of my own. The ulterior motive, or the limiting feature, whichever it is, is a variable constant. One does not always know what it is, nor what nor how much work it does; but one always knows it is there—for strength or weakness. It may be only the strength of emphasis—which is necessarily distortion; or it may be the worse strength of a simplifying formula, which skeletonizes and transforms what we want to recognize in the flesh. It may be only the weakness of what is unfinished, undeveloped, or unseen—the weakness that follows on emphasis; or it may be the weakness that shows when pertinent things are deliberately dismissed or

---

[6] Such a fiction, if not consciously so contrived, is the fiction of the organic continuity of all literature as expounded by T. S. Eliot in his essay, "Tradition and the Individual Talent." The locus is famous and represents that each new work of art slightly alters the relationships among the whole order of existing works. The notion has truth, but it is a mathematical truth and has little relevance to the arts. Used as Eliot uses it, it is an experimental conceit and pushes the mind forward. Taken seriously it is bad constitutional law, in the sense that it would provoke numberless artificial and insoluble problems.

ignored, which is the corresponding weakness of the mind strong in formula. No mind can avoid distortion and formula altogether, nor would wish to; but minds rush to the defense of qualities they think cannot be avoided, and that, in itself, is an ulterior motive, a limiting feature of the mind that rushes. I say nothing of one's personal prepossessions, of the damage of one's private experience, of the malice and false tolerance they inculcate into judgment. I know that my own essays suffer variously, but I cannot bring myself to specify the indulgences I would ask; mostly, I hope, that general indulgence which consists in the task of bringing my distortions and emphases and opinions into balance with other distortions, other emphases and better opinions.

But rather than myself, let us examine briefly, because of their differences from each other and from the three critics already handled, the modes of approach to the act of criticism and habits of critical work of I. A. Richards, Kenneth Burke, and S. Foster Damon. It is to characterize them and to judge the *character* of their work—its typical scope and value—that we want to examine them. With the objective validity of their varying theories we are not much here concerned. Objective standards of criticism, as we hope them to exist at all, must have an existence anterior and superior to the practice of particular critics. The personal element in a given critic—what he happens to know and happens to be able to understand—is strong or obstinate enough to reach into his esthetic theories; and as most critics do not have the coherence of philosophers it seems doubtful if any outsider could ever reach the same conclusions as the critic did by adopting his esthetics. Esthetics sometimes seems only as implicit in the practice of criticism as the atomic physics is present in sunlight when you feel it.

But some critics deliberately expand the theoretic phase of every practical problem. There is a tendency to urge the scientific principle and the statistical method, and in doing so to bring in the whole assorted world of thought. That Mr. Richards, who is an admirable critic and whose love and knowledge of poetry are incontestable, is a victim of the expansiveness of his mind in these directions, is what characterizes, and reduces, the scope of his work as literary criticism. It is possible that he ought not to be called a literary critic at all. If we list the titles of his books we are in a quandary: *The Foundations of Aesthetics, The Meaning of Meaning* (these with C. K. Ogden), *The Principles of Literary Criticism, Science and Poetry, Practical Criticism, Mencius on the Mind,* and *Coleridge on Imagination.* The apparatus is so vast, so labyrinthine, so inclusive—and the amount of actual literary criticism is so small that it seems almost a by-product instead of the central target. The slightest volume, physically, *Science and Poetry,* contains proportionally the most literary criticism, and contains, curiously, his one obvious failure in appreciation— since amply redressed—his misjudgment of the nature of Yeats' poetry. His work is for the most part *about* a department of the mind which includes the pedagogy of sensibility and the practice of literary criticism. The matters he investigates are the problems of belief, of meaning, of communication, of the nature of controversy, and of poetic language as the supreme mode of imagination. The discussion of these problems is made to focus for the most part on poetry because poetry provides the only great monuments of imagination available to verbal imagination. His bottom contention might, I think, be put as this: that words have a synergical power, in the realms of feeling, emotion, and value, to create a reality, or the sense of it, not contained in the words separately; and that the power and the reality as experienced in great poetry make the chief source of meaning and value for the life we live. This contention I share; except that I should wish to put on the same level, as sources of meaning and value, modes of imagination that have no medium in words—though words may call on them—and are not susceptible of verbal reformulation: the modes of great acting, architecture, music and painting. Thus I can assent to Mr. Richards' positive statement of the task of criticism, because I can add to it positive tasks in analogous fields: "To recall that poetry is the supreme use of language, man's chief co-ordinating instrument, in the service of the most integral purposes of life; and to explore, with thoroughness, the intricacies of the modes of language as working modes of the mind." But I want this criticism, engaged in this task, constantly to be confronted with examples of poetry, and I want it so for the very practical purpose of assisting in pretty immediate appreciation of the use, meaning, and value of the language in that particular poetry. I want it to assist in doing for me what it actually assists Mr. Richards in doing, whatever that is, when he is reading poetry for its own sake.

Mr. Richards wants it to do that, too, but he wants it to do a great deal else first. Before it gets to actual poetry (from which it is said to spring) he wants literary criticism to become something else and much more: he wants it to become, indeed, the master department of the mind. As we become aware of the scope of poetry, we see, according to Mr. Richards that the

. . . study of the modes of language becomes, as it attempts to be thorough, the most fundamental and extensive of all inquiries. It is no preliminary or preparation for other profounder studies. . . . The very formation of the objects which these studies propose to examine takes place through the processes (of which imagination and fancy are modes) by which the words they use acquire their meanings. Criticism is the science of these meanings. . . . Critics in the future must have a theoretical equipment which has not been felt to be necessary in the past. . . . But the critical equipment will not be *primarily* philosophical. It will be rather a command *of the methods of general linguistic analysis.*[7]

I think we may take it that *Mencius on the Mind* is an example of the kind of excursion on which Mr. Richards would lead us. It is an excursion into multi-

[7] All quoted material is from the last four pages of *Coleridge on Imagination.*

ple definition, and it is a good one if that is where you want to go and are in no hurry to come back: you learn the enormous variety and complexity of the operations possible in the process of verbally describing and defining brief passages of imaginative language and the equal variety and complexity of the result; you learn the practical impossibility of verbally ascertaining what an author means—and you hear nothing of the other ways of apprehending meaning at all. The instance is in the translation of Mencius, because Mr. Richards happens to be interested in Mencius, and because it is easy to see the difficulties of translating Chinese; but the principles and method of application would work as well on passages from Milton or Rudyard Kipling. The real point of Mr. Richards' book is the impossibility of understanding, short of a lifetime's analysis and compensation, the mechanism of meaning in even a small body of work. There is no question of the exemplary value and stimulus of Mr. Richards' work; but there is no question either that few would care to emulate him for any purpose of literary criticism. In the first place it would take too long, and in the second he does not answer the questions literary criticism would put. The literal adoption of Mr. Richards' approach to literary criticism would stultify the very power it was aimed to enhance—the power of imaginative apprehension, of imaginative co-ordination of varied and separate elements. Mr. Richards' work is something to be aware of, but deep awareness is the limit of use. It is notable that in his admirable incidental criticism of such poets as Eliot, Lawrence, Yeats and Hopkins, Mr. Richards does not himself find it necessary to be more than aware of his own doctrines of linguistic analysis. As philosophy from Descartes to Bradley transformed itself into a study of the modes of knowing, Mr. Richards would transform literary criticism into the science of linguistics. Epistemology is a great subject, and so is linguistics; but they come neither in first nor final places; the one is only a fragment of wisdom and the other only a fraction of the means of understanding. Literary criticism is not a science—though it may be the object of one; and to try to make it one is to turn it upside down. Right side up, Mr. Richards' contribution shrinks in weight and dominion but remains intact and preserves its importance. We may conclude that it was the newness of his view that led him to exaggerate it, and we ought to add the probability that had he not exaggerated it we should never have seen either that it was new or valuable at all.

From another point of view than that of literary criticism, and as a contribution to a psychological theory of knowledge, Mr. Richards' work is not heretical, but is integral and integrating, and especially when it incorporates poetry into its procedure; but from our point of view the heresy is profound —and is far more distorting than the heresies of Santayana, Brooks, and Hicks, which carry with them obviously the impetus for their correction. Because it is possible to apply scientific methods to the language of poetry, and because sci-

entific methods engross their subject matter, Mr. Richards places the whole
burden of criticism in the application of a scientific approach, and asserts it to
be an implement for the judgment of poetry. Actually, it can handle only the
language and its words and cannot touch—except by assertion—the imaginative product of the words which is poetry: which is the object revealed or
elucidated by criticism. Criticism must be concerned, first and last—whatever
comes between—with the poem as it is read and as what it represents is felt.
As no amount of physics and physiology can explain the *feeling* of things seen
as green or even certify their existence, so no amount of linguistic analysis can
explain the *feeling* or existence of a poem. Yet the physics in the one case and
the linguistics in the other may be useful both to the poet and the reader. It
may be useful, for example, in extracting facts of meaning from a poem, to
show that, whether the poet was aware of it or not, the semantic history of a
word was so and so; but only if the semantics can be resolved into the ambiguities and precisions created by the poem. Similarly with any branch of
linguistics; and similarly with the applications of psychology—Mr. Richards'
other emphasis. No statistical description can either explain or demean a
poem unless the description is translated back to the imaginative apprehension
or feeling which must have taken place without it. The light of science is
parallel or in the background where feeling or meaning is concerned. The
Oedipus complex does not explain *Oedipus Rex;* not that Mr. Richards would
think it did. Otherwise he could not believe that "poetry is the supreme use
of language" and more, could not convey in his comments on T. S. Eliot's *Ash
Wednesday* the actuality of his belief that poetry is the supreme use.

It is the interest and fascination of Mr. Richards' work in reference to
different levels of sensibility, including the poetic, that has given him both a
wide and a penetrating influence. No literary critic can escape his influence;
an influence that stimulates the mind as much as anything by showing the
sheer excitement as well as profundity of the problems of language—many of
which he has himself made genuine problems, at least for the readers of poetry: an influence, obviously, worth deliberately incorporating by reducing it
to one's own size and needs. In T. S. Eliot the influence is conspicuous if
slight. Mr. Kenneth Burke is considerably indebted, partly directly to Mr.
Richards, partly to the influences which acted upon Mr. Richards (as Bentham's theory of Fictions) and partly to the frame of mind which helped mold
them both. But Mr. Burke is clearly a different person—and different from
anyone writing today; and the virtues, the defects, and the élan of his criticism
are his own.

Some years ago, when Mr. Burke was an animating influence on the staff of
The Dial, Miss Marianne Moore published a poem in that magazine called
"Picking and Choosing" which contained the following lines:

and Burke is a
psychologist—of acute and racoon-
like curiosity. *Summa diligentia*
to the humbug, whose name is so amusing—very young
and ve-
ry rushed, Caesar crossed the Alps on the 'top of a
diligence.' We are not daft about the meaning but this
familiarity
with wrong meanings puzzles one.

In the index of Miss Moore's *Observations,* we find under Burke that the
reference is to Edmund, but it is really to Kenneth just the same. There is no
acuter curiosity than Mr. Burke's engaged in associating the meanings, right
and wrong, of the business of literature with the business of life and vice
versa. No one has a greater awareness—not even Mr. Richards—of the important part wrong meanings play in establishing the consistency of right ones.
The writer of whom he reminds us, for the buoyancy and sheer remarkable-
ness of his speculations, is Charles Santiago Saunders Peirce; one is enlivened
by them without any *necessary* reference to their truth; hence they have truth
for their own purposes, that is, for their own uses. Into what these purposes or
uses are it is our present business to inquire.

As Mr. Richards in fact uses literature as a springboard or source for scientific method of a philosophy of value, Mr. Burke uses literature, not only as a
springboard but also as a resort or home, for philosophy or psychology of moral
possibility. Literature is the hold-all and the persuasive form for the patterns
of possibility. In literature we see unique possibilities enacted, actualized, and
in the moral and psychological philosophies we see the types of possibility
generalized, see their abstracted, convertible forms. In some literature, and in
some aspects of most literature of either great magnitude or great possibility,
we see, so to speak, the enactment or dramatic representation of the type or
patterns. Thus Mr. Burke can make a thrilling intellectual pursuit of the
subintelligent writing of Erskine Caldwell: where he shows that Caldwell
gains a great effect of humanity by putting in *none himself,* appealing to the
reader's common stock: *i.e.,* what is called for so desperately by the pattern of
the story must needs be generously supplied. Exactly as thrilling is his demonstration of the great emotional rôle of the outsider as played in the supremely
intelligent works of Thomas Mann and André Gide. His common illustrations
of the pervasive spread of symbolic pattern are drawn from Shakespeare and
from the type of the popular or pulp press. I think that on the whole his
method could be applied with equal fruitfulness to Shakespeare, Dashiell
Hammett, or Marie Corelli; as indeed he does apply it with equal force both
to the field of anarchic private morals and to the outline of a secular conver-

sion to Communism—as in, respectively, *Toward a Better Life* and *Permanence and Change.*

The real harvest that we barn from Mr. Burke's writings is his presentation of the types of ways the mind works in the written word. He is more interested in the psychological means of the meaning, and how it might mean (and often really does) something else, than in the meaning itself. Like Mr. Richards, but for another purpose, he is engaged largely in the meaning of meaning, and is therefore much bound up with considerations of language, but on the plane of emotional and intellectual patterns rather than on the emotional plane; which is why his essays deal with literature (or other writings) as it dramatizes or unfolds character (a character is a pattern of emotions and notions) rather than with lyric or meditative poetry which is Mr. Richards' field. So we find language containing felt character as well as felt co-ordination. The representation of character, and of aspiration and symbol, must always be rhetorical; and therefore we find that for Mr. Burke the rightly rhetorical is the profoundly hortatory. Thus literature may be seen as an inexhaustible reservoir of moral or character philosophies in action.

It is the technique of such philosophies that Mr. Burke explores, as he pursues it through curiosities of development and conversion and duplicity; it is the technique of the notions that may be put into or taken out of literature, but it is only a part of the technique of literature itself. The final reference is to the psychological and moral possibilities of the mind, and these certainly do not exhaust the technique or the reality of literature. The reality in literature is an object of contemplation and of feeling, like the reality of a picture or a cathedral, not a route of speculation. If we remember this and make the appropriate reductions here as elsewhere, Mr. Burke's essays become as pertinent to literary criticism as they are to the general ethical play of the mind. Otherwise they become too much a methodology for its own sake on the one hand, and too much a philosophy at one remove on the other. A man writes as he can; but those who use his writings have the further responsibility of redefining their scope, an operation (of which Mr. Burke is a master) which alone uses them to the full.

It is in relation to these examples which I have so unjustly held up of the philosophical, the sociological, or psychological approaches to criticism that I wish to examine an example of what composes, after all, the great bulk of serious writings about literature: a work of literary scholarship. Upon scholarship all other forms of literary criticism depend, so long as they are criticism, in much the same way that architecture depends on engineering. The great editors of the last century—men such as Dyce and Skeat and Gifford and Furness—performed work as valuable to the use of literature, and with far less complement of harm, as men like Hazlitt and Arnold and Pater. Scholarship, being bent on the collection, arrangement, and scrutiny of facts, has the positive advantage over other forms of criticism that it is a co-operative labor, and may be completed and corrected by subsequent scholars; and it has the negative advantage that it is not bound to investigate the mysteries of meaning or to connect literature with other departments of life—it has only to furnish the factual materials for such investigations and connections. It is not surprising to find that the great scholars are sometimes good critics, though usually in restricted fields; and it is a fact, on the other hand, that the great critics are themselves either good scholars or know how to take great advantage of scholarship. Perhaps we may put it that for the most part dead critics remain alive in us to the extent that they form part of our scholarship. It is Dr. Johnson's statements of fact that we preserve of him as a critic; his opinions have long since become a part of that imaginative structure, his personality. A last fact about scholarship is this, that so far as its conclusions are sound they are subject to use and digestion not debate by those outside the fold. And of bad scholarship as of bad criticism we have only to find means to minimize what we cannot destroy.

It is difficult to find an example of scholarship pure and simple, of high character, which can be made to seem relevant to the discussion in hand. What I want is to bring into the discussion the omnipresence of scholarship as a background and its immediate and necessary availability to every other mode of approach. What I want is almost anonymous. Failing that, I choose S. Foster Damon's *William Blake* (as I might have taken J. L. Lowes' *Road to Xanadu*) which, because of its special subject matter, brings its scholarship a little nearer the terms of discussion than a Shakespeare commentary would have done. The scholar's major problem with Blake happened to be one which many scholars could not handle, some refused to see, and some fumbled. A great part of Blake's meaning is not open to ordinarily well-instructed readers, but must be brought out by the detailed solution of something very like an enormous and enormously complicated acrostic puzzle. Not only earnest scrutiny of the poems as printed, but also a study of Blake's reading, a reconstruction of habits of thought, and an industrious piecing together into a consistent key of thousands of clues throughout the work, were necessary before many even of the simplest appearing poems could be explained. It is one thing to explain a mystical poet, like Crashaw, who was attached to a recognized church, and difficult enough; but it is a far more difficult thing to explain a mystical poet like Blake, who was so much an eclectic in his sources that his mystery as well as his apprehension of it was practically his own. All Mr. Damon had to go on besides the texts, and the small body of previous scholarship that was pertinent, were the general outlines of insight to which all mystics apparently adhere. The only explanation would be in the facts of what Blake meant to mean when he habitually said one thing in order to hide and enhance another; and in order to be convincing—poetry being what it is—the facts adduced had to be self-evident. It is not a question here whether the mystery enlightened was worth it. The result for emphasis is that Mr. Damon made Blake exactly what he seemed least to be, perhaps the most intellectually consistent of the greater poets in English. Since the chief weapons used are the extended facts of scholarship, the picture Mr. Damon produced cannot be destroyed even though later and other scholarship modifies, re-arranges, or adds to it with different or other facts. The only suspicion that might attach is that the picture is too consistent and that the facts are made to tell too much, and direct, but instructed, apprehension not enough.

My point about Mr. Damon's work is typical and double. First, that the same sort of work, the adduction of ultimately self-evident facts, can be done and must be done in other kinds of poetry than Blake's. Blake is merely an extreme and obvious example of an unusually difficult poet who hid his facts on purpose. The work must be done to the appropriate degree of digging out the facts in all orders of poetry—and especially perhaps in contemporary poetry, where we tend to let the work go either because it seems too easy or because it seems supererogatory. Self-evident facts are paradoxically the hardest to come by; they are not evident till they are seen; yet the meaning of a poem—the part of it which is intellectually formulable—must invariably depend on this order of facts, the facts about the meanings of the elements aside from their final meaning in combination. The rest of the poem, what it is, what it shows, its final value as a created emotion, its meanings, if you like, as a poem, cannot in the more serious orders of poetry develop itself to the full without this factual or intellectual meaning to show the way. The other point is already made, and has been made before in this essay, but it may still be emphasized. Although the scholarly account is indispensable it does not tell the whole story. It is only the basis and perhaps ultimately the residue of all the other stories. But it must be seen to first.

My own approach, such as it is, and if it can be named, does not tell the whole story either; the reader is conscientiously left with the poem, with the real work yet to do; and I wish to advance it—as indeed I have been advancing it *seriatim*—only in connection with the reduced and compensated approaches I have laid out; and I expect, too, that if my approach is used at all it will require its own reduction as well as its compensations. Which is why this essay has taken its present form, preferring for once, in the realm of theory and apologetics, the implicit to the explicit statement. It is, I suppose, an approach to literary criticism—to the discourse of an amateur—primarily through the technique, in the widest sense of that word, of the examples handled; technique on the plane of words and even of linguistics in Mr. Richards' sense, but also technique on the plane of intellectual and emotional patterns in Mr. Burke's sense, and technique, too, in that there is a technique of securing and arranging and representing a fundamental view of life. The advantage of the technical approach is I think double. It readily admits other approaches and is anxious to be complemented by them. Furthermore, in a sense, it is able to incorporate the technical aspect, which always exists, of what is secured by other approaches—as I have argued elsewhere that so unpromising a matter as T. S. Eliot's religious convictions may be profitably considered as a dominant element in his technique of revealing the actual. The second advantage of the technical approach is a consequence of the first; it treats of nothing in literature except in its capacity of reduction to literary fact, which is where it resembles scholarship, only passing beyond it in that its facts are usually further into the heart of the literature than the facts of most scholarship. Aristotle, curiously, is here the type and master; as the *Poetics* is nothing but a collection and explanation of the facts of Greek poetry, it is the factual aspect that is invariably produced. The rest of the labor is in the effort to find understandable terms to fit the composition of the facts. After all, it is only the facts about a poem, a play, a novel, that can be reduced to tractable form, talked about, and examined; the rest is the product of the facts, from the technical point of view, and not a product but the thing itself from its own point of view. The rest, whatever it is, can only be known, not talked about.

But facts are not simple or easy to come at; not all the facts will appear to one mind, and the same facts appear differently in the light of different minds. No attention is undivided, no single approach sufficient, no predilection guaranteed, when facts or what their arrangements create are in question. In short, for the arts, *mere* technical scrutiny of any order is not enough without the direct apprehension—which may come first or last—to which all scrutinies that show facts contribute.

It may be that there are principles that cover both the direct apprehension and the labor of providing modes for the understanding of the expressive arts. If so, they are Socratic and found within, and subject to the fundamental skepticism as in Montaigne. There must be seeds, let us say—seeds, germs, beginning forms upon which I can rely and to which I resort. When I use a word, an image, a notion, there must be in its small nodular apparent form, as in the peas I am testing on my desk, at least prophetically, the whole future growth, the whole harvested life; and not rhetorically, nor in a formula, but stubbornly, pervasively, heart-hidden, materially, in both the anterior and the eventual prospect as well as in the small handled form of the nub. What is it, what are they, these seeds of understanding? And if I know, are they logical? Do they take the processional form of the words I use? Or do they take a form like that of the silver backing a glass, a dark that enholds all brightness? Is every metaphor—and the assertion of understanding is our great metaphor—mixed by the necessity of its intention? What is the mixture of a word, an image, a notion?

The mixture, if I may start a hare so late, the mixture, even in the fresh use of an old word, is made in the pre-conscious, and is by hypothesis un-ascertainable. But let us not use hypotheses, let us not desire to ascertain. By intuition we adventure in the pre-conscious; and there, where the adventure is, there is no need or suspicion of certainty or meaning; there is the living, ex-panding, *prescient* substance without the tags and handles of conscious form. Art is the looking-glass of the pre-conscious, and when it is deepest seems to participate in it sensibly. Or, better, for purposes of criticism, our sensibility resumes the division of the senses and faculties at the same time that it preens itself into conscious form. Criticism may have as an object the establishment and evaluation (comparison and analysis) of the modes of making the pre-conscious *consciously* available.

But this emphasis upon the pre-conscious need not be insisted on; once recognized it may be tacitly assumed, and the effort of the mind will be, as it were, restored to its own plane—only a little sensitive to the tap-roots below. On its own plane—that is, the plane where almost everything is taken for granted in order to assume adequate implementation in handling what is taken for granted by others; where because you can list the items of your bewilderment and can move from one to another you assert that the achieve-ment of motion is the experience of order; where, therefore, you must adopt always an attitude of provisional skepticism; where, imperatively, you must scrutinize and scrutinize until you have revealed, if it is there, the inscrutable divination, or, if it is not, the void of personal ambition; where, finally, you must stop short only when you have, with all the facts you can muster, indi-cated, surrounded, detached, somehow found the way demonstrably to get at, in pretty conscious terms which others may use, the substance of your chosen case.

From *The Double Agent. Essays in Craft and Elu-cidation* by R. P. Blackmur, pp. 269–302. Ar-row Editions. Copyright, 1935, by R. P. Black-mur. Reprinted by permission of the author.

APPENDICES

APPENDIX I

Recent Works of American Criticism

THIS list is selective. It includes works of several varieties that relate to modern American criticism: some on the backgrounds of American literature, some of literary biography, some on general problems of aesthetics and theory, some studies in the analysis of form and style. Those of the last three groups are of special value in extending the interests of the present volume. Books of historical and linguistic scholarship are not as a rule listed except where they are relevant to critical problems and methods. Books by critics discussed in the "Foreword" and "Introduction" are included except in the case of earlier critics who preceded Henry James, but books by critics whose work appears in this volume will be found listed not here but in Appendix IV. The writers included here are of American birth or residence, though a few foreign critics who have worked, taught, or been notably influential in the United States (I. A. Richards, Jacques Maritain, Alfred Korzybski, *et al.*), as well as those who have adopted American citizenship, have been added.

For fuller bibliographies of American authors and critics, the reader is referred to two standard works of reference: Volume III of *Literary History of the United States (Bibliography)*, edited by Robert E. Spiller, Willard Thorp, Thomas H. Johnson, and Henry Seidel Canby, with Howard Mumford Jones, Dixon Wecter, and Stanley T. Williams as associates (New York: The Macmillan Company, 1948); and *Contemporary American Authors: A Critical Survey and 219 Bio-Bibliographies*, by Fred B. Millett (New York: Harcourt, Brace and Company, 1940). Further reference may be made to the current annual bibliographies in *Publications of the Modern Language Association of America*, in the *Annual Bibliography of English Language and Literature* of the Modern Humanities Research Association, and in the quarterly *American Literature*, as well as in *The Reader's Guide to Periodical Literature*, *The International Index to Periodicals*, and *The Book Review Digest*.

Abbott, Charles D. *Poets at Work* (editor, 1948).
Adler, Mortimer. *Art and Prudence: A Study in Practical Philosophy* (1937).
    How to Read a Book (1940).
Aiken, Conrad. *Skepticisms: Notes on Contemporary Poetry* (1919).
Ames, Van Meter. *Aesthetics of the Novel* (1928).
    André Gide (1947).

Arvin, Newton.   See Appendix IV.
Auden, W. H.   See Appendix IV.

Babbitt, Irving.   See Appendix IV.
Baker, Carlos.   *Shelley's Major Poetry* (1948).
Baker, Howard.   *Induction to Tragedy* (1937).
Barnes, Albert C.   *The Art in Painting* (1928).
Barrett, William.   See Appendix IV.
Barzun, Jacques.   *Romanticism and the Modern Ego* (1943).
Basler, Roy P.   *Sex, Symbolism, and Psychology in Literature* (1948).
Beach, Joseph Warren.   *The Method of Henry James* (1918).
      The Comic Spirit of George Meredith (1920).
      The Technique of Thomas Hardy (1922).
      The Outlook for American Prose (1924).
      The Twentieth Century Novel: Studies in Technique (1932).
      American Fiction: 1920–1940 (1941).
Beer, Thomas.   *Stephen Crane: A Study in American Letters* (1924).
Bennett, Joseph D.   *Baudelaire* (1944).
Bentley, Eric.   See Appendix IV.
Bishop, John Peale.   *The Collected Essays of John Peale Bishop* (edited by Edmund Wilson, 1948).
Blackmur, R. P.   See Appendix IV.
Boas, George.   *Philosophy and Poetry* (1932).
      A Primer for Critics (1937).
Bogan, Louise.   See Appendix IV.
Bourne, Randolph.   See Appendix IV.
Boynton, Percy Holmes.   *Some Contemporary Americans* (1924).
      More Contemporary Americans (1927).
      The Challenge of American Criticism (1927).
      Literature and American Life (1936).
Brooks, Cleanth.   See Appendix IV.
Brooks, Van Wyck.   See Appendix IV.
Brown, E. K.   See Appendix IV.
Brownell, William Crary.   *American Prose Masters* (1909).
      Criticism (1914).
      Standards (1917).
      The Genius of Style (1924).
      Democratic Distinction in America (1927).
      The Spirit of Society (1927).
Buchanan, Scott.   *Poetry and Mathematics* (1929).
Buermeyer, Laurence.   *The Aesthetic Experience* (1924).
      Art and Education (with others, 1929).
Burgum, Edwin Berry.   *The Novel and the World's Dilemma* (1947).
Burke, Kenneth.   See Appendix IV.
Bush, Douglas.   *Mythology in the Renaissance Tradition in English Poetry* (1932, 1937).

The Renaissance and English Humanism (1939).
Paradise Lost in Our Time: Some Comments (1945).

Cairns, Huntington.   *The Limits of Art* (anthology with critical commentaries, 1947).
Calverton, V. F.   *The Newer Spirit: A Sociological Criticism of Literature* (1925).
      The New Grounds of Criticism (1930).
      The Liberation of American Literature (1932).
Campbell, Joseph.   *A Skeleton Key to Finnegans Wake* (with Henry Morton Robinson, 1944).
      The Hero with a Thousand Faces (1949).
Canby, Henry Seidel.   *Definitions* (first series, 1922; second series, 1924).
      American Estimates (1929).
      Classic Americans (1931).
      Thoreau (1939).
      Walt Whitman, An American: A Study in Biography (1943).
Cantwell, Robert.   See Appendix IV.
Cargill, Oscar.   *Intellectual America: Ideas on the March* (1941).
Chamberlain, John.   *Farewell to Reform* (1932).
Chapman, John Jay.   See Appendix IV.
Chase, Richard.   See Appendix IV.
Cheney, Sheldon.   *The New Movement in the Theatre* (1914).
      Expressionism in Art (1934).
Colum, Mary M.   *From These Roots* (1938; new edition, 1945).
Cowley, Malcolm.   See Appendix IV.
Crane, R. S.   See Appendix IV.

Daiches, David.   *The Place of Meaning in Poetry* (1935).
      New Literary Values: Studies in Modern Literature (1936).
      Literature and Society (1938).
      The Novel and the Modern World (1940).
      Poetry and the Modern World (1940).
      Virginia Woolf (1942).
      Robert Louis Stevenson (1947).
      A Study of Literature (1948).
Damon, S. Foster.   *William Blake: His Philosophy and Symbols* (1924).
      The Odyssey in Dublin (on Joyce: reprinted from *The Hound and Horn*, 1930).
      Amy Lowell: A Chronicle (1935).
Davidson, Donald.   *The Attack on Leviathan* (1938).
DeMille, George E.   *Literary Criticism in America: A Preliminary Survey* (1931).
Deutsch, Babette.   *This Modern Poetry* (1935).
De Voto, Bernard.   *Mark Twain's America* (1932).
      The Literary Fallacy (1944).

Dickinson, Thomas H.   *The Case of the American Drama* (1915).
  Playwrights of the New American Theatre (1925).
Drew, Elizabeth.   *The Modern Novel: Some Aspects of Contemporary Fiction*
    (1926).
  Discovering Poetry (1933).
  The Enjoyment of Literature (1935).
  Directions in Modern Poetry (with John L. Sweeney, 1940).
  T. S. Eliot: The Design of His Poetry (1949).
Ducasse, John.   *The Philosophy of Art* (1930).
  Art, The Critics, and You (1944).
Dudley, Dorothy.   *Forgotten Frontiers: Dreiser and the Land of the Free* (1932).
Dupee, F. W.   See Appendix IV.

Eastman, Max.   *The Literary Mind: Its Place in an Age of Science* (1931).
  Artists in Uniform: A Study of Literature and Bureaucratism (1934).
  Art and the Life of Action (1934).
  The Enjoyment of Poetry (1939).
Edgar, Pelham.   *The Art of the Novel* (1933).
  Henry James: Man and Author (1935).
Eliot, T. S.   See Appendix IV.
Elliott, G. R.   *The Cycle of Modern Poetry* (1939).
  Humanism and Imagination (1939).

Farrell, James T.   *A Note on Literary Criticism* (1936).
  The League of Frightened Philistines (1945).
  The Fate of Writing in America (1946).
  Literature and Morality (1947).
Fergusson, Francis.   See Appendix IV.
Flores, Angel.   *Henrik Ibsen* (editor, 1937).
  Literature and Marxism: A Controversy (1938).
  The Kafka Problem (editor, 1946).
Foerster, Norman.   *American Criticism: A Study in Literary Theory from Poe to
    the Present* (1928).
  *Toward Standards: A Study of the Present Critical Movement in Ameri-
    can Letters* (1930).
  Humanism and America (editor, 1930).
Follett, Wilson.   *The Modern Novel* (1933).
Fowlie, Wallace.   *Clowns and Angels* (1943).
  Rimbaud (1946).
  Jacob's Night (1947).
  The Clown's Grail (1948).
  Mallarmé (1951).
Fraenkel, Michael.   *Death is Not Enough: Essays in Active Negation* (1939).
Frank, Waldo.   *Salvos: An Informal Book about Books and Plays* (1924).
  The Re-Discovery of America (1928).
  In the American Jungle (1937).

Freeman, Joseph.   *An American Testament: A Narrative of Rebels and Roman-*
        tics (1936).
        Voices of October (with Joshua Kunitz and Louis Lozowick, 1930).
Frye, Northrop.   *Fearful Symmetry: A Study of Blake* (1947).
Frye, Prosser Hall.   *Romance and Tragedy* (1922).
        Visions and Chimeras (1929).

Gates, Lewis E.   *Studies and Appreciations* (1900).
Geismar, Maxwell.   *Writers in Crisis: The American Novel Between Two Wars*
        (1942).
        The Last of the Provincials: The American Novel, 1915–1925 (1948).
Gilman, Margaret.   *Baudelaire the Critic* (1943).
Glasgow, Ellen.   *A Certain Measure: An Interpretation of Prose Fiction* (1943).
Grabo, Carl.   *The Creative Critic* (1948).
Greene, Theodore M.   *The Arts and the Art of Criticism* (1940).
Greenlaw, Edwin.   *The Province of Literary History* (1931).
Gregory, Horace.   See Appendix IV.
Grudin, Louis.   *A Primer of Aesthetics: Logical Approaches to a Philosophy of*
        Art (1930).
        Mr. Eliot among the Nightingales (1931).
Guérard, Albert.   *Literature and Society* (1935).
        Art for Art's Sake (1936).
Guérard, Albert, Jr.   *Robert Bridges: A Study in Traditionalism* (1942).
        Joseph Conrad (1947).
        Thomas Hardy: The Novels and Stories (1949).

Hackett, Francis.   *Horizons: A Book of Criticism* (1918).
Hatcher, Harlan.   *Creating the Modern American Novel* (1935).
Hazlitt, Henry.   *The Anatomy of Criticism* (1933).
Hearn, Lafcadio.   *Appreciations of Poetry* (1916).
        Complete Lectures on Criticism, Literature, and Philosophy (1932).
Heilman, Robert B.   *This Great Stage* (on Shakespeare and *King Lear*, 1948).
Hicks, Granville.   *The Great Tradition: An Interpretation of American Litera-*
        ture since the Civil War (1933; revised edition, 1935).
        John Reed: The Making of a Revolutionary (with John Stuart, 1936).
        Figures of Transition (1939).
Hoffman, Frederick J.   *Freudianism and the Literary Mind* (1945).
        The Little Magazine: A History and a Bibliography (with Charles Allen
        and Carolyn F. Ulrich (1946; new edition, 1947).
Honig, Edwin.   *Garcia Lorca* (1945).
Horton, Philip.   *Hart Crane: The Life of an American Poet* (1937).
Hospers, John.   *Meaning and Truth in the Arts* (1946).
Howells, William Dean.   See Appendix IV.
Hughes, Glenn.   *Imagism and the Imagists* (1941).
Huneker, James Gibbons.   See Appendix IV.
Hyman, Stanley Edgar.   See Appendix IV.

James, Henry.   See Appendix IV.
Jarrell, Randall.   See Appendix IV.
Jones, Howard Mumford.   *Hamlet: With a Psychoanalytical Study* (1948).
    The Theory of American Literature (1948).
Jones, Llewellyn.   *First Impressions* (1925).
    How to Criticize Books (1928).
Josephson, Matthew.   *Zola and His Time* (1928).
    Portrait of the Artist as an American (1930).
    Jean-Jacques Rousseau (1931).
    Victor Hugo (1942).
    Stendhal, or The Pursuit of Happiness (1946).

Kazin, Alfred.   See Appendix IV.
Korzybski, Alfred.   *Science and Sanity* (1934; third edition, 1948).
Krutch, Joseph Wood.   See Appendix IV.

Langer, Suzanne K.   *Philosophy in a New Key* (1942).
Levin, Harry.   See Appendix IV.
Lewisohn, Ludwig.   *The Drama and the Stage* (1922).
    The Creative Life (1924).
    Expression in America (1932).
    The Artist and His Message (with Adolph Gillis, 1933).
Littell, Robert.   *Read America First* (1926).
Lovejoy, Arthur O.   *The Revolt against Dualism* (1930).
    The Great Chain of Being (1936).
    A Documentary History of Primitivism (with George Boas, 1936).
Lovett, Robert Morss.   See Appendix IV.
Lowell, Amy.   *Six French Poets* (1915).
    Tendencies in Modern American Poetry (1917).
    A Critical Fable (1922).
    John Keats (1925).
    Poetry and Poets (1930).
Lowes, John Livingston.   *Convention and Revolt in Poetry* (1919; new edition,
    1922).
    The Road to Xanadu: A Study in the Ways of the Imagination (on Cole-
    ridge, 1927).
    Of Reading Books (1929).
    Geoffrey Chaucer (1934).
    Essays in Appreciation (1936).

MacLeish, Archibald.   *The Irresponsibles* (1940).
    A Time to Speak: Selected Prose (1941).
    A Time to Act (1942).
Macy, John.   *The Spirit of American Literature* (1913).
    The Critical Game (1922).
March, H. M.   *The Two Worlds of Marcel Proust* (1948).

RECENT WORKS OF AMERICAN CRITICISM

799

Maritain, Jacques.   *Art and Scholasticism* (translated by F. S. Flint, 1930; trans
   lated by J. F. Scanlan, 1935, 1942).
   Art and Poetry (1943).
Masters, Edgar Lee.   *Vachel Lindsay: A Poet in America* (1935).
   Whitman (1937).
Matthiessen, F. O.   See Appendix IV.
McMahon, Philip.   *The Meaning of Art* (1930).
Mencken, H. L.   See Appendix IV.
Mercier, Louis J. A.   *The Challenge of Humanism: A Study in Comparative
   Criticism* (1933).
Miller, Perry.   *Orthodoxy in Massachusetts: A Genetic Study* (1933).
   The Puritans (edited with Thomas H. Johnson, 1938).
   The New England Mind: The Seventeenth Century (1939).
   Jonathan Edwards (1949).
   The Transcendentalists (edited, 1950).
Millett, Fred B.   *Contemporary British Literature* (with J. M. Manly and Edith
   Rickert, revised edition, 1935).
   *Contemporary American Authors: A Critical Survey and 219 Bio-Bibliog-
   raphies* (1940).
   The Rebirth of Liberal Education (1945).
Mizener, Arthur.   *The Far Side of Paradise* (on F. Scott Fitzgerald, 1951).
Monroe, Harriet.   *Poets and Their Art* (1926; new edition, 1932).
   A Poet's Life: Seventy Years in a Changing World (1938).
More, Paul Elmer.   See Appendix IV.
Moore, Marianne.   See Appendix IV.
Muller, Herbert J.   *Modern Fiction* (1937).
   Science and Criticism: The Humanist Tradition (1943).
   Thomas Wolfe (1947).
Mumford, Lewis.   *The Story of Utopias* (1922).
   Sticks and Stones: A Study of American Architecture and Civilization
   (1924).
   The Golden Day: A Study of American Experience and Culture (1926).
   Herman Melville (1929).
   American Taste (1929).
   The Brown Decades: A Study of the Arts in America: 1865–1895 (1931).
   Technics and Civilization (1934).
   The Culture of Cities (1938).
Munson, Gorham B.   *Destinations: A Canvass of American Literature since
   1900* (1928).
   Style and Form in American Prose (1929).
   The Dilemma of the Liberated (1930).

Nabokov, Vladimir.   *Nikolai Gogol* (1945).
Nahm, Milton C.   *Aesthetic Experience and Its Presuppositions* (1946).
Nathan, George Jean.   *Another Book on the Theatre* (1915).
   The Popular Theatre (1918).

The Critic and the Drama (1922).
Materia Critica (1924).
Land of the Pilgrims' Pride (1927).
Art of the Night (1928).
Testament of a Critic (1931).
The Intimate Notebooks of George Jean Nathan (1932).
Since Ibsen: A Statistical Historical Outline of the Popular Theatre Since 1900 (1933).
The Theatre of the Moment: A Journalistic Commentary (1936).

Neff, Emery. *Carlyle and Mill: Mystic and Utilitarian* (1924; 1930).
A Revolution in European Poetry: 1660–1900 (1940).
The Poetry of History (1947).
Edwin Arlington Robinson (1948).

Neider, Charles. *The Frozen Sea* (a study of Kafka, 1948).

Nuhn, Ferner. *The Wind Blew from the East: A Study in the Orientation of American Culture* (1942).

O'Brien, Justin. *The Journals of André Gide* (translator and editor, 3 vols., 1947–1949).

O'Connor, William Van. *Sense and Sensibility in Modern Poetry* (1948).
Forms of Modern Fiction (editor, 1948).
The Shaping Spirit: A Study of Wallace Stevens (1950).

Olson, Charles. *Call Me Ishmael* (a study of Herman Melville, 1947).

Parker, DeWitt. *The Principles of Aesthetics* (1920; new edition, 1946).
The Analysis of Art (1924).
The Analysis of Beauty (1926).

Parkes, Henry Bamford. *The Pragmatic Test* (1941).

Parrington, Vernon Louis. *Main Currents in American Thought: An Interpretation of American Literature from the Beginnings to 1920* (3 volumes, 1927–1930).

Pepper, S. C. *Aesthetic Quality: A Contextualist Theory* (1938).
The Basis of Criticism in the Arts (1946).

Peyre, Henri. *Writers and Their Critics* (1944).

Phillips, William. See Appendix IV.

Porter, Katherine Anne. See Appendix IV.

Pottle, Frederick. *The Idiom of Poetry* (1942; revised edition, 1946).

Pound, Ezra. See Appendix IV.

Prall, D. W. *Aesthetic Judgment* (1929).
Aesthetic Analysis (1936).

Prescott, F. C. *Poetry and Dreams* (1919).
The Poetic Mind (1922).
Poetry and Myth (1927).

Prior, Moody E. *The Language of Tragedy* (1947).

Quinn, Arthur Hobson. *A History of the American Drama from the Beginnings to the Civil War* (revised edition, 1943).

A History of the American Drama from the Civil War to the Present Day
   (revised edition, 1936).
American Fiction: An Historical and Critical Survey (1936).
Edgar Allan Poe: A Critical Biography (1941).

Rader, Melvin.   *A Modern Book of Aesthetics* (editor, 1935).
Rahv, Philip.   See Appendix IV.
Ranson, John Crowe.   See Appendix IV.
Rice, Philip Blair.   See Appendix IV.
Richards, I. A.   *The Foundations of Aesthetics* (with C. K. Ogden and James
   Wood, 1922).
   The Meaning of Meaning (with C. K. Ogden, 1923).
   The Principles of Literary Criticism (1924).
   Practical Criticism: A Study of Literary Judgment (1929).
   Mencius on the Mind (1932).
   Coleridge on Imagination (1934).
   The Philosophy of Rhetoric (1936).
   Interpretation in Teaching (1938).
   How To Read a Page (1942).
Riding, Laura.   *A Survey of Modernist Poetry* (with Robert Graves, 1927).
   Contemporaries and Snobs (1928).
Roberts, Morris.   *Henry James's Criticism* (1929).
Roditi, Edouard.   *Oscar Wilde* (1947).
Rosenfeld, Paul.   *Port of New York: Essays on Fourteen American Moderns*
   (1924).
   Men Seen (1925).
Rourke, Constance.   *American Humor: A Study of the National Character*
   (1931).
   Audubon (1936).
   Charles Sheeler: Artist in the American Tradition (1938).
   The Roots of American Culture (edited by Van Wyck Brooks, 1942).

Santayana, George.   See Appendix IV.
Schorer, Mark.   *William Blake: The Politics of Vision* (1946).
Schwartz, Delmore.   See Appendix IV.
Shafer, Robert M.   *Paul Elmer More and American Criticism* (1935).
Shapiro, Karl.   *Essay on Rime* (1945).
Sherman, Stuart Pratt.   *Americans* (1922).
   The Genius of America: Studies on Behalf of the Younger Generation
   (1923).
   The Main Stream (1927).
Shipley, Joseph T.   *The Quest for Literature: A Survey of Literary Criticism and
   the Theories of Literary Forms* (1931).
   A Dictionary of World Literature (editor, 1943).
   Encyclopedia of Literature (editor, 1946).
Shuster, George N.   *The Catholic Spirit in Modern English Literature* (1922).
   The Catholic Church and Current Literature (1929).

Sinclair, Upton. *Mammonart* (1925).
Slochower, Harry. *Three Ways of Modern Man* (1937).
    Thomas Mann's Joseph Story (1938).
    No Voice Is Wholly Lost (1945).
Smith, Bernard. *Forces in American Criticism* (1939).
Smith, Chard Powers. *Pattern and Variation in Poetry* (1932).
    Annals of the Poets (1935).
Smith, Logan Pearsall. *Words and Idioms* (1925).
    On Reading Shakespeare (1933).
    Reperusals and Re-Collections (1936).
    Milton and His Modern Critics (1940).
Spencer, Theodore. See Appendix IV.
Spingarn, J. E. See Appendix IV.
Stauffer, Donald A. *The Intent of the Critic* (editor, 1941).
    The Nature of Poetry (1946).
    Shakespeare's World of Images (1949).
    The Golden Nightingale: Essays on Some Principles of Poetry in the Lyrics of William Butler Yeats (1949).
Stearns, Harold E. *America and the Young Intellectual* (1921).
    Civilization in the United States: An Enquiry by Thirty Americans (editor, 1922).
    America Now: An Enquiry into Civilization in the United States by Thirty-Six Americans (editor, 1938).
Stein, Leo. *The A. B. C. of Aesthetics* (1927).
Stoll, E. E. *Art and Artifice in Shakespeare* (1933).
    From Shakespeare to Joyce (1944).

Tate, Allen. See Appendix IV.
Taupin, René. *L'Influence du Symbolisme français sur la Poésie américaine de 1910 à 1920* (1929).
Thorp, Willard. *Herman Melville: Representative Selections* (editor, 1938).
    The Lost Tradition of American Letters (1945).
    Moby Dick by Herman Melville (critical edition, 1947).
Tindall, William York. *D. H. Lawrence and Susan His Cow* (1939).
    Forces in Modern British Literature: 1885–1946 (1947).
    James Joyce (1949).
Trilling, Lionel. See Appendix IV.
Troy, William. See Appendix IV.
Tuve, Rosamund. *Elizabethan and Metaphysical Imagery* (1947).
Tyler, Parker. *Magic and Myth of the Movies* (1947).

Untermeyer, Louis. *American Poetry since 1900* (1923).
    Modern American Poetry and *Modern British Poetry* (successive editions, apart or combined, since 1919; latest edition, 1950, with biographies and critical introductions).

Van Doren, Carl.   *The American Novel* (1921; revised, 1940).
    Contemporary American Novelists (1922).
    The Roving Critic (1923).
    Many Minds (1924).
    American and British Literature since 1900 (with M. van Doren, 1925).
    American Literature: An Introduction (1933; republished as *What Is American Literature?*, 1933; included in *The Portable Carl van Doren*, 1945).
    Three Worlds (autobiography; 1936).
    Benjamin Franklin (three volumes, 1938).
Van Doren, Mark.   *Henry David Thoreau: A Critical Study* (1916).
    The Poetry of John Dryden (1920; reissued 1946).
    Edwin Arlington Robinson (1927).
    Shakespeare (1939).
    The Private Reader (1942).
    The Noble Voice (1946).
    Nathaniel Hawthorne (1949).

Warren, Austin.   See Appendix IV.
Warren, Robert Penn.   See Appendix IV.
Wellek, René.   *Theory of Literature* (with Austin Warren, 1949).
Wells, Henry.   *Poetic Imagery* (1924).
    The Judgment of Literature: An Outline of Aesthetics (1928).
    New Poets from Old: A Study in Literary Genetics (1940).
    The American Way of Poetry (1943).
West, Ray B., Jr.   *Writing in the Rocky Mountains* (1947).
    The Art of Modern Fiction (editor, with R. W. Stallman, 1949).
Weston, Jessie L.   *From Ritual to Romance* (1920; reissued 1946).
Wharton, Edith.   *The Writing of Fiction* (1925).
    A Backward Glance (memoirs, 1934).
Whipple, T. K.   *Spokesmen: Modern Writers and American Life* (1928).
    Study Out the Land (1943).
Wickham, Harvey.   *The Impuritans* (1929).
Wilder, Amos.   *The Spiritual Aspects of the New Poetry* (1940).
Williamson, George.   *The Talent of T. S. Eliot* (1929).
    The Donne Tradition (1930).
Wilson, Edmund.   See Appendix IV.
Winters, Yvor.   See Appendix IV.
Woodberry, George Edward.   *The Torch* (1905).
    The Appreciation of Literature (1907).
    Two Phases of Criticism (1914).
    Collected Essays (1920–1921).
    Literary Memoirs, Studies, Heart of Man, and other Papers (1922).

Young, Stark.   See Appendix IV.

Zabel, Morton Dauwen. *Literary Opinion in America: Essays Illustrating the Status, Methods, and Problems of Criticism in the United States since the War* (editor, 1937).

The Condition of American Criticism: 1939 (reprinted from *The English Journal*, 1939).

Two Years of Poetry: 1937–1939 (reprinted from *The Southern Review*, 1939).

The Contemporary Period in *A Book of English Literature* (editor, 1943).

A Literatura dos Estados Unidos (a book on the masters of American literature, in Portuguese translation, Rio de Janeiro, 1947; in Spanish translation as *Historia de la Literatura Norte-Americana*, Buenos Aires, 1950).

The Portable Conrad (editor, 1947).

The Portable Henry James (editor, 1951).

Zukovsky, Louis.   *A Test for Poetry* (1949).

See Appendix VII, page 891, for American critics and works of criticism published since 1951.

APPENDIX II

Collections of Contemporary American Criticism

THE list is selective, and titles are arranged chronologically. All important collections of American criticism of the years 1919–1951 are listed. In addition, there have been included a number of the special critical symposia published in literary journals like *The Hound and Horn, The Southern Review,* and *The Kenyon Review,* which have become a feature of contemporary critical activity. Other special numbers of this kind may be traced in *The New Republic, The Nation, The Sewanee Review, Partisan Review,* etc., during the past thirty years. When a large number of essays by foreign critics are included in the books listed below, the names of these critics are not given; when such foreign contributions are few in any given volume, their authors are named. Where collections of criticism are devoted to special programs or purposes, or where they issued from special occasions, these are briefly indicated.

A Modern Book of Criticism, edited by Ludwig Lewisohn (1919).
   Essays defining and illustrating the impressionist and liberal points of view by French critics (Anatole France, Jules Lemaître, Remy de Gourmont); German (Friedrich Hebbel, Wilhelm Dilthey, Johannes Volkelt, Richard Moritz Meyer, Hugo von Hofmannsthal, Richard Mueller-Freienfels, Alfred Kerr); English and Irish (George Moore, George Bernard Shaw, Arthur Symons, John Galsworthy, Arnold Bennett, W. L. George, Thomas MacDonagh, John Cooper Powys); and American (James Gibbons Huneker, J. E. Spingarn, H. L. Mencken, Ludwig Lewisohn, Francis Hackett, Van Wyck Brooks, Randolph Bourne).
Criticism in America: Its Function and Status, edited by J. E. Spingarn (1924).
   Essays by Irving Babbitt, Van Wyck Brooks, William Crary Brownell, Ernest Boyd, T. S. Eliot, H. L. Mencken, Stuart Pratt Sherman, J. E. Spingarn, George Edward Woodberry.
Contemporary American Criticism, edited by James Cloyd Bowman (1926).
   Essays by James Russell Lowell, Walt Whitman, J. E. Spingarn, H. L. Mencken, William Crary Brownell, Irving Babbitt, Grant Showerman, Stuart Pratt Sherman, Percy H. Boynton, Van Wyck Brooks, Sherwood Anderson, Robert Morss Lovett, Carl van Doren, Irwin Edman, Llewellyn Jones, Theodore Maynard, William McFee, John Macy, Henry Seidel Canby, Amy Lowell, Conrad Aiken, Fred Lewis Pattee, George Edward Woodberry.

American Criticism: 1926, edited by William A. Drake (1926).
Essays and reviews of the year July 1925 to July 1926 by Henry Seidel
Canby, Samuel C. Chew, Mary M. Colum, Robert L. Duffus, Waldo Frank,
Zona Gale, Herbert S. Gorman, Alyse Gregory, Albert Guérard, Joseph
Wood Krutch, Sinclair Lewis, Archibald MacLeish, Edgar Lee Masters,
H. L. Mencken, W. B. Pressey, Agnes Repplier, Edith Rickert, Cameron
Rogers, Anne Douglas Sedgwick, Gilbert Seldes, Stuart Pratt Sherman, Har-
rison Smith, Logan Pearsall Smith, C. B. Tinker, Charles K. Trueblood, Carl
van Doren, Arnold Whitredge, Edmund Wilson, P. W. Wilson.

The New Criticism, edited by Edwin Berry Burgum (1930).
Essays chiefly in aesthetic theory by American critics: J. E. Spingarn, George
Santayana, Laurence Buermeyer, DeWitt Parker, T. S. Eliot; and by English
and European critics: Benedetto Croce, Bernard Bosanquet, E. F. Carritt,
I. A. Richards, J. B. S. Haldane, J. W. N. Sullivan, Roger Fry, Ramon Fer-
nandez, Oswald Spengler, Élie Faure.

American Critical Essays, edited by Norman Foerster (1930).
Essays illustrating the history of criticism in America by Edgar Allan Poe,
Ralph Waldo Emerson, James Russell Lowell, Walt Whitman, William Dean
Howells, Henry James, Lewis E. Gates, George Edward Woodberry, William
Crary Brownell, Irving Babbitt, Paul Elmer More, Prosser Hall Frye, J. E.
Spingarn, Stuart Pratt Sherman, Van Wyck Brooks.

Humanism and America: Essays on the Outlook of Modern Civilization, edited by
Norman Foerster (1930).
Essays defending the Humanist position by Lewis Trenchard More, Irving
Babbitt, Paul Elmer More, G. R. Elliott, T. S. Eliot, Frank Jewett Mather,
Jr., Alan Reynolds Thompson, Robert Shafer, Harry Hayden Clark, Stanley
P. Chase, Gorham B. Munson, Bernard Bandler II, Sherlock Bronson Gass,
Richard Lindley Brown.

The Critique of Humanism: A Symposium, edited by C. Hartley Grattan (1930).
Essays in opposition to Humanism by C. Hartley Grattan, Edmund Wilson,
Malcolm Cowley, Henry Hazlitt, Burton Rascoe, Allen Tate, Kenneth
Burke, Henry-Russell Hitchcock, Jr., R. P. Blackmur, John Chamberlain,
Bernard Bandler II, Yvor Winters, Lewis Mumford.

A Garland for John Donne: 1631–1931, edited by Theodore Spencer (1931).
Essays on Donne on the tercentenary of his death by T. S. Eliot, Evelyn M.
Simpson, Mario Praz, John Hayward, Mary Paton Ramsay, John Sparrow,
George Williamson, Theodore Spencer.

Homage to Henry James: 1843–1916. A special number of *The Hound and
Horn,* Volume VII, No. 3 (April–May, 1934), pages 361–562. Edited by Lincoln
Kirstein (1934).
Essays on the life and work of Henry James by Marianne Moore, Lawrence
Leighton, Edmund Wilson, Francis Fergusson, Stephen Spender, Newton
Arvin, R. P. Blackmur, Alice Boughton, John Wheelwright, Robert Cant-
well, Edna Kenton, H. R. Hays, Glenway Wescott.

Proletarian Literature in the United States: An Anthology, edited by Granville

Hicks, Michael Gold, Isidor Schneider, Joseph North, Paul Peters, Alan Calmer (1935).

> Includes, besides verse, fiction, etc., essays defining the proletarian theory of literature by Obed Brooks, Edwin Berry Burgum, Alan Calmer, Malcolm Cowley, Michael Gold, Granville Hicks, Joshua Kunitz, William Phillips and Philip Rahv, Bernard Smith.

After the Genteel Tradition: American Writers Since 1910, edited by Malcolm Cowley (1937).

> Essays on American writers after 1910, chiefly 1918–1937, by John Chamberlain, Robert Cantwell, Lionel Trilling, Bernard Smith, Newton Arvin, Robert Morss Lovett, Louis Kronenberger, Peter Monro Jack, Hildegarde Flanner, Malcolm Cowley, John Peale Bishop, Hamilton Basso.

Literary Opinion in America: Essays Illustrating the Status, Methods, and Problems of Criticism in the United States since the War, edited by Morton Dauwen Zabel (1937).

> The first edition of the present volume, including a history of American criticism since Poe and Emerson by the editor, and essays of the years 1919–1937 by T. S. Eliot, Van Wyck Brooks, Irving Babbitt, Paul Elmer More, J. E. Spingarn, H. L. Mencken, John Crowe Ransom, George Santayana, Edmund Wilson, Allen Tate, Yvor Winters, Marianne Moore, Charles K. Trueblood, Theodore Spencer, Stark Young, Joseph Wood Krutch, Francis Fergusson, Robert Morss Lovett, William Troy, Robert Penn Warren, Louise Bogan, Morton Dauwen Zabel, George N. Shuster, Philip Blair Rice, Kenneth Burke, Malcolm Cowley, Horace Gregory, Newton Arvin, Robert Cantwell, William Phillips and Philip Rahv, R. P. Blackmur.

Books That Changed Our Minds, edited by Malcolm Cowley and Bernard Smith (1939).

> Essays on thinkers, scientists, and writers of the nineteenth and twentieth centuries by George Soule, Louis Kronenberger, Charles A. Beard, John Chamberlain, Rexford Guy Tugwell, C. E. Ayres, Paul Radin, Max Lerner, David Daiches, Bernard Smith, Lewis Mumford, Malcolm Cowley.

Thomas Hardy Centennial Number. A special number of *The Southern Review*, Volume VI, No. 1 (Summer, 1940), pages 1–224. Edited by Charles W. Pipkin, Cleanth Brooks, and Robert Penn Warren (1940).

> Essays on the prose and poetry of Hardy by John Crowe Ransom, R. P. Blackmur, Howard Baker, Delmore Schwartz, W. H. Auden, F. R. Leavis, Allen Tate, Bonamy Dobrée, Morton Dauwen Zabel, Katherine Anne Porter, Donald Davidson, Jacques Barzun, Arthur Mizener, Herbert J. Muller.

The Intent of the Artist, edited with an introduction by Augusto Centeno (1940).

> Discussions of creative process in the arts, by Sherwood Anderson, Thornton Wilder, Roger Sessions, William Lescaze. The essays were given as a series of lectures at Princeton University in 1938–1939.

The English Institute Annual: 1939 (1940).

> Essays read before the English Institute, September 1939, by Carleton Brown, Robert E. Spiller, Carl van Doren, James M. Osborn, Marjorie Nicolson, Howard F. Lowry, Townsend Scudder, MacEdward Leach.

William Butler Yeats Memorial Number. A special number of *The Southern Review,* Volume VII, No. 3 (Winter, 1941), pages 407–666. Edited by Cleanth Brooks and Robert Penn Warren (1941).

Essays on the work of Yeats by R. P. Blackmur, L. C. Knights, T. S. Eliot, F. O. Matthiessen, Delmore Schwartz, Horace Gregory, Donald Davidson, John Crowe Ransom, Kenneth Burke, Morton Dauwen Zabel, Allen Tate, Arthur Mizener, Austin Warren, Howard Baker, Randall Jarrell.

The English Institute Annual: 1940 (1941).

Essays read before the English Institute, September 1940, by W. H. Auden, Cleanth Brooks, William York Tindall, Norman Holmes Pearson, René Wellek, Willard Thorp, Harry Hayden Clark, Ralph Thompson, Randolph G. Adams, Walter L. Pforzheimer.

The Intent of the Critic, edited with an introduction by Donald A. Stauffer (1941).

Four essays forming a symposium on the nature and motives of modern criticism, by Edmund Wilson, Norman Foerster, John Crowe Ransom, W. H. Auden. The essays were given as lectures at Princeton University in 1940–1941.

The Language of Poetry, edited by Allen Tate (1942).

Essays on poetry based on lectures read for the Creative Arts Program at Princeton University, Spring 1941, by Philip Wheelwright, Cleanth Brooks, I. A. Richards, Wallace Stevens.

The English Institute Annual: 1941 (1942).

Essays read before the English Institute, September 1941, by Lionel Trilling, René Wellek, J. Burke Severs, Madeleine Doran, Arthur Friedman, Sculley Bradley, R. C. Bald, Fredson Bowers, Charlton Hinman.

The Shock of Recognition: The Development of Literature in the United States Recorded by the Men Who Made It, edited by Edmund Wilson (1943).

Documents by Lowell, Poe, Melville, Emerson, Whitman, Bayard Taylor, Mallarmé, Henry James, Mark Twain, John Jay Chapman, H. G. Wells, W. D. Howells, Henry Adams, T. S. Eliot, George Santayana, D. H. Lawrence, Amy Lowell, H. L. Mencken, John Dos Passos, Sherwood Anderson.

Henry James Number of *The Kenyon Review,* Volume V, No. 4 (Autumn, 1943), pp. 481–618 (1943).

A centenary collection of essays by Katherine Anne Porter, Francis Fergusson, Jacques Barzun, John L. Sweeney, F. O. Matthiessen, Austin Warren, David Daiches, Eliseo Vivas, R. P. Blackmur, with editorial note by John Crowe Ransom; prepared under the editorship of Robert Penn Warren.

Gerard Manley Hopkins, by the Kenyon Critics (1945).

Essays on Hopkins, most of which originally appeared in *The Kenyon Review* in 1944, by Austin Warren, Herbert Marshall McLuhan, Harold Whitehall, Josephine Miles, Robert Lowell, Arthur Mizener, F. R. Leavis.

The Question of Henry James. A Collection of Critical Essays, edited by F. W. Dupee (1945).

Critical essays selected to describe the critical reputation of Henry James from 1879 to 1943 by the following American critics: Thomas Wentworth

Higginson, William Dean Howells, Frank Moore Colby, Herbert Croly, Stuart P. Sherman, Joseph Warren Beach, Thomas Beer, T. S. Eliot, Van Wyck Brooks, Vernon Louis Parrington, Edna Kenton, Constance Rourke, Edmund Wilson, R. P. Blackmur, Morton Dauwen Zabel, F. O. Matthiessen, W. H. Auden, Jacques Barzun, William Troy; and by the following Europeans: Max Beerbohm, Joseph Conrad, Ford Madox Ford, Percy Lubbock, André Gide.

The Kafka Problem, edited by Angel Flores (1946).

Criticism and exposition of Franz Kafka and his works by European critics and the following Americans: Max Lerner, W. H. Auden, Austin Warren, John Kelly, Frederick J. Hoffman, Edwin Berry Burgum, T. Weiss, Charles Neider, Angel Flores, Kate Flores.

Twentieth Century English, edited by William S. Knickerbocker (1946).

Includes, besides essays on language and linguistic problems, essays on the relation of language and literature by F. B. Millett, René Wellek, Louise Pound, Archibald MacLeish, Kenneth Burke, Austin Warren, Oscar Cargill, Wylie Sypher, Walter J. Ong, Cleanth Brooks, Roy T. Basler, Walter Pritchard Eaton, George Coffin Taylor.

Accent Anthology: Selections from *Accent, A Quarterly of New Literature, 1940–1945,* edited by Kerker Quinn and Charles Shattuck (1946).

Includes critical prose by Eric Bentley, R. P. Blackmur, Marjorie Brace, Cleanth Brooks, Edwin Berry Burgum, Kenneth Burke, David Daiches, Richard Eberhart, Otis Ferguson, Wallace Fowlie, Ruth Herschberger, F. O. Matthiessen, Henry Miller, Arthur Mizener, Paul Rosenfeld, Delmore Schwartz, Harry Slochower, T. Weiss.

The Partisan Reader: Ten Years of Partisan Review, 1934–1944, edited by William Phillips and Philip Rahv. Introduction by Lionel Trilling. (1946).

Includes, besides fiction and verse, critical essays and discussions printed in the *Partisan Review,* 1934–1944, by the following American writers and critics: Edmund Wilson, Meyer Schapiro, Philip Rahv, William Troy, W. H. Auden, F. W. Dupee, Clement Greenberg, Katherine Anne Porter, Morton Dauwen Zabel, Sidney Hook, Eugene Jolas, Robert Vigneron, William Phillips, T. S. Eliot, John Dewey, Ernest Nagel, Dwight Macdonald, Wylie Sypher, Randall Jarrell, Mary McCarthy, James Burnham, Harold Rosenberg, James Johnson Sweeney, George L. K. Morris, Sherwood Anderson, R. P. Blackmur, Louise Bogan, John Dos Passos, James T. Farrell, Horace Gregory, Gertrude Stein, Wallace Stevens, Allen Tate.

A Southern Vanguard, edited by Allen Tate (1947).

Being "The John Peale Bishop Memorial Volume," and containing, besides verse and fiction, critical essays by John Peale Bishop, Malcolm Cowley, Robert Wooster Stallman, Nathan L. Rothman, Eunice Glenn, William Van O'Connor, Herbert Marshall MacLuhan, Robert B. Heilman, Louis B. Wright—all dealing with Southern writers, tradition, and history.

The Stature of Thomas Mann, edited by Charles Neider (1947).

Essays on the life, personality, and work of Thomas Mann by European and English critics as well as the following Americans: G. A. Borgese, Martin Gumpert, Charles Jackson, Erika Mann, Klaus Mann, Dorothy Thompson,

Robert Morss Lovett, Ludwig Lewisohn, Vernon Venable, Joseph Warren Beach, Lewis Mumford, Hermann J. Weigand, Conrad Aiken, Henry C. Hatfield, Reinold Niebuhr, Harry Levin, Kenneth Burke, Helen Muchnic, Agnes E. Meyer, Charles Neider, Philip Blair Rice, Philo M. Buck, Jr., Albert Guérard, H. T. Lowe-Porter.

English Institute Essays: 1946 (1947).

Essays read before the English Institute, September 1946, by Gerald E. Bentley, Douglas Bush, Louis A. Landa, Carlos Baker, Marion Witt, Arthur Mizener, René Wellek, Cleanth Brooks, Alan S. Downer, E. L. MacAdam, Jr.

Forms of Modern Fiction: Essays Collected in Honor of Joseph Warren Beach, edited by William Van O'Connor (1948).

Essays on the theory and craft of fiction by American critics: Mark Schorer, Allen Tate, Joseph Warren Beach, David Daiches, Francis Fergusson, William Troy, Ray B. West, Jr., Richard Chase, T. S. Eliot, Robert Penn Warren, Lionel Trilling, E. K. Brown, Carlos Lynes, Jr., Frederick J. Hoffman, C. W. M. Johnson, Robert Bechtold Heilman, Robert Wooster Stallman, Warren Beck, Charles Child Walcutt, Eric Bentley, Morton Dauwen Zabel, C. H. Rickword.

James Joyce: Two Decades of Criticism, edited by S. Given (1948).

Essays on Joyce by American critics: Eugene Jolas, Irene Hendry, R. Levin and C. Shattuck, James T. Farrell, Hugh Kenner, T. S. Eliot, S. Foster Damon, Vivian Mercier, William Troy, Edmund Wilson, Joseph Campbell, Frederick J. Hoffman, J. F. Hendry; and European critics: Frank Budgen, Philip Toynbee, Stuart Gilbert.

T. S. Eliot: A Selected Critique, edited by Leonard Unger (1948).

Essays of the years 1919–1947 on the poetry and prose of T. S. Eliot, including discussions by the following American critics: Conrad Aiken, Ezra Pound, Mark Van Doren, Paul Elmer More, Malcolm Cowley, Granville Hicks, Delmore Schwartz, John Crowe Ransom, Yvor Winters, Van Wyck Brooks, Ferner Nuhn, Karl Shapiro, Edmund Wilson, F. O. Matthiessen, R. P. Blackmur, Allen Tate, Cleanth Brooks, Leonard Unger, James Johnson Sweeney, C. L. Barber, Louis L. Martz.

English Institute Essays: 1947 (1948).

Essays read before the English Institute, September 1947, by Richard Chase, Donald A. Stauffer, William Carlos Williams, M. M. Mathews, M. A. Shaaber, Matthew W. Black, Hereward T. Price, Giles E. Dawson.

Criticism: The Foundations of Modern Literary Judgment, edited by Mark Schorer, Josephine Miles, and Gordon McKenzie (1948).

Essays in critical theory and practice from Aristotle and Plato to the present day, including articles and essays by the following Americans: Henry James, Joseph Wood Krutch, Constance Rourke, James T. Farrell, Arthur O. Lovejoy, Edmund Wilson, W. H. Auden, Lionel Trilling, Allen Tate, T. S. Eliot, Yvor Winters, R. P. Blackmur, John Crowe Ransom, David Daiches, Cleanth Brooks, Robert Penn Warren, Joseph Frank, W. K. Wimsatt, Jr., Edgar Allan Poe, Kenneth Burke, Paul Elmer More, Harry Levin.

Critiques and Essays in Criticism: 1920–1948. Representing the Achievement of Modern British and American Critics, selected by Robert Wooster Stallman. With a Foreword by Cleanth Brooks. (1949).

Critical theory and practice since 1920, including essays by American critics: John Crowe Ransom, T. S. Eliot, Allen Tate, Cleanth Brooks, Robert Penn Warren, Robert B. Heilman, Yvor Winters, René Wellek, Kenneth Burke, Elder Olson, Joseph Frank, Delmore Schwartz, R. P. Blackmur, Eliseo Vivas, W. K. Wimsatt, Jr. and Monroe C. Beardsley, Edmund Wilson, F. W. Dupee.

Immortal Diamond: Studies in Gerard Manley Hopkins, edited by Norman Weyand, S.J., with the assistance of Raymond Schoder, S.J. (1949).

Essays by M. C. Carroll, Arthur MacGillivray, J. L. Bonn, W. J. Ong, C. A. Burns, R. V. Schoder, M. B. McNamee, W. T. Noon, Youree Watson, R. R. Boyle.

English Institute Essays: 1948 (1949).

Essays read before the English Institute, September 1948, by Wallace Stevens, Robert B. Heilman, Northrop Frye, Leslie A. Fiedler, Edward Hubler, Craig La Drière, Ruth C. Wallerstein, W. K. Wimsatt, Jr.

Lectures in Criticism, edited by Huntington Cairns (1949).

A symposium of lectures on historical and modern theory in criticism, delivered at Johns Hopkins University in April, 1948, by R. P. Blackmur, Benedetto Croce, Henri Peyre, John Crowe Ransom, Herbert Read, and Allen Tate.

The Permanence of Yeats, edited by James Hall and Martin Steinmann (1950).

Selected critical essays on William Butler Yeats by English critics (J. Middleton Murry, F. R. Leavis, Stephen Spender, D. S. Savage, A. Norman Jeffares) and the following Americans: Edmund Wilson, R. P. Blackmur, Cleanth Brooks, John Crowe Ransom, Allen Tate, David Daiches, Arthur Mizener, Joseph Warren Beach, Austin Warren, Eric Bentley, Kenneth Burke, William York Tindall, Donald Davidson, Elder Olson, Delmore Schwartz, T. S. Eliot, W. H. Auden, Morton Dauwen Zabel, Walter E. Houghton.

Perspectives of Criticism, edited by Harry Levin (1950).

Essays in criticism on various aspects of ancient and modern literature— Volume XX of the Harvard Studies in Comparative Literature—by Jean-Joseph Seznec, William C. Greene, Harry Levin, Alfred Schwartz, Perry Miller, Walter Jackson Bate, Geoffrey Tillotson, John V. Kelleher, Renato Poggioli.

English Institute Essays: 1949 (1950).

Essays read before the English Institute, September 1949, by Moody E. Prior, Arthur Mizener, Francis Fergusson, William Charvat, Roy Harvey Pearce, Benjamin Townley Spencer, Frederick J. Hoffman.

Critics and Criticism: Ancient and Modern, edited by R. S. Crane (1951).

Essays on ancient and modern theory and practice in criticism by R. S. Crane, W. R. Keast, Richard P. McKeon, Norman F. Maclean, Elder Olson, Bernard Weinberg.

APPENDIX III

American Magazines Publishing Criticism

THIS check-list includes the most important magazines that have published the work of American critics since 1900. A number of standard magazines are included, but a point has been made of including the best of the independent journals and "little magazines" that have encouraged literary experiment and critical activity. The dates and personnel of these have been described as closely as their irregular careers permit. [A more complete account of their careers will be found in *The Little Magazine: A History and a Bibliography*, by Frederick J. Hoffman, Charles Allen, and Carolyn F. Ulrich. Princeton University Press, 1946; revised edition, 1947.] Standard magazines devoted chiefly to public affairs, politics, and fiction have not been included. Magazines published in foreign countries are included when they have been edited and contributed to by American writers.

Accent: A Quarterly of New Literature. Urbana Illinois. Founded 1940. Edited by Kerker Quinn, Kenneth Andrews, Charles Shattuck, W. R. Moses, Thomas Bledsoe, Keith Huntress, W. McNeal Lowry, and others in subsequent years. Published quarterly.

The American Caravan: A Yearbook of American Literature. New York. Begun in 1927 "in the interests of a growing American literature"; established as an annual, but issued irregularly until 1936. Edited by Van Wyck Brooks (in 1927), Alfred Kreymborg, Lewis Mumford, Paul Rosenfeld (1927–1936). Discontinued in 1936.

American Literature: A Journal of Literary History, Criticism, and Bibliography. Durham, N. C. Founded in 1929. Edited by a board of American scholars. Published quarterly.

The American Mercury. New York. Founded in 1924 by H. L. Mencken and George Jean Nathan, who served as editors 1924–1925; edited by H. L. Mencken alone, 1925–1933; subsequent editors: Henry Hazlitt, Charles Angoff, Paul Palmer, Eugene Lyons, Lawrence Spivak. Published monthly.

American Prefaces: A Journal of Critical and Imaginative Writing. Iowa City, Iowa. Founded in 1935; discontinued in 1943. Edited by Wilbur Schramm, Paul Engle, Frederick Brantley, Jean Garrigue. Published quarterly.

The American Review. New York. Founded in 1933 and edited by Seward Collins. Published ten months of the year. Discontinued in 1938.

The American Spectator: A Literary Newspaper. New York. Founded in 1932; discontinued in 1937. Edited by George Jean Nathan, Ernest Boyd, James Branch Cabell, Eugene O'Neill; later by Theodore Dreiser, Sherwood Anderson, Charles Angoff, Max Lehman. Published monthly, with some periods of irregularity.

The Arizona Quarterly: A Journal of Literature, History, Folklore. University of Arizona, Tuscon, Arizona. Founded in 1945. Edited by Frederick Cromwell and Harry Behn. Published quarterly.

Blast: An Anglo-American Quarterly. A Review of the Great English Vortex. London, England. Founded in 1914 by Wyndham Lewis and Ezra Pound; edited by Wyndham Lewis. Discontinued in 1915. Two issues only.

Blues: A Magazine of New Rhythms. Columbus, Mississippi; later New York City. Founded in 1929 and edited by Charles Henri Ford. Discontinued in 1933, after irregular publication. Issued monthly, then irregularly.

The Bookman. New York City. Edited by John Farrar, 1921–1928; by Seward Collins and Burton Rascoe, 1928–1929; by Seward Collins, 1930–1933. Published monthly. Discontinued in 1933 with the founding of *The American Review* by Seward Collins.

Books Abroad: A Quarterly Publication Devoted to Comment on Foreign Books. Norman, Oklahoma. Founded in 1928 by Roy Temple House; edited by him and later by an editorial board, centering at the University of Oklahoma. Published quarterly.

Broom: An International Magazine of the Arts. Rome; Berlin; New York City. Founded in 1921. Edited by Harold A. Loeb, Alfred Kreymborg, Slater Brown, Matthew Josephson, Malcolm Cowley. Published monthly. Discontinued in 1924.

The Catholic World: A Monthly Magazine of General Literature and Science. New York City. Founded in 1865. Various successive editors. Published monthly.

The Chicago Literary Times. Chicago. Founded in 1923. Edited by Ben Hecht, with Maxwell Bodenheim as Associate. Published biweekly. Discontinued in 1924.

The Chimera: A Rough Beast. New York City. Founded in 1942 as a quarterly; later appearances irregular. Edited by Benjamin Ford, William Arrowsmith, Fearon Brown, Frederick Morgan, Barbara Howes, and others.

Commentary. Incorporating The Contemporary Jewish Record. New York City. Founded in 1945. Published by the American Jewish Committee. Editor: Elliot E. Cohen; associate editor, Clement Greenberg. Published monthly.

The Commonweal: A Weekly Review of Literature, the Arts, and Public Affairs. New York City. Founded in 1924 and edited by Michael Williams, with George Shuster as Associate Editor, and a board of consultants; later edited by Philip Wheelwright, Philip Burnham, Harry Lorin Binsse, and others. A Catholic lay journal. Published weekly.

Contact. New York City. Founded in 1921 and edited by William Carlos Williams and Robert McAlmon until 1923; revived briefly in 1933 as *Contact: An*

American Quarterly and edited by William Carlos Williams. Published irregularly. Discontinued in 1933.

The Criterion: A Quarterly Review. London, England. Founded in 1922 and edited by T. S. Eliot. Published quarterly except during 1927–1928 when it was called *The Monthly Criterion.* Discontinued in January, 1939.

Decision: A Review of Free Culture. New York City. Founded in 1941 and edited by Klaus Mann, later with Muriel Rukeyser as Associate Editor. Published monthly. Discontinued in 1942.

The Dial. Founded in New York in 1920 as a monthly devoted to literature and the arts, after an earlier career as a weekly, later a monthly, in Chicago and in New York. Edited by Scofield Thayer, 1920–1925; by Marianne Moore, 1925–1929; with John B. Watson as an advisory director, and Stewart Mitchell, Gilbert Seldes, Alyse Gregory, Kenneth Burke, and Ellen Thayer as editorial assistants. Published monthly. Discontinued in 1929.

Direction: A Quarterly of New Literature. Peoria, Illinois. Founded in 1934. Edited by Kerker Quinn, Rhody Fisher, Howard Nutt, Nelson Bittner. Published quarterly. Discontinued in 1935. Some of the editors and the general purpose of the magazine reappeared when *Accent* was founded in 1940.

The Double Dealer. New Orleans. Founded in 1921. Edited by Julius Weis Friend, Basil Thompson, John McClure. Published monthly. Discontinued in 1926.

The Drama. Chicago. Founded in 1911. Successively edited by William Norman Guthrie, Charles Hubbard Sergel, Theodore Ballou Hinckley, Albert E. Thompson, with various boards of advisory and associate editors. Titled *The Drama Magazine,* 1930–1931. Discontinued in 1931.

Dynamo: A Journal of Revolutionary Poetry. New York City. Founded in 1934. Edited by S. Funaroff, Herman Spector, Joseph Vogel, Nicholas Wirth, Stephen Foster. Published bimonthly, with some periods of irregularity. Discontinued in 1936.

The Egoist: An Individualist Review. London, England. Founded in 1914. Edited by Dora Marsden and Harriet Shaw Weaver, with Richard Aldington, H. D. (Hilda Doolittle), and T. S. Eliot as assistant editors. Published bimonthly. Discontinued in 1919.

The Exile. Founded in 1927 and edited by Ezra Pound from Paris and Rapallo, Italy, later numbers bearing a publication imprint of Chicago. Four issues only. Discontinued in 1928.

The Explicator. Fredericksburg, Virginia; now at Lynchburg, Virginia. Founded in 1942. Edited by G. W. Arms, J. P. Kirby, L. G. Locke, J. E. Whitesell. Published monthly from October to June.

The Figure in the Carpet: A Magazine of Prose. New York City. Founded in 1927. Edited by Hansell Baugh, then by John Riordan. Called *The Salient* after December, 1928. Published monthly but later irregularly. Discontinued in 1929.

The Forum and Century. New York City. *The Forum* founded in 1886; combined with *The Century* Magazine in 1931. Last editor, Henry Goddard Leach. Published monthly. Discontinued in 1939.

The Freeman. New York City. Founded in 1920. Edited by Francis Neilson and Albert Jay Nock; Associate Editor, Van Wyck Brooks. Published weekly. Discontinued in 1924. Re-established as a biweekly in 1950.

Front: A Radical Tri-Lingual Magazine. Being an International Review of Literature. The Hague, Holland. Edited by Sonja Prins, with Foreign Editors: Xavier Abril for Spain, Masaki Ikeda for Japan, Secretariat F. O. S. P. for Russia, Norman Macleod for the United States. Published bimonthly. Discontinued in 1931.

The Frontier. Missoula, Montana (University of Montana). Founded in 1920 as "a literary magazine"; later subtitled *A Regional Literary Quarterly.* Incorporated *Muse and Mirror* in 1932, and *The Midland* in 1933. Edited by H. G. Merriam and a board of editors. Three issues a year. Discontinued in 1939.

The Fugitive. Nashville, Tennessee. Founded in 1922. Edited by Walter Clyde Curry, Donald Davidson, Merrill Moore, John Crowe Ransom, James M. Frank, Sidney Mttron Hirsch, Stanley Johnson, Alec Brock Stevenson, Allen Tate, and others, including Robert Penn Warren and Laura Riding for short periods. Published bimonthly. Discontinued in 1925.

Furioso. New Haven, Conn.; later Northfield, Minnesota. Founded in 1939 as "a magazine of verse," appearing irregularly until 1942; resumed as quarterly in 1947. First editors: James Angleton and E. Reed Whittemore; later edited by James J. Angleton, Ambrose Gordon, Jr., Carmen Angleton Hauser, W. R. Johnson, Arthur Mizener, Rosemary Mizener, Howard Nemerov, John Pauker, Irwin Touster, and Reed Whittemore. Published quarterly.

The Guardian: A Monthly Journal of Life, Art, and Letters. Philadelphia. Founded in 1924. Board of Editors: Abraham N. Gerbovoy, Madelin Leof, Abe Grosner, Herman Silverman. Published monthly. Discontinued in 1925.

The Gyroscope. Palo Alto, California. Founded in 1929 and edited by Yvor Winters, Janet Lewis, Howard Baker. Issued irregularly. Discontinued in 1931.

The Harkness Hoot: A Yale Undergraduate Review. New Haven, Conn. Founded in 1930 and edited successively by William Harlan Hale, Selden Rodman, Richard M. Bissell, Richard S. Childs, and others. Published irregularly. Discontinued in 1934.

The Harvard Advocate. Cambridge, Mass. A literary review of Harvard University. Founded in 1866 and edited by successive student editors. Published biweekly.

The Harvard Monthly. Cambridge, Mass. Founded in 1885 and edited by successive student editors. Published monthly.

The Harvard Wake. Cambridge, Mass. An irregularly published journal, founded in 1944 and edited by students of Harvard University.

Hemispheres. Brooklyn, N. Y. Founded in 1943 as "a French-American quarterly of poetry," and edited by Yvan Goll. Discontinued in 1945.

The Hound and Horn. Cambridge, Mass., later New York City. Founded as "A Harvard Miscellany" in 1927 and edited by Bernard Bandler II, R. P. Blackmur, Lincoln E. Kirstein, Varian Fry, A. Hyatt Mayor. Edited after 1931 by

Lincoln Kirstein, with Allen Tate and Yvor Winters as Regional Editors. Published quarterly. Discontinued in 1934.

The Hudson Review. New York City. Founded in 1948 and edited by William Arrowsmith, Joseph D. Bennett, Frederick Morgan. Published quarterly.

The Kenyon Review. Kenyon College, Gambier, Ohio. Founded in 1939. Edited by John Crowe Ransom, with Philip Blair Rice as Associate Editor, and with advisory boards that have included R. P. Blackmur, Allen Tate, Mark Van Doren, Eliseo Vivas, Cleanth Brooks, Robert Penn Warren, Eric Bentley, Lionel Trilling, and Roger Sessions. Published quarterly.

Larus: The Celestial Visitor, with which has been combined Tempo. Lynn, Mass. Founded in 1927 and edited by Sherry Mangan, with Virgil Thomson as French editor. Issued irregularly. Discontinued in 1928.

The Laughing Horse: A Magazine of Satire from the Pacific Slope. Berkeley, California; later at Guadalajara, Mexico, Santa Fe and Taos, New Mexico. Founded in 1922. Edited by Roy E. Chanslor, James T. Van Renssalaer, Jr., and Willard Johnson. Published quarterly; later irregularly. Discontinued in 1939.

The Left: A Quarterly Review of Radical and Experimental Art. Davenport, Iowa. Founded in 1931. Edited by George Redfield, Jay du Von, Marvin Klein, R. C. Lorenz, W. K. Jordan, with various associate editors. Published quarterly. Discontinued in 1932.

The Liberator. New York City. Founded in 1918 as successor to *The Masses.* Edited by Max Eastman, Robert Minor, Floyd Dell, Chrystal Eastman, and others, with numerous editorial associates. Published monthly. Later merged with *Workers' Monthly, Labor Herald,* and *Soviet Russia Pictorial.* Published monthly. Discontinued as *The Liberator* in 1924.

Literary America. New York City. A "journal devoted to the American scene." Founded in 1934, and edited by Kenneth Houston and S. Robert Morse. Published monthly. Discontinued in 1936.

The Literary World: A Monthly Survey of International Letters. New York City. Founded in 1934 and edited by Angel Flores and Victor Robinson, with Samuel Putnam, Pierre Loving, Clifton Fadiman, and Willy Haas among the editorial advisers. Discontinued in 1935.

The Little Review: A Monthly Devoted to Literature, Drama, Music, and Art. Chicago; New York; Paris. Founded in 1914 as a monthly; later irregular in appearance. Edited by Margaret C. Anderson; later with Jane Heap (1922–1929). Ezra Pound as Foreign Editor, 1917–1921. Discontinued in 1929.

Mainstream: A Literary Quarterly. New York City. Founded in 1947 as a journal of Marxist-Communist opinion. Editor-in-chief: Samuel Sillen, assisted by an editorial board. Published monthly. In 1948 combined with *The New Masses* to form *Masses and Mainstream.*

Manuscripts. New York City. Founded in 1922 and edited coöperatively by Sherwood Anderson, Paul Rosenfeld, William Carlos Williams, Waldo Frank, and others. Issued irregularly. Discontinued in 1923.

The Maryland Quarterly, later *The Briarcliff Quarterly.* College Park, Maryland; later at Briarcliff Junior College, New York. Founded in 1944. Edited by

Norman Macleod, Jane Woodring, Pauline Howard, Arthur O'Keefe, and others. Published quarterly.

The Masses: A Monthly Devoted to the Interests of the Working People. New York City. Founded in 1911, and edited successively by Thomas Seltzer, Horatio Winslow, Piet Vlag, and Max Eastman, with Floyd Dell, John Reed, Mary Heaton Vorse, Louis Untermeyer, Arthur Bullard among the contributing editors, and Art Young, George Bellows, Boardman Robinson, and H. J. Glintenkamp as art editors. Discontinued in 1917, but continued in *The Liberator* and *The New Masses.*

Masses and Mainstream. New York City. Founded in 1948, combining *Mainstream* and *The New Masses.* Edited by Samuel Sillen, with Herbert Apotheker, Lloyd L. Brown, and Charles Humboldt as associate editors. Published monthly.

The Measure: A Journal of Poetry. New York City. Founded in 1921 and edited by a board including Maxwell Anderson, Padraic Colum, Frank E. Hill, David Morton, Louise Townsend Nicoll, George O'Neill, Genevieve Taggard, Joseph Auslander, Elinor Wylie, Louise Bogan, and others. Published monthly. Discontinued in 1926.

Measure: A Critical Journal. Chicago. Founded in 1949. Board of editors: Daniel J. Boorstin, David Grene, Robert M. Hutchins (chairman), John U. Nef, Robert Redfield, Henry Regnery, Otto G. von Simson (managing editor). Editorial advisers: Montgomery Belgion, A. P. d'Entrèves, Jacques Maritain, Franz Joseph Schöningh. Published quarterly.

The Miscellany. New York City. Founded in 1931 and edited by F. W. Dupee, Geoffrey T. Hellman, Dwight Macdonald, George L. K. Morris. Published bimonthly. Discontinued in 1931.

Modern Philology. University of Chicago. Founded in 1905 by John Matthews Manly, its first editor; present managing editor, R. S. Crane, with a board of consultants. Published quarterly.

The Modern Quarterly. Baltimore. Founded in 1923 and edited by V. F. Calverton, with assistants: Rachel North, Mortin Levin, Savington Crampton, Samuel D. Schmalhausen, Max Eastman, Edmund Wilson, Ernest Sutherland Bates, Carleton Beals, Bruno Fischer, Diego Rivera, Thomas Benton, and others. Published quarterly except 1933–1938 when it was called *The Modern Monthly.* Discontinued in 1940.

Modern Review. Winchester, Mass. Founded in 1922 and edited by Fiskwoode Tarleton. Published quarterly. Discontinued in 1924.

The Morada: A Tri-Lingual Advance Guard Quarterly. Albuquerque, New Mexico, and Cagnes-sur Mer, France. Founded in 1929 and edited by Norman Macleod, William Flynn, C. V. Wicker, Donal McKenzie, with various contributing editors. Published quarterly. Discontinued in 1931.

The Nation. New York City. Founded in 1865 and edited by E. L. Godkin. Edited by Paul Elmer More, 1909–1914. Reorganized by Oswald Garrison Villard in 1918 and edited by him and others until 1932. Edited 1935–1938 by Joseph Wood Krutch, Max Lerner, Freda Kirchwey. After 1938 edited by Freda Kirchwey, with Margaret Marshall as Literary Editor, Joseph Wood

Krutch as Drama Critic, B. H. Haggin as Music Critic, and with Robert
Bendiner, Keith Hutchison, and others as associates. Published weekly.

Nativity: An American Quarterly. Delaware and Columbus, Ohio. Founded in
1930 and edited by Boris J. Israel. Published quarterly. Discontinued in
1931.

The New Act: A Literary Review. New York City. Founded in 1933 and edited
by H. R. Hays and Harold Rosenberg. Issued irregularly. Discontinued in
1934.

New Directions in Prose and Poetry. Norfolk, Conn. An annual founded in 1936
and edited by James Laughlin IV; devoted to new and experimental writing
and art, and including critical essays and surveys. Published annually.

The New Freeman. New York City. Founded in 1930 and edited by Suzanne
LaFollette. Published weekly. Discontinued in 1931.

The New Masses. New York City. Founded in 1926 and edited successively by
Egmont Arens, Hugo Gellert, Michael Gold, Joseph Freeman, James Rorty,
John Sloan, William Gropper, and numerous others. Published monthly,
with intervals as a weekly. Discontinued in 1948 when it was merged with
Mainstream as *Masses and Mainstream.*

The New Mexico Quarterly. University of New Mexico, Albuquerque, N. M.
Founded in 1941; after 1941 titled as *The New Mexico Quarterly Review.*
Edited successively by J. F. Zimmerman, John D. Clark, J. W. Diefendorf,
with T. M. Pearce and Dudley Wynn as active editors, 1932 and following;
Alan Swallow as Poetry Editor; and others. Published quarterly.

The New Republic. New York City. Founded in 1914 and edited by Herbert
Croly, Walter Lippmann, Francis Hackett, Randolph Bourne, Philip Littell,
and others; later by Bruce Bliven, Robert Morss Lovett, Edmund Wilson,
Stark Young, George Soule, Malcolm Cowley, and others; at present by Michael Straight, Bruce Bliven, and others. Published weekly.

The New Review: An International Notebook of the Arts. Paris. Founded in 1931;
edited by Samuel Putnam, with Peter Neagoe, Ezra Pound, Maxwell Bodenheim, Richard Thoma as associates. Published quarterly. Discontinued in
1932.

The Pacific Spectator. Palo Alto, California. Founded in 1947, with John W.
Dodds (chairman), Frederick Hard, Wallace Stegner, George R. Stewart,
Dixon Wecter as board of editors, and Edith R. Mirrielees as managing edi-
tor. Published quarterly by the Stanford University Press for the Pacific Coast
Committee for the Humanities and 26 supporting colleges and universities.

Pagany: A Native Quarterly. Boston; later New York. Founded in 1930 and edited
by Richard Johns. Published quarterly. Discontinued in 1933.

Partisan Review. New York City. Founded in 1934 as "A Bi-Monthly of Rev-
olutionary Literature" under the auspices of the John Reed Club of New
York, with Nathan Adler, Edward Dahlberg, Joseph Freeman, Philip Rahv,
William Phillips, Alan Calmer, Jack Conroy, Ben Field, Clinton Simpson,
and others on the editorial board, 1934–1937. Reorganized in 1937 with
Philip Rahv, William Phillips, Dwight Macdonald, F. W. Dupee, George
L. K. Morris, and Mary McCarthy as editors. Published quarterly, later bi-

monthly, from 1937 to 1947. As monthly beginning in 1948, but reverting to bimonthly in 1950, with William Phillips and Philip Rahv as editors, Delmore Schwartz and William Barrett as associate editors, with advisory board.

The Playboy: A Portfolio of Art and Satire. New York City. Founded in 1919 and edited by Egmont Arens. Published irregularly. Discontinued in 1924.

The Plowshare: A Magazine of the Literature, Arts, and Life Evolving in Woodstock. Woodstock, N. Y. Founded as *The Wild Hawk* in 1912, with Hervey White, Carl Eric Lindin, Allan Updegraff as editors. Published monthly; later irregularly. Discontinued in 1920. Briefly resumed in 1935.

Poetry: A Magazine of Verse. Chicago. Founded in 1912 and edited 1912–1936 by Harriet Monroe, with Alice Corbin Henderson, Ezra Pound, Eunice Tietjens, Helen Hoyt, Emanuel Carnevali, Marion Strobel, George Dillon, Jessica Nelson North, and Morton Dauwen Zabel as successive associate editors. Edited 1936–1937 by Morton Dauwen Zabel; 1937–1942 and 1946–1949 by George Dillon; 1949 by Hayden Carruth; 1950–   by Karl Shapiro.

Politics. New York City. Founded in 1942 and edited by Dwight Macdonald. Published weekly; then monthly; later irregularly. Discontinued in 1949.

The Quarterly Review of Literature. Chapel Hill, N. C., New Haven, Conn., and Annandale-on-Hudson, N. Y. Founded in 1944. Edited by Warren Carrier and T. Weiss, with T. Weiss as editor after 1946. Published quarterly.

Reedy's Mirror: A Weekly Dealing in Politics and Literature. St. Louis, Missouri. Founded in 1891 as *The Mirror;* edited as *Reedy's Mirror* from 1913 to 1920 by William Marion Reedy. Published weekly. Discontinued in 1920, and superseded by *All's Well, or The Mirror Repolished.*

The Reviewer. Richmond, Virginia. Edited by Emily Clark and Hunter Stagg as a bimonthly, 1921–1924 (with Margaret Freeman, Mary D. Street, James Branch Cabell as temporary associates). Edited by Paul Green, 1925. Absorbed by *The Southwest Review* in 1926.

S4N. Publication of the S4N Society to Promote Open-Minded Consideration of Theories and Practices of Art. Northampton, Mass., and New Haven, Conn. Founded in 1919 and edited by Norman Fitts, with Gorham B. Munson, E. E. Cummings, Thornton Wilder, Jean Toomer, Stephen Vincent Benét among the members of the editorial board. Published monthly and irregularly. Combined with *The Modern Review* in 1926 to form *The Modern S4N Review.*

The Saturday Review of Literature. New York. Founded in 1924 and edited until 1936 by Henry Seidel Canby; from 1936 to 1938 by Bernard De Voto; now edited by Norman Cousins, with Amy Loveman, John Mason Brown, and Harrison Smith as associate editors; Bennett Cerf, John T. Winterich, Mary Gould Davis, Irving Kolodin, James Thrall Soby as contributing editors; Henry Seidel Canby as chairman of Board of Directors. Published weekly.

Science and Society: A Marxian Quarterly. New York City. Founded in 1936, with Albert E. Blumberg, Edwin Berry Burgum, V. J. McGill, Margaret Schlauch, and Bernhard J. Stern as editors; now edited by Bernhard J. Stern (chairman), Samuel Bernstein, Edwin Berry Burgum, V. J. McGill, Henry F. Mins, Margaret Schlauch, Dirk J. Struik. Published quarterly.

Secession: A Quarterly. An Independent Magazine of Modern Letters. Vienna, Berlin, Reutte (Tirol, Austria), New York. Founded in 1922 and edited successively by Gorham B. Munson, Matthew Josephson, Kenneth Burke. Published monthly, then irregularly. Discontinued in 1924.

The Seven Arts: A Monthly. New York. Founded in 1916. Editor: James Oppenheim; with Waldo Frank and Van Wyck Brooks as associate editors. Discontinued in 1917, to be absorbed by *The Dial.*

The Sewanee Review: A Quarterly of Life and Letters. Sewanee, Tennessee (The University of the South). Founded in 1892 and edited successively by Telfair Hodgson, W. P. Trent, B. W. Wells, and others; by William S. Knickerbocker, 1926–1942; by Tudor S. Long in 1943; by Andrew C. Lytle, 1943–1944; by Allen Tate, 1944–1946; by J. E. Palmer, 1946– . Published quarterly.

The Smart Set: A Magazine of Cleverness. New York. Founded earlier; edited from 1912 to 1914 by Willard Huntington Wright; from 1914–1923 by H. L. Mencken and George Jean Nathan. Published monthly. The literary importance of the magazine belongs to the years 1912–1923.

The Southern Review. Baton Rouge, Louisiana (Louisiana State University). Founded in 1935, with Charles W. Pipkin as editor, Cleanth Brooks, Jr., and Robert Penn Warren as associate editors; Brooks and Warren as editors 1941–1942. Published quarterly. Discontinued in 1942.

The Southwest Review. University of Texas; Southern Methodist University. Founded as *The Texas Review* in 1912 with Stark Young as editor; later edited, 1917–1924, by Robert Adger Law; reorganized as *The Southwest Review* in 1924 and edited by Jay B. Hubbell, George Bond, and others. Published quarterly.

Story. Vienna; Majorca; New York. Founded in 1931 and edited by Whit Burnett, with Martha Foley as associate, 1931–1941. Published bimonthly.

The Symposium: A Critical Review. New York. Founded in 1930. Editors: James Burnham and Philip E. Wheelwright. Published quarterly. Discontinued in 1933.

Tambour. Paris, France. Founded in 1929 and edited by Harold Salemson. Published irregularly. Discontinued in 1930.

Theatre Arts Magazine. New York. Founded in 1916 with Sheldon Cheney as editor 1916–1921; Edith J. R. Isaacs editor from 1919 to 1946; Marion Tucker and Stark Young editors 1919–1921 and 1922–1924 respectively; Ashley Dukes, John Mason Brown, Carl Carmer, Rosamond Gilder, Morton Eustis, Stark Young, Kenneth Macgowan sometime associate editors; Charles MacArthur, editor, 1946– . Published quarterly, later monthly.

This Quarter: An International Quarterly Review of Arts and Letters. Milan, Monte Carlo, Cannes, and Paris, France. Founded in 1925 and edited by Ernest Walsh, 1925–1926, and Ethel Moorhead, 1925–1927; edited by Edward W. Titus, 1929–1932. Published quarterly. Discontinued in 1933.

The Transatlantic Review. Paris, France. Founded in 1924 and edited by Ford Madox Ford. Published monthly. Discontinued in 1925.

Transition: An International Magazine for Creative Experiment. Paris; The Hague; New York. Founded in 1927. Editors: Eugene Jolas and Elliot Paul, with

Robert Sage, Harry Crosby, Matthew Josephson, and others as associates; edited by Eugene Jolas after 1929. Published monthly, later quarterly, with periods of suspension.

Twice a Year: A Journal of Literature, the Arts, and Civil Liberties. New York City. Founded in 1938 and edited by Dorothy Norman. Published semiannually.

The University Review. University of Kansas City, Missouri. Founded in 1934; edited by Clarence Decker. Published quarterly.

Vice Versa. New York City. Founded in 1940, with Harry Brown and Dunstan Thompson as editors. Published bimonthly. Discontinued in 1942.

View. New York City. Founded in 1940, with Charles Henri Ford as editor, James Decker as managing editor, and Parker Tyler later as associate editor. Four irregular issues a year. Discontinued in 1947.

The Virginia Quarterly Review. Charlottesville, Virginia. Founded in 1925, with James Southall Wilson as editor, assisted by others. Now edited by Charlotte Kohler, with James Southall Wilson, R. K. Gooch, Thomas Perkins Abernethy, Hardy C. Dillard, and William S. Weedon as advisory editors. Published quarterly.

Voices: A Journal of Verse. Boston; later New York City. Founded in 1921 and edited by Harold Vinal. Published bimonthly.

The Wave: A Journal of Art and Letters. Chicago; later Copenhagen. Editor: Vincent Starret. Published irregularly. Discontinued in 1924.

The Western Review. Founded at Murray, Utah, in 1937 as *The Intermountain Review* by Ray B. West, Jr. In 1938 moved to Ogden, Utah, and became *The Rocky Mountain Review* with Ray B. West, Jr., as editor; George Snell and Grant H. Redford as associates; Brewster Ghiselin as poetry editor. In 1946 moved to Lawrence, Kansas, with title changed to *The Western Review,* Ray B. West, Jr., continuing as editor, R. W. Stallman and Alwyn Berland as associate editors. In 1949 moved to State University of Iowa, Iowa City, with Ray B. West, Jr., as editor; Warren Carrier and Robie Macauley as associate editors; Alwyn Berland, George Bluestone, John Hunt, Carl Hartman, E. F. McGuire, Austryn Wainhouse as assistants; Dean Cadle as business manager. Published quarterly.

The Westminster Magazine. Oglethorpe University, Georgia. Founded in 1911. Various editors. Published quarterly with periods of suspension. Absorbed *Bozart* and *Contemporary Verse* in 1935.

The Windsor Quarterly. Hartland Four Corners, Vermont. Founded in 1933 with Frederick B. Maxham and Irene Merrill as editors. Published quarterly. Discontinued in 1935.

The Yale Review: A National Quarterly. New Haven, Conn. First founded in 1879; reëstablished in 1892; reorganized in 1911 with Wilbur Cross as editor and Helen MacAfee as assistant editor, Miss MacAfee later succeeding Wilbur Cross as editor. Present editor (1950): David M. Potter, with Paul Pickrel as managing editor, Helen MacAfee as editor emeritus, and William Clyde DeVane, Edgar S. Furniss, and Arnold Wolfers as the editorial board. Published quarterly.

APPENDIX IV

Notes on Contributors

THESE notes are chiefly bibliographical in character. In addition to their books, all of the contributors to this volume have written for critical and literary journals; the titles of these are not, however, listed, except in the case of periodicals on which editorial positions have been held. Such contributions may be traced by consulting *The Reader's Guide to Periodical Literature* and *The International Index to Periodicals*. For lists of selected critical essays see Appendix V.

ARVIN, NEWTON. Born: Valparaiso, Indiana, 1900. Educated: Harvard University, B.A., 1921. Member of the English Department of Smith College since 1922: instructor, 1926–1928; assistant professor, 1928–1932; associate professor, 1932–1940; professor of English since 1940. Associate editor of *The Living Age*, 1925–1926. Editor: *The Heart of Hawthorne's Journals* (1929); *Hawthorne's Short Stories* (1946). Books of criticism and biography: *Hawthorne* (1929); *Whitman* (1938); *Herman Melville* (1950).

AUDEN, WYSTAN HUGH. Born: York, England, 1907. Educated: Gresham's School, Holt; Christ Church, Oxford University. School teacher at Malvern, 1930–1935. Worked with the G. P. O. Film Unit, 1935–1936. Traveled in France, Germany, Spain, Iceland, China, United States. Came to the United States in 1939 and presently adopted American citizenship. Has taught at University of Michigan, Haverford College, New School in New York City, and lectured in many other colleges and universities. Verse first published in *Oxford Poetry*, 1926. King's Medal for Poetry (England), 1937; Pulitzer Prize in Poetry, 1947. Books of verse: *Poems* (1930); *The Orators* (1932); *Letters from Iceland* (with Louis MacNeice, 1937); *Spain* (1937); *On This Island* (1937); *Selected Poems* (1938); *Journey to a War* (with Christopher Isherwood, 1939); *Another Time* (1940); *The Double Man* (1941); *For the Time Being* (1944); *Collected Poems* (1945); *The Age of Anxiety* (1948). Plays in verse: *The Dance of Death* (1933); *The Dog Beneath the Skin* (with Christopher Isherwood, 1935); *The Ascent of F 6* (with Christopher Isherwood, 1936); *On the Frontier* (with Christopher Isherwood, 1939). Editor of: *The Poet's Tongue* (with John Garrett, 1935); *The Oxford Book of Light Verse* (1938); *Selections from Tennyson* (1944); *The Portable Greek Reader* (1948); *Poets of the English Language* (5 volumes, with N. H. Pearson, 1950). Book of critical prose: *The Enchafèd Flood: or, The Romantic Iconography of the Sea* (1950).

BABBITT, IRVING. Born: Dayton, Ohio, 1865. Died in 1932. Educated: Harvard University, B.A., 1889; M.A., 1893; Sorbonne, Paris, 1891–1892. Instructor of French, Williams College, 1893–1894; instructor of French, Harvard, 1894–1902; assistant professor, 1902–1912; professor of French, 1912–1932. Lecturer at the Sorbonne, 1923. Editor of: Taine's *Introduction à l'Histoire de la Littérature anglaise* (1898); Renan's *Souvenirs de l'Enfance* (1902); Voltaire's *Zadig* (1905); Racine's *Phèdre* (1910), etc. Translator and editor of *The Dhammapada* (1936). Books of critical and philosophical prose: *Literature and the American College* (1908); *The New Laokoön* (1910); *The Masters of Modern French Criticism* (1912); *Rousseau and Romanticism* (1919); *Democracy and Leadership* (1924); *On Being Creative and Other Essays* (1932).

BARRETT, WILLIAM. Born: New York City, 1915. Educated: New York City schools; College of the City of New York; Columbia University, B.A., M.A., Ph. D. Taught philosophy at the University of Illinois and Brown University, 1938–1942; and English composition at College of the City of New York. Instructor for the Navy, 1942–1945; served with State Department in Italy, 1945–1946. Associate Editor of *Partisan Review*, 1946–   . Works of criticism: *Aristotle's Theory of Nature; What is Existentialism?* (1947).

BENTLEY, ERIC (RUSSELL). Born: England, 1916. Educated: Oxford University, B.A.; Yale University, Ph.D. While at Oxford acted in Shakespeare and studied production under John Gielgud and Esme Church. Has taught literature at Oxford, The University of California, Black Mountain College, The Kenyon School of English, and the University of Minnesota (Associate Professor of English since 1946). Guggenheim Fellowship, 1948. Guest director, Hedgerow Theatre, 1948; at the Abbey Theatre, Dublin, 1950. European correspondent, *Theatre Arts Magazine*, 1948–1950. Editor: *The Importance of Scrutiny* (1948); *From the Modern Repertoire* (1949). Translator: *The Private Life of the Master Race* by Bert Brecht (1944), and other works of Brecht. Books of critical prose: *A Century of Hero Worship* (1944); *The Playwright as Thinker* (in England published as *The Modern Theatre*) (1946); *Bernard Shaw* (1947).

BLACKMUR, RICHARD P. Born: Springfield, Massachusetts, 1904. Member of the editorial board of *The Hound and Horn*, 1928–1929. Assistant in Creative Arts Program, Princeton University, 1940–1943; member of the Institute of Advanced Study, Princeton, 1943–1946; Resident Fellow in Creative Writing, Princeton University, 1946–   . Books of verse: *From Jordan's Delight* (1937); *The Second World* (1942); *The Good European and Other Poems* (1947). Books of criticism: *The Double Agent: Essays in Craft and Elucidation* (1935); *The Expense of Greatness* (1940).

BOGAN, LOUISE. Born: Livermore Falls, Maine, 1897. Educated: Mount St. Mary's Academy, Manchester, N.H., 1907–1909; Girls' Latin School, Boston,

1910–1915; Boston University, 1915–1916. Visiting lecturer on poetry at University of Washington, 1948; University of Chicago, 1949; has lectured at University of Utah, University of Indiana, University of Iowa, and other colleges. John Reed Memorial Prize (*Poetry*), 1930; Helen Haire Levinson Prize (*Poetry*), 1937; Guggenheim Fellowship, 1933 and 1937; Fellow in American Letters, Library of Congress, 1944, and incumbent of the Chair of Poetry, 1945–1946; Harriet Monroe Poetry Award (University of Chicago), 1948. Poetry critic of *The New Yorker* since 1929. Books of verse: *Body of This Death* (1923); *Dark Summer* (1929); *The Sleeping Fury* (1937); *Poems and New Poems* (1941).

BOURNE, RANDOLPH SILLIMAN. Born: Bloomfield, New Jersey, 1886. Died in 1918. Educated: public schools, Bloomfield, N.J., Columbia University, B.A., 1912; M.A., 1913. Gilder Fellowship for travel and study in Europe, 1913–1914. Member of the first editorial board of *The New Republic*, 1914–1918. Contributing editor of *The Dial*, 1917–1918; of *The Seven Arts*, 1917. Editor of a symposium *Towards a Lasting Peace* (1916). Books of prose and criticism: *Youth and Life* (1913); *Arbitration and International Politics* (1913); *The Gary Schools* (1916); *Education and Living* (1917); *Untimely Papers* (edited by James Oppenheim, 1919); *The History of a Literary Radical and Other Essays* (edited by Van Wyck Brooks, 1920).

BROOKS, CLEANTH. Born: Murray, Kentucky, 1906. Educated: McTeire School, 1920–1924; Vanderbilt University, B.A., 1928; Tulane University, M.A., 1929; Exeter College, Oxford University (Rhodes Scholar), B.A., 1931 (Honors); B. Litt., 1932. A founder and editor of *The Southern Review*, 1935–1942. Assistant professor of English, Vanderbilt University, 1932–1934; assistant professor, associate professor, professor of English, Louisiana State University, 1934–1947; professor of English, Yale University, 1947–   . Visiting professor of English, universities of Texas, Michigan, Chicago. Fellow, Kenyon School of English, 1948. Books of criticism: *Modern Poetry and the Tradition* (1939); *The Well Wrought Urn: Studies in the Structure of Poetry* (1947). Books for literary study: *An Approach to Literature* (with Robert Penn Warren and Jack Purser, 1936, 1938, 1943); *Understanding Poetry* (with Robert Penn Warren, 1938, 1950); *Understanding Fiction* (with Robert Penn Warren, 1943); *Understanding Drama* (with Robert B. Heilman, 1945). Coauthor: *The Language of Poetry* (1942); *Twentieth Century English* (1946); *T. S. Eliot: A Study of His Writings by Several Hands* (1947). Editor: *The Percy Letters* (with David Nichol Smith, 1944–   ). Linguistic study: *The Relation of the Alabama-Georgia Dialect to the Provincial Dialects of Great Britain* (1935).

BROOKS, VAN WYCK. Born: Plainfield, New Jersey, 1886. Educated: Harvard University, A.B., 1908. On the editorial staff of Doubleday, Page and Co., 1907–1909; editor for The Century Company, 1915–1918. Lecturer at Leland Stanford University, 1911–1913. Assistant editor of *The Seven Arts*, 1917; associate editor of *The Freeman*, 1920–1924; founder and editor of *The American Caravan* in 1927 (with Alfred Kreymborg, Paul Rosenfeld, Lewis Mumford). Translator of works by Amiel, André Chamson, Georges Duhamel, Paul Gauguin, Léon Bazalgette, Romain Rolland. Editor of *The History of a Literary Radical* by Randolph Bourne (1920), *Journal of the First Voyage to America* by Christopher Columbus (1924), etc. Litt. D. of Columbia, Tufts, Bowdoin, Boston, Dartmouth; L.H.D., Northwestern University. Member of American Academy of Arts and Letters; National Institute of Arts and Letters; American Philosophical Society; Phi Beta Kappa. Granted the Dial Award, 1923; Pulitzer Prize in History, 1937. Books of prose and criticism: *The Wine of the Puritans* (1909); *The Malady of the Ideal* (1913); *John Addington Symonds* (1914); *The World of H. G. Wells* (1915); *America's Coming-of-Age* (1915); *Letters and Leadership* (1918); *The Ordeal of Mark Twain* (1920; revised 1932); *The Pilgrimage of Henry James* (1925); *Emerson and Others* (1927); *Sketches in Criticism* (1932); *Life of Emerson* (1932); *Three Essays on America* (1934); *The Flowering of New England* (1936); *New England: Indian Summer* (1940); *On Literature Today* (1941); *The Opinions of Oliver Allston* (1941); *The World of Washington Irving* (1944); *The Times of Melville and Whitman* (1947); *A Chilmark Miscellany* (1947).

BROWN, EDWARD KILLORAN. Born: Toronto, Canada, 1905. Educated: University of Toronto, B.A., 1926; Docteur ès Lettres, University of Paris, 1935. Lecturer, later assistant professor of English, University of Toronto, 1929–1935; professor and chairman of English, University of Manitoba, 1935–1937; professor of English, University of Toronto, 1938–1941; professor and chairman of English, Cornell University, 1941–1944; professor of English, University of Chicago, 1944–   . Alexander lecturer, University of Toronto, 1949. Translations: *Carlyle* by Louis Cazamian (1932); *Le Père Goriot* by Balzac (1946). Editor: *Representative Essays of Matthew Arnold* (1936); *Victorian Poetry* (1942); *At the Long Sault* by Archibald Lampman (with D. C. Scott, 1943). Books of criticism: *Edith Wharton: Étude critique* (Paris, 1935); *Studies in the Text of Matthew Arnold's Prose Works* (1935); *On Canadian Poetry* (1943); *Matthew Arnold: A Study in Conflict* (1948). In preparation: a biography of Willa Cather.

BURKE, KENNETH. Born: Pittsburgh, Pennsylvania, 1897. Educated: Ohio State University; Columbia University. Research worker, Laura Spellman Rockefeller Foundation, 1926–1927. Editor for the Bureau of Social Hygiene, 1928–1929. On the staff of *The Dial*, 1922–1929; music critic, 1927–1929. Visiting lecturer, University of Chicago, 1939 and 1949–1950; member of the staff of Bennington College, 1943–   . Received the Dial Award, 1928; Guggenheim Fellowship, 1935; grant of the American Academy of Arts and Letters, 1946. Has lectured at the New School for Social Research and other institutions. Fellow of the Institute of Advanced Study, 1948–1949. Translator of books by Thomas Mann, Emil Ludwig, Emile Baumann, and others. Books of narrative: *The White Oxen* (1924); *Toward a Better Life* (1932). Books of criticism and philosophical enquiry: *Counter-Statement* (1931); *Permanence and Change: Anatomy of Purpose* (1935); *Attitudes Toward History* (1937); *The Philosophy of Literary Form* (1941); *A Grammar of Motives* (1945); *A Rhetoric of Motives* (1950).

CANTWELL, ROBERT EMMETT. Born: Little Falls, Washington, 1908. Educated: Weatherwax High School, Aberdeen, Wash., 1921–1924; University of Washington, 1924–1925. Worked as factory hand, section hand, common laborer, welder's assistant. On the editorial staff of *Time*, 1935–1936; of *Fortune*, 1937; associate editor of *Time*, 1938–1945. Novels: *Laugh and Lie Down* (1931); *The Land of Plenty* (1934). Critical biography: *Nathaniel Hawthorne: The American Years* (1948).

CHAPMAN, JOHN JAY. Born: New York City, 1862. Died in 1933. Educated: St. Paul's School, Concord, N.H.; Harvard College, B.A., 1885; Harvard Law School. Admitted to Bar in 1888. Practised law briefly in New York; traveled in the West, in Europe and Russia. Edited *The Nursery*, later *The Political Nursery*, 1897. Active in New York politics, 1896–1910, in "Third Ticket" Movement, Good Government Club, etc. L.H.D., Hobart College; Phi Beta Kappa poet, Harvard, 1912; Litt. D., Yale University, 1916. Books of plays: *Four Plays for Children* (1908); *The Maid's Forgiveness* (1908); *A Sausage from Bologna* (1909); *The Treason and Death of Benedict Arnold* (1910); *Neptune's Isle and Other Plays for Children* (1916); *Cupid and Psyche* (1916); *Two Greek Plays: The Philoctetes of Sophocles and the Medea of Euripides* (1928); *The Antigone of Sophocles* (1929). Books of verse: *Homeric Scenes* (1914); *Songs and Poems* (1919). Books of political and social discussion: *Causes and Consequences* (1898); *Practical Agitation* (1900); *William Lloyd Garrison* (1913); *Memories and Milestones* (1915); *Notes on Religion* (1915); *New Horizons in American Life* (1932). Books of criticism: *Emerson and Other Essays* (1898); *Learning and Other Essays* (1910); *Greek Genius and Other Essays* (1915); *A Glance Toward Shakespeare* (1922); *Letters and Religion* (1924); *Dante* (1927); *Lucian, Plato, and Greek Morals* (1931).

CHASE, RICHARD. Born: Lakeport, New Hampshire, 1914. Educated: Dartmouth College, B.A., 1937; Columbia University, Ph. D., 1946. Instructor in English, Connecticut College, 1946–1949; assistant professor of English, Columbia University, 1949– . Books of criticism and literary history: *Quest for Myth* (1949); *Herman Melville: A Critical Study* (1949).

COWLEY, MALCOLM. Born: Belsano, Pennsylvania, 1898. Educated: Harvard University, B.A., 1920; University of Montpellier, France, on American Field Service Fellowship, 1921–1922. Free-lance writer in New York, 1923–1929. Translator of books by Paul Valéry, Maurice Barrès, Raymond Radiguet, Pierre Mac Orlan, Princess Bibesco, André Gide, and others. Guarantors Prize, *Poetry*, 1928. Associate Editor of *The New Republic*, 1929–1944; contributing editor, 1944– . Editor: *After the Genteel Tradition* (1937); *Books That Changed Our Minds* (1939); *The Portable Hemingway* (1944); *The Portable Faulkner* (1948). Books of verse: *Blue Juniata* (1929); *The Dry Season* (1941). Book of prose: *Exile's Return: A Narrative of Ideas* (1934).

CRANE, RONALD SALMON. Born: Tecumseh, Michigan, 1886. Educated: University of Michigan, B.A., 1908; University of Pennsylvania, Ph. D., 1911. Instructor of English, Northwestern University, 1911–1915; assistant professor, 1915–1920; associate professor, 1920–1924; associate professor, University of Chicago, 1924–1925; professor of English, 1925–   ; chairman, Department of English, 1935–1947. Member: American Association of Arts and Letters; Phi Beta Kappa. Managing Editor of *Modern Philology*, 1930–   . Studies of literary history: *The Vogue of Guy of Warwick from the Close of the Middle Ages to the Romantic Revival* (1915); *The Vogue of Medieval Chivalric Romance during the English Renaissance* (1919). Compiler: *A Census of British Newspapers and Periodicals, 1620–1800* (with F. B. Kaye and M. E. Prior, 1927). Editor: *The English Familiar Essay* (with W. F. Bryan, 1916); *New Essays by Oliver Goldsmith* (1927); *A Collection of English Poems: 1660–1800* (1932); *Critics and Criticism: Ancient and Modern* (1951).

DUPEE, FREDERICK W. Born: Chicago, Illinois, 1904. Educated: Yale University, Ph. B., 1927; Columbia University Graduate School. Teacher of English, Bowdoin College, 1927–1929; Bard College, 1944–1948; instructor of English, Columbia University, 1941–1944; assistant professor of English, 1948–   . An associate editor of *Partisan Review*, 1937–1940. Editor: *The Question of Henry James* (1945). Critical biography: *Henry James* (1951).

ELIOT, THOMAS STEARNS. Born: St. Louis, Missouri, 1888. Educated: Smith Academy, St. Louis, 1898–1905; Milton Academy, Mass., 1905–1906; Harvard University, B.A., 1909, M.A., 1910; The Sorbonne, 1910–1911; Merton College, Oxford, 1914–1915. Worked in London as teacher, editor, bank clerk. Assistant editor of *The Egoist*, 1917–1919. Founder and editor of *The Criterion*, 1922–1939. A director of Faber and Faber, Ltd., publishers, London, since 1923. Became a British subject in 1927. Held the Charles Eliot Norton professorship of poetry at Harvard, 1932–1933; delivered Page-Barbour Lectures, University of Virginia, 1933. Granted the Dial Award, 1922; Nobel Prize for Literature, 1948. LL.D., Edinburgh; Litt. D., Columbia, Cambridge, Bristol, Leeds, Harvard, Yale, Princeton, Oxford; Ph. D., Munich; D. ès Lettres, Aix-Marseilles. Honorary Fellow, Magdalene College, Cambridge. Fellow in American Letters, Library of Congress. Books of verse: *Prufrock and Other Observations* (1917); *Poems* (1919); *Ara Vos Prec* (1919); *Poems* (1920); *The Waste Land* (1922); *Poems: 1909–1925* (1925); *The Journey of the Magi* (1927); *A Song for Simeon* (1928); *Animula* (1929); *Ash-Wednesday* (1930); *Marina* (1930); *Triumphal March* (1931); *Poems: 1909–1935* (1936); *Old Possum's Book of Practical Cats* (1939); *Four Quartets* (1943). Books of criticism and speculation: *The Sacred Wood* (1920); *Homage to John Dryden* (1924); *For Launcelot Andrewes* (1928); *Shakespeare and the Stoicism of Seneca* (1928); *Dante* (1929); *Thoughts after Lambeth* (1931); *Charles Whibley: A Memoir* (1931); *Selected Essays: 1917–1932* (1932; new edition with additional essays, 1950); *John Dryden* (1932); *The Use of Poetry and the Use of Criticism* (1933); *After Strange Gods* (1934); *Elizabethan Essays* (1935); *Essays Ancient and Modern* (1936); *The Idea of a Christian Society* (1939); *Points of View* (edited by John Hayward, 1941); *The Music of Poetry* (1942); *The Classics and the Man of Letters* (1942); *What is a Classic?* (1945); *From Poe to Valéry* (1948). Plays in verse: *Sweeney Agonistes* (1932); *The Rock* (coauthor, 1934); *Murder in the Cathedral* (1935); *The Family Reunion* (1939); *The Cocktail Party* (1950). Translations: *Anabase* by St. John Perse (1930; new edition, 1949). Editor: *Seneca: His Tenne Tragedies* (1927); John Dryden's *Of Dramatick Poesie* (1928); *Selected Poems* by Ezra Pound (1928); Samuel Johnson's *London: A Poem, and The Vanity of Human Wishes* (1930); Baudelaire's *Intimate Journals* (1930); *Selected Poems* by Marianne Moore (1935); *Nightwood* by Djuna Barnes (1937); *Introducing James Joyce* (1941), etc. Enquiry: *Notes Towards the Definition of Culture* (1948).

FERGUSSON, FRANCIS. Born: Albuquerque, New Mexico, 1904. Educated: Harvard University, 1921–1923; Oxford University (Rhodes Scholar), B.A., 1926. Associate director of the American Laboratory Theatre, New York, 1926–1930; drama critic of *The Bookman,* 1930–1932. Lecturer and executive secretary, New School for Social Research, 1932–1934; professor of Humanities and Drama, Bennington College, 1934–1947; member of the Institute for Advanced Study, Princeton, 1948–1949; associate professor of literature, Princeton University, 1949–   . Translator: *The Electra of Sophocles* (1937). Editor: *Exiles* by James Joyce (1946). Book of criticism: *The Idea of a Theatre* (1949).

GREGORY, HORACE. Born: Milwaukee, Wisconsin, 1898. Educated: German-English Academy, Milwaukee, 1914–1919; Milwaukee School of Fine Arts, 1913–1916; University of Wisconsin, B.A., 1923. Lecturer in English, Sarah Lawrence College, 1934–   . Awarded Lyric Prize by *Poetry,* 1928; Helen Haire Levinson Prize, 1934; Russell Loines Award for poetry, American Institute of Arts and Letters, 1942. Books of verse: *Chelsea Rooming House* (1930); *No Retreat* (1933); *Chorus for Survival* (1935); *Poems: 1930–1940* (1941). Editor: *New Letters in America* (1937); *The Portable Sherwood Anderson* (1948). Translation: *The Poems of Catullus* (1931). Books of criticism: *Pilgrim of the Apocalypse: A Critical Study of D. H. Lawrence* (1933); *The Shield of Achilles: Essays on Poetry and Beliefs* (1944); *A History of American Poetry: 1900–1940* (with Marya Zaturenska, 1946).

HOWE, IRVING. Born: New York City, 1920. Educated: DeWitt Clinton High School, New York City; College of the City of New York, B.Sc.S., 1940. Professor of English, Brandeis University, 1953–60; now Professor of English, Stanford University, 1961–   . Visiting professorships of English at University of Washington, summer 1952; University of Minnesota, summer 1956; Wayne State University, Detroit, 1958–59; Seminar in American Studies, Salzburg, Austria, summer 1958. Editor of *Dissent,* 1953–   ; contributing editor, *The New Republic,* 1959–   . Lecturer, Christian Gauss seminar in criticism, Princeton University, 1953. Kenyon Review fellowship, 1953; Bollingen Foundation fellowship, 1959–60; award, National Institute of Arts and Letters, 1960. Books of criticism: *Sherwood Anderson* (1951); *William Faulkner: A Critical Study* (1953 and 1962); *Politics and the Novel* (1957). Editor: *A Treasury of Yiddish Stories* (with Eliezer Greenberg, 1957); *Modern Literary Criticism*

(1959), etc. Books of social and political criticism: *The U. A. W. and Walter Reuther* (1949); *The American Communist Party* (with Lewis Coser, 1958).

HOWELLS, WILLIAM DEAN. Born: Martin's Ferry, Belmont Co., Ohio, 1837. Died, 1920. Common schooling in Ohio; studied Latin, German, Spanish, and literature alone. Reporter and editorial writer, *Ohio State Journal*, 1856–1861. Went to Boston, 1860. Campaign biography of Lincoln, 1860. U.S. consul in Venice, Italy, 1861–1865. Assistant on *The Nation* under E. L. Godkin, 1865; subeditor, *The Atlantic Monthly*, under James T. Fields, 1866–1871; editor-in-chief, 1871–1881; associated with Harper & Brothers, 1885–1916; wrote "Editor's Study," *Harper's Monthly*, 1886–1891; moved to New York, 1891; editor, *Cosmopolitan Magazine*, 1891–1892; wrote "Easy Chair," *Harper's Monthly Magazine*, 1900–1920. Novelist, essayist, critic, dramatist, editor, diplomat. Refused professorships at Yale, Harvard, Johns Hopkins universities. Honorary degrees from Oxford, Yale, Harvard, Columbia, etc. Author of *Their Wedding Journey, A Foregone Conclusion, The Lady of Aroostook, A Modern Instance, The Rise of Silas Lapham, Indian Summer, A Hazard of New Fortunes, A Traveler from Altruria, The Kentons, The 'Leatherwood God,* and other novels. Books of criticism and literary reminiscence: *Modern Italian Poets* (1887); *Criticism and Fiction* (1891); *My Literary Passions* (1895); *Impressions and Experiences* (1896); *Literary Friends and Acquaintances* (1900); *Heroines of Fiction* (1901); *Literature and Life* (1902); *My Mark Twain* (1910); *Imaginary Interviews* (1910). Books of travel, verse, autobiography.

HUNEKER, JAMES GIBBONS. Born: Philadelphia, 1860. Died in 1921. Educated: Roth's Military Academy, Philadelphia; Philadelphia Law Academy; the Sorbonne, Paris; music under Michael Cross, Georges Matthias, Rafael Joseffy. Assistant to Rafael Joseffy in piano department of the National Conservatory of Music, New York, 1881–1891. Wrote a column on music for the *Musical Courier*, New York, 1887–1902. Music critic for the *New York Evening Recorder*, 1891–1895; for the *Morning Advertiser*, 1895–1897; for the *New York Sun*, 1900–1902; drama critic, *New York Sun*, 1902–1917; music critic, *Philadelphia Press*, 1917; *New York Times*, 1918; *New York World*, 1919–1921. Member of the National Institute of Arts and Letters; officer of Legion of Honor. Books of literary and musical criticism: *Mezzotints in Modern Music* (1899); *Chopin: The Man and His Music* (1900); *Melomaniacs* (1902); *Overtones* (1904); *Iconoclasts: A Book of Dramatists* (1905); *Visionaries* (1905); *Egoists: A Book of Supermen* (1909); *Promenades of an Impressionist* (1910); *Franz Liszt* (1911); *The Pathos of Distance* (1913); *Old Fogy* (1913); *Ivory, Apes, and Peacocks* (1915); *The New Cosmopolis* (1915); *Unicorns* (1917); *Bedouins* (1920); *Variations* (1921); *Essays* (edited by H. L. Mencken, 1929). Fiction: *Painted Veils* (1920). Autobiography: *Steeplejack* (1920).

HYMAN, STANLEY EDGAR. Born: New York City, 1919. Educated: Syracuse University, B.A., 1940. Editorial assistant, *The New Republic*, 1940; staff writer, *The New Yorker*, 1940–   Teacher of literary criticism and folk literature,

Bennington College, 1945–1946. Book of criticism: *The Armed Vision: A Study in the Methods of Modern Literary Criticism* (1948).

JAMES, HENRY. Born: New York City, 1843. Died in London in 1916. Educated in schools in New York, France, Switzerland, Germany; Harvard Law School, 1862–1863. Began adult travels to Europe, 1869; began residence in Europe and England, 1876; settled in England, 1883; adopted British citizenship, 1915. Novelist, writer of tales, critic, dramatist, writer of books of travel, autobiography, biography. Author of *Roderick Hudson, The American, The Portrait of a Lady, The Bostonians, The Princess Casamassima, The Tragic Muse, What Maisie Knew, The Awkward Age, The Spoils of Poynton, The Sacred Fount, The Ambassadors, The Wings of the Dove, The Golden Bowl,* etc. Books of literary criticism: *French Poets and Novelists* (1878); *Hawthorne* (1879); *Partial Portraits* (1888); *Essays in London and Elsewhere* (1893); *Notes on Novelists with Some Other Notes* (1914); *Views and Reviews* (collection of early essays and reviews, edited by LeRoy Phillips, 1908); *Notes and Reviews* (collection of early reviews, edited by Pierre de Chaignon la Rose, 1921); *The Art of the Novel* (collection of prefaces for his works in the New York Edition of 1907–1909; 1934); *The Scenic Art: Notes on Acting and the Drama: 1872–1901* (edited by Allan Wade, 1948). Critical biography: *William Wetmore Story and His Friends* (1903). Art criticism: *Picture and Text* (1893). Literary journal: *The Notebooks of Henry James* (edited by F. O. Matthiessen and Kenneth B. Murdock, 1947).

JARRELL, RANDALL. Born: Nashville, Tennessee, 1914. Educated: Vanderbilt University, B.S., 1936; M.A., 1939. Instructor in English, University of Texas, 1938–1942; at Kenyon College; at Sarah Lawrence College, 1946–1947; at Salzburg Seminar in American Civilization, 1949; associate professor, Woman's College of University of North Carolina, 1947–   . Acting literary editor, *The Nation,* 1946–1947. Books of verse: *Blood for a Stranger* (1942); *Little Friend, Little Friend* (1945); *Losses* (1948). Editor: *Selected Poems of William Carlos Williams* (1949).

KAZIN, ALFRED. Born: Brooklyn, New York, 1915. Educated: College of the City of New York, B.S., 1935; Columbia University, M.A., 1938. Tutor in English, College of the City of New York, 1937–1939 (summers); member of the Department of English, 1939–1942; tutor in English, Queen's College, New York, 1940; lecturer, New School for Social Research, 1941–1942, 1948–1949; lecturer, Black Mountain College, 1944. Literary editor of *The New Republic,* 1942–1943; contributing editor, 1943–1945; contributing editor, *Fortune,* 1943–1944. Visiting lecturer, Quinzaine Anglo-Américaine, Paris, 1945; visiting professor, University of Minnesota, summer 1946; lecturer, John L. Elliott Institute, 1946; Salzburg Seminar in American Studies, summer 1947. Guggenheim Fellowships, 1940, 1947. Rockefeller Foundation Fellowship for study of trade-union and army popular education movements in Great Britain, 1945. Award from National Institute of Arts and Letters, 1947. Editor: *The Portable William Blake*

(1946), *Crime and Punishment* by Dostoevsky (1946), *A Raw Youth* by Dostoevsky (1946). Book of criticism: *On Native Grounds: An Interpretation of Modern American Prose Literature* (1942).

KRUTCH, JOSEPH WOOD. Born: Knoxville, Tennessee, 1893. Educated: University of Tennessee, B.A., 1915; Columbia University, M.A., 1916; Ph. D., 1923. Assistant professor of English, Brooklyn Polytechnic Institute, 1920–1923; professor of English, Vassar College, 1924–1925; assistant professor, School of Journalism, Columbia University, 1925–1931; associate professor, 1931–1937; professor, 1937–1943; lecturer, New School for Social Research, 1932–1935; Brander Matthews Professor of dramatic literature, at Columbia University, 1943–   . Dramatic critic of *The Nation* since 1924; associate editor, 1924–1932; member of board of editors, 1932–1937. Member of the editorial board of the Literary Guild, 1925–1935. Guggenheim Fellowship, 1930. Books of criticism and literary history: *Comedy and Conscience after the Restoration* (1924); *Edgar Allan Poe: A Study in Genius* (1926); *Five Masters* (1930); *Experience and Art* (1932); *The American Drama since 1918* (1939); *Samuel Johnson* (1944); *Henry David Thoreau* (1948). Other books: *The Modern Temper* (1929); *Was Europe a Success?* (1934); *The Twelve Seasons* (1949).

LEVIN, HARRY TUCHMAN. Born: Minneapolis, Minnesota, 1912. Educated: Harvard University, B.A., 1933; University of Paris, 1934. Faculty instructor and tutor in English, Harvard University, 1939–1944; associate professor of English, 1944–1948; professor of English, 1948–   ; chairman of the Department of Comparative Literature, 1947–   . Junior fellow, Society of Fellows, Harvard University, 1934–1939; senior fellow, 1947–   . Guggenheim Fellowship, 1943. Editor: *Selected Works of Ben Jonson* (1938); *A Satire against Mankind, and Other Poems* by the Earl of Rochester (1942); *Three Tales* by Flaubert (1944); *The Portable James Joyce* (1945). Books: *The Broken Column: A Study in Romantic Hellenism* (1931); *James Joyce: A Critical Introduction* (1941); *Toward Stendhal* (1945); *Toward Balzac* (1947). In preparation: *The Gates of Horn,* a study of the classic French novel.

MATTHIESSEN, FRANCIS OTTO. Born: Pasadena, California, 1902. Died in 1950. Educated: Hackley School, Tarrytown, N.Y., 1914–1918; Yale University, B.A., 1923; Oxford University (Rhodes Scholar, New College), B. Litt., 1925; Harvard, M.A., 1926; Ph. D., 1927. D. Litt., Princeton University, 1947. Instructor of English, Yale University, 1927–1929; instructor and tutor, Harvard University, 1929–1930; assistant professor, 1930–1934; associate professor, 1934–1942; professor of English and American Literature, 1942–1950. Chairman, Board of Tutors, Harvard, 1931–1949; senior tutor, Eliot House, 1931–1933. Alexander Lecturer, University of Toronto, 1944; visiting professor, Charles University, Prague, 1947; Salzburg Seminar in American Studies, 1947; senior fellow, Kenyon School of English, 1948–1950. Member of editorial board, *The New England Quarterly*, 1937–1940. Member, Massachusetts Civil Liberties Union (president, 1940–1942); of the Harvard Teachers Union, 1935–1950. Editor: *Stories of Writers and Artists* by Henry James (1944); *Selected Poems of Herman Melville* (1944); *The American Novels and Stories of Henry James* (1947); *The Notebooks of Henry James* (with Kenneth B. Murdock, 1947); *The Oxford Book of American Verse* (1950). Books of criticism and literary history: *Sarah Orne Jewett* (1929); *Translation: An Elizabethan Art* (1931); *The Achievement of T. S. Eliot* (1935; new edition, 1947); *American Renaissance: Art and Expression in the Age of Emerson and Whitman* (1941); *Henry James: The Major Phase* (1944); *Russell Cheney: A Record of his Work* (1947); *The James Family* (1947); *Theodore Dreiser* (to be published posthumously). Book of social and political observation: *From the Heart of Europe* (1948).

MENCKEN, HENRY LOUIS. Born: Baltimore, Maryland, 1880. Educated: private schools in Baltimore; Baltimore Polytechnic, graduated, 1896. Reporter, *Baltimore Morning Herald*, 1899; city editor, 1903–1905; editor, *Baltimore Evening Herald*, 1905–1906; on staff of the *Baltimore Sun*, 1906–1910; of *Evening Sun*, 1910–1917, 1920–1935; of both *Sunpapers*, 1936–1941. Literary critic of *The Smart Set*, 1908–1923; coeditor, 1914–1923. Editor of *The American Mercury*, 1924–1933. Books of criticism: *George Bernard Shaw* (1905); *The Philosophy of Friedrich Nietzsche* (1908); *A Book of Burlesques* (1916); *A Book of Prefaces* (1917); *Damn: A Book of Calumny* (1918); *In Defense of Women* (1918); *Prejudices* (six series, 1919–1927); *Selected Prejudices* (1927); *James Branch Cabell* (1927); *A Mencken Chrestomathy* (1949). Books of speculative prose: *Notes on Democracy* (1926); *Treatise on the Gods* (1930); *Treatise on Right and Wrong* (1934). Verse: *Ventures into Verse* (1903). Plays: *The Artist* (1912); *Heliogabalus* (with George Jean Nathan, 1920). Coauthor of *Men vs. the Man* (1910); *Europe after 8:15* (1914); *A Little Book in C Major* (1916); *The American Credo* (1920); *Americana* (1925–26). Linguistic history: *The American Language* (1918; fourth revised edition, 1936); *Supplement I* (1945); *Supplement II* (1948). Dictionary: *A New Dictionary of Quotations* (1942). Autobiographies: *Happy Days* (1940); *Newspaper Days* (1941); *Heathen Days* (1943); *The Days of H. L. Mencken* (1947). Fiction: *Christmas Story* (1946). Editor: *We Moderns* by Edwin Muir (1920); *Essays* by James Gibbons Huneker (1929); *The American Democrat* by James Fenimore Cooper (1931).

MIZENER, ARTHUR. Born: Erie, Pennsylvania, 1907. Educated: The Hill School, Pottstown, Penn., graduated 1926; Princeton University, B.S. in English, highest honors, 1930; Harvard University, M.A., 1932; Princeton University, Ph.D., 1934. Instructor of English, Yale University, 1934–40; Assistant and Associate Professor of English, Wells College, 1940–45; Professor and Chairman of the Department of English, Carleton College, 1945–51; Professor of English, Cornell University, 1951–   . Book: *The Far Side of Paradise: A Biography of F. Scott Fitzgerald* (1951; new edition, 1958). Editor: *Afternoon of an Author* by F. Scott Fitzgerald (1957). To appear in 1962: *The Sense of Life*. Contributor to literary journals and reviews in America and England.

MOORE, MARIANNE CRAIG. Born: St. Louis, Missouri, 1887. Educated: Metzger Institute, Carlisle, Penn., 1896–1905; Bryn Mawr College, B.A., 1909; Carlisle Commercial College, 1910. Teacher, United States Indian School, Carlisle, 1911–1915; assistant, Hudson Park Branch, New York Public Library, 1919–1925. Editor of *The Dial,* 1925–1929. Granted the Dial Award, 1924; Levinson Prize (*Poetry*), 1933; Ernest Hartsock Memorial Prize, 1935; Shelley Memorial Award, 1940; *Contemporary Poetry's* Poetry Prize, 1944; Harriet Monroe Award in Poetry (University of Chicago), 1944; Guggenheim Fellowship, 1945; National Institute of Arts and Letters Award, 1946. Books of verse: *Poems* (1921); *Observations* (1924); *Selected Poems* (1935); *The Pangolin and Other Verse* (1936); *What Are Years?* (1941); *Nevertheless* (1944); *Collected Poems* (1951).

MORE, PAUL ELMER. Born: St. Louis, Missouri, 1864. Died in 1937. Educated: Washington University, B.A., 1887; M.A., 1892; Harvard University, M.A., 1893. Taught Sanscrit at Harvard, 1894–1895; assistant professor of Sanscrit, Bryn Mawr College, 1895–1897. Literary editor of *The Independent,* 1901; literary editor of *The New York Evening Post,* 1903; editor of *The Nation,* 1909–14. Retired to Princeton in 1914; sometime lecturer on Plato in the Department of Classics, Princeton University. Books of critical and literary essays: *Shelburne Essays* (eleven volumes, 1904–1921, of which the last four carried individual titles: *The Drift of Romanticism* [1913]; *Aristocracy and Justice* [1915]; *With the Wits* [1919]; *A New England Group and Others* [1921]); *The New Shelburne Essays: The Demon of the Absolute* (1928); *The Skeptical Approach to Religion* (1934); *On Being Human* (1936); *Selected Shelburne Essays* (1935). Poems: *Helena* (1890). Novel: *The Jessica Letters* (with Corra May Harris, 1904). Biography: *Benjamin Franklin* (1900). Books of philosophical and religious enquiry: *Nietzsche* (1912); *Platonism* (1917); *The Religion of Plato* (1921); *Hellenistic Philosophies* (1923); *The Christ of the New Testament* (1924); *Christ the Word* (1927); *The Catholic Faith* (1931).

PHILLIPS, WILLIAM. Born: New York City, 1907. Educated: College of the City of New York, B.A., 1928; New York University, M.A., 1930. Taught English at New York University, 1929–1932. An editor of *Partisan Review* since its founding in 1934. Editor: *Great American Short Novels* (1946); *The Partisan Reader: Ten Years of Partisan Review: 1934–1944* (with Philip Rahv, 1946).

PORTER, KATHERINE ANNE. Born: Indian Creek, Texas, 1894. Educated: private schools in Texas and New Orleans. Lecturer and consultant, Olivet College Writers' Conference, 1937; Fellow in Regional American Literature, Library of Congress, 1944; Fellow in American Letters, Library of Congress; writer-in-residence and lecturer on literature, Stanford University, 1948–1949; lecturer in English, University of Chicago, 1951; lecturer at numerous colleges and universities. Has lived and traveled in Mexico, Germany, France. Guggenheim Fellowships, 1931, 1938; Book of the Month Club Award, 1937; first annual gold medal for literature, Society for Libraries of New York University, 1940. Books of fiction: *Flowering Judas* (1930; new edition, 1935); *Hacienda* (1934); *Noon Wine* (1937); *Pale Horse, Pale Rider* (1939); *The Leaning Tower* (1944). Translation: *The Itching Parrot* (from the Spanish, 1942). Editor: *Katherine Anne Porter's French Song Book* (1933); *Fiesta in November* (1942).

POUND, EZRA. Born: Hailey, Idaho, 1885. Educated: University of Pennsylvania, 1901–1903; Hamilton College, Ph. B., 1905; University of Pennsylvania, M.A., 1906. "Instructor with professorial functions," University of Pennsylvania, 1905–1907; instructor at Wabash College, Crawfordsville, Indiana, for four months, 1907–1908. To Europe in 1908, traveling and living in Spain, Italy, France, England, France, Italy, 1908–1945. Returned to America, 1938, and again in 1945. Associate editor (European correspondent) of *Poetry*, 1912–1918; London editor of *The Little Review*, 1917–1919; editor of *The Exile*, 1927–1928. Books of verse: *A Lume Spento* (1908); *Personae* (1909); *Exultations* (1909); *Provenca* (1910); *Canzoni* (1911); *Ripostes* (1912); *Cathay* (1915); *Lustra* (1916); *Lustra and Other Poems* (1917); *Quia Pauper Amavi* (1919); *Umbra* (1920); *Hugh Selwyn Mauberley* (1920); *Cantos I–XVI* (1925); *Personae: Collected Poems* (1926); *Cantos XVII–XXVII* (1928); *A Draft of XXX Cantos* (1930); *Eleven New Cantos XXXI–LXI* (1934); *The Fifth Decad of Cantos* (1937); *Cantos LII–LXXI* (1940); *The Pisan Cantos* (1948); *The Cantos* (complete edition, 1948). Translations: *Sonnets and Ballate of Guido Cavalcanti* (1912, 1913, complete edition 1932); *Certain Noble Plays of Japan* (1916); *Noh, or Accomplishment* (1917); *Twelve Dialogues of Fontenelle* (1917); *Physique de l'Amour* by Remy de Gourmont (1921); *The Ta Hio* (1920); *The Analects of Confucius* (1949–1950). Operas: *Le Testament* (1919–1921; partial performance, Paris, 1926); *Guido Cavalcanti* (1931–1932). Books of criticism and literary enquiry: *The Spirit of Romance* (1910); *Gaudier Brzeska* (1916); *Pavannes and Divisions* (1918); *Instigations* (1920); *Indiscretions* (1923); *Antheil and the Treatise on Harmony* (1924); *Imaginary Letters* (1930); *How To Read* (1931); *Prolegomena* (1932); *The ABC of Reading* (1934); *Make It New* (1934); *Polite Essays* (1937); *Digest of the Analects* (1937); *Guide to Kulchur* (1938; in American edition: *Culture*, 1939); *Patria Mia* (1950). Books on economics and politics: *The ABC of Economics* (1933); *Social Credit and Impact* (1935); *Jefferson and/or Mussolini* (1935); *What is Money For?* (1938). Editor: *Des Imagistes* (1914); *Catholic Anthology* (1915); *Letters of John Butler Yeats* (1917); *Profile* (1932); *Active Anthology* (1933); *The Chinese Written Character by Ernest Fenollosa* (1936), etc; *The Letters of Ezra Pound* (1950).

RAHV, PHILIP. Born: Kupin, Ukraine, 1908. Came to America, 1922. Educated: elementary and high school, Providence, R.I. An editor of *Partisan Review* since 1934. Editor: *The Great Short Novels of Henry James* (1944); *The Bostonians* by Henry James (1945); *The Short Novels of Tolstoy* (1946); *The Partisan Reader: Ten Years of Partisan Review: 1934–44* (with William Phillips, 1946); *Discovery of Europe: The Story of American Experience in the Old World* (1947). Book of criticism: *Image and Idea: Fourteen Essays on Literary Themes* (1949).

RANSOM, JOHN CROWE. Born: Pulaski, Tennessee, 1888. Educated: Vanderbilt University, B.A., 1909; Christ Church, Oxford University (Rhodes Scholar), B.A., 1913. Member of the faculty, Department of English, Vanderbilt University, 1914–1937; professor of English 1927–1937; Carnegie Professor of English, Kenyon College, 1937–   Senior Fellow, at Kenyon School of English, 1948–   . Lecturer and visiting professor, summers, at University of New Mexico, University of Florida, University of Kentucky, University of Texas, Women's College of University of North Carolina. Bread Loaf School of English, Colorado State Teachers' College, Peabody College for Teachers. A founder and editor of *The Fugitive*, 1922–1925; editor of *The Kenyon Review*, 1939–   . Guggenheim Fellowship, 1931. Verse: *Poems About God* (1919); *Grace After Meat* (1924); *Chills and Fever* (1924); *Two Gentlemen in Bonds* (1926); *Selected Poems* (1945). Book of speculative prose: *God Without Thunder* (1930). Books of literary criticism: *The World's Body* (1938); *The New Criticism* (1941). Co-author: *I'll Take My Stand* (1930); *Who Owns America?* (1936); *The Intent of the Critic* (1941).

RICE, PHILIP BLAIR. Born: Martinsville, Indiana, 1904. Educated: University of Illinois; University of Indiana, B.A., 1925; Oxford University (Rhodes Scholar), B.A., 1928. Newspaper work in Paris and Cincinnati, 1928–1930. Instructor in philosophy, University of Cincinnati, 1930–1937; assistant professor, 1937–1938; Guy Despard Gaff associate professor of philosophy and chairman of department, Kenyon College, 1938–1948; now professor of philosophy. Associate editor, *The Kenyon Review*, 1939–

SANTAYANA, GEORGE. Born: Madrid, Spain, 1863. Came to the United States in 1872. Educated: Latin School, Boston; Harvard University, B.A., 1886; University of Berlin, 1886–1888; King's College, Cambridge University, 1896–1897. Member and professor of Philosophy, Harvard University, 1889–1912. Hyde Lecturer at the Sorbonne, 1905–1906. Returned to Europe to live in 1914—England, France, Italy. Books of philosophic and critical enquiry: *The Sense of Beauty* (1896); *Interpretations of Poetry and Religion* (1900); *The Life of Reason: Reason and Common Sense* (1905); *Reason in Society* (1905); *Reason in Religion* (1905); *Reason in Art* (1905); *Reason in Science* (1906); *Three Philosophical Poets: Lucretius, Dante, Goethe* (1910); *Winds of Doctrine* (1913); *Egoism in German Philosophy* (1916); *Philosophical Opinion in America* (1918); *Character and Opinion in the United States* (1920); *Soliloquies in England, and Later Soliloquies* (1922); *Skepticism and Animal Faith* (1923); *Dialogues in Limbo* (1925); *Platonism and the Spiritual Life* (1927); *The Realm of Essence* (1927); *The Realm of Matter* (1930); *The Genteel Tradition at Bay* (1931); *Some Turns of Thought in Modern Philosophy* (1933); *Obiter Dicta: Lectures, Essays, and Reviews* (1936); *The Realm of Truth* (1937); *The Realm of Spirit* (1940); *The Realms of Being* (1942); *The Idea of Christ in the Gospels, or God in Man* (1946); *Atoms of Thought* (1950). Verse: *Sonnets and Other Verse* (1894); *Lucifer, or The Heavenly Truce* (1898; new edition, 1924); *Poems* (1922).

Novel: *The Last Puritan* (1935). Memoirs: *Persons and Places* (1944); *The Middle Span* (1945). *The Works of George Santayana* (Triton Edition, 14 volumes, 1936–37).

SCHWARTZ, DELMORE. Born: Brooklyn, N.Y., 1913. Educated: New York University, B.A., 1935; studied at Columbia, Wisconsin, and Harvard universities. Instructor in English, Harvard University, 1940–1945; assistant professor of English Composition, 1946–1947. Associate editor of *Partisan Review*, 1943– Guggenheim Fellowship, 1939. Books of verse and narrative: *In Dreams Begin Responsibilities* (1938); *Shenandoah* (1941); *Genesis: Book One* (1943); *The World Is a Wedding* (1948); *Vaudeville for a Princess* (1950). In preparation: books on T. S. Eliot and F. Scott Fitzgerald.

SPENCER, THEODORE. Born: Villa Nova, Pennsylvania, 1902. Died in 1949. Educated: Princeton University, B.A., 1923; Cambridge University, B.A., 1925; Harvard University, Ph. D., 1928. Instructor and tutor, in English, Harvard, 1927–1933; assistant professor of English, 1933–1939; appointed lecturer, Cambridge University, 1939–1940; associate professor of English, Harvard University, 1940–1946; Boylston professor of Rhetoric and Oratory, 1946–1949. Lowell lecturer, Boston, 1942. Phi Beta Kappa poet, William and Mary College, 1942; Tufts College, 1943; Harvard, 1943. Editor: *A Garland for John Donne* (1931); *Stephen Hero* by James Joyce (1944). Books of verse: *The Paradox in the Circle* (1941); *The World in Your Hand* (1943); *An Act of Life* (1944); *Poems: 1940–1947* (1948). Books of criticism and literary history: *Death and Elizabethan Tragedy* (1936); *Studies in Metaphysical Poetry* (with Mark Van Doren, 1939); *Shakespeare and the Nature of Man* (1942).

SPINGARN, JOEL ELIAS. Born: New York City, 1875. Died in 1939. Educated: Columbia University, B.A., 1895; Ph. D., 1899; Harvard University, 1895–1896. Assistant and tutor in Comparative Literature, Columbia University, 1899–1909; adjunct professor, 1904; professor, 1909–1911. Engaged in political, military, and journalistic activities, 1911–1923; a founder and adviser of Harcourt, Brace and Co., 1919–1932; chairman of directors, Association for the Advancement of Colored Peoples, 1913–1919, treasurer until 1930, president until 1939. Editor: *Critical Essays of the Seventeenth Century* (1908–1909); *Essays of Sir William Temple* (1909); *A Renaissance Courtesy Book: The Galateo of Della Casa* (1914); *Goethe's Literary Essays* (1921); *Civilization in the United States* (1923); *Criticism in America* (1924); *Troutbeck Leaflets* (1924–1926); *The European Library* (1920–1925). Books of criticism and literary history: *A History of Literary Criticism in the Renaissance* (1899; revised edition, 1908); *The New Criticism* (1911); *Creative Criticism and Other Essays* (1917; revised edition, 1931). Verse: *The New Hesperides* (1911); *Poems* (1924). Controversy: *A Question of Academic Freedom* (1911); *A Spingarn Enchiridion* (1929).

TATE, (JOHN ORLEY) ALLEN. Born: Winchester, Clark County, Kentucky, 1899. Educated: schools in Louisville and Nashville; Georgetown University; University of Virginia; Vanderbilt University, B.A., 1922. A founder and editor of *The Fugitive*, 1922–1925. Guggenheim Fellowship, 1928–1930. Lecturer on English Literature, Southwestern University, 1934–1936; professor of English, Woman's College of the University of North Carolina, 1938–1939; resident fellow, Creative Arts Program, Princeton University, 1939–1942; fellow in American Letters, Library of Congress, 1943–   ; Chair of Poetry, Library of Congress, 1943–1944; editor, Henry Holt and Co., 1946–1948; lecturer in English, New York University, 1947–   ; visiting professor of Humanities, University of Chicago, 1949; fellow, Kenyon School of English, 1949; lecturer at writers' conferences, universities of Colorado, Utah, Indiana, Kansas, Olivet College, etc. Southern editor, *The Hound and Horn*, 1932–1934; editor, *The Sewanee Review*, 1944–1946. Caroline Sinkler Prize of the Poetry Society of South Carolina, 1928; Midland Authors' Prize (*Poetry*), 1933; award of American Institute of Arts and Letters, 1948. Books of verse: *Mr. Pope and Other Poems* (1928); *Three Poems* (1930); *Poems: 1928–31* (1932); *The Mediterranean and Other Poems* (1936); *Selected Poems* (1937); *The Winter Sea* (1944); *Poems: 1922–47* (1948). Translator: *The Vigil of Venus* (1943). Novel: *The Fathers* (1938). Editor: *I'll Take My Stand* (with others, 1930); *Who Owns America?* (with Herbert Agar, 1936); *Invitation to Learning* (with Huntington Cairns and Mark Van Doren, 1941); *Princeton Verse Between Two Wars* (1942); *The Language of Poetry* (1942); *American Harvest* (with J. P. Bishop, 1942); *A Southern Vanguard* (1947); *The House of Fiction* (with Caroline Gordon, 1950). Books of criticism: *Reactionary Essays on Poetry and Ideas* (1936); *Reason in Madness: Critical Essays* (1941); *On the Limits of Poetry: Selected Essays 1928–48* (1948); *The Hovering Fly* (1949).

TRILLING, LIONEL. Born: New York City, 1905. Educated: Columbia University, B.A., 1925; M.A., 1926; Ph. D., 1938. Instructor in English, University of Wisconsin, 1926–1927; instructor in English, Hunter College, 1927–1930; instructor in English, Columbia University, 1931–1938; assistant professor, 1938–1943; associate professor, 1943–1948; professor since 1948. Advisory editor, *The Kenyon Review*, 1942–   ; advisory editor, *Partisan Review*, 1946–   ; member of board of editors, American Men of Letters Series. Editor: *The Great Gatsby* by F. Scott Fitzgerald (1945); *The Princess Casamassima* by Henry James (1948); *The Portable Matthew Arnold* (1949), etc. Books of criticism: *Matthew Arnold* (1939); *E. M. Forster* (1943); *The Liberal Imagination: Essays on Literature and Society* (1950). Novel: *The Middle of the Journey* (1947).

TROY, WILLIAM. Born: Chicago, Illinois, 1903. Educated: Yale University, B.A., 1925; Columbia University; University of Grenoble, France (American Field Service Fellowship, 1929–1930); the Sorbonne. Taught English at the University of New Hampshire and New York University, 1932–1935; a member of the faculty of the Department of English, Bennington College, 1935–1937, 1938–1946; lecturer on literature, New School for Social Research, 1946–   . Film critic, *The Nation*, 1933–1935.

WARREN, AUSTIN. Born: Waltham, Massachusetts, 1899. Educated: Wesleyan University, Conn., B.A., 1920; Harvard University, M.A., 1922; Princeton University, Ph. D., 1926. Instructor in English, University of Kentucky, 1920–1921; instructor in English, University of Minnesota, 1922–1924; dean of St. Peter's School of Liberal and Humane Studies (summers), Hebron, Conn., 1922–1930; instructor in English, Boston University, 1926–1929; assistant and associate professor, 1929–1934; professor of English, 1934–1939; professor of English, University of Iowa, 1939–1948; professor of English, University of Michigan, 1948–   . Fellow, American Council of Learned Societies. Guggenheim Fellowship, 1949. Associate editor of *The New England Quarterly*, 1937–1940, 1942–1946; associate editor of *American Literature*, 1940–1942. Books of criticism and literary history: *Alexander Pope as Critic and Humanist* (1929); *The Elder Henry James* (1934); *Richard Crashaw* (1939); *Rage for Order* (1948). Editor: *Hawthorne* (American Writers Series, 1934). Coauthor: *Literary Scholarship* (1941); *Theory of Literature* (with René Wellek, 1948). In preparation: a study of John Donne.

WARREN, ROBERT PENN. Born: Guthrie, Kentucky, 1905. Educated: Vanderbilt University, B.A., 1925; University of California, M.A., 1927; Yale University, 1927–1928; Oxford University (Rhodes Scholar), B. Litt., 1930. Assistant professor, Southwestern University, 1930–1931; acting assistant professor of English, Vanderbilt University, 1931–1934; assistant professor of English, Louisiana State University, 1934–1936; associate professor, 1936–1942; professor of English, University of Minnesota, 1942. Chair of Poetry, Library of Congress, 1944–1945; Fellow in American Letters, Library of Congress, 1944. Visiting professor and consultant at writers' conferences at University of Iowa, Kenyon College, University of Colorado, etc. A founder and editor of *The Southern Review*, 1935–1942. Houghton, Mifflin Fellowship, 1936; Levinson Prize (*Poetry*), 1936; Caroline Sinkler Prize, Poetry Society of South Carolina, 1936; Guggenheim Fellowships, 1939 and 1947; Shelley Memorial Award, 1942; Pulitzer Prize in fiction, 1947. Books of verse: *Eleven Poems on the Same Theme* (1942); *Selected Poems* (1944). Novels and books of fiction: *Night Rider* (1939); *At Heaven's Gate* (1943); *All the King's Men* (1946); *Blackberry Winter* (1946); *The Circus in the Attic and Other Stories* (1947); *World Enough and Time* (1950). Books for literary study: *An Approach to Literature* (with Cleanth Brooks and Jack Purser, 1936 and 1938); *Understanding Poetry* (with Cleanth Brooks, 1938 and 1950); *Understanding Fiction* (with Cleanth Brooks, 1943). Editor: *A Southern Harvest* (1937); *The Rime of the Ancient Mariner* by S. T. Coleridge (1946).

WILSON, EDMUND. Born: Red Bank, New Jersey, 1895. Educated: Hill School, Pottstown, Pa.; Princeton University, B.A., 1916. On staff of *The New York Sun*, 1919–1920; managing editor of *Vanity Fair*, 1920–1921; associate and literary editor of *The New Republic*, 1926–1931; book reviewer of *The New Yorker*, 1944–1948, etc. Guggenheim Fellowship, 1935. Novels: *I Thought of Daisy* (1929); *Memoirs of Hecate County* (1946). Imaginative verse and prose: *The Undertaker's Garland* (with John Peale Bishop, 1922). Verse: *Poets, Farewell!*

(1929). Plays: *This Room and This Gin and These Sandwiches* (1937); *The Little Blue Light* (1950). Miscellany: *Notebooks of Night* (1942). Books of travel and social reporting: *The American Jitters* (1932); *Travels in Two Democracies* (1936); *Europe without Baedeker* (1947). Political-cultural history: *To the Finland Station* (1940). Criticism and literary studies: *Discordant Encounters* (1927); *Axel's Castle: A Study of the Imaginative Literature of 1870–1930* (1931); *The Triple Thinkers* (1938; revised edition, 1948); *The Boys in the Back Room* (1941); *The Wound and the Bow* (1941); *The Shock of Recognition* (1943); *Classics and Commercials: A Literary Chronicle of the Forties* (1950).

WINTERS, (ARTHUR) YVOR. Born: Chicago, Illinois, 1900. Educated: high schools in Evanston and Chicago; University of Chicago, 1917–1919; University of Colorado, B.A., M.A., both 1925; Stanford University, Ph. D., 1934. Teacher of Spanish and French, University of Idaho, 1925–1927; instructor, assistant professor, and associate professor of English, Stanford University, 1927–1948; professor of English, 1948–   . A founder and editor of *The Gyroscope* (with Janet Lewis and Howard Baker), 1928–1929; regional editor (Western) of *The Hound and Horn*, 1932–1934. Fellow, Kenyon School of English, 1949. Editor: *Twelve Poets of the Pacific* (1937); *Poets of the Pacific: Second Series* (1949). Books of verse: *The Immobile Wind* (1921); *The Magpie's Shadow* (1922); *The Bare Hills* (1927); *The Proof* (1930); *The Journey and Other Poems* (1931); *Before Disaster* (1934); *Poems* (1940); *The Giant Weapon* (1943). Criticism: *Notes on the Mechanics of the Poetic Image: The Testament of a Stone* (1925); *Primitivism and Decadence: A Study of American Experimental Poetry* (1937); *Maule's Curse: Seven Studies in the History of American Obscurantism* (1938); *The Anatomy of Nonsense* (1943); *In Defense of Reason* (1947).

YOUNG, STARK. Born: Como, Mississippi, 1881. Educated: University of Mississippi, B.A., 1901; Columbia University, M.A., 1902. Instructor in English, University of Mississippi, 1904–1907; instructor in English, University of Texas, 1907–1910; professor of General Literature, 1910–1915; professor of English, Amherst College, 1915–1921. An associate editor and drama critic of *The New Republic*, 1921–1924, 1925–1947; associate editor of *Theatre Arts Monthly*, 1921–1940; drama critic of *The New York Times*, 1924–1925. Plays: *The Blind Man at the Window* (1906); *Guenevere* (1906); *Madretta Addio, The Twilight Saint, and other One-Act Plays* (1911); *Three Plays* (1919); *The Saint* (1924); *The Colonnade* (1926); *Rose Windows* (1926). Novels and fiction: *Heaven Trees* (1926); *The Torches Flare* (1927); *River House* (1929); *The Street of the Islands* (1930); *So Red the Rose* (1934); *Feliciana* (1935). Books of dramatic criticism: *The Flower in Drama* (1923); *The Three Fountains* (1924); *Glamour* (1925); *The Theatre* (1927); *Immortal Shadows* (1948).

For books published by the above critics since 1951, see Appendix VII, page 891 and following.

APPENDIX V

A Supplementary List of Essays in Criticism: 1900–1950

THE following index of essays, articles, and reviews dates from about 1900 to the present day, and is designed both to supplement the essays printed in this book and to provide a program for the further study of modern American criticism. The list, though drastically selective, includes a wide variety of writing, ranging from popular literary journalism to historical and aesthetic scholarship. Both these types of material are shown, however, in a small number of selections, the largest part of the space being given to work of critical motivation and method. The writers listed are usually those who have shown some persistence and continuity of critical performance, though a few exceptions have been made in the case of articles of individual or special interest.

Included are discussions of the writer's and critic's roles in American life, of the function and problems of modern criticism, of its connections with political, social, scientific, and educational developments, and of its bearing on the modern cultural situation generally, as well as many discussions of specific authors and texts. Work in historical and philosophical scholarship has not as a rule been included except where it bears closely on the interests of criticism. From the work of each critic a small number of typical or relevant writings have been chosen. The reader will soon find his way to others, as well as to other critics who could not be included here. The articles listed are usually in American literary and critical journals, though a number written by Americans for foreign magazines have been admitted. Reference has also been made, in the case of critics of large output, to essays or revised versions of essays which have appeared more accessibly in book form.

The books listed in Appendices I, II, and IV take precedence over the writings in the present list as representing the work of their authors, and the reader should refer to those books in all cases. The student wishing seriously to trace the development of modern criticism in the United States will investigate the files of the magazines listed in Appendix III. Among these journals, the following will be found especially important in shaping the growth of contemporary American literature and criticism: *Accent, The American Mercury, The American Review, Broom, The Dial, The Freeman, The Fugitive, The Hound and Horn, The Hudson Review, The Kenyon Review, The Little Review, The Nation, The New Republic, New Directions, Partisan Review, Poetry: A Magazine of Verse, The Seven Arts, The Sewanee Review, The Smart Set, The Southern Review, The Symposium, Transition, The Western Review.*

The indexes and bibliographies named at the beginning of Appendix I will again be found useful in tracing further work by the critics listed below, and by others.

The titles of certain magazines in the following list have been abbreviated as follows (all others being printed in full):

A:	*Accent*	N:	*The Nation*
Am Merc:	*The American Mercury*	No Am:	*The North American*
Ant R:	*The Antioch Review*		*Review*
AR:	*The American Review*	NR:	*The New Republic*
AS:	*The American Scholar*	P:	*Poetry: A Magazine of*
At Mon:	*The Atlantic Monthly*		*Verse*
B:	*The Bookman*	PR:	*Partisan Review*
CE:	*College English*	RMR:	*The Rocky Mountain*
Century:	*The Century Magazine*		*Review*
D:	*The Dial*	Scribner's:	*Scribner's Magazine*
EHL:	*English Literary History*	Sew R:	*The Sewanee Review*
EJ:	*The English Journal*	Sou R:	*The Southern Review*
F:	*The Forum*	SRL:	*The Saturday Review of*
Harper's:	*Harper's Monthly Maga-*		*Literature*
	zine or Harper's Magazine	Sym:	*The Symposium*
HH:	*The Hound and Horn*	VQR:	*The Virginia Quarterly*
HR:	*The Hudson Review*		*Review*
KR:	*The Kenyon Review*	WR:	*The Western Review*
MP:	*Modern Philology*	YR:	*The Yale Review* (new
			series)

Aiken, Conrad, "John Keats," D, 78: 475–490 (June, 1925).

Aiken, Conrad, "The Novel as a Work of Art," D, 83: 41–44 (July, 1927).

Aiken, Conrad, "A Plea for Anonymity," NR, 84: 155–157 (September 18, 1935).

Aiken, Conrad, "A. E. Housman," NR, 89: 51 (November 11, 1936).

Aiken, Conrad, "William Faulkner," At Mon, 164: 650–654 (November, 1939).

Aiken, Conrad, "Back to Poetry," At Mon, 166: 217–223 (August, 1940).

Aiken, Conrad, "Poetry: What Direction?" NR, 104: 670–677 (May 12, 1941).

Aiken, Conrad, "American Writers Come of Age," At Mon, 169: 476–481 (April, 1942).

Anderson, Quentin, "Henry James and the New Jerusalem," KR, 8: 515–566 (Autumn, 1946).

Arendt, Hannah, "Franz Kafka: A Revaluation," PR, 11: 412–422 (Fall, 1944).

Arendt, Hannah, "What is Existenz Philosophy?" PR, 13: 34–56 (Winter, 1946).

Arendt, Hannah, "Beyond Personal Frustration: The Poetry of Bert Brecht," KR, 10: 304–312 (Spring, 1948).

Arvin, Newton, "Stuart Sherman," HH, 3: 304–313 (April–June, 1930).

Arvin, Newton, "Whitman's Individualism," NR, 71: 212–213 (July 6, 1932).

Arvin, Newton, "Society and Solitude," NR, 76: 284 (October 18, 1933).

Arvin, Newton, "Henry James and the Almighty Dollar," HH, 7: 434–443 (April–May, 1934).

Arvin, Newton, "Homage to Robert Herrick," NR, 82: 93–95 (March 6, 1935).

Arvin, Newton, "The Usableness of Howells," NR, 91: 227–228 (June 30, 1937).

Arvin, Newton, "Counterfeit Presentments," PR, 15: 673–680 (June, 1948).

Arvin, Newton, "Melville's Shorter Poems," PR, 16: 1034–1046 (October, 1949).

Auden, W. H., "Psychology and Art Today," in The Arts Today (edited by Geoffrey Grigson, London, 1935).

Auden, W. H., "Rilke in English," NR, 100: 135 (September 6, 1939).

Auden, W. H., "A Literary Transference" (on Hardy), Sou R, 6: 78–86 (Summer, 1940).

Auden, W. H., "Yeats: Master of Diction," SRL, 22: 14 (June 8, 1940).

Auden, W. H., "The Fabian Figaro" (on Shaw), Commonweal, 37: 12–13 (October 23, 1942).

Auden, W. H., "Preface to Kierkegaard," NR, 110: 683–684 plus (May 15, 1944).

Auden, W. H., "Some Notes on D. H. Lawrence," N, 164: 482–484 (April 26, 1947).

Auden, W. H., "Yeats as an Example," KR, 10: 163–181 (Spring, 1948).

Auden, W. H., "Henry James and the Artist in America," Harper's, 197: 36–40 (July, 1948).

Auden, W. H., "Criticism in a Mass Society," in The Intent of the Critic (edited by Donald A. Stauffer, Princeton, 1941).

Babbitt, Irving, "Are the English Critical?" N, 94: 282–284, 309–311 (March 21, 28, 1912).

Babbitt, Irving, "Bergson and Rousseau," N, 95: 452–455 (November 14, 1912).

Babbitt, Irving, "Humanists and Humanitarians," N, 10: 288–289 (September 2, 1915).

Babbitt, Irving, "Matthew Arnold," N, 105: 117–121 (August 2, 1917).

Babbitt, Irving, "Genius and Taste," N, 106: 138–141 (February 7, 1918).

Babbitt, Irving, "Croce and the Philosophy of Flux," YR, 14: 377–381 (January, 1925).

Babbitt, Irving, "Coleridge and Imagination," B, 70: 113–124 (October, 1929).

Babbitt, Irving, "What I Believe," F, 83: 80–87 (February, 1930).

Babbitt, Irving, "On Being Creative," B, 73: 113–122 (April, 1931).

Babbitt, Irving, "Style in a Democracy," SRL, 9: 325–326 (December 17, 1932). "The Primitivism of Wordsworth," "The Problem of the Imagination: Dr. Johnson," "Schiller as Aesthetic Theorist," "Julien Benda," and "The Critic and American Life" in On Being Creative and Other Essays (1932).

Baker, Howard, "Wallace Stevens and Other Poets," Sou R, 1: 373–396 (Autumn, 1935).

Baker, Howard, "The Contemporary Short Story," Sou R, 3: 576–596 (Winter, 1938).

Baker, Howard, "Hardy's Poetic Certitude," Sou R, 6: 49–63 (Summer, 1940).

Baker, Howard, "An Essay on Fiction with Examples," Sou R, 7: 385–406 (Autumn, 1941).

Baker, Howard, "Domes of Byzantium" (on Yeats), Sou R, 7: 639–652 (Winter, 1942).

Barrett, William, "The Talent of Jean-Paul Sartre," PR, 13: 237–246 (Spring, 1946).

Barrett, William, "The Resistance" (on the little magazine), PR, 13: 479–488 (September–October, 1946).

Barrett, William, "Writers and Madness," PR, 14: 5–22 (January–February, 1947).

Barrett, William, "Dialogue on Anxiety," PR, 14: 151–159 (March–April, 1947).

Barrett, William, "Temptations of St. Yvor" (on Yvor Winters), KR, 9: 532–551 (Autumn, 1947).

Barrett, William, "A Prize for Ezra Pound," PR, 16: 344–347 (April, 1949).

Barrett, William, "The Liberal Mind" (an exchange with Lionel Trilling and Richard Chase), PR, 16: 649–665 (June, 1949).

Barzun, Jacques, "To the Rescue of Romanticism," AS, 9: 147–158 (Spring, 1940).

Barzun, Jacques, "Truth and Poetry in Thomas Hardy," Sou R, 6: 179–192 (Summer, 1940).

Barzun, Jacques, "The American as Critic," SRL, 23: 30 plus (December 7, 1940).

Barzun, Jacques, "William James as Artist," NR, 108: 218–220 (February 15, 1943).

Barzun, Jacques, "Bernard Shaw in Twilight," KR, 5: 321–345 (Summer, 1943).

Barzun, Jacques, "James the Melodramatist," KR, 5: 508–521 (Autumn, 1943).

Barzun, Jacques, "The Critic as Statesman," At Mon, 178: 128–132 (August, 1946).

Barzun, Jacques, "Twenty-five Years of American Sensuality," N, 166: 355–357 (March 27, 1948).

Barzun, Jacques, "The Fetish of Form: An Example from Music," KR, 12: 86–98 (Winter, 1950).

Beach, Joseph Warren, "Decade of the Doomed," N, 131: 622 (December 3, 1930).

Beach, Joseph Warren, "The Novel from James to Joyce," N, 132: 634–636 (June 10, 1931).

Beach, Joseph Warren, "Thackeray Full Length," VQR, 22: 280–295 (Spring, 1946).

Beach, Joseph Warren, "The Sacred and Solitary Refuge" (on Henry James), *Furioso*, 3: 23–37 (Winter, 1947).

Beach, Joseph Warren, "Dos Passos: 1947," Sew R, 55: 406–418 (Summer, 1947).

Beach, Joseph Warren, "Sartre's Roads to Freedom," WR, 12: 180–191 (Spring, 1948).

Beach, Joseph Warren, "The Poems of Auden and the Prose Diathesis," VQR, 25: 365–383 (Summer, 1949).
> For Mr. Beach's more extended essays on modern English, European, and American novelists, see his books *The Twentieth Century Novel* (1932) and *American Fiction: 1920–40* (1941).

Bentley, Eric, "The Story of Stefan George," PR, 9: 321–330 (July–August, 1942).

Bentley, Eric, "The Theatres of Wagner and Ibsen," KR, 6: 542–569 (Autumn, 1944).

Bentley, Eric, "Romanticism: A Re-Evaluation," Ant R, 4: 6–20 (Spring, 1944).

Bentley, Eric, "The Drama at Ebb," KR, 7: 169–184 (Spring, 1945).

Bentley, Eric, "Jean-Paul Sartre, Dramatist," KR, 8: 66–79 (Winter, 1946).

Bentley, Eric, "Bernard Shaw's Politics," KR, 8: 347–371 (Summer, 1946).

Bentley, Eric, "Yeats as a Playwright," KR, 10: 196–208 (Spring, 1948).

Bentley, Eric, "The Meaning of Robert Penn Warren's Novels," KR, 10: 407–424 (Summer, 1948).

Bentley, Eric, "Chekhov as Playwright," KR, 11: 226–250 (Spring, 1949).

Bentley, Eric, "Jean-Louis Barrault," KR, 12: 222–242 (Spring, 1950).

Berryman, John, "F. Scott Fitzgerald," KR, 8: 103–112 (Winter, 1946).

Berryman, John, "The Poetry of Ezra Pound," PR, 16: 377–394 (April, 1949).

Bewley, Marius, "Kenneth Burke as Literary Critic," *Scrutiny* (Cambridge, England), 15: 254–277 (December, 1948).

Bewley, Marius, "The Poetry of Wallace Stevens," PR, 16: 895–916 (September, 1949).

Bewley, Marius, "James's Debt to Hawthorne," *Scrutiny*, 16: 178–195 (September, 1949), 16: 301–317 (Winter, 1949), 17: 14–31 (Spring, 1950).

Bishop, John Peale, "Homage to Hemingway," NR, 89: 39–42 (November 11, 1936).

Bishop, John Peale, "The Poems of Ford Madox Ford," P, 50: 336–341 (September, 1937).

Bishop, John Peale, "The Discipline of Poetry," VQR, 14: 343–356 (Summer, 1938).

Bishop, John Peale, "The Poems and Prose of E. E. Cummings," Sou R, 4: 173–186 (Summer, 1938).

Bishop, John Peale, "Myth and Modern Literature," SRL, 20: 3–4 plus (July 22, 1939).

Bishop, John Peale, "Finnegans Wake," Sou R, 5: 439–452 (Winter, 1940).

Bishop, John Peale, "The Poetry of A. E. Housman," P, 56: 144–153 (June, 1940).

Bishop, John Peale, "Poetry and Painting," Sew R, 53: 247–258 (Spring, 1945).
> For further essays and reviews see *The Collected Essays of John Peale Bishop* (edited by Edmund Wilson, 1948).

Blackmur, R. P., "Wallace Stevens," HH, 5: 223–256 (January–March, 1932).

Blackmur, R. P., "Masks of Ezra Pound," HH, 7: 177–212 (January–March, 1934).

Blackmur, R. P., "The Later Poetry of W. B. Yeats," Sou R, 2: 339–362 (Autumn, 1936).

Blackmur, R. P., "Emily Dickinson: Notes on Prejudice and Fact," Sou R, 3: 323–347 (Autumn, 1937).

Blackmur, R. P., "Henry Adams: Three Late Moments," KR, 2: 7–29 (Winter, 1940).

Blackmur, R. P., "The Shorter Poems of Thomas Hardy," Sou R, 6: 20–48 (Summer, 1940).

Blackmur, R. P., "The Enabling Act of Criticism," in *American Issues* (edited by Willard Thorp, 1941).

Blackmur, R. P., "The Sacred Fount" (on Henry James), KR, 4: 328–352 (Autumn, 1942).

Blackmur, R. P., "In the Country of the Blue" (on Henry James), KR, 5: 595–617 (Autumn, 1943).

Blackmur, R. P., "The Economy of the American Writer," Sew R, 53: 175–185 (Spring, 1945).

Blackmur, R. P., "Notes on Four Categories of Criticism," Sew R, 54: 576–589 (Autumn, 1946).

Blackmur, R. P., "In the Birdcage" (on Dostoevsky), HR, 1: 7–28 (Spring, 1948).

Blackmur, R. P., "A Burden for Critics," HR, 1: 170–185 (Summer, 1948).

Blackmur, R. P., "*Anna Karenina*: The Dialectic of Incarnation," KR, 12: 433–456 (Summer, 1950).

"D. H. Lawrence and Expressive Form," "New Thresholds, New Anatomies: Notes on a Text by Hart Crane," "The Method of Marianne Moore," "The Dangers of Authorship," "T. S. Eliot: From *Ash-Wednesday* to *Murder in the Cathedral*," and "The Critical Prefaces of Henry James" in *The Double Agent* (1935); and "A Featherbed for Critics" in *The Expense of Greatness* (1940).

Bogan, Louise, "Rilke in his Age," P, 50: 34–42 (April, 1937).

Bogan, Louise, "William Butler Yeats," At Mon, 161: 637–644 (May, 1938).

Bogan, Louise, "The Cutting of an Agate," N, 148: 234–235 (February 25, 1939).

Bogan, Louise, "The Poetry of Paul Eluard," PR, 6: 76–84 (Fall, 1939).

Bogan, Louise, "The Brontë Fantasies," NR, 105: 285–286 (September 1, 1941).

Bogan, Louise, "*Sentimental Education* Today," N, 155: 301–302 (October 3, 1942).

Bogan, Louise, "Some Notes on Popular and Unpopular Art," PR, 10: 391–401 (September–October, 1943).

Bogan, Louise, "The Time of the Assassins," N, 158: 475–476 plus (April 22, 1944).

Bogan, Louise, "The Mystic Experience," N, 161: 15 (July 7, 1945).

Bogan, Louise, "The Portrait of New England" (on James's *The Bostonians*), N, 161: 582–583 plus (December 1, 1945).

See *The New Yorker*, 1929–1950, *passim*, for reviews of current poetry.

Bourne, Randolph, "Two Generations," At Mon, 107: 591–598 (May, 1911).

Bourne, Randolph, "Theodore Dreiser," NR, 2: supp 7–8 (April 17, 1915).

Bourne, Randolph, "John Dewey's Philosophy," NR, 2: 154–156 (May 13, 1915).

Bourne, Randolph, "The Cult of the Best," NR, 5: 275–277 (January 15, 1916).

Bourne, Randolph, "The Art of Theodore Dreiser," D, 62: 507–509 (June 14, 1917).

Bourne, Randolph, "The History of a Literary Radical," YR, 8: 468–484 (April, 1919).

  For other essays by Bourne see *Untimely Papers* (edited by James Oppenheim, 1919), and *The History of a Literary Radical and Other Essays* (edited by Van Wyck Brooks, 1920).

Brooks, Cleanth, "Three Revolutions in Poetry," Sou R, 1: 151–163 (Summer, 1935), 1: 328–338 (Autumn, 1935), 1: 568–583 (Winter, 1936).

Brooks, Cleanth, "The Reading of Modern Poetry," AR, 8: 435–449 (February, 1937).

Brooks, Cleanth, *"The Waste Land:* An Analysis," Sou R, 3: 106–136 (Summer, 1937). For a revised version see *T. S. Eliot: A Study of his Writings by Several Hands* (edited by B. Rajan, 1947).

Brooks, Cleanth, "Literary History versus Criticism," KR, 2: 403–412 (Autumn, 1940).

Brooks, Cleanth, "The Poem as Organism," in *English Institute Annual: 1940* (1941).

Brooks, Cleanth, "The Language of Paradox," in *The Language of Poetry* (edited by Allen Tate, 1942).

Brooks, Cleanth, "The New Criticism: A Brief for the Defense," AS, 13: 435–449 (Summer, 1944).

Brooks, Cleanth, "The Intimations of the Ode" (on Wordsworth), KR, 8: 80–102 (Winter, 1946).

Brooks, Cleanth, "Criticism and Literary History: Marvell's Horatian Ode," Sew R, 55: 199–222 (Spring, 1947).

  See also "Metaphor and the Tradition," "Metaphysical Poetry and Propaganda Art," "The Modern Poet and the Tradition," "Yeats: The Poet as Myth-Maker," and "Notes for a Revised History of English Poetry," in *Modern Poetry and the Tradition* (1939); and "The Heresy of Paraphrase," "Criticism, History, and Critical Relativism," and "The Problem of Belief and the Problem of Cognition," in *The Well Wrought Urn* (1947).

Brooks, Van Wyck, "Highbrow and Lowbrow," F, 53: 481–492 (April, 1915).

Brooks, Van Wyck, "On Creating a Usable Past," D, 64: 337–341 (April 11, 1918).

Brooks, Van Wyck, "Mark Twain's Humor," D, 68: 275–291 (March, 1920).

Brooks, Van Wyck, "Mark Twain's Satire," D, 68: 424–443 (April, 1920).

Brooks, Van Wyck, "Henry James: The First Phase," D, 74: 433–450 (May, 1923).

Brooks, Van Wyck, "Henry James: The American Scene," D, 75: 29–42 (July, 1923).

Brooks, Van Wyck, "Henry James: An International Episode," D, 75: 225–238 (September, 1923).

Brooks, Van Wyck, "Emerson and the Reformers," *Harper's,* 154: 114–119 (December, 1926).

Brooks, Van Wyck, "What is Primary Literature?" YR, 31: 25–37 (Summer, 1941).

　　Van Wyck Brooks's three most important essays, "America's Coming-of-Age" of 1915, "Letters and Leadership" of 1918, and "The Literary Life in America," are now collected in *Three Essays on America* (1934).

Brown, E. K., "The Revival of E. M. Forster," YR, 33: 668–681 (June, 1944).

Brown, E. K., "James and Conrad," YR, 35: 265–285 (December, 1945).

Brown, E. K., "David Copperfield," YR, 37: 651–666 (June, 1948).

Brownell, William Crary, "Criticism," At Mon, 107: 548–567 (April, 1911).

Brownell, William Crary, "Standards," *Scribner's,* 61: 277–284 March, 1917), 61: 435–444 (April, 1917), 61: 619–626 (May, 1917).

　　See also the books listed in Appendix I.

Burgum, Edwin Berry, "Romanticism," KR, 3: 479–490 (Autumn, 1941).

Burke, Kenneth, "Symbolic War," Sou R, 2: 134–147 (Summer, 1936).

Burke, Kenneth, "Acceptance and Rejection," Sou R, 2: 600–632 (Winter, 1937).

Burke, Kenneth, "Semantic and Poetic Meaning," Sou R, 3: 501–523 (Winter, 1939).

Burke, Kenneth, "The Calling of the Tune," KR, 1: 272–282 (Summer, 1939).

Burke, Kenneth, "Four Master Tropes," KR, 3: 421–438 (Autumn, 1941).

Burke, Kenneth, "On Motivation in Yeats," Sou R, 7: 547–561 (Winter, 1942).

Burke, Kenneth, "The Tactics of Motivation," *Chimera,* 1: 21–33, 2: 37–53 (Spring, Summer, 1943).

Burke, Kenneth, "Container and Thing Contained," Sew R, 53: 56–78 (Winter, 1945).

Burke, Kenneth, "The Temporizing of Essence," KR, 7: 616–627 (Autumn, 1945).

Burke, Kenneth, "The Imagery of Killing," HR, 1: 151–167 (Summer, 1948). See also "The Poetic Process," "The Status of Art," "Program," "Lexicon Rhetoricae," and "Applications of the Terminology," in *Counter-Statement* (1931); and "Freud—And the Analysis of Poetry," "Twelve Propositions," "On Musicality in Verse," "Antony on Behalf of the Play," and "The Rhetoric of Hitler's *Battle,*" in *The Philosophy of Literary Form* (1941); as well as the other books listed in Appendix IV.

Burnham, James, "Marxism and Esthetics," Sym, 4: 3–30 (January, 1933).

Calverton, V. F., "The American Revolutionary Tradition," *Scribner's,* 95: 352–357 (May, 1934).

Calverton, V. F., "Literature as a Revolutionary Force," *Canadian Forum,* 15: 221–227 (March, 1935).

Canby, Henry Seidel, "Sex in Fiction," *Century,* 105: 98–105 (November, 1922).

Canby, Henry Seidel, "The Age of Experiment," *Century,* 107: 571–578 (February, 1924).

Canby, Henry Seidel, "Anon is Dead," Am Merc, 8: 79–84 (May, 1926).

Canby, Henry Seidel, "Interpreting our Literature," SRL, 5: 721–722 (March 2, 1929).

Cantwell, Robert, "No Landmarks," Sym, 4: 70–84 (January, 1933).

Cantwell, Robert, "The Influence of James Joyce," NR, 77: 200–201 (December 27, 1933).

Cantwell, Robert, "The Return of Henry James," NR, 81: 119–121 (December 12, 1934).

Cantwell, Robert, "Upton Sinclair," NR, 90: 69–71 (February 24, 1937).

Cantwell, Robert, "A Warning to Pre-War Novelists," NR, 91: 177–180 (June 23, 1937).

Cantwell, Robert, "America and the Writers' Project," NR, 98: 323–325 (April 26, 1939).

Cantwell, Robert, "The Future of American Journalism," NR, 101: 39–41 (November 8, 1939).

Cather, Willa, "The Novel Démeublé," NR, 30: supp 5–6 (April 12, 1922).

Chapman, John Jay, "Emerson Sixty Years After," At Mon, 79: 27–41 (January, 1897), 79: 222–240 (February, 1897).

Chapman, John Jay, "Literature," The Critic, 36: 53–60 (January, 1900).

Chapman, John Jay, "Learning," At Mon, 106: 125–136 (July, 1910).

Chapman, John Jay, "The Greek Genius," At Mon, 114: 70–82 (July, 1914).

Chapman, John Jay, "Lincoln and Hamlet," No Am, 209: 371–379 (March, 1919).

Chapman, John Jay, "Dante and Modern Criticism," NR, 51: 71–72 (June 8, 1927).

    Of the books by Chapman listed in Appendix IV, see especially *Emerson and Other Essays* (1898); *Learning and Other Essays* (1910); *The Greek Genius and Other Essays* (1915); and *Letters and Religion* (1924).

Chase, Richard, "History vs. the City of God" (on Arnold Toynbee), PR, 11: 45–55 (Winter, 1944).

Chase, Richard, "The Sense of the Present," KR, 7: 218–231 (Spring, 1945).

Chase, Richard, "Notes on the Study of Myth," PR, 13: 338–346 (Summer, 1946).

Chase, Richard, "The Brontës," KR, 9: 487–506 (Autumn, 1947).

Chase, Richard, "The Stone and the Crucifixion: Faulkner's *Light in August*," KR, 10: 538–551 (Autumn, 1948).

Chase, Richard, "Dissent on *Billy Budd*," PR, 15: 1212–1218 (November, 1948).

Chase, Richard, "The Progressive Hawthorne," PR, 16: 96–100 (January, 1949).

Chase, Richard, "Melville's *Confidence Man*," KR, 11: 122–140 (Winter, 1949). For Mr. Chase's fuller discussion of myth, see his *Quest for Myth* (1949); for his fuller study of Melville, see his *Herman Melville: A Critical Study* (1949).

Clark, Eleanor, "Death of a Thinker: A Note on the French Novel 1925–40," KR, 3: 322–335 (Summer, 1941).

Chevalier, Haakon M., "André Malraux: The Return of the Hero," KR, 2: 35–47 (Winter, 1940).

Collins, Seward, "Criticism in America," B, 71: 241–256 (June, 1930), 71: 400–415 (July, 1930), 72: 145–164, 209–228 (October, 1930).

Colum, Mary M., "A Critical Credo," *Scribner's,* 79: 387–392 (April, 1926).

Colum, Mary M., "The Changing Novel," SRL, 5: 1070–1071 (June 1, 1929).

Colum, Mary M., "Self-Critical America," *Scribner's,* 87: 197–206 (February, 1930).

Colum, Mary M., "Debating Humanism," SRL, 6: 1063–1064 (May 24, 1930).

Colum, Mary M., "The American Mind in Literature," F, 90: 330–334 (December, 1933).

Colum, Mary M., "On Thinking Critically," F, 91: 76–82 (February, 1934).

Colum, Mary M., "Marxism and Literature," F, 91: 145–149 (March, 1934).

Cowley, Malcolm, "A Farewell to Spain" (on Hemingway), NR, 73: 76–77 (November 30, 1932).

Cowley, Malcolm, "Farewell to the 1930's," NR, 101: 42–44 (November 8, 1939).

Cowley, Malcolm, "Remembering Hart Crane," NR, 104: 504–506 (April 14, 1941).

Cowley, Malcolm, "Robert Frost: A Dissenting Opinion," NR, 111: 312–313 (September 11, 1944).

Cowley, Malcolm, "The Case against Mr. Frost: II," NR, 111: 345–347 (September 18, 1944).

Cowley, Malcolm, "William Faulkner's Legend of the South," Sew R, 53: 343–361 (Summer, 1945).

Cowley, Malcolm, "William Faulkner Revisited," SRL, 28: 13–16 (April 14, 1945).

Cowley, Malcolm, "Walt Whitman: The Miracle," NR, 114: 385–388 (March 18, 1946).

Cowley, Malcolm, "Walt Whitman: The Secret," NR, 114: 481–484 (April 8, 1946).

Cowley, Malcolm, " 'Not Men': A Natural History of American Naturalism," KR, 9: 414–435 (Summer, 1947).

Cowley, Malcolm, "Hawthorne in the Looking Glass," Sew R, 56: 545–563 (Autumn, 1948).

See also the "Introduction" to *The Portable Faulkner* (edited by Malcolm Cowley, 1946).

Crane, Hart, "A Discussion with Hart Crane" (by Harriet Monroe), P, 29: 34–41 (October, 1926).

Crane, Hart, "Two Letters on *The Bridge,*" HH, 7: 677–682 (July, 1934).

Crane, Hart, "Modern Poetry," in *Collected Poems of Hart Crane* (1933).

Crane, R. S., "History versus Criticism in the University Study of Literature," EJ (College Edition), 24: 645–667 (October, 1935).

Crane, R. S., Foreword to "Two Essays in Practical Criticism" by Norman F. Maclean and Elder Olson, *University Review* (Kansas City), 8: 199–219 (Spring, 1942).

Crane, R. S., "Cleanth Brooks; or, The Bankruptcy of Critical Monism," MP, 45: 226–245 (May, 1948).

Crane, R. S., "The Plot of *Tom Jones*," *Journal of General Education*, 4: 112–130 (January, 1950).

Cunningham, J. V., "The Ancient Quarrel between History and Poetry," P, 74: 336–342 (September, 1949).

Cunningham, J. V., "The Poetry of Wallace Stevens," P, 75: 149–165 (December, 1949).

Daiches, David, "The Principles of Literary Criticism" (on I. A. Richards), NR, 98: 95–98 (March 1, 1939).

Daiches, David, "The Novels of Aldous Huxley," NR, 100: 362–365 (November 1, 1939).

Daiches, David, "Sensibility and Technique: Preface to a Critique" (on Henry James), KR, 5: 569–579 (Autumn, 1943).

Daiches, David, "Jane Austen, Karl Marx, and the Aristocratic Dance," AS, 17: 289–296 (July, 1948).

Daiches, David, "T. S. Eliot," YR, 38: 460–470 (March, 1949).

Daiches, David, "The Novels of Elizabeth Bowen," EJ, 38: 305–313 (June, 1949).

Daiches, David, "The New Criticism: Some Qualifications," CE, 39: 64–72 (February, 1950).

See also the books listed in Appendix I.

Damon, S. Foster, "The Odyssey in Dublin" (on James Joyce), HH, 3: 7–44 (October–December, 1929).

Davidson, Donald, "Sectionalism in the United States," HH, 6: 561–589 (July–September, 1933).

Davidson, Donald, "The Traditional Basis of Thomas Hardy's Fiction," Sou R, 6: 162–178 (Summer, 1940).

Davidson, Donald, "Yeats and the Centaur," Sou R, 7: 510–516 (Winter, 1942). For further essays, especially on Southern tradition and literature, see *The Attack on Leviathan* (1938).

Davis, Robert Gorham, "Art and Anxiety," PR, 12: 310–320 (Summer, 1945).

Davis, Robert Gorham, "History, Tragedy, and Sentimentality," SRL, 32: 13 (December 24, 1949).

Davis, Robert Gorham, "The New Criticism and the Democratic Tradition," AS, 19: 9–19 (Winter, 1949).

Deutsch, Babette, "The Future of Poetry," NR, 60: 12–15 (August 21, 1929).

Deutsch, Babette, "Understanding Poetry," AS, 10: 67–71 (January, 1941).

Deutsch, Babette, "War Poetry Then and Now," NR, 104: 565–567 (April 21, 1941).

De Voto, Bernard, "My dear Edmund Wilson," (a reply to Edmund Wilson's criticism in NR, 89: 405–408, February 3, 1937), SRL, 15: 8 plus (February 13, 1937).

De Voto, Bernard, "The Critics and Robert Frost," SRL, 17: 3–4 plus (January 1, 1938).

De Voto, Bernard, "Freud's Influence on Literature," SRL, 20: 10–11 (October 7, 1939).

De Voto, Bernard, "American Novels," At Mon, 165: 66–74 (January, 1940).

Dupee, F. W., "André Malraux," PR, 4: 24–35 (March, 1938).

Dupee, F. W., "The English Literary Left," PR, 5: 11–21 (August–September, 1938).

Dupee, F. W., "Frost and Tate," N, 160: 464 plus (April 21, 1945).

Dupee, F. W., "Difficulty as Style," AS, 14: 355–357 (July, 1945).

Dupee, F. W., "Cecil Day Lewis and Louis MacNeice," N, 161: 380 (October 13, 1945).

Dupee, F. W., "Henry James and the Play," N, 171: 40–42 (July 8, 1950).

Eastman, Max, "American Ideals in Poetry," NR, 16: 190–192 (September 14, 1918, 16: 222–225 (September 21, 1918).

Eastman, Max, "Humor and America," Scribner's, 100: 9–13 (July, 1936).

Eastman, Max, "Wit and Nonsense: Freud's Mistake," YR, 26: 71–87 (September, 1936).

Eastman, Max, "Pushkin and his English Translators," NR, 89: 187–188 (December 9, 1936).

Eastman, Max, "The End of Socialism in Russia," Harper's, 174: 302–314 (February, 1937).

Eastman, Max, "Russia and the Socialist Ideal," Harper's, 176: 374–385 (March, 1938).

Edel, Leon, "Introduction" and Notes to The Ghostly Tales of Henry James (edited by Leon Edel, 1948).

Edel, Leon, "Foreword," Introduction: "Henry James: The Dramatic Years," and Notes to The Complete Plays of Henry James (edited by Leon Edel, 1949).

Eliot, T. S., "In Memory" and "The Hawthorne Aspect" (both on Henry James), The Little Review, 5: 44–53 (August, 1918).

Eliot, T. S., "Studies in Contemporary Criticism," The Egoist (London), 5: 113–114 (October, 1918) and 5: 131–133 (November–December, 1918).

Eliot, T. S., "American Literature," The Athenaeum (London), No. 4643: 236–237 (April 25, 1919).

Eliot, T. S., "A Brief Treatise on the Criticism of Poetry," The Chapbook (London), 2: 1–10 (March, 1920).

Eliot, T. S., "The Perfect Critic," The Athenaeum (London), No. 4706: 40–41 (July 9, 1920) and No. 4708: 102–104 (July 23, 1920).

Eliot, T. S., "The Possibility of a Poetic Drama," D, 69: 441–447 (November, 1920).

Eliot, T. S., "The Function of Criticism," The Criterion (London), 2: 31–42 (October, 1923).

Eliot, T. S., "Ulysses, Order, and Myth" (on Joyce's Ulysses), D, 75: 480–483 (November, 1923).

Eliot, T. S., "A Note on Poetry and Belief," The Enemy (London), 1: 15–17 (January, 1927).

Eliot, T. S., "Literature, Science, and Dogma," D, 82: 239–243 (March, 1927).

Eliot, T. S., "Isolated Superiority" (on Ezra Pound), D, 84: 4–7 (January, 1928).

Eliot, T. S., "Literature and the Modern World," American Prefaces, 1: 19–22 (November, 1935).

Eliot, T. S., "A Note on the Verse of John Milton," *Essays and Studies of the English Association* (1936), 21: 32–40.

Eliot, T. S., "The Poetry of William Butler Yeats," Sou R, 7: 442–454 (Winter, 1942).

Eliot, T. S., "The Music of Poetry," PR, 9: 450–465 (November–December, 1942).

Eliot, T. S., "Notes Towards a Definition of Culture," PR, 11: 145–157 (Spring, 1944).

Eliot, T. S., "The Man of Letters and the Future of Europe," Sew R, 53: 333–342 (Summer, 1945).

Eliot, T. S., "The Social Function of Poetry," *The Adelphi* (London), 21: 152–161 (July, 1945).

Eliot, T. S., "What Is Minor Poetry?" Sew R, 54: 1–18 (Winter, 1946).

Eliot, T. S., "Ezra Pound," P, 68: 326–338 (September, 1946).

Eliot, T. S., "Milton," Sew R, 56: 185–209 (Spring, 1948).

See *The Criterion* (London), 1922–1939, *passim*, for editorials, essays, and reviews by T. S. Eliot during the years of his editorship.

See also the books of criticism listed in Appendix IV, especially *The Sacred Wood: Essays on Poetry and Criticism* (1920), in which appear "The Perfect Critic," "Imperfect Critics," "Tradition and the Individual Talent," "The Possibility of a Poetic Drama," "Rhetoric and Poetic Drama"; *For Lancelot Andrews* (1928), in which appear "Baudelaire in our Time" and "The Humanism of Irving Babbitt"; *Selected Essays* (1932; new edition, 1950), in which appear most of the above-named essays as well as "Dante," "Shakespeare and the Stoicism of Seneca," the three influential essays on "John Dryden," "The Metaphysical Poets," and "Andrew Marvell" which were first collected as *Homage to John Dryden* in 1924, the series on the Elizabethan dramatists, "Arnold and Pater," and, now added in 1950 from *Essays Ancient and Modern* of 1935, the papers on "Religion and Literature," "Modern Education and the Classics," and essays on Pascal and Tennyson; and for a compilation of critical passages by Eliot, *Points of View* (1941).

For a list of Eliot's writings in books and magazines, see *A Bibliographical Check-List of the Writings of T. S. Eliot*, compiled by Donald Gallup (1947).

Ellmann, Richard, "Robartes and Aherne: Two Sides of a Penny" (on Yeats), KR, 10: 177–186 (Spring, 1948).

See also the book-length study of Yeats by Richard Ellmann—*Yeats: The Man and the Masks* (1948).

Farrell, James T., "A Note on Literary Criticism," N, 142: 276–277 (March 4, 1936), 142: 314–315 (March 11, 1936).

Farrell, James T., "Ignazio Silone," Sou R, 4: 771–783 (Spring, 1939).

Farrell, James T., "The End of a Literary Decade," Am Merc, 48: 408–414 (December, 1939).

Farrell, James T., "The Faith of Lewis Mumford," Sou R, 6: 417–438 (Spring, 1941).

Farrell, James T., "The Frightened Philistines," NR, 111: 764 plus (December 4, 1944).

Farrell, James T., "Tolstoy: Husband and Writer," NR, 113: 290–292 (September 3, 1945).

> See also "The Duality of Literature," "Marx on the Relative Validity of Literature," "Individualism and the Class Struggle," "Literature and Propaganda," and "Growth and Decay in Literature," in *A Note on Literary Criticism* (1936); the title essay, "Literature and Ideology," and "The Language of Hollywood," in *The League of Frightened Philistines and Other Papers* (1945); and the title essay, "Social Themes in American Realism," "Theodore Dreiser: In Memoriam," and "The Fate of Writing in America," in *Literature and Morality* (1947).

Fergusson, Francis, "Joyce's *Exiles* and Ibsen," HH, 5: 345–353 (April–June, 1932).

Fergusson, Francis, "D. H. Lawrence's Sensibility," HH, 6: 447–463 (April–June, 1933).

Fergusson, Francis, "James's Idea of Dramatic Form," KR, 5: 495–507 (Autumn, 1943).

Fergusson, Francis, "Action as Passion: *Tristan* and *Murder in the Cathedral*," KR, 9: 201–221 (Spring, 1947).

Fergusson, Francis, "The Theatricality of Shaw and Pirandello," PR, 16: 589–604 (June, 1949).

> See also *The Idea of a Theatre* by Francis Fergusson (1949).

Fiedler, Leslie J., "The Sufferings and Greatness of Self-Love" (on Thomas Mann), PR, 14: 524–526 (September–October, 1947).

Fiedler, Leslie J., "Come Back to the Raft Ag'in, Huck Honey!" PR, 15: 664–672 (June, 1948).

Fiedler, Leslie J., "The Impotence of *Scrutiny*," N, 168: 252–253 (February 26, 1949).

Fiedler, Leslie J., "Out of the Whale" (on Melville), N, 169: 494–496 (November 19, 1949).

Fiedler, Leslie J., "The Third Thomas Hardy," N, 171: 210–211 (September 2, 1950).

Flint, F. Cudworth, "Metaphor in Contemporary Poetry," Sym, 1: 310–335 (July, 1930).

Flint, F. Cudworth, "Five Poets," Sou R, 1: 650–674 (Winter, 1936).

Flint, F. Cudworth, "Contemporary Criticism," Sou R, 2: 208–224 (Summer, 1936).

Flint, F. Cudworth, "New Leaders in English Poetry," VQR, 14: 502–518 (Summer, 1938).

Foerster, Norman, "Humanism and Religion," F, 82: 146–150 (September, 1929).

Foerster, Norman, "The Impressionists," B, 70: 337–347 (December, 1929).

Foerster, Norman, "Literary Historians," B, 71: 365–374 (July, 1930).

Foerster, Norman, "Literary Prophets," B, 72: 35–44 (September, 1930).

Foerster, Norman, "Toward a New Scholarship," SRL, 8: 1–3 (July 25, 1931).

Foerster, Norman, "The Study of Letters," in *Literary Scholarship* (1941).

Foerster, Norman, "The Esthetic Judgment and the Ethical Judgment," in *The Intent of the Critic* (edited by Donald A. Stauffer, 1941).
    Consult also the books listed in Appendix I.

Fowlie, Wallace, "Swann and Hamlet: A Note on the Contemporary Hero," PR, 9: 195–202 (May–June, 1942).

Fowlie, Wallace, "The Novel of Jules Romains," Sou R, 7: 880–892 (Spring, 1942).

Fowlie, Wallace, "François Mauriac," KR, 5: 189–200 (Spring, 1943).

Fowlie, Wallace, "Homage to Valéry," Sew R, 54: 250–257 (April–June, 1946).

Fowlie, Wallace, "Andre Bréton in the Age of Surrealism," WR, 14: 5–17 (Autumn, 1949).

Fowlie, Wallace, "Mallarmé's Island Voyage," MP, 47: 178–190 (February, 1950).

Frank, Joseph, "Spatial Form in Modern Literature," Sew R, 53: 221–240 (Summer, 1945), 53: 433–456 (Autumn, 1945), 53: 643–653 (Winter, 1945).

Frank, Joseph, "Force and Form: A Study of John Peale Bishop," Sew R, 55: 71–107 (Winter, 1947).

Frye, Northrop, "Levels of Meaning in Literature," KR, 12: 246–262 (Spring, 1950).

Gates, Lewis E., "English Literature in the Nineteenth Century," *The Critic*, 36: 69–80 (January, 1900), 36: 172–180 (February, 1900), 36: 268–275 (March, 1900).

Gates, Lewis E., "Tennyson's Relation to Common Life," *The Critic*, 36: 530–537 (June, 1900).

Gates, Lewis E., "Impressionism and Appreciation," At Mon, 86: 73–84 (July, 1900).
    See *Studies and Appreciations*, by Lewis E. Gates (1900).

Ghiselin, Brewster, "D. H. Lawrence and a New World," WR, 11: 150–159 (Spring, 1947).

Ghiselin, Brewster, "Bridge into the Sea" (on Hart Crane), PR, 16: 679–686 (July, 1949).

Gold, Michael, "Thornton Wilder: Prophet of the Genteel Christ," NR, 64: 266–267 (October 22, 1930).

Gold, Michael, "Out of the Fascist Unconscious" (on Archibald MacLeish), NR, 75: 295–296 (July 26, 1933).

Goodman, Paul, "Neo-Classicism, Platonism, and Romanticism," *Journal of Philosophy*, 31: 148–163 (1934).

Goodman, Paul, "The Shape of the Screen and the Darkness of the Theatre," PR, 9: 141–152 (March–April, 1942).

Gordon, Caroline, "Notes on Faulkner and Flaubert," HR, 1: 222–231 (Summer, 1948).

Gordon, Caroline, "Notes on Hemingway and Kafka," Sew R, 57: 215–226 (Spring, 1949).

Gordon, Caroline, "Notes on Chekhov and Maugham," Sew R, 57: 401–410 (Summer, 1949).

See *The House of Fiction,* edited by Caroline Gordon and Allen Tate (1950).

Greenberg, Clement, "Avant-Garde and Kitsch," PR, 6: 34–49 (Fall, 1939).

Greenberg, Clement, "Towards a Newer Laocoön, PR, 7: 296–310 (July–August, 1940).

Greenberg, Clement, "The Renaissance of the Little Mag," PR, 8: 72–75 (January–February, 1941).

Greenberg, Clement, "Bertolt Brecht's Poetry," PR, 8: 114–127 (March–April, 1941).

Gregory, Horace, "Wordsworth: An Evaluation," NR, 67: 25–26 (May 20, 1931).

Gregory, Horace, "Rugged Skelton," NR, 72: 333–334 (November 2, 1932).

Gregory, Horace, "The Search for a Frontier" (on Ezra Pound), NR, 75: 292–294 (July 25, 1933).

Gregory, Horace, "Two Critics in Search of an Absolute," N, 138: 189–191 (February 14, 1934).

Gregory, Horace, "The Man of Feeling" (on T. S. Eliot), NR, 79: 23–24 (May 16, 1934).

Gregory, Horace, "A Defense of Poetry," NR, 76: 237–238 (October 11, 1933).

Gregory, Horace, "The Proletarian Poet" (on Cecil Day Lewis), PR, 3: 27–28 (May, 1936).

Gregory, Horace, "W. B. Yeats and the Mask of Jonathan Swift," Sou R, 7: 492–509 (Winter, 1941).

Gregory, Horace. "Within the Private View: A Note on Rereading the Poetry of Edgar Allan Poe," PR, 10: 263–274 (May, 1943).

Gregory, Horace, "On Paul Elmer More and his *Shelburne Essays,* A, 4: 140–149 (Spring, 1944).

For the selected essays of Horace Gregory see *The Shield of Achilles: Essays on Poetry and Beliefs* (1944).

Guérard, Albert J., "Prometheus and the Aeolian Lyre," YR, 33: 482–497 (March, 1944).

Guérard, Albert J., "French and American Pessimism," *Harper's,* 191: 267–272 (September, 1945).

Guérard, Albert J., "Montherlant and the Collaborators," YR, 35: 93–98 (September, 1945).

Guérard, Albert J., "Literature and the Western Colleges," NR, 116: 27–28 (May 19, 1947).

Heilman, Robert B., "The Freudian Reading of *The Turn of the Screw,*" MLN, 62: 433–445 (November, 1947).

Heilman, Robert B., "*The Turn of the Screw* as Poem," *University Review* (Kansas City), 14: 277–289 (Summer, 1948).

Heilman, Robert B., "The Unity of *King Lear,*" Sew R, 56: 58–68 (Winter, 1948).

Hicks, Granville, "Conrad After Five Years," NR, 61: 192–194 (January 8, 1930).

Hicks, Granville, "The Twenties in American Literature," N, 130: 183–185 (February 12, 1930).

Hicks, Granville, "Ford Madox Ford: A Neglected Contemporary," B, 72: 364–370 (December, 1930).

Hicks, Granville, "Robert Herrick, Liberal," NR, 67: 129–130 (June 17, 1931).

Hicks, Granville, "The Past and Future of William Faulkner," B, 70: 17–24 (September, 1931).

Hicks, Granville, "John Dos Passos," B, 75: 32–42 (April, 1932).

Hicks, Granville, "The Failure of 'Left' Criticism," NR, 103: 345–347 (September 9, 1940).

Hicks, Granville, "Arthur Koestler and the Future of the Left," Antioch Review, 5: 212–223 (June, 1945).

Hicks, Granville, "The Intransigence of Edmund Wilson," Antioch Review, 6: 550–562 (December, 1946).

Hoffman, Frederick W., "From Surrealism to 'The Apocalpyse,'" ELH, 15: 147–165 (June, 1948).

Hook, Sidney, "Some Social Uses and Abuses of Semantics," PR, 4: 14–25 (April, 1938).

Hook, Sidney, "The Integral Humanism of Jacques Maritain," PR, 7: 204–229 (May–June, 1940).

Hook, Sidney, "The Future of Socialism," PR, 14: 23–36 (January–February, 1947).

Howe, Irving, "James T. Farrell: The Critic Calcified," PR, 14: 545–552 (September–October, 1947).

Howe, Irving, "The Critic as Stuffed Head" (on Stanley Edgar Hyman), N, 167: 22–24 (July 3, 1948).

Howe, Irving, "Edmund Wilson: A Revaluation," N, 167: 430–431 (October 16, 1948).

Howells, William Dean, "Mr. James's Masterpiece," Harper's Bazar, 36: 9–14 (January, 1902).

Howells, William Dean, "George Eliot," Harper's, 105: 963–967 (November, 1902).

Howells, William Dean, "Emile Zola," No Am, 175: 587–596 (November, 1902).

Howells, William Dean, "Frank Norris," No Am, 175: 769–778 (December, 1902).

Howells, William Dean, "Henry James's Later Work," No Am, 176: 125, 177–179 (January, 1903).

Howells, William Dean, "Certain of the Chicago School of Fiction," No Am, 176: 734–746 (May, 1903).

Howells, William Dean, "Shaw and Shakespeare," Harper's, 111: 633–635 (September, 1905).

Howells, William Dean, "Henrik Ibsen," No Am, 183: 1–14 (July, 1906).

Howells, William Dean, "The Novels of Robert Herrick," No Am, 189: 812–820 (June, 1909).

Howells, William Dean, "Mark Twain: An Enquiry," No Am, 191: 836–850 (June, 1910).

Howells, William Dean, "Mr. Henry James's Later Work," No Am, 203: 572–584 (April, 1916).

Howells, William Dean, "The Conjecture of Intensive Fiction," No Am, 204: 869–880 (December, 1916).

The above represents a small portion of Howells' output as critic and reviewer during the last twenty years of his life. His best critical work in book form is in two small volumes, *Criticism and Fiction* (1891) and *My Mark Twain* (1910). A good collection of his practical criticism is needed. His critical papers and journalism will be found listed and collated in the *Bibliography of William Dean Howells* by W. M. Gibson and George Arms.

Humphries, Rolfe, "Poet or Prophet?" (on Robinson Jeffers), NR, 61: 228–229 (January 15, 1930).

Humphries, Rolfe, "Archibald MacLeish," *Modern Monthly*, 8: 264–270, 274 (June, 1934).

Humphries, Rolfe, "Foreword, with Poems" (on Yvor Winters), P, 45: 288–291 (February, 1935).

Humphries, Rolfe, "Miss Millay as Artist," N, 153: 644–645 (December 30, 1941).

Humphries, Rolfe, "A Disciple of Aristippus" (on A. E. Housman), N, 154: 550–552 (May 9, 1942).

Humphries, Rolfe, "On the Creative Imagination," N, 157: 411–412 (October 9, 1943).

Humphries, Rolfe, "On Writers and their Critics," N, 159: 691–692 (December 2, 1944).

Huneker, James Gibbons, "Arthur Symons and his New Book," *The Lamp*, 28: 374–378 (June, 1904).

Huneker, James Gibbons, "Gerhardt Hauptmann," *The Lamp*, 29: 91–104 (September, 1904).

Huneker, James Gibbons, "August Strindberg," *The Lamp*, 29: 573–582 (January, 1905).

Huneker, James Gibbons, "Henrik Ibsen," *Scribner's*, 40: 351–361 (September, 1906).

Huneker, James Gibbons, "Anatole France," No Am, 184: 59–72 (January, 1907).

Huneker, James Gibbons, "The Baudelaire Legend," *Scribner's*, 45: 240–249 (February, 1909).

Huneker, James Gibbons, "The Genius of Joseph Conrad," No Am, 200: 270–279 (August, 1914).

Huneker, James Gibbons, "Jules Laforgue," No Am, 202: 80–91 (July, 1915).

Huneker, James Gibbons, "Dostoevsky and Tolstoy," F, 54: 201–216 (August, 1915).

Huneker, James Gibbons, "Remy de Gourmont," No Am, 205: 935–42 (June, 1917).

The above is a small selection of Huneker's critical journalism during the last twenty years of his life. His writings on literature, music, and the other arts will be found listed in Appendix IV. A convenient selection is the volume of *Essays* edited by H. L. Mencken (1929), in which see especially "The Quintessence of Shaw," "Villiers de l'Isle-Adam," "The Real Flaubert," "A Study of De Maupassant," "George Sand," and "Ibsen."

Hyman, Stanley Edgar, "Henry Thoreau in Our Time," At Mon, 178: 137–138 plus (November, 1946).

Hyman, Stanley Edgar, "The Psychoanalytic Criticism of Literature," WR, 12: 106–115 (Winter, 1948).

Hyman, Stanley Edgar, "The Critic as Narcissus," A, 8: 187–191 (Spring, 1948).

Hyman, Stanley Edgar, "Some Bankrupt Treasuries," KR, 10: 484–500 (Summer, 1948).

Hyman, Stanley Edgar, "Notes on the Organic Unity of John Peale Bishop," A, 9: 102–113 (Winter, 1949).

Hyman, Stanley Edgar, "Five Books in Search of an Author," HR, 2: 139–151 (Spring, 1949).

Hyman, Stanley Edgar, "Myth, Ritual, and Nonsense," KR, 11: 454–475 (Summer, 1949).

Hyman, Stanley Edgar, "The Deflowering of New England," HR, 2: 600–612 (Winter, 1950).

The Armed Vision by Stanley Edgar Hyman (1948) contains essays on Edmund Wilson, Yvor Winters, T. S. Eliot, Van Wyck Brooks, Constance Rourke, Maud Bodkin, Christopher Caudwell, Caroline Spurgeon, R. P. Blackmur, William Empson, I. A. Richards, and Kenneth Burke.

James, Henry, "James Russell Lowell," At Mon, 69: 35–50 (January, 1892).

James, Henry, "The Present Literary Situation in France," No Am, 169: 488–500 (October, 1899).

James, Henry, "Letters of Robert Louis Stevenson," No Am, 170: 61–77 (January, 1900).

James, Henry, "George Sand," No Am, 174: 546–554 (April, 1902).

James, Henry, "The Lesson of Balzac," At Mon, 96: 166–180 (August, 1905).

James, Henry, "The Novel in *The Ring and the Book*," Quarterly Review, 217: 68–87 (July, 1912).

James, Henry, "The Founding of *The Nation*," N, 101: 44–45 (July 8, 1915).

The above are a few of James's essays after 1890; his work as critic, journalist, and essayist will be found comprehensively indexed in LeRoy Phillips' *Bibliography of the Writings of Henry James* (new edition, 1930). James's books of criticism are listed in Appendix IV of the present volume. Of special importance are the book on *Hawthorne* (1879); the essays "The Art of Fiction," "Emerson," "Guy de Maupassant," and "Ivan Turgénieff" in *Partial Portraits* (1888); "Gustave Flaubert," "James Russell Lowell," and "Criticism" in *Essays in London and Elsewhere* (1893); "Matthew Arnold's Essays," "Mr. Walt Whitman," and "The Limitations of Dickens" in the collection of early writings called *Views and Reviews* (edited by LeRoy Phillips (1908); and the essays on Stevenson, Zola, Flaubert, Balzac, George Sand, Gabriele D'Annunzio, and "The New Novel, 1914" in *Notes on Novelists* (1914).

Jarrell, Randall, "Contemporary Poetry Criticisms," NR, 105: 88–90 (August 21, 1941).

Jarrell, Randall, "Changes of Attitude and Rhetoric in Auden's Poetry," Sou R, 7: 326–349 (Autumn, 1941).

Jarrell, Randall, "Freud to Paul: Stages in Auden's Ideology," PR, 12: 437–457 (Autumn, 1945).

Jarrell, Randall, "From the Kingdom of Necessity" (on Robert Lowell), N, 164: 74–75 (January 18, 1947).

Jarrell, Randall, "The Other Robert Frost," N, 165: 588, 590–601 (November 29, 1947).

Jarrell, Randall, "John Ransom's Poetry," Sew R, 56: 378–390 (Summer, 1948).

Jarrell, Randall, "The Profession of Poetry," PR, 17: 724–731 (September–October, 1950).

Jones, Howard Mumford, "Literary Scholarship and Contemporary Criticism," EJ, 23: 740–758 (November, 1934).

Jones, Howard Mumford, "The Limits of Contemporary Criticism," SRL, 24: 3–4, 17 (September 6, 1941).

[Cf. "Editorial," SR, 7: iv-xii (Autumn, 1941).]

Josephson, Matthew, "The Literary Life in Russia," NR, 79: 90–93 (June 6, 1934).

Kazin, Alfred, "Mr. Brooks's New England," PR, 7: 402–405 (September–October, 1940).

Kazin, Alfred, "Faulkner: The Rhetoric and the Agony," VQR, 18: 389–402 (July, 1942).

Kazin, Alfred, "The Irreducible Element," NR, 107: 259–260 (August 31, 1942).

Kazin, Alfred, "Criticism at the Poles," NR, 107: 492–495 (October 19, 1942).

Kazin, Alfred, "But What Is an American?" NR, 110: 218–220 (February 14, 1944).

Kazin, Alfred, "The Inmost Leaf" (on Melville), NR, 111: 840–841 (December 18, 1944).

Kazin, Alfred, "Introduction" to *The Portable Blake* (1947).

Kazin, Alfred, "The Indignant Flesh" (on Hemingway), *The New Yorker*, September 9, 1950, pp. 101–103.

See *On Native Grounds: An Interpretation of Modern American Prose Literature* (1942).

Kelly, John, "Franz Kafka's *Trial* and the Theology of Crisis," SR, 5: 748–766 (Spring, 1940).

Kronenberger, Louis, "T. S. Eliot as Critic," N, 140: 452–453 (April 17, 1935).

Kronenberger, Louis, "H. L. Mencken," NR, 88: 243–245 (October 7, 1936).

Kronenberger, Louis, "The Education of Henry Adams," NR, 18: 155–158 (March 15, 1939).

Kronenberger, Louis, "Virginia Woolf as Critic," N, 155; 382 plus (October 17, 1942).

Kronenberger, Louis, "Peacock," N, 155: 134–135 (August 15, 1942).

Kronenberger, Louis, "Lytton Strachey," N, 159: 158–159 (August 5, 1944).

Kronenberger, Louis, "The Perfect Trifler" (on Max Beerbohm), SRL, 30: 9–10 (June 21, 1947).

Krutch, Joseph Wood, "Realism and Drama," N, 133: 440–441 (October 21, 1931).

Krutch, Joseph Wood, "Lytton Strachey," N, 134: 199–200 (February 17, 1932).

Krutch, Joseph Wood. "Philosophical Criticism," N, 134: 407–408 (April 6, 1932).

Krutch, Joseph Wood, "The Comic Wisdom of S. N. Behrman," N, 137: 74–76 (July 19, 1933).

Krutch, Joseph Wood, "A Poem is a Poem" (on Eliot), N, 137: 679–680 (December 13, 1933).

Krutch, Joseph Wood, "The Meaning of Modern Drama," N, 141: 269–270 (September 4, 1935), 141: 291–293 (September 11, 1935), 141: 320–323 (September 18, 1935), 141: 351–353 (September 25, 1935).

Krutch, Joseph Wood, "On the Difficulty of Modern Poetry," N, 142: 283–284 (March 4, 1936).

Krutch, Joseph Wood, "What Is a Good Review?" N, 144: 438 (April 17, 1937).

Krutch, Joseph Wood, "New, Newer, Newest" (vogues in criticism), N, 171: 62–63 (July 15, 1950).

See also reviews of drama in The Nation since 1924 and his book The American Drama since 1918 (1939).

Langer, Suzanne, "The Principles of Creation in Art," HR, 2: 515–534 (Winter, 1950).

Langer, Suzanne, "The Primary Illusions and the Great Orders of Art," HR, 3: 219–233 (Summer, 1950).

Levin, Harry, "Literature and the Lively Sciences," At Mon, 155: 303–311 (March, 1935).

Levin, Harry, "Everybody's Earwicker," NR, 111: 106–107 (July 24, 1944).

Levin, Harry, "The Self-Condemned Playboy" (on Cyril Connolly), NR, 115: 49–50 (July 15, 1946).

Levin, Harry, "Stendhal in Technicolor," NR, 115: 595–597 (November 4, 1946).

Levin, Harry, "James Joyce," At Mon, 178: 125–129 (December, 1946).

Levin, Harry, "America Discovers Bohemia," At Mon, 180: 68–75 (September, 1947).

Levin, Harry, "Flaubert: Portrait of the Artist as a Saint," KR, 10: 28–43 (Winter, 1948).

Levin, Harry, "Flaubert and the Spirit of '48," YR, 38: 96–108 (September, 1948).

Levin, Harry, "Marcel Proust," At Mon, 182: 85–89 (October, 1948).

Lewis, Sinclair, "Fools, Liars, and Mr. De Voto," SRL, 17: 9, 12 (April 15, 1944).

Lovett, Robert Morss, "The Betrayal of Henry Adams," D, 65: 468–472 (November 30, 1918).

Lovett, Robert Morss, "The Function of Criticism," NR, 28: 247–249 (October 26, 1921).

Lovett, Robert Morss, "The World of Havelock Ellis," B, 67: 573–575 (July, 1928).

Lovett, Robert Morss, "Tolstoy: The Lesson of the Artist," NR, 56: 63–66 (September 5, 1928).

Lovett, Robert Morss, "William Crary Brownell," NR, 56: 204–206 (October 19, 1928).

Lovett, Robert Morss, "The Legend of Charles Dickens," NR, 56: 252–253 (October 17, 1928).

Lovett, Robert Morss, "Fuller of Chicago," NR, 60: 16–18 (August 21, 1929).

Lovett, Robert Morss, "The Centenary of Scott," NR, 72: 360–361 (November 9, 1932).

McCarthy, Mary, "Theatre Chronicle," serially in PR from 1937 to 1949.

McKeon, Richard P., "Literary Criticism and the Concept of Imitation in Antiquity," MP, 34: 1–35 (August, 1936).

McKeon, Richard P., "Education and the Disciplines," *International Journal of Ethics*, 47: 370–381 (April, 1937).

McKeon, Richard P., "Rhetoric in the Middle Ages," *Speculum*, 17: 1–32 (January, 1942).

McKeon, Richard P., "The Philosophic Bases of Art and Criticism," MP, 41: 65–87, 129–147 (November, 1943 and February, 1944).

McKeon, Richard P., "Aristotle's Conception of Language and the Arts of Language," *Classical Philology*, 41: 193–206 (October, 1946), 42: 21–50 (January, 1947).

McKeon, Richard P., "The Nature and Teaching of the Humanities," *Journal of General Education*, 3: 290–303 (July, 1949).

MacLeish, Archibald, "The Social Cant," NR, 73: 156–158 (December 21, 1932).

MacLeish, Archibald, "Public Speech and Private Speech in Poetry," YR, 27: 536–547 (Spring, 1938).

MacLeish, Archibald, "Poetry and the Public World," At Mon, 163: 823–831 (June, 1939).

MacLeish, Archibald, "The Irresponsibles," N, 150: 618–623 (May 18, 1940).

MacLeish, Archibald, "Post-War Writers and Pre-War Readers," NR, 102: 789–790 (June 10, 1940).

McLuhan, Herbert Marshall, "Poetic versus Rhetorical Exegesis," Sew R, 52: 266–276 (Spring, 1944).

McLuhan, Herbert Marshall, "The Analogical Mirrors" (on Hopkins), KR, 6: 322–332 (Summer, 1944).

McLuhan, Herbert Marshall, "The Southern Quality," Sew R, 55: 357–383 (Summer, 1947).

Macauley, Robie, "The Good Ford" (on Ford Madox Ford), KR, 11: 269–288 (Spring, 1949).

Macdonald, Dwight, "Reading from Left to Right," PR, 8: 24–33 (January–February, 1941).

Macdonald, Dwight, "Kulturbolschiwismus is Here," PR, 8: 442–459 (November–December, 1941).

Macdonald, Dwight, "The Future of Undemocratic Values," PR, 10: 321–344 (July–August, 1943).

Marshall, Margaret, "Our Critics, Right or Wrong" (with Mary McCarthy), N, 141: 468–469 (October 23, 1935), 542–544 (November 6, 1935), 595–598 (November 20, 1935), 653–655 (December 4, 1935), 717–719 (December 18, 1935).

Marshall, Margaret, "The Artist in America," N, 147: 270–271 (September 17, 1938).

Marshall, Margaret, "Writers in the Wilderness," N, 149: 576–579 (November 25, 1939), 150: 15–18 (January 6, 1940), 150: 473–475 (April 13, 1940).

Marshall, Margaret, "Katherine Anne Porter," N, 150: 473–475 (April 13, 1940).

Marshall, Margaret, "Constance Rourke: Artist and Citizen," N, 152: 726–728 (June 21, 1941).

Marshall, Margaret, "Socialism, Communism, and the West," N, 150: 473–475 (September 13, 1947).

Matthiessen, F. O., "The Crooked Road" (on Yeats), Sou R, 7: 455–470 (Winter, 1942).

Matthiessen, F. O., "James and the Plastic Arts," KR, 5: 533–550 (Autumn, 1943).

Matthiessen, F. O., "Henry James's Portrait of the Artist," PR, 11: 71–87 (Winter, 1944).

Matthiessen, F. O., "The Problem of the Private Poet" (on Emily Dickinson), KR, 7: 584–597 (Autumn, 1945).

Matthiessen, F. O., "Poe," Sew R, 54: 175–205 (Spring, 1946).

Matthiessen, F. O., "American Poetry 1920–1940," Sew R, 55: 25–55 (Winter, 1947).

Matthiessen, F. O., "Phelps Putnam," KR, 11: 61–82 (Winter, 1949).

Matthiessen, F. O., "The Responsibilities of the Critic," Michigan Alumnus Quarterly Review, 55: 283–292 (July 30, 1949).

    See also the books listed in Appendix IV, notably American Renaissance: Art and Expression in the Age of Emerson and Whitman (1941), Henry James: The Major Phase (1944), and The Achievement of T. S. Eliot (new edition, 1947).

Mencken, H. L., "James Huneker," Century, 102: 191–197 (June, 1921).

Mencken, H. L., "The Motive of the Critic," NR, 28: 249–251 (October 26, 1921).

Mencken, H. L., "The Future of English," *Harper's,* 170: 541–548 (April, 1935).

Mencken, H. L., "The American Future," Am Merc, 40: 129–136 (February, 1937).

Mencken's writings, published widely in magazines and newspapers over a space of more than forty years, and especially in *The Smart Set* and *The American Mercury* during his years of editorship and literary influence, are most conveniently consulted in the volumes listed in Appendix IV. Among his critical writings the following may be noted:

"Theodore Dreiser," "Joseph Conrad," "James Huneker," and "Puritanism as a Literary Force" in *A Book of Prefaces* (1917).

"Criticism of Criticism of Criticism," "The Late Mr. Wells," "Arnold Bennett," "The New Poetry Movement," "Six Members of the Institute," "The American Magazine," "Jack London," and "Three American Immortals" in *Prejudices: First Series* (1919).

"The National Letters," "The Sahara of the Bozart," and "The Allied Arts" in *Prejudices: Second Series* (1920).

"Huneker: A Memory," "Footnote on Criticism," "The Poet and his Art," "The Novel," and "Reflections on the Drama" in *Prejudices: Third Series* (1922).

"The American Tradition," "From a Critic's Notebook," "Toward a Realistic Aesthetic," and "The American Novel" in *Prejudices: Fourth Series* (1924).

"Journalism in America," "Souvenirs of a Book Reviewer," and "Ambrose Bierce" in *Prejudices: Sixth Series* (1927).

Selected critical essays will be found in *Selected Prejudices* (1927) and in *A Mencken Chrestomathy* (1949).

Miles, Josephine, "The Sweet and Lovely Language," KR, 6: 355–368 (Summer, 1944).

Mizener, Arthur, "The Structure of Figurative Language in Shakespeare's Sonnets," Sou R, 5: 730–747 (Spring, 1940).

Mizener, Arthur, *"Jude the Obscure* as a Tragedy," Sou R, 6: 193–213 (Summer, 1940).

Mizener, Arthur, "The Romanticism of W. B. Yeats," Sou R, 7: 601–623 (Winter, 1942).

Mizener, Arthur, "The Elizabethan Art of our Movies," KR, 4: 181–194 (Spring, 1942).

Mizener, Arthur, "Victorian Hopkins," KR, 6: 590–606 (Autumn, 1944).

Mizener, Arthur, "Scott Fitzgerald and the Imaginative Possession of American Life," Sew R, 54: 66–86 (January–March, 1946).

Mizener, Arthur, "The Novel of Manners in America," KR, 12: 1–19 (Winter, 1950).

Moore, Marianne, "The Cantos" (on Ezra Pound), P, 39: 37–50 (October, 1931).

Moore, Marianne, "If a Man Die" (on Conrad Aiken), HH, 5: 312–320 (January–March, 1932).

Moore, Marianne, "Emily Dickinson," P, 41: 219–226 (January, 1933).

Moore, Marianne, "Words for Music Perhaps" (on Yeats), P, 42: 40–44 (April, 1933).

Moore, Marianne, " 'It is Not Forbidden to Think' " (on Eliot), N, 142: 680–681 (May 27, 1935).

Moore, Marianne, "The Dial: A Retrospect," PR, 9: 52–58 (January–February, 1942).

Moore, Marianne, "Feeling and Precision," Sew R, 52: 499–507 (Autumn, 1944).

More, Paul Elmer, "Taste and Tradition," Unpopular Review," 8: 112–132 (July, 1917).

More, Paul Elmer, "Henry Adams," Unpopular Review, 10: 255–272 (October, 1918).

More, Paul Elmer, "The Modern Current in American Literature," F, 79: 127–136 (January, 1928).

More, Paul Elmer, "The Revival of Humanism," B, 71: 1–11 (March, 1930).

More, Paul Elmer, "The Cleft Eliot," SRL, 9: 233 plus (November 12, 1932).

More, Paul Elmer, "Proust: The Two Ways," AR, 1: 50–75 (April, 1933).

More, Paul Elmer, "Irving Babbitt," AR, 3: 23–40 (April, 1934).

More, Paul Elmer, "James Joyce," AR, 5: 129–157 (May, 1935).

More, Paul Elmer, "The Modernism of French Poetry," AR, 5: 329–348 (June, 1935).

Paul Elmer More's most representative writings on literature will be found in the series of volumes called Shelburne Essays, from 1904 to 1936, with the following essays especially notable:

In the First Series (1904): "The Solitude of Nathaniel Hawthorne," "The Origins of Hawthorne and Poe," and "Arthur Symons: The Two Illusions."

In the Second Series (1905): "Lafcadio Hearn," "Kipling and Fitzgerald," and "The Novels of George Meredith."

In the Third Series (1905): "The Centenary of Sainte-Beuve," "Swinburne," "Christina Rossetti," and "The Quest of a Century."

In the Fourth Series (1906): "John Keats" and "Walt Whitman."

In the Fifth Series (1908): "The Praise of Gissing," "Mrs. Gaskell," "The Centenary of Longfellow," and "James Thomson."

In the Seventh Series (1910): "Tennyson," "Criticism," "Victorian Literature," and "The Pragmatism of William James."

In the Eighth Series, titled The Drift of Romanticism (1913): "Cardinal Newman" and "Walter Pater."

In the Ninth Series, titled Aristocracy and Justice (1915): "The New Morality" and "Natural Aristocracy."

In the Eleventh Series, titled A New England Group and Others (1921): "Henry Adams," "Samuel Butler of Erewhon," and "Charles Eliot Norton."

In *New Shelburne Essays: Volume I,* titled *The Demon of the Absolute* (1928): the title essay, and "Modern Currents in American Literature," "A Note on Poe's Method," and "Henry Vaughan."

In *New Shelburne Essays: Volume III,* titled *On Being Human* (1936): the essays on Humanism, Irving Babbitt, Proust, Joyce, French Poetry listed above, and "A Scholar-Saint," "Religion and Social Discontent," and "How to Read *Lycidas*" (included in the present volume).

Muller, Herbert J., "The Worlds of Henry Miller," KR, 2: 312–318 (Summer, 1940).

Muller, Herbert J., "Pathways in Recent Criticism," Sou R, 4: 187–208 (Summer, 1939).

Muller, Herbert J., "The New Criticism in Poetry," Sou R, 6: 811–839 (Spring, 1941).

Muller, Herbert J., "The Relative and the Absolute" (an exchange with Cleanth Brooks), Sew R, 57: 357–377 (Summer, 1949).

Mumford, Lewis, "Aesthetics: A Palaver," AM, 3: 360–365 (November, 1924).

Mumford, Lewis, "The Emergence of a Past," NR, 45: 18–19 (November 25, 1925).

Mumford, Lewis, "The Writing of *Moby Dick,*" AM, 15: 482–490 (December, 1928).

Mumford, Lewis, "American Condescension and European Superiority," *Scribner's,* 87: 518–527 (May, 1930).

Mumford, Lewis, "The Image of Randolph Bourne," NR, 64: 151–152 (September 24, 1930).

Mumford, Lewis, "Thorstein Veblen," NR, 67: 314–316 (August 5, 1931).

Mumford, Lewis, "What Has 1932 Done for Literature?" At Mon, 150: 761–767 (December, 1932).

Of the books listed in Appendix I, see *The Golden Day* (1926) and *The Brown Decades* (1931).

Munson, Gorham B., "Van Wyck Brooks, his Sphere and his Encroachments," D, 78: 28–42 (January, 1925).

Munson, Gorham B., "The Dandyism of Wallace Stevens," D, 79: 413–417 (November, 1925).

Munson, Gorham B., "Embattled Humanists," B, 68: 404–410 (December, 1928).

Munson, Gorham B., "Criticism for Black Sheep," Sew R, 37: 459–477 (October, 1929).

Munson, Gorham B., "Young Critics of the Nineteen-Twenties," B, 70: 369–373 (December, 1929).

Munson, Gorham B., "American Criticism and the Fighting Hope," YR, 20: 568–582 (March, 1931).

Munson, Gorham B., "The Impracticality of the Contemporary American Writer," Sew R, 39: 257–261 (July, 1931).

Munson, Gorham B., "The Literary Profession in America," Sew R, 39: 398–406 (October, 1931).

Munson, Gorham B., "The Fledgling Years, 1916–24," Sew R, 40: 24–54 (January, 1932)

Nathan, George Jean: for his reviews and criticisms of drama since 1906 in many newspapers as well as in magazines like *The Smart Set, The American Mercury, The New Freeman,* and *Esquire,* see his published volumes, of which a selection is listed in Appendix I, as well as his recent annual on the New York theatre titled *The Theatre Book of the Year,* issued yearly since 1943.

O'Brien, Justin, "French Literature and the War," SRL, 22: 3–4 plus (June 15, 1940).

O'Brien, Justin, "On Re-reading the Modern Classics," N, 155: 579–580 (November 28, 1942).

O'Brien, Justin, "Poet on Horseback" (on Roy Campbell), KR, 4: 75–86 (Winter, 1942).

O'Brien, Justin, "Marcel Proust as a *Moraliste,*" Romantic Review, 39: 50–57 (February, 1948).

O'Connor, William Van, "André Gide and the Poet in Wartime," P, 63: 276–278 (February, 1944).

O'Connor, William Van, "This Alexandrian Criticism," AS, 14: 357–361 (July, 1945).

O'Connor, William Van, "The Direction of the Little Mag," P, 71: 281–284 (February, 1948).

O'Connor, William Van, "Wallace Stevens and Imagined Reality," WR, 12: 156–163 (Spring, 1948).

O'Connor, William Van, "The Little Magazine as a Cultural Journal," P, 72: 339–342 (September, 1948).

Olson, Elder, "Rhetoric and the Appreciation of Pope," MP, 37: 13–35 (August, 1939).

Olson, Elder, "The Argument of Longinus' *On the Sublime,*" MP, 39: 225–258 (February, 1942).

Olson, Elder, "Recent Literary Criticism," MP, 40, 275–283 (February, 1943).

Olson, Elder, "An Outline of Poetic Theory," in *Critiques and Essays in Criticism* (edited by R. W. Stallman, 1949).

Olson, Elder, "William Empson, Contemporary Criticism and Poetic Diction," MP, 47: 222–252 (May, 1950).

Parkes, Henry Bamford, "The Puritan Heresy," HH, 5: 165–190 (January–March, 1932).

Parkes, Henry Bamford, "William James," HH, 7: 6–28 (October–December, 1933).

Parkes, Henry Bamford, "The Limitations of Marxism," HH, 7: 565–581 (July–September, 1934).

Parkes, Henry Bamford, "Attitudes toward History" (on Kenneth Burke), Sou R, 3: 693–706 (Spring, 1938).

Parkes, Henry Bamford, "Some Marxist Fallacies," Sou R, 4: 474–488 (Winter, 1939).

Parkes, Henry Bamford, "Poe, Hawthorne, Melville: An Essay in Sociological Criticism," PR, 16: 157–165 (February, 1949).

Pepper, Stephen C., "The Outlook for Aesthetics," KR, 8: 179–187 (Spring, 1946).

Phillips, William, "Categories for Criticism," Sym, 4: 31–47 (January, 1933).

Phillips, William, "The Esthetic of the Founding Fathers," PR, 4: 11–21 (March, 1938).

Phillips, William, "The Devil Theory of the Dialectic," PR, 6: 82–90 (Fall, 1938).

Phillips, William, "The Intellectualists' Tradition," PR, 8: 481–490 (November–December, 1941).

Phillips, William, "Dostoevsky's Underground Man," PR, 13: 551–561 (November–December, 1946).

Porter, Katherine Anne, "A Bright Particular Faith, A.D. 1700" (on Cotton Mather), HH, 7: 246–257 (January–March, 1934).

Porter, Katherine Anne, "The Art of Katherine Mansfield," N, 145: 435–436 (October 23, 1937).

Porter, Katherine Anne, "Notes on a Criticism of Thomas Hardy," Sou R, 6: 150–161 (Summer, 1940).

Porter, Katherine Anne, "The Days Before" (on Henry James), KR, 5: 481–494 (Autumn, 1943).

Pound, Ezra, "A Few Don'ts by an Imagist," P, 1: 200–206 (March, 1913).

Pound, Ezra, "Irony, Laforgue, and Some Satire," P, 11: 93–98 (November, 1917).

Pound, Ezra, "In Explanation," "Brief Note," "A Shake Down," and "The Middle Years" (all on Henry James), Little Review, 5: 5–41 (August, 1918).

Pound, Ezra, "On Criticism in General," Criterion (London), 1: 143–156 (January, 1923).

Pound, Ezra, "Where Is American Culture?" N, 126: 443–444 (April 18, 1928).

Pound, Ezra, "Dr. Williams' Position," D, 85: 395–404 (November, 1928).

Pound, Ezra, "Small Magazines," EJ, 19: 689–704 (November, 1930).

Pound, Ezra, "Ford Madox Ford," Nineteenth Century (London), 126: 178–181 (August, 1939).

Ezra Pound's innumerable contributions to magazines and literary journals, American, English, French, and Italian, extend from 1907 to the present day. The most representative have been collected in the prose volumes listed under his name in Appendix IV, especially in *The Spirit of Romance* (1910), *Pavannes and Divisions* (1918), *Instigations* (1920), *How to Read* (1931), *The ABC of Reading* (1934), *Make It New* (1934), *Polite Essays* (1937), *Guide to Kulchur* (1938), the last-named published in America as *Culture* (1939). See also the early essay of 1913 on the possibilities of a Renaissance in American arts and literature, *Patria Mia* (published in 1950).

For representative essays, see *Make It New* (1934): "Troubadours: Their Sorts and Conditions," "Arnaut Daniel," "Notes on Elizabethan Classicists,"

"French Poets," "Henry James and Remy de Gourmont," and "Cavalcanti"; and *Polite Essays* (1937): "Mr. Housman in Little Bethel," "Hell," "The Prose Tradition in Verse," "James Joyce and Pécuchet," "Mr. Eliot's Solid Merit," "The Teacher's Mission," "How to Read," "Civilization," and "Note on Dante."

Rahv, Philip, "Franz Kafka: The Hero as Lonely Man," KR, 1: 60–74 (Winter, 1939).

Rahv, Philip, "Proletarian Literature: A Political Autopsy," Sou R, 4: 616–628 (Winter, 1939).

Rahv, Philip, "Paleface and Redskin," KR, 1: 251–256 (Summer, 1939).

Rahv, Philip, "The Dark Lady of Salem," PR, 8: 362–381 (September–October, 1941).

Rahv, Philip, "The Heiress of all the Ages" (on Henry James), PR, 10: 227–247 (May–June, 1943).

Rahv, Philip, "Concerning Tolstoy," PR, 13: 420–432 (September–October, 1946).

Rahv, Philip, "The Unfuture of Utopia," PR, 16: 743–749 (July, 1949).

Rahv, Philip, "Melville and his Critics," PR, 17: 732–735 (September–October, 1950).

See *Image and Idea* by Philip Rahv (1949) for fourteen selected essays, including some of the above, usually in revised form.

Ransom, John Crowe, "The Tense of Poetry," Sou R, 1: 221–238 (Autumn, 1935).

Ransom, John Crowe, "Yeats and his Symbols," KR, 1: 309–322 (Summer, 1939).

Ransom, John Crowe, "The Pragmatics of Art," KR, 2: 76–87 (Winter, 1940).

Ransom, John Crowe, "Yvor Winters: The Logical Critic," Sou R, 6: 558–583 (Winter, 1941).

Ransom, John Crowe, "An Address to Kenneth Burke," KR, 4: 219–237 (Spring, 1942).

Ransom, John Crowe, "The Bases of Criticism," Sew R, 52: 556–571 (Autumn, 1944).

[Cf. "Aristotle and the 'New Criticism,' " by Hoyt Trowbridge, in Sew R, 52: 537–555 (Autumn, 1944).]

Ransom, John Crowe, "On Shakespeare's Language," Sew R, 55: 181–198 (Spring, 1947).

Ransom, John Crowe, "Poetry: The Formal Analysis," KR, 9: 436–456 (Summer, 1947).

Ransom, John Crowe, "Poetry: The Final Cause," KR, 9: 640–658 (Autumn, 1947).

Ransom, John Crowe, "The Literary Criticism of Aristotle," KR, 10: 382–402 (Summer, 1948).

Ransom, John Crowe, "The Understanding of Fiction," KR, 12: 189–218 (Spring, 1950).

See also *The Kenyon Review* from 1939, *passim;* also Ransom's volumes of collected essays: in *The World's Body* (1938) especially "A Poem nearly Anonymous," "Poetry: A Note in Ontology," "The Cathartic Principle," "The Mimetic Principle," "Art and Mr. Santayana," and "Criticism, Inc."; and in *The New Criticism* (1941) "I. A. Richards: The Psychological Critic; and William Empson, his Pupil," "T. S. Eliot: The Historical Critic," "Yvor Winters: The Logical Critic," and "Wanted: An Ontological Critic."

Rice, Philip Blair, "A Modern Poet's Technique: Guillaume Apollinaire," Sym, 2: 468–483 (October, 1931).

Rice, Philip Blair, "Jeffers and the Tragic Sense," N, 141: 480–482 (October 23, 1935).

Rice, Philip Blair, "George Santayana: The Philosophei as Poet," KR, 2: 460–475 (Autumn, 1940).

Rice, Philip Blair, "Thomas Mann and the Religious Revival," KR, 7: 361–377 (Summer, 1945).

Rice, Philip Blair, "The Merging Parallels: Mann's *Doctor Faustus*," KR, 11: 199–217 (Spring, 1949).

Rice, Philip Blair, "Existentialism and the Self," KR, 12: 304–330 (Spring, 1950).

Roditi, Edouard, "Paul Valéry: Poetics as an Exact Science," KR, 6: 398–408 (Summer, 1944).

Rosenberg, Harold, "Myth and Poem," Sym, 2: 179–191 (April, 1931).

Rosenberg, Harold, "Myth and History" (on Thomas Mann), PR, 6: 19–39 (Winter, 1939).

Rosenberg, Harold, "The Profession of Poetry, or Trails through the Night for M. Maritain," PR, 9: 392–413 (September–October, 1942).

Rosenberg, Harold, "The Case of the Baffled Radical" (on Arthur Koestler), PR, 11: 100–103 (Winter, 1944).

Rosenfeld, Paul, "Carl Sandburg," B, 53: 389–396 (July, 1921).

Rosenfeld, Paul, "Sherwood Anderson," D, 72: 29–42 (January, 1922).

Rosenfeld, Paul, "Randolph Bourne," D, 75: 545–560 (December, 1923).

Rosenfeld, Paul, "D. H. Lawrence," NR, 62: 155–156 (March 26, 1930).

Rosenfeld, Paul, "An Affirmative Romantic: Phelps Putnam," B, 74: 607–613 (March, 1932).

Rosenfeld, Paul, "Authors and Politics," *Scribner's*, 93: 318–320 (May, 1933).

Rosenfeld, Paul, "Resistances to Rilke," Sou R, 4: 784–794 (Spring, 1939).

Rosenzweig, Saul, "The Ghost of Henry James," PR, 11: 436–455 (Fall, 1944). Reprinted from *Character and Personality*, XII, No. 2 (December, 1943), where it appeared as "The Ghost of Henry James: A Study in Thematic Apperception."

Rourke, Constance, "Dorothy M. Richardson," NR, 20: sup 14–15 (November 26, 1919).

Rourke, Constance, "The Genius of the Novel," NR, 29: 149–151 (January 4, 1922).

Rourke, Constance, "Our Comic Heritage," SRL, 7: 678–679 (March 21, 1931).

Rourke, Constance, "American Art: A Possible Future," *American Magazine of Art*, 28: 390–405 (July, 1935).

See the books by Constance Rourke listed in Appendix I, notably *American Humor: A Study of the National Character* (1931), and the chapters of an unfinished work which appeared as *The Roots of American Culture* (edited by Van Wyck Brooks, 1942).

Santayana, George, "Liberalism and Culture," NR, 4: 123–125 (September 4, 1915).

Santayana, George, "Materialism and Idealism in America," Living Age, 300: 583–595 (March 8, 1919).

Santayana, George, "Dickens," D, 71: 537–549 (November, 1921).

Santayana, George, "America's Young Radicals," F, 67: 371–375 (May, 1922).

Santayana, George, "An Aesthetic Soviet," D, 82: 361–370 (May, 1927).

Santayana, George, "The Genteel Tradition at Bay," SRL, 7: 502–503 (January 3, 1931), 7: 518–519 (January 10, 1931), 7: 534–535 (January 17, 1931).

Santayana, George, "Alternatives to Liberalism," SRL, 10: 761–762 (June 23, 1934).

Santayana's most important writings on aesthetics and literature appear in the following books listed in Appendix IV: *The Sense of Beauty* (1896); *Interpretations of Poetry and Religion* (1900), in which see especially the essays "Understanding, Imagination, and Mysticism," "The Absence of Religion in Shakespeare," "The Poetry of Barbarism," "Emerson," and "The Elements and Function of Poetry"; *Three Philosophical Poets: Lucretius, Dante, Goethe* (1910); *Character and Opinion in the United States* (1920); and *Obiter Scripta* (1936), in which see "The Two Idealisms," "What Is Aesthetics?" "Hamlet," "Literal and Symbolic Knowledge," and "Proust on Essences."

Schappes, Morris U., "Notes on the Concrete as Method in Criticism," Sym, 2: 315–324 (July, 1931).

Schorer, Mark, "Mythology (For the Study of William Blake)," KR, 4: 366–380 (Autumn, 1942).

Schorer, Mark, "Blake as a Religious Poet," Sew R, 54: 241–249 (April–June, 1946).

Schorer, Mark, "Technique as Discovery," HR, 1: 67–87 (Spring, 1948).

Schorer, Mark, "Fiction and the Matrix of Analogy," KR, 11: 539–560 (Autumn, 1949).

Schwartz, Delmore, "Ernest Hemingway's Literary Situation," Sou R, 3: 769–789 (Spring, 1938).

Schwartz, Delmore, "John Dos Passos and the Whole Truth," Sou R, 4: 351–367 (Autumn, 1938).

Schwartz, Delmore, "The Critical Method of R. P. Blackmur," P, 53: 28–39 (October, 1938).

Schwartz, Delmore, "The Two Audens," KR, 1: 34–45 (Winter, 1939).

Schwartz, Delmore, "*The Criterion*: 1922–1939," KR, 1: 437–450 (Autumn, 1939).

Schwartz, Delmore, "The Poetry of Allen Tate," Sou R, 5: 419–438 (Winter, 1940).

Schwartz, Delmore, "Poetry and Belief in Thomas Hardy," Sou R, 6: 64–77 (Summer, 1940).

Schwartz, Delmore, "The Fiction of William Faulkner," Sou R, 7: 145–160 (Summer, 1941).

Schwartz, Delmore, "The Isolation of Modern Poetry," KR, 3: 209–220 (Spring, 1941).

Schwartz, Delmore, "The Writings of Edmund Wilson," A, 3: 177–186 (Summer, 1942).

Schwartz, Delmore, "T. S. Eliot as the International Hero," PR, 12: 199–206 (Spring, 1945).

Shafer, Robert, "The Definition of Humanism," HH, 3: 533–557 (July–September, 1930).

Shapiro, Karl, "English Prosody and Modern Poetry," English Literary History, 14: 77–92 (June, 1947).

Shapiro, Karl, "A Farewell to Criticism," P, 71: 196–217 (January, 1948).

Shapiro, Karl, "The Meaning of the Discarded Poem," in Poets at Work (edited by Charles D. Abbott, 1948).

Shuster, George, "Thomas Hardy," Catholic World, 126: 721–729 (March, 1928).

Shuster, George, "Jacques Maritain, Revivalist," B, 70: 1–10 (September, 1929).

Shuster, George, "François Mauriac," B, 72: 466–475 (January, 1931).

Shuster, George, "Paul Bourget and Reality," B, 73: 273–283 (May, 1931).

Slochower, Harry, "Thomas Mann and Universal Culture," Sou R, 4: 726–744 (Spring, 1939).

Slochower, Harry, "John Dewey: Philosopher of the Possible," Sew R, 52: 151–168 (Winter, 1944).

Spencer, Theodore, "The Critic's Function," Sew R, 47: 552–558 (October, 1939).

Spencer, Theodore, "The Central Problem in Literary Criticism," College English, 4: 159–163 (1942).

Spencer, Theodore, "How to Criticize a Poem" (a parody), NR, 109: 816–818 (December 6, 1943).

Spingarn, J. E., "Grocer-shop Critic and Real Critic," D, 57: 96–99 (August 16, 1914).

Spingarn, J. E., "The Growth of a Literary Myth," Freeman, 7: 181–183 (May 2, 1923).

  Spingarn's important work as critic will be found in Creative Criticism and Other Essays (new and enlarged edition, 1931), in which see especially "The New Criticism," "Prose and Verse," "Dramatic Criticism and the Theatre," "Creative Connoisseurship," "The Younger Generation," "The American Critic," "The American Scholar," and "The Seven Arts and the Seven Confusions."

Stallman, Robert W., "Hardy's Hour-Glass Novel," Sew R, 55: 283–296 (April, 1947).

Stallman, Robert W., "The New Criticism and the Southern Critics," in A Southern Vanguard (edited by Allen Tate, 1947).

Stallman, Robert W., "The New Critics," in *Critiques and Essays in Criticism* (edited by Stallman, 1949).

Stauffer, Donald A., "Cooperative Criticism: A Letter from the Critical Front," KR, 4: 133–144 (Winter, 1942).

Stauffer, Donald A., "Critical Principles and a Sonnet," AS, 12: 52–62 (Winter, 1942).

Stauffer, Donald A., "Which Side Am I Supposed to Be On?: The Search for Beliefs in Auden's Poetry," VQR, 22: 570–580 (Autumn, 1946).

Stauffer, Donald A., "Poetry as Symbolic Thinking," SRL, 30: 9–10 (March 22, 1947).

Stauffer, Donald A., "W. B. Yeats and the Medium of Poetry," *English Literary History*, 15: 227–246 (September, 1948).

Stauffer, Donald A., "The Reading of a Lyric," KR, 11: 426–440 (Summer, 1949).

Stevens, Wallace, "The Noble Rider and the Sound of Words," in *The Language of Poetry* (edited by Allen Tate, 1942).

Stevens, Wallace, "The Figure of the Youth as Virile Poet," Sew R, 52: 508–529 (October, 1944).

Swallow, Alan, "An Examination of Modern Critics. 6: Yvor Winters," RMR, 9: 31–37 (Fall, 1944).

Sypher, Wylie, "The Metaphysicals and the Baroque," PR, 9: 3–17 (Winter, 1944).

Sypher, Wylie, "Connoisseur in Chaos: Wallace Stevens," PR, 13: 83–95 (Winter, 1946).

Sypher, Wylie, "Aesthetic of Revolution: The Marxist Melodrama," KR, 10: 431–444 (Summer, 1948).

Sypher, Wylie, "Gide's Cubist Novel," KR, 11: 291–309 (Spring, 1949).

Tate, Allen, "The Fallacy of Humanism," HH, 3: 234–258 (January–March, 1930).

Tate, Allen, "Irony and Humility" (on Eliot's *Ash-Wednesday*), HH, 4: 298–300 (January–March, 1931).

Tate, Allen, "New England Culture and Emily Dickinson," Sym, 3: 206–226 (April, 1932).

Tate, Allen, "The Function of the Critical Quarterly," Sou R, 1: 551–559 (Winter, 1936).

Tate, Allen, "Tension in Poetry," Sou R, 4: 101–115 (Summer, 1938).

Tate, Allen, "Hardy's Philosophic Metaphors," Sou R, 6: 99–108 (Summer, 1940).

Tate, Allen, "Literature as Knowledge: Comment and Comparison," Sou R, 6: 629–657 (Spring, 1941).

Tate, Allen, "Dostoevsky's Hovering Fly," Sew R, 51: 353–369 (Summer, 1943).

Tate, Allen, "Techniques of Fiction." Sew R, 52: 210–225 (Spring, 1944).

Tate, Allen, "A Reading of Keats," AS, 15: 55–63 (January, 1946), 15: 189–197 (April, 1946).

Tate, Allen, "Longinus," HR, 1: 344–361 (Autumn, 1948).

Tate, Allen, "Johnson on the Metaphysicals," KR, 11: 377–394 (Summer, 1949).

Tate, Allen, "Our Cousin, Mr. Poe," PR, 16: 1207–1219 (December, 1949).

  See also in *Reactionary Essays* by Allen Tate (1936) the essays "Three Types of Poetry," "Humanism and Naturalism," "The Profession of Letters in the South," and the essays on E. A. Robinson, MacLeish's *Conquistador*, Edna St. Vincent Millay, and E. E. Cummings; and in *Reason in Madness* (1941) the essays "The Present Function of Criticism," "Literature as Knowledge," "Understanding Modern Poetry," "Narcissus as Narcissus," and "Liberalism and Tradition."

  Further essays will be found in *The Hovering Fly* (1949); and a collection of essays from these three volumes, including most of those listed above, appears in *On the Limits of Poetry: Selected Essays 1928–1948* (1948).

Taupin, René, "The Classicism of T. S. Eliot," Sym, 2: 64–82 (January, 1932).

Thorp, Willard, "The Present State of American Literary Scholarship," Sew R, 53: 325–331 (Spring, 1945).

Trilling, Diana, "Men, Women, and Sex," PR, 17: 365–378 (April, 1950).

Trilling, Diana, "A Memorandum on the Hiss Case," PR, 17: 484–500 (May–June, 1950).

  For reviews and essays on current fiction, see *The Nation, passim,* 1943–1949.

Trilling, Lionel, "The America of John Dos Passos," PR, 4: 26–32 (April, 1938).

Trilling, Lionel, " 'Elements that Are Wanting,' " (on Eliot's *Idea of a Christian Society*), PR, 7: 367–379 (September–October, 1940).

Trilling, Lionel, "Sherwood Anderson," KR, 3: 293–302 (Summer, 1941).

Trilling, Lionel, "The Sense of the Past," PR, 9: 229–241 (May–June, 1942).

Trilling, Lionel, "A Note on Art and Neurosis," PR, 12: 41–48 (Winter, 1945).

Trilling, Lionel, "Sermon on a Text from Whitman," N, 160: 215–216, 218–220 (February 24, 1945).

Trilling, Lionel, "The Life of the Novel," KR, 8: 658–667 (Autumn, 1946).

Trilling, Lionel, "Manners, Morals and the Novel," KR, 12: 477–497 (Winter, 1948).

Trilling, Lionel, "Sex and Science: The Kinsey Report," PR, 15: 460–476 (April, 1948).

Trilling, Lionel, "Art and Fortune," PR, 15: 1271–1292 (December, 1948).

  See also *Matthew Arnold* by Lionel Trilling (1939) and *E. M. Forster* (1943), as well as the collection of critical papers *The Liberal Imagination* (1950), in which see especially the essays (in addition to those listed above, most of which appear here in a revised form) "The Princess Casamassima," "The Function of the Little Magazine," "Huckleberry Finn," "Kipling," "The Immortality Ode," "F. Scott Fitzgerald," and "The Meaning of a Literary Idea."

Troy, William, "Proust in Retrospect," Sym, 2: 385–392 (July, 1931).

Troy, William, "The Letters of D. H. Lawrence," Sym, 4: 85–94 (January, 1933).

Troy, William, "The D. H. Lawrence Myth," PR, 4: 3–13 (January, 1937).

Troy, William, "Thomas Mann: Myth and Reason," PR, 5: 24–32 (June, 1938).

Troy, William, "On Re-reading Balzac: The Artist as Scapegoat," KR, 2: 333–344 (Summer, 1940).

Troy, William, "Stendhal: In Quest of Henri Beyle," PR, 9: 3–22 (January–February, 1942).

Troy, William, "Paul Valéry and the Poetic Universe," QRL, 3: 232–239 (1946).

Tyler, Parker, "The Impressionism of Marcel Proust," KR, 8: 46–54 (Winter, 1946).

Unger, Leonard, "T. S. Eliot's Rose Garden: A Persistent Theme," Sou R, 7: 667–689 (Spring, 1942).

Unger, Leonard, "Keats and the Music of Autumn," WR, 14: 275–284 (Summer, 1950).

Van Doren, Carl, "Literature and a New Heroic Age," N, 107: 644–645 (November 30, 1918).

Van Doren, Carl, "On Studying Biography," N, 109: 244–245 (August 23, 1919).

Van Doren, Carl, "The Flower of Puritanism," N, 111: 649–650 (December 8, 1920).

Van Doren, Carl, "The Soil of the Puritans," Century, 105: 629–636 (February, 1923).

Van Doren, Carl, "American Realism," NR, 34: 107–109 (March 21, 1923).

Van Doren, Carl, "The American Rhythm," Century, 107: 150–156 (November, 1923).

Van Doren, Carl, "Stephen Crane," Am Merc, 1: 11–14 (January, 1924).

Van Doren, Carl, "Lucifer in Nantucket" (on Melville), Century, 110: 494–501 (August, 1925).

Van Doren, Carl, "Toward a New Canon," N, 134: 429–430 (April 13, 1932). See also "What Is American Literature?" (included in The Portable Carl Van Doren, 1945) and The American Novel (revised edition, 1940), and for collected essays The Roving Critic (1923) and Many Minds (1924).

Van Doren, Mark, "The Progress of Poetry," N, 112: 883–885 (June 23, 1921).

Van Doren, Mark, "W. H. Hudson," N, 115: 373–374 (October 11, 1922).

Van Doren, Mark, "Thomas Hardy, Poet," N, 126: 151–152 (February 8, 1928).

Van Doren, Mark, "What Is a Poet?" N, 134: 624–625 (June 1, 1932).

Van Doren, Mark, "The Art of American Fiction," N, 138: 471–473 (April 25, 1934).

Van Doren, Mark, "The Unity of Shakespeare," N, 138: 595–596 (May 23, 1934).

Van Doren, Mark, "Walt Whitman, Stranger," Am Merc, 35: 277–285 (July, 1935).

Van Doren, Mark, "The Achievements of Intellectualist Poetry," AR, 8: 449–456 (February, 1937).

Van Doren, Mark, "Good Critics Rare and Common," N, 154: 94–95 (January 24, 1942).

Van Doren, Mark, "Poets and Trimmers," Sew R, 53: 52–55 (January–March, 1945).

Van Doren, Mark, "The Divine Comedy," Sew R, 54: 349–395 (July–September, 1946).

Van Doren, Mark, "The Teaching of Literature: The Riches and the Terrors," Sew R, 55: 569–571 (October–December, 1947).

Van Doren, Mark, "The Happy Critic," N, 168: 663 (June 11, 1949).
   See also the books listed in Appendix I, notably *Henry David Thoreau* (1916), *The Poetry of John Dryden* (new edition, 1946), *Shakespeare* (1939), and for essays and studies *The Private Reader* (1942) and *The Noble Voice* (1946).

Vigneron, Pierre Robert, "Genesis of *Swann*," PR, 8: 460–475 (November–December, 1941).

Vivas, Eliseo, "The Legacy of Sigmund Freud: Philosophical," KR, 2: 173–185 (Spring, 1940).

Vivas, Eliseo, "Lawrence's Problems," KR, 3: 83–94 (Winter, 1941).

Vivas, Eliseo, "The New Naturalism," KR, 3: 445–459 (Autumn, 1941).

Vivas, Eliseo, "Henry and William" (on the Jameses), KR, 5: 580–594 (Autumn, 1943).

Vivas, Eliseo, "The Objective Correlative of T. S. Eliot," *American Bookman*, 1: 7–18 (Winter, 1944).

Vivas, Eliseo, "Kafka's Distorted Mask," KR, 10: 51–69 (Winter, 1948).

Vivas, Eliseo, "The Objective Basis of Criticism," WR, 12: 197–210 (Summer, 1948).

Warren, Austin, "The Mysticism of Richard Crashaw," Sym, 4: 135–155 (April, 1933).

Warren, Austin, "The Novels of E. M. Forster," AR, 9: 226–251 (Summer, 1937).

Warren, Austin, "Edward Taylor's Poetry: Colonial Baroque," KR, 3: 355–371 (Summer, 1941).

Warren, Austin, "Religio Poetae" (on Yeats), Sou R, 7: 624–638 (Winter, 1942).

Warren, Austin, "Myth and Dialectic in the Later Novels" (on Henry James), KR, 5: 551–568 (Autumn, 1943).

Warren, Austin, "Instress of Inscape" (on G. M. Hopkins), KR, 6: 369–382 (Summer, 1944).

Warren, Austin, "The Case of Vachel Lindsay," A, 6: 320–339 (August, 1946).
   See also *Richard Crashaw: A Study in Baroque Sensibility* (1939) and *Theory of Literature* (written with René Wellek, 1948), and for selected essays, including some of the above in revised form, *Rage for Order* (1947), especially those on George Herbert, Hopkins, Yeats, Hawthorne, Kafka, E. M. Forster, and Henry James.

Warren, Robert Penn, "T. S. Stribling: A Paragraph in the History of Critical Realism," AR, 2: 463–486 (February, 1934).

Warren, Robert Penn, "The Hamlet of Thomas Wolfe," AR, 5: 191–208 (September, 1935).

Warren, Robert Penn, "The Reading of Modern Poetry" (with Cleanth Brooks), AR, 8: 435–449 (February, 1937).

Warren, Robert Penn, "Katherine Anne Porter," KR, 4: 29–42 (Winter, 1942).

Warren, Robert Penn, "Pure and Impure Poetry," KR, 5: 228–254 (Spring, 1943).

Warren, Robert Penn, "The Love and the Separateness in Miss Welty," KR, 6: 246–259 (Spring, 1944).

Warren, Robert Penn, "Melville the Poet," KR, 8: 208–223 (Spring, 1946).

Warren, Robert Penn, "A Poem of Pure Imagination" (on Coleridge's "Ancient Mariner"), KR, 8: 391–427 (Summer, 1946).

Warren, Robert Penn, "Hemingway," KR, 9: 1–28 (Winter, 1947).

Weiss, T., "T. S. Eliot and the Courtyard Revolution," Sew R, 54: 289–307 (April–June, 1946).

Wellek, René, "Literary Criticism and Philosophy," Scrutiny (Cambridge, England), 5: 375–383 (March, 1937).

Wellek, René, "Literary History," in Literary Scholarship (1941).

Wellek, René, "Periods and Movements in Literary History," in English Institute Annual: 1940 (1941).

Wellek, René, "The Parallelism between Literature and the Arts," in English Institute Annual: 1941 (1942).

Wellek, René, "The Mode of Existence of a Literary Work of Art," Sou R, 7: 735–754 (Spring, 1942).

Wellek, René, "Six Types of Literary History," in English Institute Essays: 1946 (1947).

See also Theory of Literature (written with Austin Warren, 1948).

West, Ray B., Jr., "R. P. Blackmur," RMR, 8: 139–145 (Summer, 1944).

West, Ray B., Jr., "Ernest Hemingway," Sew R, 53: 120–135 (January–March, 1945).

West, Ray B., Jr., "Portrait of the Artist as American" (on Hart Crane), WR, 12: 247–251 (Summer, 1948).

Wheelwright, Philip, "Poetry and Logic," Sym, 1: 440–457 (Autumn, 1930).

Wheelwright, Philip, "On the Semantics of Poetry," KR, 2: 263–283 (Summer, 1940).

Wheelwright, Philip, "The Failure of Naturalism," KR, 3: 460–472 (Autumn, 1941).

Wheelwright, Philip, "The Burnt Norton Trilogy" (on T. S. Eliot), Chimera, 1: 7–18 (1942).

Wheelwright, Philip, "Poetry, Myth, and Reality," in The Language of Poetry (edited by Allen Tate, 1942).

Whipple, T. K., "Willa Cather," The Literary Review, 4: 331–332 (December 8, 1923).

Whipple, T. K., "Robert Frost," The Literary Review, 4: 605–606 (March 22, 1924).

See Spokesmen: Modern Writers and American Life (1928) for essays on

Henry Adams, E. A. Robinson, Theodore Dreiser, Robert Frost, Sherwood Anderson, Willa Cather, Carl Sandburg, Vachel Lindsay, Sinclair Lewis, Eugene O'Neill, "The Poetic Temper," and "The American Situation"; and *Study Out the Land* (1943), especially the essays "Machinery, Magic, and Art," "American Sagas," "The American Predicament," "The American Land," "The Myth of the Old West," "Dos Passos and the U.S.A.," "Jack London—Wonder Boy," "Steinbeck," "The American Way," "Poetry and Morals," and "Literature as Action."

Williams, William Carlos, "Marianne Moore," D, 78: 393–401 (May, 1925).

Williams, William Carlos, "Federico Garcia Lorca," KR, 1: 148–158 (Spring, 1939).

Williams, William Carlos, "An Approach to the Poem," in *English Institute Essays: 1947* (1948).

Williamson, George, "Libertine Donne," *Philological Quarterly*, 13: 276–291 (July, 1934).

Williamson, George, "Textual Difficulties in the Interpretation of Donne's Poetry," MP, 38: 37–72 (August, 1940).

Williamson, George, "The Structure of *The Waste Land*," MP, 47: 191–206 (February, 1950).

Wilson, Edmund, "A. E. Housman," NR, 92: 206–210 (September 29, 1937).

Wilson, Edmund, "Flaubert's Politics," PR, 4: 13–24 (December, 1937).

Wilson, Edmund, "The Myth of the Marxist Dialectic," PR, 6: 66–81 (Fall, 1938).

Wilson, Edmund, "Ernest Hemingway," At Mon, 164: 36–46 (July, 1939).

Wilson, Edmund, "H. C. Earwicker and Family" (on James Joyce), NR, 99: 203–206 (June 28, 1939) and 99: 270–274 (July 12, 1939).

Wilson, Edmund, "Dickens and the Marshalsea Prison," At Mon, 165: 473–483 (April, 1940) and 165: 681–691 (May, 1940).

Wilson, Edmund, "Archibald MacLeish and 'The Word,'" NR, 103: 30–32 (July 1, 1940).

Wilson, Edmund, "The Kipling That Nobody Read," At Mon, 167: 201–214 (February, 1941) and 167: 340–354 (March, 1941).

    See *The Dial*, 1921–1929 *passim*, *The New Republic*, 1926–1941, *passim*, and *The New Yorker*, 1944–1950, *passim*, for contributions to those magazines.

    See *Axel's Castle* (1931) for essays on "Symbolism," W. B. Yeats, Paul Valéry, Marcel Proust, Gertrude Stein, and "Axel and Rimbaud," as well as those on James Joyce and T. S. Eliot included in the present volume.

    See *The Triple Thinkers* (revised edition, 1948) for essays on "Mr. More and the Mithraic Bull," "Is Verse a Dying Technique?" "In Honor of Pushkin," "A. E. Housman," "The Politics of Flaubert," "The Ambiguity of Henry James," "John Jay Chapman," "Bernard Shaw at Eighty," "Morose Ben Jonson," and "The Historical Interpretation of Literature," as well as "Marxism and Literature" included in the present volume.

    See *The Wound and the Bow* (1941, 1947) for the essays "Dickens: The Two Scrooges," "The Kipling That Nobody Read," "Justice to Edith Wharton," "Hemingway: Gauge of Morale," "The Dream of H. C. Earwicker," "Philoctetes: The Wound and the Bow."

See *Classics and Commercials: A Literary Chronicle of the Forties* (1950) for essays and reviews on the books of the decade 1940–1950.

Wimsatt, William Kurtz, Jr., "The Intentional Fallacy" (with M. C. Beardsley), Sew R, 54: 468–488 (July–September, 1946).

Wimsatt, William Kurtz, Jr., "The Structure of the 'Concrete Universal,'" PMLA, 62: 262–280 (March, 1947).

Wimsatt, William Kurtz, Jr., "Poetry and Morals," *Thought*, 23: 281–299 (June, 1948).

Wimsatt, William Kurtz, Jr., "The Affective Fallacy" (with M. C. Beardsley), Sew R, 57: 31–55 (January–March, 1949).

Winters, Yvor, "Holiday and Day of Wrath" (on Marianne Moore), P, 26: 39–44 (April, 1925).

Winters, Yvor, "The Extension and Reintegration of the Human Spirit Through the Poetry Mainly French and American since Poe and Baudelaire," in *The American Caravan* (No. 3, 1929).

Winters, Yvor, "The Symbolist Influence" (on the French Influence on American Poetry), HH, 4: 607–618 (July–September, 1931).

Winters, Yvor, "Traditional Mastery" (on Robert Bridges), HH, 5: 321–327 (January–March, 1932).

Winters, Yvor, "Poets and Others," HH, 4: 675–686 (July–September, 1932).

Winters, Yvor, "T. Sturge Moore," HH, 6: 534–545 (April–June, 1933).

Winters, Yvor, "The Sixteenth Century Lyric in England," P, 53: 258–272 (February, 1939), 53: 320–335 (March, 1939), 54: 35–51 (April, 1939).

Winters, Yvor, "T. S. Eliot: The Illusion of Reaction," KR, 3: 7–30 (Winter, 1941), 3: 221–239 (Spring, 1941).

Winters, Yvor, "The Poetry of Gerard Manley Hopkins," HR, 1: 455–476 (Winter, 1949) and 2: 61–93 (Spring, 1949).

See *Primitivism and Decadence: A Study of American Experimental Poetry* (1937); *Maule's Curse: Seven Studies in the History of American Obscurantism* (1938) for essays on Hawthorne, Cooper, Melville, Poe, Jones Very and Emerson, Emily Dickinson, and Henry James; *The Anatomy of Nonsense* (1943) for essays on Henry Adams, Wallace Stevens, T. S. Eliot, and John Crowe Ransom; and *In Defense of Reason* (1947) for a collection of the foregoing three volumes with the addition of an essay on Hart Crane and *The Bridge*.

Young, Stark, "Ideas in Art," *Theatre Arts Monthly*, 7: 275–283 (October, 1923).

Young, Stark, "Duse," No Am, 218: 776–784 (December, 1923).

Young, Stark, "Isadora Duncan," NR, 57: 43–44 (November 28, 1928).

See *The New Republic*, 1921–47, *passim*, for reviews and articles on the drama forming a critical chronicle of the New York theatre during those twenty-six years. Some of these writings were collected in *The Flower in Drama* (1923), *The Three Fountains* (1924), *Glamour* (1925), *The Theatre* (1927), and *Immortal Shadows* (1949).

Zabel, Morton Dauwen, "Hardy in Defense of his Art: The Aesthetic of Incongruity," Sou R, 6: 125–149 (Summer, 1940).

Zabel, Morton Dauwen, "Two Years of Poetry: 1937–39," Sou R, 5: 568–60ᶠ (Winter, 1940).

Zabel, Morton Dauwen, "Rimbaud: Life and Legend," PR, 7: 268–282 (July–August, 1940).

Zabel, Morton Dauwen, "The Whole of Housman," N, 150: 684–686 (June 1, 1940).

Zabel, Morton Dauwen, "The Poet on Capitol Hill" (Archibald MacLeish), PR, 8: 1–17 (January–February, 1941) and 8: 128–158 (March–April, 1941).

Zabel, Morton Dauwen, "Conrad: The Secret Sharer," NR, 104: 567–584 (April 21, 1941).

Zabel, Morton Dauwen, "The Thinking of the Body: Yeats in the Autobiographies," Sou R, 7: 562–590 (Winter, 1942).

Zabel, Morton Dauwen, "Yeats: The Image and the Book," N, 156: 348–350 (March 6, 1943).

Zabel, Morton Dauwen, "Joseph Conrad: Chance and Recognition," Sew R, 53: 1–22 (Winter, 1945).

Zabel, Morton Dauwen, "Willa Cather," N, 164: 713–716 (July 14, 1947).

Zabel, Morton Dauwen, "Dickens: The Reputation Revised," N, 169: 279–281 (September 17, 1949).

Zukovsky, Louis, "Henry Adams: A Criticism in Autobiography," HH, 3: 333–354 (April–June, 1930), 3: 518–530 (July–September, 1930), 4: 46–72 (October–December, 1930).

Zukovsky, Louis, "American Poetry: 1920–30," Sym, 2: 60–84 (January–March, 1931).

For a selected list of critical essays by American critics since 1951, see Appendix VII, page 891 and following.

APPENDIX VI

A Note on Contemporary English Criticism

THOUGH contemporary criticism in England lies outside the scope of the present volume, its relations with American criticism are close and some of its relevant activities must be noted.

English criticism at the end of the Nineteenth Century fell into several fairly distinct categories. There was a continuation of the line that had been sponsored in the Romantic and Victorian periods by Wordsworth, Coleridge, Hazlitt, Carlyle, Ruskin, Mill, and most influentially by Matthew Arnold: it now appeared in an attenuated or popular form in the work of men like R. H. Hutton, Walter Bagehot, Walter Besant, Robert Louis Stevenson, George Saintsbury, Edmund Gosse, and a new age of literary journalism. There was also the activity, usually resisting this tradition, of the newer aesthetic critics under the leadership of Walter Pater, whose disciples numbered John Addington Symonds, Arthur Symons, Vernon Lee, Lionel Johnson, George Moore, Oscar Wilde, the youthful William Butler Yeats, and the men of the 'nineties. These asserted an alliance with the aesthetic and impressionist criticism of France and came to exert a marked influence on Americans of similar tastes—James Huneker, Lafcadio Hearn, Lewis E. Gates, Edgar Saltus, Percival Pollard. There was also the work in England of Henry James, with its marked effect on the criticism and techniques of fiction. There was likewise the special case of Bernard Shaw, who brought his social and political purposes into combination with criticism by producing the most brilliant musical and dramatic journalism of modern times and who, more than anyone else, fathered the work in America of such men as Huneker, Mencken, Nathan, and their followers. These several critical activities in England continued well into the first and second decades of the Twentieth Century.

Around 1908 or 1910 a new phase asserted itself. It derived on one side from the French and English aesthetic developments of the 'nineties and now found spokesmen in Ford Madox Hueffer (Ford), in T. E. Hulme, in the American Ezra Pound, and the men who made Hueffer's magazine *The English Review* (in 1908–1909), the Imagist movement, Wyndham Lewis' *Blast*, Vorticism, A. R. Orage's journal *The New Age*, and the new poetry of 1910–1920 their centers of activity. The emphasis here was on a new discipline in the form and style of poetry and fiction, on a reassertion of classical principles and models (particularly as advocated by Hulme and Pound), on an antiprovincial alliance with French and European standards, and on a renewed interest in both classical and experimental forms of writing. Against this activity stood a revival of traditionalism among the "Georgian" poets and critics, whose spokesmen were Robert Bridges, Lascelles Abercrombie, Laurence Binyon, G. K. Chesterton, Edward Thomas, Harold Monro, and J. C. Squire. The combat between these factions showed the basic issues and positions in English criticism in the decade 1910–1920.

A fresh stimulus to the historical and textual study of literature also came, after 1900, from academic quarters. Here the name to be emphasized is that of A. C. Bradley, whose famous book on *Shakespearean Tragedy* appeared in 1904 and initiated a new age in the interpretation of Shakespeare and classical English literature in the work of such university men as Gilbert Murray, W. P. Ker, Herbert J. C. Grierson, H. W. Garrod, W. W. Greg, John Dover Wilson, G. Wilson Knight, and C. M. Bowra.

By 1920 the work and influence of T. S. Eliot had asserted itself, notably with the publication of his first book of critical essays, *The Sacred Wood* in 1920, and presently, after 1922, through his editorship of *The Criterion*. In the course of the next thirty years his role in English poetry and criticism became dominant. The work of John Middleton Murry in his earlier years, particularly during his brief editorship of *The Athenaeum* (1919–1920) and his later editorship of *The Adelphi*, also counted in this decade, as did the art criticism of Clive Bell and Roger Fry, with their resistance to the Ruskinian tradition of critical moralism and their insistence on the formal and structural properties of the plastic arts. Another important factor made its appearance in the new semantic, analytical, and interpretational investigation of literature and the related arts that was carried on by I. A. Richards, C. K. Ogden, and their disciples following the publication of a series of influential volumes by these men—*The Foundations of Aesthetics* (1922), *The Meaning of Meaning* (1923), *Principles of Literary Criticism* (1924), and *Practical Criticism* (1929). Contrasting with these experimental and revisionist programs was a continuing activity in criticism of a more personal, belletristic order in the hands of writers like Lytton Strachey, Virginia Woolf, E. M. Forster, Percy Lubbock, Katherine Mansfield, Aldous Huxley, Desmond MacCarthy, Peter Quennell, Harold Nicolson, and the Sitwells. But the serious critical activity of the 1920's was dominated by T. S. Eliot and by I. A. Richards, whose differing but in some respects complementary ideas found issue in the work of followers (or dissenters) like Herbert Read, Edwin Muir, Edgell Rickword and Bertram Higgins during their editorship of *The Calendar of Modern Letters* (1925–1927), and the Cambridge group that included Richards' pupil William Empson, and F. R. Leavis at Downing College.

In the 1930's the work of Eliot, Richards, Empson, Muir, and Read continued, but perhaps the most important single activity was that which centered at Cambridge in the work of F. R. Leavis and his magazine *Scrutiny*, founded in 1932. This journal, originating in the programs laid down by Eliot and Richards, soon developed a purpose and standard of its own, emphasizing the formal and stylistic analysis of literature but also insisting on the relevance of critical standards to culture and education in arguments that descend from the tradition of Bentham, Coleridge, Arnold, and Mill. The books of Leavis and his collaborators—Q. D.

Leavis, L. C. Knights, Denys Thompson, D. W. Harding, and Martin Turnell among them—as well as the quarterly issues of *Scrutiny*, form the outstanding critical program in England during the past two decades. Psychological and psychoanalytical method in criticism has also had its sponsors, in Herbert Read and Ernest Jones notably; so has the Marxist theory of literature, especially in books by Christopher Caudwell, John Strachey, Ralph Fox, R. D. Charques, and Alick West.

The literary monthly *Horizon* (1940–1949), under the editorship of Cyril Connolly, formed a center of original work in writing and criticism during the 1940's, with the younger generation of English talents—W. H. Auden, Stephen Spender, George Orwell, Louis MacNeice—contributing to its pages. That activity is still in progress in 1950; and while the work of Eliot, Richards, and Leavis remains paramount in the critical developments of the past quarter-century, a generation of younger critical talents, usually recognizable as continuators of the ideas or methods of these men, has become evident in the years since 1945.

The following is a short selective bibliography of books of English criticism in the Twentieth Century, with emphasis on those of the period from 1920 to the present day:

Abercrombie, Lascelles.   *Thomas Hardy: A Critical Study* (1912).
    Principles of English Prosody (1923).
    The Idea of Great Poetry (1925).
    Romanticism (1926).
    Poetry: Its Music and Meaning (1932).
    Principles of Literary Criticism (1932).
Aldington, Richard.   *Literary Studies and Reviews* (1924).
Auden, W. H.   See Appendix IV.
Barfield, Owen.   *Poetic Diction: A Study in Meaning* (1928).
Bates, H. E.   *The Modern Short Story: A Survey* (1942).
Bell, Clive.   *Art* (1914).
Bennett, Joan.   *Four Metaphysical Poets* (1944).
    Virginia Woolf (1943).
Bentley, Eric.   See Appendix IV.
Blunden, Edmund.   *Nature in English Literature* (1929).
    Votive Tablets: Studies chiefly Appreciative of English Authors and Books (1931).
    The Mind's Eye: Essays (1934).
    Shelley (1946).
Bodkin, Maud.   *Archetypal Patterns in Poetry* (1934).
Bowen, Elizabeth.   *Collected Impressions* (1950).
Bowra, C. M.   *The Heritage of Symbolism* (1943).
    The Creative Experiment (1949).
Bradbrook, M. C.   *Joseph Conrad: Poland's English Genius* (1942).
    Ibsen, the Norwegian: A Revaluation (1946).

Bradley, Andrew C.   Shakespearean Tragedy (1904).
   Oxford Lectures on Poetry (1909, 1926).
Bridges, Robert.   Milton's Prosody, with a Chapter on Accentual Verse (revised, 1921).
   Collected Essays and Papers (1927–1930).
Bronowski, J.   The Poet's Defense (1939).
   A Man without a Mask (on Blake, 1947).
Burdett, Osbert.   The Beardsley Period (1925).
   Critical Essays (1927).
Caudwell, Christopher.   Illusion and Reality (1937).
   Studies in a Dying Culture (1939).
Cecil, David.   Hardy the Novelist (1946).
Charques, R. D.   Contemporary Literature and Social Revolution (1933).
Collingwood, R. G.   The Principles of Art (1938).
Connolly, Cyril.   Enemies of Promise (1939).
   The Unquiet Grave (by "Palinurus," 1945).
   The Condemned Playground: Essays 1927–1944 (1946).
Conrad, Joseph.   Notes on Life and Letters (1921).
   Prefaces to his Works (edited by Edward Garnett, 1937).
Crankshaw, Edward.   Joseph Conrad: Some Aspects of the Art of the Novel (1936).
Day Lewis, Cecil.   A Hope for Poetry (1934).
   The Poetic Image (1947).
Dobrée, Bonamy.   The Lamp and the Lute (1929). Modern Prose Style (1934).
Eliot, T. S.   See Appendix IV.
Empson, William.   Seven Types of Ambiguity (1930).
   Some Versions of Pastoral (1935; American edition: English Pastoral Poetry, 1938).
Ford, Ford Madox (Hueffer).   The Critical Attitude (1911).
   Henry James: A Critical Study (1913).
   Joseph Conrad: A Personal Remembrance (1924).
   The March of Literature (1938).
Forster, E. M.   Aspects of the Novel (1927).
   Abinger Harvest (collected essays, 1936).
Fox, Ralph.   The Novel and the People (1937).
Frazer, James M.   The Golden Bough: A Study in Magic and Religion (shorter version, 1922).
Fry, Roger.   The Artist and Psychoanalysis (1924).
Garrod, H. W.   The Profession of Poetry (1929).
   Poetry and the Criticism of Life (1931).
   The Study of Poetry (1936).
Gaunt, William.   The Aesthetic Adventure (1945).
Gilby, Thomas.   Poetic Experience: An Introduction to the Thomist Aesthetic (1934).
Gosse, Edmund.   Books on the Table (1921).

Aspects and Impressions (1922).

Selected Essays (1928).

Granville-Barker, Harley. *Prefaces to Shakespeare* (2 volumes, 1947).

Graves, Robert. *On English Poetry* (1922).

Poetic Unreason and Other Studies (1925).

A Survey of Modernist Poetry (with Laura Riding, 1927).

The Reader Over Your Shoulder (with Alan Hodge, 1943).

Grierson, H. J. C. *Metaphysical Lyrics and Poems of the Seventeenth Century* (edited, 1921).

The Background of English Literature (1925).

Hopkins, Gerard Manley. *The Letters of Gerard Manley Hopkins to Robert Bridges and The Correspondence of Gerard Manley Hopkins and Richard Watson Dixon* (edited by Claude Colleer Abbott, 2 volumes, 1935).

The Notebooks and Papers of Gerard Manley Hopkins (edited by Humphry House, 1937).

Further Letters of Gerard Manley Hopkins (edited by Abbott, 1938).

Housman, A. E. *The Name and Nature of Poetry* (1933).

Hulme, T. E. *Speculations* (edited by Herbert Read, 1924).

Ker, W. P. *The Art of Poetry* (1920).

Collected Essays (edited by Charles Whibley, 2 volumes, 1925).

Form and Style in Poetry (1928).

Knight, G. Wilson. *The Wheel of Fire* (1930).

The Imperial Theme (1931).

The Shakespearean Tempest (1932).

The Burning Oracle (1939).

The Starlit Dome (1941).

The Olive and the Sword (1941).

Knights, L. C. *How Many Children Had Lady Macbeth?* (1933).

Explorations: Essays in Criticism (1946).

Lawrence, D. H. *Psychoanalysis and the Unconscious* (1921).

Fantasia of the Unconscious (1922).

Studies in Classic American Literature (1923).

Pornography and Obscenity (1929).

Assorted Articles (1930).

Leavis, F. R. *Mass Civilization and Minority Culture* (1930).

New Bearings in English Poetry (1932).

How to Teach Reading: A Primer for Ezra Pound (1933).

For Continuity (1933).

Culture and Environment (with Denys Thompson, 1933).

Towards Standards of Criticism: Selections from "The Calendar of Modern Letters," 1925–1927 (edited, 1933).

Determinations: Critical Essays (edited, 1934).

Revaluation: Tradition and Development in English Poetry (1936).

Education and the University (1943).

The Great Tradition (1948).

See also *The Importance of Scrutiny* (essays collected from *Scrutiny*, 1932–1948, edited by Eric Bentley, 1948).

Leavis, Q. D.   *Fiction and the Reading Public* (1932).

Lewis, C. S.   *The Personal Heresy* (with E. M. W. Tillyard, 1939).

Liddell, Robert.   *A Treatise on the Novel* (1947).

Listowell, W. F.   *A Critical History of Modern Aesthetics* (1933).

Lubbock, Percy.   *The Craft of Fiction* (1921).

Lucas, F. L.   *Authors Dead and Living* (1926).
      The Decline and Fall of the Romantic Ideal (1936).

MacCarthy, Desmond.   *Portraits* (1931).
      Criticism: Collected Essays (1932).

MacNeice, Louis.   *Modern Poetry: A Personal Essay* (1938).
      The Poetry of W. B. Yeats (1941).

Mansfield, Katherine.   *Novels and Novelists* (1930).

Maugham, W. Somerset.   *The Summing Up* (1938).

Mégroz, R. L.   *Joseph Conrad's Mind and Method* (1931).
      Modern English Poetry: 1882–1932 (1933).

Meynell, Alice.   *Hearts of Controversy* (1917).
      The Second Person Singular and Other Essays (1921).

Moore, George.   *Avowals* (1919).
      Conversations in Ebury Street (1924).

Moore, T. Sturge.   *Art and Life* (1910).
      Armour for Aphrodite (1929).

Mortimer, Raymond.   *Channel Packet* (1942)

Muir, Edwin.   *We Moderns* (1918).
      Latitudes (1924).
      Transition: Essays on Contemporary Literature (1926).
      The Structure of the Novel (1928).
      The Present Age from 1914 (1939).
      Essays on Literature and Society (1948).

Murry, J. Middleton.   *Aspects of Literature* (1920).
      Countries of the Mind: Essays in Literary Criticism (1922).
      The Problem of Style (1922).
      Keats and Shakespeare (1925).
      D. H. Lawrence: Two Essays (1932).
      Shakespeare (1936).

Orage, A. R.   *Readers and Writers* (1922).
      The Art of Reading (1930).
      Selected Essays and Critical Writings (edited by Herbert Read and Denis Saurat, 1935).

Orwell, George.   *Inside the Whale* (1940).
      Dickens, Dali, and Others (1946; in England as *Critical Essays*, 1946).

Peacock, Ronald.   *The Poet in the Theatre* (1946).

Potter, Stephen.   *The Muse in Chains* (1937).

Pritchett, V. S.   *In My Good Books* (1942).
      The Living Novel (1946).

Why Do I Write? (an exchange with Elizabeth Bowen and Graham Greene, 1948).

Quennell, Peter. *Baudelaire and the Symbolists* (1929).

Rajan, B., ed. *Focus* (No. 3: *T. S. Eliot: A Study of his Writings by Several Hands*, 1947).

   Focus (No. 4: *The Novelist as Thinker*, 1948).

Read, Herbert. *Reason and Romanticism: Essays in Literary Criticism* (1926).

   English Prose Style (1928).

   Phases of English Poetry (1928).

   The Sense of Glory: Essays in Criticism (1929).

   Julien Benda and the New Humanism (1930).

   Wordsworth (1930).

   Form in Modern Poetry (1932).

   In Defense of Shelley and Other Essays (1936).

   Art and Society (1937).

   Collected Essays in Literary Criticism (1938).

   Poetry and Anarchism (1938).

Richards, I. A. See Appendix I.

Rickword, Edgell. *Rimbaud: The Boy and the Poet* (1924).

   Scrutinies (essays by various critics, two series, edited, 1928 and 1931).

Roberts, Michael. *New Signatures* (edited, 1932).

   New Country: Prose and Poetry by Various Authors (edited, 1933).

   A Critique of Poetry (1934).

   The Modern Mind (1937).

   T. E. Hulme (1938).

Rylands, George. *Words and Poetry* (1928).

Saintsbury, George. *Collected Essays: 1875–1920* (4 volumes, 1923–1924).

   Prefaces and Essays (1933).

Sassoon, Siegfried. *George Meredith* (1948).

Saurat, Denis. *Blake and Modern Thought* (1929).

Savage, D. S. *The Personal Principle: Studies in Modern Poetry* (1944).

   The Withered Branch (1950).

Scarfe, Francis. *Auden and After: The Liberation of Poetry: 1930–1941* (1942).

Scott-James, R. *The Making of Literature: Some Principles of Criticism* (1938).

Shaw, George Bernard. *The Quintessence of Ibsenism* (1891).

   The Perfect Wagnerite (1898).

   Dramatic Opinions and Essays (1906).

   The Sanity of Art (1908).

   Music in London: 1890–94 (three volumes, 1932).

   Our Theatres in the Nineties (three volumes, 1932).

   Pen Portraits and Reviews (1932).

Sitwell, Edith. *Aspects of Poetry* (1934).

   A Poet's Notebook (1943).

Smith, Logan Pearsall. See Appendix I.

Sparrow, John. *Sense and Poetry* (1934).

Spender, Stephen. *The Destructive Element: A Study of Modern Writers and Beliefs* (1935).
    Life and the Poet (1942).
Spurgeon, Caroline. *Leading Motives in the Imagery of Shakespeare's Tragedies* (1930).
    Shakespeare's Imagery and What It Tells Us (1935).
Starkie, Enid. *Baudelaire* (1933).
    Arthur Rimbaud (1938; revised, 1947).
Stonier, G. W. *Gog Magog, and Other Critical Essays* (1933).
Strachey, John. *Literature and Dialectical Materialism* (1934).
Strachey, Lytton. *Landmarks in French Literature* (1912).
    Books and Characters (1922).
    Portraits in Miniature (1931).
    Characters and Commentaries (1933).
Strong, L. A. G. *Common Sense about Poetry* (1931).
    The Sacred River: An Approach to James Joyce (1949).
Swinnerton, Frank. *The Georgian Scene: A Literary Panorama* (1934).
Symons, Arthur. *The Symbolist Movement in Literature* (1899).
    Studies in Seven Arts (1906).
    The Romantic Movement in English Poetry (1909).
    Charles Baudelaire: A Study (1920).
    Collected Works (16 volumes, 1924).
Thompson, Denys. *Reading and Discrimination* (1936).
Tillotson, Geoffrey. *Essays in Criticism and Research* (1942).
Tillyard, E. M. W. *Poetry Direct and Oblique* (1934).
Traversi, D. A. *Approach to Shakespeare* (1939).
Turnell, Martin. *The Poetry of Crisis* (1938).
    The Classical Moment: Studies of Corneille, Molière, Racine (1947).
    The Novel in France (1950).
Vines, Sherard. *Movements in Modern English Poetry and Prose* (1927).
West, Alick. *Crisis and Criticism* (1937).
West, Rebecca. *The Strange Necessity: Essays and Reviews* (1928).
Whitehead, Alfred North. *Science and the Modern World* (1925).
    Symbolism: Its Meaning and Effect (1927).
Wilde, Oscar. *Intentions* (1891).
    A Critic in Pall Mall (edited by E. V. Lucas, 1922).
Williams, Charles. *The English Poetic Mind* (1932).
Wilson, John Dover. *What Happens in Hamlet* (1935).
    The Fortunes of Falstaff (1944).
Woolf, Virginia. *The Common Reader* (1925).
    The Second Common Reader (1932).
    The Death of the Moth and Other Essays (1942).
    The Moment and Other Essays (1948).
    The Captain's Death-Bed and Other Essays (1950).
Yeats, William Butler. *Ideas of Good and Evil* (1903).
    Discoveries: A Volume of Essays (1907).

The Cutting of an Agate (1912).
Per Amica Silentiae Lunae (1918).
Essays (1924).
A Vision (1925; revised edition, 1938).
Autobiographies: Reveries over Childhood and Youth and The Trembling of the Veil (1926).
The Oxford Book of Modern Verse (edited, 1936).
Letters on Poetry from W. B. Yeats to Dorothy Wellesley (1940).

Several anthologies will be found useful in the study of English criticism in the Twentieth Century:

English Critical Essays: Twentieth Century, edited by Phyllis M. Jones (1933).
Contains essays by Robert Bridges, George Saintsbury, Alice Meynell, A. C. Bradley, George Moore, W. P. Ker, A. C. Benson, E. K. Chambers, Max Beerbohm, J. A. Chapman, H. W. Garrod, Desmond MacCarthy, E. M. Forster, Lytton Strachey, Lascelles Abercrombie, R. W. Chapman, G. M. Young, Charles Williams, T. S. Eliot, J. Middleton Murry, Bonamy Dobree, Herbert Read, F. L. Lucas, Virginia Woolf.
Scrutinies I, edited by Edgell Rickword (1928).
Essays on writers of the earlier Twentieth Century by Edgell Rickword, Edwin Muir, Dorothy Edwards, Douglas Garman, D. H. Lawrence, Robert Graves, Bertram Higgins, Thomas McGreevy, W. J. Turner, John Holms, Roy Campbell.
Scrutinies II, edited by Edgell Rickword (1931).
Essays on English writers of the 1920's by Alec Brown, Bertram Higgins, Mary Butts, Jack Lindsay, Peter Quennell, Edgell Rickword, Sherard Vines, Christopher Saltmarshe, William Empson, Gilbert Armitage, Brian Penton, Montagu Slater, Constant Lambert.
Towards Standards of Criticism, edited by F. R. Leavis (1933).
Selections from *The Calendar of Modern Letters,* 1925–1927, by Douglas Garman, Bertram Higgins, Samuel Hoare, J. F. Holms, Edwin Muir, Peter Quennell, C. H. Rickword, Edgell Rickword, and other contributors to that magazine.
Determinations: Critical Essays, edited by F. R. Leavis (1934).
Essays from *Scrutiny* on earlier and modern English literature by James Smith, William Empson, D. W. Harding, F. R. Leavis, L. C. Knights, John Spiers, W. A. Edwards, Ronald Bottrall, Denys Thompson, Michael Oakeshott, J. L. Russell.
Turnstile One, edited by V. S. Pritchett (1948).
A Literary Miscellany from *The New Statesman and Nation* that includes critical articles by Rebecca West, James Joyce, Raymond Mortimer, H. N. Brailsford, David Garnett, Leonard Woolf, Arthur Marshall, Desmond Mac-Carthy, Desmond Shawe-Taylor, Lytton Strachey, Cyril Connolly, R. H. S. Crossman, Robert Lynd, D. H. Lawrence, Derek Verschoyle, C. E. M. Joad.

Virginia Woolf, Harold Laski, E. M. Forster, Harold Nicolson, Stella Benson, Peter Quennell, G. W. Stonier, Logan Pearsall Smith.

Focus, edited by B. Rajan (1945 and following).

A series of volumes of critical studies: *One* is devoted to articles on Kafka and Rex Warner by D. S. Savage, G. W. Stonier, Tom Harrisson, Julian Symons, Kathleen Raine, and others. *Two* contains articles on the realistic novel of the 1930's by D. S. Savage, George Orwell, George Woodcock, Walter Allen, and Arthur Barea, as well as essays on Auden and Eliot. *Three* is entitled *T. S. Eliot: A Study of his Writings by Several Hands*, with essays by Cleanth Brooks, E. E. Duncan Jones, Helen L. Gardner, B. Rajan, Philip Wheelwright, Anne Ridler, M. C. Bradbrook, and Wolf Mankowitz. *Four* is entitled *The Novelist as Thinker*, with essays on Aldous Huxley, Evelyn Waugh, Christopher Isherwood, L. H. Myers, Sartre, and Mauriac by various critics. *Five* is devoted to *Modern American Poetry*. Future titles in the series will be *The Yeats Companion*, *The Critic and Psychoanalysis*, and *The Writer and Politics*.

The Importance of Scrutiny, edited by Eric Bentley (1948).

Selections from *Scrutiny* during the years 1932-1948 by F. R. Leavis, James Smith, D. A. Traversi, L. C. Knights, R. G. Cox, Marius Bewley, D. W. Harding, R. C. Churchill, W. H. Mellers, R. G. Leinhardt, Edgell Rickword, R. O. C. Winkler, H. A. Mason, Boris Ford, Martin Turnell, Q. D. Leavis, and other contributors.

There remains the question of the influence that European criticism—French, Italian, German, Russian—has had on American criticism in the Twentieth Century. The matter cannot be surveyed here, but it must be noted that this influence has been in some cases strong and fairly continuous. It began, so far as modern developments are concerned, with the interest of Henry James, William Dean Howells, and their contemporaries in the French masters of the Nineteenth Century—Sainte-Beuve, Taine, Renan, Schérer, Lemaître, Brunetière; continued through the influence of Baudelaire, Gautier, Mallarmé, Anatole France, and the aesthetic critics on Francis Grierson, Lafcadio Hearn, James Huneker, and the American impressionists of 1890–1920; became marked in the influence exerted by Remy de Gourmont on Ezra Pound and T. S. Eliot; and has persisted to the present day through the work of such Frenchmen as Paul Valéry, André Gide, Henri Brémond, Ramon Fernandez, Jacques Maritain, Etienne Gilson, Charles Péguy, and their contemporaries of the past thirty years.

The Italian influence has been chiefly that of Benedetto Croce and his theory of creative expressionism, which acted chiefly in America in the work of J. E. Spingarn and his program for a "new criticism" around 1910. Mario Praz has been the most important link between Italian and English and American criticism since 1930.

The influence of Germany and Austria has been strongest in the case of the psychological and psychoanalytical theory and methods of Freud and Jung during the past forty years. The Russian influence—Plekhanov, Trotsky, and other literary spokesmen of the Soviet regime—has been a paramount factor in the growth of a Marxist interpretation of literature in the United States since 1910, with Marx, Engels, and the founding fathers of communist theory behind it.

The tracing of these affiliations and connections is a task which the student of modern American criticism will inevitably encounter, and for whose furtherance abundant evidence exists in the books and journals of the past fifty years.

APPENDIX VII: 1962

A: American Books of Criticism since 1951

THE following list of books of American criticism, most of them published since the last edition of *Literary Opinion in America* appeared in 1951, has been designed to cover representative work in the field since that date for those who wish to pursue the subject. The titles are necessarily selective: the output of critical work continues to be very large and no given short list of it can be more than suggestive. The present works by 113 critics include books published since 1951 by the writers whose essays appear in this book, as a supplement to Appendix IV, as well as by other critics, much of whose work has appeared in book form only during the past decade, thus supplementing Appendix I. All the critics are American. The titles listed under their names deal for the most part with the problems of American literature and criticism, and chiefly with the modern aspects of these. Historical and documentary scholarship is usually omitted here. A few works dealing with the relation of literature or criticism to such fields as philosophy, aesthetics, history, music, art, and anthropology are included; also several studies of foreign literature. Even under individual authors' names, however, the choice of titles has been selective; work outside the field of literary criticism or history has generally been omitted. In order to hold the list within limits some writers on literature have not been included—regrettably so, since much of their work is of value; but the user of this book will soon be led to these writers through cross references or bibliographical indexes. Though the emphasis here is on work in criticism some other titles have been included: studies in American history and social movements, some in literary biography and memoir-writing, some in political problems as they bear on American writing, a few in more technical or specialized fields of enquiry. The aim here, as in the other appendixes and in the body of the book itself, has been to show American writing and criticism in their larger bearings while emphasizing primarily their critical problems and purposes.

The reference works and bibliographies listed under Appendix I on page 793, and also under Appendixes IV, page 822, and V, page 840, will be found useful in amplifying the present list of titles. A valuable recent aid is the *Bibliographical Supplement* (edited by Richard M. Ludwig and published by the Macmillan Company, New York, in 1959) to the bibliography included as Volume III of *A Literary History of the United States* (originally published by Macmillan in 1948). Mr. Ludwig's volume brings the original bibliography down to the year 1957, and covers both past and contemporary American writers and subjects.

Current annual indexes or bibliographies, especially those issued every year by the Modern Language Association of America (PMLA) and the quarterly journal *American Literature,* will carry his book down to the present. The monthly and annual issues of the *Cumulative Book Index* will also be of value.

Aaron, Daniel. *Writers of the Left: Episodes in American Literary Communism* (1961).

Aiken, Conrad. *A Reviewer's ABC: Collected Criticism of Conrad Aiken from 1916 to the Present* (1958).

Aldridge, John W. *After the Lost Generation: A Critical Study of the Writers of Two Wars* (1951).

In Search of Heresy: American Literature in an Age of Conformity (1956).

Auden, W. H. *Making, Knowing, and Judging* (the inaugural lecture by the Professor of Poetry delivered before the University of Oxford on June 11, 1956), (1956).

Baker, Carlos H. *Hemingway: The Writer as Artist* (1952).

Barrett, William. *Irrational Man: A Study in Existential Philosophy* (1958).

Barzun, Jacques. *Berlioz and the Romantic Century* (1950).

The Energies of Art: Studies of Authors Classic and Modern (1956).

The House of Intellect (1959, 1961).

Classic, Romantic, and Modern (1961). (A revised edition of *Romanticism and the Modern Ego,* 1943.)

Beach, Joseph Warren. *The Method of Henry James* (revised edition, 1954).

The Making of the Auden Canon (1957).

Obsessive Images: Symbolism in the Poetry of the 1930's and 1940's (edited by William Van O'Connor, 1960).

Bentley, Eric. *Bernard Shaw: A Reconsideration* (1950).

Bernard Shaw: 1856–1950 (amended edition, 1957).

In Search of Theatre (1953).

The Dramatic Event: An American Chronicle (1954).

What is Theatre? A Query in Chronicle Form (1956).

Bewley, Marius. *The Complex Fate: Hawthorne, Henry James, and Some Other American Writers* (1952).

Blackmur, R. P. *The Lion and the Honeycomb: Essays in Solicitude and Critique* (1950, reissued 1955).

Language as Gesture: Essays in Poetry (1952).

Form and Value in Modern Poetry (1952, reissued 1957).

Anni Mirabiles 1921–1925: Reason in the Madness of Letters (1956).

Blair, Walter. *Mark Twain and Huck Finn* (1960).

Blotner, Joseph L. *The Political Novel* (1955).

Bogan, Louise. *Achievement in American Poetry: 1900–1950* (1951).

Selected Criticism: Prose, Poetry (1955).

Bradbury, John M. *The Fugitives: A Critical Account* (1958).

Brooks, Cleanth. *Literary Criticism: A Short History* (with William K. Wimsatt, Jr., 1957).

Brooks, Van Wyck. *The Confident Years: 1885–1915* [the concluding volume of the five volumes of *Makers and Finders: A History of the Writer in America*] (1952).
The Writer in America (1953).
Scenes and Portraits: Memories of Childhood and Youth (1954).
Days of the Phoenix: The Nineteen-Twenties I Remember (1957).
From a Writer's Notebook (1958).
The Dream of Arcadia: American Writers and Artists in Italy: 1760–1915 (1958).
Howells: His Life and World (1959).
From the Shadow of the Mountain: My Post-Meridian Years (1961).

Brown, E. K. *Rhythm in the Novel* (1950).
Willa Cather: A Critical Biography (completed by Leon Edel, 1953).

Burke, Kenneth. *Permanence and Change: An Anatomy of Purpose* (revised edition, 1954).
The Rhetoric of Religion: Studies in Logology (1961).

Campbell, Harry M., and Ruel E. Foster. *William Faulkner: A Critical Appraisal* (1951).

Campbell, Joseph. *The Masks of God: Primitive Mythology* (1959).
The Masks of God: Oriental Mythology (1962).

Cantwell, Robert. *Famous American Men of Letters* (1956).

Cargill, Oscar. *The Novels of Henry James* (1961).

Chase, Richard. *Emily Dickinson* (1951).
Walt Whitman Reconsidered (1955).
The American Novel and Its Tradition (1957).
The Democratic Vista: A Dialogue on Life and Letters in Contemporary America (1958).
Walt Whitman (1961).

Coffman, Stanley K. *Imagism: A Chapter for the History of Modern Poetry* (1951).

Coughlan, Robert. *The Private World of William Faulkner* (1954).

Cowley, Malcolm. *Exile's Return: A Literary Odyssey of the 1920's* (revised edition, 1951).
The Literary Situation (1954).
Writers at Work: The Paris Review Interviews (edited, 1958).

Crane, Ronald S. *The Language of Criticism and the Structure of Poetry* (1953).

Daiches, David. *Willa Cather: A Critical Introduction* (1951).
Critical Approaches to Literature (1956).
Literary Essays (1956).
The Novel and the Modern World (revised edition, 1960).

Denny, Margaret, and William H. Gilman, editors. *The American Writer and the European Tradition* (1950).

Deutsch, Babette.   *Poetry in Our Time* (1952).
Edel, Leon.   *Henry James: The Untried Years 1843–1870* (1953).
    The Psychological Novel: 1900–1950 (1955).
    Literary Biography (1957).
    Willa Cather: The Paradox of Success (1959).
    Henry James (1960).
    Henry James: The Conquest of London (1962).
    Henry James: The Middle Years (Forthcoming, 1962 or 1963).
Eliot, T. S.   *Poetry and Drama* (1951).
    The Three Voices of Poetry (1953).
    The Literature of Politics (1955).
    American Literature and the American Language (1953).
    The Frontiers of Criticism (1956).
    On Poetry and Poets (1957).
Ellmann, Richard.   *Yeats: The Man and the Masks* (1949, reissued 1956).
    The Identity of Yeats (1954).
    James Joyce (1959).
Farrell, James T.   *Reflections at Fifty, and Other Essays* (1954).
Fenton, Charles A.   *The Apprenticeship of Ernest Hemingway* (1954).
Fergusson, Francis.   *The Idea of a Theatre: A Study of Ten Plays* (1953).
    The Human Image in Dramatic Literature (1957).
    Dante's Drama of the Mind: A Modern Reading of the Purgatorio (1958).
Feidelson, Charles, Jr.   *Symbolism and American Literature* (1953).
Fiedler, Leslie A.   *An End to Innocence* (1955).
    Love and Death in the American Novel (1960).
Fishman, Solomon.   *The Disinherited of Art: Writer and Background* (1953).
Foster, Richard.   *The New Romantics: A Reappraisal of the New Criticism* (1962).
Fowlie, Wallace.   *The Age of Surrealism* (1950).
    Rimbaud's Illuminations: A Study in Angelism (1953).
    Mallarmé (1953).
    Mid-Century French Poets: Selections, Translations, and Critical Notices (1955).
    Paul Claudel (1957).
Friedman, Melvin.   *Stream of Consciousness: A Study in Literary Method* (1955).
Frohack, W. M.   *The Novel of Violence in America* (revised edition, 1957).
Geismar, Maxwell.   *Rebels and Ancestors: The American Novel 1890–1915* (1953).
    American Moderns: From Rebellion to Conformity (1958).
Gregory, Horace.   *James Whitcomb Riley: A Victorian American* (1951).
    Amy Lowell: Portrait of the Poet in Her Time (1958).
    The World of James McNeill Whistler (1959).
    The Dying Gladiators, and Other Essays (1961).
Guerard, Albert J., Jr.   *André Gide* (1951).
    Conrad the Novelist (1958).

Hicks, Granville.   *The Living Novel: A Symposium* (edited, 1957).
Hoffman, Frederick J.   *The Twenties* (1955).
Howe, Irving.   *William Faulkner: A Critical Study* (1952).
    Politics and the Novel (1957).
Humphrey, Robert.   *Stream of Consciousness in the Modern Novel* (1954).
Hyman, Stanley Edgar.   *The Critical Performance: An Anthology of American
        and British Literary Criticism of Our Century* (edited, 1956).
    Poetry and Criticism: Four Revolutions in Literary Taste (1961).
    The Tangled Bank: Darwin, Marx, Fraser, and Freud (1962).
Jarrell, Randall.   *Poetry and the Age* (1953).
    A Sad Heart at the Supermarket (1962).
Josephson, Matthew.   *Life Among the Surrealists* (1962).
Kazin, Alfred.   *The Inmost Leaf: A Selection of Essays* (1959).
    Contemporaries (1962).
Kenner, Hugh.   *The Poetry of Ezra Pound* (1951).
    Wyndham Lewis (1954).
    Dublin's Joyce (1956).
    Gnomon: Essays on Contemporary Literature (1958).
    The Invisible Poet: T. S. Eliot (1959).
Knight, Grant C.   *The Critical Period in American Literature: 1890–1900*
        (1951).
    The Strenuous Age in American Literature: 1900–1910 (1954).
Krieger, Murray.   *The New Apologists for Poetry* (1956).
Kronenberger, Louis.   *Kings and Desperate Men* (1942, reissued 1960).
    The Pleasure of Their Company (1946).
    The Thread of Laughter: Chapters on English Stage Comedy (1952).
    The Republic of Letters (1955).
Krutch, Joseph Wood.   *"Modernism" in Modern Drama: A Definition and Esti-
        mate* (1953).
    *The Measure of Man: On Freedom, Human Values, Survival, and the
        Modern Temper* (1954).
    The American Drama Since 1918: An Informal History (revised edition,
        1957).
Langer, Suzanne K.   *Feeling and Form: A Theory of Art* (1953).
    An Introduction to Symbolic Logic (second revised edition,
        1953).
    *Philosophy in a New Key: A Study in the Symbolism of Reason, Rite,
        and Art* (third edition, 1957).
    Problems of Art: Ten Philosophical Lectures (1957).
    *Reflections on Art: A Source Book of Writings by Artists, Critics, and
        Philosophers* (edited, 1958).
Levin, Harry.   *The Overreacher: A Study of Christopher Marlowe* (1952).
    Symbolism and Fiction (1956).
    Contexts of Criticism (1957).
    The Power of Blackness: Hawthorne, Poe, Melville (1958).
    The Question of Hamlet (1959).

Lewis, R. W. B.   *The American Adam: Innocence, Tragedy, and Tradition in the Nineteenth Century* (1955).

Lyde, Marilyn Jones.   *Edith Wharton: Convention and Morality in the Work of a Novelist* (1959).

Lynn, Kenneth.   *The Dream of Success* [a study of Dreiser, Jack London, David Graham Phillips, Frank Norris, and Robert Herrick] (1955).

Macdonald, Dwight.   *Memoirs of a Revolutionist* (1957).

MacLeish, Archibald.   *Poetry and Opinion: The Pisan Cantos of Ezra Pound: A Dialogue on the Role of Poetry* (1950).
   Yeats and the Belief in Life (1958).
   Poetry and Experience (1960).

McCarthy, Mary.   *Sights and Spectacles: 1937–1956* (1956).
   On the Contrary (1961).

McCormick, John.   *Catastrophe and Imagination: An Interpretation of the Recent English and American Novel* (1957).

Maritain, Jocques.   *Creative Intuition in Art and Poetry* (1953).
   The Situation of Poetry: Four Essays on the Relations between Poetry, Mysticism, Magic, and Knowledge (1954).
   Reflections on America (1958).
   On the Use of Philosophy: Three Essays (1961).

Matthiessen, F. O.   *Theodore Dreiser* (1951).
   The Responsibilities of the Critic (1952).

Mencken, H. L.   *A Carnival of Buncombe* (edited by Malcolm Moos, 1956).
   Minority Report: H. L. Mencken's Notebooks (1956).
   H. L. Mencken on Music (1961).

Miller, James E., Jr.   *The Fictional Technique of Scott Fitzgerald* (1957).
   A Reader's Guide to Herman Melville (1961).

Miller, Perry.   *American Thought: The Civil War to World War I* (1954).
   The Raven and the Whale: The War of Words and Wits in the Era of Poe and Melville (1956).

Miner, Ward L.   *The World of William Faulkner* (1952).

Moore, Marianne.   *Predilections* [literary and critical essays] (1955).

Muller, Herbert J.   *The Spirit of Tragedy* (1956).
   Science and Criticism: The Humanistic Tradition in Contemporary Thought (1956).

Nevius, Blake.   *Edith Wharton: A Study of Her Fiction* (1953, reissued 1961).

Norman, Charles.   *The Magic Maker: E. E. Cummings* (1958).

O'Connor, William Van.   *The Shaping Spirit: A Study of Wallace Stevens* (1950).
   The Age of Criticism: 1900–1950 (1952).
   The Tangled Fire of William Faulkner (1954).
   A Casebook on Ezra Pound (edited with Edward Stone, 1959).

Olson, Elder.   *The Poetry of Dylan Thomas* (1954).
   Tragedy and the Theory of Drama (1961).

Peyre, Henri.   *The Contemporary French Novel* (1955).
   Observations on Life, Literature, and Learning in America (1961).

Phillips, William.   Art and Psychoanalysis (1957).

Porter, Katherine Anne.   The Days Before [literary and other essays] (1952).

Pound, Ezra.   Lavoro ed Usura: Tre Saggi (1954).

    Impact: Essays on Ignorance and the Decline of American Civilization (edited by Noel Stock, 1960).

Rahv, Philip.   Image and Idea: Twenty Essays on Literary Themes (revised edition, 1957).

Ransom, John Crowe.   The Kenyon Critics: Studies in Modern Literature (edited, 1951).

    Poems and Essays (selected, 1955).

Ray, Gordon N.   Vanity Fair: One Version of the Novelist's Responsibility (1950).

    The Buried Life: A Study of the Relations Between Thackeray's Fiction and His Personal History (1952).

Rice, Philip Blair.   On the Knowledge of Good and Evil (1955).

Richards, I. A.   Speculative Instruments (1955).

Santayana, George.   Persons and Places (three volumes, 1944–53).

    Atoms of Thought: An Anthology of Thoughts (1950).

    Dominations and Powers: Reflections on Liberty, Society, and Government (1951).

    Essays in Literary Criticism (selected and edited by Irving Singer, 1956).

    The Idler and His Works, and Other Essays (edited by Daniel Cory, 1957).

Schorer, Mark.   Sinclair Lewis: An American Life (1961).

Sievers, W. David.   Freud on Broadway: A History of Psychoanalysis and the American Drama (1955).

Slatoff, Walter Jacob.   Quest for Failure: A Study of William Faulkner (1960).

Smith, Henry Nash.   Virgin Land: The American West as Symbol and Myth (1950).

Spencer, Benjamin T.   The Quest for Nationality: An American Literary Campaign (1957).

Tate, Allen.   The Forlorn Demon: Didactic and Critical Essays (1953).

    The Man of Letters in the Modern World: Selected Essays 1928–1955 (1955).

    Collected Essays (1959).

Thorp, Willard.   American Writing in the Twentieth Century (1960).

Tindall, William York.   James Joyce: His Way of Interpreting the Modern World (1950).

    The Literary Symbol (1955).

    A Reader's Guide to James Joyce (1959).

Trilling, Lionel.   The Opposing Self: Nine Essays in Criticism (1955).

    Freud and the Crisis of Our Culture (1955).

    A Gathering of Fugitives (1957).

Unger, Leonard.   The Man in the Name: Essays on the Experience of Poetry (1956).

Van Doren, Mark.   *Introduction to Poetry* (1951).
> *Don Quixote's Profession* (1958).
> *The Happy Critic, and Other Essays* (1961).

Van Ghent, Dorothy.   *The English Novel: Form and Function* (1953, reissued 1961).

Vickery, Olga W.   *The Novels of William Faulkner: A Critical Interpretation* (1959).

Vivas, Eliseo.   *Creation and Discovery: Essays in Criticism and Aesthetics* (1955).

Waggoner, Hyatt Howe.   *The Heel of Elohim: Science and Values in Modern American Poetry* (1950).
> *William Faulkner: From Jefferson to the World* (1959).

Walcutt, Charles Child.   *American Literary Naturalism: A Divided Stream* (1956).

Warren, Austin.   *New England Saints* (1956).

Warren, Robert Penn.   *Selected Essays* (1958).

Wellek, René.   *A History of Modern Criticism: 1750–1950.* Vol. I: *The Later Eighteenth Century* (1955). Vol. II: *The Romantic Age* (1955). [Other volumes to follow.]

Wheelwright, Philip.   *The Burning Fountain: A Study in the Language of Symbolism* (1954).

Williamson, George.   *A Reader's Guide to T. S. Eliot: A Poem-by-Poem Analysis* (1953).

Wilson, Edmund.   *The Shores of Light: A Literary Chronicle of the Twenties and Thirties* (1952).
> *A Literary Chronicle: 1922–1950* [selected essays] (1956).
> *A Piece of My Mind: Reflections at Sixty* (1956).
> *Patriotic Gore: Studies in the Literature of the American Civil War* (1962).

Wimsatt, William K., Jr.   *The Verbal Icon: Studies in the Meaning of Poetry* (1954).
> *Literary Criticism: A Short History* (with Cleanth Brooks, 1957).

Winters, Yvor.   *In Defense of Reason* (new edition, 1951).
> *The Function of Criticism: Problems and Exercises* (1957).
> *On Modern Poets* (1959).

Young, Philip.   *Ernest Hemingway* (1954).
> *Ernest Hemingway* (1960).

Young, Stark.   *The Pavilion: Of People and Times Remembered, of Stories and Places* (1951).
> *The Flower in Drama* and *Glamour: Theatre Essays and Criticism* (revised edition, two volumes in one, 1955).
> *Immortal Shadows: A Book of Dramatic Criticism* (new edition, 1958).

Zabel, Morton Dauwen.   *Craft and Character: Text, Method, and Vocation in Modern Fiction* (1957).

B: *Selected Essays in American Criticism: 1951–1962*

THE following selection of essays by forty American critics date (with a few exceptions) from 1951 to 1962, and are appended as a list of suggested readings for those who wish to supplement the essays included in *Literary Opinion in America*. Had it been possible, in the present edition, to amplify the book to cover the past twelve years, the additional essays would have been selected from such a list as this. The list is again selective. Recent work by critics already represented in the book is included, as well as essays by other critics; and the list is not offered as a comprehensive survey of the field. The reader will first wish to supplement his readings from the books listed in the preceding part of this appendix. The essays listed below are suggestive only. Where a critic is best represented in his published books only one or two of his writings are included here; for some authors, several more essays are listed. The reader will be led to other essays through the indexes listed under Appendix I on page 793, and in the files of the magazines listed under Appendix V on pages 841–42.

Bentley, Eric, "Trying to Like O'Neill," Kenyon Review, 14: 476–92 (1952).

Bewley, Marius, "The Poetry of Wallace Stevens," Partisan Review, 16: 895–915 (September, 1940).

Bewley, Marius, "Scott Fitzgerald's Criticism of America," Sewanee Review, 62: 223–46 (April, 1954).

Bewley, Marius, "Henry James and Life," Hudson Review, 11: 167–85 (Summer, 1958).

Blackmur, R. P., "Harmony and True Liberalism: Henry Adams' *Mont Saint-Michel and Chartres*," Sewanee Review, 55: 1–27 (1952).

Blackmur, R. P., "The Virgin and the Dynamo," Magazine of Art, 45: 147–53 (April, 1952).

Brooks, Cleanth, "The State of Criticism: A Sampling," Sewanee Review, 65: 484–98 (Summer, 1957).

Burke, Kenneth, "Form and Persecution in the *Oresteia*," Sewanee Review, 60: 377–96 (Summer, 1952).

Burke, Kenneth, "Symbol and Association," Hudson Review, 9: 212–25 (Summer, 1956).

Chase, Richard, "Cable and his *Grandissimes*," Kenyon Review, 18: 373–83 (1956).

Chase, Richard, "Radicalism Today," Partisan Review, 24: 45–54 (Winter, 1957).

Chase, Richard, "The Fate of the Avant-Garde," Partisan Review, 24: 363–75 (Summer, 1957).

Cowley, Malcolm, "Defeat and Triumph" [on Edwin Arlington Robinson], New Republic, 119: 26–30 (December 6, 1948).

Coxe, Louis O., "E. A. Robinson: The Lost Tradition," Sewanee Review, 62: 247–66 (1954).

Dupee, F. W., "The Other Dickens," Partisan Review, 27: 111–22 (Winter, 1960).

Edel, Leon, Introduction to The Sacred Fount by Henry James (New York, 1953).

Edel, Leon, "Willa Cather's The Professor's House: An Enquiry into the Use of Psychology in Literary Criticism," Literature and Psychology, 4: 66–79 (November, 1954).

Eliot, T. S., "Virgil and the Christian World," Sewanee Review, 61: 1–14 (January, 1953).

Eliot, T. S., "The Frontiers of Criticism," Sewanee Review, 64: 525–43 (Fall, 1956).

Ellmann, Richard, "Joyce and Yeats," Kenyon Review, 12: No. 4: 618–38 (1950).

Ellmann, Richard, "The Art of Yeats: Affirmative Capability," Kenyon Review, 15: 357–85 (1954).

Fergusson, Francis, "The Golden Bowl Revisited," Sewanee Review, 63: 13–28 (Winter, 1955).

Fergusson, Francis, "The Search for New Standards in the Theatre," Kenyon Review, 17: 581–96 (Fall, 1955).

Fergusson, Francis, "Three Allegorists: Brecht, Wilder, and Eliot," Sewanee Review, 64: 544–73 (Fall, 1956).

Fiedler, Leslie A., "Archetype and Signature: A Study of the Relationship between Biography and Poetry," Sewanee Review, 60: 253–73 (April, 1952).

Fiedler, Leslie A., "The Novel and America," Partisan Review, 27: 41–62 (Winter, 1960).

Flint, R. W., "The Four Quartets Reconsidered," Sewanee Review, 56: 69–81 (1948).

Fowlie, Wallace, "Mallarmé as Ritualist," Sewanee Review, 59: 228–53 (April, 1951).

Fowlie, Wallace, "Claudel as Dramatist," Sewanee Review, 64: 218–37 (Spring, 1956).

Guerard, Albert J., "The Nigger of the 'Narcissus'," Kenyon Review, 19: 205–32 (Spring, 1957).

Howe, Irving, "This Age of Conformity," Partisan Review, 21: 7–33, 238–40 (January; March, 1954).

Jarrell, Randall, "Reflections on Wallace Stevens," Partisan Review, 18: 335–44 (May, 1951).

Jarrell, Randall, "Walt Whitman: He Had His Nerve," Kenyon Review, 14: 63–79 (1952).

Jarrell, Randall, "An Age of Criticism," Partisan Review, 19: 185–210 (March, 1952).

Frank, Joseph, "The Metaphysic of Modern Art," Partisan Review, 17: 174–88 (February, 1950).

Frank, Joseph, "God, Man, and Jean-Paul Sartre," Partisan Review, 19: 202–10 (March, 1952).

Frank, Joseph, "Nihilism and *Notes from Underground*," Sewanee Review, 69: 1–33 (Winter, 1961).

Kazin, Alfred, "On Melville as Scripture," Partisan Review, 17: 67–75 (January, 1950).

Kazin, Alfred, "The Stillness of *Light in August*," Partisan Review, 24: 519–38 (Fall, 1957).

Kenner, Hugh, "Joyce and Ibsen's Naturalism," Sewanee Review, 59: 75–96 (Winter, 1951).

Kenner, Hugh, "The Sacred Book of the Arts," Sewanee Review, 64: 574–90 (Fall, 1956).

Levin, Harry, "Observations on the Style of Ernest Hemingway," Kenyon Review, 13: 581–609 (1951).

Levin, Harry, "Crisis in Criticism," Comparative Literature, 7: 144–55 (Spring, 1955).

Lewis, R. W. B., "American Letters: A Projection," Yale Review, 51: 211–226 (Winter, 1962).

Macdonald, Dwight, "By Cozzens Possessed," Commentary, 25: 36–47 (January, 1958).

McCarthy, Mary, "The Will and Testament of Ibsen," Partisan Review, 23: 74–80, 287–88 (Winter–Spring, 1956).

Mizener, Arthur, "The Novel of Manners in America," Kenyon Review, 12: 1–19 (1950).

Mizener, Arthur, "A Dance to the Music of Time: the Novels of Anthony Powell," Kenyon Review, 22: 79–92 (Winter, 1960).

Olson, Elder, "William Empson: Contemporary Criticism and Poetic Diction," Modern Philology, 47: 222–52 (May, 1950).

Podhoretz, Norman, "Edmund Wilson: The Last Patrician," The Reporter, 19: 25–28 (December 25, 1958) and 20: 32–35 (January 8, 1959).

Rahv, Philip, "Myth and the Powerhouse," Partisan Review, 20: 635–48 (Fall, 1953).

Rahv, Philip, "Fiction and the Criticism of Fiction," Kenyon Review, 18: 276–99 (Spring, 1956).

Ransom, John Crowe, "Poetry of 1900–1950," Kenyon Review, 13: 445–54 (1951).

Ransom, John Crowe, "Emily Dickinson," Perspectives USA, 15: 5–20 (1956).

Schorer, Mark, "Fiction and the Matrix of Analogy," Kenyon Review, 11: 539–60 (1949).

Schorer, Mark, "Pride Unprejudiced," Kenyon Review, 18: 72–91 (Winter, 1956).

Sillen, Samuel, "The Challenge of Randolph Bourne," Masses and Mainstream, 6: 24–32 (December, 1953).

Tate, Allen, "Is Literary Criticism Possible?", Partisan Review, 19: 546–57 (September, 1952).

Tate, Allen, "The Angelic Imagination: Poe and the Power of Words," Kenyon Review, 14: 455–75 (1952).

Tate, Allen, "Reflections on American Poetry 1900–1950," Sewanee Review, 64: 59–70 (Winter, 1956).

Trilling, Diana, "A Letter of Introduction to Lawrence," Partisan Review, 25: 32–48 (Winter, 1958).

Trilling, Lionel, "W. D. Howells and the Roots of Modern Taste," Partisan Review, 18: 516–36 (September, 1951).

Warren, Austin, "Emily Dickinson," Sewanee Review, 65: 565–586 (1957).

Warren, Robert Penn, "Nostromo," Sewanee Review, 59: 363–91 (Summer, 1951).

Wellek, René, "The Criticism of T. S. Eliot," Sewanee Review, 64: 398–443 (Summer, 1956).

Wellek, René, "The Main Trends of Twentieth Century Criticism," Yale Review, 51: 102–18 (Autumn, 1961).

Wilson, Edmund, "The James Branch Cabell Case Reopened," New Yorker, 32: 140–68 (April 21, 1956).

Wilson, Edmund, "The Ordeal of George Washington Cable," New Yorker 33: 172–216 (November 9, 1957).

C: Further Suggestions

COLLECTIONS or anthologies of American criticism, listed up to 1951 in Appendix II of this book (pp. 805–11), have continued to appear during the past twelve years in considerable number; and while a full index of them cannot be included here, some of their types may be indicated. Symposia on individual American writers have continued. Among them are: *Mark Twain: Selected Criticism,* edited by Arthur L. Scott (1955); *The Stature of Theodore Dreiser: A Critical Survey of the Man and His Work,* edited by Alfred Kazin (1955); *William Faulkner: Two Decades of Criticism,* edited by Frederick Hoffman and Olga W. Vickery (1951); *F. Scott Fitzgerald: The Man and His Work,* edited by Alfred Kazin (1951); two on Hemingway—*Ernest Hemingway: The Man and His Work,* edited by John K. McCaffrey (1950), and *Hemingway and His Critics,* edited by Carlos Baker (1961); *O'Neill and His Plays: Four Decades of Criticism,* edited by Oscar Cargill, N. Bryllion Fagin, and William J. Fisher (1961); and *The Achievement of Wallace Stevens,* edited by Ashley Brown and Robert Haller (1962). Another kind of critical collection has appeared in recent years—the so-called "casebook" or "controlled research" symposium on individual authors or literary works. Two recent examples dealing with American writers are *A Casebook on Ezra Pound,* edited by William Van O'Connor and Edward Stone (1959) and *A Casebook on Henry James's "The Turn of the Screw,"* edited by Gerald Willen (1960).

Collections of work from individual magazines have also continued to appear— *The Kenyon Critics: Studies in Modern Literature,* edited by John Crowe Ransom, two further installments of *The Partisan Reader,* edited by Philip Rahv and

William Phillips, a selection of writings from *The Hudson Review,* edited by Frederick Morgan, etc. Among more general anthologies of American criticism during the past twelve years are *American Literary Criticism 1900–1950,* edited by Charles I. Glicksberg (1951); *Critiques and Essays on Modern Fiction 1920–1951,* edited by John W. Aldridge (1952); *Essays in Modern Literary Criticism,* edited by Ray B. West, Jr. (1952); *The Achievement of American Criticism,* edited by Clarence A. Brown (1954); *The Critical Performance: An Anthology of American and British Literary Criticism of Our Century,* edited by Stanley Edgar Hyman (1956); *Twelve Original Essays on Great American Novels,* edited by Charles Shapiro (1958); *Literary Criticism in America,* edited by Albert D. Van Nostrand (1957); and *The Living Novel: A Symposium,* edited by Granville Hicks (1957); which includes discussions of American and other fiction.

American critical magazines, here listed to cover the years up to 1951 in Appendix III (pp. 812–21), have also continued to multiply. Among recently established journals are *Modern Fiction Studies* (1955), *Twentieth Century Literature* (1955), *Victorian Studies* (1957), *Nineteenth-Century Fiction* (1951), which includes essays on Twentieth Century fiction, *The Modern Drama* (1958), *The Chicago Review* (1946), *The Texas Quarterly* (1958), *The University of Minnesota Review* (1958), *Criticism: A Quarterly for Literature and the Arts* (1959), *The Literary Review* (1958), *The Carleton Miscellany* (1959), *The Evergreen Review* (1957). A number of the journals listed as currently published in Appendix III have been suspended during the past decade, but the above-named and others have taken over some of their fields of interest or established special fields of their own.

The best indexes of criticism published in magazines continue to be *The Reader's Guide to Periodical Literature* and *The International Index to Periodicals.* *The Book Review Digest* supplies other information in its monthly and collective issues; and the most comprehensive listings of current American scholarship and criticism are those published in annual or quarterly installments by the *Publications of the Modern Language Association* (PMLA) and the journal *American Literature.*

HARPER TORCHBOOKS / The University Library

HARPER TORCHBOOKS / The Academy Library

HARPER TORCHBOOKS / The Bollingen Library

Elliott Coleman, *Ed.*	LECTURES IN CRITICISM: *By R. P. Blackmur, B. Croce, Henri Peyre, . Crowe Ransom, Herbert Read, and Allen Tate* TB/2003
C. G. Jung	PSYCHOLOGICAL REFLECTIONS. Edited by Jolande Jacobi TB/2001
C. G. Jung	SYMBOLS OF TRANSFORMATION: *An Analysis of the Prelude to a Case of Schizophrenia.* Illustrated. *Vol. I,* TB/2009; *Vol. II,* TB/2010
C. G. Jung & Carl Kerényi	ESSAYS ON A SCIENCE OF MYTHOLOGY: *The Myth of the Divine Child and the Divine Maiden.* Illustrated TB/2014
Erich Neumann	AMOR AND PSYCHE: *The Psychic Development of the Feminine: A Commentary on the Tale by Apuleius* TB/2012
Erich Neumann	THE ORIGINS AND HISTORY OF CONSCIOUSNESS. *Vol. I,* illustrated, TB/2007; *Vol. II,* TB/2008
St.-John Perse	SEAMARKS. Translated by Wallace Fowlie TB/2002
A. Piankoff	THE SHRINES OF TUT-ANKH-AMON. Edited by N. Rambova. Illustrated TB/2011
Jean Seznec	THE SURVIVAL OF THE PAGAN GODS: *The Mythological Tradition and Its Place in Renaissance Humanism and Art.* Illustrated TB/2004
Heinrich Zimmer	MYTHS AND SYMBOLS IN INDIAN ART AND CIVILIZATION. Illustrated TB/2005

HARPER TORCHBOOKS / The Cloister Library

W. F. Albright	THE BIBLICAL PERIOD FROM ABRAHAM TO EZRA TB/102
Tor Andrae	MOHAMMED: *The Man and His Faith* TB/62
Augustine/Przywara	AN AUGUSTINE SYNTHESIS TB/35
C. K. Barrett, *Ed.*	THE NEW TESTAMENT BACKGROUND: *Selected Documents* TB/86
Karl Barth	CHURCH DOGMATICS: *A Selection.* Edited by G. W. Bromiley, with Introduction by H. Gollwitzer TB/95
Karl Barth	DOGMATICS IN OUTLINE TB/56
Karl Barth	THE WORD OF GOD AND THE WORD OF MAN TB/13
Nicolas Berdyaev	THE BEGINNING AND THE END TB/14
Nicolas Berdyaev	THE DESTINY OF MAN TB/61
Anton T. Boisen	THE EXPLORATION OF THE INNER WORLD: *A Study of Mental Disorder and Religious Experience* TB/87
J. H. Breasted	DEVELOPMENT OF RELIGION AND THOUGHT IN ANCIENT EGYPT. Intro. by John Wilson TB/57
Martin Buber	ECLIPSE OF GOD: *The Relation Between Religion and Philosophy* TB/12
Martin Buber	MOSES: *The Revelation and the Covenant* TB/27
Martin Buber	THE PROPHETIC FAITH TB/73
Martin Buber	TWO TYPES OF FAITH: *The Interpenetration of Judaism and Christianity* TB/75
Rudolf Bultmann	HISTORY AND ESCHATOLOGY: *The Presence of Eternity* TB/91
R. Bultmann, et al.	KERYGMA AND MYTH: *A Theological Debate.* Ed. by H. W. Bartsch TB/80
Rudolf Bultmann & K. Kundsin	FORM CRITICISM: *Two Essays on New Testament Research.* Translated & edited by Frederick C. Grant TB/96
Jacob Burckhardt	THE CIVILIZATION OF THE RENAISSANCE IN ITALY. Illustrated Edition. Introduction by B. Nelson and C. Trinkaus. *Vol. I,* TB/40; *Vol. II,* TB/41
Edward Conze	BUDDHISM: *Its Essence and Development.* Foreword by Arthur Waley TB/58
Frederick Copleston	MEDIEVAL PHILOSOPHY TB/76
F. M. Cornford	FROM RELIGION TO PHILOSOPHY: *The Origins of Western Speculation* TB/20
H. G. Creel	CONFUCIUS AND THE CHINESE WAY TB/63
Adolf Deissmann	PAUL: *A Study in Social and Religious History* TB/15
C. H. Dodd	THE AUTHORITY OF THE BIBLE TB/43
Johannes Eckhart	MEISTER ECKHART: A Modern Translation TB/8
Mircea Eliade	COSMOS AND HISTORY: *The Myth of the Eternal Return* TB/50
Mircea Eliade	THE SACRED AND THE PROFANE: *The Significance of Religious Myth, Symbolism, and Ritual Within Life and Culture* TB/81
Morton S. Enslin	CHRISTIAN BEGINNINGS TB/5
Morton S. Enslin	THE LITERATURE OF THE CHRISTIAN MOVEMENT TB/6
G. P. Fedotov	THE RUSSIAN RELIGIOUS MIND: *Kievan Christianity, the 10th to the 13th Centuries* TB/70
Ludwig Feuerbach	THE ESSENCE OF CHRISTIANITY. Introduction by Karl Barth; Foreword by H. Richard Niebuhr TB/11
Harry E. Fosdick	A GUIDE TO UNDERSTANDING THE BIBLE TB/2
Henri Frankfort	ANCIENT EGYPTIAN RELIGION: *An Interpretation.* Illustrated TB/77
Sigmund Freud	ON CREATIVITY AND THE UNCONSCIOUS: *Papers on the Psychology of Art, Literature, Love, Religion.* Edited by Benjamin Nelson TB/45
Maurice Friedman	MARTIN BUBER: *The Life of Dialogue* TB/64
Edward Gibbon	THE TRIUMPH OF CHRISTENDOM IN THE ROMAN EMPIRE [J. B. Bury Edition, illus., Chapters 15-20 of "The Decline and Fall"] TB/46

3

HARPER TORCHBOOKS / The Science Library